Communicating
FOR SUCCESS

CHERYL HAMILTON

Tarrant County College, Northeast Campus

BONNIE CREEL

Tarrant County College, Northeast Campus

Allyn & Bacon

Boston   Columbus   Indianapolis   New York   San Francisco   Upper Saddle River
Amsterdam   Cape Town   Dubai   London   Madrid   Milan   Munich   Paris   Montreal   Toronto
Delhi   Mexico City   Sao Paulo   Sydney   Hong Kong   Seoul   Singapore   Taipei   Tokyo

Editor-in-Chief, Communication: *Karon Bowers*
Editorial Assistant: *Stephanie Chaisson*
Senior Development Editor: *Carol Alper*
Development Manager: *David Kear*
Associate Development Editor: *Angela Pickard*
Media Producer: *Megan Higginbotham*
Marketing Manager: *Blair Tuckman*
Project Manager: *Barbara Mack*
Managing Editor: *Linda Mihatov Behrens*
Project Coordination and Electronic Page Makeup: *Nesbitt Graphics, Inc.*
Senior Operations Specialist: *Nick Sklitsis*
Operations Specialist: *Mary Ann Gloriande*
Interior Design: *Dorling Kindersley*
Cover Designer: *Joel Gendron*
Cover Images: *Ants © Martin Gallagher/Corbis; Apple © Image Source Photography/veer*
Manager, Photo Rights and Permissions: *Zina Arabia*
Manager, Visual Research: *Beth Brenzel*
Image Permission Coordinator: *Cynthia Vincenti*
Photo Researcher: *Sarah Evertson*

10 9 8 7 6 5 4

Photo credits appear on page 449, which constitutes an extension of the copyright page.

Library of Congress Cataloging-in-Publication Data

Hamilton, Cheryl.
  Communicating for success/Cheryl Hamilton, Bonnie Creel.
    p. cm.
ISBN 0-205-52475-3
1. Business communication. 2. Oral communication. 3. Public speaking. 4. Success.
I. Creel, Bonnie. II. Title.
  HF5718.H2835 2010
  651.7--dc22

                          2009045254

Allyn & Bacon
is an imprint of

PEARSON

www.pearsonhighered.com

ISBN-13: 978-0-205-52475-4
ISBN-10: 0-205-52475-3

In memory of
Dr. George Thomas Tade:
Distinguished scholar, insightful teacher,
gracious mentor, cherished friend—
and communicator without equal.

Brief Contents

Contents

UNIT I
BUILDING COMMUNICATION FOUNDATIONS

1 Getting Started in Communication *3*

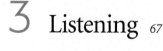

UNIT II

INTERPERSONAL AND SMALL GROUP COMMUNICATION

6 Building Interpersonal Relationships *151*

9 **Becoming Effective Group Members and Leaders** *233*

12 Informative Speaking *315*

13 Adding Visuals and Practicing Your Presentation *345*

14 Persuasive Speaking *375*

Have you ever wondered why your relationships don't go as planned? Or why you didn't get the promotion you were expecting? Or why you feel so nervous when speaking in front of others? Or why the team you were on got caught up in arguing and failed to complete the project in a timely fashion? Communication skills and competencies determine your success in every phase of your lives, from family and friends, to job success, to working in teams and giving oral presentations. We designed *Communicating for Success* to give you specific skills and the theory behind those skills to help you improve the quality of your communication and thus the quality of your life. Just as the ants on the cover of our textbook used their communication skills to get the apple, you can help achieve your relationship, career, team, and speaking goals by improving your communication skills.

Communicating
FOR SUCCESS

CHERYL HAMILTON
BONNIE CREEL

30

COMM

LEARNING OBJECTIVES
focus on the
goals for each chapter.

LEARNING **OBJE**

1.6 What commu
skills covered
chapter relate
specifically to
career?

SPOTLIGHTS
feature current
communication
findings.

SPOTLIGHT O

BUSINESS
No matter whether
in business as comm
tion, or an organizat
skills are extremely
success. In addition
with co-workers and
are likely to interact
with members of ot
Throughout this t
lighting how specific
from each chapter a
cation in business. I
may be one of the
determiners of man
relationships (Hubb
2005). Yet one stud
1990) found that 7.
ployees felt their ma
advantage of them,
believed their mana
trusted. [See Chapte
building trust and re

CAREER MOMENTS
look at job
information.

CAREER MOM

You may be taking th
at your college or un
course in Communic
According to John
regarded outplaceme
and Christmas,

The two requireme
dates to possess are
tion of communicat
Outlook, 2006, C

Challenger reports
that are particularly l
jobs that will be in g
speech and acting;
tions; physical thera

CAREER FOCUS

The communication skills you need to launch a successful career may be one of the most tangible benefits of taking this course. We are committed to making this introductory communication course relevant to your future career by offering a safe environment for you to explore career decisions and see how communication plays a role in all career choices and in all careers.

Each chapter concludes with a special two-page **CAREER** feature, complete with information and activities to help you find your own road to success. The career spread highlights three career fields: business, education, and healthcare. *MyCommunicationLab*, the online website for this text (www.mycommunicationlab.com; access code required), includes an electronic version of the career-related activities in these three fields as well as activities for students wishing to pursue careers in psychology/counseling and the STEM fields of science, technology, engineering, and math.

CONNECTING TO
activities allow you to apply your newly learned communication skills.

31

N AND YOUR CAREER

late the information in this chapter directly to your career. Each chapter
 section containing: a *Spotlight on* feature that takes a current look at a
 relates to the specific fields of business, education, and healthcare; a
ature that relates communication skills from the chapter to success in the
Connecting to feature that includes specific activities to further expand your
e same three fields. Whether you are interested in one of these fields or
 of the products and services of these fields, these features and activities
.

CONNECTING TO . . . BUSINESS

Are you considering a career in business? Surveys continue to rank communication skills as the most important skills for workplace success (*Job Outlook* 2008). Success depends on employees who can effectively communicate. Run a computer search on a college database like EBSCOhost or LexisNexis or even Google with search words like *engineering and oral communication skills* to find sample articles.

ACTIVITY The important role that ethics plays in business communication and technology has raised difficult ethical questions. Answer either **yes** or **no** to the following ethics questions and discuss your answers in small groups.

1. Is it wrong to use company e-mail for personal reasons? YES/NO
2. Is it wrong to use office equipment to help children/spouse do schoolwork? YES/NO
3. Is it wrong to play computer games on office equipment during the workday? YES/NO
4. Is it wrong to use office equipment to do Internet shopping? YES/NO
5. Is it unethical to blame an error you made on a technological glitch? YES/NO
6. Is it unethical to visit pornographic Web sites using office equipment? YES/NO
7. Is a $50 gift to a boss unacceptable? YES/NO
8. Is it OK to accept a $200 pair of football tickets? YES/NO
9. Can you accept a $75 prize won at a raffle at a supplier's conference? YES/NO
10. Is it wrong to take sick days when you aren't really ill? YES/NO

*Adapted from a *Wall Street Journal* Workplace-Ethics Quiz (1999).

MUNICATION SKILLS

TION

er in which level of education
ide to work—elementary, middle
high school, or college—effective
nication skills are part of what it
o be a successful teacher. Since
e had teachers who were both
ve and effective role models,
w firsthand the importance of
nication.
ghout this text, we will be spot-
how specific concepts or skills
ch chapter apply to communi-
 education. For example, re-
rs have found that when
rs use *immediacy behaviors*
and nonverbal behaviors that
e feelings of closeness), stu-
ot only have a better attitude
the classroom but actually learn
ntly more (Menzel & Carrell,
[See more about this concept
ter 5.]

HEALTHCARE

No matter where you work in the healthcare field, communication skills are essential for success in your work. In addition to communicating with patients and their family members, you will be interacting with co-workers and professionals from other health areas, with superiors and subordinates, and with people in other healthcare organizations involved in your patient's care.

Throughout this text, we will be spotlighting how specific concepts or skills from each chapter apply to communication in healthcare. For example, Sharf (1984) found that the use of *medical jargon* by healthcare professionals often interferes with patients' ability to understand the scope of their health problems and the side effects that may accompany their treatments. [You will learn more about this type of verbal encoding in Chapter 4.]

CONNECTING TO . . . EDUCATION

Are you considering a career in education? You have had exposure to excellent educators and effective communicators who can serve as models for your own teaching career if you are interested in one. Communication skills are part of what it means to be a successful teacher. From the manner in which you deliver information to the relationships you are able to form with your students, you will be called upon to use a wide variety of communication skills every day.

ACTIVITY

Meet in a small group with other students who are planning careers in teaching or are interested in teaching.

- Discuss communication skills that you consider to be important for effective teaching and communication behaviors that you consider to be undesirable. Be as specific as possible.

- As a group, identify the top five "effective" behaviors and the five most "ineffective" communication behaviors. Be prepared to report these to the class or to write about them if your teacher asks you to.

CONNECTING TO . . . HEALTHCARE

Are you considering a career in healthcare? Healthcare is a career area that will be in great demand for the foreseeable future due to the aging of our population and new jobs from advanced technologies. Even people who expect to work in accounting, law, marketing, and other business-oriented fields may find themselves employed by a healthcare organization.

ACTIVITY Meet with a group of other students who are planning careers in healthcare and do the following:

- Take turns sharing stories (health narratives) about your own experiences in healthcare settings.
- Think about an instance in which you have interacted with a healthcare professional. In what ways were the communication behaviors of the health professional effective or ineffective?

- If the communication was effective, what specific behaviors of the healthcare professional helped to create that outcome?
- If the communication was ineffective, where was the *noise*? How could you reframe your experience from the healthcare professional's perspective?

▶ Log onto MyCommunicationLab.com to access Connecting to Psychology and Connecting to Science, Technology, Engineering, and Math—both with related activities.

S WANT!

uirement
that a
e curricula.
e highly
er, Gray,

candi-
founda-
s (*Jobs*

majors
s for the
ure:
onal rela-
g.

Whether you will be taking this one course or will decide to major or minor in communication, learning and applying the theories and skills presented in this text and in class discussions will benefit you in your professional life. In each chapter of this text you will find a *Career Moment* box that will highlight how the skills in that chapter are especially related to particular careers in which you may be interested.

Law is only one of many professions where communication skills are essential.

GAINING COMMUNICATION COMPETENCE

Being instructors ourselves, we appreciate the importance of a textbook that is well organized and written with effectively designed resources for both instructors and students. Meaningful and researched activities for both individual and group participation, both self-directed and instructor-assigned, are essential in a good textbook. *Communicating for Success* meets all these requirements and more. At the beginning of each chapter, two-part **LEARNING OBJECTIVES** are posed as questions and cover concepts that will be presented as well as skills and outcomes that students should be able to demonstrate after studying the material. These learning objectives and skills are in sync with the standards established by the National Communication Association (www.natcom.org), various state guidelines, accepted professional standards, and individual communication professors.

LEARNING **OBJECTIVES**

1.1 What are the basic terms in the definition of communication, why is each so important, and what are the types of communication contexts included in this course?

1.2 What are the differences between the action, interaction, and transaction models of communication?

1.3 What are the elements of the transaction communication model, how does each work, and what are the resulting communication principles?

1.4 How do culture, gender, technology, and ethics affect our communication successes or failures?

1.5 What are the basic communication competencies and skills that can be gained from a communication course and what specific benefits result from studying communication?

1.6 What communication skills covered in this chapter relate specifically to your career (see highlighted fields of business, education, and healthcare)?

After studying this chapter you should be able to . . .
- Identify context and account for the effect of context on daily communication.
- Identify the elements of the basic com and recognize when each is used effe
- Pinpoint the competencies of an effec and realize the role of culture, gender, ethics on communication effectivenes
- Reframe situations from others' persp one source of noise in personal intera

CHAPTER

The **OBJECTIVES** are numbered which makes it easy for you to locate the specific material in the text and identify the competencies taught in the course.

These **OBJECTIVES** appear again, one at a time, in the margin when that topic is being discussed.

Communication Defined

Definitions are used to clarify ideas, concepts, and words. Although you use communication every day and may think there is no need to define the concept, a simple definition shows its complexity and the difficulties involved in communicating successfully. According to *Webster's New World Dictionary, third edition*, the word *communicate* is derived from the Latin word *communicare* which means "to impart, share, to make common." Building on this definition, in this book we will define **communication** as the transactional process by which people, interacting in a particular context, negotiate the meanings of verbal and nonverbal symbols in order to achieve shared understanding. Embedded in this definition are a number of terms that have important implications for understanding the communication process—transactional process, context, negotiated meaning, and shared understanding. Let's look at each of these in more detail.

LEARNING **OBJECTIVE**

1.1 What are the basic terms in the definition of communication, why is each so important, and what are the types of communication contexts included in this course?

Following each major section in the chapter is an exercise called **APPLY WHAT YOU KNOW**, which involves thinking critically about how the material relates to specific ideas or situations involving communication.

APPLY **WHAT YOU KNOW**
COMMUNICATION COMPETENCIES AND BENEFITS

Apply what you know about communication competencies and benefits by answering the following:

- Think of an attempt at communication that went wrong. Briefly describe what happened.

- Explain which communication competency discussed earlier was likely missing and responsible for the misunderstanding or communication problem.

- Which communication benefit would make the greatest change in your life? And why?

CHAPTER SUMMARY

Understanding the basic communication process is the first step toward becoming a competent communicator. You can determine your knowledge of the communication process by checking the skills and learning objectives presented in this chapter.

Summary of **SKILLS**

Check each skill that you now feel qualified to perform:

☐ I can identify context in both its narrow and broad perspectives and account for the effect of context on my daily communication.

☐ I can identify the elements of the basic communication model and recognize those that I use effectively and those that need improvement.

☐ I can pinpoint the competencies of an effective ethics play an important role in communication

☐ I can "reframe" situations from others' perspectiv interactions that I plan to correct.

> At the end of each chapter, a **SUMMARY OF LEARNING SKILLS** and **OUTCOMES** enables you to check the extent to which you have achieved the learning objectives and skills for the chapter.

Summary of LEARNING **OUTCOMES**

1.1 *What are the basic terms in the definition of communication, why is each so important, and what are the types of communication contexts included in this course?*

• Communication is defined as a transactional process by which people, interacting in a particular context, negotiate the meanings of verbal and nonverbal symbols in order to achieve shared understanding.

• The basic terms include transactional process, context (from a broad and narrow perspective), verbal and nonverbal symbols, and shared understanding.

• Each of these terms represents an important part of the communication process. Without terms for each component, it would be difficult to think about and discuss communication or identify the communication components needing improvement in our own communication.

• Types of communication contexts of special interest in this course include intrapersonal, interpersonal, group, organizational, public, and mass communication contexts.

• Determine your confidence levels by taking McCroskey's PRCA-24 survey in the *Developing Skills* feature in this chapter.

1.2 *What are the differences between the action, interaction, and transaction models of communication?*

• The action model views the communication process as a linear, or one-way, transmission of messages beginning with the sender and ending with the receiver; it does not involve feedback.

• The interaction model views communication as a circular process and involves feedback and frame of reference.

• The transaction model believes that both communicators create meaning simultaneously rather than in a linear or circular fashion and adds context to the model. It is the transaction model that gives the most complete view of communication.

1.3 *What are the elements of the transaction communication model, how does each work, and what are the resulting communication principles?*

• The elements of the transaction model include the sender/receiver (or Person A/B), the message, encoding/decoding, frame of reference, code, channel, feedback, context, and noise.

• A description of how each element of the transaction model works can be found on pages 13–17.

Theory Practical feature on page 20. Additional principles include that communicators have unique frames of reference; make sure their codes are congruent; use feedback to indicate how messages are received; and do their best to control the context.

1.4 *How do culture, gender, technology, and ethics affect our communication successes or failures?*

• The values, beliefs, attitudes, rules, and norms shared by the peoples of a particular culture tend to differ from culture to culture and can affect communication success or failure. Major cultural differences discussed include the individualistic/collectivistic distinction, the high-context/low-context distinction, and ethnocentrism.

• Gender differences, such as instrumental/expressive preferences, can affect communication success.

• When technology is a lean medium carrying only one communication code (as e-mail does), it has a greater chance of failure; however, when technology is a rich medium (such as television), it has a greater chance of success.

• People who are not ethical and do not follow a system of moral principles that governs their conduct when communicating with others are more likely to experience communication failure.

1.5 *What are the basic communication competencies and skills that can be gained from a communication course and what specific benefits result from studying communication?*

• Competent communicators do each of the following: accept personal responsibility for their communication behavior; are ethical; are able to adapt their communication to varied situations and, therefore, possess cognitive complexity and perspective taking; use verbal and nonverbal symbols effectively; use effective interpersonal skills; create and maintain successful relationships; are effective team participants and leaders; and are effective listeners.

• There are many benefit skills, including increase participation, improved sional success, and imp

1.6 *What communication skills covered in this ch specifically to yo ness, education,*

Spotlight on tures highlight business, edu

> Each chapter includes a list of **KEY TERMS** along with a page reference where it is discussed in the chapter.

> A **GLOSSARY** at the end of the book includes definitions for all key terms.

proval toward a person, idea, or an event. Speaker are especially interested in audience attitudes towa the topic, the speaker, and the event

Attribution How we explain the events in our lives in an attempt to control and understand the future

Attribution theory A theory that describes how the ical listener processes information and uses it to explain behaviors of self and others

Avoiding stage The fourth stage of relationship deter ration, which is usually brief and involves limited communication with no depth or breath; face-to-f communication is averted when possible

Audience-centered Focusing on the audience membe and whether they are understanding rather than or yourself and the impression you are making

Audience demographics Those bits of information th constitute the statistical characteristics of the audienc

Authoritarian leader One who essentially makes the decisions and imposes them upon the group

Basic design principles Contrast, repetition, alignme and proximity that will improve the appearance, cl ity, and professionalism of all types of text and graphic visual aids

Begging the question A flaw in reason that occurs if you try to prove that a claim is true by using the cl

KEY TERMS

action model	p. 11	ethics	p. 25	interpersonal communication	p. 7	psychological noise	p. 19
androgynous	p. 23	ethnocentrism	p. 23	intrapersonal communication	p. 7	public communication	p. 7
channel	p. 15	expressive communication	p. 23	lean medium channel	p. 24	receiver	p. 13
co-culture	p. 21	external noise	p. 18	low-context cultures	p. 22	reframe	p. 28
collectivistic cultures	p. 22	feedback	p. 16			rich medium channel	p. 24
communication	p. 5	frame of reference	p. 14	mass communication	p. 8	rules	p. 18
computer mediated communication	p. 24	gender	p. 23	message	p. 14	self-monitoring	p. 28
context	p. 6	group communication	p. 7	models	p. 11	semantic noise	p. 19
Coordinated Management of Meaning Theory (CMM)	p. 21	high-context cultures	p. 22	negotiated meaning	p. 8	sender	p. 13
culture	p. 21	individualistic cultures	p. 22	noise	p. 18	sex	p. 23
decoding	p. 14	instrumental communication	p. 23	nonverbal code	p. 15	symbols	p. 8
dyad	p. 7	interaction model	p. 12	norms	p. 18	transaction model	p. 12
encoding	p. 14	internal noise	p. 19	organizational communication	p. 7	transactional process	p. 5
environment	p. 6			physiological noise	p. 19	verbal code	p. 15

BALANCE OF SKILLS AND THEORY

When we first began teaching we soon learned two things—we loved teaching and we were excited by the field of communication. Now, years later, we still love teaching a subject that has such application to people in all phases of their lives. People aren't born with good communication skills; they learn them by observing the successes of others and through practice and hard work.

We also recognize that learning communication skills is only part of what makes up the heart and soul of the study of communication. Understanding the theory upon which the skills are built will enrich your learning and give you the big picture. Therefore, *Communicating for Success* offers unique theory and skills features in each chapter to give you a balanced understanding of communication.

209

INDIVIDUAL VERSUS GROUP DECISIONS

DEVELOPING SKILLS
HOW TO ORGANIZE A SERVICE-LEARNING PROJECT

musts and *wants* with the wants ranked in importance. In Step 4, you will generate possible solutions (projects)—cleaning up the park could be one of them. Then in Step 5, you will apply the criteria to select the best project.
- *Get permission* from the community organization in charge as well as your professor and college volunteer department and plan steps to meet any requirements.
- *Actively participate* by completing the project (in this case, cleaning up the park).
- *Analyze what occurred and what your group did* (take pictures to show in a final PowerPoint presentation to the class).
- *Share your results* with the park service and/or community, possibly suggesting solutions for keeping the park clean.
- *Ask the community organization in charge to evaluate your group's project* and send the evaluation to your professor. A simple evaluation form will include three or four questions on a five-point continuum. Questions could

Sheila and her group members aren't the only ones uncertain about service-learning projects. Volunteerism and service learning are often confused. The National Commission on Service-Learning offers this definition ("What Is," 2004): "Service-learning is a teaching and learning approach that integrates community service with academic study to enrich learning, teach civic responsibility, and strengthen communities."

It's important to realize that service learning is not a volunteer program where individuals from a class or campus complete a certain number of hours of volunteer work. Volunteerism is great, but it is not service learning. In other words, when students pick up trash in a park along a riverbed, they are volunteering and providing community service—but this is not service-learning. To make the park project into a service-learning project for a communication course, your group would need to do some or all of the following:
- *Use the group problem-solving process* discussed later in this chapter (see pp. 218–227) to select a project (possibly the park project) and organize it. For example, in Step 3, your group would list and rank criteria considered important in picking a service-learning project. Sample criteria might include selecting a project that: fits within the time and resources of team members, will be fun, provides a benefit to people in the community (nation, or world), is legal, is approved by the professor and campus officials, and so on. Then the criteria will be grouped into

DEVELOPING SKILLS boxes present a variety of interesting and helpful ideas for extending learning beyond the concepts contained in the text material.

298

SELECTING A TOPIC AND GATHERING SUPPORTING MATERIALS **CHAPTER 11**

DEVELOPING **SKILLS**
HOW TO AVOID PLAGIARISM

With so many plagiarism cases in every field today, it may be that people are just not clear on what plagiarism really is. **Plagiarism** is using the ideas or words of another person (whether from a print or online source) without giving credit. Even if you cite a source, if you use the information verbatim without using quotation marks to indicate the quoted content, it is still plagiarism. A survey of medical students by Rennie and Crosby (2001) found that 56 percent of them admitted that they had used information copied/pasted from another source word-for-word and, although they listed the reference, did not use quotation marks around the copied information. Without the quotation marks, you are saying to the reader that the words are your own. Changing one or two words does not qualify as a paraphrase either—it is still plagiarism. You may have access through your college to online software such as *Turnitin.com* that allows students to check for plagiarism in speech outlines and written materials before submitting them.

In case you are not clear on what plagiarism is and what it is not, take a look at a portion of a student's outline on President Ronald Reagan's First Inaugural Address in 1980. The student was having so many problems keeping plagiarism out of her outline that we took one of her actual sources and prepared several versions of it to help her and her classmates identify plagiarism (Hamilton, 2007). Consider which of the following speaker versions are plagiarized and which are not. Before you look at the actual answers, compare your answers with those of a classmate.

Actual source material: "More than anything else, it was Reagan's exceptional communication skills that enabled him to gain control of the political agenda and change the temperature of the time" (Giuliano, 2004, p. 46).

Speaker versions (from speech outline):
A. It was Reagan's outstanding communication skills that allowed him to gain control of the political agenda and change the temperature of the time (Giuliano, 2004).
❏ Plagiarized   ❏ Not plagiarized

B. I've read several of Reagan's speeches, and I believe that it was Reagan's amazing communication skills that allowed him to gain control of the political agenda and change the temperature of the time.

D. Reagan's communication skills are well known and it is those skills "that enabled him to gain control of the political agenda and change the temperature of the time" (Giuliano, 2004, p. 46).
❏ Plagiarized   ❏ Not plagiarized

E. Reagan managed to stay on top of the political scene by using outstanding communication skills
❏ Plagiarized   ❏ Not plagiarized

APPLY **WHAT YOU KNOW**
GROUPS AND SERVICE-LEARNING PROJECTS

Apply what you know about groups and service-learning projects by completing the following activities:
- Brainstorm a list of criteria (guidelines) that your group could use in evaluating which service-learning project to select if assigned one by your professor: for example, "a project that

We also take seriously the value of helping you to understand how scholars contribute to our understanding of communication through the development of useful theories. Therefore, each chapter includes a feature oriented toward **MAKING THEORY PRACTICAL**, in which an important theory that informs our understanding of the material in that chapter is presented in an interesting way and shows you that theory has practical application to your everyday life.

MAKING THEORY **PRACTICAL**
COORDINATED MANAGEMENT OF MEANING THEORY

If a close friend knows that you have been ill or experiencing stressful life circumstances, his "How are you?" might be construed as an expression of concern. According to CMM, this is because there are many levels of meaning that we consider when making sense out of a particular situation or context:

• Our *self-concept*—view of self in this situation;

• The *relationship* with the other person;

• The specific *episode* where the conversation takes place such as an interview, a personal conversation, or polite conversation made in passing;

• The meaning of the *speech act*—was it a compliment, an insult, just information, etc.;

> Each chapter includes a special
> **MAKING THEORY PRACTICAL** feature
> that presents an important theory
> in an interesting way and shows
> you how theory can be applied
> to your everyday life.

When you pass an acquaintance in the hall as you are going to class, your conversation probably goes something like this:

• "Hey! How are you?"

• "I'm fine. How are you?"

• "Fine, thanks."

Have you ever stopped to think about why you do not interpret "How are you?" to be a request for information about your physical health or psychological state? How do you and your conversational partner know how to interpret this exchange?

Theorists
Communication scholars Barnett Pearce and Vernon Cronen developed the **Coordinated Management of Meaning Theory** (CMM) to explain how people create, coordinate, and manage meaning-making in conversations with each other. The theory focuses on the "rules" we follow when sending messages to others and when interpreting messages that we receive:

• *Constitutive rules* are those that enable us to understand what other persons are likely to mean by their choices of verbal or nonverbal symbols.

• *Regulative rules* guide us toward appropriate behaviors for the situation.

Levels of Meaning
Sometimes "How are you?" really is a request for information about how you are feeling physically or psychologically.

MAKING THEORY **PRACTICAL**
LISTENING STYLES PROFILE

• *Action-oriented listeners* are interested in organized, structured presentations. They want the purpose spelled out clearly and accurately and are interested in what actions are recommended because they like to do something with the information they hear.

• *Content-oriented listeners* revel in details, facts, and evidence and are very concerned with accuracy of the facts presented. They are more interested in the message than the message giver.

• *Time-oriented listeners* hate to waste time. They aren't interested in details but instead want a quick, to-the-point, "sound bite" approach to the message. Time is money to them, and they don't want to waste it.

When you listen to others, whether at a formal presentation or informally with colleagues, family, or friends, are you aware of your listening style? Are you more *people-*, *action-*, *content-*, or *time-oriented*? Here's a clue—which of the following thoughts sound more like you?

• "Great. I really relate to that personal example!"

• "So, what's the bottom line—am I supposed to guess the purpose?"

• "Now this is what I like—details!"

• "I don't have all day—get to the point."

Original Theorists
The Listening Styles Profile (LSP-16) developed by Kitty Watson, Larry Barker, and James Weaver (1995) was revised by Barker and Watson in 2000. The LSP is not actually called a theory although it has many of the characteristics of a theory. According to Littlejohn and Foss (2008), communication theories "provide a set of useful tools for seeing the everyday processes and experiences of communication through new lenses" (p. 3). The researchers found that it is possible to divide our listening styles into four significantly different types and that 60 percent of people prefer listening with a single style (Weaver, Richendoller, & Kirtley, 1995).

Listening Styles (Watson, et al.)
• *People-oriented listeners* are relationship-oriented. They pay attention to people's feelings and emotions and look for personal information. They are interested in discovering common ground between themselves and the speaker.

PRACTICAL USES
Being able to identify your own listening styles will help you understand why you have problems listening to certain types of messages and allow you to adapt to situations that are not ideal for your preferred listening style. For example, a content-oriented listener will find it difficult to pay attention to a people-oriented speaker giving personal examples rather than detailed and documented facts.

The Listening Styles Profile also gives us a practical way of identifying and responding to the listening styles of others and, thereby, improving our communication with them. For example, if you know you will be speaking with a time-oriented listener, mention that you know the person has time constraints and then make sure to begin with the summary followed by supporting reasons—brief and to-the-point. On the other hand, if you know that the listener is more people-oriented, make sure to establish a common ground by offering personal information and showing you care about the listener's feelings. In other words, what type of information is appropriate to convey may vary, depending on the listening styles of others. This is one reason that effective speakers use a variety of supporting materials in an attempt to relate to everyone in the audience.

Source: Watson, K., Barker, L., & Weaver, J. (1995). The listening styles profile (LSP-16): Development and validation of an instrument to assess four listening styles. *International Journal of Listening, 9*(1), 1–13.

PROBLEM–SOLUTION APPROACH

We use a problem–solution approach to learning to help you see the connection between the communication situations you encounter as a part of everyday life and what you learn about communication in this course. As you read the chapter you are challenged to analyze a communication scenario in light of the insights you have just gained.

SCENARIO

The semester had barely begun, and already Blanca was having doubts about her ability to succeed in college. She realized that a significant part of the problem was undoubtedly due to the "culture shock" she was experiencing. She was excited to have the opportunity to study in the United States, especially because she was planning a career in international business. But things were quite different here than they were at home. Even though she had always considered Mexico City to be very cosmopolitan, and even though she spoke fluent English, Blanca was puzzled by how her American peers behaved.

She was especially confused about how men and women talked to each other in social settings. There was a level of familiarity in the way they interacted that seemed inappropriate, especially when they weren't even close friends. She was anxious about a LAN party Julie was holding in their dorm room on Tuesday evening—all she knew was that she should bring her laptop and that a group of men and women would be playing a computer game together on a local area network (LAN). Even though she enjoyed gaming, Blanca had never been to a LAN party and was worried about how to interact with Julie's friends, especially the men.

Her relationship with her roommate was also troubling. Julie was certainly nice enough and was very considerate in helping to keep their dormitory room neat and clean. But several times Blanca had made a suggestion about how they might decorate their room, and each time Julie had flatly said, "No, I don't like that." By contrast, when Julie had asked Blanca her opinion about the bedspreads she had chosen, Blanca had said, "Those are very nice," even though she found the dark color depressing. Overall, she found herself becoming uncharacteristically withdrawn as she tried to figure out how she could adapt to the way people communicated in her new home.

Julie had noticed that Blanca seemed to have lost some of her excitement and enthusiasm since they first met as they moved into their dorm room. She had been ha[...] being paired with an international stude[...] when she discovered that Blanca's fluen[...] they wouldn't have the communication [...] about. Julie wondered if Blanca was just homesick or was ha[...] if Julie had done something to offend her. They certainly ha[...] making decisions about how to decorate their room; she wa[...] had similar tastes in color and design. She couldn't think of [...] might have done; she had treated Blanca just as she would [...] wanted to make her relationship with Blanca work and hope[...] Blanca make friends and enjoy her experience in America. M[...] help Blanca feel more a part of the group. Yes, Julie thought[...] just what we need.

> Each chapter begins with a true-to-life SCENARIO that illustrates a common communication problem that may seem familiar to you.

> You are prompted to think about the problem as you read.

Julie and Blanca are having some communication difficulties, aren't they? As you read this chapter, look for specific communication concepts that would be helpful in analyzing interactions between Julie and Blanca. Pay particular attention to how culture, gender, ethics, and technology may be affecting their communication. See if you can identify two communication goals for each person that would go a long way in helping them improve the situation.

SOLVE IT NOW! ⟩ P. 34

> Each chapter ends with a SOLVE IT NOW feature that invites you to apply what you have learned in solving the scenario's problem.

SOLVE IT NOW!

Taking into consideration all that you learned about communication from this chapter, how would you analyze the communication difficulties between Julie and Blanca in our opening scenario?*

- Which two or three *communication concepts* if known by Julie and Blanca would help them more accurately communicate with each other?

- Where in the *communication model* are Julie's and Blanca's difficulties occurring? Select and explain at least two locations for each person (such as *noise*).

- Which of the special concepts—*culture, gender, ethics,* or *technology*—do you think are causing the most communication difficulties between Julie and Blanca? Why?

- Which *communication goals* would you recommend that Julie and Blanca implement that would go a long way in helping them improve their situation? Why?

*(Check your answers with those located in MyCommunicationLab, Scenario Analysis for Chapter 1)

LOOKING AT TECHNOLOGY, GENDER, CULTURE, AND ETHICS

Communicating for Success approaches the study of technology, gender, culture, and ethics in communication by integrating these topics within the appropriate discussions in each chapter. Unlike many texts that offer an isolated chapter on culture and gender, *Communicating for Success* introduces these themes in Chapter 1 and explores their importance throughout each of the remaining chapters. Because concepts have been introduced early in the course, you are more able to integrate and apply them to your own life and in a variety of communication contexts.

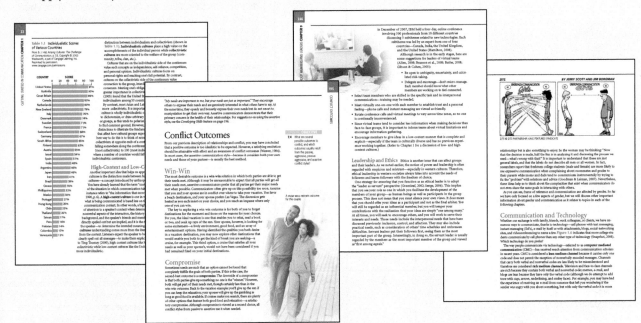

SAMPLE SPEECHES ON VIDEO

Annotated sample speeches illustrate the concepts and skills covered in the public speaking chapters. Video versions of these sample speeches are available on www.mycommunicationlab.com.

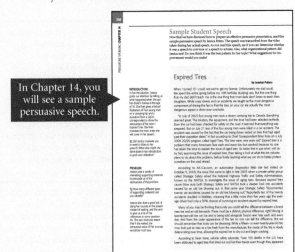

In Chapter 14, you will see a sample persuasive speech.

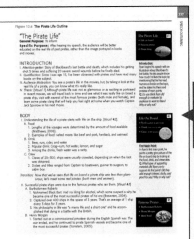

In Chapter 12, you will see a detailed format outline that shows the various parts of the outline and how they function.

Resources in Print and Online

NAME OF SUPPLEMENT	AVAILABLE IN PRINT	AVAILABLE ONLINE	INSTRUCTOR OR STUDENT SUPPLEMENT	DESCRIPTION
Instructor's Manual (ISBN: 0205757359)	✗	✗	Instructor Supplement	Prepared by Pamela Hayward, Augusta State University, and Leonard M. Edmonds, Arizona State University, the Instructor's Manual includes a wealth of resources for each chapter. There is an annotated Instructional Outline, which can be used for organizing and developing lectures. Discussion Questions, designed to stimulate class discussion, can also be used for assignments, essay questions, or as review questions for an exam (sample answers are provided). In addition, there are engaging In-Class/Out-of-Class Activities and suggestions for Additional Resources. Available for download at www. pearsonhighered.com/irc (access code required).
Test Bank (ISBN: 0205757243)	✗	✗	Instructor Supplement	The Test Bank, prepared by Shellie Michael, Volunteer State Community College, consists of more than 600 thoroughly reviewed assessments. Each chapter contains a blend of multiple choice, completion, matching sequences, and essay questions. Each question is referenced by a correct answer/grading criteria (for essay questions only), page reference, learning objective, and skill designation. Available for download at www.pearsonhighered.com/irc (access code required).
MyTest (ISBN: 0205737307)		✗	Instructor Supplement	This flexible, online test generating software includes all of the questions found in the printed Test Bank, allowing instructors to create their own personalized exams. Instructors can also edit any or all of the existing test questions and even add new questions. Other special features of this program include random generation of test questions, creation of alternate versions of the same test, scrambling of question sequence, and test preview before printing. Available at www.pearsonmytest. com (access code required).
PowerPoint™ Presentation Package (ISBN: 0205757367)		✗	Instructor Supplement	This text-specific package, prepared by Karen Wolf, Suffolk Community College, provides a basis for your lecture with PowerPoint™ slides for each chapter of the book. Each presentation is consistent with the guidelines for visual aids presented in Chapter 13. Available for download at www.pearsonhighered.com/irc (access code required).
Pearson Allyn & Bacon Introduction to Communication Video Library	✗		Instructor Supplement	Pearson Allyn & Bacon's Introduction to Communication Video Library contains a range of videos from which adopters can choose. The videos feature a variety of topics and scenarios for communication foundations, interpersonal communication, small group communication, and public speaking. Please contact your Pearson representative for details and a complete list of videos and their contents to choose which would be most useful for your course. Some restrictions apply.
Lecture Questions for Clickers for Introduction to Communication (ISBN: 0205547230)		✗	Instructor Supplement	Prepared by Keri Moe, El Paso Community College, this assortment of questions and activities covering culture, listening, interviewing, public speaking, interpersonal conflict and more is presented in a user-friendly PowerPoint™. These slides will help liven up your lectures and can be used along with the Personal Response System to get students more involved in class discussion. Available for download at www.pearsonhighered.com/irc (access code required).
Digital Media Archive for Communication, Version 3.0 (ISBN:0205437095)	✗		Instructor Supplement	The Digital Media Archive CD-ROM contains electronic images of charts, graphs, tables, and figures, along with media elements such as video and related web links. These media assets are fully customizable to use with our pre-formatted PowerPoint™ outlines or to import into the instructor's own lectures (available for Windows and Mac).
A Guide for New Teachers of Introduction to Communication: Interactive Strategies for Teaching Communication, Fourth Edition (ISBN: 0205750001)	✗	✗	Instructor Supplement	Prepared by Susanna G. Porter, Kennesaw State University, with a new chapter on using MyCommunicationLab by Heather Dillon, Urbana, Illinois, this guide is designed to help new teachers effectively teach the introductory communication course. It is full of first-day-of-class tips, great teaching ideas, a guide to Pearson resources, and sample activities and assignments. Available at www.pearsonhighered.com/irc (access code required).

NAME OF SUPPLEMENT	AVAILABLE IN PRINT	AVAILABLE ONLINE	INSTRUCTOR OR STUDENT SUPPLEMENT	DESCRIPTION
Preparing Visual Aids for Presentations, Fifth Edition (ISBN:020561115X)	✗		Student Supplement	Prepared by Dan Cavanaugh, this 32-page visual booklet provides a host of ideas for using today's multimedia tools to improve presentations, including suggestions for planning a presentation, guidelines for designing visual aids and storyboarding, and a walkthrough that shows how to prepare a visual display using PowerPoint™ (available for purchase).
Pearson Allyn & Bacon Introduction to Communication Study Site (Open access)		✗	Student Supplement	The Pearson Allyn & Bacon Introduction to Communication Study Site features practice tests, learning objectives, and weblinks. The site is organized around the major topics typically covered in the Introduction to Communication course. These topics have also been correlated to the table of contents for your book (available at www.abintrocommunication.com).
Public Speaking in the Multicultural Environment, Second Edition (ISBN:0205265111)	✗		Student Supplement	Prepared by Devorah A. Lieberman, Portland State University, this booklet helps students learn to analyze cultural diversity within their audiences and adapt their presentations accordingly (available for purchase).
The Speech Outline: Outlining to Plan, Organize, and Deliver a Speech (ISBN:032108702X)	✗		Student Supplement	Prepared by Reeze L. Hanson and Sharon Condon of Haskell Indian Nations University, this workbook includes activities, exercises, and answers to help students develop and master the critical skill of outlining (available for purchase).
Multicultural Activities Workbook Prince (ISBN:0205546528)	✗		Student Supplement	Prepared by Marlene C. Cohen and Susan L. Richardson of George's Community College, Maryland, this workbook is filled with hands-on activities that help broaden the content of speech classes to reflect diverse cultural backgrounds. The checklists, surveys, and writing assignments all help students succeed in speech communication by offering experiences that address a variety of learning styles (available for purchase).
Speech Preparation Workbook (ISBN: 013559569X)	✗		Student Supplement	Prepared by Jennifer Dreyer and Gregory H. Patton of San Diego State University, this workbook takes students through the stages of speech creation–from audience analysis to writing the speech–and includes guidelines, tips, and easy to fill-in pages (available for purchase).
Study Card for Introduction to Speech Communication (ISBN: 0205474381)	✗		Student Supplement	Colorful, affordable, and packed with useful information, the Pearson Allyn & Bacon Study Cards make studying easier, more efficient, and more enjoyable. Course information is distilled down to the basics, helping students quickly master the fundamentals, review a subject for understanding, or prepare for an exam. Because they're laminated for durability, they can be kept for years to come and pulled out whenever students need a quick review (available for purchase).
VideoLab CD-ROM (ISBN:0205561616)	✗		Student Supplement	This interactive study tool for students can be used independently or in class. It provides digital video of student speeches that can be viewed in conjunction with corresponding outlines, manuscripts, note cards, and instructor critiques. A series of drills to help students analyze content and delivery follows each speech (available for purchase).
MyCommunicationLab		✗	Instructor & Student Supplement	MyCommunicationLab is a state-of-the-art, interactive, and instructive solution for communication courses. Designed to be used as a supplement to a traditional lecture course or to completely administer an online course, MyCommunicationLab combines a Pearson eText, multimedia, video clips, activities, research support, tests and quizzes to completely engage students. See next page for more details.

Designed to amplify a traditional course in numerous ways or to administer a course online, **MyCommunicationLab** for Introductory Communication courses combines pedagogy and assessment with an array of multimedia activities—videos, speech preparation tools, assessments, research support, and multiple newsfeeds—to make learning more effective for all types of students. Now featuring more resources, including a video upload tool, this new release of **MyCommunicationLab** is visually richer and even more interactive than the previous version—a leap forward in design with more tools and features to enrich learning and aid students in classroom success.

TEACHING AND LEARNING TOOLS

Special Content to Enrich The Text: Log on to see suggested solutions to the *Solve It Now!* feature, and answers to the *Apply What You Know* questions. You can also find an electronic version of the career activities for the three highlighted careers (business, education, and healthcare) as well as psychology and the STEM fields (science, technology, engineering, and math).

NEW VERSION! Pearson eText: Identical in content and design to the printed text, a Pearson eText provides students access to their text whenever and wherever they need it. In addition to contextually placed multimedia features in every chapter, our new Pearson eText allows students to take notes and highlight, just like a traditional book.

Videos and Video Quizzes: Interactive videos provide students with the opportunity to watch video clips that portray different communication scenarios, interviews with well-known communication scholars, and sample speeches including both professional and student speeches. Many videos are annotated with critical thinking questions or include short, assignable quizzes that report to the instructor's gradebook.

Self-Assessments: Online self assessments including SCAM, PRCA-24, and assessments that test introversion, shyness, and communication competence, as well as Pre- and Post-tests for every chapter, help students to learn about different communication styles and assess their own. The tests generate a customized study plan for further assessment and focus students on areas in which they need to improve. Instructors can use these tools to show learning over the duration of the course.

UPDATED! MyOutline: MyOutline offers step-by-step guidance for writing an effective outline, along with tips and explanations to help students better understand the elements of an outline and how all the pieces fit together. Outlines that students create can be downloaded to their computer, emailed as an attachment, printed, or saved in the tool for future editing. Instructors can either select from several templates provided or they can create their own outline template for students to use.

UPDATED! **Topic Selector:** This interactive tool helps students get started generating ideas and then narrowing down topics. Our Topic Selector is question-based, rather than drill-down, in order to help students really learn the process of selecting their topic. Once they have determined their topic, students are directed to credible online sources for guidance with the research process.

NEW! **ABC News RSS Feed:** MyCommunicationLab provides an online feed from ABC news, updated hourly, to help students choose and research group assignments and speeches.

NEW! **MySearchLab:** Pearson's MySearchLab™ is the easiest way for students to start a research assignment, speech, or paper. Complete with extensive help on the research process and four databases of credible and reliable source material, MySearchLab ™ helps students quickly and efficiently make the most of their research time.

CUTTING EDGE TECHNOLOGY

NEW! **MediaShare:** With this new video upload tool, students are able to upload group assignments, interpersonal role plays, and speeches for their instructor and classmates to watch (whether face-to-face or online) and provide online feedback and comments at time-stamped intervals. Structured much like a social networking site, MediaShare can help promote a sense of community among students.

NEW! **Audio Chapter Summaries:** Every chapter includes an audio chapter summary, formatted as an MP3 file, perfect for students reviewing material before a test or instructors reviewing material before class.

NEW! **Quick and Dirty Tips Podcast:** Through an agreement with Quick and Dirty Tips, MyCommunicationLab now features a RSS Feed of *The Public Speaker's Quick and Dirty Tips for Improving Your Communication Skills*, which covers topics such as conflict, negotiation, networking, pronunciation, eye contact, overcoming nervousness, interviewing skills, accent modification, and more!

ONLINE ADMINISTRATION

No matter what course management system you use—or if you do not use one at all, but still wish to easily capture your students' grades and track their performance—Pearson has a **MyCommunicationLab** option to suit your needs. Contact one of Pearson's Technology Specialists for more information and assistance.

A **MyCommunicationLab** access code is no additional cost when packaged with selected Pearson Communication texts. To get started, contact your local Pearson Publisher's Representative at www.pearsonhighered.com/replocator.

ACKNOWLEDGMENTS

We would like to thank the following reviewers and focus group participants for their helpful comments and suggestions:

Amy M. Atchley, *Baton Rouge Community College*

Kaylene Barbe, *Oklahoma Baptist University*

Vernita M. Batchelder, *Edison State College*

Jeffery L. Bineham, *St. Cloud State University*

Maryanna Brannan Richardson, *Forsyth Technical Community College*

Ellen B. Bremen, *Highline Community College*

Pam Broyles, *Southern Nazarene University*

Timothy R. Cline, *College of Notre Dame of Maryland*

Alice Crume, *Kent State University*

Lynne Derbyshire, *University of Rhode Island*

Deborah Hatton, *Sam Houston State University*

Pamela A. Hayward, *Augusta State University*

Laura Janusik, *Rockhurst University*

Jean M. Kapinsky, *Northcentral Technical College*

James J. Kimble, *Seton Hall University*

Nancy R. Levin, *Palm Beach Community College*

David Mathes, *South Mountain Community College*

Miriam C. McMullen-Pastrick, *Penn State Erie, The Behrend College*

Shellie Michael, *Volunteer State Community College*

Robert E. Mild, Jr., *Fairmont State University*

Yolanda D. Monroe, *Gadsden State Community College*

Mary Moore, *NorthWest Arkansas Community College*

Kay Mueller, *Des Moines Area Community College*

Tami McCray Olds, *Northern Virginia Community College, Loudoun*

Butch Owens, *Navarro College*

Trudi Peterson, *Monmouth College*

Paul Potter, *Hardin-Simmons University*

Jolinda Ramsey, *Alamo Community College*

Dan Rogers, *Cedar Valley College*

Thomas Ruddick, *Edison Community College*

Michelle Bacino Thiessen, *Rock Valley College*

Sharlene Thompson, *James Madison University*

Rebecca Wolniewicz, *Southwestern College*

The editorial and production teams at Pearson/Allyn & Bacon were very helpful and deserve a special thanks, especially Carol Alper, Senior Development Editor, who held our hands through the entire process as well as Karon Bowers, Editor-in-Chief, Communication; David Kear, Development Manager; Sarah Evertson, Photo Researcher; Sarah Bylund, Permissions Assistant; Sarah D'Stair, Permissions Researcher; Barbara Mack, Project Manager—Production; Dee Josephson, Project Manager—Nesbitt Graphics; Roberta Sherman, Production Supervisor.

We would also like to thank our colleague Debbie Blankenship for her excellent suggestions and ideas and Alma Martinez-Egger for her help with research and activities—thanks, ladies; our student speakers Ryan Elliott, Jessica Peters, and Keith Royal for their excellent speeches available for viewing on MyCommunicationLab, and our many students for using our materials and making helpful suggestions.

Finally, we would like to thank the many talented individuals who prepared the array of supplemental materials listed in the supplements section in this preface. We appreciate their contributions that help to complete this integrated teaching and learning package.

Cheryl Hamilton
Bonnie Creel
Fort Worth, Texas

About the Authors

The authors of *Communicating for Success* are colleagues at Tarrant County College, a large urban college district with an enrollment of more than 47,000 students on five campuses. The authors have taught a wide array of Communication courses to a diverse student population. In addition to their favorite courses—fundamentals, business communication, and public speaking—they have taught more than twenty credit courses including rhetoric and Western civilization, interviewing, leadership training, anxiety reduction, intercultural communication, discussion and small group communication, voice and diction, theatre appreciation, health communication, and graduate persuasion. They have also presented workshops and given presentations on a variety of communication topics to numerous business and community groups including the National Property Management Association and the U.S. Postal Department. Both authors are active in their communities and in various volunteer projects including service-learning projects with their students. In addition, they enjoy mentoring and sharing with colleagues, adjunct teachers, and their many students.

 Cheryl Hamilton received her bachelor's degree in Speech and Drama from Eastern Illinois University in Charleston, Illinois; a master's degree in Interpersonal and Small Group Communication from Purdue University in West Lafayette, Indiana; and a doctorate in Higher Education and College Teaching in 1999 from the University of North Texas in Denton, Texas. In addition to *Communicating for Success,* Professor Hamilton has written two other texts, including *Communicating for Results: A Guide for Business and the Professions*, Ninth Edition and *Essentials of Public Speaking,* Fourth Edition. She has presented over forty papers at professional conventions including the National Communication Association, the Southwest Educational Research Association, and the Western Communication Association. In addition, Professor Hamilton is active in college affairs where she has served on numerous local and district committees, chaired the faculty senate, and served as president of the faculty association. And, of course, Professor Hamilton loves teaching. She has received several teaching awards, including the Chancellor's Award for Exemplary Teaching.

 Bonnie Creel received her bachelor's degree in Speech Education and her masters degree in Speech Communication from Texas Christian University and is currently working on her dissertation to complete her doctorate in Communication from Texas A&M University. Professor Creel specializes in communication for health care professionals and has taught special sections of the basic course for nurses and other healthcare providers. Professor Creel loves teaching and working with students. She has served as coach/coordinator for the College Bowl team on campus. She also was instrumental in developing the Cornerstone Honors Program for the college district and taught multiple courses in the program. In addition to other citations for her teaching, she received the Chancellor's Award for Exemplary Teaching.

Communicating
FOR SUCCESS

1 Getting Started in Communication

CHAPTER SUMMARY 〉 P. 32

LEARNING OBJECTIVES

1.1 What are the basic terms in the definition of communica-tion, why is each so important, and what are the types of communication contexts included in this course?

1.2 What are the differences between the action, interaction, and transaction models of communication?

1.3 What are the elements of the transaction communication model, how does each work, and what are the resulting communication principles?

1.4 How do culture, gender, technology, and ethics affect our communication successes or failures?

1.5 What are the basic communication competencies and skills that can be gained from a communication course and what specific benefits result from studying communication?

1.6 What communication skills covered in this chapter relate specifically to your career (see highlighted fields of busi-ness, education, and healthcare)?

After studying this chapter you should be able to . . .

- Identify context and account for the effect of context on daily communication.
- Identify the elements of the basic communication model and recognize when each is used effectively.
- Pinpoint the competencies of an effective communicator and realize the role of culture, gender, technology, and ethics on communication effectiveness.
- Reframe situations from others' perspectives and identify one source of noise in personal interactions.

SCENARIO

The semester had barely begun, and already Blanca was having doubts about her ability to succeed in college. She realized that a significant part of the problem was undoubtedly due to the "culture shock" she was experiencing. She was excited to have the opportunity to study in the United States, especially because she was planning a career in international business. But things were quite different here than they were at home. Even though she had always considered Mexico City to be very cosmopolitan, and even though she spoke fluent English, Blanca was puzzled by how her American peers behaved.

She was especially confused about how men and women talked to each other in social settings. There was a level of familiarity in the way they interacted that seemed inappropriate, especially when they weren't even close friends. She was anxious about a LAN party Julie was holding in their dorm room on Tuesday evening—all she knew was that she should bring her laptop and that a group of men and women would be playing a computer game together on a local area network (LAN). Even though she enjoyed gaming, Blanca had never been to a LAN party and was worried about how to interact with Julie's friends, especially the men.

Her relationship with her roommate was also troubling. Julie was certainly nice enough and was very considerate in helping to keep their dormitory room neat and clean. But several times Blanca had made a suggestion about how they might decorate their room, and each time Julie had flatly said, "No, I don't like that." By contrast, when Julie had asked Blanca her opinion about the bedspreads she had chosen, Blanca had said, "Those are very nice," even though she found the dark color depressing. Overall, she found herself becoming uncharacteristically withdrawn as she tried to figure out how she could adapt to the way people communicated in her new home.

Julie had noticed that Blanca seemed to have lost some of her excitement and enthusiasm since they first met as they moved into their dorm room. She had been happy to learn that she was being paired with an international student, and especially pleased when she discovered that Blanca's fluency in English meant that they wouldn't have the communication barriers she had worried about. Julie wondered if Blanca was just homesick or was having trouble in a class, or if Julie had done something to offend her. They certainly hadn't had any trouble in making decisions about how to decorate their room; she was glad that she and Blanca had similar tastes in color and design. She couldn't think of anything offensive she might have done; she had treated Blanca just as she would treat any friend. She wanted to make her relationship with Blanca work and hoped that she could help Blanca make friends and enjoy her experience in America. Maybe the LAN party would help Blanca feel more a part of the group. Yes, Julie thought with a smile—this party is just what we need.

Julie and Blanca are having some communication difficulties, aren't they? As you read this chapter, look for specific communication concepts that would be helpful in analyzing interactions between Julie and Blanca. Pay particular attention to how culture, gender, ethics, and technology may be affecting their communication. See if you can identify two communication goals for each person that would go a long way in helping them improve the situation.

SOLVE IT NOW! ⟩ P. 34

Lack of communication can cause problems in all phases of life. How we communicate with those whose ideas differ from ours is something that concerns each of us every day. Like Julie and Blanca in the opening scenario, we all have had times when we failed to communicate. The purpose of this text, *Communicating for Success*, is to explore in detail the many communication difficulties that occur in our personal and career lives and to offer practical goals for solving them. Look for specific application of communication concepts spotlighting the career fields of business, education, and healthcare near the end of each chapter as well as additional career fields included online. You will find this information valuable whether you are planning a career in one of these fields or are a consumer of the services related to these careers. Practical solutions to communication difficulties presented in this text will come not only from research and theory developed by scholars in the communication discipline but also from many other disciplines. Don't be surprised to find your major area of study included as well. Each chapter will end by summarizing specific communication skills that you should feel comfortable using to solve problems and maximize your communication abilities at home and in the workplace.

Communication Defined

Definitions are used to clarify ideas, concepts, and words. Although you use communication every day and may think there is no need to define the concept, a simple definition shows its complexity and the difficulties involved in communicating successfully. According to *Webster's New World Dictionary, third edition*, the word *communicate* is derived from the Latin word *communicare* which means "to impart, share, to make common." Building on this definition, in this book we will define **communication** as the transactional process by which people, interacting in a particular context, negotiate the meanings of verbal and nonverbal symbols in order to achieve shared understanding. Embedded in this definition are a number of terms that have important implications for understanding the communication process—transactional process, context, negotiated meaning, and shared understanding. Let's look at each of these in more detail.

LEARNING OBJECTIVE

1.1 What are the basic terms in the definition of communication, why is each so important, and what are the types of communication contexts included in this course?

Communication Is a Transactional Process

By saying that communication is a *process*, we mean that it is continuous and ongoing. It is not a static or individual event, nor is it the end result of an interaction. It does not start when you open your mouth to speak, and it does not end when you finish speaking. In fact, the process begins before you speak (involving previous history with the other person and assessments of the person's gender, cultural background, position, and so on). It may not involve actual "speaking" at all as in the case of nonverbal communication, and its effects may continue long after the interchange is over (with something said or implied continuing to impact our feelings and actions).

By defining communication as **transactional**, we convey two meanings. First, communication is transactional because it involves an *exchange*—communicators exchange symbols (words, gestures, or vocal tones) to create meaning. Second, communication is transactional because both parties are responsible for the outcome of the interaction, and both are affected by it. When communication is successful, it is not because one party has done something particularly well; it is because both parties have contributed to a satisfactory exchange. When communication is unsuccessful, that, too, is the responsibility of both people, and both are affected by the failure. For example, when you and a friend are exchanging information and ideas, you simultaneously affect each other's knowledge as well as your perceptions of each other and the situation. You also affect how each of you perceives your own personal competence as individuals and human beings. When you think about it, it is awesome to recognize the power that each of us has to influence other people's lives—even their perception of who they are—by the ways we choose to communicate with them.

Communication Occurs in a Context

Our definition of *communication* includes the idea that people engage in interactions within a particular *context*. **Context** refers to the situation in which the communication takes place and affects how we communicate and even the success or failure of our communication. Context may be viewed from either a narrow or a broad perspective:

Taking a narrow perspective, *context* refers to the specific environment or climate in which a communication occurs. Holm (1981) defines **environment** as including "time, place, physical and social surroundings" (p. 22); therefore, environment is neither the actual message nor the communicators; it is what surrounds the communicators. For example, consider your usual style of interacting with your friends. You may prefer to meet in the evenings, possibly in a favorite gathering spot in a dorm where you can dress informally and lounge on your favorite chairs or even stretch out on the carpet. No doubt your conversations are relatively informal, possibly filled with the current slang and nicknames that you have developed for each other. Imagine, however, how the social environment and your communication would change if a guest from out of town or your parents were present in the group one night. When the environment changes, the communication within the context changes.

What constraints would the environment of a space shuttle place on communication?

Taking a broad perspective, *context* refers to the diverse categories of communication usually covered in communication courses such as group communication and public speaking. It is very unlikely that you would use the same style of communication in a group or public speaking context that you used with your friends in the preceding example—a more formal approach is expected. Each of the following broad contexts poses different expectations and affects both the way communication is organized and the way people interact:

- The **intrapersonal** context is "self-talk" communication that occurs within you. Instead of being the least important type of communication, intrapersonal communication is the foundation for all other types. For example, a person with low self-concept and/or high communication anxiety (both based on the intrapersonal context) will have difficulty with other types of communication—especially interpersonal relationships, group interaction, and public speaking. Chapter 2 covers the relationship between self-concept and perception and how both affect your communication with others.

- The **interpersonal** context refers to communication that occurs "between people." Communication scholars generally study interpersonal communication by looking at interactions that occur in **dyads**—two people communicating with each other, such as in a personal relationship and in most interview situations. Chapters 6 and 7 take a detailed look at understanding, developing, and managing interpersonal relationships and the effect self-disclosure and conflict have on such relationships. Effective interviewing from both the interviewee and the interviewer perspective is discussed in Appendix A.

- **Group** communication is yet another context (sometimes referred to as "multiple dyads") in which typically three to seven people interact with each other in order to accomplish a meaningful objective. Group success—whether involving family, friends, or job-related teams—depends on the task, relational, and procedural skills of all members. Chapters 8 and 9 provide a detailed look at successful communication within groups and teams, including participant roles, effective leadership, and the six-step problem-solving process.

- The **organizational** context is a particularly interesting area of study for communication scholars because of its complexity—there are individuals, dyads, and groups communicating with other individuals, dyads, and groups. Dyads account for approximately half of all organizational communication (Panko & Kinney, 1992). In this text, we are interested in the organizational context as it relates to workplace careers. Each chapter connects specific communication skills to careers in business, education, and healthcare, and a special feature called Career Moment offers helpful advice as you plan your future.

- The **public** context, which is represented by oral presentations, is a "one-to-many" situation in which a single speaker addresses a defined audience that might range from fairly small to extremely large. Chapter 5 discusses how to interpret audience feedback. Chapters 10–14 contain specific suggestions on how to organize and research, prepare, practice, and deliver

effective oral presentations. These chapters contain numerous tips to help you deliver a presentation successfully and confidently.

- By contrast, the **mass communication** context is one in which a single individual or company sends a message to a few or thousands of receivers who are not immediately present. Feedback, when it occurs, is often delayed and takes many different forms, such as letters to the editor, votes for a candidate, or even the purchase of various items. Mass communication is a context that has significance for us because it powerfully affects us in our daily lives. Although mass communication falls outside of the scope of this text, computer-mediated communication (CMC), which involves communicating via technology, will be discussed.

In communication, context always matters. Since context is a very important concept in the discussion of communication, you will find it mentioned throughout this text. Whether we view it from a narrow or a broad perspective, the context in which communication occurs has important implications for how the interaction takes place.

Communication Involves Negotiated Meanings of Symbols

Another part of our communication definition states that communicative partners "negotiate the meanings of verbal and nonverbal symbols" they use. A **symbol** is something—such as a word, vocal tone, gesture, or behavior—that represents or stands for something else—such as an idea, concept, or feeling. Symbols can be verbal—such as a spoken word—or nonverbal—such as a gesture or behavior. Whether you are using facial expressions and gestures in a game of charades as you attempt to explain the title of a movie or are discussing a serious problem with a coworker, you are creating meaning by using symbols.

The problem with using symbols is that we don't always recognize the same meanings for them; each of us uses our own background, experiences, and culture in choosing meanings or symbols. Consider the following examples:

- *Example 1*: You may express grief by becoming quiet and introspective. Since your other family members express grief by talking about it, your behavior (which is a symbol) communicates to them that you aren't sharing their grief, and they become angry.

- *Example 2*: Two colleagues in a large company—one from the United States and the other from France—are attending a long, conflict-filled meeting. The American gives the A-OK gesture (which is a symbol) made by forming the forefinger and thumb into a circle not knowing that in France the symbol means you are "worthless—a real zero" (Axtell, 2007).

- *Example 3*: When a chunk of foam flew off the space shuttle *Columbia* during takeoff in the fatal 2003 mission, management labeled it as an "action" (which is a symbol) instead of an "in-flight anomaly," which may have masked the seriousness of the situation (CAIB, 2003, p. 137). To most NASA employees, "action" meant that this incident was not a safety concern because losing some foam during flight was a normal occurrence.

Since symbols usually do not have universally understood meanings, the task for communicators is to *negotiate meaning* for the symbols they use. Just as you may negotiate with a salesperson before settling on a satisfactory price for your new car, communicators, in order to be successful, must be able to negotiate with each other meanings for various symbols in order to accomplish their goal of mutual understanding.

Communication Involves Shared Understanding

The last part of our definition of communication involves "shared understanding"—the ideal goal of communication. Shared understanding simply means that both parties in the process perceive as clearly and as accurately as possible the ideas and emotions that each intends to communicate to the

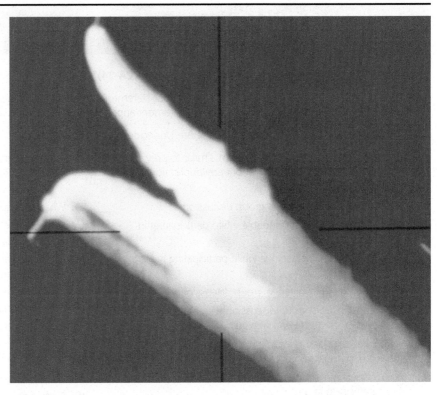

"We are convinced that the management practices overseeing the Space Shuttle Program were as much a cause of the accident as the foam that struck the left wing." (CAIB, 2003, p. 11)

other. This, of course, is not always an easy task. To complicate matters, some people have as their goal that their partner will not merely understand what they are communicating but also agree with their perspective. This is not only difficult; it may not always be desirable. It is true that some communicators do aim at agreement; for example, members of Congress debate issues for the purpose of persuading each other to adopt a favored policy. However, in our relationships with family, friends, and co-workers, there will always be times when it should be acceptable to disagree. In other words, we can "agree to disagree" as long as each has the sense that the other understands his or her perspective. To accomplish this end, symbols must be effectively chosen and their meanings successfully negotiated.

Let's end our definition of *communication* by discussing something that bothers many of us—our level of confidence when communicating. The different contexts discussed above produce different levels of confidence or anxiety for each of us. For example, you might feel confident talking with individuals one-on-one, but feel a high level of anxiety when giving an oral presentation before an audience. If you would like to know which communication contexts cause you anxiety and which instill the most confidence, take the PRCA-24 (Personal Report of Communication Anxiety) by James McCroskey (1982) found on MyCommunicationLab—the Web site that accompanies your text—or in the *Developing Skills* box on p. 10. This survey can be only as accurate as you are honest in answering the questions. Don't answer how you wish you were or how you may have reacted once or twice; instead, answer the way you would typically respond if you found yourself in the context described. Once you have completed the survey, your totals will give you an indication of your anxiety levels in group, meeting, dyadic, and public speaking situations.

DEVELOPING **SKILLS**
HOW TO DETERMINE YOUR ANXIETY/CONFIDENCE LEVEL

Personal Report of Communication Apprehension (PRCA-24)*

Directions: This instrument is composed of twenty-four statements concerning feelings about communicating with other people. Please indicate the degree to which each statement applies to you by marking whether you:

(1) Strongly Agree   (2) Agree   (3) Are Undecided   (4) Disagree   (5) Strongly Disagree

Although many of the statements will seem similar to previous statements, your answers might be different. There are no wrong or right answers. Don't worry about any duplication. Work quickly and honestly. Record your impression of how you see yourself at this point in your life.

_____ 1. I dislike participating in group discussions.

_____ 2. Generally, I am comfortable while participating in a group discussion.

_____ 3. I am tense and nervous while participating in group discussions.

_____ 4. I like to get involved in group discussions.

_____ 5. Engaging in a group discussion with new people makes me tense and nervous.

_____ 6. I am calm and relaxed while participating in a group discussion.

_____ 7. Generally, I am nervous when I have to participate in a meeting.

_____ 8. Usually I am calm and relaxed while participating in meetings.

_____ 9. I am very calm and relaxed when I am called upon to express an opinion at a meeting.

_____ 10. I am afraid to express myself at meetings.

_____ 11. Communicating at meetings usually makes me uncomfortable.

_____ 12. I am very relaxed when answering questions at a meeting.

_____ 13. While participating in a conversation with a new acquaintance, I feel very nervous.

_____ 14. I have no fear of speaking up in conversations.

_____ 15. Ordinarily I am very tense and nervous in conversations.

_____ 16. Ordinarily I am very calm and relaxed in conversations.

_____ 17. While conversing with a new acquaintance, I feel very relaxed.

_____ 18. I'm afraid to speak up in conversations.

_____ 19. I have no fear of giving a speech.

_____ 20. Certain parts of my body feel very tense and rigid while I am giving a speech.

_____ 21. I feel relaxed while giving a speech.

_____ 22. My thoughts become confused and jumbled when I am giving a speech.

_____ 23. I face the prospect of giving a speech with confidence.

_____ 24. While giving a speech, I get so nervous I forget facts I really know.

Scoring: Four subscale scores and a total apprehension score are calculated as follows:

Group =   Begin with 18 points. Subtract your scores for questions 1, 3, and 5. Then add the scores for 2, 4, and 6.

Meeting = Begin with 18 points. Subtract your scores for questions 7, 10, and 11. Then add the scores for 8, 9, and 12.

Dyadic = Begin with 18 points. Subtract your scores for questions 13, 15, and 18. Then add the scores for 14, 16, and 17.

Public = Begin with 18 points. Subtract your scores for questions 20, 22, and 24. Then add the scores for 19, 21, and 23.

Overall = Add the Group total + Meeting total + Dyadic total + Public total. (Totals will range between 24 and 120)

Total Scores:

_____ Group

_____ Meeting

_____ Dyadic

_____ Public

_____ Overall

Analysis: For each subscale total, your scores can range from a low of **6** to a high of **30**. Overall totals range between **24** and **120**. _Any subtotal above 18 or an overall score above 65 indicates some anxiety_. The lower your scores, the less anxiety you have. If you have _MyCommunicationLab_ bundled with your text (or have decided to purchase it as an add-on), you can transfer your scores to the online version of the PRCA-24 located on MyCommunicationLab and it will calculate your scores for you.

*Adapted from James C. McCroskey, _An Introduction to Rhetorical Communication: A Western Rhetorical Perspective_, 9th ed., Fig. 3.1, p. 40: Personal Report of Communication Apprehension (PRCA-24) and Fig. 3.2, p. 41: How to Score the PRCA-24. Published by Allyn and Bacon/Merrill Education, Boston, MA. Copyright © 2006 by Pearson Education. Adapted by permission of the publisher.

APPLY **WHAT YOU KNOW**
CONTEXT AND THE PRCA

If you haven't taken the PRCA-24 yet, please do so now. Once you have taken and scored the survey, you will have data on four different contexts–group, meetings, dyadic, and public. The lower your scores, the more confident you are. Use the data to answer the following questions:

- Any subtotal score of 18 or above indicates some anxiety. According to the survey, which contexts cause you the most anxiety?
- Do the survey results accurately describe you? Why or why not?

Now that we have defined communication and taken a look at various contexts, we are ready to take a detailed look at the basic communication process.

Basic Communication Process

One way to understand the communication process is by looking at a communication model. **Models** are visual representations of the basic elements of real processes. They provide a practical roadmap to effective communication. Three basic models describe the way our view of communication has changed over the years. We will take a brief look at each type of model, note the differences between them, and then—because the transaction model includes all the elements—take a detailed look at the basic communication process, using the transaction model as our guide.

Communication Models: A Brief Overview

Three communication models best describe how our thinking about communication has evolved over the years—the action model, the interaction model, and the transaction model. Each model has improved upon its predecessors by introducing elements of the process of communication that more accurately describe what happens when people interact. If Julie in our opening scenario had known the concepts in these models, she would have had a better understanding of her problem and how to solve it. Let's take a brief look at each model.

LEARNING **OBJECTIVE**

1.2 What are the differences between the action, interaction, and transaction models of communication?

Action Models The earliest models of communication—the **action models**—viewed the communication process as a linear or one-way transmission of messages beginning with the sender and ending with the receiver (Laswell, 1948; Shannon & Weaver, 1949). Models in this tradition identified many important elements of the communication process to be discussed in detail later (see **Figure 1.1**). A *sender encodes* the symbols that represent ideas and feelings into a *message* and sends it via *code* (verbal and nonverbal symbols) through a *channel* (method of transmitting code, such as a telephone) to a *receiver* who *decodes* (interprets) the message, often in the presence of *noise* (internal or external

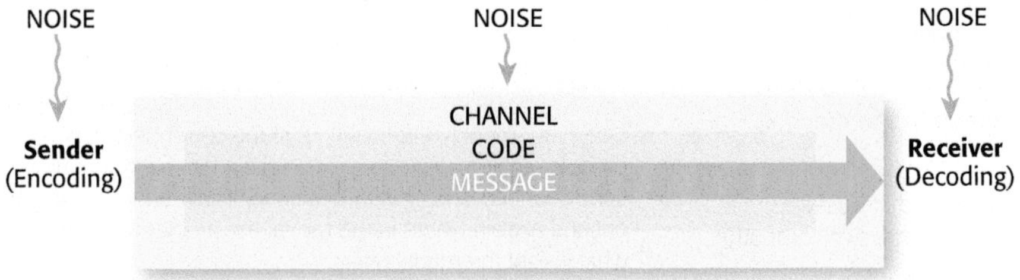

Figure 1.1 Action Model of Communication

NOISE   NOISE   NOISE

Sender   CHANNEL   **Receiver**
(Encoding)   CODE   (Decoding)
                   MESSAGE

Figure 1.2 Interaction
Model of Communication

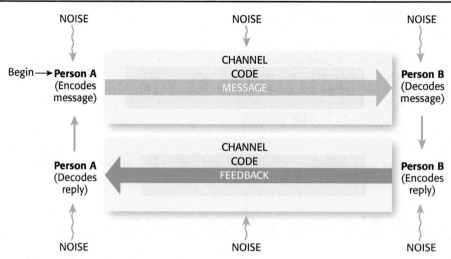

distractions). One obvious element that is missing from the action model is *feedback*. Without a response from the receiver, how can a sender be sure that effective communication has occurred?

Interaction Models

A more complete model of communication was illustrated by **interaction models** (first introduced by Schramm in 1965), which viewed communication as a *circular process* involving *feedback* (see **Figure 1.2**). In the interaction models, the message from Person A (the sender) is picked up by Person B (the receiver), who decodes the message and encodes a reply (called *feedback*); the reply is then picked up by Person A (the original sender) who responds back as well; and so on. Schramm also introduced the concept that people communicate using their own background and experiences (now called *frame of reference*). Even so, this model was not as complete as the transaction model discussed on page 13.

Transaction Models

Transaction models (introduced by Barnlund in 1970) are more recent and more complete models of the communication process. These models view communication as a *transactional* process—meaning that both parties are responsible for the creation of meaning, and each party affects and is affected by the other. Transaction models also recognize that the activities of sending and receiving do not occur separately and are not necessarily circular. Instead, both communicators send and receive *simultaneously,* as the arrow in **Figure 1.3** indicates. Since the transaction model includes not only the elements of the previous models but also several new elements and ways of looking at communication—such as the importance of context—it is the most useful to us in analyzing our own communication. Therefore, we will refer to the transaction model as we discuss the elements of the basic communication process in the next section.

APPLY **WHAT YOU KNOW**
COMMUNICATION MODELS

To apply what you know about communication models, complete the following:

- Draw and label a communication model that illustrates the way you communicate with a specific friend, significant other, or parent.

- Does your model indicate where in the communication process problems tend to occur? Take a recent communication misunderstanding with the friend, significant other, or parent and explain where in the model the problem occurred and what insight the model offers.

Figure 1.3 Transaction Model of Communication

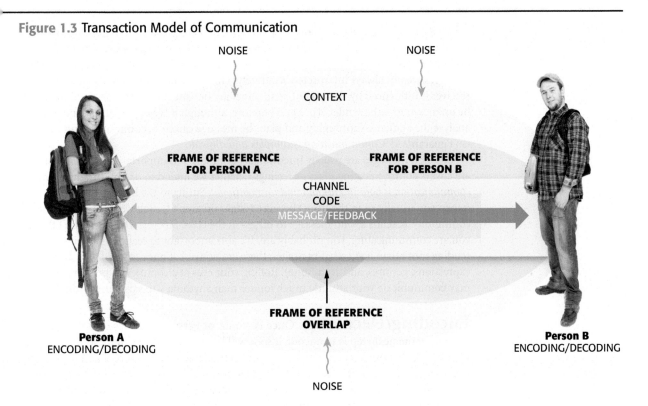

Elements of the Transaction Communication Model

Now that we have seen an overview of the communication models, let's use the transaction model—the most complete model—to identify and discuss each element of the basic communication process: sender/receiver, message, encoding/decoding, frame of reference, code, channel, feedback, context, and noise. As you read about each element, think about where in the communication process most of your own communication problems occur.

Sender/Receiver It is from the transaction model that we get the most accurate view of what really happens when people communicate. As you recall, in the action model, the **sender** (Person A) is the person who initiates the communication process, and the **receiver** (Person B) is the person toward whom a message is aimed. In the interaction model, both persons send and receive, but they do so in a circular manner. The transaction model enhances the view of the sender/receiver by depicting communication as a *simultaneous process*. For example, when patients describe their symptoms to healthcare professionals, the professionals monitor language and physical cues that enable them to understand how patients are feeling, both physically and emotionally, about their health. At the same time, patients are monitoring the healthcare professionals' responses to determine whether the professionals are listening and understanding the content of the messages, whether they find any of the content alarming, and whether more talk and elaboration on the situation is needed. Even in the public speaking setting, which may seem to be adequately depicted in the linear action model, speakers are constantly attending to the reactions of audience members to determine whether the message requires adaptation in order to achieve the desired effect.

LEARNING **OBJECTIVE**

1.3 What are the elements of the transaction communication model, how does each work, and what are the resulting communication principles?

Message   The **message** is the idea, thought, or feeling that a communicator wishes to convey to others. It is important to realize that once the message is sent, the sender is no longer in control. In fact, Corman, Trethewey, and Goodall (2007) note that even clear messages are not always interpreted accurately. This is because "interpretation by a receiver is influenced by an array of factors that are outside the control of—and may even be unknown to—the sender" (p. 11). Therefore, although it is essential for a sender to analyze the audience thoroughly and plan the message carefully, communication success isn't guaranteed. *Communication is complex and difficult.*

Although messages are usually intentionally sent, it is also important to realize that we are always communicating ideas or feelings whether we intend to or not. In other words, *communication is both intentional and unintentional.* Sitting in the back of the room (when you usually sit in the front) because today you aren't feeling well and don't want to communicate, sends a loud message to others in the class. So even when you don't think you are communicating, you probably are. It's also important to realize that you are sending more than just verbal messages; there are nonverbal ones as well (such as facial expressions, gestures, and vocal tone). Rolling your eyes at a comment a person just made may communicate your attitude much louder than anything you say with words.

Encoding/Decoding   Once Person A or Person B decides on a message to be sent, the next step is to encode it so it will be clear and meaningful to the receiver. **Encoding** is the process the sender goes through in choosing the verbal and nonverbal symbols to use. When the receiver attempts to interpret or make sense of the symbols conveyed in the message, the process is called **decoding**. Of course, we have all been angry enough at least once in our lives that we spoke without thinking. We didn't pick our words, tone, and gestures carefully; we didn't think about how our message would affect the other person; we let our anger speak for us. The problem with speaking without planning is that *communication is irreversible.* Once the words are spoken, we can't recall them. True, we can try to smooth them over with comments like, "You know I didn't mean that!" or "You know I really love you." However, words can be like weapons, and, once a person has been wounded by one, the hurt and doubt remain long after the conversation is over.

Another problem involved in encoding and decoding is that communicators tend to formulate and interpret messages using their own background and experiences (called frame of reference). Because no two of us have the exact same background and experiences, there are bound to be misunderstandings—as illustrated in the next section.

Frame of Reference   Communicators bring to each interaction their own **frames of reference**, their individual perspectives and views of the world. Each of us has a frame of reference that is unique; no two of us see the world in precisely the same way. Fortunately, there are areas in which the sender's frame of reference overlaps with the receiver's. This area of overlap includes what both parties have in common, and, no matter how different we are, there are always commonalities. This overlap is important because the things we have in common give us a starting point for communicating with each other (see the frame of reference overlap in the transaction model, Figure 1.3).

Your frame of reference depends upon many factors, including your self-concept, values and goals, beliefs and attitudes, expectations, culture, gender, age, and past experiences—in short, everything that goes into making you who you are. While all of these factors are important, the ones that often have the greatest potential for misunderstandings are culture and gender differences, which will be discussed later in this chapter.

Code

Code includes the verbal and nonverbal symbols that communicators use to convey their messages. Keep in mind that the code is not the message itself; code consists of the symbols that carry the message. As communicators encode, they have two different types of codes from which to choose—verbal and nonverbal. **Verbal code** consists of language symbols including written or spoken words. **Nonverbal code** encompasses two types of non-language symbols—*visual cues,* such as gestures, posture, facial expressions, and eye contact; and *vocal cues* that accompany word symbols, such as tone of voice, volume, rate, and pitch. Although senders and receivers can use either verbal or nonverbal code or a combination of both, *successful communicators make sure their codes are congruent*—that all codes are sending the same message. Many of us are experts at sending conflicting (non-congruent) messages. We say one thing verbally, but vocally indicate something different with our tone of voice, and visually indicate yet a third meaning with our facial expressions and gestures.

So which code do people pay the most attention to when interpreting the meaning of a message? It depends on the message, the person, and the context. If the message deals mainly with straightforward and factual material, then the verbal code may be the only one needed for an accurate interpretation (Lapakko, 1996). However, when the message is complicated, vague or emotional, both the verbal and nonverbal codes are needed for an accurate interpretation (see the discussion of a "rich" channel in the section below). In some situations, communicators pay more attention to the nonverbal code (visual and vocal cues) to figure out what others really mean. After analyzing 23 studies, Philpott (1983) found that 69 percent of the variance in meanings between communicators came from the nonverbal code, and only 31 percent of the variance came from the actual words spoken—the verbal code. In these studies, people paid more attention to the nonverbal code than they did to the verbal code when interpreting messages (see **Figure 1.4**). Although the exact level of importance of verbal versus nonverbal codes depends on the situation, the message and the people involved, as Burgoon & Hoobler (2002, p. 247) suggest, "[T]he ability to encode and decode nonverbal messages is critically important to successful communication."

Figure 1.4 Interpreting Meanings
Philpott found that research subjects used the following percents of verbal and nonverbal codes when interpreting messages. Which do you consider the most important for accurate interpretation of meaning?

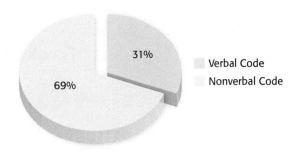

31%

69%

Verbal Code

Nonverbal Code

Channel

The person who wishes to send a message must next select a **channel**—the means or method of transmitting the code. When you think about channels, it is useful to begin by considering the ways that you receive messages from your environment. At the most basic level, you receive information through your five senses: seeing (visual), hearing (auditory), smelling (olfactory), tasting (gustatory), and feeling (tactile) channels. For a receiver to get a message, one or more of these senses must be engaged.

Another way to think about channels is to consider the various media that may be used to activate the five senses. For example, if you wish to send a verbal message to someone, you may do so using oral speech, which can be accomplished in the face-to-face channel, or by using a telephone as the channel. If the message is an important one that must be received by the larger population (an advertisement or political message, for example), you may use the radio or television as the medium to convey an oral message. However, you might wish to send your verbal message in writing, in which case you could use the channels of letters, e-mails, text messages, or any of the print media. You can undoubtedly think of other channels.

The channel you choose matters because your choice of channel conveys its own message. For example, in August, 2006, Radio Shack (an electronics retailer) notified over 400 employees by e-mail that their jobs had been eliminated. The company had publicly announced the projected layoffs nearly three weeks earlier, and employees were briefed in a series of meetings that layoff notices would be delivered via e-mail. However, many employees, news writers, and management experts questioned the appropriateness of using e-mail as a channel for such an announcement, commenting that it could be seen as "dehumanizing" (Associated Press, 2006).

As the photo indicates, sometimes we must write a letter or an e-mail because the person we wish to contact is not available for a telephone call or face-to-face interaction. In addition, there are other factors to consider when choosing a channel (Timm, 1986):

- *Message importance.* The more important or critical the message, the more essential it is to use the face-to-face channel.

- *Receiver needs and abilities.* Some receivers are good decoders and can effectively interpret e-mail and phone messages; others need both the verbal and nonverbal codes found in face-to-face messages.

- *Feedback importance.* The face-to-face channel is best for complicated messages and messages that need immediate feedback. Although e-mail and the telephone are fast, only the face-to-face channel gives immediate feedback.

- *Cost.* A fax or e-mail often costs less than long-distance calls or face-to-face meetings.

- *Formality desired.* In most cases, newsletters or memos are more formal than face-to-face interactions, which are more formal than e-mail.

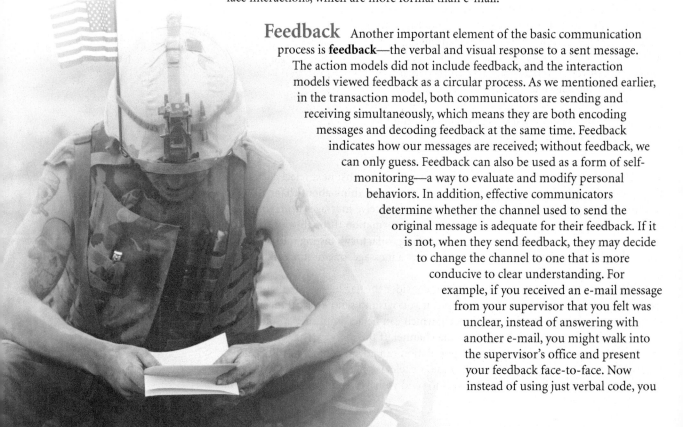

Sometimes your choice of channel for sending a message is limited by circumstances.

Feedback Another important element of the basic communication process is **feedback**—the verbal and visual response to a sent message. The action models did not include feedback, and the interaction models viewed feedback as a circular process. As we mentioned earlier, in the transaction model, both communicators are sending and receiving simultaneously, which means they are both encoding messages and decoding feedback at the same time. Feedback indicates how our messages are received; without feedback, we can only guess. Feedback can also be used as a form of self-monitoring—a way to evaluate and modify personal behaviors. In addition, effective communicators determine whether the channel used to send the original message is adequate for their feedback. If it is not, when they send feedback, they may decide to change the channel to one that is more conducive to clear understanding. For example, if you received an e-mail message from your supervisor that you felt was unclear, instead of answering with another e-mail, you might walk into the supervisor's office and present your feedback face-to-face. Now instead of using just verbal code, you can clarify your message by using both verbal and nonverbal codes. With instant access to facial expressions and eye contact—and by receiving an immediate answer to any questions—you have improved the chances for successful communication.

Although feedback definitely improves our chances of successful communication because we can better determine how our messages have been received, feedback also increases the chance of encoding and decoding errors. In fact, if not used with care, feedback can lead to communication misunderstandings rather than shared meanings. Just because one communicator is good at encoding and decoding, doesn't mean that the other one is. Think of your family members and friends. Aren't some of them much easier to communicate with than others? Do you know of a work colleague who can't seem to correctly interpret instructions or a supervisor who encodes instructions so poorly that they are almost impossible to follow? Obviously, feedback is needed.

When giving or receiving feedback, here are some suggestions to keep in mind:

- *Make any feedback you give brief and specific.* Detailed and overly general feedback is more likely to be misunderstood and less likely to be useful. Commenting, "That was a good presentation" may be brief, but it is too general to be of any value. Saying, "Your presentation had an excellent attention-getter and preview of main points. I could see that your audience was really listening" is more helpful.

- *When giving feedback, pay particular attention to the receiver's nonverbal reactions.* Although the receivers may not say anything, their understanding and attitude toward the feedback is usually obvious by their nonverbal reactions. If you observe a possible problem, adjust your feedback or ask questions.

- *Don't assume that your feedback was clearly understood; follow-up and plan for possible failure.* Thinking ahead about how your message may be misunderstood or fail to affect the receivers the way you intend is an important start. It is also good to follow up with a written note or e-mail message that contains a brief summary of the key points and any actions you and the other person agreed to implement. However, as mentioned earlier, once your feedback is sent, you are no longer in control; it may take on a life of its own. The receiver may completely misunderstand what you intended. Plan what to do if your feedback fails—such as schedule a face-to-face meeting, back off and let things cool down, or give a sincere apology.

- *When receiving feedback, use paraphrasing to verify meaning.* A brief summary in your own words of the other person's comments allows corrections to be made if any are needed.

APPLY **WHAT YOU KNOW**
COMMUNICATION CHANNELS AND FEEDBACK

Now that you are familiar with communication channels and feedback, expand your knowledge by answering the following questions:

- When your opinion is requested and you are allowed to give feedback—whether in the workplace, with friends, or with family members—how does this affect your self-concept and feelings of satisfaction? Do you think this is true of all people? Why or why not?

- What channel do you think would work best if you had negative feedback to give a friend? To someone in one of your classes you have known only a brief time? To a family member you haven't seen for a year? If you chose different channels for each situation, explain why; if your channel choices were the same, explain why.

Context As mentioned earlier, *context* refers to the situation in which a communication event takes place and can be viewed from a narrow perspective (the time, place, or physical or social environment in which the communication occurs) or a broad perspective (ranging from intrapersonal and interpersonal to group or public communication). Because neither the action nor interaction model dealt with context, the transaction model gives a more complete version of what actually happens during a communication situation. In Figure 1.3 the context in which Person A and Person B are communicating is represented by the large outer oval.

Effective communicators do their best to control the context because they know it can either help or harm the success of their communication. For example, holding an important meeting right after lunch is probably not wise, especially if PowerPoint will be used in a darkened room. Why? Because the audience is likely to doze off. Arranging a meeting in an extremely large space like an auditorium when you are expecting 30 to 40 people is probably not wise either. Why? Because it will look like the meeting isn't important since so few people came. And planning a private conversation with a close friend in a busy, noisy place probably won't work either. Why? Because there will be too many distractions for an intimate discussion.

Another way to think of context is to consider the expectations, rules, and norms that various communication contexts carry with them: *Communication is affected by rules and norms.* **Rules** are standards of acceptable behavior in a given situation that are explicitly spelled out; **norms** are standards of acceptable behavior that are implied. For example, your exchanges with your classmates during class time are quite different from the interactions that you have outside of class; a significant reason for this is because the rules and norms that govern what is considered acceptable in each situation are different. Meeting with a physician is another example of a context where rules and norms are important. A physician's communication with a patient who is hospitalized in a semi-private room is different from the exchanges that occur in the privacy of the medical office. Another example would be the type of conversation that is considered appropriate between friends attending a funeral versus the conversation at a local diner. Although the "rules" of interaction in any of these contexts are usually not explicitly stated, they play an important role in how people communicate, how they are viewed by others, and how they negotiate meaning. The rules and norms we are discussing are spelled out in more detail by the theory of Coordinated Management of Meaning (Pearce, 2005) that appears in the *Making Theory Practical* feature later in the chapter.

Noise A final component of the communication process that was included even in the early models of communication is the element of **noise**, which is anything that interferes with successful sending and receiving of messages or hinders creation of shared meaning. Generally speaking, there are two broad categories of noise—external and internal. **External noise** refers to distractions in your environment, such as loud sounds or unusual movement that distract you. These noises either make it difficult to compose your thoughts as you speak to others or make it difficult to decode the messages you are receiving. **Internal noise** is anything that is happening within you that gets in the way of effective sending or receiving. Internal noise can be subdivided into three types:

- **Physiological noise** is any aspect of your physical condition that compromises your effectiveness as a communicator—either as a sender or as a receiver. Hunger, fatigue, pain, illness, and physical impairment are examples of sources of internal physiological noise.

- **Psychological noise** refers to factors related to your thoughts and emotions that get in the way of effective sending or receiving of messages. If you are worried about an exam in your next class, you may not be able to attend well to your professor's lecture. If you are feeling neglected by a friend, you may dwell on that emotion rather than the content of the message she is currently trying to convey.

- **Semantic noise** occurs when people use language for which meanings are not shared. If you have ever been in an argument with someone only to find out that you didn't really disagree but simply understood a particular word differently, you have experienced semantic noise. The topic of how we draw meaning from language will be discussed in greater depth in a later chapter.

For now, consider the many places at which noise can occur in the communication process. Noise could happen in the message if you were not sure what you were trying to communicate. Noise could occur in the code if you chose symbols that did not have the same meaning to you that they had to your partner. Noise could be in the channel if you chose to send a message in writing that would have been better delivered face-to-face. And, as our discussion of frames of reference should illustrate, noise can be within yourself when your perspective differs from that of your conversational partner.

The purpose of presenting you with a model of communication was to help you to be more conscious of what is happening when you communicate with others. If you fully understand the components of the model and how they interact with each other, you should also be able to diagnose communication problems when they occur. Even more helpful would be if your understanding of the process enabled you to prevent problems from arising.

APPLY **WHAT YOU KNOW**
COMMUNICATION PROCESS

Apply what you know about the communication process by answering the following:

- Think of an example where communication misunderstanding occurred because of faulty encoding or decoding (usually based on frame of reference differences). The example may include you or someone you know. Give plenty of details.

- Explain the difference between the message, code, and channel. Give an example to clarify your answer.

- When you are attending a college class, which types of noise create the main distractions for you? Give examples to illustrate your answer.

Now that we have defined communication and looked at the basic elements in the communication process, let's further explore the communication model by looking at several specific areas where frame of reference differences are likely to cause communication misunderstandings.

MAKING THEORY **PRACTICAL**
COORDINATED MANAGEMENT OF MEANING THEORY

When you pass an acquaintance in the hall as you are going to class, your conversation probably goes something like this:

- "Hey! How are you?"
- "I'm fine. How are you?"
- "Fine, thanks."

Have you ever stopped to think about why you do not interpret "How are you?" to be a request for information about your physical health or psychological state? How do you and your conversational partner know how to interpret this exchange?

Theorists

Communication scholars Barnett Pearce and Vernon Cronen developed the **Coordinated Management of Meaning Theory** (CMM) to explain how people create, coordinate, and manage meaning-making in conversations with each other. The theory focuses on the "rules" we follow when sending messages to others and when interpreting messages that we receive:

- *Constitutive rules* are those that enable us to understand what other persons are likely to mean by their choices of verbal or nonverbal symbols.

- *Regulative rules* guide us toward appropriate behaviors for the situation.

Levels of Meaning

Sometimes "How are you?" really is a request for information about how you are feeling physically or psychologically.

If a close friend knows that you have been ill or experiencing stressful life circumstances, his "How are you?" might be construed as an expression of concern. According to CMM, this is because there are many levels of meaning that we consider when making sense out of a particular situation or context:

- Our *self-concept*—view of self in this situation;
- The *relationship* with the other person;
- The specific *episode* where the conversation takes place such as an interview, a personal conversation, or polite conversation made in passing;
- The meaning of the *speech act*—was it a compliment, an insult, just information, etc.;
- The *cultural aspects* of the context—whether eye contact is appropriate, for example.

PRACTICAL USES

In the conversation examples given in greetings between a stranger and someone you know, the *episode* and *relationship* levels are most directly involved. The constitutive and regulative rules are different for each situation. In the first instance, the episode is an accidental encounter, and the relationship is that of a stranger—resulting in a familiar routine exchange. In the second example, in the context of an episode of recent distress, a close friend's question would likely have a different motivation and suggest a different interpretation.

As you can see, the Coordinated Management of Meaning Theory pays particular attention to two parts of our communication model: the *context* in which communication takes place and the *frames of reference* of the communicators. If you and your conversational partner are operating from the same understanding of the rules and from the same levels, it is much easier to communicate.

You can use the ideas of the CMM to figure out what might be causing you to have trouble "coordinating meaning" with another person—and to appreciate the times when you manage meanings well.

Source: Pearce, W. B., & Cronen, V. E. (1980). *Communication, Action and Meaning: The Creation of Social Realities.* New York: Praeger.

Exploring the Communication Model: Frames of Reference

LEARNING **OBJECTIVE**

1.4 How do culture, gender, technology, and ethics affect our communication successes or failures?

In addition to the basic elements of the communication process that we have just covered, there are some special areas where frame of reference differences affect the success of our communication—culture, gender, technology, and ethics. As you read this section, see which concepts have caused you communication problems in the past.

Communication and Culture

Culture can be defined as a system of values, beliefs, attitudes, rules, and norms shared by a group of people. People are also members of **co-cultures**, which are smaller groups of people who are bound by shared values, beliefs, attitudes, rules, and norms that interact with those of the larger culture. For example, within the larger culture of the United States, many different co-cultures exist whose members are bound together by virtue of such characteristics as ethnicity, religion, gender, sexual orientation, geographic region, and/or socio-economic status. As you can see, you may belong to several co-cultural groups, and often you may find that the values of one of your co-cultural identities conflict with those of another.

Fifty years ago, you could expect to live in a community that was fairly homogeneous. In today's world, you have many opportunities to interact with people from different cultural and co-cultural groups with different frames of reference. Intercultural scholar Stella Ting-Toomey (1999) likens our awareness of these differences to how we view an iceberg (**Figure 1.5**).

What you see when you look at an iceberg is merely the tip. However, the foundation for that tip lies well beneath the water. So it is with intercultural communication. Above the water, we observe the verbal and nonverbal symbols and behaviors. Below the "waterline"—beneath the obvious differences—is where we find the values, beliefs, attitudes, rules and norms that create the differing verbal and nonverbal behaviors we observe in other cultures. These are the aspects of culture that create cultural diversity. At the base of the iceberg lies "universal human need," that binds us to each other as human beings and offers commonalities for communication.

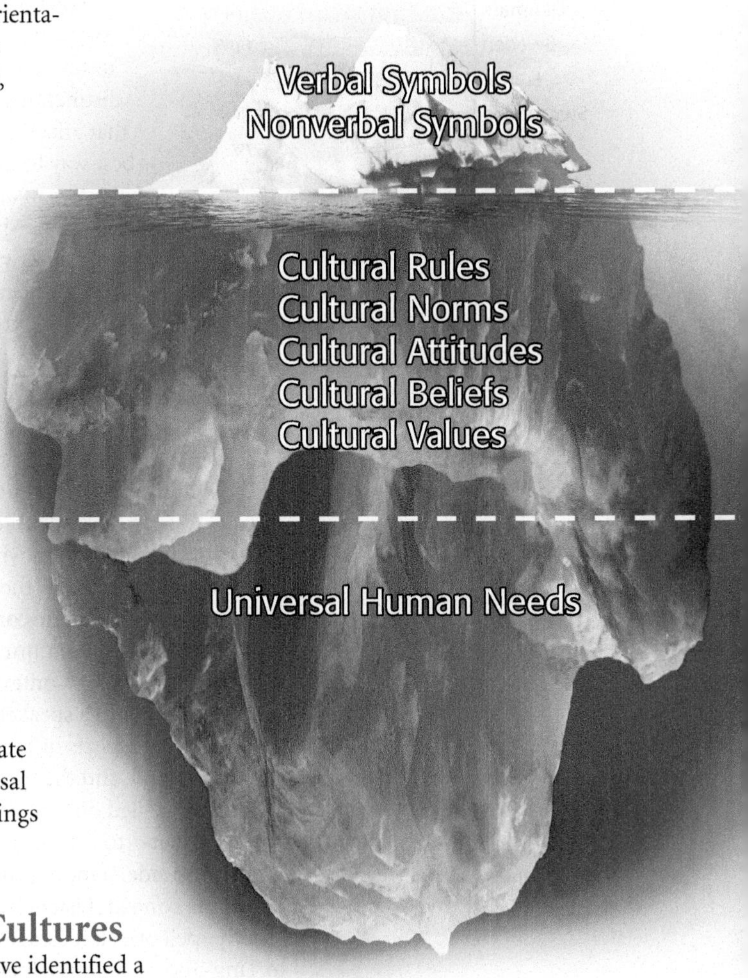

Figure 1.5 Cultural Iceberg

Adapted from Stella Ting-Toomey, *Communicating Across Cultures.* Copyright © 1998 by Guilford Publications, Inc. Reprinted by permission.

Verbal Symbols
Nonverbal Symbols

Cultural Rules
Cultural Norms
Cultural Attitudes
Cultural Beliefs
Cultural Values

Universal Human Needs

Individualistic and Collectivistic Cultures

Scholars in the field of intercultural communication have identified a number of ways in which cultural values differ (Hall, 2002; Hofstede, 1984, 2005). One of the most often cited differences between cultures is the

Table 1.1 Individualistic Scores of Various Countries

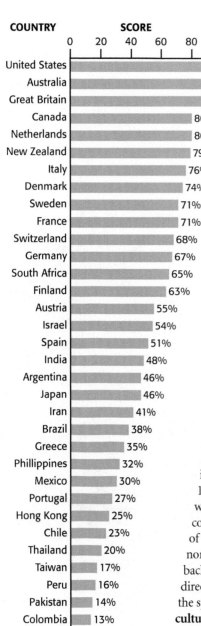

COUNTRY	SCORE
United States	91%
Australia	90%
Great Britain	89%
Canada	80%
Netherlands	80%
New Zealand	79%
Italy	76%
Denmark	74%
Sweden	71%
France	71%
Switzerland	68%
Germany	67%
South Africa	65%
Finland	63%
Austria	55%
Israel	54%
Spain	51%
India	48%
Argentina	46%
Japan	46%
Iran	41%
Brazil	38%
Greece	35%
Phillipines	32%
Mexico	30%
Portugal	27%
Hong Kong	25%
Chile	23%
Thailand	20%
Taiwan	17%
Peru	16%
Pakistan	14%
Colombia	13%
Venezuela	12%

distinction between individualism and collectivism (shown in **Table 1.1**). **Individualistic cultures** place a high value on the accomplishments of the individual person while **collectivistic cultures** are more oriented to the welfare of the group (community, tribe, clan, etc.).

Cultures that are on the individualistic side of the continuum value such concepts as independence, self-reliance, competition, and personal opinion. Individualistic cultures focus on personal rights and reaching one's full potential. By contrast, cultures on the collectivistic side of the continuum value connection to the group, interdependence, cooperation, and consensus. Meeting one's obligations and fitting in are of greater importance in collectivistic cultures. Geart Hofstede (2005) found that the United States ranks the highest in individualism among 53 countries and regions of the world. By contrast, most Asian and Latin American countries are more collectivistic. It is important to understand that no culture is wholly individualistic or collectivistic. It is dangerous to dichotomize, or draw arbitrary distinctions between people or groups, as this tends to polarize people and make it difficult to find common ground. However, it is useful to make these distinctions to illustrate the fundamental differences in values that affect how cultural groups express their differences. Perhaps the best way to do this is to think of extreme individualism and extreme collectivism at opposite ends of a continuum, with cultural groups falling somewhere along the continuum between the extremes of 1 (most collectivistic) to 100 (most individualistic). Table 1.1 shows where a number of countries would fall on the collectivistic/individualistic continuum.

High-Context and Low-Context Cultures

Another important idea that helps us appreciate the differences among cultures is the distinction made between high-context and low-context cultures—a concept introduced by anthropologist Edward T. Hall (1976). You have already learned that the term "context" refers to the characteristics of the situation in which communication takes place. Context used in this instance refers to "the information that surrounds an event" (Hall & Hall, 1990, p. 6). A **high-context culture** is one in which people's understanding of what is being communicated is based less on the words spoken and more on the communication context. In other words, a high-context culture pays a great deal of attention to a speaker's context when determining meaning—such as the nonverbal aspects of the interaction, the history of the situation, family background, and the speaker's friends and memberships. Meanings are not directly spelled out but are implied, and it is the responsibility of the receiver—not the speaker—to determine the intended meaning. By contrast, in **low-context cultures** understanding comes more from the literal meaning of spoken words than from the context. Listeners expect the speaker to be responsible for meaning and to clearly spell out all messages—to make them explicit and well-organized. According to Ting-Toomey (2000), high-context cultures like Mexico and Japan tend to be collectivistic while low-context cultures like the United States and Canada are more individualistic.

You may be wondering how the notions of individualism/collectivism and high-context/low-context cultures are relevant to our study of communication. They are significant because senders and receivers from different cultures have different expectations and encode and decode messages differently, which often lead to misunderstandings. Considering the individualism/collectivism idea helps us to understand why people from some individualistic cultures feel that it is their right to express their opinions on any subject, while people from other collectivistic cultures are apt to think that the group's perspective should be expressed and that their role should be to listen. The point is that culture is a major determiner of one's frame of reference because it affects one's view on what is considered acceptable or unacceptable in communicating with others. Also, in cultures where there is a great deal of diversity, meanings are more difficult to interpret because communicators do not have as much in common.

Ethnocentrism and Culture
One of the challenges for all communicators is to resist the tendency toward **ethnocentrism**, which is the assumption that one's own cultural perspective is superior to all others. It is almost impossible to escape ethnocentrism; we are so profoundly a product of our own culture that we don't recognize the extent to which it affects our behavior and our judgment. It is understandable that we each regard our own cultural traditions as "normal" and question the logic behind another's cultural traditions. However, if we are ever to live in harmony, it is essential that we understand that other groups' traditions are just as logical to them as ours are to us. We should be proud of our own heritage and the accomplishments of our own cultural group but recognize that learning about and respecting other cultural perspectives broadens our own frame of reference.

Communication and Gender

As previously discussed, within a culture there are many co-cultures. Co-cultures are identified as such when the shared values, beliefs, attitudes, rules, and communication behaviors of people in a particular group are so similar to each other (yet different enough from other groups) that they create a very real level of diversity. Many scholars treat gender as a co-culture. Although we often think of sex and gender as equivalent terms, **sex** is actually a biologically based characteristic whereas **gender** refers to cultural and psychological consequences of social roles and personal identity. The terms "male" and "female" are used to distinguish between the sexes; the terms "masculine," "feminine," or "**androgynous**" (referring to a balance between traditional masculine and feminine characteristics) are used to distinguish the genders. You will hear much more about these areas in later chapters.

It's no shock to any of us that men and women are different and communicate somewhat differently. Scholars in many fields of study have investigated these differences, and some have concluded that the differences are significant enough to treat interactions between men and women as a type of cross-cultural communication. One of the key differences is with respect to the goals each gender has for communicating. Scholars often describe men as **instrumental communicators** (Wood, 2009), meaning that their purpose is generally to accomplish some goal or solve a problem, and communication is used as a means to that end. Therefore, the man may be thinking: "In a conversation with a woman, when a problem's solved, why does the woman still want to continue the conversation?" (Ivy & Backlund, 2008, p. 40). Women, on the other hand, are often described as **expressive communicators**, meaning that their purpose involves making the process of reaching a goal a quality experience, and communication is not only used to build and maintain harmonious

ZITS   **BY JERRY SCOTT AND JIM BORGMAN**

ZITS © ZITS PARTNERSHIP, KING FEATURES SYNDICATE

relationships but is also something to enjoy. So the woman may be thinking: "Now that the decision is made, half the fun is in analyzing it and discussing the process we used—what's wrong with that?" It is important to understand that these are just general labels, and that the labels do not describe all men or all women. In fact, researchers report that freshmen college students (male and female) are more likely to use expressive communication when complaining about roommates and grades to their parents while moms and dads tend to communicate instrumentally by trying to fix the "problem" with solutions and advice (Goodman & Leiman, 2007). Nevertheless, these ideas help us to think about the complexities that exist when communicators do not even share the same goals in interacting with others.

As you can see, frame of reference and communication are affected by gender. So far we have only focused on a few aspects of gender, but we will discuss other important information about gender and communication as it relates to topics in each of the following chapters.

Communication and Technology

Whether our exchange is with family, friends, work colleagues, or clients, we have numerous ways to communicate, thanks to technology—cell phones with text messaging, instant messaging (IM's), e-mail by itself or with attachments, blogs, social-networking sites, and videoconferencing to name a few. **Figure 1.6** indicates that more college students communicate by cell phones than any other type of technology (Snapshot, 2008). Which technology do you prefer?

The way people communicate via technology—referred to as **computer mediated communication (CMC)**—has received much attention from communication scholars in recent years. CMC is considered a **lean medium channel** because it carries only one code and does not permit the reception of nonverbally encoded messages. Channels that carry both verbal and nonverbal codes are less likely to be misunderstood and therefore are considered **rich medium channels**. Television and face-to-face channels are rich because they contain both verbal and nonverbal code; memos, e-mail, and blogs are lean because they have only the verbal code (although we do attempt to add tone with caps, arrows, underlining, and smiley faces). For example, you may have had the experience of receiving an e-mail from someone that left you wondering if the sender was angry with you about something, but with only the verbal code it is more

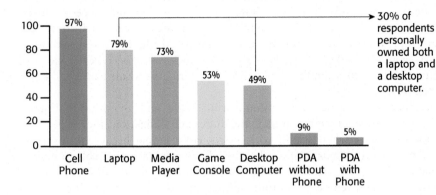

Figure 1.6 Student Technology

difficult to decode accurately. Later you may have discovered that the sender was merely in too great a hurry to write more than a few words and had no idea that the message sent sounded angry. The more codes operating in a channel, the less chance you will have for communication breakdown.

Although technology has expanded the ways we communicate, we see that it has also increased the ways we can be misunderstood. It makes sense that the informal, abbreviated language that is appropriate for text messages sent by cell phones makes a negative impression when used in an e-mail thank-you note sent to an interviewer. Every type of technology has both strengths and weaknesses when it comes to communication, and effective communicators work to avoid potential problem areas. For example, social-networking sites like *Facebook* and *MySpace* often have been used as a way to let off steam to friends. However, now these sites are being viewed by interviewers (Needleman, 2008) and even college admissions officers (Hechinger, 2008). In a recent survey, 38 percent of college admissions officers who looked at student online information reported that "what they saw 'negatively affected' their views of the applicant" (p. D6). Hechinger advises those who use *Facebook* or *MySpace* to avoid including any offensive language, illegal behaviors, or negative comments about colleges. Because technology can affect the success of our interactions with others, each of the following chapters will address technology as it relates to specific chapter content.

Communication and Ethics

Ethics can be defined as a system of moral principles that governs the conduct of people in relationship to others. When dealing with the notion of ethical communication, a key issue is honesty. For example, were Julia and Blanca in our opening scenario being honest with each other? You may think that what constitutes honesty is self-evident: If you speak the truth, you are being honest and, therefore, ethical; if you don't speak the truth, you are lying, and therefore, communicating unethically. However, the issue is much more complicated than that, since ethical communication is also communication that concerns itself with the needs of others. It is especially interesting to note the relationship between culture and ethics. The standards for what is considered honest/dishonest may vary depending upon the degree to which a culture is high context or low context. For example, in

Mexico there is a conception of a more personal truth rather than an objective truth. The goal is to preserve harmonious relationships, which means that "truth" may be expressed differently depending upon the situation and the people involved (Novinger, 2001, pp. 132–133). In high-context cultures such as the United States, what people think of as a "white lie" is not considered a lie at all; to speak too bluntly would be to disregard others' feelings, which would be a greater violation of ethical communication than not telling "the truth, the whole truth, and nothing but the truth."

Another key issue of ethical communication is the "code of ethics" that many professions have adopted to stipulate the duties and obligations they expect their members to follow when dealing with others. For example, because Johnson & Johnson adhered to their ethics code called *The Credo,* they were able to make a difficult and costly decision to recall 31 million bottles of Tylenol when it was determined that seven deaths in four Chicago suburbs were the result of capsules laced with cyanide (Trevino & Nelson, 2004). Texas Instruments not only has an ethics code, they also give employees a business card with an ethics hot-line number to call and quick test of seven criteria to use when determining whether a behavior is ethical (Ethics Quick Test, 2009):

- Is the action legal?
- Does it comply with our values?
- If you do it, will you feel bad?
- How will it look in the newspaper?
- If you know it's wrong, don't do it.
- If you're not sure, ask.
- Keep asking until you get an answer.

The nursing profession has two ethics codes: the American Nurses Association Code of Ethics for Nurses and the International Council of Nurses Code of Ethics (Berman, Snyder, Kozier, & Erb, 2008, pp. 86–87). The National Communication Association has its own *Credo for Communication Ethics* in **Figure 1.7** (Credo, 2009) which outlines a number of ethics principles for communicators, such as truthfulness, accuracy, and honesty. It expressly condemns distortion, intimidation, coercion, intolerance, and hatred.

APPLY **WHAT YOU KNOW**
CULTURE, GENDER, TECHNOLOGY, AND ETHICS

Apply what you know about the special areas (culture, gender, technology, or ethics) discussed in the above section and answer the following questions:

- Which area do you feel most often causes others communication problems; the most serious

communication problems; the most personal problems? Why?

- Give an example of a time that culture, gender, technology, or ethics caused you a communication problem.

Now that we have defined *communication,* explored the basic elements in the communication process, and looked at the effects that culture, gender, technology, and ethics have on communication, it shouldn't be too difficult to determine the communication competencies needed in the workplace and in everyday life.

Figure 1.7 NCA Credo

NCA Credo for Ethical Communication, available at www.natcom.org. Reprinted by permission of the National Communication Association.

NCA National Communication Association

NCA Credo for Ethical Communication

Questions of right and wrong arise whenever people communicate. Ethical communication is fundamental to responsible thinking, decision making, and the development of relationships and communities within and across contexts, cultures, channels, and media. Moreover, ethical communication enhances human worth and dignity by fostering truthfulness, fairness, responsibility, personal integrity, and respect for self and others. We believe that unethical communication threatens the quality of all communication and consequently the well-being of individuals and the society in which we live. Therefore we, the members of the National Communication Association, endorse and are committed to practicing the following principles of ethical communication:

- We advocate truthfulness, accuracy, honesty, and reason as essential to the integrity of communication.

- We endorse freedom of expression, diversity of perspective, and tolerance of dissent to achieve the informed and responsible decision making fundamental to a civil society.

- We strive to understand and respect other communicators before evaluating and responding to their messages.

- We promote access to communication resources and opportunities as necessary to fulfill human potential and contribute to the well-being of families, communities, and society.

- We promote communication climates of caring and mutual understanding that respect the unique needs and characteristics of individual communicators.

- We condemn communication that degrades individuals and humanity through distortion, intimidation, coercion, and violence, and through the expression of intolerance and hatred.

- We are committed to the courageous expression of personal convictions in pursuit of fairness and justice.

- We advocate sharing information, opinions, and feelings when facing significant choices while also respecting privacy and confidentiality.

- We accept responsibility for the short- and long-term consequences for our own communication and expect the same of others.

A Practical Look at Communication: Competencies and Benefits

LEARNING **OBJECTIVE**

1.5 What are the basic communication competencies and skills that can be gained from a communication course and what specific benefits result from studying communication?

The overall goal of the course in which you are enrolled and of this text is to help you to become a more competent and skilled communicator in any setting. Multiple times each semester students tell us how they wished they had taken this communication course much sooner because it would have helped them in so many aspects of their lives—college, personal, and career. So although this course covers information and theory, it also has a definite practical side. If you work hard reading and applying the concepts covered, you can expect to gain competencies and skills that you can use throughout your life and reap the benefits of these skills.

The specific competencies and skills used throughout this text were adapted from the National Communication Association (Morreale, Rubin, & Jones, 1998), various state guidelines, professional standards, and communication professors. Each chapter begins with a list of learning objectives and skills to guide you in reading the chapters and ends with a check sheet of competencies and skills for you to assess what you have learned and can actually use. Which competencies and skills listed here will be the most beneficial to you?

Competent Communicators

- *Accept responsibility for their own communication behavior.* Being able to evaluate and correct any behavior that leads to communication problems is a skill that competent communicators work hard to achieve. [Identifying problems begins with the communication model in Chapter 1; Chapter 2 gives insight into perception and how it affects our behavior.]

- *Are ethical communicators.* The true measure of competence in communication is the ability to get one's needs met as well as meeting the needs of others while using only ethical communication. [General ethical suggestions are included throughout the text; specifics on plagiarism and ethical presentations are covered in Chapters 11 and 13.]

- *Achieve shared meaning in differing cultural, gender, technological, and ethical situations.* Being able to encode and decode from another person's perspective as well as **reframe** (express) a situation from a frame of reference other than your own are important communication skills especially when there are cultural, gender, technological, or ethical differences between those communicating. [Each chapter will add to our understanding on culture, gender, technology, and ethics.]

  - *Use verbal and nonverbal symbols effectively.* Being aware of the importance of selecting words carefully, adding the appropriate nonverbal element to a message, and striving to improve pronunciation, grammar, and articulation affect the success of your communication. [See Chapters 4 and 5 for verbal and nonverbal specifics.]

    - *Listen effectively.* Knowing how to avoid barriers to listening, overcoming poor listening habits such as getting defensive, and knowing when and how to use informational, critical, and empathic listening places competent communicators well ahead of the norm. [See Chapter 3 for listening specifics.]

    - *Apply successful interpersonal skills.* Using interpersonal skills such as **self-monitoring** (being aware of your own behaviors and how others respond to them) and mindfulness—rather than mind*less*ness—are just a few interpersonal skills used by competent communicators. [See Chapters 6 and 7 for specifics.]

      - *Create and maintain successful relationships.* Being able to determine your needs and your communication style and knowing how to get your needs met while meeting the needs of others is a communication skill that can affect your personal life and your career. [See Chapters 6 and 7 for specifics.]

      - *Effectively participate in and lead teams to solve problems and manage conflict.* Being able to participate in and/or lead a team, whether at home or at work, involves learning specific communication skills such as working with people and effective organization. [See Chapters 8 and 9 for group and leadership specifics.]

Spike Lee earned a degree in Communication from Indiana University where he learned the skills of a competent communicator.

- *Speak effectively.* Knowing how to manage your speaker anxiety; select topics and analyze your audience; research, organize, and prepare; and deliver an effective presentation are definitely communication skills worth learning. [See Chapters 10–14 for specifics.]

Communication competencies and skills aren't the only practical element of this course; studying communication results in several valuable benefits including awareness of your thought processes, empowerment toward action, improved relations with others, professional success, and increased value as a citizen.

Benefits of Studying Communication

- *Increased Self-Awareness.* Communication begins with an individual's thought processes. Most of us have found ourselves reflecting on an event in our life and wondering, "Why did I say or do that?" The study of communication can help you explore aspects of yourself that you may not have considered before. In the process of investigating these ideas, you will acquire greater understanding of your motivations, feelings, and capabilities.

- *Empowered Participation.* Although some people may have natural abilities when it comes to communication, most people have learned the communication skills needed to be competent communicators. By learning these skills, they empowered themselves. It is such a wonderful feeling of self-confidence and pride to know that you have taken more control over your life and can communicate effectively without having to worry or experience high anxiety. If you work on the skills presented in each chapter, by the end of the course you will be empowered to take an active role in many different situations.

- *Improved Relationships.* Communication involves relationships with other people that are important and necessary parts of what it means to be human. You will have the opportunity to learn ways to develop more satisfying relationships, accomplish goals in working with others, and take part in professional, social, and civic arenas that will enrich your life and allow you to realize your full potential as a citizen and as a human being.

- *Enhanced Professional Success.* If you have ever looked at job postings in your newspaper or on the Web, you will have noticed that "excellent communication skills" are required or desired by most employers. It is easy to understand why this would be true for positions in sales, training, public relations, or any job that requires that you interact with clients or customers on a regular basis. However, even in jobs where you would be primarily working alone, you will sometimes be required to interact with co-workers, often in ways that you cannot anticipate until you are actually on the job.

Of course, your first professional challenge is actually to get the job. People who are skilled communicators are more likely to handle job interviews successfully. In fact, the interview is aimed more at demonstrating that you possess the ability to interact well with others than it is at identifying your technical qualifications—which are, after all, outlined on your written resume. Once you have landed the job, effective communication is necessary for you to keep the job. In fact, the more you advance in your career, the more you will be expected to communicate effectively, including making various kinds of presentations. In addition to helping you get a job and keep it, your ability to communicate effectively will put you in the position of

COMMUNICATION **AND YOUR CAREER**

LEARNING OBJECTIVE

1.6 What communication skills covered in this chapter relate specifically to your career?

Now it's time to relate the information in this chapter directly to your career. Each chapter ends with a career section containing: a *Spotlight on* feature that takes a current look at a chapter topic as it relates to the specific fields of business, education, and healthcare; a *Career Moment* feature that relates communication skills from the chapter to success in the workplace; and a *Connecting to* feature that includes specific activities to further expand your knowledge of these same three fields. Whether you are interested in one of these fields or will be a consumer of the products and services of these fields, these features and activities should interest you.

SPOTLIGHT ON **THE VALUE OF COMMUNICATION SKILLS**

BUSINESS

No matter whether you are interested in business as commerce, an occupation, or an organization, communication skills are extremely important to your success. In addition to communicating with co-workers and supervisors, you are likely to interact with the public and with members of other organizations.

Throughout this text, we will be spotlighting how specific concepts or skills from each chapter apply to communication in business. For example, *trust* may be one of the most important determiners of manager-employee relationships (Hubbell & Chory-Assad, 2005). Yet one study (Kanter & Mirvis, 1990) found that 72 percent of employees felt their managers were taking advantage of them, and 66 percent believed their managers could not be trusted. [See Chapter 6 for specifics on building trust and relationships.]

EDUCATION

No matter in which level of education you decide to work—elementary, middle school, high school, or college—effective communication skills are part of what it means to be a successful teacher. Since you have had teachers who were both ineffective and effective role models, you know firsthand the importance of communication.

Throughout this text, we will be spotlighting how specific concepts or skills from each chapter apply to communication in education. For example, researchers have found that when instructors use *immediacy behaviors* (verbal and nonverbal behaviors that produce feelings of closeness), students not only have a better attitude toward the classroom but actually learn significantly more (Menzel & Carrell, 1999). [See more about this concept in Chapter 5.]

HEALTHCARE

No matter where you work in the healthcare field, communication skills are essential for success in your work. In addition to communicating with patients and their family members, you will be interacting with co-workers and professionals from other health areas, with superiors and subordinates, and with people in other healthcare organizations involved in your patient's care.

Throughout this text, we will be spotlighting how specific concepts or skills from each chapter apply to communication in healthcare. For example, Sharf (1984) found that the use of *medical jargon* by healthcare professionals often interferes with patients' ability to understand the scope of their health problems and the side effects that may accompany their treatments. [You will learn more about this type of verbal encoding in Chapter 4.]

CAREER MOMENT **WHAT EMPLOYERS WANT!**

You may be taking this course to satisfy a degree requirement at your college or university. There are many reasons that a course in Communication is included in so many core curricula.

According to John Challenger, chief executive of the highly regarded outplacement consultancy firm of Challenger, Gray, and Christmas,

> The two requirements that employers will always want candidates to possess are real world experience and a solid foundation of communication, technology and analytical skills (*Jobs Outlook*, 2006, October 27).

Challenger reports that there are certain college majors that are particularly beneficial in preparing students for the jobs that will be in greatest demand in the near future: speech and acting; foreign languages and international relations; physical therapy, accounting, and engineering.

Whether you will be taking this one course or will decide to major or minor in communication, learning and applying the theories and skills presented in this text and in class discussions will benefit you in

Law is only one of many professions where communication skills are essential.

your professional life. In each chapter of this text you will find a *Career Moment* box that will highlight how the skills in that chapter are especially related to particular careers in which you may be interested.

CONNECTING TO . . . **BUSINESS**

Are you considering a career in business? Surveys continue to rank communication skills as the most important skills for workplace success (*Job Outlook* 2008). Success depends on employees who can effectively communicate. Run a computer search on a college database like EBSCOhost or LexisNexis or even Google with search words like *engineering and oral communication skills* to find sample articles.

ACTIVITY The important role that ethics plays in business communication and technology has raised difficult ethical questions. Answer either **yes** or **no** to the following ethics questions and discuss your answers in small groups.

1. Is it wrong to use company e-mail for personal reasons? YES/NO
2. Is it wrong to use office equipment to help children/spouse do schoolwork? YES/NO
3. Is it wrong to play computer games on office equipment during the workday? YES/NO
4. Is it wrong to use office equipment to do Internet shopping? YES/NO
5. Is it unethical to blame an error you made on a technological glitch? YES/NO
6. Is it unethical to visit pornographic Web sites using office equipment? YES/NO
7. Is a $50 gift to a boss unacceptable? YES/NO
8. Is it OK to accept a $200 pair of football tickets? YES/NO
9. Can you accept a $75 prize won at a raffle at a supplier's conference? YES/NO
10. Is it wrong to take sick days when you aren't really ill? YES/NO

*Adapted from a *Wall Street Journal* Workplace-Ethics Quiz (1999).

CONNECTING TO . . . **EDUCATION**

Are you considering a career in education? You have had exposure to excellent educators and effective communicators who can serve as models for your own teaching career if you are interested in one. Communication skills are part of what it means to be a successful teacher. From the manner in which you deliver information to the relationships you are able to form with your students, you will be called upon to use a wide variety of communication skills every day.

ACTIVITY

Meet in a small group with other students who are planning careers in teaching or are interested in teaching.

- Discuss communication skills that you consider to be important for effective teaching and communication behaviors that you consider to be undesirable. Be as specific as possible.

- As a group, identify the top five "effective" behaviors and the five most "ineffective" communication behaviors. Be prepared to report these to the class or to write about them if your teacher asks you to.

CONNECTING TO . . . **HEALTHCARE**

Are you considering a career in healthcare? Healthcare is a career area that will be in great demand for the foreseeable future due to the aging of our population and new jobs from advanced technologies. Even people who expect to work in accounting, law, marketing, and other business-oriented fields may find themselves employed by a healthcare organization.

ACTIVITY Meet with a group of other students who are planning careers in healthcare and do the following:

- Take turns sharing stories (health narratives) about your own experiences in healthcare settings.
- Think about an instance in which you have interacted with a healthcare professional. In what ways were the communication behaviors of the health professional effective or ineffective?
- If the communication was effective, what specific behaviors of the healthcare professional helped to create that outcome?
- If the communication was ineffective, where was the *noise*? How could you reframe your experience from the healthcare professional's perspective?

▶ Log onto MyCommunicationLab.com to access Connecting to Psychology and Connecting to Science, Technology, Engineering, and Math—both with related activities.

being noticed by those who can make the decision to promote you. Improved communication skills leads to improved upward mobility.

- *Improved Citizenship.* Imagine for a moment that your city council is deliberating the possibility of implementing a plan that you think would be detrimental to your neighborhood. What can you do about it? Many people in situations like this do little more than to bemoan their fate in conversations with neighbors. Other people, however, decide to make their voices heard. These people are not content to feel powerless. They recognize that it is not only their right as citizens to speak to their elected representatives: it is their responsibility.

As citizens, we have an obligation to be informed about the issues that have an impact on our lives and our communities. However, it is not enough to be informed; we must also communicate with other citizens and with decision makers in order to influence the outcomes of public debate. People who are less skilled in communication are often reluctant to participate in private or public discussion of issues, which essentially means that they have no "voice." Working to improve your communication skills can give you a voice and can, therefore, enable you to function more effectively in your role as a citizen.

APPLY **WHAT YOU KNOW**
COMMUNICATION COMPETENCIES AND BENEFITS

Apply what you know about communication competencies and benefits by answering the following:

- Think of an attempt at communication that went wrong. Briefly describe what happened.

- Explain which communication competency discussed earlier was likely missing and responsible for the misunderstanding or communication problem.

- Which communication benefit would make the greatest change in your life? And why?

CHAPTER SUMMARY

Understanding the basic communication process is the first step toward becoming a competent communicator. You can determine your knowledge of the communication process by checking the skills and learning objectives presented in this chapter.

Summary of **SKILLS**

Check each skill that you now feel qualified to perform:

- ❑ I can identify context in both its narrow and broad perspectives and account for the effect of context on my daily communication.
- ❑ I can identify the elements of the basic communication model and recognize those that I use effectively and those that need improvement.
- ❑ I can pinpoint the competencies of an effective communicator and realize that culture, gender, technology, and ethics play an important role in communication effectiveness.
- ❑ I can "reframe" situations from others' perspectives and can identify at least one source of "noise" in my own interactions that I plan to correct.

Summary of LEARNING **OUTCOMES**

1.1 *What are the basic terms in the definition of communi-cation, why is each so important, and what are the types of communication contexts included in this course?*

- Communication is defined as a transactional process by which people, interacting in a particular context, negotiate the meanings of verbal and nonverbal symbols in order to achieve shared understanding.

- The basic terms include transactional process, context (from a broad and narrow perspective), verbal and non-verbal symbols, and shared understanding.

- Each of these terms represents an important part of the communication process. Without terms for each compo-nent, it would be difficult to think about and discuss com-munication or identify the communication components needing improvement in our own communication.

- Types of communication contexts of special interest in this course include intrapersonal, interpersonal, group, organi-zational, public, and mass communication contexts.

- Determine your confidence levels by taking McCroskey's PRCA-24 survey in the *Developing Skills* feature in this chapter.

1.2 *What are the differences between the action, interaction, and transaction models of communication?*

- The action model views the communication process as a linear, or one-way, transmission of messages beginning with the sender and ending with the receiver; it does not involve feedback.

- The interaction model views communication as a circular process and involves feedback and frame of reference.

- The transaction model believes that both communicators create meaning simultaneously rather than in a linear or circular fashion and adds context to the model. It is the transaction model that gives the most complete view of communication.

1.3 *What are the elements of the transaction communica-tion model, how does each work, and what are the re-sulting communication principles?*

- The elements of the transaction model include the sender/receiver (or Person A/B), the message, encod-ing/decoding, frame of reference, code, channel, feed-back, context, and noise.

- A description of how each element of the transaction model works can be found on pages 13–17.

- Important communication principles to remember are communication is a simultaneous process; complex and difficult; intentional and unintentional; irreversible; and affected by rules and norms explained in the *Making*

Theory Practical feature on page 20. Additional principles include that communicators have unique frames of refer-ence; make sure their codes are congruent; use feedback to indicate how messages are received; and do their best to control the context.

1.4 *How do culture, gender, technology, and ethics affect our communication successes or failures?*

- The values, beliefs, attitudes, rules, and norms shared by the peoples of a particular culture tend to differ from cul-ture to culture and can affect communication success or failure. Major cultural differences discussed include the individualistic/collectivistic distinction, the high-context/ low-context distinction, and ethnocentrism.

- Gender differences, such as instrumental/expressive pref-erences, can affect communication success.

- When technology is a lean medium carrying only one communication code (as e-mail does), it has a greater chance of failure; however, when technology is a rich medium (such as television), it has a greater chance of success.

- People who are not ethical and do not follow a system of moral principles that governs their conduct when communicating with others are more likely to experi-ence communication failure.

1.5 *What are the basic communication competencies and skills that can be gained from a communication course and what specific benefits result from studying communication?*

- Competent communicators do each of the following: accept personal responsibility for their communication behavior; are ethical; are able to adapt their communi-cation to varied situations and, therefore, possess cogni-tive complexity and perspective taking; use verbal and nonverbal symbols effectively; use effective interpersonal skills; create and maintain successful relationships; are effective team participants and leaders; and are effec-tive listeners.

- There are many benefits to learning communication skills, including increased self-awareness, empowered participation, improved relationships, enhanced profes-sional success, and improved citizenship.

1.6 *What communication skills covered in this chapter relate specifically to your career (see highlighted fields of busi-ness, education, and healthcare)?*

- *The Spotlight on, Career Moment,* and *Connecting to* features highlight the value of communication in the fields of business, education, and healthcare.

 Taking into consideration all that you learned about communication from this chapter, how would you analyze the communication difficulties between Julie and Blanca in our opening scenario?*

• Which two or three *communication concepts* if known by Julie and Blanca would help them more accurately communicate with each other?

• Where in the *communication model* are Julie's and Blanca's difficulties occurring? Select and explain at least two locations for each person (such as *noise*).

• Which of the special concepts—*culture, gender, ethics,* or *technology*—do you think are causing the most communication difficulties between Julie and Blanca? Why?

• Which *communication goals* would you recommend that Julie and Blanca implement that would go a long way in helping them improve their situation? Why?

*(Check your answers with those located in MyCommunicationLab, Scenario Analysis for Chapter 1)

The next chapter will look at the role that self-concept and perception play in the success or failure of our communication with others.

KEY TERMS

action model	p. 11	ethics	p. 25	interpersonal communication	p. 7	psychological noise	p. 19
androgynous	p. 23	ethnocentrism	p. 23	intrapersonal communication	p. 7	public communication	p. 7
channel	p. 15	expressive communication	p. 23	lean medium channel	p. 24	receiver	p. 13
co-culture	p. 21	external noise	p. 18	low-context cultures	p. 22	reframe	p. 28
collectivistic cultures	p. 22	feedback	p. 16	mass communication	p. 8	rich medium channel	p. 24
communication	p. 5	frame of reference	p. 14	message	p. 14	rules	p. 18
computer mediated communication	p. 24	gender	p. 23	models	p. 11	self-monitoring	p. 28
context	p. 6	group communication	p. 7	negotiated meaning	p. 8	semantic noise	p. 19
Coordinated Management of Meaning Theory (CMM)	p. 18	high-context cultures	p. 22	noise	p. 18	sender	p. 13
culture	p. 21	individualistic cultures	p. 22	nonverbal code	p. 15	sex	p. 23
decoding	p. 14	instrumental communication	p. 23	norms	p. 18	symbols	p. 8
dyad	p. 7	interaction model	p. 12	organizational communication	p. 7	transaction model	p. 12
encoding	p. 14	internal noise	p. 19	physiological noise	p. 19	transactional process	p. 5
environment	p. 6					verbal code	p. 15

SKILL BUILDERS

1. Divide into groups and develop an original model of communication. Your model could take the form of a drawing, a skit, or a demonstration using the members of your group and/or objects to represent components of the model. Be prepared to present your model to the class.

2. Critically Evaluating What You Read
According to Paul & Elder (2003, p. 10), **critical thinking** is "that mode of thinking—about any subject, content, or problem—in which the thinker improves the quality of his or her

thinking by skillfully taking charge of the structures inherent in thinking and imposing intellectual standards upon them."

Instructions for this assignment: Find an article that relates to a term or concept from the chapter and analyze the "logic" of it using the template below. Your instructor may assign a paper based on your analysis below.

1) The main **purpose** of this article is: (State as accurately as possible the author's purpose for writing the article.)

_____

2) The key **question** that the author is addressing is: (Figure out the key question in the mind of the author when s/he wrote the article?) _____

3) The most important **information** in this article is: (Figure out the main facts, experiences, or data the author is using to support her/his conclusions.) _____

4) The main **inferences/conclusions** in this article are: (Identify the key conclusions the author comes to and presents in the article.) _____

5) The key **concept(s)** we need to understand in this article is/are: (Figure out the most important ideas you would have to understand in order to understand the author's line of reasoning.) _____

6) The main **assumption(s)** underlying the author's thinking is/are: (Figure out what the author is taking for granted that might be questioned.) _____

7) If we take this line of reasoning seriously, the **implications** are: (What consequences are likely to follow if people agree with the author's line of reasoning?) _____

8) If we fail to take this line of reasoning seriously, the **implications** are: (What consequences are likely to follow if people ignore the author's line of reasoning?)
_____

9) The main **points(s) of view** presented in this article is/are: (What is the author looking at, and how is s/he seeing it?) _____

3. As you think about the differences between **high-context** and **low-context cultures**, consider how you think these values might affect the way messages are encoded. For the following scenarios, encode the message the way you think would be typical for a person from a high-context culture, and then contrast that with the way you think a person from a low-context culture would choose to encode the same message.

- Two people (a dating couple) are at a party. One of them wants to leave and go somewhere else.

- A business owner is approached by a sales representative from a company that wishes to supply goods or services to the business owner. The business owner is not interested in the sales representative's product.

- A patient wants to tell a healthcare provider that prescribed treatments are not working and may be creating new health problems.

Now, using the same three scenarios, consider how **gender** might affect the way messages are encoded. For each scenario, encode the message the way you think would be typical for a man, and then contrast that with the way you think a woman would choose to encode the same message. How do you think this may relate to the concepts of high/low-context? What conclusions would you draw?

*Adapted from page 10 of Paul, R., & Elder, L. (2003). *The Miniature Guide to Critical Thinking: Concepts & Tools*. Dillon Beach, CA: The Foundation for Critical Thinking.

EXPLORE SOME MORE . . .

1. Looking for a good book that relates to communication and life? We suggest you read the following:

- *The Tipping Point: How Little Things Can Make a Big Difference* by Malcolm Gladwell (2002, Back Bay Books).

- *Communication Skills for Pharmacists* by Bruce Berger (2005, APhA Publications).

- *Messages: The Communication Skills Book* by Matthew McKay, Martha Davis, and Patrick Fanning (2009, Hew Harbinger Publications).

2. If you haven't seen the following movies, watch them and see how many ways each of them relates to this chapter on communication—especially what parts of the communication models appear in these movies:

- *Patch Adams* (1998)
- *Lost in Translation* (2003)
- *Spanglish* (2004)
- *Lackawanna Blues* (2005)
- *The Devil Wears Prada* (2006)
- *Wall-E* (2008)
- *Couples Retreat* (2009)

2 Using Perception to Understand Self and Others

After studying this chapter you should be able to . . .
- Recognize the importance of accurate perception in your everyday communication.
- Analyze and improve the accuracy of your self-concept.
- Analyze and improve your perception of others by pinpointing the perceptual errors that cause you the most trouble.
- Develop the skills of self-reflection, mindfulness, and perception checking.

CHAPTER SUMMARY P. 63

SCENARIO

Zach was puzzled. He and his brother, Tony, had been sharing an apartment for several months, and during that time they had fallen into a kind of routine. Typically, Zach got home from school and his part-time job around 7:00 p.m., and Tony soon after. They usually grabbed a bite to eat at a neighborhood restaurant where two of Zach's friends worked and where they watched sports while eating. Sometimes, Zach's friends came over when they were not working, and the four of them ordered a pizza and watched whatever game was on TV while they waited for it to be delivered. Later they went to their own rooms to study, talk on the phone, or occupy their time on their computers. Typically they ended the night prowling around the kitchen for whatever snack food they could find and exchanged commentary on a variety of topics before they turned in for the night. On the weekends, they played a golf game or went out with Zach's friends to the lake. Occasionally, Zach and Tony double-dated, though neither had a serious relationship with anyone in particular.

Recently, however, Zach noticed that Tony often did not return to the apartment until much later, and usually he had already eaten something when he got home. Sometimes he went straight to his room and got on the computer, and often he was already gone the following morning before Zach had gotten up for the day. Last weekend, Tony had declined to play golf with Zach and his friends, opting for a day at the school library. The weekend before, Tony had gone on a camping trip with friends from his work without inviting Zach.

Although Zach and Tony rarely argued about anything, Zach began to wonder if he had done something that had irritated Tony. In thinking about it, he remembered a comment Tony had made a couple of weeks before about how it would be nice if Zach would occasionally contribute some groceries; Zach had taken the hint and bought some soft drinks and chips the next day. Zach found himself building an angry argument in his head about how Tony rarely did anything to help keep the apartment reasonably clean.

When Tony came home that night, Zach angrily responded to Tony's "Hey, how's it going? You want to go grab something to eat?"

"Maybe we could eat here, if this place wasn't such a trash heap. You know, it would help if you were around sometimes to pick stuff up and load the dishwasher occasionally."

"Whoa! Where did that come from?" Tony replied. "I'll get around to cleaning up some as soon as I've finished my term paper in English and my business management project. It's not like I've had a lot of time, what with school and the extra hours I've had to pull at work. Since when did you become Mr. Clean?"

For some reason, this comment really angered Zach who retorted, "What's with you, anyway? It's like you don't even live here anymore. You don't even want to play golf or hang out on the weekends."

Tony tried not to get angry, "Like I said: I've been way busier than usual. Besides, it's not like you don't have plenty of friends to eat with and hang with during the weekends. I can't see how my not being around makes any difference."

Have you ever found yourself in a situation similar to Zach and Tony's? No matter how close our relationships with others might be, there are times when our understanding of what is happening differs from theirs. Very frustrating, isn't it? The main issue between Zach and Tony is *perception*—our topic for Chapter 2. As you read this chapter, see if you can determine which perceptual difficulties caused Tony in this scenario the most problem and which caused Zach the most difficulties. Select one or two communication goals for each that would improve their communication effectiveness as decoders.

SOLVE IT NOW! ⟩ P. 64 ⟩

The factors that shape our perceptions are significant because they are at the heart of how successfully we communicate. Most of the time, when we think about becoming more effective communicators, what we really mean is that we want to become better at *encoding* messages (i.e., improving the clarity or persuasiveness of our ideas). However, successful communication depends as much—perhaps even more—on how competent we are at *decoding* the messages others send to us. For that reason, Chapters 2 and 3 will focus, respectively, on the decoding processes of *perception* and *listening*. Each chapter will discuss difficulties we encounter in being accurate perceivers and listeners and will offer valuable skills we can use to solve these difficulties and improve our communication as receivers.

Perception: Definitions and Steps

LEARNING **OBJECTIVE**

2.1 What is the definition of perception, and what are the three basic steps involved?

As our opening scenario illustrates, communication is directly affected by our perceptions. **Perception** is the process by which individuals become aware of, organize, and interpret information received though their senses. As this definition indicates, perception doesn't happen all at once—it is a process that involves at least three steps. First, we *select* available data by "becoming aware of" or registering a small amount of stimuli in the environment; second, we *organize* this data into a form that we can more easily use and remember; and third, we *interpret* the data by adding meaning and making predictions. These steps may progress slowly, or they may occur in very quick succession—even in a matter of seconds. Let's expand our definition of *perception* by looking at each of these steps in more detail.

Step 1: Selecting Available Data

At any given moment, you are being bombarded by stimuli. As you are reading this sentence, for example, your *visual sense* is activated as you observe the words on the page. However, if you stop and listen, you will notice that there are also sounds in your environment that stimulate your *auditory sense*: you may have music on in the background, there may be sounds emanating from the light fixture overhead, or there may be any number of other sounds from people or objects in your immediate vicinity or in the distance. In addition, though you may not have noticed, there may be aromas in the room that can be detected by your *olfactory sense*. If you concentrate a little more, you might notice that your *gustatory sense* is able to discern taste, even if you are not currently eating or drinking anything. Furthermore, your *tactile sense* is at work, registering such stimuli as the touch of fabric on your skin and the temperature of the air in the room.

Figure 2.1 Which circle pops out for attention?

The conscious effort of choosing which stimulus from all those present in the environment to pay attention to is called **selection**. Below are some of the factors that determine why we choose to attend to one stimulus and ignore others. Each of these factors affects our own communication as receivers and can be useful when communicating as senders in various contexts—such as public speaking, where getting and keeping attention is crucial:

- *A stimulus that is more intense* than another is more likely to "pop-out" and catch your ear or eye (Kosslyn & Rosenberg, 2006). For example, louder voices and richer colors are more noticeable than quiet voices and muted hues (**Figure 2.1**).

- *A stimulus that changes* in some way—the sudden movement of something that was at rest, for example—may increase your awareness.

- *A stimulus that is novel or unexpected* is more likely to draw your attention. For example, the presence of a female in an otherwise all-male crowd might cause you to take notice.

- *A stimulus that has the potential to meet our needs* at a given moment will certainly attract our attention. For instance, if you are very hungry, you are more suscepti-ble to the aromas of cooking food than you might be if you had just eaten a hearty meal. Also, you are more likely to notice the sandwich shop located in the middle of the block if you are hungry (although you may have passed this same shop many times before without realizing it was there). And you are much more likely to tune in to your teacher's lecture if you know there will be a quiz at the end of it.

On the other hand, even with awareness and training, there are some physical and psychological factors that limit or distort our selection of stimuli. For example:

- *It is impossible to pay attention to two stimuli or tasks at the same instant* (Kosslyn & Rosenberg, 2006, pp. 158–159). Although we like to think we are good at multi-tasking or that our driving is not affected by talking on a cell phone, we are wrong. We can only attend to one task or stimulus at a particular instant and must divide our attention by shifting back and forth between them (Rodriguez, Valdes-Sona, & Freiwald, 2002). For example, it may be the swerving car that draws our attention from the cell phone back to the road—hopefully in time to avoid a collision. This divided attention usually causes us to perform less effec-tively on one or both of the tasks unless a particular task has become automatic.

- *Our personal filters may unconsciously distort accurate awareness of selected stimuli.* Not only do we selectively choose stimuli, we may unknowingly selectively distort them. **Selective distortion** is the process of an individual's expectations or fears deceiving the senses into reporting a false stimulus as real. Consider this example:

> A realtor walks into a deserted building to measure it for renovation. As she closes the door, the wind blows a crumpled piece of paper past her. She screams and runs back outside yelling that the building has rats. Even after she

is shown the paper by her colleague, who offers a more plausible version of what happened, the woman refuses to go back into the building until it is fumigated.

The realtor is positive that she saw a rat—if pressed, she could probably recall how large it was and the length of its tail. Yet her expectations (based on past experiences or fears) gave her a distorted view of reality.

Summarizing Step 1 of the perception process, we can see that not only do we selectively attend to a small amount of the available stimuli in any situation, but that the stimuli we do select may be limited and/or distorted by sensory and psychological factors.

We have to conclude by looking at the first step in the perception process that *we are not perfect decoders.* Unfortunately, the next step in perception also contains some decoding problems.

Is multitasking possible? Can you pay attention to driving while talking on a cell phone? If you said yes, think again.

APPLY **WHAT YOU KNOW**
PERCEPTION AND MULTITASKING

"I multitask" is a comment people make with pride. But can nurses, mothers, teachers, and business professionals or any of us really multitask or are we just good at breaking down stimuli and tasks into small pieces and moving back and forth between them? Apply what you know to these questions:

- When a student works on math problems for a class while listening to music—is this multitasking? Would this be the same

as a student who is listening to music in preparation for a music appreciation exam while also working on math problems for a class? Why or why not?

- What about an employee working on an important project while answering e-mail—can these tasks be done simultaneously? What do you think happens to the employee's concentration each time a new e-mail arrives—would the quality of work and the level of concentration be affected? Why or why not?

Step 2: Organizing Data into a Usable Form

What do the following symbols mean to you: "Тоате фиинцеле умане се наск либере ши егале ын демнитате ши ын дрептурь?" Unless you can read the Cyrillic alphabet used in eastern Slavic countries, just attending to this stimulus isn't very helpful, is it? Once we choose to pay attention to a particular stimulus (Step 1 of the perception process), the next step is to organize the data into a usable form. **Organization** involves discovering the recognizable patterns in the stimulus and recoding them in a form that is simple enough to remember and use. You might have suspected that the above symbols represented words, but you would not be able to organize them into meaningful communication; however, a Russian or Romanian would likely have no problem. Translated into English, the Cyrillic words read: "All human beings are born free and equal in dignity and rights" (Lazarev, 2007).

In order to communicate and make sense out of our environment, it is important for humans to organize and group stimuli into usable patterns. There are several ways we do this, depending on the type of stimuli. Two of the most useful ways of organizing data involve laws of organization and stereotyping.

Laws of Organization

Laws of Organization   One of the first ways humans discover the recognizable patterns in a stimulus is almost automatically initiated by their brains. Gestalt psychologists discovered several ways the brain groups visual and vocal stimuli into patterns and called them **laws of organization** (Kosslyn & Rosenberg, 2006, p. 146). *Gestalt* is a German word meaning "whole"; gestalt psychologists were interested in how the whole became more than a "sum of its parts" (i.e., how a flock is more than a sum of 50 individual birds (p. 13)). We will look at three laws of organization:

- **Proximity**—Objects that are close together tend to be grouped together.

  How many groups are in each item? A: ■■　■■　■■■　■■　B: ■■■■■■■■■

  How many groups of sounds are in this item? tap-tap, pause, tap-tap, pause, tap-tap

- **Similarity**—Objects that look similar tend to be grouped together.

  How many groups are in each item? A: ■■□□■■□□■■　B: ABCXYZ

  How many groups of sound waves do you see?　ᨠᨠᨠᨠ

  How many objects are here?　✳

- **Closure**—Incomplete figures tend to be closed or filled in to represent a whole object.

  What object do you see here?　⌐　　⌐

  　　　　　　　　　　　　　∨

Since the initial development of Gestalt theory, knowledge of perceptual grouping has expanded widely. For example, artists and advertisers know that size, distance, color, texture, shapes, spatial relations, motion, and figure-ground cues are just a few additional factors that also affect organization of data. Let's look at two specific ways that organizing data may cause possible decoding issues:

1. **Ambiguous Figures**—Figure-ground contrast allows figures to be organized so that they can be viewed in more than one way. Psychologists refer to these figures as ambiguous figures (Kosslyn & Rosenberg, 2006, p. 146). Take a look at **Figure 2.2**. In example a, do you see a variety of dark shapes, or do you see a word? In example b, do you see a person playing an instrument such as a saxophone or do you see a woman's face? In example c, there are three different people—do you see a young woman, an old woman, and a man with a mustache?

2. **Visual illusions**—What your eyes tell you is true is not always as it appears to be. For example, take a look at the objects in **Figure 2.3**. Look at the horizontal lines in example a. If your eyes tell you that the horizontal lines are not parallel, your eyes are wrong. The placement of the white and black squares is causing a visual illusion. Which line in example b is shorter: the top or bottom? Although the bottom line definitely looks shorter, both lines

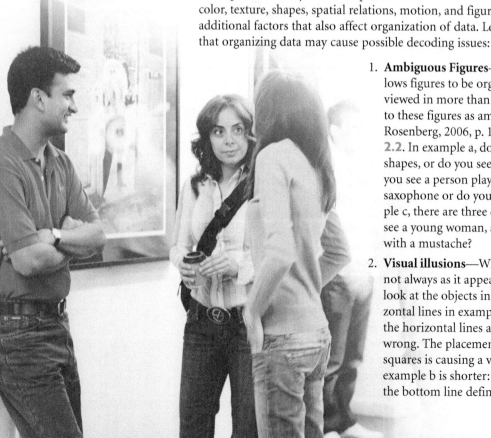

Even in the noisy yet interesting environment of a crowded party, we humans organize and group stimuli into usable patterns.

(a)

(b)

(c)

Figure 2.2 Ambiguous Figures Talk with your classmates and see which objects they saw first. Why didn't everyone see the same objects first? Once you can see each object, is one still dominant? *What you see depends on how you organize or attend to the stimuli in the figures.*

are identical in length. How about the curved objects in example c—which is obviously smaller: the blue or the pink object? You probably chose the blue on the right (pull back from the page to make it look even smaller). Yet, if you look very carefully, you can see that the objects are identical in size. And finally, count the black dots in example d. Actually, all of the dots are white, but if you look at a white surface first, then look at the object, blink, and move your eyes around the object, several black dots will appear—a visual illusion.

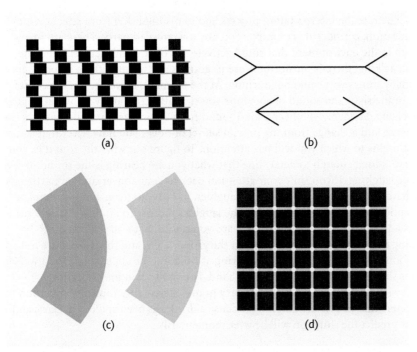

(a)

(b)

(c)

(d)

Figure 2.3 Visual Illusions If our eyes were like a camera that takes a picture of what is really there, would magicians be able to fool us so easily?

Even though you probably will find Figures 2.2 and 2.3 intriguing, you may be wondering how these visual illusions apply to communication. We use these same principles to generalize and organize our impressions of people to make sense of their behaviors and to communicate with them. For example, if we see a person whom we think has a certain characteristic (e.g., "quiet") but we know little else about the person, we will gain *closure* by assigning other characteristics to that person that fit into the same cluster. If we consider "quiet," "intelligent," and "friendly" to cluster together, "we may then attribute intelligence to that person without any firsthand evidence" (Trenholm & Jensen, 2006, p. 181).

APPLY **WHAT YOU KNOW**
PERCEPTION AND ORGANIZATION

To apply what you know about perception and organization, answer these critical thinking questions:

- There are many factors that cause us to choose to attend to one stimulus while ignoring others: for example, if the stimulus is novel; if the stimulus has motion; or if the stimulus is intense. Select two factors and give an example of each.

- How could you use *proximity* and *similarity* as organizational tools to make it easier to remember information about class-mates? Give a specific example.

Step 3: Interpreting the Data by Adding Meaning and Making Predictions

Having selected a particular stimulus to which you will pay attention, and having figured out exactly what that stimulus is, your next step is to interpret the stimulus. **Interpretation** is the process of attaching meaning to words, acts, or events in our environment and using the meaning to make predictions about future events or behaviors. In other words, we go beyond the data we have collected and the stereotypes we used to store our impressions and assign meanings and make predictions.

To illustrate the interpretation process and to distinguish it from selection and organization, consider this example: You are at a crowded party. There are many stimuli in the environment that could activate any of your five senses: There are people talking, there is music, there are fragrances and aromas, there is food, and there are many things you could be touching. At the moment, however, you are conscious only of the sight and sound of someone you find attractive and with whom you are conversing. Suddenly you hear a loud sound from across the room. Because the sound is intense and a change from the previous level of noise, you now select that sound as the stimulus to which you will pay attention. To figure out what the sound is, you observe it long enough to determine that what you are hearing is the sound of several people laughing. If you shift your attention back to your conversational partner, you will have only partially perceived the laughter. In order to form a more complete perception, you must interpret what the laughter means. To do that, you will need to select and organize other stimuli. Perhaps you notice that everyone seems to be looking at one person in the middle of the group, Gary, and that Gary does not appear to be joining in the laughter. He is glaring at Mike and he appears to have a wet spot on his shirt and an empty glass in his hand. For clarity, you may store your impressions of Gary in a "harmless party prank" stereotype. Your interpretation might be merely that people are laughing because a drink has been spilled on Gary, and you might predict the situation will be over momentarily.

Because people's frames of reference are never exactly the same, we may interpret an event quite differently from someone else. Using the scenario above as an example, what additional interpretation might we draw from observing the laughing party-goers?

- Assume for a moment that your friend Sonya notices the laughter, the stain on the shirt, and Gary's frown. Because of her negative past experiences with both Gary and Mike, she stores her observations in the stereotype of "trouble-maker." Her interpretation of the situation may be that Mike likely spilled the drink on Gary on purpose and that Gary is hot-headed and likely to use this as an excuse to start a fight. Although you may think Gary is involved in a harmless party prank, Sonya thinks that Gary is a trouble-causer. She motioned to a mutual friend to join you and she says she thinks it would be a good idea for all three of you to get out before things get ugly.

- With a third interpretation, however, the mutual friend says, "Oh, it's no big deal. Gary is just embarrassed about spilling his drink."

Here we see three people and three different interpretations of what happened as well as predictions of what may happen next. We might question whether all three were observing the same event. It's no wonder that perceptual differences cause misunderstandings.

APPLY **WHAT YOU KNOW**
PERCEPTUAL DIFFERENCES

Apply what you know about interpreting data and making predictions by answering the following questions:

- Consider this chapter's opening scenario about Zach and Tony. Do you think Zach's perception and interpretation of

events is more a result of active or subjective perception? Explain your choice.

- What role does Zach's frame of reference contribute to his interpretation of Tony's behavior?

Factors That Lead to Differences in Perception

LEARNING **OBJECTIVE**

2.2 What are the three major factors in perception that help explain why people perceive things differently (and sometimes erroneously)?

Although we have already discussed many factors that can cause errors in perception, let's review three of the major factors that help explain why people perceive things differently (and sometimes erroneously): physiological, psychological, and cultural factors.

Physiological Factors in Perceptual Errors

Our perceptions begin at the physiological level where our sensory organs are activated and send messages to our brain. Therefore, there are **physiological factors** (any impairment of a sensory organ) that affect our perceptions by interfering with accurate perception of stimuli. Poor vision or hearing, for example, may cause us to err in perceiving sights and sounds. Potential vision problems include near- or far-sightedness, color blindness (see *Spotlight on* feature later in chapter), and light sensitivity—when you walk into a dark room on a sunny day and are "blinded," how long does it take for you to adjust? Within 30 minutes, most people's eyes are 100,000 times more sensitive to light (Kosslyn & Rosenberg, 2006, p. 139). Or you may have difficulty (as many people do) distinguishing colors such as red and brown that look alike when viewed from a distance (Johnson, 1995).

Our other senses may not be so reliable either. Take smell, for example: some people are 20 percent more sensitive to smell than are others (Rabin & Cain, 1986). Our hearing varies also. People who like to listen to loud music, use portable music players with ear buds, are musicians, or work in a loud environment may have a significant hearing loss in later years since hearing loss is usually a gradual occurrence (Perusse, 2008).

Other physiological factors that play a role in perception include gender, physical characteristics, and health. Researchers are actively engaged in studying how a man's cerebral cortex processes emotional stimuli differently than a woman's (Alter, et al., 2003; Hess, et. al., 2000; Schirmer & Simpson, 2008). In addition, a physically fit person may assess the weight of an object differently from a less able-bodied friend. Also, there is considerable difference in the degree of sensitivity to stimuli from person to person. Do you know someone who is perpetually cold even when you find the room temperature quite comfortable? If you are ill, hungry, or tired, you probably perceive many things differently from the way you might if you were healthy, well-fed, and well-rested.

Psychological Factors in Perceptual Errors

In addition to physiological factors, there are many **psychological factors** that enter into how we perceive others and how others perceive us. People who are experiencing *strong emotions*—sorrow, anxiety, fear, anger, joy—undoubtedly perceive events differently from those who are not caught up in those emotions, and differently from the way they themselves would if they were not experiencing those feelings. Your *outlook on life* (generated by your personality traits) will color your perceptions as well. People who are generally more optimistic may interpret events more favorably than those who tend to be pessimistic about life. Your *present circumstances* will also affect how you perceive events. For example, when you feel confident about yourself and about your relationship with someone else, you may interpret comments differently from the way you do when you feel insecure about yourself or the relationship. Have you found that your *moods* may cause you to interpret things differently from day to day? What you found funny yesterday may be annoying today. No doubt you can think of many other psychological variables that affect how you are likely to perceive words, acts, or events.

Cultural Factors in Perceptual Errors

The *culture* or *co-culture* with which you identify exerts a powerful influence on your perception. From simple things, such as whether a food item is spicy or bland, to more complex issues, such as what sorts of behaviors are acceptable or unacceptable, your perceptions are strongly related to the norms of your cultural group. Do body odors offend you? For members of some cultural groups, the normal smells of the human body are just that—normal. People in these groups find the American obsession with personal hygiene mystifying! We will discuss some of the differences in cultural expectations more thoroughly in Chapters 3 and 5, but for now consider the perceptual differences shown by **Figure 2.4**—the top ten values of three different cultural groups: Arab countries, Japan, and the United States. After looking at the differences in the values on each list, is it any wonder that communication errors occur? You can probably think of many other ways in which perceptions you have about many things differ from the perceptions of friends of yours with different cultural heritages.

Figure 2.4 **The top 10 values of three cultural groups**

Arab Countries:	**Japan:**	**United States:**
1. Family security	1. Belonging	1. Freedom
2. Family harmony	2. Group harmony	2. Independence
3. Parental guidance	3. Collectiveness	3. Self-reliance
4. Age	4. Age and seniority	4. Equality
5. Authority	5. Group consensus	5. Individualism
6. Compromise	6. Cooperation	6. Competition
7. Devotion	7. Quality	7. Efficiency
8. Patience	8. Patience	8. Time
9. Indirectness	9. Indirectness	9. Directness
10. Hospitality	10. Hospitality	10. Openness

Source: From F. Elashmawi and P. R. Harris. *Multicultural Management,* p. 72. Copyright © 2000 by Elsevier. Reprinted by permission.

APPLY **WHAT YOU KNOW**
CULTURE AND PERCEPTUAL ERRORS

Apply what you know about perception by answering these questions relating to culture:

- Although there is some agreement in the top ten values held by Arab and Japanese peoples (Figure 2.4), how do you explain the fact that not one of the American values appears in the other two lists?

- If an international problem-solving team composed of members from all three groups of people were selected to solve a serious problem with another country, discuss at least two perceptual differences that could likely cause misunderstandings. If you were the leader of the team, what could you do to minimize any misunderstandings, and why do you think your approach has a chance of working?

Now that we have talked in general terms about the perception process and factors that lead to differences and errors in perception, we will turn our attention to two very important entities in our perception: ourselves and others. Our understanding of ourselves and our perception of the other person with whom we are communicating are the principal factors that determine not only how we send messages but, most particularly, how we receive and decode messages.

Perception and Self

Successful communication requires successful perception on the part of those involved. As we discussed in Chapter 1, intrapersonal communication deals with how we perceive ourselves; interpersonal communication deals with how we perceive others. How you perceive yourself plays a large role in how successfully you communicate with others.

LEARNING **OBJECTIVE**

2.3 What is the definition of self-concept, how does it relate to perception and communication, and what are some of the major barriers in forming an accurate self-concept?

Self-Concept Defined

Your overall understanding of who you are is referred to as your **self-concept.** Self-concept is a kind of umbrella term that includes many other concepts. For example, a **self-image** is the picture you have of yourself—not only how you look, but how you interact with others. Another important element of your self-concept is your **self-esteem**, which refers to the degree to which you see yourself as valuable and worthwhile. We often talk about how some people seem to have an "inferiority complex," meaning that they tend to see others as more competent and worthy than themselves. We generally believe that it is a good thing to have "positive self-esteem,"

DEVELOPING **SKILLS**
HOW TO DETERMINE YOUR PERSONALITY TYPE*

One reason our perceptions of objects, ideas, and other people differ is that our *personality types* differ. To get an indication of your personality type, complete the following survey, based on Jung's Typology and the Myers-Briggs Type Indicator (MBTI). When answering these questions, don't think of a single situation; instead, consider generally how you would answer each question regardless of the situation.

Choose either *a* or *b* for each question below—select the one that is more like you:

1. I would rather:
   a. Solve a new and complicated problem
   b. Work on something I've done before

2. I like to:
   a. Work alone in a quiet place
   b. Be where "the action" is

3. I want a boss who:
   a. Establishes and applies criteria in decisions
   b. Considers individual needs and makes exceptions

4. When I work on a project, I:
   a. Like to finish it and get some closure
   b. Often leave it open for possible change

5. When making a decision, my most important considerations are:
   a. Rational thoughts, ideas, and data
   b. People's feelings and values

6. On a project, I tend to:
   a. Think it over and over before I begin to work
   b. Start working right away, thinking as I go

7. When working on a project, I prefer to:
   a. Maintain as much control as possible
   b. Explore various options

8. In my work, I prefer to:
   a. Work on several projects at a time, learning as much as possible from each
   b. Have one project that is challenging and keeps me busy

9. I often:
   a. Make lists and plans whenever I start something and hate to alter them
   b. Avoid plans and just let things progress as I work on them

10. When discussing a problem with colleagues, it is easier for me:
    a. To see "the big picture"
    b. To grasp the specifics of the situation

11. When I listen to someone talk, I usually:
    a. Consider it an interruption
    b. Don't mind answering it

12. The word that describes me better is:
    a. Analytical
    b. Empathetic

13. When working on assignments, I tend to:
    a. Work steadily and consistently
    b. Work in bursts of energy with "down time" in between

14. When I listen to someone talk, I try to:
    a. Relate it to my experience and see if it fits
    b. Assess and analyze the message

15. When I come up with new ideas, I generally:
    a. "Go for it"
    b. Like to contemplate them some more

16. When working on a project, I prefer to:
    a. Narrow the scope so it is clearly defined
    b. Broaden to include related aspects

17. When I read something, I usually:
    a. Confine my thoughts to what is written
    b. Read between the lines and relate words to other ideas

18. When making a decision in a hurry, I often:
    a. Feel uncomfortable and wish for more information
    b. Am able to do so with available data.

19. In a meeting, I tend to:
    a. Continue formulating my ideas as I talk about them
    b. Speak out only after I have carefully thought the issue through

20. At work, I prefer spending a great deal of time on issues of:
    a. Ideas
    b. People

21. In meetings, I am most often annoyed with people who:
    a. Come up with many sketchy ideas
    b. Lengthen the meeting with many practical details.

22. I tend to be:
    a. A morning person
    b. A night owl

23. My style in preparing for a meeting is:
   a. To be willing to go in and be responsive
   b. To be fully prepared and sketch out an outline of the meeting.

24. In meetings, I would prefer for people to:
   a. Display a fuller range of emotions
   b. Be more task-oriented

25. I would rather work for an organization where:
   a. My job was intellectually stimulating
   b. I was committed to its goals and mission

26. On weekends, I tend to:
   a. Plan what I will do
   b. Just see what happens and decide as I go

27. I am more:
   a. Outgoing
   b. Contemplative

28. I would rather work for a boss who is:
   a. Full of new ideas
   b. Practical

In numbers 29–32, select the word in each pair that is more appealing to you:

29. a. Social
   b. Theoretical

30. a. Inventiveness
   b. Practicality

31. a. Organized
   b. Adaptable

32. a. Active
   b. Concentration

Scoring A: Put the letter of your answer to each question in the blanks below:

1. ____	9. ____	17. ____	25. ____
2. ____	10. ____	18. ____	26. ____
3. ____	11. ____	19. ____	27. ____
4. ____	12. ____	20. ____	28. ____
5. ____	13. ____	21. ____	29. ____
6. ____	14. ____	22. ____	30. ____
7. ____	15. ____	23. ____	31. ____
8. ____	16. ____	24. ____	32. ____

Scoring B:

1. Circle answers below if you find them in the list above. For example, if you answered *a* to 1, you would locate 1a below next to INtuition and circle it; if you answered *b* to 1, you would locate 1b next to Sensing and circle it.

2. In each bracketed group of two characteristics listed below, the line with the most circled answers is most like you. Circle the bold letter representing your style located in front of each bracketed pair.

I or E { Introversion—2a, 6a, 11a, 15b, 19b, 22a, 27b, 32b
{ Extroversion—2b, 6b, 11b, 15a, 19a, 22b, 27a, 32a

S or N { Sensing—1b, 10b, 13a, 16a, 17a, 21a, 28b, 30b
{ INtuition—1a, 10a, 13b, 16b, 17b, 21b, 28a, 30a

T or F { Thinking—3a, 5a, 12a, 14b, 20a, 24b, 25a, 29b
{ Feeling—3b, 5b, 12b, 14a, 20b, 24a, 25b, 29a

J or P { Judging—4a, 7a, 8b, 9a, 18b, 23b, 16a, 31a
{ Perceiving—4b, 7b, 8a, 9b, 18a, 23a, 26b, 31b

3. Your MBTI is made up of all four circled bold letters (i.e., ENFP)—write them below.

Your Final Style: _____

Source: From Daft & Marcic, *Understanding Management,* 5th ed., pp. 401–404. Copyright © 2006 South-Western, a part of Cengage Learning, Inc. Reprinted by permission. www.cengage.com/permissions.

***Note:** The above test prepared by Marcic and Daft is a quick self-test only to give you an idea of how the MBTI works and not the licensed instrument.

although certainly there are people who seem to have an inflated impression of their own value, as is true when someone is arrogant or habitually criticizes or demeans others. A *healthy self-esteem* would be illustrated by people who have confidence in their own worth but also recognize the worth of others.

Barnlund's "6-Person" Concept: A "Self" Orientation

To illustrate how perception and self-concept play definite roles in the success of your communication, let's revisit the transaction model of communication covered in Chapter 1 (see Figure 1.3). As you recall, a *transaction* is an exchange in which both parties are responsible for the outcome and in which both parties affect and are affected by the other. Dean Barnlund (1970) was a communication theorist who advocated the transactional process of communication and illustrated the problems involved by referring to his "6-person" concept. According to Barnlund, when two people are talking, there are actually six separate entities involved. Each person communicates from within an understanding of who he or she is—which is perception of self or self-concept. At the same time, each person has a view of the other person; perception of others is filtered by our frames of reference and personality. Further, each person has a perception of how he or she is viewed by the other person—in other words, "who you think they think you are," which is a *reflected appraisal*.

Let's go back to our opening scenario for this chapter involving Zach and Tony. Following Barnlund's 6-person concept, when Zach and Tony are communicating, the following six entities are involved:

- Person 1 = Zach's view of Zach (Zach's Zach)
- Person 2 = Tony's view of Tony (Tony's Tony)
- Person 3 = Zach's view of Tony (Zach's Tony)
- Person 4 = Tony's view of Zach (Tony's Zach)
- Person 5 = Zach's view of how Tony sees him (Zach's Tony's Zach)
- Person 6 = Tony's view of how Zach sees him (Tony's Zach's Tony)

So it's no wonder that Zach and Tony were having communication difficulties in the opening scenario.

Plus-2 Concept: An "Other" Orientation[1]

Being aware that there are actually six entities involved in interpersonal interaction may improve our communication by making us aware of the inherent complexity of the process. However, all six of these entities are egocentric or "self" oriented. In other words, when I am talking with you, there is *my* view of myself, *my* view of you, and *my* view of how you see *me*—"self" oriented. And you are equally as self-oriented.

For a complete picture, we need to add two more entities to our 6-person concept. These two entities give us an "other" orientation to add to our self-orientations—thus the "Plus-2." When I add "my view of how you see yourself," and you add "your view of how I see myself," we have added more than understanding; we have added empathy. **Empathy** occurs when you put yourself in other people's frames of reference—try to walk in their shoes or see the situation through their eyes. This view makes cooperation, problem-solving, and communication much easier; perception is now less self-oriented and more other-oriented. Now when Zach and Tony are

[1]The Plus-2 Concept was developed specifically for this text by Cheryl Hamilton—one of your authors.

communicating, there are actually 8 entities—the two new entities include:

- Person 7 = Zach's view of how Tony sees himself (Zach's Tony's Tony)
- Person 8 = Tony's view of how Zach sees himself (Tony's Zach's Zach)

Whereas we were beginning to get overwhelmed with 6 entities, now that we have added plus-2, it all starts to make more sense and seem less frantic. By emphasizing the other person, the pressure seems more manageable; perception seems more valuable. Empathy is covered in much more detail in Chapter 3, including empathic listening responses.

Barriers to an Accurate Self-Concept

It is important to have an accurate self-concept when we communicate because when we interpret the meaning of others, we filter it through our understanding of who we are. However, there are many things that may cause us to have problems in accurately perceiving ourselves. See if any of the following problems relate to you and your self-concept:

"What do you think I think about what you think I think you've been thinking about?"

Self-Concept Is a Reflection of Appraisals from Others

We do not come into this world with a ready-built self-concept. Our understanding of who we are results from how and what others communicate to us throughout our lives. We develop a self-concept from the inferences or **reflected appraisals** we perceive from what others say to us or how they behave towards us (Edwards, 1990). In other words, the way we think others see us is often the way we see ourselves. From infancy, we receive messages about whether we are worthwhile, based on the ways that our parents and caregivers respond to our needs. Imagine crying when you were young and no one coming versus having several people running to you at even the smallest peep. As our contact with other significant people increases, we receive additional messages about who we are from teachers, other adults, and peers—whether we are pretty, smart, athletic, musically gifted, and so on. Eventually we develop a fairly stable self-concept.

Self-Concept Is Resistant to Change

One problem in accurate self-perception is that our self-concepts, once they are stable, tend to *resist change*. Even if your understanding of yourself is distorted, it is the concept with which you are comfortable, so you tend to cling to it. Therefore, developing a fairly stable self-concept is both a good thing and a bad thing. Certainly it is a good thing to have a strong self-concept so that you are not confused about who you are or overly willing to accept others' appraisals of you. On the other hand, a strong self-concept can be a problem. If others tell us something that contradicts what we believe to be true about ourselves, how do we handle those messages? Typically, we ignore contradictory messages, or explain them away. "He's just being nice," we say, or "That can't be true; I know I'm not attractive." Consider the example of people who suffer from eating disorders. Everyone they know tells them that they are dangerously underweight, but in their mind—their self-image—they are not just overweight, they are *fat*. They may hear what others tell them as efforts to undermine what they see as a healthy weight-loss or as jealousy. Clearly, an inaccurate self-concept can have dangerous consequences.

Self-Concept Involves Self-Serving Bias

Another problem in accurate self-perception is the **self-serving bias** (Duval & Silva, 2002), which occurs when we tend to accept responsibility for positive outcomes in our life but deny responsibility for negative outcomes. When you make a good grade on an exam, you are most likely to attribute that to your superior intellect or your diligence in preparing for the exam; when you do poorly on an exam, you are likely to find others to blame. Another example of the self-serving bias at work is found in the tendency we have to think of ourselves as among those who fall into the "above average" category. For example, a study of 1,255 college students found that 99 percent judged themselves to be either "very honest" or "honest," and 62 percent felt that other people would rate them as "very honest" (Rakovski & Levy, 2007). However, 60 percent of these same students admitted to performing dishonest acts.

Self-Concept Involves Self-Fulfilling Prophecy

Another problem that leads to a distortion in our perception of ourselves is called **self-fulfilling prophecy**—which occurs when we predict the outcome of an anticipated event and then engage in behaviors that insure that outcome. When you say, "I can't possibly pass this exam, so I may as well not waste my time studying for it," you are setting yourself up for the self-fulfilling prophecy. Chances are that you will then decide not to study for the exam and, as a result, will do poorly on it. Then you will point to the outcome and declare, "See! I knew I wouldn't do well. I know myself." But did you really know yourself, or did you simply choose the behaviors that led to the failing grade?

Self-Concept Clings to Stagnant Thinking

Another challenge to accurate self-perception lies in the tendency to cling to **stagnant thinking**. As we discussed above, our self-concept, once it is fairly stable, resists change. However, human beings do change. If you think back to the sort of person you were in grade school, you can likely identify several ways in which you have changed as you have matured. Perhaps you used to be less confident than you are now. Or you might have discovered abilities that you didn't know you had until recently. If we cling too much to our self-concept, we limit what we can come to know of ourselves because we avoid trying out new activities or exploring new ways of thinking about ourselves. Because you were not proficient in playing soccer in kindergarten does not mean that you do not have any athletic ability; it may just mean that soccer is not your sport!

An accurate self-conception is difficult to achieve

Self-Concept Is Affected by Self-Talk

All of these problems in accurately perceiving ourselves are compounded by our **self-talk**—the intrapersonal messages we send to ourselves. These messages powerfully affect the choices we make in everything, including how we communicate. "I know I'll fumble my responses in this job interview" is exactly the kind of self-talk that leads to the self-fulfilling prophecy. "I've never been good at meeting people" perpetuates stagnant thinking.

Psychologist Albert Ellis, founder of the therapeutic approach known as **Rational-Emotive Behavior** Therapy or cognitive restructuring (Ellis, 1994, 2004), points out that our self-talk is often self-defeating, and that this is due to our tendency to hold certain "irrational beliefs." For example, many people refuse to try something new because they believe that they must be competent in all they do. When you think about this idea, you can see that this is wholly irrational, and yet, how often do you berate yourself when you are not successful at something you are trying to do? Some people think that they must always be loved and approved of, which causes them to feel deeply hurt when they encounter someone who does not seem to like them. In reality, you will meet many people in your life who are not particularly attracted to you, but this does not mean that you are not lovable or worthwhile. The problem with holding any of these irrational beliefs (Dr. Ellis and his protégés identified twelve of them) is that they lead to distortions in how we view ourselves, our competence, and our essential worthiness. For more information on self-talk, see Use Cognitive Restructuring in Chapter 10.

This child's self-concept will be formed in part from the messages he receives from others about who he is.

Self-Concept and Impression Management Can Create Ethical Issues

Whether we realize it or not, we strive to create a special image of ourselves in our interactions with others. This process of **impression management** involves choices that we make about how we speak and behave in order to affect what others think of us (Rosenfeld, 1997). Some scholars refer to this as "facework," meaning that we choose which "face"—which aspect of our personality—we will reveal to a given person at a given time (Ting-Toomey, 2000; Ting-Toomey & Kurogi, 1988). If we are ethical communicators, we do not try to manipulate others' impressions of us by pretending to be something we are not. However, we are complicated creatures; we do not have just one "self." Each of us embodies many different traits, sometimes even traits that are opposites. You may know, for example, that you have a quiet self, but that you also have a more boisterous and sociable side. You may recognize that you are often very responsible, but that you have a more carefree and fun-loving "face" as well. You reveal different faces to different people according to the type of relationship you hope to develop with each person. It is not dishonest to be somewhat different in different relationships, but it is unethical to pose as something you are not in order to win someone's favor through deception. For more on face and face negotiation theory, see the *Making Theory Practical* feature in Chapter 6.

APPLY **WHAT YOU KNOW**
PERCEPTION AND SELF

Now that you are aware of the terms and information used to explain self-concept, consider these questions:

- How would you describe your self-concept—including how healthy and accurate you judge it to be?

- Think of some aspect of your self-concept that may be a product of stagnant thinking or negative self-talk. How can you determine whether change is needed?

LEARNING **OBJECTIVE**

2.4 What are the barriers to accurate perception of others, and how does each barrier affect our communication success?

Perception and Others

As important as our self-concept is in determining how we decode the messages of others, our accuracy in perceiving others is equally crucial. Unfortunately, there are many barriers to accurate perception of others. Which of these perception problems have affected you and your communication?

First Impressions

One problem we have in perceiving others accurately is that we tend to adhere to **first impressions**. We cannot avoid forming first impressions; they are a natural part of sizing up another person to determine whether communication with them is desirable or not. Interviewers certainly form first impressions. One of the first studies on interviewers and first impressions (Blakeman et al., 1971, p. 57) found that positive first impressions (formed in the first five minutes) resulted in a job offer 75 percent of the time; however, negative first impressions resulted in no job offer 90 percent of the time. More recent research reinforces the power of first impressions (Burgoon & Hoobler, 2002; Zunin & Zunin, 1994). The problem arises when we cling to our first impressions to such a degree that we fail to alter those impressions even when new information is received—which might happen as we come to know the person better. We may decide, based on a first impression, that the person is not worth getting to know better at all and choose to have no further interaction. If so, we will have no way to confirm or reject the first impression. It is important to be open to new information and new ways of perceiving.

Stereotyping

Often the inaccuracy in our first impressions is complicated by our tendency to stereotype. **Stereotyping** is what we do when we make assumptions about people based on our perceptions of the groups to which they belong. More specifically, stereotyping (which relates to the organizational principle of similarity) occurs when we store our perceptions of a person by inserting them into a larger, more generalized category. Sometimes these categories (which were learned from experiences, friends, family, and the media) require some thought; usually, however, they come to us almost automatically. Although stereotyping generally has a negative connotation, it does help order our lives, saves time, and allows us to function in situations where we may have limited information. Stereotyping—like first impressions—can serve as a kind of "first hunch" about how to approach communication with a person from a particular group.

However, stereotyping can cause real problems if we fail to realize that our perceptions are not "reality" but are "filtered views of reality." It can also cause us to forget that all people are unique.

We typically think of stereotypes as they relate to how we react to people from different cultural or social groups from our own. As a member of one race, you may have perceptions of what people from another race are likely to believe or how they are likely to behave; you then assume that a particular individual from that race will embody all the characteristics you believe to be true of that racial group. Stereotypes are not limited to race, though; they include beliefs we may hold about people of particular age groups, occupations, social classes, geographic regions, gender, political persuasion, or other connections.

This Southwest Airlines ticket agent knows how important first impressions are to company success.

Perceptual Constancy

Another problem we have with accurately perceiving others is that we seek perceptual constancy. **Perceptual constancy** refers to a desire for consistency between what we have experienced in the past and what we are experiencing in the present. If my first impression of you is that you are an honest individual, then I am going to expect you to be honest in all of our interactions. This tendency is related to the problem of **halo effect**, which occurs when a positive assessment of a person with respect to one central trait leads to the assumption of other positive traits, whether observed or not. For example, attractive people are often assumed to possess other traits that are considered socially desirable, such as friendliness, honesty, or successfulness. The **devil effect** is the reverse of the halo effect (Cook, Marsh, & Hicks, 2003). The halo and devil effects are related to stereotyping and the organizational principle of closure discussed earlier.

Fundamental Attribution Error

The fundamental attribution error is discussed in more detail in *Making Theory Practical*. The term *attribution* refers to how we assign cause. When something happens, or someone behaves in a particular way, we ask ourselves, "Why did this happen? What caused her to do that?" Our attributions are the explanations we develop for the event or behavior. The **fundamental attribution error** occurs when we overestimate the effects of character traits and underestimate the effects of the situation in explaining another's behavior. This problem in perceiving others is similar to the self-serving bias that interferes with our perception of ourselves. While we tend to attribute our successes to our personal qualities and blame our failures on others or on situations beyond our control, we tend to do the reverse when explaining the successes and failures of others. When a friend does poorly on an exam, we attribute that to his lack of diligence as a student; when he does well, we attribute it to luck.

Projection

Projection is our tendency to attribute to others the similar traits, motivations, and reactions that we possess. In the field of psychology, projection is the term used generally to refer to a defense mechanism that causes a person to attribute his own negative trait or motivation to someone else as a way to feel less ashamed of that trait (Lewis, Bates, & Lawrence, 1994). For example, dishonest people are often quick to assume dishonesty in others. In this context, however, we are not using the term to refer only to negative traits or behaviors. Projection occurs any time we assume that others think, feel, and act the same way and for the same reasons that we do. We conclude that another person is happy about an event because we would be if it were to happen to us. Or we presume that someone else is angry about something because the person is acting the way we would act if we were angry. However, human beings vary too widely in how they think or act in response to similar situations for us to make assumptions.

APPLY **WHAT YOU KNOW**
PERCEPTION AND OTHERS

Expand your knowledge of perception and others by answering the following questions:

- Give an example of when you or someone you know made a fundamental attribution error. How serious was this error in perception, and what, if anything, was done to remedy it?

- Which perceptual barriers give you the most trouble with strangers—first impressions or projection? With close friends? Give examples to clarify your answers.

MAKING THEORY **PRACTICAL**
ATTRIBUTION THEORY

Imagine this situation:

Both you and a team member come to the team's final preparation meeting but have not completed your assignments. Your failures are actions or behaviors that will be interpreted by the team members as they search for understanding. One theory that helps to explain the process your teammates will use in the above situation is called Attribution Theory (Littlejohn & Foss, 2008).

Do you attribute the failures of others to their personal qualities but blame your own failures on the situation or on other people?

Theorist

Attribution Theory, launched by psychologist Fritz Heider's book *The Psychology of Interpersonal Relations* (1958), describes how individuals process information and use it to explain behaviors of self and others.

Three Basic Steps

According to Heider, attribution theory involves three basic steps:

- Step 1. We *perceive* an action/behavior/comment.
- Step 2. We *judge* the intent of the action/behavior/comment.
- Step 3. We *attribute* a reason or motivation for the action/behavior/comment.

Unfortunately, research indicates that "people are often illogical and biased in their attributions" (Littlejohn & Foss, p. 71). Although the team members in this situation may think they are being logical and careful, their judgments will likely be made quickly and be over-generalized. While each member assesses the event or behavior and the verbal and non-

verbal cues associated with it, personal psychological factors are affecting their interpretations. These factors include frames of reference, gender and cultural differences, emotional state, listening skills (discussed in Chapter 3), and what Heider calls the *perceptual style* of each member (i.e., an optimistic person is more likely than a pessimistic one to give others and self the benefit of the doubt). Also, keep in mind that once an attribution is made, we tend to stick with it even if later evidence sheds doubt on it.

Fundamental Attribution Error

As your team members strive to understand your behavior, they are likely to assume that what happened was a result of specific things you did or failed to do—in other words, your failure was your fault. As mentioned earlier in this chapter, this tendency to overestimate the role that a person's character plays in behavior while underestimating the role of the situation is called the *fundamental attribution error* (Ross, 1977). The fundamental attribution error also suggests that when *you* describe the situation, you will join the other team members and likely consider the other person's failure as "his fault" (poor attitude or poor study habits). However, when describing your own failure, you are more likely to attribute your failure to "the situation" (faulty alarm or illness) rather than to a personal characteristic. Does this sound reasonable? In other words, *your* date's unhappiness was due to a slip of the tongue caused by your not getting enough sleep the night before; your friend's girlfriend problems are due to his poor communication skills.

PRACTICAL APPLICATION

So the next time you, your friends, or your team (or family) members attempt to assign a reason or motivation to an event or behavior, think about the insights that attribution theory and the fundamental attribution error offer. When differences in interpretation occur (often leading to arguments), remember the role that personal psychological factors play in our attributions. We are not as "unbiased" as we like to think.

Source: Heider, Fritz. *The Psychology of Interpersonal Relations.* New York: Wiley, 1958.

Developing Perceptual Skills

LEARNING **OBJECTIVE**

2.5 What are the perceptual skills used to improve self-concept, and how are those skills used to improve perception with others?

We can see, then, that there are many barriers to being able to accurately perceive others. However, without accurate perceptions, our responses to others will often be inappropriate; they may even create conflict when there is no real reason for it to exist. Therefore, it is important to consider some perceptual skills that may be useful in improving the accuracy of our perceptions of both ourselves and others.

Using Perceptual Skills to Improve Self-Concept

Obviously, there are many roadblocks to building a strong yet accurate self-concept. If your self-esteem is low in some areas of your life, or you are uncertain about the accuracy of your self-image, or perhaps you haven't really thought much about your self-image—you may want to try the following two tips for improving self-concept: self-reflection and feedback.

Self-Reflection
If we are to improve the accuracy of our self-concept, it is helpful for us to cultivate self-reflection. To use **self-reflection** is to have conscious awareness of what we are doing and thinking at the moment—it is an introspective process that includes the following:

- *Awareness of our self-talk.* Hansen and Allen in *The One Minute Millionaire* (2002) suggest that because so many people use negative self-talk, it is a good idea to place a rubber band around your wrist and snap it each time you think or say something negative. You will be amazed at how many times you snap the band in just a single day—by the end of the day, most people have a red welt around their wrist.

- *Recognition of using a self-serving bias, self-fulfilling prophecy, or irrational beliefs.* When you are interpreting the words or acts of others are you aware of when you are using the filter of the self-serving bias? Are you aware of when you are setting yourself up for a self-fulfilling prophecy? Can you recognize when you are succumbing to irrational beliefs? The self-reflective person learns to challenge those beliefs (e.g., "She may not like me, but that does not make me unlovable") and to assess in a realistic way the validity of the messages received from others.

- *Recognition of using impression management in an unethical manner.* As mentioned earlier, although you do not always present the same "face" to every person you know, you should consider how your behaviors are or are not authentic reflections of who you are. No one likes to find out that the person they thought they could trust is actually a different person from the image that was presented. Deception is not ethical; it causes people to make relationship choices based on faulty information. The self-reflective person is aware of the difference between impression management used to present a polished image and impression management used to manipulate.

Seeking Feedback
Another way to improve accuracy in your perception of yourself is to seek feedback. You can ask others to give you an honest appraisal of your strengths and weaknesses. It is, of course, important that you seek this type of information only from people whose opinions you value and who have proven to be insightful and constructive in the past. You are under no obligation to accept the opinions of others as being the final word on who you are! However, be careful that you do not ask for such feedback if you are not open and willing to consider it carefully. It is

not fair to others—and may be damaging to your interpersonal relationships—to ask for honest opinions and then become defensive or angry about what you hear. If you are looking for honest feedback, you could ask: "What do you think about this outfit for my job interview on Monday?" However, if you are only looking for agreement, it might be better to say: "You do like this outfit, don't you?" This type of comment is a fairly clear message that you are asking for approval, not constructive criticism. Seeking feedback can be very beneficial, but it is not a good strategy if you do not have a trusted respondent or are unwilling to use the feedback in a constructive way.

Using Perceptual Skills to Improve Your Perception with Others

Not only can perceptual skills help us improve our self-concept, they can help us in our communication with others. Valuable perception skills include mindfulness, reframing, and perception checking.

Mindfulness

Deliberately paying attention (conscious awareness) to your thought processes in a nonjudgmental way (Kabat-Zinn, 2007) is referred to as **mindfulness**. Being mindful will enable you to identify those moments when you may be swayed by one or more perceptual barriers discussed earlier. When you meet someone from a different social group or culture from your own, being mindful will cause you to recognize the tendency to operate from stereotypes and remind you to keep an open mind. When you are mindful, you will be able to catch yourself projecting your own perspective onto someone else. Communication scholars Burgoon, Berger, and Waldron (2000) express mindfulness this way:

> Communication that is planful, effortfully processed, creative, strategic, flexible, and/or reason-based (as opposed to emotion-based) would seem to qualify as *mindful*, whereas communication that is reactive, superficially processed, routine, rigid, and emotional would fall toward the *mindless* end of the continuum (p. 112).

While mindfulness occurs at the intrapersonal level, *shared mindfulness* is important at the interpersonal level when two or more people are working together to make effective decisions often in crisis situations (Krieger, 2005).

Experts are more successful when they can reframe their knowledge from the novice's perspective.

Reframing

One step past mindfulness is the skill of **reframing,** in which you recast a situation from the perspective of the other person, not just from your own perspective. Although it is easy to imagine what probably happened from your own frame of reference, looking at the same situation from the other person's frame of reference (i.e., reframing the situation) is much more difficult. Even if you think your version of events is the correct one, try to see the situation as though you were the other person. This exercise will help you become more open to other points of view and to other people—thus becoming a better communicator.

Perception Checking

An even more active step toward improving your perception of others is to cultivate the skill known as perception checking. A **perception check** is a verbal request for feedback to determine whether your interpretation of someone's nonverbal behavior is accurate.

To illustrate how the skill of perception checking, when used correctly, can be beneficial to you, consider this example. Suppose you notice that a classmate does not respond to your "hello" when you enter the classroom. If she customarily returns your greetings, you will probably wonder why she didn't do the same this time. You decide that the most likely explanation is that she is miffed because you didn't return her call the night before. Wouldn't it be helpful to know what her behavior really meant before responding? This is where a perception check would be helpful in avoiding a potential crisis in your relationship.

Use Perception Checking Correctly: For a perception check to be effective, it is important that you consider exactly what to say. Many people would say, "What's wrong?" And chances are good that the response they would receive is "Nothing." If this has ever happened to you, you probably know what follows. Often this opening to dialogue leads to even more conflict. The problem is that you have put the other person in a defensive position by assuming that there *is* something wrong, and that whatever is wrong is their responsibility. Let's look at a better way to get the feedback you need to make an accurate perception.

Include Four Basic Steps: Effective perception checks require *four basic steps* (the first two occur in your mind; the last two are spoken):

- Step 1: Determine the exact behavior that triggered your perception.
- Step 2: Identify your initial interpretation of the behavior but consider other possible interpretations as well.
- Step 3: Describe (in an open and non-accusatory manner) the specific behavior you observed along with two or three possible interpretations.
- Step 4: Ask the other person to verify or correct your interpretations.

Your perception check in the above example might proceed like this:

- Step 1: Rachel ignored me completely when I said "hello"—I can't believe she did this!
- Step 2: I'm afraid she's mad at me because I didn't return her call the night before; however; it's possible that she is preoccupied with something or didn't even hear me.
- Step 3: "Rachel, I noticed that you didn't respond when I said hello, which isn't like you. I wondered if you were just preoccupied, or maybe you didn't hear me, or if you are upset because I didn't have time to return your call last night?"
- Step 4: "Is everything okay?"

Understand Reasons for Each Step: At first, this formula for an effective perception check may seem too mechanical and awkward. However, there are good reasons for each of the suggested steps.

- *Reason for Step 1*: Determining the specific behavior that has triggered your perception requires you to recognize that a behavior is different from an interpretation. Too often we accuse others of "acting" angry. But anger is not a behavior; it is the interpretation that an observer draws from someone's behavior. The behavior is the frown, the stomping out of the room, or the slamming of the door.
- *Reason for Step 2:* Identifying the interpretation you have drawn, recognizing why you have drawn it, and exploring the range of other possible interpretations forces you to acknowledge that any nonverbal behavior may have many different meanings. Too often, we make the dangerous assumption that there is only one plausible reason for people to act the way they do. Furthermore, we fail to recognize that our interpretations are *ours* and are based on something personal, such as the reluctant admission that we may have done something that would justify someone else's

PERCEPTION **AND YOUR CAREER**

2.6 What perception skills covered in this chapter relate specifically to your career?

The communication and perception skills covered in this chapter can be of special importance to you as you search for and develop a career. The *Spotlight on, Career Moment*, and *Connecting to* features relate communication skills from the chapter to success in the specific fields of business, education, and healthcare.

SPOTLIGHT ON **THE IMPORTANCE OF PERCEPTION**

BUSINESS

Employers are interested in learning how your attitudes and personality affect your perceptions of colleagues, projects, and ideas.

For example, Herb Kelleher, former president and CEO of Southwest Airlines, claims that Southwest keeps their winning atmosphere by hiring "attitudes" not just people. When hiring, they look for seven traits: "cheerfulness, optimism, decision-making ability, team spirit, communication, self-confidence, and self-starter skills" (Krames, 2003, p. 180).

Many companies use personality tests "to hire, evaluate, or promote employees" (Daft & Marcic, 2006, p. 385), including Hewlett-Packard, J. C. Penney, Toys "R" Us, Dow Chemicals, American MultiCinema (AMC), and Marriott Hotels.

EDUCATION

According to the *Handbook of Instructional Communication* (Mottet, Richmond, & McCroskey, 2006), approximately 20 percent of college students experience communication apprehension (CA)—fear of communicating with other people—they perceive the instructor and other students as dangerous.

Students who perceive communication as enjoyable generally sit in the front or in the middle of the classroom, students with high CA are likely to sit in the back or along the sides of the classroom, which instructors generally ignore (p. 63).

To make class less fearful for high CAs, the *Handbook* offers these recommendations:

• Encourage participation,

• Avoid randomly calling on students,

• Avoid alphabetical seating.

HEALTHCARE

Is it possible that what children perceive in food ads on television makes them eat more? New research conducted by the University of Liverpool (Liverpool, UK, 2007) indicates the answer is yes.

One study of 5- to 7-year-old children found that they consumed 14–17% more calories in snack foods after watching food ads than after watching toy ads.

Another study of 9- to 11-year-olds found that they consumed 84–134% more calories in snack foods after watching food ads than after watching toy ads. None of the foods available for the children to eat were foods in the ad.

The Kaiser Family Foundation (Kavilanz, 2007) found that 34% of ads targeting children between the ages of 8–12 were for junk food (candy and snacks).

CAREER MOMENT **PERSONALITY TESTS**

College counselors use personality tests like the Myers-Briggs Type Indicator (MBTI) to help students select careers in which their abilities and personality match the job requirements. The self-test included in our *Developing Skills* feature for this chapter is only an indication of your scores for **I**ntroversion/**E**xtroversion; **S**ensing/**IN**tuition; **T**hinking/**F**eeling; and **J**udging/**P**erceiving scales. In each paired opposite, there is one word that describes you best—thus your style is represented by four letters (such as ISTJ or ENFP). We recommend that you go to your counseling department and take the complete licensed MBTI and let them suggest careers that would be a match for your abilities and personality (Daft & Marcic, 2006):

Many companies use personality tests in an effort to match the worker with the best job assignment (Overholt, 2004a; 2004b). For example, if the job requires creativity, but you prefer facts, details, and rules, you would probably be miserable. Yet you might make a good developer or manager. Overholt recommends that during your search of the company you find out whether they use assessments during hiring. If so, go to a bookstore or library and find a book about the specific assessment tool.

Also, keep in mind that although personality plays a role in job success, you can learn to be a good communicator regardless of your particular personality characteristics. Just by taking a single course in communication and applying the skills presented, you can improve your choices, abilities, and communication confidence and make yourself more desirable to employers.

Sensing-Thinking
Accounting
Computer programming
Engineering

Sensing-Feeling
Supervising
Counseling
Selling

Intuitive-Thinking
Systems design
Law/management
Teaching business

Intuitive-Feeling
Public Relations/politics
Advertising
Human resources

CONNECTING TO ... **BUSINESS**

Are you aware of the following "Big Five" personality factors (Daft & Marcic, 2006, p. 383):

1. *Extroversion*—are you "sociable, talkative, assertive, and comfortable" with others?
2. *Agreeableness*—are you "good-natured, cooperative, forgiving, and trusting"?
3. *Conscientiousness*—are you "dependable, persistent, and achievement oriented"?
4. *Emotional stability*—are you "calm and secure or tense and insecure"?
5. *Openness to experience*—are you "creative and imaginative"?

ACTIVITY Rate yourself on each statement: 1 (low) to 5 (high)*

Extroversion

1 2 3 4 5   I am usually the life of the party.
1 2 3 4 5   I feel comfortable around people.

Agreeableness

1 2 3 4 5   I am kind and sympathetic.
1 2 3 4 5   I have a good word for everyone.

Conscientiousness

1 2 3 4 5   I am systematic and efficient.
1 2 3 4 5   I am always prepared for meetings.

Emotional Stability

1 2 3 4 5   I am happy when others receive recognition.
1 2 3 4 5   I am a relaxed, cheerful person.

Openness

1 2 3 4 5   I enjoy trying new things.
1 2 3 4 5   I look for creative solutions.

Interpretation: Higher scores = effective employee; lower scores = self-assessment needed.

CONNECTING TO ... **EDUCATION**

As students, you know that your perceptions may not always be the same as your professors' perceptions. But students' perceptions can affect how much they learn. According to Professor C. Roland Christensen (2006), teachers play an important catalytic role in what their students perceive and potentially in what they learn in two important areas:

1. *Students learn more if they perceive the instructor as open and caring* (p. 647).
2. *Students learn more if they perceive the instructor as relaxed and patient* (p. 650).

ACTIVITY Join 3 or 4 other students who have an interest in education and discuss the following questions:

1. Recall teachers you have had in the past who aided positive student perceptions or negative student perceptions.

2. Share your descriptions of an "open and caring" professor and contrast it with the description of a "closed and indiffer-

ent" professor. Why do students learn more when an instructor is open and caring?

3. Describe a "relaxed and patient" professor and contrast the description with a "rushed and impatient" professor. Why do students learn more when an instructor is relaxed and patient?

CONNECTING TO ... **HEALTHCARE**

What if today was your first day on the job as an ER nurse or other healthcare professional? You would need to be a competent communicator and realize that the perceptions of patients, family members, and healthcare workers are not always the same (Scotti, Driscoll, Harmon & Behson, 2007). When the perceptions of these three groups do not overlap, chaos and problems are likely to occur for all involved.

ACTIVITY In groups of four to six people, read the following scenario and answer the questions that follow.

This is Rob's first day as a nurse in the ER. When the intercom calls, "Rob to room #4 for code red stat!," he enters the room to see a three-year-old boy with lower abdomen trauma screaming and kicking. The ER doctor is busy tending to the wounds while other healthcare workers assist. The parents are screaming, "Save my baby!" A physician calls, "Please, leave and let us do our job!" Rob sees the head

nurse point toward the family, and it is apparently Rob's role to deal with them.

1. Describe this chaotic situation from the *perceptions* of the following people: the child, parents, and healthcare staff.

2. What should Rob do and not do to spread calm and provide an overlap of perceptions to those in the room?

* Adapted from Daft & Marcic, 2006, p. 384.

▶ Log onto MyCommunicationLab.com to access Connecting to Psychology and Connecting to Science, Technology, Engineering, and Math—both with related activities.

behavior. By taking time to perform the first two steps, we are accomplishing mindfulness in our communication. Also we are being self-reflective, acknowledging our own role in the formation of the perception.

- *Reason for Step 3*: Describing the specific behavior you have observed along with several non-accusatory interpretations allows you to check the accuracy of your perception. It also allows the other person to know exactly what he or she did that confused you. Sometimes people are not as aware as they should be about how their behaviors communicate (as in the cartoon on page 51). When you tell them what has caused you to wonder about the meaning of their behavior and possible interpretations you have reached about that behavior, you are, in effect, helping them to understand that their behaviors do communicate.

- *Reason for Step 4*: The request for feedback is simply an invitation to dialogue. It lets the other person know that you are genuinely interested in hearing their perspective and that you are striving to achieve shared meaning instead of misunderstanding. There are many ways to ask for feedback; you could simply say, "What's up?" or you could elaborate by saying, "I'd really like to know, so I don't misunderstand."

Your initial attempts at performing effective perception checks may feel strange and uncomfortable, but there is always a period of awkwardness when you are learning a new skill. It is also true that when you first use a perception check with someone with whom you have a longstanding relationship, your efforts may surprise them. After all, this isn't the normal routine. However, over time, perception checks will become second nature to you, and they have the potential to greatly improve communication within your relationships.

Finally, for successful perception checking, we have two additional suggestions: First, do not wait until there seems to be a potential crisis brewing to try out your new skill. The best time to learn a new approach is in situations that have a low-risk threshold. Perhaps you see your friend smiling broadly. Practice your new skill by saying, "Wow, you sure do have a big smile on your face! Did you get some good news or are you just in a good mood today? What's going on?" Practicing in these types of situations will enable you to draw on your new skill with less awkwardness when there are potentially more serious issues to confront.

Second, you do not need to check every perception. It would be quite annoying if you performed a perception check every time you observed a behavior—not to mention time-consuming, since nonverbal behaviors are nearly constant! However, when someone does something that has potential significance to how you perceive them or to how you perceive your relationship, a perception check is deserved. Misunderstandings lead to conflicts that can have potentially devastating effects on relationships.

APPLY **WHAT YOU KNOW**
PERCEPTUAL SKILLS

Apply what you know about perceptual skills by identifying each of the following situations (select from: A = Self-reflection, B = Reframing, or C = Perception checking) and give reasons why you feel that your answers are correct:

- Josue, who is discussing the recent football game with some friends, acknowledges Chase with a frown when he walks up to the group. Later that day, Chase finds Josue alone and says, "You frowned when you saw me earlier today. Were you reacting to something someone said or are you still angry that I took your parking spot yesterday when I was late for an exam? What was going on?" Chase's question to Josue is an example of _____.

- Dana sees one of her classmates, Amy, in the cafeteria. Since she does not see anyone else she knows, she decides to greet Amy in hopes that she will be invited to join her. However, Amy just looks up from her book and says, "Hi," and then returns to her reading. Dana is offended by Amy's rudeness until she stops to consider that Amy might be studying for an exam. Dana's consideration of this possibility is an example of _____.

- Joe and Sally were having a disagreement. In the middle of the argument, Joe realized that Sally was right, but that he was still arguing because he couldn't stand to be wrong. Joe's awareness of his behavior is an example of _____.

CHAPTER SUMMARY

Understanding and using accurate perceptions of self and others requires knowledge and skill. Most people have inaccurate perceptions of themselves and others which lead to communication misunderstandings. You can determine your knowledge of perception by checking the skills and learning outcomes presented in this chapter.

Summary of **SKILLS**

Check each skill that you now feel qualified to perform:

❑   I can recognize the importance of accurate perception for communication and its effect on my daily communication.

❑   I can more accurately analyze my self-concept and recognize areas that need improvement.

❑   I can pinpoint two or three perceptual errors that cause me trouble and plan to improve them so I can more accurately perceive others.

❑   I can use the perception skills of self-reflection, mindfulness, and perception checking.

Summary of LEARNING **OUTCOMES**

2.1 *What are the definitions of perception and stereotyping, and what are the three basic steps involved in perception?*

- *Perception* is defined as the process by which individuals become aware of, organize, and interpret information received though their senses.

- *Stereotyping* occurs when we store our perceptions of a person by inserting them into a larger, more generalized category. We do this to save time and to add order to our lives. Problems occur, however, when we go beyond the known data to make predictions and forget that our perceptions are only filtered views of reality—not reality itself.

- The basic steps involved in perception include:
  Step 1: Selecting available data;
  Step 2: Organizing data into a usable form;
  Step 3: Interpreting the data by adding meaning and making predictions.

2.2 *What are the three major factors in perception that help explain why people perceive things differently (and sometimes erroneously)?*

- Physiological factors (e.g., poor vision or hearing), psychological factors (e.g., emotions or outlook on life), and cultural factors (e.g., your cultural heritage and values) are three reasons that people perceive things differently and often erroneously.

- You can determine your personality type by taking the sample Myers-Briggs Type Indicator (MBTI) in the *Developing Skills* feature in this chapter.

2.3 *What is the definition of self-concept, how does it relate to perception and communication, and what are some of the major barriers in forming an accurate self-concept?*

- *Self-concept* is defined as your overall understanding of who you are and includes your self-image and your self-esteem.

- The way your self-concept relates to communication is found in the explanation of the 6-Person Concept and the Plus-2 concept on page 50.

- Important barriers to an accurate self-concept include the fact that self-concept is a reflection of the appraisals we receive from others; is resistant to change; involves a self-serving bias; involves a self-fulfilling prophecy; clings to stagnant thinking; is affected by self-talk; and can cause ethical issues.

2.4 *What are the barriers to accurate perception of others, and how does each barrier affect our communication success?*

- Barriers to accurate perception include first impressions, perceptual constancy, fundamental attribution error, and projection.

- Each of these barriers can cause faulty perception and communication errors if we continue to cling to first impressions even after new information is received, see things that are no longer there just because we seek consistency with earlier times, overestimate character traits while underestimating the situation when explaining a person's behavior, or attribute to others similar traits, motivations, and reactions that we possess. For details, see the *Making Theory Practical* feature in this chapter.

2.5 *What are the perceptual skills used to improve self-concept, and how are those skills used to improve perception with others?*

- Perceptual skills used to improve self-concept include self-reflection and feedback.

- Perceptual skills used to improve perception of others include mindfulness, reframing, and perception checking.

2.6 *What perception skills covered in this chapter relate specifically to your career (see highlighted fields of business, education, and healthcare)?*

- The *Spotlight on, Career Moment,* and *Connecting to* features highlight the value of communication in the fields of business, education, and healthcare.

SOLVE IT NOW!

Taking into consideration all that you learned about perception from this chapter, how would you analyze the communication difficulties between Zach and Tony in our opening scenario?*

- Which of the three steps in the perception process do you think is responsible for most of the perception problems between Zach and Tony? Support your answer with reasons.
- Identify two main perception problems that Zach was experiencing and give your suggestions for how he can minimize them.

- The opening scenario is from Zach's perspective. What role do you think Zach's reframing of the situation from Tony's perspective would play in the communication between Tony and Zach?
- Which perceptual skills do you think would make good *communication goals* for Zach and Tony and would go a long way toward helping them improve their communication now and in the future? Why?

*(Check your answers with those located in MyCommunicationLab, Scenario Analysis for Chapter 2)

The next chapter will look at the role that listening plays in the success or failure of our communication with others.

KEY TERMS

6-person concept	p. 50	interpretation	p. 44	projection	p. 55	self-concept	p. 47
ambiguous figures	p. 42	laws of organization	p. 42	proximity	p. 42	self-esteem	p. 47
closure	p. 42	mindfulness	p. 58	psychological factors	p. 46	self-fulfilling prophecy	p. 52
devil effect	p. 55	organization	p. 41	rational-emotive behavior	p. 53	self-image	p. 47
empathy	p. 50	perception	p. 39	reflected appraisal	p. 51	self-reflection	p. 57
first impressions	p. 54	perception checking	p. 58	reframing	p. 58	self-serving bias	p. 52
fundamental attribution error	p. 55	perceptual constancy	p. 55	selection	p. 40	self-talk	p. 52
halo effect	p. 55	physiological factors	p. 45	selective distortion	p. 40	similarity	p. 42
impression management	p. 53					stagnant thinking	p. 52
						stereotyping	p. 54
						visual illusions	p. 42

SKILL BUILDERS

1. Divide into groups and complete the following exercise involving King Arthur, Lancelot, Guinevere, and a disgruntled knight who is an enemy of the king. The history of King Arthur goes something like this:

King Arthur introduces his wife to his faithful knight, Lancelot. When the king leaves on an important mission, he makes Lancelot promise to watch over and protect Guinevere. The friendship between Lancelot and Guinevere grows into an attraction that soon gets out of hand. Feeling shame and fearing the imminent return of the king, they agree to meet one last time. An enemy of the king follows Lancelot and plans a trap so they will be discovered.

Instructions On paper, each group member should rank the four people involved in the story from the *most* acceptable behavior to the *least* acceptable. When everyone

is finished, discuss your rankings and work as a group to get unanimous agreement. When you are finished with the exercise, discuss the reason for any disagreements and why your perceptions were different or the same.

2. Using the same groups from Activity 1 above, have each group member complete the *Developing Skills* (on pages 48–49). During the following class period, take a few minutes to compare the results of each member's personality type. Discuss the differences and similarities of personality types found in your group and discuss what effect, if any, personality might have had on possible group disagreements in Activity 1.

3. Critically Evaluating What You Read
Using the critical evaluation form in Chapter 1, select and evaluate an article from the *CROW: Course Resources on the Web* supported by the Associated Colleges of Illinois

(http://jonathan.mueller.faculty.noctrl.edu/crow/topictheself.htm). Although any article on this page will work, you will especially enjoy Jonathan Mueller's article, "The Forgotten Origins of the Self-serving Bias." Be prepared to share your observations with your classmates.

4. Consider American involvement in the Iraq war and differing perceptions as discussed in this chapter. Regardless of your personal opinion, be as objective as possible in discussing the war from several of the following perceptions:

- Republican Senator
- Democratic Senator
- Military person completing a tour in Iraq
- Iraqi citizen
- Liberal American citizen
- Conservative American citizen
- College student aged 18–25
- College student aged 26 and older

EXPLORE SOME MORE . . .

1. Looking for a good book that relates to perception and life? We suggest you read *Personality Plus* by Florence Littauer (Monarch Books, 2004) or *21 Days to Creating Your Dream Life* by Stephen Mark (Dream Board Publications, 2008).

2. If you haven't seen the following movies, watch them and see how many ways each of them relates to this chapter on perception:

- *Bagdad Café* (1987)—a German tourist named Jasmin, who has a positive attitude and self-concept, changes the lives of those involved in the Bagdad Café (a truck stop and motel located in the Mojave Desert) even though their perceptions of her were negative at first.

- *Crash* (2004)—when the lives of a diverse group of Los Angeles strangers collide, their mostly inaccurate perceptions and stereotypes of each other make an interesting story that directly relates to this chapter on perception.

- *The Devil Wears Prada* (2006)—includes some excellent examples of self-concept and how strangers, potential employers, and friends perceived the main character, Andrea (played by Anne Hathaway), first as a journalist and later as a fashion assistant for the editor of *Runway* magazine.

- *The Doctor* (1991)—played by William Hurt, shows an arrogant surgeon's perceptions of patients before his own illness and how those perceptions change after he becomes ill and experiences fears of death and the indignities of being treated with indifference by doctors and hospital staff.

- *My Big Fat Greek Wedding* (2002)—when a Greek woman marries a man who is not Greek, cultural differences and perceptions abound! As you watch this movie, see how "mindfulness" plays a role in the conflicts.

3 Listening

LEARNING **OBJECTIVES**

3.1 What is the definition of listening, and what are the stages involved in effective listening as well as several memory tips to improve listening?

3.2 Why is listening important, and what specific benefits does listening offer in our everyday lives?

3.3 What are the major barriers that complicate effective listening for most people, what are four poor listening habits, and what role does a person's listening style inventory play in listening effectiveness?

3.4 What is informational listening, in what listening situations is it needed most, and which specific skills are suggested for its effective use?

3.5 What is critical listening, in what listening situations is it needed most, and which specific skills are suggested for its effective use?

3.6 What is empathic listening, in what listening situations is it needed most, and which specific skills are suggested for its effective use?

3.7 What communication skills covered in this chapter relate specifically to your career (see highlighted fields of business, education, and healthcare)?

After studying this chapter you should be able to . . .
- Incorporate several memory tips to improve your listening.
- Identify and avoid major barriers to effective listening.
- Pinpoint poor listening habits that you have and make and follow a plan to overcome them.
- Recognize and use at least two listening skills needed in the informational, critical, and empathic contexts.

CHAPTER SUMMARY ⟩ P. 92 ⟩

SCENARIO

Samantha sighed as she walked into her English Composition class and took a seat near the back of the room. It had been a long day already, beginning with her car not starting and her need to call a taxi to get to school. "I wonder who I can call to give me a ride home," she thought, "and how am I going to get my car to the mechanic?" She settled into her desk and opened her backpack to take out her materials for class.

"Hey, Sam, how's it going?" asked Scott, as he dropped into the desk beside her. "Did you get your essay written?"

"Essay?" Samantha's face registered alarm. "I thought we were just supposed to start writing in our journals."

"Well, I don't know. He said something about having it done today, and our class schedule says our journals aren't due until mid-term. He said we should make sure it was typed and double-spaced, so I figured he wanted us to write it up as an essay."

"Great!" Samantha muttered. "This is a wonderful way to start off the semester. Our first assignment, and I've already messed up. I heard him say that, but I thought he just meant that he wanted us to type and double-space our journals."

Professor Perkins entered and walked to the front of the room. "I hope you have the rough draft of your essays ready to turn in," he said. "Please pull those out and pass them to the front of the room while I take roll."

Scott shook his head and frowned. "Gee, if I had known it was a rough draft, I wouldn't have stayed up late polishing it. That was a waste of time."

Samantha was miserable for the rest of the class, wondering if she should meet with Professor Perkins afterwards to explain why she had not done the assignment. "His instructions really weren't clear," she thought. "He just gave us too much information for the first day of class." Her thoughts turned again to the problem of her car, which reminded her that she needed to drive across town to the discount bookstore to see if they still had used copies of her Spanish text. When class was adjourned, Samantha asked Scott, "Hey, is there any chance you could give me a ride home?"

"Sure," Scott said, "but I have to go to the Administration Building to pay for my parking permit first. That won't take long, though."

"That's okay, because I think I will drop by Professor Perkins's office for a couple of minutes."

"Let's just meet out front, then."

Samantha walked to the Faculty Office Building and found Professor Perkins in his office. Samantha showed him that she had written a journal entry as she had thought she was supposed to do. Professor Perkins agreed that he would accept her assignment with points deducted for being late if she could e-mail it to him before the end of the day. Samantha's spirits lifted a bit with this one thing that had finally gone somewhat okay today. Her mood changed, though, as she sat outside the English Building waiting for Scott. He should have been there by now. Her cell phone rang.

"Where are you? And what took you so long?" Scott asked impatiently.

"I'm in front of the English Building."

"Well, I'm in front of the Administration Building, where we agreed to meet. You said you'd only be a couple of minutes and I've been waiting more like a half an hour."

Samantha started to retort that Scott had just misunderstood, but stopped short when she realized that he was doing her a favor. "I'm sorry," she apologized. "I'll come right now to where you are. I guess I just wasn't listening."

Does this scenario sound like you or someone you know? As you read this chapter, see if you can determine how many of the problems in the scenario were directly or indirectly the result of poor listening, which character in this story is most in need of listening improvement, and what both should do as decoders to improve the situation.

SOLVE IT NOW! ⟩ P. 93

We are focusing on the decoder in this chapter (as we did in Chapter 2) because the role of decoding is often overlooked when people attempt to improve their communication. We tend to be much more concerned about encoding (how we are going to effectively convey our own ideas) than decoding (how we are going to understand the ideas of others). Following the oft-quoted prayer of St. Francis of Assisi, "Grant that I may seek not so much to be understood as to understand," this chapter will concentrate on the important decoding skill of listening.

What Is Listening?

If we were to ask Samantha and Scott whether they consider themselves to be good listeners, each would likely say, "Yes." Yet, if we were to ask them to judge the listening ability of the other person, they probably wouldn't be as positive. While most of us tend to think we are better listeners than most, we also take our own listening for granted—it just comes naturally. Actually, effective listening requires much skill and training.

"Listening" Defined

First, let us make sure we understand what is meant by listening. **Listening** is the active process of constructing meaning from spoken messages through attention to the verbal and nonverbal codes that accompany the messages. Notice that our definition says that *listening is an active process*. Listening is not the passive activity that many of us assume it to be. There is a big difference between *hearing* and *listening*. You do not have to exert any effort to hear; hearing is going to happen any time you are in the presence of sound waves, assuming that you have a fully functioning ear drum. Listening requires you to do something with those sound waves. *Listening requires effort.*

Of course to listen, we will need a verbal message. However, there is more to listening than just paying attention to the words that are spoken. Good listeners also know how important it is to tune into the visual and vocal nonverbal messages that accompany the verbal code. It is these nonverbal messages (discussed in Chapter 1) that help us more accurately interpret the message.

Next, let's look at the definition in more detail to determine the basic stages we go through when listening.

LEARNING **OBJECTIVE**

3.1 What is the definition of listening, and what are the stages involved in effective listening as well as several memory tips to improve listening?

Stages of Listening

Understanding the listening process is easier when you are aware of the basic stages of listening—attending, understanding, responding, and remembering. After reading Chapter 2, you already know the first three steps of listening because they are the same as the three steps in perception—see if you recall these:

- First, we *select* available data by "becoming aware of" or registering a small amount of the stimuli in the environment—in listening we call this the *attending stage*. When we listen we attend to things that are of interest or importance to us and tune out other less interesting or less important stimuli. Such factors as our age, gender, culture, and biases also determine the stimuli to which we attend. In our opening scenario, do you think that Samantha's apparent failure to attend to all of the assignment was due in part to the fact that the first day of class presented so many competing stimuli?

- Second, we *organize* this data into a form that we can more easily use and remember—in listening we call this the *understanding stage*. There are many factors that make this stage difficult, such as frame-of-reference differences, different meanings for words and actions, attitudes toward the speaker, and even listener fatigue or infor-mation overload. Some of Samantha's listening problems in our opening scenario occurred in the understanding stage—see if you can identify at least one of them.

- Third, we *interpret* the data by adding meaning and making predictions—in listening, we call this the *responding stage*. Unless senders know what meaning you derived from each message, they have no way to correct any misperceptions that will get in the way of achieving the shared meaning that is the goal of effec-tive communication. Listeners respond in various ways. If the situation is too formal for a verbal response, they will likely show their agreement, disagreement, or confusion by nonverbal facial expressions (such as nodding their heads or frowning) or by vocal sounds (such as laughter, groans, or sighs). In our discus-sion of nonverbal communication in Chapter 5, we will discuss how to interpret audience reactions.

In addition to *attending* to spoken messages, *understanding* their meaning, and *responding* to the messages, listeners, in the fourth stage, *remember* what they have heard. Now this may be the hardest part of the whole process. Do you doubt that remembering is really part of listening? Consider this: Have you ever told others that you wanted them to do something, only to have them fail to do it and then claim that they "just forgot"? How do you respond to this? If you are like most people, you either accuse that person directly (or complain to someone else) that the person "didn't listen." It seems clear that, to most of us, remembering and listening are linked. However much we may claim that our forgetfulness is due to age or a lack of talent that some people are presumably just born with, the fact is that, much of the time, our "forgetfulness" is really the result of not fully listening.

Researchers tell us that even when listeners really try to remember, most will remember only about 10–25 percent the next day or a week later (Wolff, Marsnik, Tracey, & Nichols, 1983). Of course, we are more likely to remember information that is related to our interests, well organized, repeated, delivered effectively, and accompanied with quality visual aids. Even so, poor listeners fail to use the most important memory aid—transferring information from short-term to long-term memory (Schab & Crowder, 1989; Miller, 1994). **Short-term memory** is memory that holds information for 30 seconds or less; **long-term memory** is memory that lasts a lifetime. Consider this example: Your roommate asks you to pick up three items at the store, but, by the time you get there, you have forgotten what you went for. This happens when you don't transfer information from short-term to long-term memory. Although memory is only one of the four stages of listening, it is certainly an important one. The *Developing Skills* feature on the next page will provide some specifics on how to improve your memory.

APPLY **WHAT YOU KNOW**
YOUR LISTENING ABILITY

Now that you are aware of the definition of listening and the basic stages in the listening process, consider the following questions:

- How would you describe your listening ability: poor, average, good, or excellent?

- To verify your opinion, take one of the Listening Quizzes from Randall's ESL Cyber Listening Lab at www.esl-lab.com or the listening quiz from The Consulting Team at http://mmanning.com/Quiz-Listening.htm. Report your quiz results.

- Do you agree with the quiz results? Why or why not? Give at least one example to support your opinion.

Importance of Listening

LEARNING OBJECTIVE

3.2 Why is listening important, and what specific benefits does listening offer in our everyday lives?

Now that you know what listening is and the elements or stages that constitute this essential communication skill, you may be wondering why a whole chapter is devoted to the topic. "After all," you may be thinking, "listening is something that I do all the time. Surely all the listening I have to do will make me a good listener." Actually, the fact that you do so much listening in your everyday life is one of the reasons that we need to examine the subject a little more closely. Many scholars have estimated the amount of time people spend in various communication activities and have concluded that listening occupies much more of our time than any other activity. For example, employees at work spend around 60 to 80 percent of their time listening (Wolvin & Coakley, 1981) while college students spend around 24 percent of their time listening and 26 percent in related forms of listening as indicated in **Figure 3.1** (Janusik & Wolvin, 2007). Despite the amount of listening you do, most of you would probably agree that practice does not always mean perfection. Almost any improvement we can make in our listening skills has the potential to yield very real benefits.

Figure 3.1 Pie chart of percent of time students spend communicating

Listening Helps Us Develop and Maintain Relationships

Listening is an important part of developing and maintaining relationships. You know that when any relationship is in its early stages, you do a lot of concentrated listening in order to get to know each other and reduce any uncertainty you have about the other. Unfortunately, once a relationship is established, the amount of quality listening begins to decline. When people lament that they are being "taken for granted," oftentimes this is related to the feeling that the other person is no longer really listening. Indeed, good listeners are valued and cherished as friends and life-mates.

Daily Communication
Time college students spend communicating includes...

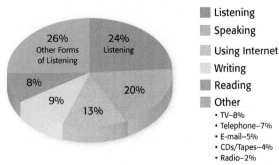

- Listening
- Speaking
- Using Internet
- Writing
- Reading
- Other
  - TV–8%
  - Telephone–7%
  - E-mail–5%
  - CDs/Tapes–4%
  - Radio–2%

DEVELOPING **SKILLS**
HOW TO IMPROVE YOUR MEMORY

Although poor listening habits are a result of poor decoding skills, to improve your memory you will need to focus on your *encoding* skills as well. This feature provides two encoding TIPS for improving your memory:

Memory TIP #1

Learn to transfer important information from your short-term memory (STM) to your long-term memory (LTM). Our STM is intended to hold only small amounts for short-term storage. Miller (1994) suggested that short-term memory holds between 5–9 bits or chunks of information—a bit could be a letter, number, sound, word, or sentence. More recent research suggests that most of us can hold only 4 bits or chunks in our short-term memories without getting overloaded (Cowan, 2001). Not only does our STM hold a small amount of information, but, unless we take notes or rehearse this information in some way within 30 seconds, we will forget it (Kosslyn & Rosenberg, 2006). It is important for listeners to learn how to transfer information from their STM to their LTM. Try using the following three steps when listening to speakers:

- First, *identify key words* as you listen. Don't be tempted to listen for or remember complete sentences. Instead, narrow each key idea down to only one to four words to help you recall the complete idea later. Speakers who use PowerPoint slides make it easier to identify key words.

- Second, w*rite down the key words* if you have paper handy. If no paper is available, locate each word (or image of the word) on a body part. For example, remember that *STM = 30 seconds* by locating it on your left foot and

LTM = lifetime on right foot; or when going shopping, locate bread on the left foot, jelly on the right foot, and milk on the right hand. You can also locate items using a familiar room (bread on window, jelly on window ledge, milk on door knob, and so on). These memory techniques were used by ancient Greek and Roman orators such as Cicero and Quintilian and discussed in Quintilian's *De Institutione Oratoria.* A story is also told about Simonides, a Greek lyric poet, who had just left a banquet hall when the ceiling collapsed burying the guests and making the bodies impossible to identify. Simonides was able to recall where each guest was seated, thereby locating the bodies for family members (Boorstin, 1983, pp. 480–481).

- *Third, constantly summarize the key words in your mind,* referring back to your notes when necessary. This form of rehearsal, which transfers information from STM to LTM, will not keep you from laughing at jokes and appreciating other facts and supporting materials presented. In fact, by using these three steps, you are probably paying closer attention than usual. Since you can think so much faster than the typical speaker talks, you have plenty of spare time to transfer information to your LTM and still daydream just a bit.

Memory TIP #2

Learn to retrieve stored information from your LTM. Research on how to improve the memories of witnesses to crimes (Fisher & Geiselman, 1992) resulted in memory techniques and principles that allowed "witnesses to recall 63% more information than was obtained with the standard police interview format" (Kosslyn & Rosenberg, p. 319). Try some of these following techniques when trying to remember stored information (Kosslyn & Rosenberg):

- *Recall the context where you learned the information.* You will recall more LTM if you can remember where you were when you learned the stored information. Think of details such as the occasion, the weather, any strong emotions you may have felt, and so on. For example, you probably remember where you were and what you were doing when you first heard about the terrorist attacks on the twin towers in New York City. Also, you have likely experienced a random smell or sound that brought back a long forgotten memory.

- *Concentrate.* It is important to keep from becoming distracted because recalling information from LTM is hard work. Find a quiet place, and focus on the task at hand.

- *Expect to try several times.* Don't give up if your first attempt at remembering an item doesn't work. Researchers have found that you are more likely to remember something if you try several times to remember it (Roediger & Thorpe, 1978). That is why it is easier to learn things for an exam if you spend several times working on it rather than "cramming" the night before.

- *Grasp any fragments.* To help recall specific details, think about what characteristics fit with the information. If you are trying to recall a person's name, think about the person's characteristics (features, size, style of clothes, ethnic background) and the characteristics of the name (was it short or long; was it unusual; what was the first letter; and so on). These fragments of information will likely lead you to the actual name.

If you concentrate on these two memory tips at least twice each week while you are taking this course, by the time the semester is finished, you will have an improved memory. First, you will be better able to remember information while listening (because you can transfer it from STM to LTM). Second, you will be better able to retrieve information stored in your LTM.

Listening Helps Us in Our Careers

Listening is something that will be expected of you in any job or career you might choose. At the very least, your supervisor will expect you to be able to follow directions and will attribute your failure to do so to your "not listening." A survey of industrial salespeople found failure to listen as the main reason for lack of job success (Ingram, Schwepker, & Hutson, 1992). In some careers, listening to customers or clients will be part of your daily work. The best salespeople know that listening to customers is essential in determining what products or services will best meet the customer's needs, not to mention helping to determine what sales strategy has the potential to be most persuasive. Customers in one survey ranked listening as the most important skill needed by salespeople (Boyle, 1999). See *Spotlight on The Value of Listening* later in this chapter for more specifics.

Listening Helps Us Become Better Citizens

Listening is also necessary if we are to be informed and responsible citizens, capable of making the decisions that will affect our family and our community. In our country, people who seek political office know that they must appeal to the citizenry in order to win elections. You will be asked throughout your lifetime to hear persuasive messages and cast your vote according to your beliefs about what candidates and what policies seem to be most supportable. Poor listeners are often frightened by these messages, largely because they fear that they cannot comprehend what is being said. They experience a phenomenon known as **receiver apprehension**. It is possible to experience receiver apprehension in any type of listening situation, but it is certainly common whenever the speaker seems to have an abundance of knowledge about topics that are not part of our own day-to-day experience. In our country, people who are uninformed about political issues are not uninformed because of an absence of information. In fact, they may be overwhelmed by all the information that is available, and they may choose to screen it out in order to avoid having to do any real thinking about it. This, of course, is not a desirable approach for citizens of a representative democracy to adopt. Learning how to listen in these situations is part of the process of earning the privileges granted to us by our governmental system.

Listening Helps Us Develop and Maintain Our Mental Health

One of the first things commentators mentioned after the Virginia Tech shootings in April, 2007, was, "Didn't anyone know the gunman was in serious trouble? Didn't anyone really listen to him?" Listening helps us develop and maintain our mental health. According to *Corrections Today* (Walker & Sakai, 2006) Hawaiian inmates are taught the life skill of listening as part of emotional intelligence training. The success of the program is indicated by one inmate who said, "We were given a gift, the gift of learning to listen" (p. 61).

When people really listen to us, they listen without thinking about personal views, make no judgments, and speak only to clarify what we are saying. This level of listening, called **focused listening** (Farquharson, 2006), offers "empathy, sympathy, creativity, and even compassion" (p. 61). When someone listens to us at this level, we feel validated and important because the listener was willing to take the time required to really listen to us;

as a result, our self-esteem and positive mental outlook are improved, whether we are children, teens, adults, or elderly. According to NIACE (National Institute of Adult Continuing Education), "Speaking and listening are important for developing fulfillment, identity and self-esteem" (Eldred, 2007, p. 7).

APPLY **WHAT YOU KNOW**
IMPORTANCE OF LISTENING

Apply what you know about the importance of listening to these critical thinking questions:

- In which area or areas in your life do you use listening the most effectively (in personal relationships, in a job or career, as a citizen in society, or in maintaining your

mental health)? Give at least two personal examples to explain your answers.

- In which area in your life are your listening skills in need of the most improvement (in relationships, in a job or career, as a citizen, or in maintaining your mental health)? Give a personal example to explain your answer.

LEARNING **OBJECTIVE**

3.3 What are the major barriers that complicate effective listening for most people, what are four poor listening habits, and what role does a person's listening style inventory play in listening effectiveness?

Barriers to Listening

One way to improve listening skills is to become aware of some major listening barriers. Once we are aware of them, we can minimize them. Although there are many barriers to listening, we will look at those that cause the most serious problems: noise, information processing, cultural differences, gender orientation, and poor listening habits. Vocabulary, which is also a barrier to listening, is covered in Chapter 4. As you read, see which of these barriers have complicated your listening effectiveness.

Noise

Noise, which can be divided into three types, is definitely a barrier to listening. Noise can be external, internal, or semantic.

External Noise
One obvious complicating factor to effective listening is the presence of external noise. As we learned when we discussed the communication model, **external noise** refers to the literal noises that exist in our environment. Sometimes your attention will shift to other sounds in the environment, particularly if the sounds seem to have greater importance to you at the moment. You have undoubtedly also experienced the problems that arise in trying to carry on a conversation with someone in a setting where there are other sights and sounds around you. Striking up a conversation with someone in a club where a loud band is playing is an exercise in futility. In such a situation, you would probably suggest that you move to a quieter place in order to be able to *hear* each other, not to mention actually *listen* to each other.

Internal Noise
A second type of noise, *internal noise*, is even more difficult to overcome than external noise. You will recall that **internal noise** refers to any number of things that you may be experiencing physiologically or psychologically that cause you to have difficulty focusing on messages. It is difficult to listen to another person when you are ill, angry, worried, or even excited about something. The presence of such conditions or thoughts can cause your attention to shift to something other than the message the speaker is trying to convey.

In *Turn Off That Racket!* (2002), composer Philip Glass offers the following suggestions for quieting internal noises:

- Don't focus on petty matters. They can clog your brain.
- Throw useless information out the window.
- Don't dwell on any thought or emotion.
- Approach listening with an open mind (Glass, 2002).

For advice on how to get ready to listen in the classroom, see the section on Informational Listening later in this chapter.

Semantic Noise A third type of noise that can complicate effective listening is **semantic noise.** This is the problem that occurs when people hold different understandings of words. This idea will be discussed more thoroughly when we look closely at verbal communication. For now, realize that words often mean very different things to different people. Some words trigger emotional responses in people that can create a kind of internal noise that interferes with listening. A person who has recently experienced the death of a loved one may respond to any form of the word "death" in a way that precludes their hearing anything else the speaker is saying. People hear words such as "liberal" or "conservative" in sharply different ways, depending on their frames of reference.

Information Processing

Information barriers include both the amount of information received and how fast we can process it. Sometimes there is just too much information coming from too many directions for us to process effectively—we call this **information overload**. It is sometimes difficult to sort through all the messages available to us to determine which ones are important, relevant, or credible. If you have ever found yourself shutting down completely and not listening or attending to any of the messages, you were reacting to information overload. Although shutting down is one way to resolve the problem of information overload, such a strategy does not lead to good listening.

Another information barrier relates to how fast we process information. Scholars have determined that no matter how fast a speaker can talk, listeners are capable of processing several times the amount of information contained in the message. In fact the average person speaks only 100–150 words per minute; yet you as a college student easily can process 600 and more words per minute, if anyone could speak that rapidly (Wolvin & Coakley, 1988, p. 208). At first glance, this might seem to be an advantage for us in the attempt to listen well. However, since we can grasp what is being said so rapidly, we have some "spare" time while the speaker catches up. Instead of using this spare time to summarize the material or analyze the speaker's evidence, most of us tend to think of other topics or daydream.

When listening to people from different cultures, greater attention and concentration are required.

Cultural Differences

In the previous chapters, our discussion of culture looked at the dimensions of low-context/ high-context differences. When determining the meaning of a message, people from **low-context cultures** pay careful attention to the actual words and only minor attention to the context in which the message occurs. On the other hand, people from **high-context cultures** pay less attention to the actual words and more to the context, such as the groups to which the speaker belongs (community, family, or organizations), the speaker's status and age, the background and history of the topic or situation, and the speaker's nonverbal gestures and expressions. High-context cultures consider words as dangerous tools and are very concerned that words not cause a loss of face for the speaker or the audience members—therefore, the fewer words, the better. Low-context cultures are more concerned with telling it like it is and have less concern with saving face.

So how does listening differ among cultures? Not all cultures view listening in the same way. High-context cultures such as Japan and Mexico believe that it is the listener's responsibility to achieve understanding. As a result, they expect messages and instructions to be brief and even fairly vague and are insulted when too much information is given. On the other hand, low-context cultures such as Canada and the United States believe that it is the speaker's responsibility to make sure the listener understands. As a result, they expect messages to be detailed and carefully spelled out and are frustrated when messages are too brief. According to Brownell (2006), "Listening in cross-cultural contexts takes greater attention and concentration than it does when interacting with members of your own language community" (p. 376).

Gender Orientation

Gender differences can also cause listening problems. For example, research shows that men talk longer and more often than women, are more likely to interrupt, use communication for competitive purposes, listen to solve problems, respond to conversations with minimal responses, tell stories instead of asking questions, use "I" more than "we," and are listened to more by both genders (Tannen, 1995; Wood, 2009). Women, on the other hand, use communication for cooperative purposes, listen to show understanding and enhance relationships, decode nonverbal communication better than men, ask more questions, interrupt less, give more personal examples, and use "we" more than "I" (Tannen, 1995; Wood, 2009). Both men and women managers use tag questions (such as "Don't you agree") at the end of comments often to soften their comments and invite participation (Calnan & Davidson, 1998; Wood, 2009).

Although it is obvious that differences in listening do exist between men and women, the reason why is not as obvious. Before we can determine whether these listening differences are sex-linked (biological) or culturally based (learned behaviors), more research is needed. In any case, if we are to improve our listening, we need to be aware of these differences. It may be that the context of the communication should determine the listening style we choose. Heath (1991) found that androgynous people (people who use both "male" and "female" characteristics as needed) are the most successful in the workplace and at home. If we understand the communication principles discussed in this text and are considerate and flexible in their use, our gender differences will become less of a problem.

Poor Listening Habits

All of us have developed certain unproductive listening habits that prevent us from attending to and understanding the messages that senders try to convey to us. Poor listening habits are the result of poor decoding skills. Once you identify that you have one or more of these poor listening habits, it is possible to make necessary changes that will result in improved communication. See which of the following poor listening habits cause you the most difficulty and probably should be changed: imitation listening, selective and insulated listening, defensive listening, or combative listening.

Imitation Listening
Imitation listening is false listening. This is what you are doing when you pretend to listen by exhibiting behaviors that are commonly associated with good listening, while simultaneously attending to some other stimulus in the environment or to your intrapersonal dialogue. Nodding your head, making eye contact, making occasional noises that sound like you are affirming the speaker's message—all of these are the hallmarks of imitation listening. Perhaps you can recall a time when a professor called your name in the middle of a lecture to ask what you thought about the ideas just presented. The need to say, "I'm sorry, could you repeat what you just said?" is a dead giveaway that you have not been actively listening. If you are often guilty of imitation listening, consider how uncomfortable you feel when you have been "caught," as well as how you feel when you realize that the person you are taking with is also an imitation listener who has apparently not heard a word you have said.

Selective Listening and Insulated Listening
Selective listening and insulated listening are two closely related unproductive listening habits that you may be guilty of at times. Listening to only part of a message is known as **selective listening**. An example of this would be asking your roommate if you can borrow the car for the evening. However, when he says, "Sure," you stop listening. You don't hear him also say to be sure to fill the tank because he has to leave for an interview early in the morning and to leave the car keys on the kitchen counter when you return so he won't have to wake you. When your friend wakes you the next morning and is upset that the tank is empty and the keys are nowhere to be found, you may insist that he never said any of that.

Sometimes a message may contain information that we would rather not have to deal with, so we use **insulated listening** and don't hear what we don't want to hear. For example, when a physician has to deliver bad news to a patient or family member, the listener is often unable to hear the whole message because of the emotional turmoil. Many physicians learn that it is best to deliver the bare essentials and then allow some time for the message to sink in before attempting to expand on the information (Buckman,1992; Friedrichsen & Milberg, 2006). It is a good thing when speakers take this approach, although not all speakers do. Therefore, listeners need to be aware of the possibility that they may have failed to hear the whole message and take steps to clarify their understanding.

DRABBLE: © Kevin Fagan/ Dist. by United Feature Syndicate, Inc.

Defensive Listening
Have you ever known people who seem to be easily offended and tend to interpret innocent remarks as though they were criticisms? Perhaps the problem is that they are **defensive listeners**. Sometimes people have

insecurities within their self-concepts that make them feel that it is necessary to be on guard with other people. Other times, the nature of a relationship may be such that one person feels that he or she is generally the target of criticism from the other. Whatever the causes may be, defensive listening is a barrier to shared meaning. If this describes you, it may be useful to examine the source of your feelings that cause you to defend yourself from the verbal messages of others. If you determine that you may be hypersensitive and a defensive listener, it may be difficult for you to establish high-quality interpersonal relationships. Your friend or partner may find it easier not to say anything to you rather than risk offending you, which makes the relationship hard to maintain.

Combative Listening

Combative listening occurs when a person listens very intently to senders' messages for the purpose of attacking them, often by using their own words against them as soon as they are finished speaking. These listeners often make an elaborate display of their listening while disguising their readiness to attack. This form of listening has great usefulness for prosecuting attorneys and debaters, but it is damaging to interpersonal relationships. Certainly, close listening is a desirable skill; in this case, it is the *attitude* of the listener that is called into question. Listening should be approached as an act aimed at understanding the other person's meanings, not as an opportunity for combat. It might help to determine which poor listening habits you have that need changing. Use the *Making Theory Practical* feature in this chapter to analyze your listening style. In order to overcome the above barriers to effective listening we need to recognize that not all listening situations are the same. Just as carpenters need tools and skills to effectively address a variety of situations in construction, so listeners need a variety of tools and skills to effectively address various listening situations in communication. We will cover three main types of listening (informational, critical, and empathic), discuss what situations require each type of listening, and suggest specific skills needed for successful use of each listening type.

APPLY **WHAT YOU KNOW**
LISTENING BARRIERS AND STYLES

Now that you are aware of poor listening habits and varying listening styles, answer at least one the following set of questions:

- What do you consider to be the two main listening problems of college students? Of parents? Of professors?

Discuss your thinking by giving examples to illustrate your answers.

- Are you more of a people-, action-, content-, or time-oriented listener? Support your answer with at least two personal examples.

3.4 What is informational listening, in what listening situations is it needed most, and which specific skills are suggested for its effective use?

Informational Listening

Informational listening is the type of listening that is required when the sender's goal is to convey information, and the receiver's goal is to comprehend the information. A classroom is a context in which informational listening should be the goal. Other informational listening situations include the workplace (where training frequently occurs, as supervisors explain how tasks are to be accomplished) and the medical consultation (where physicians or other healthcare professionals explain the causes and processes of illness and the procedures required for treatment).

In order for informational listening to be effective, several skills or behaviors are needed. For the purposes of this discussion, we will use the classroom as our model context, though the skills discussed here have applicability to other informational listening situations as well.

MAKING THEORY **PRACTICAL**
LISTENING STYLES PROFILE

- *Action-oriented listeners* are interested in organized, structured presentations. They want the purpose spelled out clearly and accurately and are interested in what actions are recommended because they like to do something with the information they hear.
- *Content-oriented listeners* revel in details, facts, and evidence and are very concerned with accuracy of the facts presented. They are more interested in the message than the message giver.
- *Time-oriented listeners* hate to waste time. They aren't interested in details but instead want a quick, to-the-point, "sound bite" approach to the message. Time is money to them, and they don't want to waste it.

When you listen to others, whether at a formal presentation or informally with colleagues, family, or friends, are you aware of your listening style? Are you more *people-*, *action-*, *content-*, or *time-oriented*? Here's a clue—which of the following thoughts sound more like you?

- "Great. I really relate to that personal example!"
- "So, what's the bottom line—am I supposed to guess the purpose?"
- "Now this is what I like—details!"
- "I don't have all day—get to the point."

Original Theorists

The Listening Styles Profile (LSP-16) developed by Kitty Watson, Larry Barker, and James Weaver (1995) was revised by Barker and Watson in 2000. The LSP is not actually called a theory although it has many of the characteristics of a theory. According to Littlejohn and Foss (2008), communication theories "provide a set of useful tools for seeing the everyday processes and experiences of communication through new lenses" (p. 3). The researchers found that it is possible to divide our listening styles into four significantly different types and that 60 percent of people prefer listening with a single style (Weaver, Richendoller, & Kirtley, 1995).

Listening Styles (Watson, et al.)

- *People-oriented listeners* are relationship-oriented. They pay attention to people's feelings and emotions and look for personal information. They are interested in discovering common ground between themselves and the speaker.

PRACTICAL USES

Being able to identify your own listening styles will help you understand why you have problems listening to certain types of messages and allow you to adapt to situations that are not ideal for your preferred listening style. For example, a content-oriented listener will find it difficult to pay attention to a people-oriented speaker giving personal examples rather than detailed and documented facts.

The Listening Styles Profile also gives us a practical way of identifying and responding to the listening styles of others and, thereby, improving our communication with them. For example, if you know you will be speaking with a time-oriented listener, mention that you know the person has time constraints and then make sure to begin with the summary followed by supporting reasons—brief and to-the-point. On the other hand, if you know that the listener is more people-oriented, make sure to establish a common ground by offering personal information and showing you care about the listener's feelings. In other words, what type of information is appropriate to convey may vary, depending on the listening styles of others. This is one reason that effective speakers use a variety of supporting materials in an attempt to relate to everyone in the audience.

Source: Watson, K., Barker, L., & Weaver, J. (1995). The listening styles profile (LSP-16): Development and validation of an instrument to assess four listening styles. *International Journal of Listening, 9*(1), 1–13.

Prepare to Listen

The first step to being an effective informational listener is to come prepared to listen. In the classroom, having read the assigned material before coming to class can improve your ability to listen by reducing the potential for receiver apprehension that occurs when the topic being discussed is unfamiliar to you. Coming prepared to listen also means arriving after having had sufficient rest and nutrition to enable you to shut out hunger and fatigue as sources of internal physiological noise. The typical college student gets 6 to 7 hours of sleep per night but should be getting 9 hours. Where do you fit in? (Hosek, Phelps, & Jensen, 2004; "Help for sleep-deprived students," 2004). It is also important to eliminate sources of internal psychological noise, though this is not as easily accomplished as it is to get enough sleep and eat a proper meal. As one student suggested, "You need to put your thoughts on pause." It may help to recognize that during the class period there is little you can do about the things that concern you in your private life. If you make a commitment to listen, promising yourself that you will deal with your problems at a given point after classes are over for the day, you may find it easier to focus in the present moment.

Which of these students appears to be the most prepared to listen?

Avoid Prejudging

Informational listening requires that you avoid prejudging the speaker. Certainly there are some speakers who are more appealing to you as human beings. However, the quality of information is not necessarily linked to the appeal of a person providing the information. There may be speakers whose competence you question for good reason—we are not suggesting that you overlook such deficiencies, for it would be foolish not to take that into account. However, when your reaction to a speaker is based on personal biases or prejudices, or when you simply find the speaker's personality not one to which you are naturally drawn, you need to be especially careful that you do not let those preconceptions prevent you from hearing the message as it was intended.

Mentally Organize, Summarize, and Link Information

It is wise to make good use of the lag created by the phenomenon of processing rate discussed earlier and make the best use of your time by mentally organizing, summarizing, and linking new materials presented. In the classroom, your professor may have already prepared the lesson in an outline format with the main parts clearly expressed; you may even have the advantage of having a PowerPoint presentation that accompanies the lecture and clearly spells out the main points and subpoints of the lecture. However, you should not allow the presence of any visual aids to permit you to become a lazy listener! Merely copying the material from the slides into your notebook does not constitute active and engaged listening. If you are fortunate enough to have those aids, stay committed to the listening process by continually working to make connections between what you are writing and what you have previously learned.

Personalize Information While Listening

One way to improve your informational listening is to find ways to personalize the information you are receiving. This means that you should try to find ways in which the material is relevant to your own life and experience. Not only will this help you listen to the material in the present moment, but it will allow you to remember it in the future. Of course, as you relate the material to your life, be careful that you don't shift your attention from the speaker to your personal situation to such an extent that you succumb to internal psychological noise.

Take Skillful Notes

Every student knows the importance of taking notes. However, not all note taking is equally beneficial. Skillful note taking requires some effort, but it yields great dividends. Skillful note takers know that it is impossible to write down every word the speaker says. Attempting to do so invariably results in falling behind and missing important ideas as you struggle to write the previous idea down. It is wise to develop a system of abbreviations for the most commonly used words in a particular subject area; the shorter the abbreviation the better, though you certainly want to make sure that it is not so cryptic that you fail to remember its meaning later. For example, in a communication class, the word "communication" will obviously be used again and again. You could abbreviate this word as "comm.," but even that is unnecessarily long. A capital letter "C" should suffice. There are also common abbreviations for words such as "within" and "because," and there are mathematical symbols to represent such words or phrases as "greater than," "less than," "increase," "decrease," "therefore," and others. Develop your own system and constantly seek to perfect it. Some note takers find that it is helpful to take notes as they read the text in preparation for class, and to use only half of the page for those notes, highlighting key terms. Then, while taking class notes, they locate the appropriate term in their reading notes and add additional notes in the space next to the term. There are many note taking systems and strategies recommended by people who are experts in the development of study skills; check your local bookstore or online resources that might be useful to you. You should also investigate the resources available to you on your campus to help you improve in this vital academic skill.

Informational listening requires active participation on the part of the patient.

Ask Questions and Paraphrase

Perhaps the best way to improve your informational listening skills is to stay active and engaged throughout the class. Participation in a discussion requires you to listen to the contributions of others. Two skills that are particularly beneficial for informational listening are questioning and paraphrasing. **Questioning** is a type of cross-examination used to gain understanding or additional information. The types of questions that get you the most information—such as open-ended and follow-up questions—are discussed in Appendix A on Interviewing. **Paraphrasing** is used to clarify or confirm your understanding. A paraphrase is essentially a statement, sometimes phrased in the form of a question, which reflects to the sender the gist of what you heard her/him say. A good paraphrase is not a verba-tim restatement of the speaker's words; it is a restatement in your own words. "What I understand you to be saying is . . ." is an example of a paraphrase. If your under-standing is not accurate, the sender has a chance to clear up any misunderstanding which, of course, means that you have a chance to achieve shared meaning. Whether you are asking questions, paraphrasing, volunteering an answer to a question that has been posed, or simply making a comment about something that is being discussed, active and engaged participation in class will help you to attend, under-stand, respond, and remember—the important components of effective listening identified earlier in this chapter.

APPLY **WHAT YOU KNOW**
INFORMATIONAL LISTENING SKILLS

Apply what you know about informational listening skills by answering these questions:

- Which of the skills for informational listening (select at least two) do you think would have kept the misunderstanding

between Samantha and Scott in our opening scenario from happening? Explain your thinking.

- Do you think these same skills would help the typical college student? Why or why not?

LEARNING **OBJECTIVE**

3.5 What is critical listening, in what listening situa-tions is it needed most, and which specific skills are suggested for its ef-fective use?

Critical Listening

Every day we are subjected to persuasive messages. Whether these messages are con-veyed by advertisements in the media, political candidates, or campus speakers trying to get us to adopt their beliefs, we are asked to listen in order to make decisions about actions we will take. Unlike situations requiring informational listening where our goal is to comprehend information, persuasive situations require critical listening. In **critical listening** situations the speaker's goal is to persuade us, therefore, our goal must be to evaluate the credibility of the speaker and of the message. If we fail to make the shift from informational to critical listening, we are likely to blindly accept the information, making us an easy target for persuaders who may not have our best interests in mind.

Skillful persuaders know that they must be credible and that their messages must be believable if they are to achieve their goal. Nearly 2,500 years ago, the great Greek philosopher Aristotle theorized about rhetoric in his book *The Art of Rhetoric* and included the elements necessary for a speaker to be persuasive. He posited that speakers must attend to *ethos, logos,* and *pathos* appeals. Skillful critical listeners must pay attention to how speakers use these elements in order to judge whether the message and the speaker are worthy of belief.

Listening Critically to Speaker Ethos

Ethos refers to speaker credibility. In order for a speaker to be viewed as a person worthy of belief, the listener must perceive the speaker to be someone who demon-strates three important characteristics: competence, character, and charisma.

- *Competence* is the listener's perception that the speaker is knowledgeable about the subject.

- *Character* is the listener's perception that the speaker is someone who can be trusted, who is fair and honest, and who is motivated by interest in the listener's needs rather than merely her/his own vested interests.

- *Charisma* is the listener's perception that the speaker possesses traits that the listener admires or respects. Charisma is also related to the degree to which the listener perceives that there is enough common ground (similar values or experiences) between the speaker and the listener for the listener to identify with the speaker in some important respects.

A good critical listener will observe how speakers demonstrate credibility in their persuasive messages:

- *Speakers who are competent* will make good use of evidence to back up their claims and show sound reasoning. Competent speakers are also more likely to present both sides of an issue—showing that they are aware of arguments opposing their view and explaining why those arguments are inaccurate or so minimal as to be unimportant.

- *Speakers who have good character* will cite the sources of their evidence and will use sources that are not biased. Any persuader may have a personal stake in achieving their persuasive objectives, but a speaker of good character will also be concerned with the listener's needs. For example, salespeople clearly are motivated by the need to earn an income, which can only happen if they are able to sell a product. However, honest salespeople will not misrepresent the product and will take care to learn about the customer's needs in order to guide buyers to products that are most suitable for them.

- *Speakers who have charisma* will use their "charm" to draw others to them by the force of their personality. They may also appeal to our emotions, as we will discuss in greater detail shortly. For now, though, it is important to recognize that a speaker's charisma often carries a lot of weight in our responses to persuasive messages. Good critical listeners will not allow charisma to be the most important factor in judging a speaker as credible.

Critical listeners evaluate the evidence and the credibility of the sales person and their pitch.

Listening Critically to Speaker Logos

In addition to judging the credibility of the speaker, the critical listener will also judge the credibility of the message. When you listen for the evidence that supports any claim the speaker makes as well as the sound reasoning from that evidence, you are listening for the speaker's **logos**. In later chapters on public speaking, we will deal more specifically with forms of evidence. For now, it may be helpful to note that *evidence* refers to supporting material such as definitions, explanations, examples, illustrations, expert testimony, comparisons, and statistics. It is not enough, however, that speakers have evidence; they must also demonstrate sound reasoning from that evidence. In other words, having examined the data, speakers must draw conclusions from the evidence that are logically correct and do not exhibit fallacious reasoning.

Fallacies are flaws in reasoning. They occur when the conclusions drawn from evidence do not necessarily support the argument being made. Philosophy courses often include the study of formal and informal logic, including the systems that allow analysis of just how arguments break down. Some of the most common fallacies are presented in **Table 3.1** to give you a sense of how speakers often draw conclusions that do not necessarily follow from the evidence. Although these fallacies are covered in detail in Chapter 14, we will take a brief look at three of them to demonstrate how important it is to listen critically to logos:

- **Ad hominem,** or "against the person," is the type of reasoning that occurs when the speaker attacks a person instead of the person's argument. For example, when a speaker says that you should not believe an opponent because of some personal circumstance or trait that is irrelevant to the topic, the speaker is hoping to divert your attention from the merits of the opponent's argument. "You cannot believe Ms. Jones's statement that her proposal will save tax dollars; after all, she has been married three times!"

- **Ad verecundiam** is an inappropriate appeal to authority in which speakers claim that their arguments are true because some esteemed person claims they are true, even though the issue at hand is out of that authority's area of expertise. When athletes endorse products that are not related to their sports, a potential *ad verecundiam* fallacy exists. A classic example of this fallacy is in the advertisements where a movie star proclaims, "I am not a doctor, but I play one on television."

- **Hasty generalization** occurs when a conclusion is based on only isolated examples or too few examples. In other words, when the sample used by the speaker is too small to be representative of the population it comes from, hasty generalization is likely. For example, consider the following argument:

  —Last year in our own city a student was caught carrying a handgun.

  —A survey of one inner-city school found that 3 percent of students bring handguns to school.

  —It is obvious that our state needs to install metal detection equipment in every school in the state.

  Unless the above conclusion is supported with more inclusive research, it is certainly a hasty generalization.

Although we have presented only a few of the many fallacies that exist, you should have a better idea of the importance of listening critically to the claims, the evidence, and the reasoning that speakers use in the attempt to persuade you—all of which are part of the logos of the message.

Table 3.1 Types of Fallacious Reasoning

Fallacy	Definition
Ad hominem	Attacking the person instead of the person's argument
Ad populum	Claiming an idea is true because everyone knows that it is true
Ad verecundiam	Claiming an idea is true because an esteemed person says it's true
Begging the question	Claiming that an idea is true because it is—no evidence; just assumption
False dichotomy	Using "either-or" reasoning without admitting any middle ground
Hasty generalization	Supporting an argument with isolated or too few examples
Post hoc	Claiming that event A caused event B because B followed A
Red herring	Offering a fact to distract from the actual topic or argument
Slippery slope	Taking a certain step automatically will lead to another undesirable step
Straw man	Attacking a bogus argument rather than an actual argument

Listening Critically to Speaker Pathos

Another important component of successful persuasion is the use of **pathos**, or appeals to emotion. Aristotle observed that, in order to move people to action, speakers must appeal to listeners' emotions. We will look in detail at effective emotional appeals in our discussion of persuasive speaking later in Chapter 14. For now, be aware that emotional appeals must be used ethically.

Unfortunately, examples abound of persuaders who use emotional appeals as their primary "evidence." The goal appears to be to entice listeners to suspend their rational thought processes so that they will agree to do things that they would not do if they were really listening critically. We have all seen the advertisements that try to persuade us that popularity is virtually guaranteed if we only purchase the advertiser's product. Some speakers fabricate similarities with their audience members, such as a speaker who attempts to win over his golfing audience by referring to himself as a "golf fanatic" though he has played golf only a few times. Others use emotionally loaded terms and exaggeration of "costs, problems, or negative consequences" (Herrick, 1995, p. 230) to play on their audiences' emotions. For example, "We've received hundreds of calls in violent opposition to this new city ordinance" could be used to get city members emotionally stirred up. However, critical listening could uncover some exaggerations—for example, asking questions such as What was the exact number of phone calls? Is this number more or less than typically received by city hall? What does "violent opposition" mean?

Even more disturbing is the speaker who goes beyond suggestion, loaded words, and exaggeration to total fabrication. Consider, for example, a televangelist who uses images of children from other countries in obvious poverty in order to increase contributions when in fact the ministry serves only local needs or a salesperson who claims a product will cure a serious disfiguring acne condition, when it is no more than a normal antibiotic. As good critical listeners, we need to look through the emotional appeals and make sure that the speaker's arguments are, in fact, truthful and accurate before we adopt a belief and/or take an action such as parting with our financial resources. Unfortunately, many viewers are not effective critical listeners, and the stories about elderly people on fixed incomes who have given everything they have to unscrupulous persuaders are legion.

Using Critical Listening Skills

So what skills are helpful for developing good critical listening? The most obvious include the following:

- *Researching* speaker statements may be necessary *before making decisions*, particularly when the speaker is not readily accessible for interaction.

- *Evaluating* the credibility of the speaker and of the message is an important step. When the speaker offers forms of proof as evidence, the listener should evaluate each piece of evidence for its credibility.

- *Probing* personal observations given by the speaker as evidence is something the critical listener should do to determine if there are other factors that might account for its occurrence.

- *Questioning* is another crucial listening skill. For example, a speaker may make an assertion of something that appears to be a fact but may be, instead, an inference. An **inference** is a conclusion that is drawn from something you observe and requires evidence to support its accuracy. Therefore, when a speaker makes a claim without offering evidence

to back it up, the critical listener needs to question, "How do you know this?" Questions about the sources of statistics, the credentials of experts cited, and the details about examples that are offered are all part of the critical listener's tool kit.

- *Paraphrasing*, as always, allows you to clarify and confirm your understanding of the speaker's message.

APPLY **WHAT YOU KNOW**
CRITICAL LISTENING AND FALLACIOUS REASONING

Apply what you know about critical listening to answer these questions:

- "Bob's car was broken into while he was in class. This campus needs to double security patrols." This is an example of which fallacy: ad populum, hasty generalization, ad verecundiam?

- "Jamerson couldn't possibly make a good mayor—her first company ended in bankruptcy" is an example of the *ad populum* fallacy—true or false?

- Listen to several commercials on radio or television, or locate several ads in a newspaper or magazine. Identify at least one common fallacy from Table 3.1. Explain whether you think this fallacy was used deliberately or by mistake.

So far, we have covered two important listening situations: informational and critical. In the informational situation, the sender's goal is to convey information; the listener's goal is to comprehend it. In the critical situation, the sender's aim is to persuade; the listener's goal is to judge the credibility of the speaker and the message. One important listening situation remains—empathic listening.

LEARNING **OBJECTIVE**

3.6 What is empathic listening, in what listening situations is it needed most, and which specific skills are suggested for its effective use?

Empathic Listening

The **empathic listening** situation is encountered when a sender's goal (usually a friend or colleague) is to get help to cope with or solve a problem, and your goal is to listen with empathy and see the world from the sender's frame of reference. It is important to note that in order to be empathetic, you do not necessarily need to agree with the sender's view of the problem. It is also not necessary that you have had a similar problem in your own life. Your goal is not to project yourself into the other person's situation; it is to keep yourself out of it and, at least for the moment, experience the world through your friend's perspective.

Empathy is not the same as *sympathy*. To feel sympathy for someone is to feel sorry for their predicament. When you are empathetic you do not feel *for* someone; you feel *with* them. This is not an easy thing to do, but it is an important aspect of developing and maintaining close relationships with other people.

The key to effective empathic listening lies in the responses you offer as you listen to your friend talk. Let us examine some of the possible responses that occur when listening empathically—supporting, interpreting, paraphrasing, questioning, judging, and advising.

Use Supporting Responses

In place of giving judging responses that discount the speaker's feelings, good empathic listeners offer **supporting responses** which show that they are concerned and willing to invest the time and energy required to listen. Statements such as, "I can imagine that this would be very painful to you," or "Is there anything I can do to help? I would be glad to listen," are responses that communicate to the sender that you are supportive of his or her right to feel a particular way. As mentioned earlier, using supporting responses does not necessarily mean that you are in agreement with a person's feelings—merely that you recognize those feelings. Supporting responses may also be nonverbal; a touch on the arm, eye contact that lets the speaker know that you are completely focused on him or her at that moment, head nods and the occasional "mm-hmm" that convey attentiveness are all ways that you can demonstrate support.

Use Interpreting Responses

Supporting responses are very helpful for effective empathic listening; however, they are not enough. **Interpreting responses** offer the speaker another way to view some aspect of the situation. Sometimes as you listen to a friend, you will realize that she has possibly exaggerated the significance of an event or misinterpreted an action or a remark made by another person. People often go to others with a problem because they recognize that the other person is not emotionally embroiled in the situation and may be able to see things more objectively; sometimes we all need a "sounding board" to test out our perceptions. By providing interpreting responses, the listener can help the speaker *reframe* the situation or consider alternative interpretations. However, there are two important suggestions for offering good interpreting responses:

- *Word your response so it sounds like a possibility rather than a certainty.* "Oh, you have just misunderstood," suggests that you have a more accurate view than your friend does. Most people would react defensively to such a statement, given that they are the ones who know the whole story. It is preferable to phrase your interpreting response as a suggestion: "That is so out of character for him; is it possible that something is happening in his life now that would account for that behavior?" The speaker then has the opportunity to consider this possible reframing of the situation or to explain why his or her own perspective is, in fact, accurate.

- *Make sure the timing of your response is correct.* All too often a listener may jump in with an alternative interpretation very early in the empathic listening situation. A friend may confide that she is worried that her boyfriend is on the verge of ending their relationship because he hasn't made time to see her in a few days. You may immediately recognize that there are many possible explanations for that behavior, such as "Maybe he is just really busy right now." However, when you offer this alternative interpretation before you have heard any more information, your friend may wonder whether you are defending her boyfriend rather than understanding her concern. Therefore, a good rule of thumb is that you should not offer an alternative way to frame your friend's situation until you have a clear understanding of how she frames it. You should not offer the interpreting response until you have earned the right to be heard.

When the principles of timing and wording are observed, an interpreting response can be a very helpful way for you to demonstrate that you are attempting to fully understand the speaker's frame of reference.

Use Questioning Responses and Paraphrasing Responses

You may be wondering at this point, "How do you earn the right to be heard?" The answer lies in those two very important listening skills that have already been discussed as essential to informational and critical listening: questioning and paraphrasing.

What type of response does this parent seem to be using?

Questioning Responses

Remember that your goal in empathic listening is to see the world through the other person's frame of reference. In order to do this, you must get enough information to fill in the picture you have of the situation. You do this by asking questions. The ability to ask good questions is crucial, but it is also not always easy. Good listeners pay close attention to what has been said as well as to what has not been said. The key to formulating good questions is to keep in mind that you are trying to fill in the missing pieces of the picture. As you listen to the speaker, you should constantly ask yourself, "What else do I need to know in order to fill in this picture?" Good questions build on answers; they probe for additional information that will help you to fully understand the speaker's perspective.

Paraphrasing Responses

Paraphrasing, as we discussed earlier, is reflecting to the speaker what you heard him or her say. In fact, paraphrasing is often referred to as **reflective listening.** It is as if you are holding up a mirror so the speaker can understand how you heard what he said. Paraphrasing is important because it allows you to confirm the accuracy of your understanding or to correct your misunderstanding. It is also beneficial to the speaker because it allows him to see how his communication is being perceived. In addition, it provides evidence that you are, in fact, truly listening. There are two types of paraphrases that are used in empathic listening: content and feelings.

Content Paraphrasing

The first type, referred to as a **content paraphrase**, occurs when you "say back" to the speaker the information that was contained in his or her statement. However, be sure to:

- Put the paraphrase in your own words, not a verbatim repetition of the speaker's remarks.
- Include the whole message in your paraphrase. You should not fixate on one portion of the message and ignore other important parts of it. For example, assume that your friend says, "My boss told me that unless I start increasing my sales, I am going to lose my job, and then I won't have any way to pay my rent and car insurance." If you were to respond, "So it costs you a lot to pay rent and your car payment?" you would be missing an important aspect of the speaker's concern. A better paraphrase would be, "So you are getting a lot of pressure at work and you need to keep your job so you can meet your obligations; is that correct?"

Even empathetic listening with friends requires careful questioning and paraphrasing.

Feelings Paraphrasing

The second type of paraphrase, the **feelings paraphrase**, is achieved by reflecting to the speaker the emotions that you detect underneath the content of the message. In the example above, you would be paraphrasing your friend's feelings if you said, "It sounds like you are pretty worried about your job right now." Good empathic listeners use both types of paraphrases and, in doing so, increase their ability to see the world through the speaker's frame of reference.

Avoid Judging and Advising Responses

Although judging and advising responses are often used in empathic listening situations, we suggest that you avoid them when at all possible. The **judging response** occurs when you try to make a person feel better with platitudes or by minimizing their concerns with comments such as, "Don't worry; everything will be okay," "You shouldn't feel that way," or "That's not a problem." Although these statements are intended to comfort the speaker, what really happens is that they set you up as the "judge" of what constitutes a problem and may even communicate that you don't think the person's problems are important. Most people do not appreciate being judged or having their concerns minimized, even when the intent is to be reassuring. Although there may be times when responses of this sort can help to defuse a particularly strong statement of distress, most of the time the judging response should be avoided.

The **advising response** occurs when you propose a solution to your friend's problem. You may reason that your friend did, after all, come to you for help with a problem; surely the best thing you can do is to fix his problem for him. To make this assumption would be a mistake. Consider for a moment the dangers of offering advice. Should your friend accept your advice, only to have it fail to accomplish his goals, you would then be held responsible for that failure. By the same token, if your friend takes your advice and it works, you may well find that you are consulted every time your friend faces a new problem that he feels incapable of solving. Few of us would enjoy having the responsibility for other people's lives in this manner.

There may be times when a person does need advice. For example, if your friend is on the verge of making a decision that could potentially result in an outcome that would be physically harmful, you may not have time to employ the empathic listening techniques discussed here. As a general rule, however, you would be wise to adopt this philosophy about giving advice: *When people come to you asking for help with a problem, they do not need your right answers; what they need are the right questions, so they can find their own right answers.*

This principle suggests that people are benefited more by the type of listening that allows them to solve their own problems. A good empathic listener, when asked, "What should I do?" will avoid giving advice. A good empathic listener will, instead, use the questioning and paraphrasing responses to guide a friend in discovering alternatives that are available. The good empathic listener will use questions and paraphrases to assist a friend in evaluating the feasibility of the options identified as possibilities, until the friend has decided the option that he or she is most willing to invest in.

This approach takes the responsibility for others' decisions away from the listener. It also empowers speakers to take charge of their own lives. For most people, to be truly listened to is a rare thing; it builds trust and confidence in the quality of the relationship. In that way, good empathic listening is a gift we offer to others.

APPLY **WHAT YOU KNOW**
EMPATHIC LISTENING

Remember the opening scenario with Samantha and Scott? Assume that you are a friend of Samantha's, and that she has just expressed her frustrations about her day described earlier to you and has asked you what she should do (or pick Scott, if you prefer). To apply what you know about empathic listening, complete the following:

- Write a supporting response and an interpreting response that you might make.

- Now write a judging response and an advising response that you might make.

- Which one of these responses is more like the responses you usually make to your friends or family members?

- What problems, if any, do you see with your usual responses? What strengths do you see? Give an example for each.

LISTENING **AND YOUR CAREER**

LEARNING OBJECTIVE

3.7 What listening information and skills covered in this chapter relate to your career?

The communication and listening skills covered in this chapter can be of special importance to you as you search for and develop a career. The *Spotlight on*, *Career Moment*, and *Connecting to* features relate communication skills from the chapter to success in the specific fields of business, education, and healthcare.

SPOTLIGHT ON **THE VALUE OF LISTENING**

BUSINESS

You may find yourself working for a global company and a member of a virtual team whose members communicate with each other through the Internet and never meet face-to-face at all. In situations like these, where cultural differences are likely, the technology involved makes listening both more important and more difficult.

Some global listening tips include the following (Brownell, 2006; Reisner, 1993; Varner & Beamer, 1995):

- *Use humor,* carefully—not all cultures find the same content humorous.

- *Cultivate diverse viewpoints*—acknowledge the role of ambiguity in creating ideas.

- For clarity of ideas, both high- and low- content cultures should present information in a low-content manner without taking meanings for granted.

- *Answer e-mail carefully and quickly* to show that you are attentive.

EDUCATION

Listening training begins in preschool with "zip it, lock it, put it in your pocket." Education-world.com in "Build Listening Skills with Asian Folktales" (2007) suggests teaching listening to children from PreK through 8th grade by using such Asian folktales as:

- "Kings for Breakfast: A Hindu Legend"

- "The Gifts of Wali Dad: A Tale of India and Pakistan"

- "Too-too-moo and the Giant: A Tale of Indonesia"

At the same time, teachers could use maps to locate each country, show each country's flag, and have students act out the tales from each country.

Empathic listening is especially important to use in the classroom. According to Judith Schubert (2007), when listening, educators should (1) give complete attention, (2) avoid being judgmental, (3) focus on feelings and not just facts, and (4) use restatements to clarify (p. 228).

HEALTHCARE

To encourage an attitude of partnership with patients, healthcare professionals must focus more on listening to patients by using these listening skills (Kelner & Bourgeault, 1993):

- To get more information in less time, use *specific questions* that limit responses to *yes*, *no*, or single words.

- To encourage elaboration, use *silence* and *open-ended questions* such as "Tell me about your symptoms."

- When answers are incomplete, use *follow-up* or *probing questions*.

- To check understanding, use *paraphrasing*.

- To show you are listening, use *active listening techniques* such as eye contact, head-nods, and verbal utterances such as "mm-hmm."

- To ensure that patient concerns have been addressed, use *clearinghouse questions* ("Is there anything else that is troubling you?") See Appendix A for more questions.

CAREER MOMENT **LISTENING AND YOUR CAREER**

Our *Spotlight on the Value of Listening* looked at the importance of listening in the fields of business, education, and healthcare. No matter what career you wish to pursue, listening and communication skills are essential. Although 80 percent of executives in one study selected listening as the most important skill in the workplace, 28 percent of them also listed listening as the most lacking skill in the workplace (Salopek, 1999). Employers are looking for people with listening awareness and listening skills. This means that just by taking this course in communication, you have improved your employability.

Now consider another possibility—what about a minor in communication? A communication minor fits with many major fields of study such as business, law, criminal justice, education, international relations, psychology, health care, and hotel management—just to name a few. Communication skills are also important in the science fields. The Accreditation Board for Engineering and Technology (ABET) now includes communication skills (including listening) as a standard for evaluating college engineering programs in the United States (Williams, 2002). If you aren't convinced that communication is important in your chosen career field, use your college's databases to search for professional articles on communication skills written by people in your profession. The more communication training you receive, the better your skills in the workplace.

CONNECTING TO . . . BUSINESS

Are you considering a business or professional career? Listening skills are extremely important in the business world because we spend more of our time listening—up to 80 percent in a day (Wolvin & Coakley, 1981). Up to 60 percent of worker errors are estimated to be the result of poor listening (Cooper, 1997). Another study found that, although executives ranked listening as the most important skill in the workplace, they also ranked listening as the skill most lacking (Salopek, 1999).

ACTIVITY Go to Randall's ESL Cyber Listening Lab at www.esl-lab.com and take one of the tests in the General Listening Quizzes columns to test your listening skills. After taking the quiz, write a short paragraph explaining (1). The score you received on the quiz and what it shows about your listening, (2) Whether you agree with the quiz score based on your listening experiences in the workplace, and (3) What you learned about your listening habits from this chapter.

CONNECTING TO . . . EDUCATION

Are you considering a career in education? Listening skills are part of what it means to be a successful teacher. But not all teachers use effective listening skills, do they?

According to McCroskey, Richmond, & McCroskey (2006), teachers often reduce students' willingness to communicate by their poor use of immediacy (verbal, vocal, and visual behaviors) (p. 112).

ACTIVITY Complete the Teacher Immediacy Measure (Richmond & McCroskey, 1998) by indicating how well the following statements apply to "your teacher's communication with you": 1 = Never; 2 = Rarely; 3 = Occasionally; 4 = Often; 5 = Very Often

___ 1. Uses hands and arms to gesture while talking
___ 2. Uses a monotone or dull voice while talking
___ 3. Looks at you while talking to you
___ 4. Frowns while talking
___ 5. Has a very tense body position while talking
___ 6. Moves away while talking to you
___ 7. Uses a variety of vocal expressions while talking
___ 8. Touches you on the shoulder or arm while talking
___ 9. Smiles while talking to you
___ 10. Looks away from you while talking to you
___ 11. Has a relaxed body position while talking
___ 12. Is "stiff" while talking

___ 13. Avoids touching you while talking to you
___ 14. Moves closer while talking to you
___ 15. Is animated while talking
___ 16. Looks bland or neutral when talking
Scoring:
(1) Total scores for items 2, 4, 5, 6, 10, 12, 13, 16.
(2) Total scores for items 1, 3, 7, 8, 9, 11, 14, 15.
(3) Start with 48 points; add total from (1) and subtract total from (2).
(4) Scores above 74—high immediacy. Score below 32—low immediacy. Scores of 32–74—moderate immediacy.

CONNECTING TO . . . **HEALTHCARE**

Are you considering a career in healthcare? Healthcare is a career area that is projected to be in great demand for the foreseeable future mainly due to the aging of our population. In addition, advanced technologies in medicine and health have opened up new jobs in the field. Even people who expect to work in accounting, law, marketing, and other business fields may find they will be employed by a healthcare organization.

ACTIVITY Form a group of at least three students who are interested in careers as health professionals, and create a scenario that would involve a patient who is seeing a nurse for the first time.

After you have created your scenario, roleplay an interaction between the patient and the nurse that focuses on the listening skills of the nurse. Take turns playing the role of the nurse, working especially to use empathic listening skills or to illustrate the nurse doing a poor job of listening. Discuss the differences between the effective and ineffective scenarios.

▶ Log onto MyCommunicationLab.com to access Connecting to Psychology and Connecting to Science, Technology, Engineering, and Math—both with related activities.

CHAPTER SUMMARY

Becoming an effective listener is hard work, but it is definitely worth the effort. You can determine your knowledge of listening by checking the skills and learning objectives presented in this chapter.

Summary of **SKILLS**

Check each skill that you now feel qualified to perform:
- ❏ I can incorporate several memory tips to improve my listening.
- ❏ I can identify and avoid several major barriers to effective listening.
- ❏ I can pinpoint poor listening habits that I have and make and follow a plan to overcome them.
- ❏ I can recognize and use at least two listening skills needed in the informational, critical, and empathic contexts.

Summary of LEARNING **OUTCOMES**

3.1 *What is the definition of listening, and what are the stages involved in effective listening as well as several memory tips to improve listening?*

- *Listening* is the active process of constructing meaning from spoken messages through attention to the verbal and nonverbal codes that accompany it.

- The basic stages of listening are attending to, understanding, responding, and remembering.

- Memory tips from *Developing Skills* feature include Tip #1: Transferring short-term memory to long-term memory; and Tip #2: Recalling stored information.

3.2 *Why is listening important, and what specific benefits does listening offer in our everyday lives?*

- College students spend more time listening (53%) than they do reading, speaking, or writing all together.

- Listening helps us develop and maintain our mental health, our relationships, and our careers and helps us become better citizens.

3.3 *What are the major barriers that complicate effective listening for most people, what are four poor listening habits, and what role does a person's listening style inventory play in listening effectiveness?*

- It is difficult to listen effectively because of various complicating barriers such as types of noise, information processing, cultural differences, gender orientation, and poor listening habits.

- Poor listening habits include imitation listening, selective versus insulated listening, defensive listening, and monopolizing.

- The Listening Styles Profile discussed in the *Making Theory Practical* feature includes four listening styles—people-oriented, action-oriented, content-oriented, and time-oriented that determine listening effectiveness.

3.4 *What is informational listening, in what listening situations is it needed most, and which specific skills are suggested for its effective use?*

- Informational listening is required when the sender's goal is to convey information and the receiver's goal is to comprehend that information.

- Situations that require informational listening include the classroom, workplace, and medical consultation.

- Informational listening skills include: preparing to listen; avoiding prejudging; mentally organizing, summarizing and linking information; personalizing information; building a better vocabulary; taking skillful notes; and asking questions and paraphrasing.

3.5 *What is critical listening, in what listening situations is it needed most, and which specific skills are suggested for its effective use?*

- Critical listening is required in persuasive situations.

- Situations that require critical listening are those that involve listening to advertisements, political candidates, or persuasive speakers where the analyzing of the speaker's ethos, logos, and pathos appeals requires careful judgment.

- Critical listening skills include researching, evaluating, probing, questioning, and paraphrasing.

3.6 *What is empathic listening, in what listening situations is it needed most, and which specific skills are suggested for its effective use?*

- Empathic listening is required in interpersonal contexts.

- Situations that require empathic listening include encounters with a friend or family member where their problem requires you to see the world from their frame of reference.

- Empathic listening skills involve four skills to use (supporting, interpreting, questioning, and paraphrasing responses) and two responses to avoid (judging and advising responses).

3.7 *What communication skills covered in this chapter relate specifically to your career (see highlighted fields of business, education, and healthcare)?*

- The *Spotlight on, Career Moment,* and *Connecting to* features highlight the value of listening in the fields of business, education, and healthcare—additional fields are included online.

SOLVE IT NOW!

Taking into consideration all that you learned about listening from this chapter, how would you analyze the communication difficulties between Samantha and Scott in our opening scenario?*

- In which stage of listening did most of Samantha's listening difficulties occur?
- What specific barriers and/or poor listening habits seemed to cause decoding

difficulties for Samantha and Scott? Identify at least two for each person.

- Which type of listening was required in the opening scenario—informational, critical, or empathic—and why was it not used successfully?
- What specific communication goals would you recommend for Samantha and Scott that would improve their listening skills now and in the future?

*Check your answers with those located in MyCommunicationLab, Scenario Analysis for Chapter 3

The next chapter will look at the role that verbal skills play in the success or failure of our communication with others.

KEY TERMS

ad hominem	p. 84	fallacies	p. 83	listening	p. 78	pathos	p. 85
ad verecundiam	p. 84	feelings paraphrase	p. 88	insulated listening	p. 77	questioning	p. 81
advising response	p. 89	focused listening	p. 73	internal noise	p. 74	receiver apprehension	p. 73
combative listening	p. 78	hasty generalization	p. 84	interpreting response	p. 87	reflective listening	p. 88
content paraphrase	p. 88	high-context cultures	p. 76	judging response	p. 88	selective listening	p. 77
critical listening	p. 82	imitation listening	p. 77	listening	p. 69	semantic noise	p. 75
defensive listeners	p. 77	inference	p. 85	logos	p. 83	short-term memory	p. 70
empathic listening	p. 86	information overload	p. 75	long-term memory	p. 70	stages of listening	p. 70
ethos	p. 82			low-context cultures	p. 75	supporting responses	p. 86
external noise	p. 74	informational		paraphrasing	p. 81		

SKILL BUILDERS

1. Divide into groups and rewrite the opening scenario with Samantha and Scott so their conversation shows effective listening and communication. Be prepared to read your new scenario to the class.

2. Critically evaluating what you read. Using the critical evaluation form from Chapter 1, select and evaluate an article from the online listening newsletter called *Sssh! Listen Up!* (www.highgain.com/newsletter). Be prepared to share your observations with your classmates.

3. Critically evaluating what you hear. Use the critical listening suggestions for speaker ethos, logos, and pathos covered in this chapter as you listen to one of the following speeches available at www.americanrhetoric.com: Christopher Reeve's address to the Democratic National Convention in 1996 (use search words "Christopher Reeve and DNC"); Barbara Bush's commencement address at Wellesley College in 1990; Mary Fisher's speech, "A Whisper of AIDS," at the Republican National Convention in 1992; or Barack Obama's address to the people of Berlin on July 24, 2008. Also, if your college subscribes to the *eLibrary* database, find a transcript of a radio or television program by a controversial talk-show host to critique. In all of these

speeches, be sure not to let your personal political leanings get in the way of an objective critique. Be prepared to turn in your written critique if requested.

4. As you think about gender and listening, consider some of the main differences between the way men and women listen discussed in the text. How you think these differences might affect the way messages are encoded by men and women? For the following scenarios, encode the message the way you think would be typical for a man, and then contrast that with the way you think would be typical for a woman.

- Two people (a dating couple) are at a party. One of them wants to leave and go somewhere else.
- A male business owner is approached by a female sales representative from a company that wishes to supply goods or services to the business owner. The business owner is not interested in the sales representative's product.
- A male patient wants to tell a female healthcare provider that prescribed treatments are not working and may be creating new health problems. How do you think this may relate to the concepts of high/low context? What conclusions would you draw?

4 Verbal Communication

After studying this chapter you should be able to . . .

- Pinpoint weaknesses in the way you use language and work to minimize at least two of them.
- Notice the power of your words in shaping perceptions and attitudes and replace several ineffective words with more powerful ones.
- Select at least one major obstacle to effective verbal communication in your life and locate a journal article to expand your understanding of it.
- Implement one or more suggested verbal skills to correct a major obstacle to verbal communication in your life and ask for feedback on your successes.

CHAPTER SUMMARY 〉 P. 116

SCENARIO

Gabe tossed his backpack on the floor and dropped into the empty chair across the library table from Katelynn. "Thanks a lot," he muttered.

"Thanks a lot for what?" Katelynn inquired.

"For convincing me to take this stupid British Lit class," Gabe replied.

"I don't remember 'convincing' you to do anything. You asked me, 'Who are the good teachers in the English department?' and I just answered your question."

"Well, Katie, I hate to tell you this, but Dr. Gordon is not a good teacher. And I think the word you used was 'brilliant.' He is not brilliant. He's nutty," Gabe exclaimed.

"He is not nutty and his class is not stupid." she retorted.

"Maybe I'm just not brilliant enough to recognize brilliance," Gabe offered, recognizing that he had begun to irritate Katelynn and needed to lighten the mood. "But even then, it takes a lot more than brilliance to make a good teacher."

"So what don't you like about him?" Katelynn inquired.

"Well, for one thing, it would be nice if he would use words everyone can understand," Gabe suggested. "Plus, you told me the class wasn't difficult, but he's got us turning in a paper every week."

"But that's why the class isn't difficult. It's not like they are major research papers," Katelynn pointed out. "They're mostly just short papers to make sure students keep current with the reading, which is really very helpful."

"That's because you're an English major; only English majors would like all that writing. I'm just trying to take something to satisfy the Core requirements," Gabe explained. "I don't know why you told me this would be an interesting class."

"But British Lit is interesting," Katelynn insisted.

"Chaucer is interesting?" Gabe asked incredulously. "How is a story written in some weird form of English about a random group of people on a trip to some saint's shrine interesting?"

Katelynn smiled reassuringly. "You're just a little overwhelmed. It'll all make more sense once you understand the Middle English morphology."

Gabe looked skeptical. "I don't even understand what you just said. And I'm not just a little overwhelmed; I'm totally doomed."

Katelynn laughed. "Besides, did you know that J. K. Rowling used one of those tales as inspiration for a story that occurs in some of her *Harry Potter* books?"

"Really? Hmm. That actually is kind of interesting. Maybe you're right and it will get better," Gabe shrugged. "But I might still need you to translate."

As you read this chapter, see if you can determine what specific verbal problems Katelynn and Gabe displayed in the opening scenario and what goal each should seek as communication encoders to improve their communication success.

SOLVE IT NOW! ⟩ P. 117 ⟩

While reading our opening scenario, were you able to find several communication problems? You were probably looking for decoding problems since our last two chapters (perception and listening) focused on human *decoding* abilities. However, in both this chapter and the next, we will switch our concentration from decoding to *encoding* and focus on how well we put our ideas into verbal and nonverbal code.

The Nature of Language

Consider these words by Steven Pinker (1994), a cognitive psychologist, who—like the noted linguist Noam Chomsky—argues that humans are born with an innate ability to create language: "As you are reading these words, you are taking part in one of the wonders of the natural world. For you and I belong to a species with a remarkable ability. . . . That ability is language." It is hard to argue with the notion that the ability to create and use language is, indeed, remarkable. It is to a great degree the central distinction between humans and other animals.

Language and Verbal Communication Defined

Let's start by defining some key terms. **Language** is a more-or-less formally established collection of symbols that has meaning for a specific group of people, whereas **verbal communication** is the exchange of meanings by the use of the written or spoken symbols of a language system. We refer to a single verbal symbol as a **word**, which is a speech sound or series of speech sounds combined into a single unit conveying an assigned meaning. Most language systems also have a **lexicon**, or formal system of written characters representing the spoken words of a language system (**Figure 4.1**) By one estimate (Gordon, 2005), there are currently 6,912 "living" languages—those that are still in use by at least a small number of people. Of these, 497 are catalogued as "nearly extinct."

Not all languages exist in spoken form; there are a number of extinct languages that we know about only because of written records, and we have no idea how those written symbols might have sounded when spoken. On the other hand, some

4.1 What is language, what are the four rules that govern its use, what are the denotative versus connotative meanings of language, and how is language affected by culture and gender?

Albanian—sq	Hungarian—hun
Basque—eu	Icelandic—is
Belarusian—be	Italian—ita
Beton—br	Latvian—lv
Bulgarian—bg	Lithuanian—lt
Catalan—ca	Macedonian—mk
Croatian—hr	Norwegian—no
Czech—cs	Polish—pol
Danish—da	Portuguese—por
Dutch—nld	Romanian—ron
English—eng	Russian—rus
Estonian—et	Saami—se
Finish—fi	Serbian—sr
French—fra	Slovac—sk
Gaelic—ga	Slovenian—sl
Galician—gl	Spanish—spa
German—deu	Swedish—sv
Greek—el	Ukrainian—ukr

Figure 4.1
Language Map of Europe

Source: A Language Map of Europe. Sample from Culture: A Geographical Perspective by C. A. Heatwole at http://www.emsc.nysed.gov/ciai/socst/grade3/geograph.html. Reprinted by permission of Eupedia, www.eupedia.com

languages do not exist in written form. Many Native American languages, for example, are only spoken, which is possible when the population that uses a particular language is small and in close geographic proximity. Unfortunately, this is also the reason that many Native American languages are on the verge of extinction; the number of speakers is decreasing each year. Currently, linguists are attempting to preserve the Native American languages by making audio-recordings of the few remaining speakers and developing a system of written symbols for each language. It is also true that not all languages use words: American Sign Language and British Sign Language are examples of languages that use visual cues as symbols to convey meaning rather than spoken sounds or written symbols.

Language and the Human Ability to Think

All animals seem to be capable of some form of communication, and certain animals—such as apes, whales, and dolphins—seem to have complex systems of noises and behaviors that send messages to others in their group. In fact, there is some evidence that the songs of humpback whales include a hierarchical syntax (Suzuki, Buck, & Tyack, 2006). However, human use of language is much more sophisticated with its reference to abstract objects and use of cognition. Cognition—the power to think—is dependent on the ability to use language. Think about this for a moment: Could you think about your life in the way you do if you did not have language to label your experiences? Could you analyze what you see and decide what actions are necessary to achieve your goals if you did not have words to describe your experiences and to compare them to the experiences of others? A bird builds a nest, and each generation of fledglings builds nests in about the same way. Humans, however, can build a structure, observe its strengths and weaknesses, problem-solve to correct its deficiencies, and then communicate the building experience with others. Future generations can improve on building methods and erect structures that serve their needs better. This **time-binding** characteristic of humans—the ability to accumulate and communicate knowledge of the past in order to live in the present and shape the future—is dependent upon our capacity to use language effectively (Korzybski, 1950).

We have discussed these ideas about language to emphasize the awesome significance of this ability of humans to communicate verbally. Because most of us have no memory of learning to speak our native language, and only a slight memory of how we learned to read, we take our use of language for granted. And it is because we learned to use our language with hardly any awareness of rules that we do not appreciate the rule-governed nature of language, the power of language, or the difficulties in using language ineffectively. An exploration of these issues will help us to develop the ability to be effective verbal encoders.

Language Is Rule-Governed

Language is governed by rules. As you acquire the ability to use your native language or to become fluent in a second language, you must adapt to the rules that are part of that language system.

- **Phonological rules** deal with how words sound when spoken. The word "table," for example, sounds different when pronounced by English language rules than it does when spoken in French. Even within the English language, a word may be spelled the same but pronounced differently to represent different meanings. For example, the word *tear* is pronounced as [tir] when it is used to mean a drop of liquid from a person's eye. The same word is pronounced as [ter] when it is used to mean a *rip* in a piece of clothing. The same spelling, but different meaning and different pronunciations—no wonder the English language can be frustrating to learn.

- **Semantic rules** dictate the range of meanings that a particular language group assigns to a word. When you look up a word in the dictionary, you are essentially trying to learn the semantic rules for that word in your language. For example, how many different meanings can you think of for the word *run*? Check additional meanings by looking in the dictionary.

- **Syntactic rules** have to do with how words are combined in sentences. In English, you would refer to "my aunt's pen," but according to the syntactic rules of French, the equivalent phrase, *la plume de ma tante*, orders the words differently: "the pen of my aunt" is the literal translation.

- **Pragmatic rules** are unstated rules that we come to understand largely through context and are absorbed over time as we observe how the members of our culture use language. Pragmatic rules allow us to understand the real meaning that we are expected to attach to a phrase or sentence. For example, how do you know that a sarcastic remark is actually saying the opposite of what it appears to be saying and that it is intended as humor? Young children do not understand the pragmatic rules that govern the interpretation of sarcasm until middle childhood at the earliest (Pexman, et al., 2005), so they are likely to interpret the sarcastic comment literally. Over time, most of us begin to figure out the pragmatic rules, even though they may never be specifically described or explained to us.

Language Is Symbolic

Once we have mastered the basic rules of our language and have developed a vocabulary that is adequate for our daily use, we tend to think that the words we use have the same meaning for others that they do for us. When someone misunderstands what we say, we enjoy hauling out the *Webster's Unabridged Dictionary* and verifying that we have used the word according to one of the **denotative meanings**—dictionary definitions—contained therein. But we fail to understand that the **connotative meanings**, the personal meanings based on the images and emotions aroused by a word, are the meanings that people respond to. In other words, we fail to recognize that *words have no meaning unless people assign them meaning.*

Therefore, language is **symbolic**—words don't mean, they are merely symbols that represent ideas, feelings, objects, or events in our experience. Words are arbitrary; that is, there is no reason that any particular word must represent a particular idea or object. To be sure, we have a starting point for understanding each other in the denotative meanings of words. However, a quick glance at any page in the dictionary (which is where we store our semantic rules for the denotative meanings of the written symbols in our lexicon) reveals that many words have numerous denotative meanings. For example, in one common dictionary, the entry for the word *doctor* contains 13 denotative definitions. The definitions range from nouns ("medical practitioner") to verbs ("to tamper with"). This means that there are 13 possible ways for someone to misunderstand your denotative meaning when you use the word "doctor" in communication.

But let us suppose that you and your listener both understand that the denotative meaning you are using is "medical practitioner." Can you be sure you have achieved the goal of shared meaning that is at the heart of our efforts to communicate? It is important to realize that the denotative meanings are not

There are 13 denotative definitions for the word *doctor*.

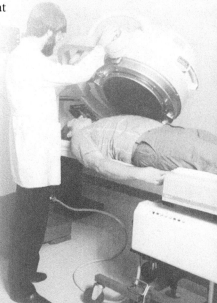

the meanings people respond to; they respond to the connotative meanings. Recall that we defined "connotative meaning" as one's personal meaning, the images and emotions that are aroused when a word is said or heard. What image comes into your mind when you hear the word *doctor*? More than likely, it is the image of someone very like your own doctor. More importantly, what emotions are aroused in you when the word "doctor" is used? If you are someone who has a near reverential awe of people trained in medicine, your emotions are likely to be positive. But what if you have been the victim of medical malpractice? So, you see, even when you think you are using a very commonly understood term, the possibility is great that you and your communication partner may not share the exact meaning.

Language and Culture

The personal meanings attached to words, as well as to how language is used, are very much a product of one's frame of reference. As we learned in Chapter 1, cultural values are a significant part of your frame of reference. People from high-context cultures have different expectations about verbal encoding than people from low-context cultures. The biggest difference is in the directness of verbal expression. Members of relatively low-context cultures value "straight talk." They prefer messages that are briefer and get to the point, and they are more likely to attach greater weight to the denotative meanings of words. Conversely, members of high-context cultures are more likely to encode messages in a less direct manner, concerned that blunt expression may offend the listener or be considered rude. A low-context person is likely to tell you, without mincing words, that s/he is not interested in what you are proposing, while a high-context person will couch the rejection of your idea in less potentially harsh language: "That is an interesting idea, but I am not certain. Let me think about it and get back to you."

Another cultural difference in verbal encoding can be found in the extent to which formality is expected. Americans, particularly younger generations, are generally much less formal in addressing each other than are people of the same generation from many other cultures. First names are more quickly adopted. You may even have some professors who ask you to use their first names—something that would have been frowned on in years past and is unheard of in some other countries. Some languages are even structured to require formality. The Spanish language, for example, has different words for the pronoun *you*, and the use of *tu* or *usted* is dependent upon the intimacy of the relationship between the parties involved in a conversation. Another word, *vos*, is used in some Latin American countries as a form of *you* that is even more casual or intimate than *tu*. In Argentina, for example, it is used instead of *tu*, while in Chile it is rarely used; in Guatamala, it is used to speak to family members or close friends, but a man would never use it to address another man. Effective communicators are aware of how language expectations differ from culture to culture.

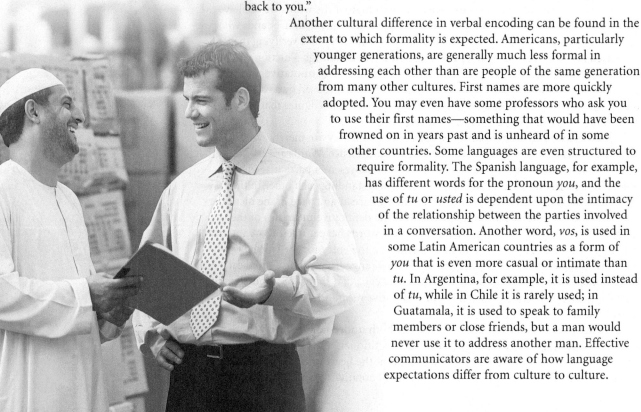

Once the pleasantries are over, will the bluntness of the man from the low-context culture and the indirectness of the man from the high-context culture cause problems?

Language and Gender

Men and women also tend to differ in the way they use verbal language. It is not inaccurate to say that women tend to be more high-context than men for the reasons we discussed in Chapter 1. Men and women have different goals in communicating: men tend to aim at accomplishing tasks while women strive to maintain harmony in relationships (Wood, 2009). Therefore, women often adopt a language style that is less power-oriented. A woman is more likely to use more words to express the same ideas, and she may add qualifiers, polite forms, and tag questions to soften what would otherwise be a straightforward message: "I hope you don't mind, but I think it might be best if we take a different approach to this; don't you agree?" While men may also use tag questions to encourage participation from others (Calnan & Davidson, 1998), they generally do so less often than women. Also men are more likely to talk more often and longer, interrupt other speakers with comments, and use conversation for competitive purposes (Tannen, 1995; Wood, 2009). Being aware of gender expectations and differences will improve your communication success. (See more on language and gender in the Overcoming Obstacles later in this chapter).

APPLY **WHAT YOU KNOW**
LANGUAGE, RULES, AND MEANING

Apply what you know about language by answering the following critical thinking questions:

- There are so many different meanings for the words we use that it is no wonder communication is difficult. Describe a time when you experienced communication misunderstanding because of a word meaning difference. The misunderstanding may have occurred at home, in the classroom, with a friend, on a date, or when visiting a different location or country.

- Which of the following is the best example of a connotative meaning for the word *home*? Explain your choice.

  a. Living quarters
  b. The house where your whole family comes together for gatherings on special occasions because they all enjoy being together
  c. The peaceful sanctuary to which you retreat at the end of the day
  d. All of the above are connotative meanings
  e. Only B and C are connotative meanings

- In your experience, does gender or culture play a larger role in verbal misunderstandings? Give an example to explain your choice.

The Power of Language

As you can see, the meanings of words do not reside in the words: culture, gender, the nature of the situation, and other aspects of our frame of reference all exert influence on how language is interpreted. Although words themselves have no meaning, the meanings that are attached to the words do have power. Language has the power to influence our perceptions, to reflect our perceptions to others, and to affect the perceptions others have of us. Let's look at how language achieves all of these functions.

LEARNING **OBJECTIVE**

4.2 What are the three main ways that language exerts power in our everyday lives, and how does the theory of linguistic relativity fit in?

Language Has Power to Influence Our Perceptions of Others

One of the more controversial issues related to the nature of language is the question of just how much the symbols and the structure of a language affect the perceptions of the language-user. The fine points of the controversy are beyond the scope of this text, but the position around which the debate revolves is articulated in the Sapir-Whorf hypothesis, which says that a culture's language affects how members of that culture think as well as their perceptions of self and others. Read more about this theory in the *Making Theory Practical* box in this chapter.

Note this example of the power of language in the medical field: Many years ago people noticed that there were certain children who seemed to have an overabundance of energy. Eventually, these children began to be described as "hyperactive." Over time, some people became convinced that hyperactivity could be traced to biochemical processes in the bodies of those children. This, of course, led to the development of a number of treatment modalities—both pharmaceutical and behavioral—designed to overcome this tendency in some children. Shortly after that, the numbers of children medically diagnosed by teachers and counselors as "hyperactive"—known by the current term *attention deficit hyperactivity disorder* or *ADHD*—increased significantly (Brown, 2000). By 2000, more than 3.8 million school-aged children had been diagnosed with hyperactivity, and two million of them were taking the drug Ritalin ("Parents," 2000). Why these statistics are true is the topic of considerable debate; the explanations range from genetic predisposition, to the deterioration of our environment and our food sources, to ineffective parenting. But ask yourself these questions: What effect might the development of medical terminology have on the perceptions of parents, teachers, and counselors? And what role might those perceptions have on the ways that people respond to the "overly energetic" child? Consider also that researchers have found that gifted children, who may show high activity levels and problems paying attention in environments lacking stimulation, are often misdiagnosed as having ADHD (Rinn & Nelson, 2009).

Racist language and sexist language are other examples of how perceptions may be influenced by the words we use. **Racist language** and **sexist language** can be defined as the intentional use of terms to imply the inferiority of persons who are not members of the dominant culture. The notion of a dominant culture is not related to numbers; it is related to where the majority of the power resides. In America, although inroads by women and minorities have been made in the past several decades, white males are still generally regarded as the dominant members of the culture. Racist and sexist language, then, would be any verbal expression that suggests that people from nonwhite cultural origins or women are not as capable or as worthy of respect as a white male would be. Racist and sexist language is not limited to the use of epithets. Referring to a person's race, ethnicity, or gender when those characteristics are irrelevant, which is called **marking**, is also an example of racist or sexist use of the language. For instance, if a person were to mention having been treated by a "woman doctor" in the emergency room, of what relevance is it that the physician was a female? What does that example of marking imply?

Setting aside for the moment the effects of racist and sexist language on the people to whom it refers, what is the effect of tolerating the use of racist and sexist verbal messages on the culture as a whole? The Sapir-Whorf hypothesis discussed in the *Making Theory Practical* box that follows would suggest that attitudes about women and people of color are perpetuated by the acceptance and widespread use of racist and sexist language.

APEX
DICTIONARIES
CO.

CLOWSED
BAK AT TOO

Parker

Cartoon by Dave Parker, Catalogue Reference: dpan1020
© Dave Parker/www.cartoonstock.com

MAKING THEORY **PRACTICAL**
THE THEORY OF LINGUISTIC RELATIVITY (OR THE SAPIR-WHORF HYPOTHESIS)

This Inuit father and son who are seal hunting have more than 15 words to describe snow.

Have you ever considered that your thoughts, attitudes, perceptions, and even your outlook on life might be in part a result of the language you speak? Italian journalist Luigi Barzini (1983) uses these terms to describe the characteristics of the world's major Western nations:

1. *imperturbable*

2. *mutable*

3. *quarrelsome*

4. *flexible*

5. *careful*

6. *baffling*

When you look at these characteristics, do any nations come readily to mind? In order, Barzini lists them as: (1) British; (2) German; (3) French; (4) Italian; (5) Dutch; and (6) American. It does make you think, doesn't it? How many of our national characteristics are due to our language?

Theorist
The **theory of linguistic relativity** (also called the Sapir-Whorf hypothesis) is based on the work of two linguists—Edward Sapir (1921) and his student Benjamin Whorf (1956). The theory asserts that the way a culture (or nation) thinks is related to the grammatical structure of the language that the culture speaks. According to Sapir: "We see and hear

and otherwise experience very largely as we do because the language habits of our community predispose certain choices of interpretation" (Whorf, p. 134).

Over the years, many examples have been offered to explain what this hypothesis means. Whorf points to the interesting observation that the Native American Hopi language does not contain terms to differentiate between past, present, and future. According to the hypothesis, this indicates that the Hopi view of time will be different from the view shared by cultural groups who see time demarcated in this way. The Sapir-Whorf hypothesis would argue that if a culture does not possess a label for a concept, that concept does not exist in that culture. Another example is the Eskimo dialect called Inuit, which has more than 15 words for *snow*. Do you think this Inuit father and son, shown seal hunting in the photo, think about snow the same as those of us with languages that have very few words for snow?

Another way to analyze language and its effect on our thinking is to consider labels used to describe various people or situations. Consider the term *gifted*. Why was this term developed to communicate about children of exceptional intellectual ability? More importantly, when the label *gifted* is used to describe a student, how does this affect our perception of that person or our perception of all the other people who do not carry that label? What label would you use to describe children who are the opposite of gifted in their reading ability? How about *challenged, poor, slow, reading disabled* or *remedial reader*? If you were placed in a low reading group as a child, how would you probably have described yourself, and how would this label affect your desire to work harder to improve your reading skills? Could a label also affect a teacher's perception of a child? The theory of linguistic relativity would definitely say, "yes." On the other hand, if a child is found to have dyslexia, does this diagnosis take away the stigma of being a "poor" reader?

PRACTICAL APPLICATION
With the Internet as large as it is and virtual groups used in many corporations, you may well find yourself working with people around the world or in other parts of your own country. When problems occur, think about the languages used by your group members and consider if language itself might be responsible for some of the differences. At least it should give you a new perspective and perhaps some additional flexibility.

Sources: Sapir, *Language*, 1921; Whorf, *Language, Thought, and Reality*, 1956.

Language Has Power to Reflect Attitudes

When you send a verbal message to someone, you obviously intend to convey some content. However, the way you encode that message carries with it another type of message. **Relational messages** are those that convey information about how you view your relationship with the other person with respect to power and connection. In other words, in addition to providing information, your verbal message tells the other person whether you perceive that you have greater, lesser, or equal control, and whether you regard yourself to be closely or loosely connected to the other person.

To be sure, some aspects of a relational message are dependent upon the nonverbal code you use as you convey the verbal message—we will discuss these elements in greater detail in Chapter 5. For example, while the actual wording of your message is significant, your facial expression and tone of voice are important cues that suggest how a message should be interpreted. Consider this scenario: You are at a party with your friend, and you decide that you are ready to leave. How do you encode this message to your friend? You could say, "I want to go." Or you might say, "Would it be alright with you if we leave?" Another possibility is to say, "Hey, man, if you're having fun, I'd be glad for you to stay, but I'm not enjoying this much, so I think I might leave. Are you okay with that?" What message about how you view the power relationship between you and your friend is communicated by each of these ways of encoding the message? What does each message imply about how close you feel to your friend?

Does the clown's button change your perception?

Some types of messages express **affiliation**, or belongingness with others. By the same token, sometimes we use language to convey **disaffiliation**, or a lack of connection with others. Unless we are careful, our relational messages that convey disaffiliation may actually hurt the receiver (see **Figure 4.2**).

Language Has Power to Affect Others' Perceptions of Us

A recent radio advertisement for a vocabulary improvement program claims, "Like it or not, people judge you by the words you use." The idea that others form impressions of you based on the way you use language may annoy you, but, if you are honest, you will acknowledge another person's use of language is a factor in the impressions you form of them as well. Do you have the same impression of someone who uses correct grammar that you have of someone who consistently violates the rules of standard usage?

Your language conveys information about, among other things, your intelligence and your educational level (Figure 4.2). Of course, the use of high-level vocabulary with people whose educational level is not the equal of yours may have the effect of conveying that you regard yourself as their superior. On the other hand, using overly simplistic vocabulary may convey condescension. Effective verbal communicators adapt their vocabulary to take into consideration their goals as well as the needs of the listener.

Your choice of language can also be a clue about your personality and your emotional state. If you frequently make use of superlatives in your speech, you create a very different image of yourself than you would if your language choice is less effusive. Are you someone who often makes statements such as "That was the most amazing thing I have ever seen!" Or are you more likely to say, "I found that unusually interesting"? Are you more likely to say, "I'm disappointed," or would you more typically say, "I'm devastated." The emotional

Relational Messages That Hurt	Relational Messages That Hurt Less
I'm not surprised that you lied to me again!	I want to trust you, so please tell me the truth even if you think it's not what I want to hear.
You are just being totally emotional.	I understand your reaction, but maybe there's another way to look at it.
All you care about is yourself.	I would really like to have my view considered as well as yours.
You can't help it that you aren't pretty (handsome)—it runs in your family.	Only models are really beautiful—thank goodness it's what's inside that really counts.
If you really wanted to lose weight, you would.	I envy those people who find losing weight an easy task.
I can't talk to you—you take everything I say personally.	My comment wasn't directed to you; I'm sorry if you took it personally.

Figure 4.2 Relational Messages That Convey Disaffiliation May Actually Hurt the Receiver

strength of a word like "ecstatic" is considerably greater than would be communicated by the word "glad." Both words are suitable in certain situations, but the consistent use of the more superlative terms may lead emotionally restrained people to think of you as a person who tends to exaggerate.

Your language choices powerfully communicate your attitudes toward yourself and toward other people—which can affect how others view your character. Consider the use of profanity. In certain social groups, profane language is very common. Adopting profanity when in the company of those people is one way that you communicate your desire to be affiliated with their group. On the other hand, using profanity in public situations where your speech is heard by both associates and strangers may well be interpreted as an expression of hostility or lack of concern for others' comfort or their impressions of you. "I don't care if this bothers you, I don't respect you, and I don't care what you think of me" are legitimate interpretations of what you are saying and who you are.

Language, as you should now recognize, is a very powerful means of communication. It is a tool, and, as with all tools, its effectiveness depends on how well you use it to accomplish your goals. Verbal communication is very much a matter of choice. The act of speaking implies intentionality. It is helpful, then, to consider some of the factors that may interfere with choosing the appropriate verbal code to achieve your objectives.

APPLY **WHAT YOU KNOW**
LANGUAGE POWER

As mentioned earlier, the number of children medically diagnosed as "hyperactive" and suffering from "attention deficit hyperactivity disorder" increased significantly once these terms were created. Apply what you know about the power of language and answer these critical thinking questions:

- Do you think parents and/or teachers respond differently to overly energetic children once they are given the label "hyperactive" or diagnosed with having "attention deficit hyperactivity disorder"? What effect would one of these labels have on the way children perceive themselves? Do you think it would be a relief to have a label to describe one's behavior, or would it likely lead to a negative self-concept?

- Give a personal example of a label applied to you (or someone you know) and how that label affected your self-perception or the way others perceived you.

LEARNING **OBJECTIVE**

4.3 What are the obstacles to effective use of language that give people the most problems, and how can reading related journal articles expand our knowledge of language and verbal communication?

Obstacles to Effective Verbal Encoding

A competent handyman possesses and knows how to use a variety of tools. If you lack a hammer and need to drive a nail into sheetrock, you could use the heel of your shoe, but the chances are that the job would take longer, be less competently achieved, and require multiple attempts. To extend the analogy further, you might even cause irreparable damage to the wall. So it is with words. If you are "at a loss for words" because of an insufficient vocabulary, you have limited your communication options.

Insufficient Vocabulary

It is difficult to quantify the size of a person's vocabulary, largely because studies that attempt to do so run into trouble in defining exactly what will be considered a word. For example, should you count every form of a word and every denotative meaning of a word as a separate word? D'Anna, Zechmeister, and Hall (1991) estimate that the average college student possesses a vocabulary of about 16,785 words. This would seem to be more than enough words to meet your communication needs. However, you have undoubtedly had the experience of hearing unfamiliar words in a professor's lecture. What do you typically do in that situation? Do you ask for the terms to be defined? Do you write them down and look them up later, in order to add them to your vocabulary? Or do you stop listening altogether, figuring that there is little possibility that you will be able to comprehend anything else the professor says? The problem with the last strategy is that you will limit your ability to be a competent decoder of language, and you will limit your ability to encode meaningful messages when you are in situations where those terms are required. So, would you say that your vocabulary is as well developed as it needs to be for successful communication?

Jargon

Another obstacle to successful verbal encoding relates to jargon. Every professional or co-cultural group has its own **jargon**, which is the specialized vocabulary that group uses as a form of shorthand requiring fewer words. Knowing how to use the jargon correctly is important if you hope to achieve affiliation with the people in that group. On the other hand, using jargon with those outside of the group can cause misunderstanding or no understanding at all. Here are a few examples:

Jargon used by this work group speeds their communication; the same jargon outside the group could bring communication to a halt.

- College students will likely have no problems understanding this statement: "I can't afford a W in this class—it will really hurt my cume." However, if you didn't know that a "W" means "withdrawal from a course" and "cume" means "cumulative grade point average," this statement wouldn't make much sense.

- If you have a close group of friends or business colleagues who send text messages or talk on a chat line, you have probably developed your own jargon. Can you interpret this message from one computer geek to another? "Did you put the jumpers on the right pins? Maybe that's why the drive won't change to master." Answer: When you get a new hard drive for your computer, there are little "pins" covered with plastic "jumpers" that you have to configure in a certain way; if you want the hard drive to be used as the boot-up drive, you make it the "master." Did that work, or do you need an interpretation of the interpretation?

- Another example of jargon is used in the medical profession (as well as the legal profession) where vocabulary is heavily based on Latin. Since most patients are not familiar with the Latin root words used in prefixes and suffixes, the practitioner's use of medical terminology is often frightening to them. Like many students faced with incomprehensible professorial mutterings, patients may hesitate to ask for a translation or may give up listening altogether. Surely, this is not the communication goal of the healthcare provider. Even outside of the medical setting, healthcare workers may find themselves automatically using the familiar jargon when conversing with friends and family.

Using jargon outside your specific group could be interpreted as a sort of "showing off" or condescension. So what do you think? Is your knowledge and use of jargon a help or hindrance when you communicate with others?

Euphemisms

Euphemisms also serve as obstacles to effective verbal encoding. **Euphemisms** are words or phrases used in place of other words or phrases that might be considered offensive, unpleasant, or taboo. Words often change meaning over time. For example, in the nineteenth and early twentieth centuries, scientists used the terms *idiot*, *imbecile*, and *moron* to distinguish among the IQ levels of developmentally disabled individuals (IQ scores of 0–25, 26–50, and 51–70, respectively). As these words took on negative connotations, the word *retarded* replaced them (along with the descriptors *profoundly*, *severely*, *moderately*, and *mildly*). Currently these words are primarily used as derogatory descriptions, sometimes in jest, of normal people that one does not like or with whom one disagrees. In the meantime, the term *retarded* has been replaced by the more euphemistic terms *developmentally disabled*, *developmentally challenged*, *differently abled*, and *specially abled*.

George Carlin doing his famous monologue on the evolution of shell shock.

Euphemisms abound in our daily life. They are prevalent in bureaucracies such as business, education, and the military. Were you a victim of "downsizing"? Does your child's report card tell you that "he is an energetic child"? Did the soldiers "neutralize the target," and was there "collateral damage"? What are the effects of all of this euphemizing?

Sometimes, the use of a euphemism is for the very reasonable purpose of not shutting down communication. If you couch your thoughts in terms that are more palatable to the listener, you maintain the ability to keep the channels of communication open. But sometimes euphemisms create a lack of clarity in your message. Do Johnny's parents think that the teacher delights in his energetic nature, or do they recognize that the teacher is trying to call attention to his inability to focus on the task at hand? There is also reason to wonder if some uses of euphemistic language are intentional attempts to obscure reality or to manipulate public perception. The comedian George Carlin developed a famous monologue about the evolution of "shell shock" in World War I into "battle fatigue" in World War II to "Post-Traumatic Stress Disorder" today. He contends that the way we view and treat people who suffer from psychological distress after participation in war is different because the terms we use soften the reality of their experience.

Euphemisms, then, may facilitate communication. However, they may also create barriers to communication when they obscure or limit the listener's ability to understand the intended meaning of the message. What about you? Is your use of euphemisms affecting your communication success?

APPLY **WHAT YOU KNOW**
LANGUAGE AND EUPHEMISMS

Apply what you know about verbal encoding obstacles, and answer these critical thinking questions:

- Do you agree that labeling the psychological distress experienced by some war veterans as "Post-Traumatic Stress Disorder" or PTSD causes people (maybe even the government) to treat the condition less seriously than if it were referred to as "shell shock"?

- What are some euphemisms for *death* or any form of the word *die* that you or your family use? How do these euphemisms affect your communication?
- Make a list of three to five other euphemisms used in our society. Which ones appear to be beneficial, and which ones could lead to societal problems?

Trigger Words

Sometimes communication is affected by the use of **trigger words**, which are verbal expressions that arouse emotions to such an extent that internal psychological noise is created. Sometimes a word triggers a listener's emotions because it links to that person's most deeply held convictions. Saying words such as *liberal, conservative, homosexual, illegal immigrant, feminist,* or *atheist* may be justified as entirely relevant to the topic, but when speaking to someone whom you do not know well, you may inadvertently create an emotional distraction that gets in the way of achieving shared meaning. Trigger words are highly individual, though, so avoiding them is sometimes like walking through a minefield. As is true in all communication, the better you know your listener, the better you should be able to anticipate what words are likely to generate the response you are aiming for. Are you aware of one or more trigger words that you should avoid using when speaking to a parent or friend?

Abstracting and Allness

One problem in verbal encoding is created by the nature of the process of verbal encoding itself. According to Alfred Korzybski, the founder of the system of language study called General Semantics, when we make a statement about a subject, we are **abstracting**. In other words, we select for discussion only certain aspects of the subject we are describing and, necessarily, leave out others. This is inevitable; you can never say everything there is to say about any subject. For example, if you were to say that the waffle you are eating is crispy, you would have selected only one aspect of your breakfast to discuss; however, you could add dozens of other pieces of information about size, shape, texture, composition, etc. Most of these additions would be irrelevant to your purposes at that time, so there would be no need to mention them at all. The point is this: to say that your waffle is crispy is not a statement that captures the totality of the waffle's essence.

Unfortunately, when we make statements about people, objects, or events in our world, our statements (abstractions) also fail to capture the totality. "She is nice," we say, and the listener hears what is assumed to be an accurate statement about the woman in question. But is she always nice? Is niceness all there is to say about her? In other words, our statements too often convey **allness**, which is the implication that the verbal expression has captured the totality of a person, object, or event. You may say, "Well, of course I realize that there is more that could be said." But are you sure that your listener makes the mental jump to recognize that there is more that could be said?

The problem of allness is especially demonstrated in the tendency to stereotype, which we discussed in Chapter 2. When you say, "She is white," the statement seems to imply that enough has been said to accurately describe the person. Compounding the problem is that if the listener is predisposed to think about white people in a particular way, your statement has preconditioned the listener to assume that a range of characteristics will be found to be true of the woman being discussed. Such language use fails to recognize the uniqueness of all human beings. How about you? Does your communication include unnecessary or distracting use of allness?

Polarizing Terms

General semanticists also point to the problem of **polarizing terms**. When we polarize, we are asserting that the thing discussed must be either of one kind or of its opposite. To polarize does not allow anything in the middle. Sometimes polarization is implied; if I say that someone is honest, I have eliminated the possibility that s/he may not be honest in all dealings. (Note that the issue of allness is involved here as well.) However, often we make polarizing statements where the two conditions are explicitly stated. "If you don't fly, you'll have to stay home." "You either join the family business and show you are for the family, or you're against the family." Polarizing statements are frequently made in the political arena, often creating the possibility of the fallacy of false dichotomy (discussed in Chapter 3). "You're either for us, or you're against us." "America: Love it or leave it." The semanticist S. I. Hayakawa (1949) notes that, to some extent, the use of the "two-valued orientation" of polarizing terms serves a purpose. "It is hardly possible to express strong feelings or to arouse the interest of an apathetic listener without conveying to some extent this sense of conflict," he says, but the discussion of solutions to problems should recognize that there are usually many options available between the two extremes. What polarizing terms do you use that could cause communication misunderstanding?

Imprecise Language and Relative Terms

One of the most important barriers to creating shared meaning and successful verbal encoding is our tendency to use **imprecise language**. Words or phrases that lack sufficient clarity to guide interpretation are probably the most common reasons for misunderstandings to arise. When you tell someone that you will be there "in a while," what does this mean? **Relative terms**, which derive their meaning only by specifying their relationship to other factors, are one type of imprecise verbal encoding. For example, if you tell me that your favorite restaurant is "inexpensive," how should I interpret this? *Inexpensive* is an imprecise word; its meaning is relative to other factors, including the expense of other restaurants of its type as well as the cost of a meal at the sorts of restaurants that you typically frequent. What you consider "inexpensive" might be "pricey" for me. Think about any imprecise language that you may have used in your typical conversations.

We have covered a number of obstacles that interfere with effective use of language. Many more could be listed and described—in fact, there are many excellent journal articles on language and verbal communication. Don't shy away from reading an interesting article just because it sounds too complicated. The *Developing Skills* box on page 112 includes some helpful suggestions on reading journal articles.

Saying that this waffle is crispy is an abstraction of its many characteristics rather than a statement of its totality. What else could you say about this waffle?

APPLY **WHAT YOU KNOW**
VERBAL ENCODING OBSTACLES

Apply what you know about verbal encoding obstacles by responding to the following critical thinking problems:

- Select a verbal encoding obstacle (vocabulary, jargon, euphemisms, trigger words, allness, polarizing, or imprecise language) that occurs the most often in your communication with others or creates the most serious difficulties for you.

- Describe a personal situation involving the obstacle, and tell how it hampered your communication effectiveness.

- Suggest a possible communication goal or tool that could help lessen the negative impact of the obstacle.

- Find a research article that offers information on the obstacle and give a brief summary of the article and its application to your communication, if any.

LEARNING OBJECTIVE

4.4 What are the communication skills that can be used to overcome verbal encoding obstacles and improve communication effectiveness?

Overcoming Obstacles to Effective Verbal Encoding

Like the competent handyman, the competent communicator needs a number of tools in order to do the job efficiently and effectively. For each of the obstacles we have discussed earlier, we offer a strategy or skill that you can use to overcome it as long as you are willing to work at it a bit.

Expanding a Poor Vocabulary

For communicators, developing a better vocabulary is essential. Even though you can often infer the meaning of words from the context in which they are used, it is wise to jot down the terms and look them up in a dictionary as soon as possible; you should then make certain to use the words repeatedly within a short period of time until you can claim them as part of your own working vocabulary. There are also many books and commercially prepared programs that can assist you in improving your vocabulary.

Not only will a better vocabulary improve your ability to decode verbal messages, it will also give you an arsenal of words to choose from so that you can select the word that is best suited to your goal and your listener. When you wish to communicate that you are happy, what word will you choose? There are qualitative differences between being *satisfied, contented, pleased, delighted, joyful, elated,* and *ecstatic.*

Avoiding Jargon

Be careful about your use of jargon. There is no doubt that you must be able to adopt the vocabulary of your professional group when communicating with your associates at work. Failure to do so would mark you as not fully competent in your field. However, using jargon with people who are not part of that group can lead them to misunderstand you or to form the impression that you are trying to impress them with your superior knowledge. It can actually alienate your listeners.

Using Euphemisms with Care

Using euphemisms, as we have suggested, is often very appropriate. While you may personally dislike the whole notion of "political correctness," there is little doubt that the use of insensitive terms can erect communication barriers between you and your intended listener. At the same time, using euphemisms can be construed as an attempt to deceive others as to your true intent. It can also prevent your listener from understanding the full meaning of your statements.

Being Alert to Trigger Words

Be cautious about choosing language that may function as triggers, creating strong emotional reaction where none is intended. Consider this example: A common pattern in Joe's and Sally's communication is that Sally will say "we need to talk," and then Joe will roll his eyes and sigh. For Joe, "we need to talk" are trigger words that almost ensure that the conversation will not go well. Just by being aware that "we need to talk" triggers a negative emotion in Joe would give Sally the opportunity to use different words and lead to a more positive outcome. Careful language selection is especially important when you are communicating with someone you do not know very well and whose opinions and life experiences are likely to vary from yours. When your language choice creates internal psychological noise in your listener, shared meaning is harder to achieve.

Racist and sexist language is another example of verbal encoding that can trigger strong emotional response. No matter what your race or sex, it is unlikely that you would appreciate language that implies that you are somehow inferior in intelligence, ability, or character to someone else. All of us may find ourselves in a minority group at one time or another. One of your authors remembers vividly a class she once had that consisted of twenty-three women and only four men. Early in the semester, a disturbing trend toward "male-bashing" began to develop, leading the men in the class to feel "ganged-up on." One older man, in particular, began to respond defensively to statements made by one of the more vocal women in the class—a woman who had been divorced and had a low opinion of men in general. The class decided to discuss the issue of sex-based stereotypes from the perspective of the men, who noted that they were less willing to listen to the women's opinions because of the language they used. In this instance, the dominant group was female. Were their comments sexist? The men surely thought so.

Using Dating and Indexing

General semanticists would urge you to be conscious of your abstracting and the problems associated with "allness." In other words, it is important to recognize that your statements about a subject are never all that could be said. Of course, it is helpful if your listeners are also conscious of this process, but you cannot always be sure that they are. It is helpful to add language that can account for this inherent problem in verbal encoding. **Dating** and **indexing** are two strategies that are helpful in achieving this goal. When you add a date to a statement, you make reference to when the statement was true in your experience. When you index, you acknowledge the differences that may exist between people within a group or between people at different points in time. For example, instead of saying, "Holland is the best place in the world for a vacation," you might index your statement as: "My trip to Holland was the best vacation I have ever experienced." Rather than offer the observation that "*The New York Times* is biased," you could index that statement by noting that a particular columnist tends to write from a particular point of view, while acknowledging that other columnists offer a different perspective. An additional way to improve these statements is to acknowledge that your perceptions are exactly that: your perceptions. What is good acting? Well, what do *you* mean by "good acting"? Might others have different criteria? What is biased reporting? Would someone else regard this as "biased" reporting?

Overcome *allness* by using dating and indexing when describing your latest vacation.

DEVELOPING **SKILLS**
HOW TO READ A JOURNAL ARTICLE

During this course, you may be asked to read a number of journal articles that relate to the field of communication, or you might be interested in reading more about topics in the text that relate to your own interests and fields of study. If you are reading articles in professional journals for the first time, you may find them overwhelming and confusing. This *Developing Skills* box offers suggestions on how to approach articles in professional journals (Wanzer, et al., 2006).

In the communication field, journal articles are published by the **National Communication Association** (natcom.org). Journals are also published by **regional associations**—Central (csca-net.org), Eastern (ecasite.org), Southern (ssca.net), and Western (westcomm.org)—and **state associations,** which

you can access at natcom.org. (Go to About us, Partnerships & initiatives, State associations.)

Remember that journal articles present only a small step in knowledge—they are a work in progress, not a final conclusion. Instead of "facts" you are more likely to find "concepts" and "ways of thinking." To guide you in taking notes as you read, we suggest that you use the Critical Evaluation form called Critically Evaluating What You Read, located at the end of Chapter 1 in the *Skill Builders* section. The more journal articles you read, the easier the task will become and the more interesting facts you will be able to add to your knowledge and your classroom discussions.

Most journal articles follow a similar format and include the following areas:

- *A descriptive title;*

- *An abstract* that summarizes the article;

- *An introduction or literature review* that summarizes recent research on the topic;

- *A methodology section* that describes the actual research conducted—quantitative or qualitative;

- *A results and/or discussion section* that discusses the conclusions and applications.

Communication Education
Vol. 58, No. 3, July 2009, pp. 303–326

R Routledge
Taylor & Francis Group

R U Able to Meat Me: The Impact of Students' Overly Casual Email Messages to Instructors

Keri K. Stephens, Marian L. Houser & Renee L. Cowan[1]

Out-of-classroom communication (OCC) in the form of email has increased considerably in the past few years. This study uses Interaction Adaptation Theory (IAT) to inform and frame the impact of using overly casual email messages with instructors. Study one used an experimental method to determine that message quality (casual vs. formal messages) accounted for between 48% and 64% of the variance explained in affect toward the student, student credibility, and message attitude. Message quality also significantly impacted on an instructor's willingness to comply with a simple request for a face-to-face meeting. Study two further examined these findings using a comparative analysis of both instructors and students. Findings reveal that instructors are bothered more than students by overly casual email messages. Instructors attribute students' use of overly casual emails more heavily to training issues, while students attribute this to technology use. Two specific email violations that bother instructors more than students are emails not signed by the message sender and messages that include shortcuts like "RU" instead of "are you". Finally, it appears that instructor generational differences have little impact on these descriptive findings.

Literature Review

Theoretical Lens for Student Email Perceptions

Interaction Adaptation Theory (IAT) (Burgoon et al., 1995) helps explain how individuals choose to respond to communication in either a matching or complementary manner. The matching response or "norm of reciprocity" (Gouldner,

Method

Study one experimentally manipulated message quality and familiarity to address their effects on instructor affect for the student, perceived student credibility, message attitude, and willingness to comply.

Participants

There were 152 instructors who participated in the experimental phase of this study. Criteria-based sampling was used, along with network sampling to solicit college-level instructors with at least one semester of experience. The participants were randomly assigned to experimental conditions, resulting in a sample that included 100 females, 45 males, and 7 unidentified. They represented a variety of positions including full-time instructors ($n=40$), part-time instructors ($n=28$), adjunct faculty ($n=16$), assistant professors ($n=24$), associate professors ($n=17$), full professors ($n=12$), those with other titles ($n=12$), and unreported ($n=3$). Their average position tenure was 8.8 ($SD=7.81$) years and their average age was 38.0 ($SD=11.71$) years. These were predominately communication-course instructors ($n=110$), yet other disciplines were also represented. Because of the focus on email in this study, it is also important to note that they were fairly heavy email users, yet text messaging varied considerably. See Table 1 for detailed demographic details that provide this data based on age of the instructor.

Results

First, the data were inspected for outliers and correlations between the dependent measures. Three multivariate outliers were identified following the procedures

---

When reading a journal, the following steps are suggested:

- Since you can usually get a real feel for the contents of an article simply by reading the title, begin by analyzing the title.

- Then, read the abstract looking for the specific problem being investigated. Reading the abstract is also a fast way to tell if the paper is relevant to your search.

- Next, read the introduction or review of literature for the review of previous research–this is especially important if you are unfamiliar with the subject. Key researchers are mentioned, and you may want to locate one or more of these articles as well.

- Make sure that you are clear on the key question that the research or authors are addressing—sometimes referred to as the rationale—and the main assumptions underlying the study.

- Even if you are not interested in research and are unfamiliar with research terminology, look in the methodology or method section for the participants and basic procedure used.

- Finally, read the results and/or discussion sections to see what conclusions were reached by the study and whether the conclusions agree or disagree with previous studies. Also note what application can by drawn from the study, if any.

Being Cautious of Extremes

Be alert to language use that tends to suggest that people, objects, or events can be categorized as being either of one type or another. As we discussed in Chapter 3, recognizing categorization is a responsibility of good critical listeners when they decode others' messages, but it is also a responsibility of good encoders. To counteract this problem, it is helpful to recognize that most things fall along a continuum between two extremes. In fact, few things are ever properly placed at the extremes. Take, for example, the statement above that "You're either for us, or you're against us." Is it possible that a person could be in favor of some aspects of your policy but opposed to others? Your verbal encoding should reflect your awareness of the potential for a wide range of perspectives on the subject.

Defining and Describing with Care

Precision in language use can best be achieved by learning the skills of **operational definitions** and **behavioral descriptions**. When you define something operationally, you add language to describe what you mean by the terms you use. When you use a behavioral description, you add language to specify the exact actions to which you are referring. These two skills are really quite similar, except that operational definitions are concerned more with the meanings of terms, while behavioral descriptions are useful in clarifying the actions you are seeing or wish to see.

For example, consider this statement that a physician might make to a patient: "I need you to take responsibility for this." What does the doctor mean by "take responsibility"? Does this mean that the patient should accept blame for what has happened to his or her health? Or does this mean that the patient needs to be willing to take control of the treatment regimen? The statement could be improved by either rewording or by providing an operational definition: "By this I mean . . ." Let us assume that the meaning is that the patient is to take control of the treatment regimen. What are the actions that the doctor expects the patient to perform? "I need you to write out a schedule for taking each of your medicines, I want you to make notes each night about any reactions you have had, and I would like you to call my nurse a week from today to report any new symptoms, including when you have experienced them and your judgment of their severity."

We use statements frequently that appear to be neutral observations but are actually expressions of our own views. "Good acting," "biased reporting," "expensive restaurants," and "good teachers" are all very much a matter of one's frame of reference. Operational definitions and behavioral descriptions can enable you to communicate with greater precision and clarity about what you mean when you make pronouncements of those sorts. These skills and strategies may mean that you have to add some more language, but they maximize the potential for achieving shared meaning.

Perhaps the best overall approach to being a more effective verbal encoder is found in the notion of being less "word-centered" and more "person-centered." You must always take into consideration your goals and intentions as well as the needs of your listener. The words you choose—and make no mistake about it, you are *choosing* the words—should be appropriate to the

Operational definitions help this building contractor communicate with greater precision and clarity.

(Text continues on page 116.)

LANGUAGE **AND YOUR CAREER**

4.5 What language skills covered in this chapter relate specifically to your career?

The language skills covered in this chapter can be of special importance to you as you search for and develop a career. The *Spotlight on, Career Moment*, and *Connecting to* features relate communication skills from the chapter to success in the specific fields of business, education, and healthcare.

SPOTLIGHT ON **LANGUAGE AND COMMUNICATION**

BUSINESS

Because of the power of language, it is especially important in the business world to select words carefully. In his book *Words That Work*, Frank Luntz (2007) warns that "It's not what you say, it's what people hear" (p. xxi). For example, when Alka-Seltzer changed its slogan to include the novel and vivid words "Plop, plop, fizz, fizz, oh what a relief it is" people finally understood how many Alka-Seltzer to take and sales doubled (p. 15). Here are some words that have tested well in today's market:

- Instead of *honest* or *credible*—say *accurate*.
- Instead of *responsible* or *professional*—say *accountable*.
- Instead of *evidence*—say *facts*.
- Instead of *capitalism*—say *free market system*.
- Instead of *peace of mind*—say *security*.
- Instead of *used*—say *pre-owned*.

EDUCATION

Educators and colleges have to be careful about their language choices as well. Not only do their language choices affect how students perceive them, but they also affect the perceptions of parents, community members, local businesses, and those who contribute to scholarships and special programs. A recent article in the *Chronicle of Higher Education* (Stanley, 2008) gave two examples of language use:

- It's difficult to know what to call classes for students who need remedial training. Titles used in the past such as *remedial education* or *developmental education* implied "deficits and low standards." A new title that implies progress—*transitional studies*—has been much more successful.
- Hennepin Technical College in Brooklyn Park, Minnesota, saved its *Automated-Packaging Program* by changing the name to *Automation Robotics Engineering Technology*. After the change, "enrollment skyrocketed" (B24).

HEALTHCARE

Patient care information is usually transmitted verbally between healthcare professionals and can result in loss or misinterpretation of data. In addition, research indicates that many nurses prefer to communicate with narratives while most doctors tend to communicate with specifics (Beyea, 2004). The SBAR model is suggested as a way to improve verbal communication between styles (nurses' example adapted from p. 1054):

- **S**—First, explain patient's current **situation**; "Mrs. L's blood pressure is 90 over 40; her pulse is 120."
- **B**—Put the situation into context by briefly summarizing patient's **background**; "She underwent a laparoscopic appendectomy this morning."
- **A**—Offer an **assessment** of the current condition; "I think she may be actively bleeding."
- **R**—Conclude with a **recommendation**; "I am concerned and would like you to come see her now."

CAREER MOMENT **VOCABULARY IN THE WORKPLACE**

Regardless of your career choice, oral and written communication skills will be essential to your success. Therefore, increasing your vocabulary is also important. As Mark Twain said, "The difference between the almost right word and the right word is a really large matter—'tis the difference between the lightning-bug and the lightning" (Bainton, 1890, pp. 87–88).

Consider the following average vocabulary results from employees of 39 manufacturing companies—the maximum score is 272 (Shand, 1994):

Position in company	Vocabulary score
Presidents and VPs	236
Managers	168
Superintendents	140
Supervisors	114
Floor bosses	86

Your vocabulary and word choices will be noticed in job interviews, committee discussions, and personal discussions and will make a difference in your positions and promotions.

Don't wait—begin to add to your vocabulary today. Underline unknown words in this textbook (check our glossary at the end of the text) and other books or journal articles that you read. Write the definitions of these words in the margins, so you will see the word and the definitions regularly. Use the new words in sentences, and use them every chance you get.

CONNECTING TO ... **BUSINESS**

Are you considering a business or professional career? If so, you know that one of the most frequent forms of written communication is the memo. David and Baker (1994) found that effective memos have common features:

- They typically begin by announcing the topic;
- They adopt a "problem-solution" scheme;
- They use clear, direct language and politeness strategies to allow face-saving;
- They are honest about the situation and avoid using language that is accusatory.

ACTIVITY

1. Divide into pairs or small groups and construct a memo that a manager or supervisor might send to deal with one of the following situations:

- Employees in your workplace are engaging in behaviors that create too much noise in the hallways.
- The funding source for your organization has made cutbacks that will require a substantial reduction in salaries.

- There is a concern about safety as employees enter and exit the parking garage (or, alternatively, safety on the floor of a manufacturing plant).
- Parking fees will be increased.

2. Discuss factors that might cause an employee to be resistant to the reminder or the change being addressed in one of these memos.

CONNECTING TO ... **EDUCATION**

Are you considering a career in education? Giving instructions is especially daunting for teachers of children who are developmentally delayed or who have disabilities. The following strategies were suggested by Muriel Saunders (2001):

- Say child's name, wait until s/he looks at you; give instructions one step at a time;
- Emphasize important words and minimize use of adjectives and adverbs;
- Tie desired behavior to a desirable result: "We will have story time when you put your work in your basket;"
- Verbally affirm the child when an objective is achieved.

ACTIVITY Working individually or in small groups, assume that you are teaching a classroom that includes a child who has difficulty processing verbal messages because of language delay or learning disabilities. Construct verbal messages for the following situations:

- You want the child to clean up a learning area cluttered with multiple types of materials that need to be put in specific places.
- You want a classroom of children to line up in preparation to go outside.

CONNECTING TO ... **HEALTHCARE**

Are you considering a career in healthcare? Healthcare practitioners know that a central concern in treating patients is "compliance" or "adherence." Safeer and Keenan (2005) found that most healthcare materials are written at a tenth-grade level, while the average adult reads at the eighth-grade level. Further, they discovered that physicians usually overestimate their patients' literacy level and use unclear jargon.

ACTIVITY Visit Internet Web sites for one or two common health conditions, such as asthma, diabetes, or coronary artery disease.

1. As you read explanations of the health condition, note the differences in language used. If you find terms that you don't understand in either site, consult a dictionary.

2. In recent years, *compliance* has been replaced by *adherence* in healthcare language. Look these words up in the dictionary and note any differences in their denotative and connotative meanings. Why might healthcare practitioners currently prefer the word *adherence*?

▶ Log onto MyCommunicationLab.com to access Connecting to Psychology and Connecting to Science, Technology, Engineering, and Math—both with related activities.

situation, your intention, and your relationship with your listener. Furthermore, you must always keep in mind the key concept discussed earlier in this chapter: Words have no meaning; people have meanings.

APPLY **WHAT YOU KNOW**
OVERCOMING VERBAL ENCODING OBSTACLES

Apply what you know about overcoming obstacles to effective verbal encoding by completing these critical thinking activities:

- List four sets of trigger words and tell who is most likely to be affected negatively by each set (such as a family member, coworker, man, woman, educator, or other).

- Suggest two or three alternative word sets that could replace each set of trigger words. Be sure to explain why you think the new words would be more acceptable.

- Identify at least two words that trigger you in a negative way and two that trigger you in a positive way. What makes these words so powerful?

CHAPTER SUMMARY

Becoming an effective verbal communicator is hard work, but it is definitely worth the effort. You can determine your knowledge of language by checking the skills and learning objectives presented in this chapter.

Summary of **SKILLS**

Check each skill that you now feel qualified to perform:

❑ I can pinpoint weaknesses in the way I use language and plan to work to minimize at least two of them.
❑ I can identify the power of my words in shaping perceptions and attitudes and plan to replace several ineffective words with more powerful ones.
❑ I will select at least one major obstacle to effective verbal communication in my life and locate a journal article to expand my understanding of it.
❑ I will implement one or more suggested verbal skills to correct a major obstacle to verbal communication in my life and ask for feedback on my successes.

Summary of LEARNING **OUTCOMES**

4.1 *What is language, what are the four rules that govern its use, what are the denotative versus connotative meanings of language, and how is language affected by culture and gender?*

- Language refers to a more or less formally established collection of spoken words and/or symbols that has meaning for a specific group of people.

- The four rules that govern the use of language include the phonological, semantic, syntactic, and pragmatic rules.

- The denotative meaning of a word refers to the dictionary definitions for the word. The connotative meaning of a word refers to your personal meanings for that word based on the images and emotions that word arouses in you.

- Since words are merely symbols that represent ideas, feelings, objects, or events in our experience, they are affected by many factors, including our culture and gender.

4.2 *What are the three main ways that language exerts*

power in our everyday lives, and how does the theory of linguistic relativity fit in?

- Language exerts power on our perceptions, reflects our attitudes toward others, and affects others' perceptions of us.

- The theory of linguistic relativity discussed in the *Making Theory Practical* feature asserts that the way a culture (or nation) thinks is related to the grammatical structure of the language that the culture speaks.

4.3 *What are the obstacles to effective use of language that give people the most problems, and how can reading related journal articles expand our knowledge of language and verbal communication?*

- The obstacles that give people the most problem in their verbal encoding include insufficient vocabulary, jargon, euphemisms, trigger words, abstracting and allness, polarizing terms, and imprecise language.

- The tips from the *Developing Skills* feature give advice on making sense of journal articles and show how reading journal articles expands your knowledge (especially of new or confusing concepts) and keeps you up-to-date with findings and applications on language and verbal communication topics discussed in this chapter. *Note*: If you want to impress your professor or classmates during class discussions, supplying information gained from journal articles is the way to do it.

4.4 *What are the communication skills that can be used to overcome verbal encoding obstacles and improve communication effectiveness?*

- Communication skills used to overcome communication obstacles in effective use of language include: expanding your vocabulary, avoiding jargon, using euphemisms with care, being alert to trigger words, being conscious of abstracting and allness, using dating and indexing, and defining and describing with care.

4.5 *What language skills covered in this chapter relate specifically to your career (see highlighted fields of business, education, and healthcare)?*

- The *Spotlight on, Career Moment,* and *Connecting to* features highlight the value of listening in the fields of business, education, and healthcare.

SOLVE IT NOW!

Taking into consideration all that you learned about verbal communication from this chapter, how would you analyze the communication difficulties between Katelynn and Gabe in our opening scenario?*

- Is it the denotative or the connotative meanings of their words that caused the most difficulty in Katelynn and Gabe's communication? Give a specific example to support your answer.

- How strong a role, if any, did gender play in their communication difficulties? Why?

- List any examples you can find of the following terms, and explain how each may have contributed to the misunderstanding between Katelynn and Gabe: trigger words; euphemisms; jargon; allness; polarizing terms; relative terms or imprecise language.

- What specific *communication goals* would you recommend for Katelynn and Gabe that would improve their verbal skills now and in the future?

*(Check your answers with those located in MyCommunicationLab, Scenario Analysis for Chapter 4)

KEY TERMS

abstracting	p. 108	disaffiliation	p. 104	operational definitions	p. 113	sexist language	p. 102
affiliation	p. 104	euphemisms	p. 107	phonological rules	p. 98	symbolic language	p. 99
allness	p. 108	imprecise language	p. 109	polarizing terms	p. 109	syntactic rules	p. 99
behavioral descriptions	p. 113	indexing	p. 111	pragmatic rules	p. 99	theory of linguistic relativity	p. 103
connotative meaning	p. 99	jargon	p. 106	racist language	p. 102	time-binding	p. 98
dating	p. 111	language	p. 97	relational messages	p. 104	trigger words	p. 108
denotative meaning	p. 99	lexicon	p. 97	relative terms	p. 109	verbal communication	p. 97
		marking	p. 102	semantic rules	p. 99		

SKILL BUILDERS

1. Using *Google* or one of the electronic databases available through your college library, search for journal articles that contain information on language and verbal communication. Begin your search using the key words *language, obstacles and language*, or *verbal communication*. Be sure to look for articles relating to communication and your major field of study. Report at least one interesting finding to the class.

2. For two or three minutes, role-play two people discussing a current political or campus issue. One person should use several obstacles to verbal communication such as abstract-

ing, allness, euphemisms, sexist language, and trigger words. The other person should reply using verbal skills such as indexing, time-binding, and dating. When time is up, exchange roles and continue the discussion for another two or three minutes.

3. How much do you think your language has influenced the way you think? In small groups, share examples to support your position. Try to find at least one example in the business, education, and healthcare fields.

5 Nonverbal Communication

LEARNING OBJECTIVES

5.1 What is the key concept and definition of *nonverbal communication*?

5.2 What makes nonverbal communication so important, and what is its nature?

5.3 What are the basic categories of nonverbal communication and the types in each category?

5.4 What are the seven functions of nonverbal communication (each beginning with the letter "R"), and what is each called?

5.5 What are several suggestions for improving nonverbal encoding and monitoring your nonverbal skills?

5.6 What nonverbal communication skills covered in this chapter relate specifically to your career (see highlighted fields of business, education, and healthcare)?

After studying this chapter you should be able to . . .

- Pinpoint your strengths and weaknesses when it comes to using nonverbal communication and work to minimize at least two weaknesses.
- Recognize the different categories of nonverbal communication and demonstrate improvement in using nonverbal behaviors that effectively support your verbal messages.
- Identify major functions of nonverbal communication and decide when each would be most appropriate to use in your own daily communication.
- Improve your own nonverbal encoding by implementing several of the suggested nonverbal skills.

CHAPTER SUMMARY 〉 P. 148

Elena anxiously waited in the Atrium Club's dining room for the evening's serving staff to arrive. Eleven people were on duty tonight, several of them longtime employees who would probably be unhappy with the changes in policy that management had sent down and that she was about to announce. When everyone had found a place around the table, she took a deep breath and began.

"I want to make this as brief as possible because I know you all have duties to perform before we open. Several of you will be working the private party arriving at 5:30 and need to get this room set up. Also, I want to have plenty of time for questions, so let's get started. Management has announced some new procedures for us. First, requests for any changes in your assigned shifts need to be made in writing to management no less than 10 days in advance. Since they will need time for processing, you may not know if your request has been granted until a week before. Obviously, the earlier you make your request, the better. Also, your request is more likely to be approved if you already have someone lined up to cover your shift."

Elena wasn't surprised at their reactions: several groaned; Evan frowned; Amy and Mark exchanged unhappy glances; and Marcie's brow furrowed as she took a small notebook out of her purse, wrote something on an open page, and pushed it across to Evan. Evan nodded, and Marcie closed the notebook and pulled it back.

"Management has also decided," Elena hesitated, and then continued, "that no one will be allowed to work triple shifts on weekends anymore. That means that no one can get by with working only on weekends."

Evan interrupted, "I don't think that is fair for those of us who are trying to earn a living while also going to school."

Elena nodded and said, "I understand that. But weekends are high-volume, and management wants more of you to have a chance at the better tips. They feel that some senior staff members are hogging those nights. You may not understand it, but they really are just trying to be fair to everyone."

Mark rolled his eyes, Evan shook his head in exasperation, but Quincy smiled and said, "Hey, I'm good with that. It's about time I get to make the big bucks all you old-timers keep pulling down!" Several people laughed. Marcie sighed, looked down at the floor, and crossed her arms.

"Any questions?" Elena asked, looking at her watch. No one responded, so she dismissed the meeting. Evan stormed out, and others followed quickly. Marcie looked serious as she tried to find a place in her purse for the notebook. As she rose to go, Elena took the opportunity to speak to her privately.

"Marcie, I noticed that you were pretty upset about the new rules."

Marcie looked surprised. "Me? No, not really. They seem fair to me."

"Well, I noticed you exchanging notes with Evan, and then you sat back in your chair with your arms across your chest, and you wouldn't even look at me."

Marcie looked directly at Elena. "I'm sorry. You misunderstood. I wasn't trying not to look at you. The note I wrote to Evan was to make sure he was still willing to cover for me when I have to sit for my Nursing Boards. I'm afraid I got a little distracted, thinking about how I was going to get enough studying time in between now and Boards. Frankly, I'm not at all upset about the weekend thing; I really do need next weekend for studying."

"Well, you sure looked to me like you were ticked off," Elena insisted.

"I promise you, I am not. I can easily work with the new rules. I'm sorry if I came across as angry. Besides, I know you didn't make the rules; you're just the messenger. There really isn't any reason for anyone to feel hostile toward you."

"Well, that was definitely the vibe I was getting."

Marcie smiled reassuringly. "Don't worry; they'll get over it. Some people just don't like change."

What do you think? As you read this chapter, keep the opening scenario in mind and see if you can identify the categories and types of nonverbal communication that caused Elena's confusion and decide what communication goals would help her be more successful in her communication.

SOLVE IT NOW! 〉 P. 149

If you feel confused just by reading the chapter opener, imagine how Elena felt after talking with Marcie. As she tries to assess how her message was received by her employees, she has a decision to make—should she trust the nonverbal reactions she observed, or should she believe Marcie's explanation?

What Is Nonverbal Communication?

When people communicate, they send more than just verbal messages—they also send multiple nonverbal messages. In fact, it's possible that the nonverbal messages communicate with more effect than the verbal ones.

Key Communication Concepts

In Chapter 4, we presented a key communication concept: *Words have no meaning; people have meanings.* Meanings, as we have learned, are **co-constructed**, which simply means that the messages exchanged in communication are not embedded in the language used but are created by people interacting within a particular context from within each person's frame of reference. In fact, much of our understanding of what has transpired in our communication with another person is not dependent on language at all. It is, to a large degree, the result of our interpretation of all the nonverbal aspects of the event. What nonverbal interpretations of each other do you think the businessman and the backpacker are making in the photo on the next page?

In this chapter, we consider another key communication concept: *You cannot not communicate.* In case you think you have spotted a typographical or grammatical error in this statement, you have not. The statement means exactly as it sounds:

LEARNING **OBJECTIVE**

5.1 What is the key concept and definition of *nonverbal communication*?

You cannot **not** communicate. You can try not to communicate, but the very act of trying not to communicate does, in fact, communicate. You don't need to say anything at all; silence communicates. In fact, you don't even have to be there; absence communicates. *Anything you do—or do not do—has the potential to communicate if someone attaches meaning to it.*

Nonverbal Communication Defined

In asserting this principle, we are pointing out the importance of **nonverbal communi-cation**, which includes any symbolic behavior, other than written or spoken language, that is either intentionally or unintentionally sent and is interpreted as meaningful by the receiver. The nonverbal symbols people use are influenced by social, cultural, and psychological aspects of their frames of reference, as are the meanings that are drawn from those behaviors. Note the part of this definition that relates to intentionality. Does it seem fair to you that even when you don't intend to communicate, your actions may still "count" as communication? In fact, there is much controversy in scholarly circles about that very idea. However, it is important to remember that *it isn't the mes-sage you intend to send that matters; it's the message that is received*. This notion takes a

What message is each of these people sending nonverbally to the other?

"receiver-oriented" view of communication. It acknowledges that, when a person draws meaning from your behavior, that meaning comes more from their interpretation of your behavior than from whatever you might have intended to communicate.

Consider this example. You receive an e-mail from someone, but, being pressed for time, you wait to reply so that you will have time to respond thoughtfully. However, the recipient is unaware of your reason for the delay. What messages may you have communicated unintentionally by not responding immediately?

You can see that nonverbal communication can be very tricky. In Chapter 2, we discussed how you can be a better *decoder* of other people's nonverbal communication through the use of perception checks. However, it is also important that you become a good *encoder* of nonverbal messages you send so that your nonverbal behaviors do, indeed, accurately convey your ideas, thoughts, and feelings. Therefore, it is important to consider the nature of nonverbal communication and to learn the range of behaviors and other factors that comprise this type of communication.

APPLY **WHAT YOU KNOW**
NONVERBAL COMMUNICATION

Apply what you know about nonverbal communication by answering the following critical thinking issues:

• Think of a time when what you intended to communicate was not the message that the other person received. Explain the situation, what you said, and what was interpreted.

• Thinking back on the situation, was your response to the mis-interpretation the best one for successful communication? Why or why not?

The Nature of Nonverbal Communication

LEARNING **OBJECTIVE**

5.2 What makes nonverbal communication so important, and what is its nature?

In Chapter 4, we explored the nature of verbal communication, focusing on how language functions as a tool that we use in order to share meaning with others. As we mentioned earlier, language is only part of how we communicate—another very important part relates to the nonverbal aspects of our messages. In fact, as we will see below, in some situations the nonverbal element may play a larger role than the verbal one.

Nonverbal Communication Aids Meaning

When nonverbal communication was introduced as part of the communication model in Chapter 1, we learned that how much attention people pay to nonverbal communication when interpreting the meaning of any particular message depends on the type of message, the person, and the context. When a message is simple and factual, the verbal code may be all that is needed for an accurate interpretation of meaning (Lapakko, 1996). However, when the message is emotional, vague or complicated, when the communicators are involved in conflict, or the context is noisy, then an accurate interpretation of meaning requires the addition of the nonverbal code including both its vocal and visual aspects. To show the importance of nonverbal communication, imagine this situation: You are a child, and there is a terrible storm raging outside your home with hail, lightning, and strong winds. Although it is the middle of the afternoon, the sky has gone completely black. Your mother attempts to calm you by saying, "Don't worry, dear. The storm will be over soon," but she has a worried look on her face, and her voice is quivering. Which would you pay more attention to: your mother's assuring words (language) or the nonverbal elements of the black sky, your mother's worried look, and her quivering voice? Even though you trust your mother, her words would probably carry less weight in this situation than the nonverbal elements.

Researchers have long known the impact of nonverbal communication on meaning. For example, as early as 1973, Michael Argyle reported that "with initially equated signals the nonverbal messages outweighed the verbal ones at least 5 to 1, and where they were in conflict the verbal messages were virtually disregarded" (p. 78). Even when the verbal and nonverbal messages are not in conflict, no more than 30 to 35 percent (approximately one-third) of the meaning receivers take from a conversation comes from the sender's verbal message (Birdwhistell, 1970; Philpott, 1983; Burgoon, 1994)—and it may be much less in some situations. So that means that 65 to 70 percent (approximately two-thirds) of the meaning of a message may come from its nonverbal elements (see **Figure 5.1**). Although we may think that what we say is more important than how we say it, research shows this assumption is not always true. Although some messages may be simple and straightforward, most of our messages are not. It's not surprising then, that nonverbal researchers Burgoon and Hoobler (2002) point out: "The ability to encode and decode nonverbal messages is critically important to successful communication" (p. 247).

Figure 5.1 Percent of Meaning: Two-thirds of meaning may come from nonverbal elements

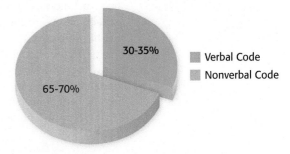

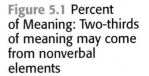

30-35%

65-70%

Verbal Code

Nonverbal Code

Nonverbal Communication Is Ambiguous

Nonverbal communication is often **ambiguous,** or unclear. It is not always easy to determine how it should be interpreted. There are several primary reasons for the ambiguity of nonverbal messages.

Multiple Meanings

First, most nonverbal behaviors have *multiple meanings*. Of course, as we learned in Chapter 4, this is also true of verbal symbols. However, with language we at least have the advantage of a dictionary definition to serve as a starting point for determining meaning. There are no valid "dictionaries" of nonverbal symbols. Occasionally you will find a book or an article in a magazine that purports to unlock the "hidden meanings" of a variety of nonverbal behaviors. Often these are aimed at helping you to decipher what is happening in the minds of customers or bosses or potential romantic partners. However, there is so much variability in what behaviors mean that it is unwise to place too much confidence in these types of interpretations.

Intentionality

Another factor that contributes to the ambiguity of nonverbal behaviors is the issue of *intentionality* discussed earlier. It is often difficult to determine whether a person exhibited a behavior with the intent of sending a message, or whether the behavior was an unconscious action that had no real message behind it. Additionally, people will sometimes claim that no message was intended when, in fact, one was. Some people like to disavow any responsibility for their nonverbal behaviors, asserting that the problem lies with the receiver for "reading too much" into an action. No doubt there are times when a person is hypersensitive to the nonverbal cues of others, but there are also times when the sender making this claim is pretending innocence or when the sender is simply not aware of the power of his or her own behaviors to generate meaning.

Culture Bound

A third reason that nonverbal behaviors are ambiguous is that nonverbal communication is highly **culture bound**. A behavior that is typically used to convey a particular meaning in one culture may be interpreted quite differently by people in another culture. For example, gestures that use arm waving are considered normal in some Middle Eastern countries; but in Asian countries, where minimal gestures are the norm, arm waving is likely viewed as lacking dignity and control (Le Roux, 2002, p. 47). We will have more to say about this idea as we explore the various categories of nonverbal behaviors. For now, though, it is important to recognize that each of us is a descendant of people from some cultural group, and our families may still adhere to certain cultural norms about what is and is not acceptable behavior.

Even if we are aware of the inherent ambiguity of nonverbal behaviors, the fact is that we all rely on nonverbal cues as a way to gauge what someone is communicating to us. If someone says, "No, I am not angry!" in a loud and forceful way, do we believe the verbal message? Probably not. The reason for this is that we tend to think that verbal symbols are consciously chosen while nonverbal behaviors are not—suggesting that the nonverbal is more revealing of another's "real" meaning. Recognizing this can help us become better decoders of nonverbal communication by helping us remember that we need to avoid making assumptions and to explore (through well-worded perception checks) the speaker's actual intent. However, this idea can also help us become better encoders by forcing us to recognize the power of our nonverbal behaviors as interpreted by others.

Nonverbal Learning Disorder A fourth reason that nonverbal behaviors are ambiguous relates to a nonverbal learning disorder (NLD). People with this disorder misinterpret nonverbal messages or don't pick up on them at all. These people, like the gentleman in the cartoon, may miss entirely any visual information that accompanies the verbal message although they interpret our words as accurately as those without NLD (Carton, Kessler, & Pape, 1999). This oversight means, of course, that they may miss the most important parts of what we are trying to communicate with our subtle facial expressions or gestures. Although the cartoon is humorous, NLD is not because it causes many problems in intimate and work relationships (Rourke, Young, & Leenaars, 1989).

Nonverbal Communication Based on Expectations Even though nonverbal behaviors are ambiguous and difficult to interpret, we still have certain nonverbal expectations of others depending on our gender, culture, general frames of reference, and the specific context. For example, what are your expectations of people riding on an elevator? How many of the following "rules" fit your expectations when on an elevator with strangers: face the front, avoid direct eye contact, don't touch unless the elevator is crowded and even then keep your arms down at your sides or in front of you; maintain two to three feet distance between you and others unless the elevator is crowded; and no talking unless asking for a certain floor. How would you feel if these expectations were violated? For example, how would you feel if you were the only person on the elevator when another person gets on and comes to your corner and stands within a foot of you instead of going to the opposite side of the elevator? Expectancy violations theory, developed by Judee Burgoon (1983; see also Burgoon & Hoobler, 2002), predicts what happens when our expectations are violated by people we know and like or by people we don't know or don't like. See the *Making Theory Practical* feature in this chapter for a detailed discussion of expectancy violations theory.

"What is it, boy? Want to go outside?"

© Mike Baldwin/Cornered/www.cartoonstock.com

APPLY **WHAT YOU KNOW**
NONVERBAL EXPECTATIONS

Apply what you know about nonverbal expectations by answering the following critical thinking issues:

- Think of some of your main nonverbal expectations in two or three of the following contexts: an elevator, movie theater, library, expensive restaurant, college classroom, local mall, or place of worship.

- Which expectations are most often violated and by whom? Share your answers with a classmate.

Categories of Nonverbal Communication

LEARNING **OBJECTIVE**

5.3 What are the basic categories of nonverbal communication and the types in each category?

You may think you have a fairly good idea of what is encompassed by the term *nonverbal communication*. However, there are likely many aspects of this type of communication that you have not considered very consciously. If you are to become

MAKING THEORY **PRACTICAL**
EXPECTANCY VIOLATIONS THEORY

Have you ever wondered why you experience a positive reaction to some people yet find other people really irritating, even if you have just met them for the first time? For example, would you judge the following behaviors as positive, mildly negative, or irritating?

- A stranger who stands too close while waiting in line.

- An acquaintance who makes direct eye contact without looking away.

- A classmate who touches your arm and hand repeatedly while talking to you.

Theorist
According to Judee K. Burgoon (1983; 1993; see also Burgoon & Hoobler, 2002), such reactions can be explained by the expectancy violations theory. We all have expectations of people's nonverbal behaviors. These expectations vary somewhat depending on the context/situation, the characteristics of the person, and our prior knowledge of the person. When people meet our expectations, we usually judge them in a positive way even though we may not consciously notice a specific behavior—everything just feels right. However, when people violate our expectations, we are conscious of the violation and often judge them less

favorably—although Burgoon says that violations can be judged positively.

The more unexpected the violation the more it serves as a distraction, causing us to pay more attention to the behavior and to spend more time evaluating it. Whether the violation is judged ultimately as negative or positive depends on whether we perceive the outcome as having more costs or more benefits to us. According to Burgoon, if expectations are low enough, a person can violate them in a positive manner by exceeding them. In fact, when a person exceeds our expectations, we perceive more benefits and rewards and are more likely to judge the person in a positive way and to even overlook later violations.

Sometimes, nonverbal behaviors are difficult to determine. In that case, "ambiguous behavior by a valued communicator will be taken as positive, but such behavior by an unrewarding communicator will be taken as negative" (Littlejohn & Foss, 2008, p. 156).

PRACTICAL USES
One way we can use expectancy violation theory is in improving our cultural and global communication. Different cultures have different social norms and nonverbal expectations. If you live in an area with a culturally diverse population or are planning to travel to other countries, being aware of differing nonverbal expectations could really improve communication success. Take touching, for example. According to Andersen and Wang (2009), people from Greece, Italy, and most Latin American countries expect a high level of touching. On the other hand, people from China and Japan consider touching outside the family to be embarrassing and would consider it to be a violation of their expectations. Arab Muslims expect to touch and be touched using only the right hand—"the left hand, which is reserved for toilet use, is considered a social insult" (p. 267). The more you research possible differences in nonverbal expectations, the better your communication may become.

Source: Judee K. Burgoon, "Nonverbal Violations of Expectations", 1983. In J. M. Wiemann & R. P. Harrison (Eds.). *Nonverbal Interaction* (pp. 11–77). Beverly Hills, CA: Sage.

a competent nonverbal communicator, you need to know the vocabulary. The main categories of nonverbal communication include: kinesics, proxemics, haptics, chronemics, artifacts, and paralanguage. Each one of these categories contains several types of nonverbal communication.

Kinesics

Most people think that a good synonym for nonverbal communication is "body language." Indeed, the things you do with your body are a significant part of the way you communicate outside of language. We will start, then, with body language—including eye contact, facial expression, posture, gestures, and movement—which scholars refer to as **kinesics**. Kinesics are so important to communication that researchers Gottman and Levenson (2000) were able to watch married couples interact and predict with 93 percent accuracy which couples would divorce and which would still be married 14 years later. In another longitudinal study lasting 6 years, researchers were able to predict which newlywed couples would divorce after watching them discuss a topic of marital disagreement for only 3 minutes (Carrere & Gottman, 1999).

Eye Contact **Eye contact**, or **gaze**, is the way we make visual connection with another through the use of our eyes. No doubt you have heard the oft-repeated saying that "the eyes are the mirror of the soul." Eye contact and aversion of eye contact are powerful ways that we establish or reject social connection with another person. The type of gaze used tells others such things as whether or not we are interested in a person or in a topic of conversation. It can communicate our desire for power over the other person or our belief that we already hold power over him or her. We look into another's eyes in order to discern emotions or to convey empathy. We accept or reject with our eyes.

As is true of most nonverbal behaviors, eye contact is highly culture bound. In Western cultures, the expectation is that a speaker will maintain eye contact with the listener; failure to do so may raise the listener's suspicion if it is construed as a sign of dishonesty or a sign of discomfort with the subject being discussed. At the same time, listeners are also expected to maintain eye contact with the speaker; aversion of gaze may be interpreted as an unwillingness to interact or a lack of respect for the speaker or lack of interest in his topic. However, both speakers and listeners in Western cultures are expected to break eye contact, though speakers are allowed to do so more frequently than listeners; indeed, excessive gaze on the part of a speaker can be seen as a sign of hostility or intrusiveness. Eye contact norms in other cultures, however, may be quite different. Japanese listeners, for example, may be more likely to focus on the speaker's neck or may shut their eyes altogether to signal total concentration. In many Muslim countries, looking at a member of the opposite sex for more than a few seconds in the initial moments of an encounter may be seen as displaying sexual interest and is, therefore, frowned upon or forbidden. People from Hispanic and Middle Eastern countries generally favor very direct and engaged eye contact. The important issue here is that we run the risk of having our intentions misunderstood if our eye contact differs from the culturally determined preferences of our conversational partner.

Eye contact behaviors are also related to gender. For example, research indicates that women look at others more often and sustain their gazes for longer periods of time than men do (Bente, Donaghy, & Suwelack, 1998; Hall, 1984).

Facial Expression A second type of kinesics refers to **facial expression**, the movement or position of the muscles of your face. Facial muscles are amazingly mobile. We can widen or narrow our eyes, stretch or compress our lips, raise one or both of our eyebrows, flare our nostrils, and combine several of these and other muscular movements at the same time.

We look at another's facial expression in order to gain important social information about that person's mood or emotional state. You have probably heard the term "poker face" to describe someone who makes a conscious effort to avoid revealing any sort of emotion that might reveal important information to an observer. Controlling facial expression is possible, though often the attempt to do so is obvious, and the perception that you are trying to mask your emotions is, itself, interpreted as meaningful. In most cases, facial expressions occur involuntarily. Researcher Paul Ekman (1994; 2003) found that even people who are unusually good at controlling facial expressions often produce **microexpressions**, fleeting movements of the face that may last only a fraction of a second; brief though they may be, microexpressions can be detected by sensitive observers.

While facial expressions are regarded as a significant means by which information about one's emotional state is conveyed, they are still subject to the ambiguity that is true of nonverbal communication in general. One complicating factor is that your *physiognomy*, or facial features, may convey messages independent of your actual emotions. For example, some people have wrinkles between the eyebrows that make them appear to be scowling even when they are feeling positive or neutral emotions. A naturally occurring upward tilt at the corners of your mouth may give others the impression that you are always on the verge of laughter. It is important to be aware of how your facial features affect others' impressions of you, as you may be inadvertently sending inaccurate or mixed messages without any effort or intent.

Facial expressions may be less culture bound than other categories of nonverbal behavior. Ekman and Friesen (1969; 1971; 1999) were able to isolate six facial expressions that they originally claimed are generally read quite accurately across all cultures: happiness, sadness, fear, anger, surprise, and disgust. In later work, Ekman (1994) notes that fear and surprise are often confused, as are anger and disgust, because those pairs of emotions are expressed through the use of the same facial muscles.

Even though some emotions may be expressed consistently across all or most cultures, there are significant differences among cultures with respect to how often facial expressions are used and how overt or pronounced they may be in order to be judged as appropriate. These differences in the extent to which cultures permit the expression of emotions by nonverbal means are known as cultural **display rules.** For example, Asian cultures tend to favor suppression of facial expression, particularly when it is likely to reveal a negative emotion (Andersen & Wang, 2009). In most Asian cultures, exaggerated facial movements are regarded as indicative of a lack of self control and are also problematic because they may cause discomfort for the listener who feels embarrassed by the sender's excessive display of emotion. On the other hand, Americans tend to use and prefer greater facial animation. There are, however, also differences related to gender, as women are more likely to use more exaggerated facial expressions than men when talking to friends. Even those who speak using American Sign Language add meaning to their signs with facial expressions.

One problem that has often been noted in discussions about the use of e-mail as a communication medium is that nonverbal cues are not available to the receiver. In face-to-face (FTF) communication, you have a greater ability to gauge the moods and intent of the other person because you have access to nonverbal cues. The lack of ability to see facial expression is particularly significant, so over time a system of "emoticons" has been developed. No doubt you are familiar with the happy face/ sad face symbols that use colons, dashes, and parentheses to signal to your reader the mood you are in as you write the message. Did you know, however, that the symbols used by Japanese e-mailers are different? The happy face is (^_^) and the sad face is (;_;). One writer has suggested that this may indicate that the Japanese place greater emphasis on the involvement of eyes in facial expression while Americans emphasize the mouth.

Posture

The position, alignment, and carriage of your body, which is referred to as **posture**, is another important type of kinesic cue. Whether you carry yourself in an erect posture or you tend to slouch can convey a great deal about your personality, your mood, and your confidence level. People who cross their arms across their chests and sit back in their chairs may seem to be communicating a desire to distance themselves from others, while those who sit upright, leaning forward and with arms positioned to their sides seem to be saying, "I'm open to communicating with you."

Effective communicators are aware of how members of other cultures view postures and body placement differently. For example, a teacher who sits on the desk in an attempt to look relaxed may be viewed by students from Muslim cultures as "extremely rude" (Le Roux, 2002, p. 44). If the teacher's legs are crossed so that the bottom of the foot is facing the class, students from Thai culture would be offended possibly for two reasons: first, the head is considered a sacred part of the body, and the teacher is sitting where others may rest their head; second, the bottom of the feet are shown only when an insult is intended (as experienced by the sister of one of your authors).

Gestures

Gestures, movements involving the arms and hands, are often what people think of first when they hear the term *body language*. You have probably known people who seem to "talk with their hands," but you are probably not aware of just how often you use gestures yourself. Gestures can be used to emphasize what you are saying verbally, or they may convey meanings of their own without the need for words at all. These meanings, however, are often culture specific. For example, the gesture created by using your index finger and thumb to form a circle while allowing your other three fingers to extend outward means "OK" in America and is also widely used by scuba divers to communicate underwater. However, in France it means "zero," in Japan it means "money," and in Italy and Spain it is an obscene sexual reference. In Brazil it is an insult referring to the anus, and in Saudi Arabia it

At the University of Texas, the longhorn salute means something very different than it would in some other cultures.

is an insult referring to the "evil eye." In the United Kingdom, placing this gesture next to your head is an insulting way to suggest that someone, such as a driver who has cut you off, is lacking in sense.

The cultural meanings attached to various gestures can, obviously, lead to misunderstanding in interpersonal contexts. However, in political contexts, misinterpretations can have serious consequences. There are many examples of misunderstandings created by gestures used by world leaders. One of the most dramatic is the instance of Soviet Premier Khrushchev visiting the United States at a time when Cold War tension between the old Soviet Union and the United States was at its height. Khrushchev greeted the assembled press by shaking clasped hands over his head (Bash & Webel, 2008). This gesture is commonly used in Russia as an acknowledgment of the bonds of friendship, whereas in the United States, it more commonly is used to claim victory in battle. Thus, it was interpreted by many pundits at the time as an expression of Khrushchev's view that the USSR would prevail over the United States.

Body Movements

Your body movements also have communicative potential. For example, a purposeful stride has a very different meaning to an observer than does an aimless shuffle. People who fidget a lot, or who repeatedly alter their body position when sitting, may convey impatience or a level of anxiety or discomfort in communicating with others.

It should be clear from the discussion of kinesics that the many ways we use our bodies do constitute an important form of nonverbal communication. However, there are many other ways that we communicate without or beyond language.

APPLY **WHAT YOU KNOW**
NONVERBAL COMMUNICATION AND KINESICS

Expand what you know about nonverbal communication and kinesics by finding a public place where you can sit off to the side and "people watch." Write a summary of the following observations:

- Observe at a distance how others use eye contact, facial expression, and gestures and see if you can imagine the tone of the conversation between people without knowing what they are saying.

- What specific differences, if any, do you notice in the way men and women communicate? Parents and children? Elderly and young adults?

- What nonverbal cultural behaviors (different from your own) did you observe?

Proxemics

The anthropologist Edward T. Hall studied the ways that people use social distance in interaction—a process known as **proxemics**. Proxemics can be explained in two ways: zones and territories.

Zones

In studying the norms for the North American culture, Hall (1983) identified four "proxemic zones" that are generally observed depending upon the context and the relationship between the people interacting.

- **Intimate Zone** from 0–1.5′—reserved for closest friends or contexts requiring confidentiality
- **Personal Zone** from 1.5′–4′—used by good friends or when you wish to communicate affiliation with another

- **Social Zone** from 4´–12´—used with acquaintances or expected in the conduct of business with strangers, such as in job interviews; also the space preferred as a minimum distance between you and another co-worker as you are engaged in your daily tasks
- **Public Zone** from 12´ and beyond—typical of the distance between a speaker and audience in public speaking situations

Each of these zones can be seen as having a "close phase" and a "far phase," illustrating that there is considerable difference between, for example, four feet and twelve feet. North Americans would generally feel more comfortable with a job interview in the close phase of the social zone than in the far phase, but they would probably prefer greater distance between their chair at work and the chair of their co-worker.

Since Hall's proxemic zones (**Figure 5.2**) are specific to the North American culture, they may not apply to people in many other cultures. For example, most Latin and Middle Eastern cultures tend to prefer a closer orientation between people. While standing close may feel like an invasion of personal space to Americans, the Saudi person might regard the American's choice of a wider distance as standoffish. Of course, context is always an important consideration. Proxemics will differ within cultures, depending upon age, sex, and perceived status and relationships between the communicators. Other factors include the nature of the verbal message being relayed

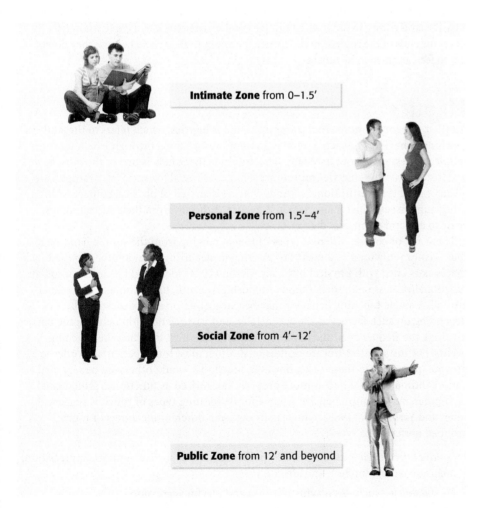

Figure 5.2 Hall's proxemic (social distance) zones

Intimate Zone from 0–1.5´

Personal Zone from 1.5´–4´

Social Zone from 4´–12´

Public Zone from 12´ and beyond

and the context in which the message occurs, including noise in the environment and time of day. For example, although Japanese people generally require even more distance than Americans in order to show respect, during rush hour in Tokyo, they are "literally jammed into subways and trains" (Andersen & Wang, 2009, p. 266). Communicators must acknowledge and adapt to cultural differences in proxemic preferences if they wish to avoid misunderstanding.

Territories A closely connected, but different, concept related to space involves **territoriality**, the space you claim for yourself in a given situation. This idea is similar to the notion of "personal space," but it is not exactly the same. Personal space is often likened to a "bubble" that you carry with you into all situations, defining the space you require between yourself and another. Some people are comfortable with as little as two feet between themselves and others, while others need greater personal space. Of course, our comfort level also depends upon the nature of our relationship with the other person. Territory, however, is the area that you have staked out for yourself in a particular place, and it is considered at least rude and possibly aggressive for others to invade that territory. For example, consider your customary desk in your classroom; unless your teacher created a seating chart, you more than likely staked your claim on that desk early in the term. By the third or fourth class period, regular attendees came to know that that was "your" desk, so that, if someone else should occupy it now, you might find yourself commenting, "Hey, why are you in my chair?" Sometimes we claim a particular territory in order to get our personal space needs met. People who prefer to sit on the ends of the rows or in the corner, for example, may do so because they do not like to feel hemmed in by others.

Haptics

Another category of nonverbal communication is **haptics**, which refers to the study of touching behavior. The tactile sense is an important channel through which we communicate messages to others. Many scholars argue that touch is one of the most basic and instinctive ways that we communicate and is essential for survival. Examples are given of infants in institutional settings who are deprived of physical contact with other humans; evidence suggests that they may withdraw from their surroundings, cease to eat, and ultimately die.

There are, of course, different types of touch, ranging from the simple handshake that is commonly used as a means of meeting or departing from another, to the touch that is associated with physical intimacy. Heslin (1974) identified five levels of touch: functional/professional, social/polite, friendship/warmth, love/intimacy, and sexual arousal. A single touching behavior may be categorized on any of these levels, depending on such factors as the age, gender, and past relationship between the parties involved, the frequency of the touch, as well as the context in which the touching occurs. For instance, healthcare professionals often must touch patients in order to provide treatment; in these cases, however, touch that would otherwise be regarded as a more intimate level 4 or 5 is more properly categorized as functional/professional.

Another, more comprehensive scheme for delineating types of touch is suggested by Jones and Yarbrough (1985), who classify eighteen different meanings of touch grouped under seven types:

- *Positive affect touch*—used to express positive emotions such as support, appreciation, inclusion, sexual interest, and affection
- *Playful touch*—includes playful affection and playful aggression

- *Control touch*—used to gain compliance, get attention, or announce a specific response
- *Ritualistic touch*—such as a greeting or a departure
- *Hybrid touch*—which shows either greeting or departure affection
- *Instrumental touch*—related to performing one's task, such as touch used by heath-care providers
- *Accidental touch*—which occurs completely by accident

One of the more interesting aspects of this system of categorizing touch is its recognition of the way that touch communicates the two components of relational messages: power and connection. A single touch may be interpreted as expressive of either or both of these. For example, if a manager touches a subordinate on the shoulder, the intent may have been to gain compliance with a request; however, the subordinate may interpret it to be an expression of personal interest. It is easy to see how such events can lead to claims of sexual harassment.

Cultures differ with respect to what is regarded as appropriate touch. In Arab countries, for example, men may embrace each other in greeting and walk hand-in-hand, which is seen merely as an expression of friendship and good will. The same behavior in America is likely to be interpreted as an indication of an intimate relationship. By the same token, many Arab cultures would frown upon a man touching a woman in public, while in the United States this is widely acceptable (Hofstede, 2001). Again, the age, gender, and relationship between the parties, the frequency of the touch, and the context in which it occurs are all factors that affect how a given touch is perceived within any given culture, but it is true that there are some cultures that are more "high contact" than others. These cultures are generally more comfortable with frequent touch of longer duration among most people in many different contexts. People from "low-contact" cultures would find such behavior too intrusive, requiring as it does the violation of personal or intimate space. Conversely, high-contact cultures are likely to view low-contact communicators as cold and aloof, or to perceive a lack of interest or sincerity.

Chronemics

Are you reading this text at this moment because you have set aside this specific time for the purpose of studying and preparing for your Communication class? Will you continue reading until you are finished with this chapter, or are you likely to put it down at some time, whether you have finished or not, because you have some other activity scheduled at that time? If friends drop by or call you on the telephone while you are reading, will you discontinue your study in order to interact, or will you ask if you can get back to them when you have time to talk? What do all of these examples of how you use time communicate to others?

The study of how we conceptualize, arrange, and use time is known as **chronemics**. It is an important category of nonverbal communication because, whether we intend it to do so or not, our use of time does

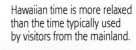

Hawaiian time is more relaxed than the time typically used by visitors from the mainland.

communicate to others. Consider, for example, what your professor communicates to you by spending fifteen minutes lecturing on one topic, while only mentioning another topic in passing. Or think about what punctuality means to you.

The way we use time is often dependent upon our perceptions of our relationship with another person, and it also communicates those perceptions to others. For example, if you are trying to make a good impression on someone you think may be a candidate for a romantic relationship, you are likely to be more concerned about being punctual for a date than you may be after the relationship is more firmly established. In the workplace, a superior would feel free to interrupt a subordinate's work if there was an issue to be discussed, but the subordinate would be expected to request time in order to discuss an issue with a superior. When a patient makes an appointment to see a physician, it is generally understood that the patient will be expected to spend some time waiting; however, for a patient to be late to the appointment may mean that s/he will have to reschedule. These examples illustrate how expectations about the use of time send relational messages about power and connection.

As is true of most categories of nonverbal communication, our understanding of time and how it is used is culture bound. One important difference is illustrated in the distinction that intercultural scholars make between *monochromic* ("M-Time") cultures and *polychromic* ("P-Time") cultures. In M-Time cultures—which tend to be more individualistic and low-context, such as the United States and Northern Europe—time is conceived of as a commodity that must be managed. It is segmented and arranged into distinct units, and activities are scheduled with definite time parameters. People in M-Time cultures worry about spending time, wasting time, and finding more time. There are specific times for sleeping, eating, working, and pursuing leisure activities, and schedules and appointments are expected to be rigidly adhered to. Punctuality is valued. P-Time cultures, on the other hand, see time as a more fluid notion. Of course, there are things to accomplish, but relationships matter more than schedules, so people are expected to be flexible in their management of time. These cultures—which tend to be more collectivistic and high-context, such as Latin American, African, and most Asian nations—are more tolerant of interruptions and changes in plans, and there really is no concept of being "late." Appointments are merely approximations, and no apology is expected for not arriving "on time." A good example of the difference between M-Time and P-Time cultures is found in Hawaii, where there is a sort of collision of cultures, including people from Asia and the Pacific Rim, people from the American mainland, and people who are indigenous to the islands. It is not uncommon to hear people clarify the time for an event by adding "Hawaiian time" or "haole time," the latter term (pronounced: HOW-le) sometimes used derisively to refer to non-natives, especially Caucasian westerners. It is understood that if an event is scheduled in haole-time, you are expected to be there at the time stated, but if it is Hawaiian-time, there is a great deal of latitude.

The understanding of time obviously varies among people within a particular culture. You no doubt have friends who are members of your own cultural group— or even of your own family—whose habits with respect to punctuality may differ from your own. Culture is not the only factor that influences behavior. However, no matter what the reasons might be, it is important to reflect upon how your use of time communicates to others. If, for example, you know that your chronic tardiness is regarded as disrespectful or inconsiderate by someone with whom you often interact, it might be useful to consider what your motivations might be in persisting in that behavior. Are you, in fact, not concerned with the impression you make on that person? Is it possible that the feelings of others, or of this person in particular, are not of concern to you? Or are you, perhaps, intending to communicate the message, "I will not be controlled"? Unlike some types of nonverbal communication, the management of time is one that is relatively easily controlled through conscious effort.

Artifacts

One of the most consciously manageable forms of nonverbal communication is found in our **artifacts**, which are the objects we surround ourselves with and display to others. If you are reading this text in a room in your home, look around at the furnishings and decorative items on display and consider what those things would reveal about you to someone who does not know you at all. If you are somewhere else, consider your clothing and accessories and the messages they convey to others. Unless someone else chooses all your personal belongings for you, you are— whether you consciously intend to or not—communicating information about yourself to others by displaying these artifacts.

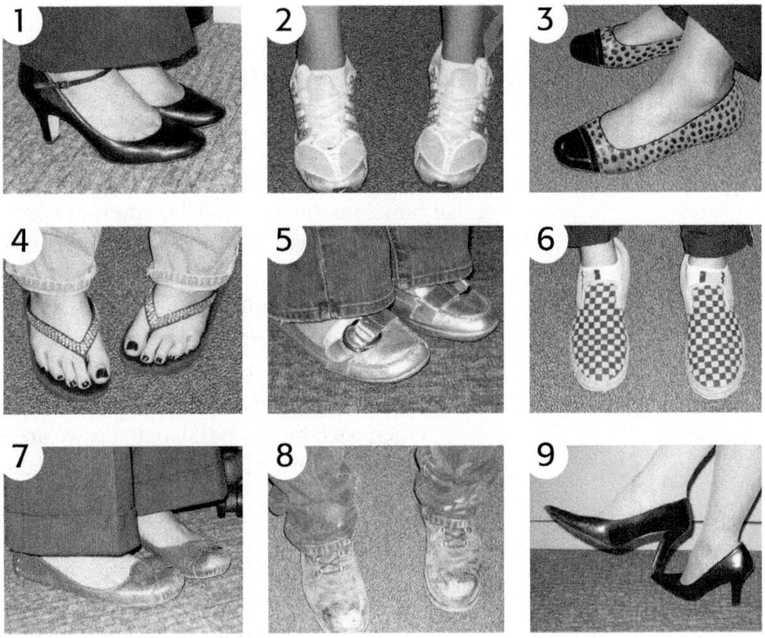

Figure 5.3 What messages do these shoes send about their owners?

Do you doubt this? Consider how long it takes you to shop for clothing. If your only objective was to cover your body, you should be able to go into any store that sells clothing and find any garment that fits and be done with it. However, chances are that you spend a great deal of time trying on many things that all fit well enough, looking for the ones that are "you." You are looking for the garments that convey the message you want to send to others through your clothing. You are concerned with the image you project and the impression you will make. Perhaps you wish to be regarded as trendy, or maybe you want others to think you are affluent or powerful. Some people choose clothing, cars, or shoes (**Figure 5.3**) that communicate that they are creative or that they refuse to conform to others' expectations. Of course, the message you send does have consequences; if your clothing communicates disdain for the occasion or the feelings of others, it is reasonable to expect others to respond with disapproval— such as demonstrated in the photo of the businessman and back packer in the beginning of this chapter.

Artifacts, of course, are strongly related to culture. The ways you dress or furnish your home are significantly influenced by the expectations—and sometimes the rules— of your cultural or co-cultural group. Religious strictures may dictate the types of clothing that can be worn in public. Sometimes people who are not actually members of a particular cultural or co-cultural group choose to dress in ways that demonstrate their affinity with that group; of course, this practice is sometimes interpreted as a sign that the person is a "wannabe," which may merely amuse others.

APPLY **WHAT YOU KNOW**
NONVERBAL CATEGORIES

Apply what you know about nonverbal communication categories by answering the following critical-thinking questions:

- Elena always dreads it when the restaurant supply rep comes by her office to talk about new items on the market. Instead of sitting in the seat across from her desk, he stands and leans across the desk to speak with her. She is thinking about closing her door and pretending to be out when he is scheduled to come today. Which of the following nonverbal categories is causing the problem?

a. Kinesics

b. Proxemics

c. Haptics

d. Chronemics

- How would you suggest that Jantzen handle her problem and still be an effective communicator? Give at least two suggestions and support your answers by referring to content from any of the first five chapters.

Paralanguage

You have probably heard someone say that her understanding of something was not because of "what was said" but because of "how it was said." The kinesic, proxemic, haptic, chronemic, and artifactual components of a message are part of the impression of how something is said; however, in situations where verbal messages are spoken, the "tone of voice" is especially significant. We are referring here to **paralanguage**, which means the combination of the aspects of voice production that accompany spoken language, and which may enhance or modify the meaning of the words uttered. Another term that is often used for this idea is *vocalics*, and the study of how the voice functions alongside language (note: the prefix *para-* means "alongside") is known as *paralinguistics*.

When we consider paralanguage, we are looking at a very wide range of vocal behaviors, all of which are essentially related to one or more of the four chief attributes of the human voice: pitch, rate, volume, and vocal quality.

Musicians aren't the only ones who pay attention to pitch; effective speakers vary their pitch to achieve good vocal variety.

Pitch
Pitch refers to the relative highness or lowness of a vocal tone as it occurs on a musical scale. Scientifically, pitch is created by the frequency of the sound waves produced by your vocal folds when they vibrate. The range of pitches you can produce is, to a large degree, determined by your physical characteristics; men's voices are, in general, capable of producing lower pitches than women can produce because their vocal folds are longer and thicker. Singers and speakers who have trained their voices are able to produce a wider range of pitches because they have learned how to control the tension they apply to their vocal folds (also called "vocal cords"). Most people speak within a pitch range that is appropriate for their sex and physical size, but occasionally you will hear people whose voices seem incongruent with their physical characteristics. This can be distracting and can lead to inaccurate perceptions of the speaker. For example, a grown woman whose voice sounds like that of a young girl may find it difficult to be taken seriously.

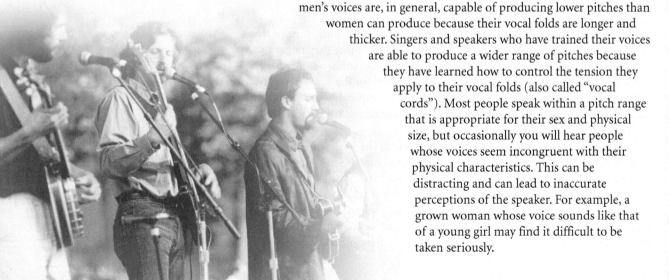

The key issue related to pitch as it pertains to nonverbal communication is the degree to which you vary your pitch, known as "inflection." You may have encountered people who speak in a monotone, which means that they vary their pitch only slightly, if at all. The monotone speaker conveys a lack of energy, enthusiasm, and interest in what s/he is saying. If you have been subjected to a long lecture by a teacher who speaks in a monotone, you may have wondered why you should be interested since the teacher apparently is not. Excessive use of inflection, however, can communicate emotional instability. To demonstrate an effective speaking voice, vary your pitch enough to hold the listener's attention and to communicate confidence in and enthusiasm for what you have to say.

Rate
Your speech **rate** is measured by the number of words uttered per minute. This definition is actually misleading because it does not take into account the effect that pausing has on a listener's subjective perception of a speaker's rate. On average, English speakers in the United States speak about 150 words per minute. However, this rate varies from one geographic region to the next. People in New York City tend to speak faster than people in the southern United States. The circumstances of the speaking context will also affect speaking rate.

To analyze how rate functions nonverbally and affects how others interpret your messages, consider your impressions of people who talk more slowly than average, relative to the standards for your cultural or social group. Slowness of speech often conveys slowness of thought. Conversely, the person who speaks at a slightly more rapid rate than average is generally perceived as someone who "knows what he is talking about." A slow rate coupled with a monotone is likely to communicate lethargic physical and mental processes, while a rapid rate accompanied by extreme variation in pitch may be interpreted as indicative of a high degree of emotional excitement. The effective communicator speaks at a rate that allows listeners to comprehend the verbal message but also holds their attention.

Volume
The term **volume** refers to the relative loudness or softness of a speaking voice. Volume, which is measured in "amplitude," depends upon the intensity of the force applied to the breath stream as it moves past the vocal folds. People who speak too loudly may, over time, actually damage their speech mechanisms. They are also likely to be perceived as overbearing or aggressive. However, people who speak too softly run the risk of not being heard at all and of conveying an unwillingness to communicate; they may be perceived as shy or lacking in confidence. Loudness is also related to emphasis, which is achieved by raising the pitch, reducing the rate, and increasing the volume as you speak the emphasized syllable or word. When you stress a word in a sentence, you are giving the listener clues to what you perceive is important for them to hear and remember. Like pitch and rate, volume should be appropriate for the situation and for the intent of the speaker. If you often sense that people pull back when you speak, perhaps your volume is excessive; by the same token, if people often say, "Huh?" when you speak, you may need to increase your volume.

Vocal Quality
Vocal quality depends upon the manner of production of your voice. Good vocal quality is accomplished when a speaker provides good support for the breath stream by proper use of the abdominal muscles and diaphragm, maintains a relaxed throat, and achieves good resonation of the vocal tone. If you speak with good vocal quality, people are likely to pay attention to what you say, instead of being distracted by qualities such as nasality, breathiness, stridency, or hoarseness. Not only is your message more likely to be heard, but your vocal quality will generate positive

impressions of you. Speakers with poor vocal quality may unwittingly send inaccurate messages about themselves that affect how listeners perceive them and their message.

For example, people who speak with excessive nasality are often perceived to be whining, and women who speak with excessive breathiness—especially when combined with high pitch—are often thought to be "ditzy."

Articulation and Diction

In addition to the four principal attributes of the human voice just outlined, there are other paralinguistic behaviors that have the potential to communicate nonverbally. **Diction**, or the manner in which each speech sound is uttered, can significantly affect whether you are understood or the impression you create. Speaking too fast can cause poor articulation, though poor articulation usually results from speakers' not applying enough energy and effort to the enunciation of the vowel sounds and the articulation of the consonant sounds of their language. Slurring occurs when you run sounds together so that each speech sound is not fully articulated. Sometimes poor diction is the result of leaving out sounds, making "What are you doing?" sound like "Wachadoon?" This style of diction may be appropriate in highly casual contexts with people you know well, but sloppy diction makes it almost impossible for non-native speakers to understand you. In more formal situations, such as a job interview, it can communicate, "I'm a sloppy person." Excessively precise diction can feel artificial or pretentious in some situations, though, so the goal should be speech that is appropriately articulated for the context.

Vocal Dysfluencies

Effective speech is *fluent*, meaning that it flows smoothly without significant interruptions. However, many people experience **vocal dysfluencies** or **vocal interferences**, which are behaviors that interrupt the fluency of the spoken message. Some vocal dysfluencies are the result of speech disorders such as stuttering or stammering. Mild forms of these conditions are often normal parts of language acquisition and are eventually outgrown, but more serious forms may require focused work with a speech pathologist to learn to manage or overcome them. Other factors can cause dysfluencies or interferences. False starts, where several efforts must be made to generate the desired phrasing of a thought, may convey a lack of clarity about the message you are trying to convey. Hesitations or repetitions of sounds may be created by a heightened emotional state, such as nervousness, excitement, or anger. Sometimes vocal dysfluencies or interferences are a matter of habit. For example, repeated clearing of the throat may start as a way to cope with seasonal allergy symptoms, but may become an unfortunate habit that is, at best, annoying to the listener and, at worst, likely to be interpreted as a lack of truthfulness or a lack of comfort with what you are saying.

Fillers

Another type of vocal dysfluency that deserves special mention is the matter of **fillers**, which are words or phrases that are inserted into a sentence—usually to replace a natural pause—that contribute nothing to the verbal meaning of the sentence. The list of these verbal habits includes such words or phrases as *you know, I mean, ok, and uh, right?, see?,* and others. You may be wondering why fillers are not part of the category of verbal communication; they are, after all, words. However, their inclusion as examples of nonverbal communication is because fillers are not used to convey substantive meaning. They really do function as sounds that take the place of a pause. Sometimes they act as "place-holders," letting the listener know that you are not yet relinquishing your turn at talking but need a moment to find the next word to communicate your idea. In other cases, they function as vocal punctuation marks. But too often they act as nothing more than verbal mannerisms, used by habit, frequently as a part of the process of demonstrating affiliation with a particular social group. Perhaps the filler that best illustrates this is the word *like*. A part of the dialect that was once isolated to a group of affluent teen girls in the San Fernando Valley of California, *like* was one of the words that gained almost overnight exposure with the 1983 release of the film *Valley Girl*. (Others include *as if, duh, whatever, totally*, and *fer sure*.) Now it is seemingly ubiquitous, being spoken by males and females of all cultures and socio-economic groups in the United States. As a means of expressing belongingness during your teen years, it serves a purpose. Unfortunately—like many habits once they are acquired—it often finds its way into oral speech in situations where it is not appropriate. Furthermore, as a speech pattern used by anyone older than eighteen, it can be seriously damaging to one's credibility, suggesting immaturity and a deficiency in one's vocabulary.

Dialect

"Valley Girl" is an example of a **dialect**, which is a variation in a spoken language specific to a particular social or cultural group or geographic region. You do not have to travel far in the United States to recognize that English doesn't sound exactly the same from place to place, or even among co-cultural groups within the same city. Dialects vary primarily in vocabulary, pronunciation, and syntax/grammar. Different words are used in New York, Indianapolis, and Atlanta to talk about soft drinks (*soda, pop*, and *coke*, respectively). In Boston, the "r" sound is often eliminated when it is part of a word (so that *park* becomes "pahk") but added when it is not (*idea* becomes "idear"). Grammatical constructions in the rural South differ from the standards of General American Speech; "He don't understand" is used instead of "He doesn't understand." The reason that dialect is a nonverbal component of communication rather than verbal is because beyond the meaning of the words you are using, you are also communicating something by the use of your dialect. Stereotyping is a factor in the interpretation of the use of a dialect. Rural Southerners are often thought to be less well-educated than residents of the Northeast, and their dialect has come to symbolize that difference. However, even well-educated Southerners may speak with their regional dialect, which means that they may be sending inaccurate messages about themselves to people who hold those stereotypes. Does this mean they should change their speech? The answer to this question will depend upon the individual's goals. It may be useful to cultivate the General American Dialect that is typical of, for example, network newscasters. It is widely spoken and does not carry the negative stereotypes of either substandard or pretentious speech. Being "bi-dialectical" can be advantageous. Similarly, people for whom English is a second language may find that their accent often creates communication problems for them in negotiating life in America. Students who wish to work on issues of dialect and accent may find courses in improving voice and diction beneficial.

What regional dialect might you expect this man to have, and would it affect your perception of him?

Paralanguage can also be related to written verbal messages. This is particularly true when using Computer Mediated Communication. When you type an e-mail message, you may find yourself using a variety of ways to embed "nonverbal" messages into what is seemingly restricted to verbal code. The emoticons that are used to suggest facial expression, for example, may also be useful in suggesting tone of voice. "Shouting," which is accomplished through the use of all capital letters, actually is symbolic of increased volume. E-mailers who typically type in all capital letters are actually violating the rules of "Netiquette." Using colored fonts, underlining, and boldface are all ways to inject paralinguistic elements into CMC.

There are other ways that we communicate nonverbally apart from kinesics, proxemics, haptics, chronemics, artifacts, and paralanguage. For example, your appearance—height, weight, skin and hair color, and body type—inadvertently sends messages. The way you arrange a room communicates to others. However, these six categories are sufficient for us to consider in thinking about how our nonverbal messages work with verbal messages to create meaning.

APPLY **WHAT YOU KNOW**
NONVERBAL AND PARALANGUAGE

Paralanguage is the vocal element of nonverbal communication. Apply what you know about paralanguage by answering the following questions:

- Which vocal element bothers you the most when used by others: Using vocal fillers like "um," a high whiny pitch, inap-

propriate volume, or a speaking rate that is too fast or too slow? Why?

- Which of the above vocal elements causes you the most difficulty? Give an example.

LEARNING **OBJECTIVE**

5.4 What are the seven functions of nonverbal communication (each beginning with the letter "R", and what is each called?

Functions of Nonverbal Messages

Now that we know the various ways we communicate nonverbally, let's look specifically at the seven functions nonverbal communication performs for us when we communicate— the "7 R's". Nonverbal communication allows us to *replace, repeat, reinforce, regulate, reveal, reverse,* and *reflect* verbal messages (based on original research from Ekman, 1965).

Nonverbal Messages Can *Replace* Verbal Messages

As we have seen in our discussion of gestures, there are some actions of the hands and arms that have specific meaning in a particular culture or co-culture. These gestures, called **emblems**, do not require a verbal message in order to be understood. They replace verbal messages. The thumbs-up sign, clapping hands, or the index finger placed vertically in front of rounded lips ("Shhhh" is conveyed, even if you do not make the sound "shh") are readily understood in American culture. Interestingly, the way an audience claps hands in applause at the end of a performance is also emblematic. In the United States, slow rhythmic hand-clapping at the end of a performance may be a kind of sarcastic message; the audience is saying, "We know it is polite to applaud, but we didn't really think this was a good performance." In Mexico and other Latin American countries, though, the same applause is a signal of a desire for an encore.

Nonverbal Messages Can *Repeat* Verbal Messages

Sometimes our nonverbal behaviors repeat the verbal message. Behaviors that complement the meaning intended by the words are known as **illustrators**. If you are describing something as being "long and smooth," you might use a gesture that demonstrates the length and suggests the smoothness; at the same time you might use pitch and rate paralinguistically ("smooooth!") to further illustrate what you are saying. If you wrinkle your forehead as you say that something is confusing, your facial expression has illustrated further the ideas you are expressing. Hugging someone as you say, "Hey, that's okay. I'm not upset," is a way to use haptics to repeat the verbal message.

Nonverbal Messages Can *Reinforce* Verbal Messages

Often, our gestures, facial expression, and paralanguage serve to reinforce our verbal message. Ever wonder why Oprah Winfrey has remained so popular for so many years? According to Karen Bradley, a communication specialist in nonverbal communication from the University of Maryland, Oprah reinforces her verbal message with her nonverbal body movements, making her appear "entirely authentic" (Argetsinger & Roberts, 2007) to her audience. Using nonverbal behaviors to emphasize a verbal message involves **accentors**. We may not be as effective as Oprah, but if we pound a fist on the table, look directly into the listener's eyes, and increase our volume as we say, "I mean this!" we are accenting, or reinforcing, our meaning.

Oprah uses nonverbal gestures to reinforce her verbal messages.

Nonverbal Messages Can *Regulate* Verbal Messages

We also use nonverbal behaviors to regulate verbal communication. The use of nonverbal behaviors to control the flow of verbal messages is accomplished by **regulators**. Your eye contact and head nods encourage another person to continue to speak; similarly, you could use many gestures, facial expressions, and body movements to indicate to the other person that you are ready for him or her to stop talking so that you might have a turn.

Nonverbal Messages Can *Reveal* the Emotions Behind Verbal Messages

Sometimes our nonverbal behaviors reveal emotions that are behind our own spoken messages or reveal the emotions we feel in response to another's message. These are known as **affect displays**. It is easy to see how facial expression is implicated in affect displays since it is to the other person's face that we often turn to determine how he or she is feeling. However, our eye contact, posture, body movement, haptics, proxemics, artifacts, and paralanguage can also serve as displays of emotion or mood.

Nonverbal Messages Can *Reverse* Verbal Messages

In some instances, nonverbal behavior can actually reverse (or contradict) the meaning of a verbal message. For example, when we say something sarcastically or signal to a listener with paralanguage, facial expressions, or gestures that we mean the opposite of what our words would seem to mean, we are using **contradictors**.[1] "Oh, right. That's a great idea," we say, with just the right inflection and rolling eyes to indicate that we really think the idea is terrible. Use of such contradictors gives an aware listener a clear view of how we really see the idea.

---

[1] Although researchers do not have a term for this function of nonverbal communication (as they do for emblems, illustrators, accentors, regulators, and affect displays), we are giving it the term "contradictors."

Figure 5.4 Ways to improve your nonverbal encoding

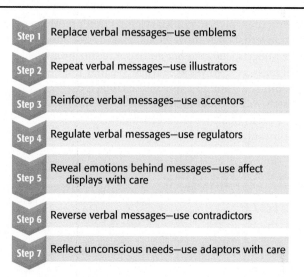

Step 1   Replace verbal messages—use emblems

Step 2   Repeat verbal messages—use illustrators

Step 3   Reinforce verbal messages—use accentors

Step 4   Regulate verbal messages—use regulators

Step 5   Reveal emotions behind messages—use affect displays with care

Step 6   Reverse verbal messages—use contradictors

Step 7   Reflect unconscious needs—use adaptors with care

Nonverbal Messages Can *Reflect* Unconscious Needs

Many nonverbal behaviors are, to some degree or another, consciously chosen. However, sometimes we exhibit nonverbal behaviors that are not sent intentionally and are displayed without our conscious awareness. These **adaptors** may reflect unconscious needs. Involuntarily shivering when you feel a draft, licking your lips when your body senses that they are dry, or sniffing your nose in response to your cold symptoms are all examples of how you adapt to your body's needs in response to conditions in the environment. You may also manipulate one part of your body with another, such as when you smooth your hair or wring your hands without any conscious awareness of what you are doing. Although these behaviors are nonconscious, and although they may not be intended to communicate anything, an observer may well attach meaning to them. You may be leaving the impression that you are anxious or uncomfortable. That, of course, is the challenge of nonverbal communication: How can you improve your competence as an encoder of nonverbal messages so that the meanings others attach to your behaviors are accurate? See **Figure 5.4**.

APPLY **WHAT YOU KNOW**
NONVERBAL FUNCTIONS

Apply what you know about nonverbal communication functions by answering the following questions:

- When communicating or giving a presentation, what *adaptors* do you use and what unconscious needs do these adaptors reflect?

- When communicating, are you more likely to use *illustrators* or *emblems* and why? Give an example.

LEARNING **OBJECTIVE**

5.5 What are several suggestions for improving nonverbal encoding and monitoring your nonverbal skills?

Improving Nonverbal Encoding

If you are fortunate, you will have some relationships in which other people take the time to check out their perceptions of what you mean by your nonverbal behaviors. You already know from your study of Chapter 2 the value of perception checking. However, all too often, other people will simply interpret your behavior and assume that they are correct, and they will respond accordingly.

Use Self-Monitoring

Becoming a better nonverbal encoder begins with being aware of what you are doing nonverbally and how others are responding to your behavior. This notion of **self-monitoring** is particularly relevant to this discussion. It is important that you take responsibility for your nonverbal behaviors to the extent that you do have choices. It is true that some nonverbal behaviors arise without conscious intent. However, some people like to disavow any awareness of how their behaviors communicate to others, preferring to blame others for choosing to attach meaning to those behaviors. But if you are honest, you will recognize that you regularly "read" the behaviors of others and interpret them as meaningful indicators of their intention and emotion. It is certainly possible to be too attuned to your nonverbal behaviors to the point that you begin to see yourself as a "performer" in relationships. You can attempt to generate a particular facial expression, for example, in order to manipulate how others perceive you. This is not the way to be an authentic person, and others may eventually doubt whether you are someone whose sincerity can be trusted. Somewhere between performance and obliviousness, there is a space where knowing what you are doing and how others are responding can guide you in choosing how to encode nonverbally. Once you can monitor your own nonverbal responses, you are ready to see if you can observe them in others and use those observations to improve your interpretations of others' messages. The *Developing Skills* section on page 144 explains several important categories of nonverbal messages for you to learn to observe in yourself and others.

Self-monitoring is important, but don't get so involved that you see yourself as a "performer" instead of a communicator.

Check for Cultural Meanings

A second important principle for improving your ability as a nonverbal encoder is to be aware of the different cultural meanings behind nonverbal behaviors. We have attempted in this chapter to point out the wide variation in the nonverbal norms and practices of other cultures. However, sometimes people wonder whose responsibility it is to adapt to the other's cultural preferences. We have heard "when in Rome, do as the Romans do," which suggests that when we are visitors in another culture, we should work to conform to their practices. However, it is important to remember that many of the people with whom you interact are not sufficiently informed about the subject of intercultural communication to make those adaptations easily. The culturally competent communicator is not the person who insists that others adapt to his or her cultural preferences. Cultural competence requires that we remain open to understanding the perspectives of others and make whatever adaptations are necessary in order to encourage shared meaning.

Check for Context

Awareness of the context is always an important concern when considering what nonverbal behaviors will be most effective in communicating your meaning. Refusing to understand that certain behaviors are appropriate in some situations but not appropriate in others is the mark of a person who is either immature, naïve, or wholly self-absorbed. Although it may seem to you that basing judgment of others' characters or intentions on external factors such as clothing or behavior is unfair, these factors are important ways that we gather the information that enables us to interact with others—or to determine whether we wish to interact at all. In Chapter 2, we discussed the

DEVELOPING **SKILLS**
HOW TO READ OTHERS' NONVERBAL MESSAGES

Much of what we know about people we learn from their nonverbal communication. Wouldn't it be beneficial if we could more accurately interpret their nonverbal messages? Yes, but reading nonverbal messages isn't easy. In fact, most people—even experienced professionals—are only about 50 percent accurate when they try it (Ekman & O'Sullivan, 1991; Miller & Stiff, 1993). Training does help somewhat (Crews, et al., 2007), but even Joe Navarro, an ex-FBI agent who has spent his entire work-life detecting deception, says that people are no more than 60 percent accurate even with training at determining the reason for a person's nonverbal reactions (Navarro & Karlins, 2008).

According to Navarro, the most reliable nonverbal behaviors are those that come from the limbic part of the brain—the emotional center that relates to survival—and includes the freeze, flight, and fight responses. "They are hardwired into our nervous system, making them difficult to disguise or eliminate" (Navarro & Karlins, 2008, p. 23). An example would be jumping at a loud noise right behind you. Other freeze, flight, and fight examples that you may have noticed include:

- **Freezing responses** indicate definite discomfort and are shown by a sudden stopping motion especially if there was other previous motion such as jiggling a foot or tap-ping a pencil; suddenly interlocking the feet or ankles or pointing the toes inward; locking feet behind legs of chair and holding a stiff posture.

- **Flight postures** indicate that the person wants to go or is anticipating some type of action. Flight postures include pointing feet in a different direction than where the person is talking, one foot points forward but the other foot points to the left or right, putting weight on toes and off heels in a "starter" position, leaning away from a person or crossing legs to serve as a barrier, clasping the knees and leaning forward when sitting, removing hands from view.

- **Fight postures** or outward aggressive behaviors are less acceptable in society today and are often replaced by such nonverbal responses as rubbing your eye, entering another person's space, or arms akimbo, or leaning forward on spread fingertips while maintaining direct eye contact.

When we experience something that makes us feel uncomfortable, we use what Navarro calls *pacifying behaviors* that stimulate nerve endings and calm us (p. 35). In this chapter we call such behaviors *adaptors* (see p. 142).

Even if a person can control the freezing, flight, and fight reactions, it is unlikely that they can also control the pacifying behaviors they unconsciously use when they feel uncomfortable. When you see adaptors being used, something just before has stressed or caused the person to feel uncomfortable. Some possible pacifiers include:

- The need to light a cigarette, chew gum, or eat comfort food.

- Touching or stroking the nose or the neck below the Adam's apple; playing with a necklace or adjusting a tie.

- Rubbing or massaging the back of the neck, forehead, or cheek.

- Puffing out the cheeks or rubbing the inside of the mouth with the tongue.

- Taking deep breaths or repeated yawning.

- Rubbing the tops of legs when sitting.

- Lifting or flipping the hair to ventilate back of neck for women; running a finger around the shirt collar to ventilate the neck for men.

Nonverbal messages should be used carefully and be considered as potential clues to meaning, not as "the ultimate" answer. Practice recognizing and using some of the nonverbal responses mentioned earlier. For example, what might the nonverbal gestures and feet positions tell you about the men in the photo at the top of the page?

dangers of stereotyping but also pointed out the need to start with a "first best guess" about another person in order to guide our communication choices. It is doubtful that there are any among us who do not make judgments of these sorts, and, in fact, it would probably be foolhardy not to. As a competent nonverbal encoder, you must be aware of how the context should be used as a guide in making behavioral choices.

Check for Personal Differences

It is also crucial that you are aware of the receiver's needs and responses. This idea has already been implied in the previous three principles, but it deserves a more specific focus here. It is difficult for some people to accept the idea expressed earlier that "it isn't the message you intend to send that matters; it's the message that's received that matters." This idea is clearly one that reminds us that, if we are to share meaning, we must always take into account the other person.

Ask for Feedback

Finally, we recommend a skill that has appeared in various forms in earlier chapters of this text: *Request feedback*. If you are tuned in to what you are doing and how others are responding, there are likely to be times when you sense that the other person's response to you may be based on a misunderstanding of what you intended to communicate. Perhaps it is because of cultural or gender differences. Perhaps it is because of internal psychological noise within either you or your partner. Perhaps it is because of other aspects of your frames of reference.

At times, your request for feedback will be very much like a perception check. You may observe a quizzical expression on the other person's face in response to some nonverbal behavior on your part. You would start with a description of that observation, and then proceed to suggest two possible interpretations and ask for their perception. At other times, you may find yourself wondering how you "come across" to others. If you have a trusted friend whose opinion you value—and a relationship with that person that will not cause you to become defensive in the presence of honest, constructive feedback—perhaps you could receive useful information to help you identify areas for improvement.

The poet Robert Burns wrote in his poem "To a Louse" a verse that is familiar to most of us: "O would some power the gift to give us/ To see ourselves as others see us." Burns goes on to point out that seeing ourselves as others see us would free us from many blunders. Competent communicators recognize that no matter what we do or do not do, our behaviors do have the power to communicate. It is up to us to decide whether we are going to work to choose behaviors that convey to others the meanings we intend to send.

APPLY **WHAT YOU KNOW**
IMPROVING NONVERBAL ENCODING

Apply what you know about improving nonverbal encoding by answering the following questions:

- Do you think Marcie was aware of the nonverbal signals she was sending to Elena? If so, how do you know? If not, what suggestions would you give Marcie to improve her communication?

- Think of a personal instance where different cultural meanings caused nonverbal misunderstanding and briefly explain it; or describe an example from the media or politics where different cultural meanings caused nonverbal misunderstanding and briefly describe it. What nonverbal skill is needed to keep the misunderstanding from happening again?

NONVERBAL SKILLS **AND YOUR CAREER**

5.6 What nonverbal communication skills covered in this chapter relate specifically to your career.

The following *Spotlight on, Career Moment,* and *Connecting to* features take a look at how important nonverbal skills are in the workplace and specifically to careers related to business, education, and healthcare.

SPOTLIGHT ON **NONVERBAL COMMUNICATION**

BUSINESS

Nonverbal communication definitely plays an important role during a job interview. According to Alison Doyle (n.d.) in an article for *About.com*, the following nonverbal behaviors are important:

- Look the interviewer directly in the eyes.
- Smile when appropriate.
- Keep your tone of voice polite and even.
- Sit up straight but lean slightly forward to look interested.
- Show that you are listening and don't interrupt.
- Show a relaxed, calm, friendly attitude.
- Avoid chewing gum, having cold hands (warm them with hot water in the restroom right before the interview) or sweaty hands (wipe them with a tissue in your pocket), or smelling of cigarettes.

EDUCATION

Effective teachers know how to use immediacy behaviors—nonverbal communication to make students feel close to and liked by them. Immediacy behaviors include direct eye contact, smiling and nodding of the head, maintaining relaxed gestures and posture, standing close to the students rather than sitting behind a desk, and using an expressive, friendly vocal tone when speaking. Research has found the following positive results from using immediacy behaviors (Mottet, et al., 2007):

- Students tend to learn more and enjoy it more.
- Faculty evaluations are more positive.
- Instructors are judged as more effective teachers.
- Instructors are judged to be more competent, trustworthy, and caring even when their workload demands violate student expectations.

HEALTHCARE

Gladwell (2005a) summarized research dealing with malpractice lawsuits and determined that it is not the number of mistakes, the amount of information given to patients, or the knowledge level of the physician/surgeon that determines how likely they are to be sued. Instead, it is how well they use nonverbal communication when talking with their patients. Physicians who have never been sued:

- Spend more time with their patients (on an average just three minutes longer).
- Are liked by their patients and even laugh with them.
- Make "orienting" comments to let the patient know what will be covered in the visit.
- Show that they are listening with comments, eye contact, and facial expressions.
- Show respect for the patient by using a friendly tone of voice instead of a dominant tone.

CAREER MOMENT **NONVERBAL SKILLS AND YOUR CAREER**

When you are being interviewed for a position or for a promotion, first impressions are critical. In the same way, the first impressions you make when dealing with customers have a lot to do with your success in sales. Because first impressions are based mostly on nonverbal communication, nonverbal skills are essential to a successful career. Interviewers and customers pay attention to your appearance, handshake, eye contact, smile and facial expressions, posture, and friendliness—to name just a few nonverbal elements. Before you have even said a word, they have formed a first impression of you.

Are you a person who makes a good first impression, or do people have to get to know you before they form a positive impression of you? If you aren't sure, take the First Impressions

Quiz from Quintessential Careers (quintcareers.com). The link to the quiz is located at the end of this chapter in the *Skill Builders* section. If you are serious about your career, you may also want to take a communication course in nonverbal communication or interviewing if your college offers these courses. Not only will these courses look good on your resume, you will discover valuable skills to use throughout your career.

CONNECTING TO **BUSINESS**

Are you considering a business or professional career? Nonverbal behaviors are culture bound. We live in a time of increasing globalization, so it is important to become more aware of the ways in which nonverbal norms differ in business and political settings.

Hillary Elfenbein, in her research on intercultural nonverbal communication, focused on the ability to train people to improve their Emotion Recognition Accuracy (ERA) when looking at the facial expressions of others. In a recent study, Elfenbein (2006) found that, with training and feedback, subjects were able to improve their ERA.

ACTIVITY

- Pair up with a person from a culture different from your own or choose someone other than a classmate (a co-worker, neighbor, or student in another class).

- Explain to your partner that you will ask questions about his or her culture and periodically summarize your perception of the emotion they are communicating.

- If your partner is willing and interested, offer to reverse roles. When your partner offers an opinion about what your emotion is, be sure to ask what you were doing that caused him or her to form that impression.

- If possible, discuss with your partner what each of you has learned from this exercise.

CONNECTING TO **EDUCATION**

Are you considering a career in education? If so, you will want to learn to use effective nonverbal immediacy behaviors in the classroom. Immediacy behaviors increase the feeling of liking and closeness between you and your students and result in increased student involvement and satisfaction (see the *Spotlight* feature on p. 146).

Rester and Edwards (2007) found that there are often negative consequences to using excessively high levels of immediacy behaviors and that a student's interpretations of a teacher's immediacy behaviors vary according to the sex of the teacher and of the student and the setting of the interaction.

ACTIVITY Divide into small groups with others who are interested in education and consider the following:

- What nonverbal behaviors seem to be most important in communication between teachers and students?

- What constitutes "excessive" use of immediacy behaviors? How does the sex of the teacher and of the student make a difference in the appropriateness of such behaviors?

- How does the setting in which teacher-student communication takes place make a difference in the appropriate versus excessive use of immediacy behaviors?

- Do you think age makes some immediacy behaviors more or less appropriate? Give an example.

CONNECTING TO **HEALTHCARE**

If you are interested in healthcare, it is important to monitor your own and your patients' nonverbal messages. Lepper, et al. (1995) developed a model of four conditions: (1) Both (physician and patient) expect patient involvement; (2) Neither expects patient involvement; (3) Only the physician expects patient involvement; (4) Only the patient expects patient involvement.

When expectations of patients and practitioners differ, information exchanged is less complete, conflict may ensue, and patient adherence to treatment is diminished.

ACTIVITY Answer the following questions, either alone or working with a partner or small group:

- What sorts of nonverbal behaviors signal to a patient that the healthcare practitioner would like the patient to be actively involved in health decisions? Contrast those with behaviors that express the opposite expectation.

- What sorts of nonverbal behaviors signal to clinicians that the

patient desires involvement? Contrast those with behaviors that express the opposite expectation.

- Reflect on a recent medical visit in which you were a patient. How did nonverbal communication between you and the clinician affect that outcome?

▶ Log onto MyCommunicationLab.com to access Connecting to Psychology and Connecting to Science, Technology, Engineering, and Math—both with related activities.

CHAPTER SUMMARY

As this chapter has stressed, knowledge of nonverbal communication is required for successful communication. Use of nonverbal encoding is a skill that requires effort. Your relationships with family, friends, and colleagues are enhanced through your use of nonverbal communication. You can determine your knowledge of nonverbal communication by checking the skills and learning objectives presented in this chapter.

Summary of **SKILLS**

Check each skill that you now feel qualified to perform:

❏ I can pinpoint my strengths and weaknesses when it comes to using nonverbal communication in my everyday life and will work to minimize at least two weaknesses.

❏ I can identify the major categories and types of nonverbal communication and demonstrate improvement in using nonverbal behaviors that effectively support my verbal messages.

❏ I can explain the seven major functions of nonverbal communication (the 7 R's) and have identified two or three that need personal improvement.

❏ I can improve my own nonverbal communication by implementing several of the suggested nonverbal skills.

Summary of LEARNING **OUTCOMES**

5.1 *What is the key concept and definition of nonverbal communication?*

- The key concept of nonverbal communication is "You cannot *not* communicate."

- Nonverbal communication is defined as any symbolic behavior, other than written or spoken language, that is either intentionally or unintentionally sent, and is interpreted as meaningful by the receiver.

- It is important to remember that it isn't the message you intend to send that matters; it's the message that is received that counts.

5.2 *What makes nonverbal communication so important, and what is its nature?*

- Although language is extremely important to meaning, nonverbal communication is even more important. In fact, 65 to 70 percent of the meaning of a message comes from its nonverbal elements.

- On the other hand, the nature of nonverbal communication is often ambiguous (due to multiple meanings, uncertainty about intent, and cultural heritage) and our interpretations of it are often determined by our expectations, explained in the *Making Theory Practical* feature in this chapter.

5.3 *What are the basic categories of nonverbal communication and the types in each category?*

- There are six basic categories of nonverbal communication: kinesics, proxemics, haptics, chronemics, artifacts, and paralanguage.

- *Kinesics* or body language includes such types as eye contact, facial expression, posture, gestures, and body movement; *proxemics* or social distance includes such types as proxemics zones and territories; *haptics* includes

communicating through touch; *chronemics* includes our understanding of time; *artifacts* includes communication through artifacts we display for others; and *paralanguage* includes such types as pitch, rate, volume, vocal quality, and vocal fillers like "uh."

5.4 *What are the seven functions of nonverbal communication (each beginning with the letter "R"), and what is each function called?*

- The seven functions of nonverbal communication allow us to replace, repeat, reinforce, regulate, reveal, reverse, and reflect verbal messages.

- Gestures that replace messages are called *emblems*, that repeat a message are called *illustrators*, that reinforce a message are called *accentors*, that regulate messages are called *regulators*, that reveal emotions behind the messages are called *affect displays*, and that reflect unconscious needs are called *adaptors*.

5.5 *What are several suggestions for improving nonverbal encoding and monitoring your nonverbal skills?*

- Improving nonverbal encoding includes using self-monitoring; checking for cultural meanings, context, and personal differences; and asking for feedback.

- To find more on self-monitoring and other interesting topics from the chapter, use the *Developing Skills* feature in this chapter as a reference.

5.6 *What nonverbal communication skills covered in this chapter relate specifically to your career (see highlighted fields of business, education, and healthcare)?*

- The *Spotlight on, Career Moment*, and *Connecting to* features highlight the value of nonverbal communication in the fields of business, education, and healthcare.

SOLVE IT NOW!

Taking into consideration all that you learned about communication from this chapter, what advice would you give Elena in our opening scenario? *

• Do you think Elena presented her "bad" news in the correct manner? Why or why not?

• What specific nonverbal behaviors did Elena observe? Do you think she interpreted them correctly? Why or why not?

• What does expectancy violations theory say about the way Elena read the nonverbal reactions of her staff?

If you were Elena, would you accept what Marcie "said" about her feelings of the new rules, or would you put more credibility in her nonverbal "behaviors"? Explain your reasoning.

*(Check your answers with those located in MyCommunicationLab, Scenario Analysis for Chapter 5)

The next chapter will look at the role of interpersonal communication in the success or failure of our relationships.

KEY TERMS

accentors	p. 141	dialect	p. 139	haptics	p. 132	proxemics	p. 130
adaptors	p. 142	diction	p. 138	illustrators	p. 140	rate	p. 137
affect displays	p. 141	display rules	p. 128	kinesics	p. 127	regulators	p. 141
ambiguous	p. 124	emblems	p. 140	microexpressions	p. 128	self-monitoring	p. 143
artifacts	p. 135	eye contact	p. 127	nonverbal		territoriality	p. 132
chronemics	p. 133	facial expression	p. 128	communication	p. 122	vocal dysfluencies	p. 138
co-constructed	p. 121	fillers	p. 138	paralanguage	p. 136	vocal interferences	p. 138
contradictors	p. 141	gaze	p. 127	pitch	p. 136	vocal quality	p. 137
culture bound	p. 124	gestures	p. 129	posture	p. 129	volume	p. 137

SKILL BUILDERS

1. Use *Google* or one of the electronic databases available through your college library to search for Web sites and articles that contain information on cultural differences in nonverbal behaviors—begin with the search words *culture and nonverbal*. Be prepared to report at least one interesting finding to the class (especially if it differs from the information included in this chapter).

2. To determine whether you make a good first impression, take the *First Impressions Quiz* on the Quintessential Careers Web site at www.quintcareers.com/first_impressions_quiz. html. You can either take the quiz online and have it scored for you, or print off the 40 questions and use the First Impressions Quiz Scoring Guide prepared by Randall S. Hansen. If you score 80 or above, you make a great first impression; a score of 60–79 means you are all right but need to stand out more; a score under 60 means you are not making a good first impression, and work is needed. Use the guidelines in this chapter to improve your nonverbal skills and improve your first impressions.

3. If you are fortunate enough to have *MyCommunicationLab* bundled with your text (or have decided to purchase it as an add-on), check out the many features of Allyn & Bacon's online site that will help you throughout the course:

• *Access to the ebook* (online version) of this text.

• *Pre- and post-test practice quizzes* that record your scores and direct you to the appropriate sections in the ebook to reread content on any missed questions.

• *Research sources* to augment your school's databases and help you with speech topics.

• *Help with your speeches,* including topic selection, organization, and source citations using MLA, APA, or other style sheets for mistake-free source citations.

6 Building Interpersonal Relationships

After studying this chapter you should be able to . . .

- Determine where your relationships fall on a continuum from impersonal to interpersonal communication and adjust them as needed.
- Identify your inclusion, control, and openness needs; evaluate whether your interpersonal relationships are fulfilling those needs; and adjust your personal relationships if needed.
- Improve your interpersonal relationships by gathering needed information, developing conversation principles, and using appropriate self-disclosure.
- Build and enhance successful interpersonal relationships at home and at work by applying the communication tips provided from at least one of the theories covered in this chapter.

CHAPTER SUMMARY 〉 P. 173

SCENARIO

Jared was confused. At first, he had not been drawn to Alicia. They had little in common, their cultural backgrounds were different, and, based on her comments in class, they held wildly opposing political beliefs. Now he realized she was very intelligent and had a wicked sense of humor, and he admired her for always critically evaluating issues before she formed an opinion—even when their opinions diverged.

The first time they had had an opportunity to talk one-on-one instead of within a group was the night they agreed to meet at a local coffee shop to put the finishing touches on a joint presentation for their Contemporary Political Rhetoric class. Their meeting began with some good-natured teasing about his "bleeding-heart liberalism" and her "heartless conservatism." The conversation turned to the factors that had contributed to the development of their political stances, and from there to each talking about family background and personal experiences. Even though he normally talked very little in one-on-one situations due to high feelings of anxiety, Jared found himself telling Alicia, in great detail, about an event that had adversely affected his family and caused him a great deal of pain. He appreciated how empathically she had listened, and her attention may have inspired him to say more than he really intended. In fact, it was right after his disclosure that Alicia mentioned how late it was getting and that she still had homework to complete.

Their class presentation had gone well, but when Jared suggested afterward that they go out and celebrate, Alicia had declined. She explained, with what had appeared to be great sincerity, that she would "really love to" but that she had a major chemistry exam the following day. They had been in class two more times since then, and, in both cases, Alicia had barely acknowledged his presence. She always seemed to be absorbed with taking notes, and, when class ended, she was among the first to rush out. Jared wondered if she was ignoring him and, if so, why, or did she simply have something pressing after class each day.

He had never divulged to anyone the painful personal experience he had shared with Alicia at the coffee shop, and he had genuinely thought that their conversation had been the start of a different sort of relationship. What had he done wrong?

Few things bring as much joy to us as an authentically high-quality interpersonal relationship, and few things are as painful as a failing one or personal anxiety that makes relationships difficult to achieve. As you read the information on relationships in this chapter, see if you can analyze Jared's problem in the opening scenario and determine what communication goals might help him manage his anxiety in order to understand and improve his relationship with Alicia.

SOLVE IT NOW! ⟩ P. 174 ⟩

Think of your previous relationships. Which ones brought you joy and which ones caused you pain? Do you think relationships are worth the effort? At this point, Jared may be thinking that they aren't.

When we look at relationships, we are looking at patterns of communication. Effective communication is the fuel that drives the development and maintenance of relationships, and ineffective communication is a significant factor—usually the most significant factor—in the disintegration of a relationship. In this chapter, we will discuss how and why we engage in interpersonal relationships and explore some guidelines for building and enhancing satisfying relationships. In the next chapter, we will examine how relationships develop and learn some *do's* and *don'ts* for handling interpersonal conflict. These two chapters are by no means an exhaustive treatment of these subjects but are an introduction to a topic that is relevant to us all. Interpersonal relationships are, after all, at the center of our lives.

Interpersonal Communication

LEARNING **OBJECTIVE**

6.1 What is the definition of interpersonal communication, and what are the differences between impersonal and interpersonal communication?

We often overlook the importance of communication in the management of interpersonal relationships until something goes awry. When a relationship is going well, most people are not conscious of making choices in their communication behaviors. When trouble looms, however, they become acutely aware that "things aren't working so well" and realize that communication may be at fault. If, like Jared in the opening scenario, you have anxiety when communicating interpersonally, retake the PRCA presented in Chapter 1 (see *Skill Builder #2* at the end of this chapter for more on this assessment) and identify specific communication skills from this chapter that might help you gain confidence in relationships.

General Definition

So what exactly is **interpersonal communication?** It is the exchange of verbal and nonverbal symbols in order to initiate, develop, and maintain (as well as terminate) relationships between people who relate to each other as unique individuals. When communication scholars examine interpersonal communication, they usually focus on the **dyad**, meaning that they are particularly interested in what happens in one-on-one communication. This does not mean that interpersonal communication is not taking place among groups of three or more close friends. It simply means that the most fruitful way to look at the dynamics of interpersonal communication, even in larger groups, is to study the situation as a series of multiple dyads in interaction with each other.

Impersonal versus Interpersonal Communication

Not all dyadic communication is interpersonal; there is a distinction between interpersonal and impersonal communication. Interpersonal communication, as the definition above points out, occurs when people relate to each other as unique individuals—no formal roles are involved, just direct, person-to-person communication. By contrast, in **impersonal communication**, the people involved relate to each other only as the occupiers of the roles or positions they hold. For example, communication between shoppers and clerks seldom moves beyond the impersonal. It is helpful to think of these two types of communication as falling along a continuum with *impersonal*

Figure 6.1 Impersonal versus Interpersonal Conversation between Student and Professor

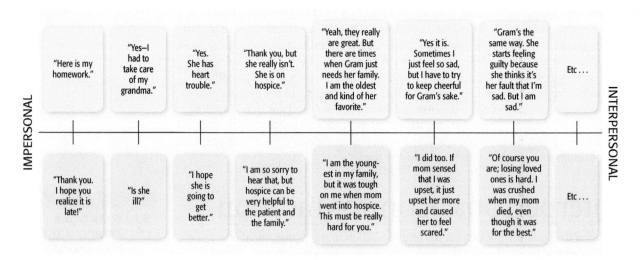

communication on the left side of the midpoint and *interpersonal communication* on the right, as the conversation between a student and professor in **Figure 6.1** illustrates.

If you want to build a quality interpersonal relationship, it is important to know the difference between impersonal and interpersonal communication. Impersonal comments aren't the building blocks needed for a relationship; interpersonal comments are. As you can tell by noticing all the failed relationships around you, building a relationship takes skills that begin with knowing what kind of comments to make. You will probably note from the student–professor interaction that fully interpersonal communication has not yet occurred. The conversation became more interpersonal as the professor and student discussed the impact of their relatives' illnesses. More personal information is yet to be disclosed, as indicated by the boxes with "Etc. . . ." It is important to recognize that the relationship between this teacher and student cannot be characterized as genuinely interpersonal until their interactions consistently involve such depth of disclosure. Most student–teacher relationships do not move to such intensely interpersonal levels, although exceptions do occur. The book *Tuesdays with Morrie* (Albom, 1997) illustrates a deep interpersonal relationship that endured between the author Mitch Albom and his beloved professor to the end of the professor's life.

APPLY WHAT YOU KNOW
IMPERSONAL COMMUNICATION

Now that you see the difference between impersonal and interpersonal communication, check your understanding by answering the following questions:

- Was the communication between Jared and Alicia impersonal or interpersonal? How do you know? Was it the same for both students?

- Does this concept shed any light on Jared's problem? Why or why not?

- In what situations do you typically use impersonal communication; in what situations do you typically communicate interpersonally? Give a specific example of each. How do you determine when each is appropriate?

Interpersonal Relationships: Getting Needs Met

Interpersonal levels of communication are required to develop interpersonal relationships, but the question arises: Why do we bother to form such relationships? The answer: To get our needs met and to gain personal rewards.

Personal Needs and Wants

Although the idea of forming relationships in order to satisfy needs may seem cynical, it is a major reason we develop and continue in relationships. It is also the reason we end relationships. We may not be aware of a specific need as we enter into a relationship, but if we look at what drives our decisions to stay in or get out of relationships, we will see that the underlying issue is **need**. William Schutz, in his concept called **FIRO-B** (1958; 1992), suggests three basic interpersonal needs: inclusion, control, and openness (which Schutz originally called *affection*). **Inclusion** is the need to feel that we belong and need to interact with others. **Control** refers to the need to feel that we have some influence over our own lives as well as the lives of others. **Openness** is the need for emotional connection with others by disclosing our inner thoughts and feelings.

Schutz points out that while we all have three needs, we do not all have the same degree of need for each. The levels may vary somewhat depending on the situation. The particular combination of our own levels of need for inclusion, control, and openness comprise our "fundamental interaction and relationship orientation," and our "behaviors" are related to that orientation. (Hence, the acronym for Schutz's concept: FIRO-B.) In other words, we each have a basic approach to how we relate to other people, and this approach is expressed in our communicative verbal and nonverbal behaviors.

In order for people to respond to each other's interpersonal inclusion, control, or openness needs, they must recognize what those needs are. For example, communication would be difficult if you were a person needing a great deal of solitude, but your relational partner needed a high level of interaction with others. On the other hand, if you both had the same levels of control, you would either be competing for control or finding that there was no one to take control. In the same way, it would be difficult to find pleasure in the company of another if you liked openness and wanted to disclose feelings, but your partner was a withholder who felt uncomfortable with such displays. To determine your inclusion, control, and openness levels, take the survey in the *Developing Skills* feature on page 156.

To better understand your scores from the survey, let's take a more detailed look at each interpersonal need: inclusion, control, and openness.

Inclusion Needs (Extrovert–Introvert)

If you have high inclusion needs (a score of 0–7 on the survey on page 156), you are referred to as an **extrovert**. If your inclusion needs are low (a score of 23–30), you are called an **introvert**. If you are somewhere in the middle with characteristics of both (a score of 8–22), you are referred to as an **ambivert** (**Figure 6.2**).

LEARNING OBJECTIVE

6.2 How does a person's desire to get needs met relate to interpersonal relationships? What is meant by inclusion, control, openness, and contradictory needs; and which theory offers insight into needs fulfillment?

People have three basic needs—inclusion, control, and openness—in varying degrees.

DEVELOPING SKILLS
HOW TO DETERMINE YOUR NEEDS

Have you considered how your personal needs control your behaviors with others—especially in a close relationship? To determine your three basic interpersonal needs, take the following survey.*

Directions: On a scale of 0, 1, 2, 3, 4, 5, 6 rate yourself on how well the following statements describe you from **0** (does not describe me at all) to **6** (totally describes me).

Survey: **Score:**

1. I seldom engage in conversations or activities with people in groups. _____
2. I certainly don't seek to become a group member or participate in group activities. _____
3. I might participate in an activity with one or two friends, but only if asked. _____
4. I feel very uncomfortable around groups and prefer being alone to being in a large group. _____
5. If forced to participate in groups in a classroom or job setting, I would try to transfer to another class or job. If impossible, I would drop the class or quit the job. _____
6. I would never volunteer for a position that requires making decisions or taking charge. _____
7. If asked to take the primary leadership role, I would definitely decline. _____
8. If asked, I might work with someone on a project as long as the other person was in charge. _____
9. I am more comfortable being a follower than being a leader. _____
10. If my job required taking a leadership role, I would find another job. _____
11. I would never volunteer to share my thoughts or feelings with others. _____
12. I see no advantage to sharing thoughts and feelings with others unless the person is a really close friend. _____
13. I might share a thought with someone I know well, but only if asked. _____
14. I am more comfortable listening to other people's ideas and feelings than sharing my own. _____
15. If a class or job required sharing feelings, I would find a different class or job. _____

Scoring directions:

1 Your total for numbers 1–5 are an indication of your inclusion needs with a total of 0–7 indicating characteristics common to those with high inclusion needs (extrovert) and a total of 23–30 indicating characteristics common to those with low inclusion needs (introvert).

2 Your total for numbers 6–10 are an indication of your control needs with a total of 0–7 indicating characteristics common to those with high control needs (dominant) and a total of 23–30 indicating characteristics common to those with low control needs (submissive).

3 Your total for numbers 11–15 are an indication of your openness needs with a total of 0–7 indicating characteristics common to those with high openness needs (discloser) and a total of 23–30 indicating characteristics common to those with low openness needs (withholder).

4 A total of 8–22 indicates more moderate inclusion, control, or openness needs which may mean that you tend to be flexible and find it easier to communicate with and accept others.

Use this survey to identify possible strengths and problem areas. You may wish to apply the interpersonal techniques discussed in this and the next chapter to any problem areas you uncover.

* NOTE: This survey is an indicator of your inclusion, control, and openness needs but is different from Shutz's 54-question FIRO-B. This 15-item scale created by your authors is not an official scale, has not been checked for reliability, and should be used only as an indicator of possible needs.

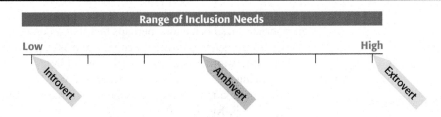

Figure 6.2 Inclusion Needs

Although you can estimate where you would fall on this continuum by your scores from the survey on page 156, it may interest you to know that there are several personality tests, including the Myers-Briggs Type Indicator (MBTI), that are used to measure more specifically where a person lies on the inclusion spectrum. Being at either extreme is regarded as unhealthy: the extreme extrovert would be incapable of being alone while the extreme introvert would be a recluse—neither of which is conducive to good social relationships. Although there is no "best" type of person to be, many cultures value extroversion, as shown in the following studies:

- Sloan, et al. (2004) found that 61% of college students at an American university studying to be elementary school teachers were extroverts.

- In a study of Malaysian university students, Ishak, et al. (2002) found that 83 percent of those majoring in law or administration were extroverts while 63 percent of engineering majors were extroverts.

- On the other hand, a study by Wu, et al. (2007) found that 43 percent of Chinese applicants to a dental school were found to be extroverts, and 57 percent were introverts.

It may be to one's advantage to be an ambivert because people who blend both types may find it easier to be comfortable in relationships with either extroverts or introverts. However, the real issue is this: *Whichever you are, do your communication behaviors enable you to consistently get your needs met?*

Your behaviors are the means by which you express your needs. If you think about the behaviors that are expected of extroverts and introverts in American culture (**Figure 6.3**), you will see some real differences (adapted from Knapp & Daly, 2002).

If you want to be more inclusive and less introverted, a good first step is to venture into social situations with a friend. You cannot gain communication skills without being in social settings, any more than you could learn to swim without going into the

Behaviors of Introverts	Behaviors of Extroverts
Wait to be spoken to; avoid self-disclosure	Initiate conversations; disclose about self
Prefer small groups; quiet environments	Enjoy crowds; noisy environments
Enjoy being alone	Prefer being with people
Ask questions only when really interested	Ask questions to show interest in others
Answer questions in brief, token manner	Answer questions in detail
Use less mutual, sustained eye contact	Engage in mutual, sustained eye contact
Use muted facial and vocal expressions	Use animated facial and vocal expressions
Use small gestures	Use large gestures
Avoid entering other's personal space	Enter into other's personal space
Move if others enter their personal space	Allow others into their personal space
Experience fairly high speech anxiety	Experience fairly low speech anxiety

Figure 6.3 Behaviors of Introverts vs. Extroverts

"Do you mind if I say something helpful about your personality?"

water. Once there, make a concerted effort to practice appropriate social behaviors, perhaps focusing on one or two at a time, such as direct eye contact and asking questions. Another strategy is to plan ahead by practicing good conversation-openers on page 163.

When talking with introverts, here are three valuable tips (Pawlik-Kienlen, 2007):

- Schedule a time—this allows the introvert to prepare his or her thoughts, especially if the topic is a big or important one.

- Use nonverbal communication to communicate— for example, touching the hand, patting the shoulder, or even giving a kiss on the cheek.

- Don't interrupt once the other person begins talking—the distraction may cause him or her to leave.

Control Needs (Dominant–Submissive)

The unsuccessful negotiation of control needs will doom most relationships, no matter how successfully other needs are met. Using your scores from the *Developing Skills* feature on page 156, we term those who are high in their need for control (a score of 0–7) as **dominant** and those whose control needs are low (a score of 23–30) as **submissive** (**Figure 6.4**).

Being at either extreme is regarded as unhealthy: the extreme extrovert (called an *autocrat*) would require total personal control while the extreme introvert (called an *abdicrat*) would abdicate or "give up" all control. When control is related to cultures, the term *power distance* is used. Cultures with a high power distance, such as Arab and Latin American countries, the Philippines, Malaysia, and India, "accept the unequal distribution of power as normal" (Littlejohn & Foss, 2008, p. 173). Dominance is expected from some members, and other members of the culture are expected to be submissive, or at least to exhibit submissive behaviors. In countries with low power distance, such as Poland, New Zealand, and the United States, people are less likely to take a submissive role and more likely to search for equality and appreciate empowerment practices (Marchese, 2001).

Keep in mind, though, that while behaviors are important, we are talking here about needs. Just as a shy person may actually wish to be included, so some people who typically behave in submissive ways may still desire some measure of control over their lives. However, the key question remains: *Wherever you fall on the control continuum, do your verbal and nonverbal behaviors enable you to consistently get your needs met?* Remember that your behaviors signal to others what your needs are and indicate how you would like others to respond to you.

Figure 6.4 Control Needs

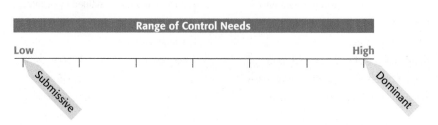

Range of Control Needs

Low   High

Submissive   Dominant

Openness Needs (Discloser–Withholder)

People who have a high need for openness (a survey score of 0–7) are termed **disclosers** while those whose need for openness is low (a score of 23–30) are called **withholders** (see **Figure 6.5**). To determine where you stand, refer to your scores in the preceding *Developing Skills* feature.

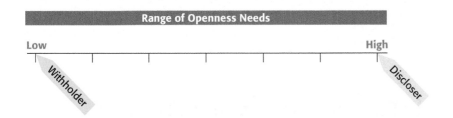

Range of Openness Needs

Low · · · · · · High

Withholder

Discloser

Figure 6.5 Openness Needs

Withholding observations, feelings, and thoughts not only hampers the growth of relationships, it is also not good for your mental health (Petrie, et al, 1998). As with inclusion and control, neither end of the openness continuum is as healthy as more moderate levels. Both extreme disclosure and extreme withholding make others feel uncomfortable and make it difficult to get your needs and wants met. A moderate amount of disclosure is recommended in most relationships and usually produces more satisfaction (Daft & Marcic, 2006; Petronio, 1991).

If you wish someone to be open with you, begin by disclosing an observation, feeling, or thought. The other person will likely disclose an observation, feeling, or thought back to you—disclosure tends to be reciprocal (Kreps, 1990). Your first disclosures will probably be fairly impersonal, but, as the relationship grows, the disclosures will become more personal.

Although this man enjoys cooking alone, he also has the contradictory need of being with others.

Contradictory Needs (Dialectics)

Although inclusion, control, and openness are significant factors that we may desire at times and that certainly affect how we communicate in relationships, there are times we may prefer their opposites. Sometimes we want to be alone; sometimes we prefer others to take control; and sometimes we prefer to withhold disclosures. This interplay of contradictory needs (i.e., I want closeness but I want my own space; I want to be known as "we" but I need to be "me") is referred to as **dialectical tension** (Baxter & Montgomery, 1996; Thompson, 2000). You can see how this tension complicates getting our needs met. In close relationships, we expect our relational partner to "know" what we need—yet we may have conflicting needs and may not be sure of them either. This makes predicting attitudes and behaviors of others difficult and increases our feelings of uncertainty. It should be clear that in order to have a solid and satisfying interpersonal relationship, the needs of both parties must be taken into consideration. It is often challenging to find ways to communicate so that you can accomplish that goal. Understanding the complexity of human needs is but one step toward meeting that communication challenge.

APPLY **WHAT YOU KNOW**
SIGNALING YOUR NEEDS

Demonstrate your knowledge of needs by completing the following:

- Imagine that you are in a relationship in which the other person makes most of the major decisions. Although this arrangement was fine while you were going to college full-time, now that you have only one semester left, you want to take more control of the everyday decisions. You realize that

your behavior in the past has signaled submission; what steps can you take to more accurately convey your true needs without alienating your partner?

- Under what circumstances might a person with high control needs choose to consistently use submissive behaviors? Can you think of an actual case to illustrate your view?

LEARNING **OBJECTIVE**

6.3 How does a person's desire to gain rewards and minimize costs relate to interpersonal relationships, and which theory offers insight into rewards and costs?

Interpersonal Relationships: Gaining Rewards and Minimizing Costs

Getting our interpersonal needs met is not the only reason we establish relationships. We also engage in interpersonal relationships to gain rewards and minimize costs. A look at Thibaut and Kelley's **social exchange theory** (1959; summarized in Roloff, 1981) will give you a good insight into how this concept affects your decisions to stay in or get out of relationships.

According to Thibaut and Kelley, the issue of rewards and costs affects our decisions to initiate, develop, and maintain relationships. In fact, human relationships are very much like economic relationships. In economics, each party possesses resources that the other desires. If you crave a latte, there is a sales assistant somewhere who would be glad to supply it for a price. If the latte tastes good, your exchange was successful; you would both be glad to engage in a similar transaction in the future. So it is with relationships. You possess certain "resources" that are desired by another person, and that person possesses resources that you find attractive. Your relationship, then, in part is based on the exchange of resources.

If this seems a calculating way to look at relationships, consider your own relationships for a moment. What rewards do you receive from being in these relationships? For example, being in an interpersonal relationship might offer you companionship, financial security, status, affection, information, personal validation, access to other relationships, and a host of other benefits that you value. At the same time, as Thibaut and Kelley point out, there are also costs associated with being in relationships. Time, money, privacy, freedom, loss of status, and loss of other relationships are just a few of the sacrifices you might make in order to sustain a relationship. As long as you perceive that the rewards are greater than or at least equal to the costs, you will find the relationship to be reasonably satisfying. However, if you perceive that the costs exceed the rewards, you will most likely choose to downscale or terminate the relationship.

There are times when you might tolerate temporary costly periods with the belief that rewards will follow. For example, as the spouse of a graduate student, you might be willing to endure several years of financial struggle, additional household responsibilities, and loneliness because of the hope that, once the degree is in hand, life as a couple will be easier and the rewards many. However, when a relationship is more costly than rewarding to either partner, especially when improvement seems unlikely, chances are the relationship will not last.

There are some exceptions, of course. You may know someone who has remained in a relationship despite repeated instances of physical, sexual, emotional, or psychological abuse. Consider the victim of domestic abuse. Perhaps the person perceives one or more of the following rewards for staying in the relationship: keeping the family intact for the children, having financial security, not having to find a job with no career skills, not risking the disapproval of family or religion, or not having to face the unknown. In many cases, *the perceived reward for staying in a relationship is greater than the perceived cost of getting out.* It is not until something transpires to force a reevaluation of the reward/cost ratio that the victim is finally able to summon the courage to leave.

Most of the time, we do not consciously think of our relationships as a balancing of rewards and costs, particularly when all seems to be going well. However, if you have found yourself in the middle of a troubled time in a relationship, you may recall asking yourself, "Is this relationship worth it?" Essentially, at that moment, you were mentally assessing the reward/cost ratio. Using social exchange theory is one way we can assess why we choose to be in some relationships and not in others.

APPLY **WHAT YOU KNOW**
REWARDS VERSUS COSTS

Now that you are aware of the rewards-versus-costs concept presented by social exchange theory, consider these questions:

- If you had a friend who was a victim of domestic abuse, do you think helping him or her think through the reward/cost aspects of the relationship would be helpful? Why or why not?

- It's easy to say that each of us has a moral and legal obligation to report child abuse to local authorities, but how can we be sure that it really is child abuse and not a different type of parent-child relationship than we are used to or think is best? Google *reporting child abuse* to find related Web sites with valuable information and be prepared to share it with your classmates.

Gathering Information and Using Effective Conversation

You have spotted someone who appears to be a viable candidate for a relationship; however, you know little-to-nothing about the person and are uncertain whether the two of you would be compatible. What should you do? First, you would gather information to reduce uncertainty; then you would engage in good conversation.

Gathering Information to Reduce Uncertainty

Before you initiate relationships with others, you need to gather enough information to reduce uncertainty about them and be able to predict their actions and behaviors. According to **uncertainty reduction theory,** when people search for information to reduce uncertainty, they are likely to use three strategies (Berger & Calabrese, 1975; Berger, 1997). Have you used any of these?

- **Passive strategy** Initially, most people will adopt a passive strategy, sitting back and observing, noting how the person customarily interacts with others. If you like what you see, you may expand your observation to watch the person in a different setting in order to gather additional information.

- **Active strategy** Your next step might be an active strategy of soliciting information from people who are acquainted with the person. Do their impressions match yours?

LEARNING **OBJECTIVE**

6.4 How does gathering information about a person reduce relationship uncertainty; how does effective conversation improve interpersonal relationships; and what are some conversational principles and openers?

If not, why might their impressions differ? You might also use the Internet and Google the person to see if they have pages on *Facebook* or *MySpace*. How people describe themselves can be very enlightening.

- **Interactive strategy** Eventually you will be ready to employ an interactive strategy where you engage the person in conversation to find out for yourself if the potential exists for a rewarding relationship. What you learn from interacting with someone will ultimately be more important than what you learn from observation or from others.

Using these three strategies to gather information should help you reduce uncertainty in two ways. First, the more you know about people the better able you will be to make predictions about their future behavior. Second, gathering information about people will help you understand why they behave as they do. For more specifics on uncertainty reduction theory see the *Making Theory Practical* feature in Chapter 10.

Once you have gathered enough information to decide you would like to get to know a certain person better, the next step is to initiate a conversation with them. And sometimes initiating and conducting a conversation can be intimidating.

Using Effective Conversation

If you aren't naturally gifted in the art of conversation, remember that the most important thing is to listen. Think about the best conversationalists you know. What sets them apart? Isn't it their ability to listen more than what they say? As you will recall from Chapter 3, good listening is marked by effective use of questions and paraphrases. Therefore, when you hear conversational partners say something that suggests a logical probe, use it to get them to elaborate. The probe may take the form of either a question or a paraphrase. "You seem to be really familiar with that band. How many times have you heard them?" "It sounds like you basically have no allegiance to any particular football team, but you like to collect the shirts." By listening and responding with questions and paraphrases, you draw the other person out and exhibit your interest.

Conversational Principles

Using probes and questions while listening is a vital skill for generating good conversation; however, since no one enjoys being interrogated, eventually you will be expected to provide information about yourself and your interests as well. Grice's **conversational principles** (Arundale, 2005; Grice, 1975; Littlejohn & Foss, 2008) state that effective contributions to the conversational dialogue must meet the following criteria:

- Contributions must have *quality*—meaning that they must be truthful; not deceptive, false, or manipulative. Although it may take time to realize that the other person's contribution contains deception, once suspected, your perception of the speaker will change and conversation will likely end.

- Contributions must have *quantity*—meaning that there must be enough information to be judged effective without having so much that it overwhelms the other person. For example, self-disclosure that is too personal or detailed is not appropriate for most conversations and will usually make the other person uncomfortable. On the other hand, if you are asked a question and your response is comprised of only a few words, this will likely bring an end to the conversation.

- Contributions must have *relevancy*—meaning that it is not acceptable to abruptly switch to a new and unrelated topic. In the ebb and flow of conversation, new topics will be introduced, but they should emerge from the previous topic. If however, a conversation takes a turn that is uncomfortable, and you want to change the subject, it is less obtrusive to return to a previous topic than it is to suddenly jump to one that is unrelated to anything that has gone before. Saying, "You mentioned earlier that . . ." is a more natural way to change the topic than it would be to respond to a critical remark about your favorite political figure by saying, "Say, do you know what our next assignment will be?" (There may be exceptions to this rule, however. If your intent is to signal clearly, though indirectly, that the developing topic is uncomfortable to you, but you wish to defuse the moment in a humorous way, a well-timed "How about those Cubbies!" may be effective. Times do change, but the old maxim about avoiding discussions of sex, religion, and politics until the relationship is well enough developed to support those topics is probably always going to be good advice.)

- Conversations must have *manner*—meaning they should be organized and clear; not ambiguous. However, if the previous comment or question is considered to be too personal to answer or might hurt the person's feelings, it is possible to indicate this indirectly in your comment. For example, suppose you were asked what grade you made on the midterm exam by a person who tells you she made a "D." Although you missed only one question on the exam, you reply, "Oh, it was better than I made on the last exam" or "Oh, you know what they say about people who discuss grades or politics."

Anytime you violate one of these maxims, be sure to do so in a way that shows that you still intend to be cooperative and are still interested in the conversation.

Conversation Openers While adhering to the principles above, here are some suggested conversation openers.

- An honest compliment (about something the person is wearing or a beautiful or different hair style) but not a corny compliment such as, "Your eyes look like pearls."

- References to the event or place you are in, such as, "I see you are wearing a Rams t-shirt. Do you think the Rams have a chance to make it to the Super Bowl this year?"

- A current topic in the news (Olympics, bus crash, etc.) but not something personal, such as which political candidate the person favors.

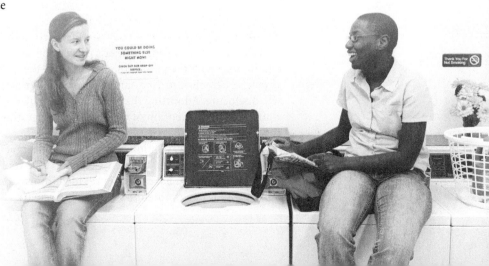

- Where the person is from ("Are you a native of this area?"), but watch for facial expressions that might show that the topic is too personal.

- Reference to the weather (if it is unusual); the person's major field of study (if she or he is a college student); a favorite singer, movie, teacher or hobby (if something the person said earlier makes this appropriate).

- Suggested ways to lead into the preceding questions were adapted from Peck (1996):

That was interesting. Tell me more about . . .	What is your viewpoint on . . .
Based on your experience, what do you think about . . .	Have you ever been . . .
	I was interested in knowing how you . . .
How do you feel about . . .	I am really impressed with . . .
I was wondering if you know . . .	I'd like to hear your feelings about . . .
With your background . . .	How are you connected with . . .

APPLY **WHAT YOU KNOW**
UNCERTAINTY REDUCTION AND SUCCESSFUL CONVERSATIONS

Now that you have a good idea of how to use uncertainty reduction and initiate conversations, check your understanding by completing the following:

- Evaluate how Jared used uncertainty reduction in developing his relationship with Alicia. Which strategies did he use and how effective were they?

- Which conversation principle and conversation opener would improve your conversations the most? Give an example to support your answer.

LEARNING **OBJECTIVE**
6.5 What is self-disclosure; what are some suggestions for improving self-disclosure; and which theory offers insight into self-disclosure?

Improving Self-Disclosure

If your initial conversation develops into one that is rather lengthy, and certainly if you continue to interact in later conversations, you will eventually find the need to engage in some degree of **self-disclosure**, or revelation of personal information about yourself to others. Although self-disclosure was mentioned earlier as one of our basic needs, it warrants a more thorough discussion.

True Self-Disclosure

Not all statements about yourself are included in the concept of self-disclosure. It is the level of risk to your partner's perception of you and, therefore, to your relationship with the person that determines the degree to which your message rates as true self-disclosure. Announcing that you like action movies or Thai food is not self-disclosure. Admitting that you have a predilection for Thai food may affect your partner's perception of you, possibly suggesting to some people that you are adventurous, but it is unlikely to have any significant effect on your relationship. Additionally, your revelation must be a conscious act for it to rise to the level of true self-disclosure. If you accidentally let it slip that you got your term paper from an Internet site, you have clearly provided information about yourself that is significant, but an unintentional revealing remark is not true self-disclosure either.

Comments that include some personal risk would be considered true self-disclosure. A comment such as, "I really appreciated your speech on the effects of cancer. I had cancer two years ago and experienced some of the effects you mentioned," includes some risk because personal comments disturb some people.

Self-Disclosure and Culture/ Gender/Technology/Ethics

Culture, gender, technology, and ethics all play a role in our disclosures. Let's take a brief look at each factor.

Culture
If you have had the interpersonal experience of communicating with people from a different culture, especially if you don't speak their language, you know that reducing uncertainty requires a great deal of information. Getting that information can be quite exhausting and even may seem impossible. According to Igor Klyukanov (2005), "We must acknowledge uncertainty as an unavoidable aspect of intercultural communication and, because it is unavoidable, deal with it" (p. 42). He goes on to note that creativity can arise from uncertainty as well as intolerance and prejudice.

Obviously, self-disclosure is a behavior that is culture bound. Some cultures are categorized as "open" cultures because the people in those cultures favor talking openly and candidly about self, even when the subject of discussion is highly personal. America is one of those cultures; in fact, Americans are among the most "open" people on the planet. American media question celebrities about their personal flaws, and the public feels that it has a right to know. Even average citizens are willing to volunteer information on television about their reactions to a tragedy—something that would be regarded as an invasion of privacy in many other cultures. People in more relatively "closed" cultures, such as Asian cultures, feel that disclosure is not needed. For example, Chinese people consider self-disclosure to be in poor taste, and Japanese people are unlikely to disclose true feelings that might offend another since saving face is so important (Caputo, et al, 2000). For more on the importance of saving face, see the *Making Theory Practical* feature on page 166.

Gender
Men and women differ in both the amount and the types of self-disclosure with which they feel comfortable in everyday interaction (Wood & Inman, 1993). Women regard self-disclosure as a necessary factor in the development and maintenance of friendships. They are willing to divulge personal information more readily than men (Riessman, 1990) in face-to-face situations and on the Internet (Punyanunt-Carter, 2006). Men, on the other hand, favor shared activities as the primary means by which they form friendships. Men are less likely to talk to other men about personal issues, especially those that might cause them to feel emotionally vulnerable. Perhaps because they know that women are generally more comfortable with the language of emotions, most men do realize that intimate relationships require some measure of self-disclosure. However, even in intimate relationships, men may find it easier to self-disclose as a part of or after a shared activity.

Technology
The most obvious technology that relates to disclosure and interpersonal relationships is use of the Internet and CMC (computer-mediated communication). Consider the following research results (Antheunis et al, 2007; Barak & Gluck-Ofri, 2007; McKenna & Bargh, 2000; Walther et al, 2001):

MAKING THEORY **PRACTICAL**
FACE NEGOTIATION THEORY

In Japan, the presentation of a business card is a significant event, requiring the use of both hands.

When you speak to people, are you concerned with allowing them to save face?

How do you feel when someone betters you but gives you no way to save face?

Saving face is of greater concern for some cultures than others. Individualistic/low-context cultures, such as the United States and Great Britain, are less concerned with saving face for themselves or others because face is usually determined by personal achievements. On the other hand, for collectivistic/high-context cultures, such as Japan and China, face—which is derived from honor of the family, organization, or team rather than personal honor—is considered a virtue (see Chapter 1 for more details on individualism and context). Stella Ting-Toomey and her colleagues developed the *face negotiation theory* as a way to predict how different cultures go about the process of saving face (1985, 1988).

Theorist

According to theorist Stella Ting-Toomey, saving face involves "communicative behaviors that people use to regulate their social identity and to support or challenge the other's social dignity" (Ting-Toomey & Kurogi, 1998,

p. 188). Therefore, "face" refers to an individual's image of self-respect in the eyes of others, and "facework" refers to the process of managing face—creating and protecting your own face; supporting or challenging the face of others. Ting-Toomey identifies two types of facework (Littlejohn & Foss, 2008, p. 173):

• *Preventive facework*—"involves communication designed to protect a person from feelings that threaten personal or group face." For example, when approaching a group to make a request, you might say: "Excuse me. I am so sorry to interrupt you—I can see you are hard at work."

• *Restorative facework*—"is designed to rebuild one's face after loss has already occurred." For example, in a meeting after making a critical comment to a member, you might say: "That didn't sound at all like I intended it to. Your past ideas have been extremely valuable to this group, and I'm looking forward to hearing what you have to say."

Regardless of whether you are from a collectivistic or an individualistic culture, it is important to recognize how other cultures view you—especially if you will be dealing with them in business, education, or healthcare situations. Normally, collectivistic cultures value relationships and are very careful that any disclosure will not cause a loss of face; individualistic cultures tend to be more concerned with telling it like it is and disclosing the "truth" than in saving face. Since the need to save face occurs more often in conflict situations, face negotiation theory has special value for these situations.

PRACTICAL APPLICATION

In interpersonal relationships, face negotiation theory has important applications. Ting-Toomey offers the following advice (Ting-Toomey, 1992; 2000; Hall, 2002):

When dealing with collectivistic cultures:

• Learn to be less direct when expressing your views (tentative statements are better than blunt ones: "Yes, but . . .," "Don't you think . . .," "Perhaps . . .," or "I'm not completely sure, but . . ."

• Compliment the group rather than the individual.

• Make greater use of intermediaries or mediators who allow members to save face.

• Don't back people to the wall—allow a way out, a way to save face.

• Not all problems have to be solved directly. If the situation is viewed as threatening to face, a cooling-off period may be needed. Or discuss the problem indirectly through storytelling, describing a situation that another company, team, or relationship experienced and how it was resolved.

• Work on respect and trust.

When dealing with individualistic cultures:

• Learn to be more open when expressing ideas or opinions, and work to keep the problem separate from relationships and personal feelings.

• Compliment the individual rather than the group.

• Realize that assertion is different from aggression. Assertive discussions allow all members to defend their positions without losing face.

• Begin dialogue with a clear thesis statement; then give examples and evidence.

• Use paraphrasing and perception checking to make sure you understand the other side's position.

• Work on respect and trust.

Source: Ting-Toomey, S., & Kurogi, A. (1998). Facework competence in intercultural conflict: an updated face-negotiation theory. *International Journal of Intercultural Relations*, 22, 187–225.

- People communicating with others by computer (whether text only or visually) ask more questions and disclose more than people communicating face-to-face.

- Self-disclosure is used as a method to reduce uncertainty when online.

- People communicating on instant messaging software offer more intimate disclosure than people communicating face-to-face.

- Discussion forums (on impersonal topics such as motorcycles) include much less disclosure than do support forums (on personal topics such as loss and bereavement).

- People with communication anxiety not only find it easier to make relationships online, but find they gain a new confidence that makes face-to-face communication easier as well.

- Strong friendships and even romantic relationships are formed online, and many of them turn into real-life relationships.

Ethics

Is it ethical to tell a friend that his wife is cheating on him? Is it ethical for a relational partner to keep things from the past to him or herself—such as having been jailed for a DWI? Is it unethical for an employer to omit telling employees that their building has dangerous levels of asbestos? Or for a doctor to leave out just how serious the cancer is? Or for a professor to omit telling a student until after the drop date has passed that he or she is failing the class? Or for a person to divulge personal information about another on a TV talk show? Many of these questions are difficult to answer even if we consider ourselves to be ethical. There is a fine line between disclosing and withholding information, regardless of the type of relationship. According to Jaska and Pritchard (1994), ethical issues are often a matter of *discretion*: "Simply speaking out truthfully about what we know can cause needless harm or suffering. It can also betray confidences or show a lack of respect for individual privacy" (p. 201). In some cases, disclosing information may be a matter of *confidentiality* that may have legal ramifications—such as a journalist's withholding the source of an article, a spouse's testifying against a partner in a legal trial, or a friend's honoring a request to keep comments private. On the other hand, whether to disclose information may depend on the other person's "*right to know*" (Jaska & Prichard). Government regulations on food labels, information about toxic chemicals, and warnings about unsafe working conditions are examples. Is there a definite answer for when disclosure is ethical and when it is not? Unfortunately no. We are each responsible for deciding what to disclose and whether an issue requires discretion, confidentiality, or the right to know. Disclosure is a difficult decision to make, especially when the information you are disclosing is about yourself.

Disclosure and the Model of Social Penetration

In the development of interpersonal relationships, self-disclosure is used to achieve intimacy. **Intimacy** refers to the closeness in a relationship that is achieved by the mutual sharing of intellectual, emotional, or physical aspects of oneself. It is possible to be intimate in only one of these dimensions—to be physically intimate, for example, without being intellectually or emotionally close. The most profound relationships in our lives, however, are those in which we reach a level of trust that allows us to be vulnerable in all three areas. Such intimacy is developed through self-disclosure.

The amount and type of self-disclosure in which you engage will always depend upon the nature of the relationship. Altman and Taylor's **model of social penetration** (1973) provides a way to consider the process of disclosure as you work toward achieving intimacy with someone. The model depicts the layers—with varying widths and depths—through which self-disclosure passes in developing relationships (**Figure 6.6**).

Communication in the outer layer is relatively superficial. Initially, you tend to offer only low-risk facts and opinions. Your goal is to increase the **breadth of disclosure** in your communication, establishing a range of topics you can discuss with your relational partner without revealing the "real you" that you are still keeping safe in the core (layer 4). Facts about your line of work or area of study, about your tastes in music and preferences in food, or about your general impressions of the context in which you are communicating (class, workplace, or party) reveal something about you without revealing too much. At the same time, you acquire information about the other person that can enable you to form a judgment about whether a relationship with this person might be sufficiently rewarding to justify further communication. If you determine that this person is a promising relational partner, your self-disclosure will move into the next layer.

To summarize:

- Layer 1, the outer layer, is represented by the first few dates of a romantic couple where communication is mostly impersonal (Littlejohn & Foss, 2008, p. 203). They talk about the topics represented by the outside ring of this layer. The remaining topics, the Xs near the "holes" in the top layer, will be addressed later in the relationship.

- Layer 2 involves further exploratory exchange in which the facts and opinions you offer are more risky. You are working toward greater **depth of disclosure** in your communication. You begin to reveal your attitudes and beliefs, seeking to assess whether there is sufficient similarity between the two of you to serve as a basis for a more substantial relationship. Your communication is less impersonal and more interpersonal. Using the romantic couple example, layer 2 represents dating that continues well after the first few dates.

- Layer 3 is considerably more intimate, meaning that both breadth and depth are present. Not only can you talk about a large range of topics, but you feel comfortable revealing more about your beliefs, values, and especially your feelings. Unless both people in the relationship feel that the potential rewards of the relationship outweigh the costs, this level will be avoided (Littlejohn & Foss, 2008). Using the romantic couple example, layer 3 occurs when the couple decides to date each other exclusively and begin thinking about a possible future together.

- Layer 4 reveals the essence of who you are—the core. Only in your most intimate relationships will you venture into communication that penetrates to your core. Almost always there will still be information that you are unwilling to share. Shameful secrets and experiences that are too painful to recount may always remain hidden, as exposing these could disrupt the relationship and, possibly, leave you unacceptably vulnerable. It is probably not possible, and possibly not desirable, for anyone to be a totally "open book." Despite this, intimate relationships are achievable, though not without taking risks in disclosure. Using the romantic couple example, layer 4 represents marriage or a long-term partnership.

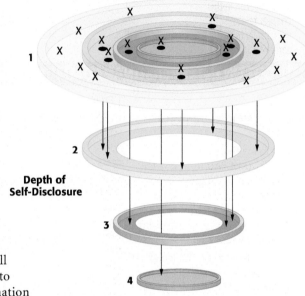

Figure 6.6 Model of Social Penetration

Breadth of Self-Disclosure

Depth of Self-Disclosure

X = Topics of discussion
Layer 1 = Superficial Exchange
Layer 2 = Exploratory Exchange
Layer 3 = Significant Exchange
Layer 4 = Intimate Exchange

Appropriate Self-Disclosure
As the model of social penetration suggests, there are guidelines for appropriate self-disclosure that should be followed if relationships are to flourish:

- Self-disclosure should *proceed gradually*. It is unwise to reveal too much too soon. Furthermore, to do so is potentially alienating; you risk making others so uncomfortable that you drive them away. The best course of action when you reveal something that is somewhat risky is to wait a while before revealing more, observing how your partner handles the information. If the other person does not respond with disapproval or divulge the information to others, you can then develop enough trust to enable you to risk further self-disclosure. Sometimes people divulge amazingly personal information about themselves to others when they feel sure that they will never see that person again. Your seatmate on a cross-country flight might feel safe in recounting his marital woes and struggles with addiction as a sort of catharsis, or release of pent-up emotions. Depending upon your temperament, you might find this interesting or even enjoyable, or you might find it extremely annoying or uncomfortable.

RELATIONSHIPS **AND YOUR CAREER**

LEARNING **OBJECTIVE**

6.6 What information and skills covered in this chapter relate specifically to your career?

Developing interpersonal relationships will be of special importance to you in your career. The following *Career* features take a look at interpersonal relationships in the workplace specifically as they relate to careers in business, education, and healthcare.

SPOTLIGHT ON **INTERPERSONAL COMMUNICATION & DISCLOSURE**

BUSINESS

How important are relationships in the workplace:

- According to the Metropolitan Life Insurance Co. (MetLife.com, 2006), the highest percent of employees (58 percent) ranked "the quality of coworker and/or customer relationships" as highly important when selecting and remaining with an employer (Sec1:8).

- A study by Feeley et al. (2008) found that it was possible to predict the likelihood of turnover of employees by their friendships. Specifically, researchers found that employees who were actively connected with a greater number of coworkers (but not necessarily close to them) were "less likely to leave" (p. 56). In other words, employee retention is related more to the number of friendships (acquaintances) a person has than to the closeness of those relationships.

EDUCATION

Graduates with learning disabilities (LD) who are looking for employment have a special problem with the rewards and costs of disclosure. According to Madaus (2008), the need for employees to disclose disabilities in order to receive protection under the Americans with Disabilities Act (ADA) is especially risky if the disorder is not visually obvious. Once they disclose their disability, their public image is damaged, and they have lost face. The accommodations they received while in college may not translate into the workplace. Madaus studied 500 graduates from three universities and found that 73 percent indicated that their LD "affected their work in some way," but only 55 percent "disclosed to an employer at some time"—either during the interview or after being hired—and only 12 percent asked for an accommodation (p. 295).

HEALTHCARE

In *Communicating about Health* (2000, p. 58), Athena du Pre discusses "doorknob disclosures." Although the doctor is ready to hear everything the minute the session begins, most patients have to work up to embarrassing conditions or worries. They start off with minor conditions and are just getting ready to disclose the real reason for the visit as the doctor is preparing to leave the room—a hand already on the doorknob.

Du Pre offers two suggestions for avoiding doorknob disclosures:

- *Patients*: Hint that you have a serious problem early in the session with a comment like, "Later, I have something really embarrassing to tell you" (p. 58).

- *Healthcare provider*: Before beginning the exam, invite the patient to "share all concerns"—but show them you mean it by listening and looking concerned.

CAREER MOMENT **INTERPERSONAL SKILLS IN THE WORKPLACE**

What skills and qualities do you think employers in your field consider essential? If you are like most people, you will say, "It has to be knowledge of the field." But you would be wrong!

Each year, the National Association of Colleges and Employers (see naceweb.org) surveys employers nationwide about their hiring expectations for the coming year. NACE also asks employers to rank, on a 5-point scale, the skills and qualities that they find most important when interviewing and hiring a candidate. In order, here are the top hiring skills for 2009 (*Job Outlook* 2009): communication skills, strong work ethic, teamwork skills, initiative, analytic skills, computer skills, flexibility/adaptability, *interpersonal skills,* and problem-solving skills.

Another survey of CFOs from Fortune 1000 companies asked the CFOs to list the most important personal attributes needed by graduates (Collier & Wilson, 1994). The four attributes, in order, were ethics, *interpersonal skills,* oral communication skills, and written communication skills. The skills you learn in this course—including interpersonal skills discussed in this chapter and in the following chapter on relationships—will be of great value in your career.

CONNECTING TO **BUSINESS**

If you are considering a career in business, you will likely find your interpersonal skills stretched to the max when personality differences occur. In an article entitled "When Personalities Clash," Judith Sills (2006) offers the following advice:

- *Resist recruiting allies*—telling the problem to others may make the problem seem larger.
- *Focus on strengths*—dwell on the positive contributions of this irritating person.
- *Get out of the way*—remove yourself from contact with agitating personalities.
- *Look in the mirror*—search for the "source of your response" to this personality type (p. 62).

ACTIVITY

1. In small groups of people interested in business, share your personal experiences of working with irritating co-workers. Make a list of the most annoying personality styles and compare them with those discussed in this chapter.

2. Which one or two pieces of advice offered by Sills does your group think is the most likely to work? Provide examples.

3. Be prepared to share your ideas with other groups.

CONNECTING TO **EDUCATION**

If you are considering a career in education, it might interest you to know the five main motives that students have for disclosing with their instructors (Mottet et al, 2004): (1) *relational motive*—desire for an interpersonal relationship; (2) *functional motive*—the desire to gain more course information; (3) *participatory motive*—desire to show course-related knowledge; (4) *excuse-making motive*—desire to explain why assignments are late; (5) *sycophantic motive*—desire to ingratiate self with instructor.

ACTIVITY

1. In small groups of people interested in education, write out at least two comments a student might make that demonstrate each motive (e.g., "I really like your tie" would indicate the sycophantic motive).

2. Which of these motives are important to student learning and why?

3. Be prepared to share your results with another group or the class.

CONNECTING TO **HEALTHCARE**

If you are considering a career in healthcare, you have probably heard people say, "Don't get too close to your patients—don't get emotionally involved." This is what they told Robin Williams in the movie *Patch Adams* when he wanted to develop doctor/patient interpersonal relationships. Today, the importance of having a relationship with your patients is known and taught. Berman, et al. in *Fundamentals of Nursing* (2008, p. 474) offer the following advice for developing relationships: listen attentively; help to identify what the person is feeling; put yourself in the other person's shoes; be honest; be genuine and credible; handle problems with ingenuity; be aware of cultural differences; maintain client confidentiality; and know your role and limitations.

ACTIVITY These suggestions sound good, but how do you accomplish them?

1. In small groups, compare these with the theories and advice given in this chapter. What discrepancies, if any, do you see?

2. Take the first two items and discuss how to communicate your caring to the patient. Make a list of the verbal and nonverbal behaviors you would use.

▶ Log onto MyCommunicationLab.com to access Connecting to Psychology and Connecting to Science, Technology, Engineering, and Math—both with related activities.

- Appropriate self-disclosure is also *reciprocal*, meaning that it is not one-sided. There is an inherent imbalance created when one party is an open communicator and the other is hidden. In the first place, the hidden communicator possesses a great deal of power over the other, as there is always the potential that information may be intentionally or unintentionally leaked to others. It may sound cynical, but when there is some **reciprocity**, both parties are in possession of information about the other, which serves as mutual "leverage." Even in trusting relationships, imbalance of self-disclosure prevents authentic intimacy. It is hard to feel genuinely close to someone when you have no sense that the other person knows who you really are. It is probably also worth noting that reciprocity is something that usually occurs without any conscious formation of intent. In other words, when someone discloses to you, you probably unconsciously recognize the need to balance that disclosure with similar disclosure of your own. This reciprocity can be a good and proper thing in developing relationships, or it may cause you to reveal information before you are truly ready to do so. In the hands of an unethical communicator, the principle of reciprocity can be used to manipulate.

- The third guideline, and perhaps the most important, is that you should always *weigh the risks*. Mindless communicators just react without thinking. Mindful communicators make choices, and self-disclosure should be a choice. This does not mean that you must always be on guard, pondering for long periods of time the reward/cost ratio of every communicative act. It does mean that it is useful to consciously assess the nature of your relationship, the degree to which trust in the other person is warranted, the goals you have for the relationship, and the potential for a particular act of self-disclosure to undermine those goals. Too much self-disclosure is risky; too little self-disclosure hampers the development of relationships. Mindful and effective interpersonal communicators achieve a balance.

APPLY **WHAT YOU KNOW**
IMPROVING SELF-DISCLOSURE

Now that you have a good idea about the importance of self-disclosure to effective relationships, check your understanding by answering the following questions:

- Based on face negotiation theory, how do you think other cultures view your culture and how accurate is their view? Give an example to explain your answer.

- Discuss a time when you had to make a decision on whether to disclose something with a friend or acquaintance. Based on information in this chapter, was your decision an ethical one? Was it an appropriate one? Why or why not?

CHAPTER SUMMARY

As this chapter indicates, building successful relationships requires knowledge and skill. You can determine your knowledge of relationships by checking the skills and learning objectives presented in this chapter.

Summary of **SKILLS**

Check each skill that you now feel qualified to perform:

❏ I can pinpoint where one or more relationships in my life fall on a continuum from impersonal to interpersonal and adjust them as needed.

❏ I can identify my inclusion, control, and openness needs, evaluate whether my interpersonal relationships are fulfilling those needs, and adjust my relationships if needed.

❏ I can improve my interpersonal relationships through one of the following: gathering needed information, developing conversational principles, or improving my use of appropriate self-disclosure.

❏ I can build and enhance my interpersonal relationships at home and at work by applying the communication tips provided from at least one of the theories covered in this chapter.

Summary of LEARNING **OUTCOMES**

6.1 *What is the definition of interpersonal communication, what are the differences between impersonal and interpersonal communication?*

- Interpersonal communication is the exchange of verbal and nonverbal symbols in order to initiate, develop, and maintain (as well as terminate) relationships between people who relate to each other as unique individuals. When we think of interpersonal communication, we usually think of dyads.

- When communication is impersonal, the people involved communicate only from the roles or positions they hold—there is no personal sharing. However, when people communicate interpersonally, they share personal thoughts and feelings.

6.2 *How does a person's desire to get needs met relate to interpersonal relationships? What is meant by inclusion, control, openness, and contradictory needs; which theory offers insight into needs fulfillment?*

- We engage in interpersonal relationships to get our inclusion, control, and openness needs met. See the *How to* feature to determine your needs and wants based on the FIRO-B concept.

- *Inclusion needs* allow us to interact with others and make us feel like we belong; they range from extrovert to introvert.

- *Control needs* are fulfilled when we feel that we have some influence over our own lives as well as the lives of others; they range from submissive to dominant.

- *Openness needs* are fulfilled when we make emotional connection with others by disclosing our inner thoughts and feelings; they range from the withholder to the discloser.

6.3 *How does a person's desire to gain rewards and minimize costs relate to interpersonal relationships, and which theory offers insight into rewards and costs?*

- Our decisions whether to initiate, develop, and maintain interpersonal relationships depend on the rewards and costs associated with the relationships.

- Social exchange theory explains that as long as we perceive that the rewards outweigh the costs of the relationship, we will be reasonably satisfied with the relationship. However, if we perceive that the costs exceed the rewards, we are likely to downscale or terminate the relationship.

6.4 *How does gathering information about a person reduce relationship uncertainty; how does effective conversation improve interpersonal relationships; and what are some conversational principles and openers?*

- If we know enough about people to predict their actions and behaviors, we may feel comfortable enough to initiate a relationship. If we don't know enough, we need to gather information until we have reduced our uncertainty. According to uncertainty reduction theory, we use three strategies to gather information to reduce uncertainly: passive, active, and interactive.

- Another way to improve our interpersonal relationships is to enter into effective conversation. The key to effective conversation is careful listening.

- According to conversational principles, an effective conversation must have quality, quantity, relevancy, and manner. Suggestions for conversational openers are located on pages 162–164.

6.5 *What is self-disclosure; what are some suggestions for improving self-disclosure; and which theory offers insight into self-disclosure?*

- Self-disclosure occurs when you share or reveal personal information about yourself to others. True self-disclosure involves some risk and is a conscious act, not accidental. Culture, gender, technology, and ethics all play a role in what we disclose.

- Some suggestions for improving appropriate self-disclosure include the following: it should be a gradual process, it should be reciprocal, and it should be weighed before disclosing.

- Face saving across cultures is discussed in the *Making Theory Practical* feature in this chapter.

- The model of social penetration suggests that we view disclosure in layers like the layers of an onion. The outer layer includes superficial disclosures such as impersonal disclosures. Layer 2 involves some exploration with low-risk attitudes and beliefs. Layer 3 includes some affection and feelings. Layer 4 is where we reveal the essence of who we are.

6.6 *What information and skills covered in this chapter relate specifically to your career (see highlighted fields of business, education, and healthcare)?*

- The *Spotlight on, Career Moment,* and *Connecting to* features highlight the value of listening in the fields of business, education, and healthcare—additional fields are included online.

SOLVE IT NOW!

Taking into consideration all that you learned about interpersonal relationships from this chapter, how would you analyze Jared's communication in our opening scenario? *

- Was Alicia's behavior unexpected, or was Jared misreading it?

- What role, if any, did Jared's communication anxiety about relationships play in the scenario?

- Which of the theories discussed in the chapter give the best advice for Jared—FIRO-B, social exchange, uncertainty reduction, conversation principles, or social penetration? Why?

- What specific communication skills would you recommend for Jared to improve his relationships now and in the future?

*(Check your answers with those located in MyCommunicationLab, Scenario Analysis for Chapter 6)

The next chapter will look into interpersonal relationships in more detail. It will cover the stages relationships go through as they develop and deteriorate and suggest how to manage conflict when it occurs in relationships.

KEY TERMS

active strategy	p. 161	discloser	p. 159	interpersonal communication	p. 153	reciprocity	p. 172
ambivert	p. 155	dominant	p. 158	intimacy	p. 168	self-disclosure	p. 164
breadth of disclosure	p. 168	dyad	p. 153	introvert	p. 155	social exchange theory	p. 160
control	p. 155	extrovert	p. 155	model of social penetration	p. 168	submissive	p. 158
conversational principles	p. 162	FIRO-B	p. 155	need	p. 155	uncertainty reduction theory	p. 161
depth of disclosure	p. 168	impersonal communication	p. 153	openness	p. 155	withholder	p. 159
dialectical tension	p. 159	inclusion	p. 155	passive strategy	p. 161		
		interactive strategy	p. 162				

SKILL BUILDERS

1. Critically Evaluating

Using the critical evaluation form from Chapter 1, select and evaluate an article on *interpersonal communication* or one of the specific theories, such as FIRO-B, social exchange theory, or uncertainty reduction theory, obtained from a communication journal. (You may wish to check for articles in library databases, such as *Communication and Mass Media Complete* in EBSCOHost.) Be prepared to share your observations with your classmates.

2. Do you recall the PRCA-24 communication apprehension quiz you took at the beginning of the semester? Take a look at your scores again (see the *Developing Skills* feature in Chapter 1). If your total score was above 65 or any subtotal was above 18, then you suffer some anxiety in communicating with others; a total score over 80 or any subtotal over 24 indicates you had high anxiety at the time you took the survey. High-anxiety communicators are likely to experience difficulties in their careers as well as in their personal relationships. To revisit your PRCA-24 scores do the following:

- Being as objective and honest as possible, answer the following questions indicating the degree to which each statement now applies to you. Answer using this scale (but don't try to remember what you said before):

    (1) Strongly Agree (2) Agree (3) Are Undecided
    (4) Disagree (5) Strongly Disagree
    ____13. While participating in a conversation with a new acquaintance, I feel very nervous.
    ____14. I have no fear of speaking up in conversations.
    ____15. Ordinarily I am very tense and nervous in conversations.
    ____16. Ordinarily I am very calm and relaxed in conversations.
    ____17. While conversing with a new acquaintance, I feel very relaxed.
    ____18. I'm afraid to speak up in conversations.

____ To total subscale begin with 18 points. Subtract your scores for questions 13, 15, and 18. Then add the scores for 14, 16, and 17.

- Compare your dyadic subtotal (which is the best indicator of relationship anxiety) to your previous score. Do you see any differences in your dyadic score? If not, you might want to skip ahead and read the section on anxiety in Chapter 10. Keep in mind that the lower your scores, the more confident you are.
- Based on the information in this chapter on building relationships, what two steps could you take to increase your communication confidence when working in small groups?

3. A national survey of college students indicated that 30% of students never or only sometimes ask questions or contribute to class discussions (Job Outlook 2007). Yet both of these types of disclosure are important to student learning. Make a list of ten major reasons that college students do not ask questions or contribute to class discussions. Do you think that knowledge of the content from this chapter would help students overcome any of these reasons? If so, list the specific content that would help.

4. In small groups, practice your knowledge of needs of extroverts/introverts by deciding which of the following jobs would be best for each style communicator. Be prepared to support your decisions with specific reasons:

- Personnel recruiter
- Technical writer
- Copy editor
- Sales manager
- Lawyer
- Accountant
- Computer software engineer
- Counseling psychologist
- Nurse
- Automotive Repairperson
- Educator
- Postal Service Mail Carrier
- Employment interviewer
- Graphic designer
- Public relations specialist
- Elementary school teacher

EXPLORE SOME MORE . . .

1. Watch the following movies for examples of interpersonal relationships:

• *The Doctor* (1991)—played by William Hurt, shows how an arrogant surgeon's relationships change with his family and patients after he becomes ill and experiences fears of death and the indignities of being treated with indifference by doctors and hospital staff. See how the movie ends with Hurt introducing a new group of interns to real-life experiences.

• *Patch Adams* (1998)—played by Robin Williams, shows how "Patch," a medical student (who was once a psychiatric

patient), struggles to convince the medical world that patients need more than sterile medical care; they need doctors who communicate interpersonally with them and establish caring relationships with them.

2. Looking for a good book on interpersonal communication? We suggest you read *Tuesdays with Morrie* (Albom, 1997) which illustrates a profoundly interpersonal relationship between the author, Mitch Albom, and his beloved professor that endured to the end of the professor's life.

7 Developing and Managing Interpersonal Relationships and Conflict

After studying this chapter you should be able to . . .
- Evaluate your relationships to determine which stage of development or deterioration is involved and make changes for improvement as needed.
- Identify any conflict escalators present in your relationships and minimize their effects as well as assess your conflict style for handling them.
- Communicate assertively by using confirming messages and improve the resolution of conflict in your relationships by using the win-win outcome.
- Manage relationships and conflict in a flexible manner, depending on the people and issues involved.

CHAPTER SUMMARY 〉 P. 197 〉

SCENARIO

Gina McDowell was on the couch, leafing aimlessly through *People* magazine, while her husband Patrick sat across the room in his favorite chair, making entries into his electronic calendar.

They had agreed to discuss their deteriorating marital relationship tonight, but neither one was willing to begin or even to look at each other, for that matter. Neither Patrick nor Gina could understand how their relationship had gone from "enormous fun" to this awkward, hostile stage. "Maybe it's my fault," sighed Gina. "I should be able to handle children and have enough energy left over for Patrick—that is, if he would pay even half as much attention to me as he does to his job." "I should start this discussion," thought Patrick, "but I just hate it when Gina rolls her eyes every time I try to tell her how I feel."

Why Gina is angry but hasn't explained to Patrick: I don't even know who I am anymore. I've lost the "Gina" I used to be; now I'm "Mrs. McDowell" and "Mommy." I love those titles, but I miss my professional identity and the sense of competence and power that I experienced in my work. My brain has turned to mush after reading nothing more stimulating than *The Very Hungry Caterpillar* for months now. Yes, we agreed that one parent should remain in the home as long as the children were young; this is so important for children. But I can't help resenting Patrick's freedom to think only of his work while I handle all of the household and child-rearing responsibilities. It's almost like Patrick has "abandoned" me. Not only does he work long hours, but he's preoccupied when he is at home. I also feel shut out of financial decisions because Patrick earns all the money. It's degrading to have to go to him every time I need to spend some money. That certainly keeps me from having any romantic feelings for Patrick. Besides, I'm so exhausted at the end of the day. Anyway, Patrick probably doesn't find me sexy any more.

Why Patrick is angry but hasn't explained to Gina: Why doesn't Gina realize that I'm "stretched to the max"? Surely she realizes that I have to work long hours to make up the loss of her income. Our children have had a bigger impact on the family budget than I realized they would. These long hours are hard on me, especially since I don't really enjoy my work all that much. My new management role has taken me out of the creative end of architecture, which is my real love. What I really want to do is open my own firm, but I don't see how I can make a career change at this moment without jeopardizing the family's financial security. Why doesn't Gina understand that I work so hard because I love her and the children? And when I try to help out at home, I can't seem to do anything right. She is always criticizing me for something. I admit that I "tune her out" when she starts in on me. This certainly keeps me from feeling romantic; our sexual intimacy has all but vanished. What's the use of discussing that—or anything—as long as every discussion turns into an argument?

"Would you like some coffee?" asked Gina without looking at Patrick. Finally, the discussion was beginning.

This relationship is in real trouble, isn't it? Wouldn't it be nice if Gina and Patrick could actually tell each other why they feel the way they do? As you read in this chapter about the specific stages of relationship development and deterioration and ways to manage conflict in relationships, see how many specific communication goals and tips you can find to help Gina and Patrick. By analyzing their difficulties and helping them, you should be able to find effective ideas to apply to your own relationships.

SOLVE IT NOW! ⟩ P. 200 ⟩

Of course, each relationship is unique, and no description of a "typical" relationship can cover all situations. However, you will hopefully recognize enough of yourself and your relational experiences within these pages to help you succeed in your current and future relationships.

Relationship Stages

LEARNING **OBJECTIVE**

7.1 What are the five stages of relationship development and the five stages of relationship deterioration?

Technology has changed the way relationships occur in today's world. Although most relationships still develop face-to-face, strong relationships and even romantic relationships are also formed online. McCown and colleagues (2001) found that 80 percent of Internet users surveyed from the United States established casual relationships online. Approximately 21 percent of these relationships were close or romantic, and one-third of the close relationships translated into contact offline—most in face-to-face meetings. Another study reported that 16 million Americans have used online dating Web sites, and 3 million adults—17 percent of online daters—have developed long-term relationships including marriage (Madden & Lenhart, 2006). Researchers are finding that people are satisfied with their online relationships and disclose feelings in basically the same way they do in their face-to-face relationships (Barraket & Henry-Waring, 2008; Pornsakulvanich, et al., 2008).

Regardless of whether your relationships occur face-to-face or online, if they are high-quality relationships, they do not just happen overnight. Instead they develop, are maintained, and sometimes deteriorate through a series of predictable stages that may take several months or last a lifetime. One of the most influential models of relationship stages was proposed by interpersonal scholar Mark Knapp and his colleagues (Knapp & Vangelisti, 2008). Knapp's model is especially applicable to intimate relationships, such as those you enjoy with close friends or romantic partners. As we mentioned in Chapter 6, **intimacy** refers to the closeness in a relationship that is achieved by the mutual sharing of intellectual, emotional, or physical aspects of oneself.

Although Knapp's model can be used to analyze different types of relationships, please note that this model doesn't work well for analyzing family relationships. Although you may have achieved fairly high levels of intimacy with one or more members of your family of origin, those relationships differ from friendships and romantic relationships in ways that are significant enough to make Knapp's model unsuitable. For example, you choose your friendships and romantic relationships, but you did not choose your family. Furthermore, in family relationships, certain roles are inescapable; as many a woman will tell you, your children may grow up and get married and start families of their own, but they will always be your children. It is also true that both the quality and the quantity of self-disclosure differ in a family relationship. For example, most close relationships require you to reveal the pivotal moments in your life; however, less discussion is needed when you are communicating with family members who were part of those moments. Even when you talk about the significance those moments had for you, a family member who was present may have a different "take" and may contest your version of the events—something that is much less likely to occur in nonfamilial relationships. For these and many other reasons, relationships with family cannot be viewed through the same lens you use to examine your other intimate relationships.

Knapp's model consists of ten stages, five of which are descriptive of the way people "come together," and five of which illustrate how relationships "come apart" (see **Figure 7.1**). Movement through the stages does not always follow a straight line. At any point, people may choose to retreat to a previous stage as they wrestle with how to define the relationship, or they may stabilize at that point for a short period of time or forever. Understanding each stage that relationships go through as they develop and deteriorate can help us manage our own relationships.

Stages of Relationship Development

Think of a fairly new relationship you are in at the moment. Whether this relationship involves a friend or colleague, or is of a more intimate nature, it is likely to be in one of the following stages:

Figure 7.1 Stages of Relationship Development and Deterioration

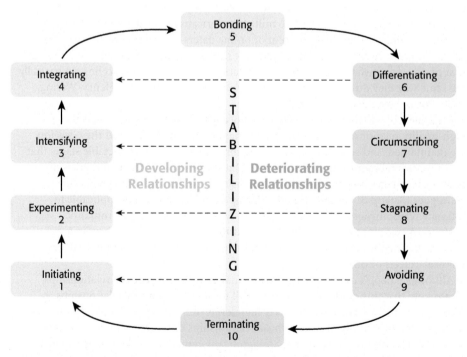

Adapted from Mark L. Knapp and Anita L. Vangelisti. *Interpersonal Communication and Human Relationships* 6th ed., Fig. 2.1, p. 48. Published by Allyn & Bacon-Merrill Education, Boston, MA. Copyright © 2009 by Pearson Education. Adapted by permission of the publisher.

Initiating Stage

The **initiating stage**, as the name suggests, is the beginning of a relationship. This stage is very brief, lasting only long enough for the parties to form a quick first impression of each other, to determine if additional communication is desired by both, and to assess how best to move forward. You may have been thrown together through circumstance, or you may have identified the other person as someone you would like to get to know. In either case, your goals for this stage are fairly simple: You wish to convey to the other person that you are likable, approachable, and available for communication; and you seek to determine if the feeling is mutual. Although the initiating stage may be brief, it creates a high level of anxiety for many of us—especially when it comes to verbal conversation openers (see Chapter 6 for suggestions). Your nonverbal communication is likely to include extending your hand to be shaken, engaging in eye contact, and maintaining a smile or pleasant expression on your face. At the same time, you will be monitoring the other's verbal and nonverbal responses, especially noting any indication that something you have done has not been well received. For example, if the other person backs off slightly, this may signal that you have invaded his or her personal space.

Experimenting Stage

The **experimenting stage** is the point at which you float conversational trial balloons on low-risk topics in search of areas of mutual interest. You engage in "small talk," an act that may seem superficial but is, in fact, a necessary and valuable communication skill. Effective self-disclosure should be gradual; this is not the stage during which revelation of one's deepest, darkest secrets is appropriate. Low-risk facts and opinions are called for here, as you are only now entering the outer layer of the *model of social penetration* discussed in Chapter 6. If the responses you receive to new trial topics are monosyllabic with no reciprocation, you are likely to decide that this is a relationship that is going nowhere, and you will move to terminate it: "So, do you come here often?" "No." "So, where do you usually spend your Saturday nights?" "Different places." "Like where?" "It depends." "I see. Well, it's been nice talking to you. I just spotted someone I need to talk to. Have a good evening."

In the above example, no sort of true relationship was formed. However, when two people participate in small talk, both answering and asking questions, a type of relationship is created: you are developing **acquaintances**. In your lifetime, you will likely cultivate a great many acquaintances. Some may eventually become more deeply interpersonal, but even when they go no further—and most will not—these relationships are important in helping you get your inclusion needs met. For example, hearing your name called as you walk between buildings on campus gives you a sense of belonging. See the *SpotLight on* feature near the end of this chapter to see the role that acquaintances play in employee satisfaction and retention.

Intensifying Stage

A relationship begins to become truly interpersonal in the **intensifying stage**, as your communication moves toward greater depth and breadth. Whether the relationship is one that is likely to become a close friendship or one that has romantic possibilities, this is the most exciting time in relational development. Indeed, you feel exhilaration as you explore the ways in which you are both similar and complementary, build trust through self-disclosure, share stories of your past, and build new experiences that will become stories in the future. In fact, some people are prone to cycle through relationships, discarding old ones and forming new ones over and over again, because they are addicted to the euphoric feelings that are characteristic of the intensifying stage.

Your verbal communication in this stage features **meta-communication**, which is communication about communication. In other words, you begin to talk explicitly about the relationship and the behaviors exhibited by each other that are especially admired or appreciated in such comments as, "Thanks for listening to me without judging." You may also attempt to define the relationship, sometimes by discussing it directly and sometimes in a statement you make to someone else in your partner's presence, such as, "Hey, Nathan. I want you to meet my *girlfriend*, Mara."

Your nonverbal behaviors provide additional evidence that this relationship is much more intensely interpersonal than most (Guerrero & Anderson, 1991). Touch, for example, increases dramatically. Affection is expressed in a variety of ways. You no longer wait until you happen to bump into each other; you arrange times to be together. You are likely to take great care with your personal appearance, trying to look your best anytime you are with your friend or partner, and especially when you are going to be around the other's family or special friends. Knapp notes that in this stage you also express affection by doing favors for the other and by exchanging "intimacy trophies," which include objects that convey to the other that you were thinking of him or her even when you were apart. You might say, "I saw this, and it made me think of you."

Integrating Stage
In the **integrating stage**, partners truly do come together. Others regard you as a social unit. If someone encounters you alone, they may ask, "Where's . . .?" Your social circles merge, as each of you forms secondary relationships with the people who matter to the other. There are many nonverbal behaviors that occur in this stage. For example, if your partner finds one of your friends objectionable, you will likely reduce the amount of time spent with that person. In addition, you may find yourself taking on characteristics of the other person—one of the most striking aspect of this stage (Knee et al., 2003). You may also find yourself adopting the speech habits of your partner, including inflectional patterns, verbal expressions, and stock phrases. Another behavior of the integrating stage occurs when you develop routines that allow you to spend almost every moment together when not at work or school or with your family. You call each other frequently just to "check in" and catch up on what may have happened to the other in the two hours since your last call.

Intimacy trophies show you were thinking of the other person.

There are also many verbal behaviors that occur in this stage as well. The pronouns *I, you, my,* and *your* are replaced by *we, us,* and *our.* This is noticeable when someone asks you what you are doing this weekend, and your response is, "*We* are going to. . ." Similarly, common property is claimed, as you are likely to ask, "Where is *our* car parked?" even though the car was the other person's long before you met. Although this language usage began to develop in the intensifying stage, it is solidly established now. It really isn't an overstatement to say that in the integrating stage of relational development, you become a different person from what you were. You may give up some interests if they are not shared by your partner—you used to love the theatre, but now you haven't seen a play in ages. At the same time, you develop enthusiasm for one of your partner's interests, despite the fact that prior to meeting him/her you knew nearly nothing about it. For example, you couldn't have identified the favorite team's colors before, but now you know the team's three-deep roster. Think back to one or more relationships that attained this level of intimacy, and you will probably see that those relationships may have been some of the most significant factors in shaping who you have become up to this point.

Bonding Stage

You enter the **bonding stage** when you make a formal public statement of commitment to the relationship. Once this formal public statement is made, dissolving the relationship becomes more complicated, partly due to legal and/or religious sanctions. On the other hand, marriages and commitment ceremonies provide greater incentive for the partners to work to make the relationship successful. That "little piece of paper" seems to make partners feel more secure. Although they probably don't verbalize it, prior to the marriage or commitment ceremony partners are aware that any disagreement could result in the end of the relationship. As one woman put it, "I always felt that he had one foot out the door." Of course, even after marriage or a commitment ceremony, spouses and partners can and do leave. But most people who take their vows seriously are more willing to stay and work it out than they might have been before. As a result, they feel safer to disagree and to stand up for their own needs, knowing that a few arguments are unlikely to permanently affect the relationship.

Another change that occurs in the bonding stage relates to expectations. Behaviors that were once tolerated may now be regarded as disrespectful to the relationship. For example, before marriage or a commitment ceremony, if one cohabiting partner liked to spend a couple of nights a week hanging out with friends, the other partner typically felt reluctant to object. However, after the marriage or commitment ceremony, the partner is likely to interpret spending time with friends without their being present as a preference for the friend—something that is no longer acceptable unless such instances are reduced significantly.

APPLY **WHAT YOU KNOW**
STAGES OF RELATIONSHIP DEVELOPMENT

To apply what you know about the stages that relationships go through as they develop (the initiating, experimenting, intensifying, integrating, and bonding stages) answer these critical thinking questions:

- Think of one of the many relationships that you have developed since becoming an adult (preferably a relationship that

has now ended but that you don't mind talking about) and briefly describe the various development stages that you experienced.

- What did you learn from this development experience that has helped you with later relationships?

Stages of Relationship Deterioration

It would be nice to be able to say about a relationship that "they lived happily ever after," but we all know that relationships sometimes do come apart. The intensity with which relationships begin to deteriorate depends upon many factors, including the stage at which the dissolution begins. If a relationship has not progressed past the experimenting stage, the decision to discontinue is accomplished by merely avoiding contact with the other person (notice the arrows between the relationship stages and deterioration stages on Figure 7.1 (see page 180) that indicate back-and-forth movement). However, once a relationship has advanced to the integrating or bonding stage, dissolution often begins with significant conflict and advances through several **stages of deterioration** that include differentiating, circumscribing, stagnating, avoiding, and terminating.

Differentiating Stage

The **differentiating stage** resembles the integrating stage in that communication involves high levels of self-disclosure and expression of deeply held feelings. However, while feelings about the relationship in the integrating stage were mostly positive, those in the differentiating stage become more negative. Instead of centering on how the partners are a unit and are similar to each other, differentiating communication focuses on their individuality and their differences. Points of incompatibility assume great significance, and the conflicts that emerge in negotiating these tensions are seen as threatening to the relationship. The desire for connection that marked the fusing of personalities in the integrating phase is replaced by the need for autonomy.

In the differentiating stage, verbal messages are used to criticize the partner and reinforce perceptions of difference: "I don't know how you could think that. I don't see it that way at all." "Why would you do that? I would never do that." The personal pronouns shift from *we* to *I* and *you*. The "I" messages are used to assert one's needs, while the "you" messages are often accusatory or blaming. Nonverbal messages may run the gamut from hostile facial expressions and the withholding of touch to the "silent treatment."

The differentiating phase is undeniably scary. However, it may be a very healthy stage of development, particularly if one or both partners gave up too much of themselves to meet their needs for connection in the integrating phase. What is needed is an understanding of the partner's differences and the willingness to embrace them as opportunities to enhance the relationship. This requires superior communication and conflict management skills. If the couple can find ways to negotiate differences, the relationship can stabilize and even emerge stronger than before. However, if the conflicts cannot be resolved, the relationship will continue on a downward path.

Circumscribing Stage

In the **circumscribing stage**, the partners figuratively "draw a circle around" the topics that cannot be discussed. Experience has shown them that little is accomplished by continuing to bring up the topics that divided them in the differentiating stage. In order to avoid the overt conflict, touchy topics are placed "off limits." The partners seem to tacitly agree that "we won't talk about your lack of helpfulness around the house," "we won't talk about my overspending," and "we certainly won't talk about the relationship." Since the restraints placed on communication do not encourage the open expression of feelings or the renegotiation of needs, the relationship shrinks in intimacy; both breadth and depth are lost. Safe topics—those about which the partners agree—are still allowed, and these permit the partners to interact in public in ways that disguise the troubled relationship from others. The conflict is still there, but it has gone underground.

Restoring the relationship becomes more difficult in the circumscribing stage because of the constraints on communication. Often a third party may be required to help the partners reconnect. When this is successful, the couple may re-experience on a smaller scale some of the joy they experienced back

"We met, fell madly in love, got engaged, had a lovely wedding and honeymoon. Then things turned sour, we grew bitter, separated and divorced. It was quite a busy weekend!"

in the intensifying phase. The key to achieving this sort of success is for the couple to learn how to communicate again and, eventually, how to address their conflicts in productive ways. If this is not accomplished, the relationship is likely to continue to decline.

Stagnating Stage

Couples in the **stagnating stage** settle into a communication pattern that allows little room for growth or movement in the relationship. The breadth and depth of their communication resembles interaction in the experimenting stage, as it focuses primarily on superficial topics, often centered on the minutiae of daily life: "Did you have a good day at work?" "We need to get a plumber in to look at that sink." "What time are we supposed to be at the Bowmans' house?" Nonverbally, the partners express little enthusiasm for anything.

As we consider the stagnating stage it becomes apparent that the relational partners are surely not getting their inclusion, control, or openness needs met unless the needs are very low on all three dimensions. For that reason, it would be tempting to conclude that such a relationship will soon end. However, the reality is that, in many cases, the couple will stay in this stage indefinitely. In such cases, it is not unusual for one or both partners to turn to other people in order to meet their interpersonal needs. Extramarital affairs are an obvious case in point. However, there are other ways to accomplish the fulfillment of social needs. Some people turn to friends to serve as social companions or confidants. Others throw themselves into volunteer work or immerse themselves in the lives of their children or grandchildren. Sadly, there are also people who simply give up and endure.

Avoiding Stage

While some people remain in the stagnation stage, others make the decision to head toward termination, going first through the **avoiding stage**. This is usually, though not always, a relatively brief stage. The goal is to limit the channels of communication so that face-to-face interaction is limited. Even telephone conversations may be avoided so that feelings aren't inadvertently "leaked" through paralanguage. Communication is more likely to take the form of written notes, text messages, or e-mails, and then only when it is necessary to communicate. When it is impossible to avoid face-to-face communication, the partners are likely to create psychological distance by eliminating eye contact and offering very concise messages and brief responses. There is obviously no depth left and minimal breadth.

The final stage of relationship deterioration involves leave-taking.

Terminating Stage

The **terminating stage** usually follows soon after avoiding is entered. The end of the relationship is generally accompanied by some sort of leave-taking statement. Sometimes, those statements take the form of an expression of sadness that the relationship has run its course. In other cases, the statement may reflect residual hostility toward the partner. It is always painful when relationships end, but there are some relationships that probably should end. Even superior communication and conflict management skills do not guarantee that a relationship can be rescued. Even when termination is the only rational decision, the end of a relationship is accompanied by grief. You may wonder if it is possible to start over and attempt to "do it right this time." Sometimes it is possible. If both parties take time to examine the reasons for the relational decline, and if both parties are willing to own up to their own complicity, sufficient personal growth can be achieved to justify making another try. However, keep in mind that since *communication is irreversible*, all of the experiences you shared the first time are now part of each partner's frame of reference. Everything that happened in the past remains a part of your memory, even if you decide to move on to a new relationship.

As previously noted, movement among the stages of development and deterioration does not always proceed in a straight line. Although we may move back and forth between stages, generally speaking, we do not skip stages. To attempt to do so leaves important relational work undone. Propelling a relationship prematurely to bonding, for example, may result in an almost immediate flurry of differentiating. You wake up in the morning and wonder, "Who is this person lying beside me?" You have good reason to wonder, as you did not take the opportunity to use the intensifying and integrating stages to gauge whether there was sufficient compatibility to support a committed relationship. Even the stagnating phase accomplishes necessary work to allow termination to be experienced as an appropriate choice.

APPLY **WHAT YOU KNOW**
STAGES OF RELATIONSHIP DETERIORATION

To apply what you know about the stages that relationships go through as they deteriorate (the differentiating, circumscribing, stagnating, avoiding, and terminating stages) answer these questions:

- Take the relationship you described earlier (the one that has ended) or a different relationship if you prefer and

briefly describe the various deterioration stages that you experienced.

- What did you learn from this deterioration experience that has helped you with later relationships?

LEARNING OBJECTIVE

7.2 What is the definition of *conflict*, what are several conflict escalators to avoid, and what theory explains why conflict often results from e-mail messages?

Relationships and Conflict

Few things in this world can be asserted with absolute certainty, but one of those is this: People are different from each other. When you think about it, the fact that some relationships last a long time is more amazing than that most do not. Human beings are complicated creatures, and bringing two of them together increases those complications exponentially. We are all a mixture of needs—often contradictory and seldom easy to reconcile even within ourselves. It should not be surprising that conflict with another person is a common experience for all of us.

Although conflict in interpersonal relationships is inevitable, conflict resolution in work and personal relationships is possible. Conflict resolution is a skill that begins with understanding what conflict is and what may cause it to escalate perhaps out of control.

Conflict Defined

Conflict is an "expressed struggle between at least two interdependent parties who perceive incompatible goals, scarce rewards, and interference from the other party in achieving their goals" (Wilmot and Hocker, 2007, p. 9). According to this definition, in order for conflict to exist, it must be expressed. The anger you feel toward your close friend who chooses to spend time with a new romantic interest instead of with you is not conflict unless you express it. You may experience internal conflict, expressing your feelings intrapersonally as you sort out reward/cost ratios and dialectical tensions, but it is not relational conflict unless your friend is also aware of your feelings.

Conflict Escalators

The definition of conflict provides us with a basis for understanding the sources of conflict escalation, which include unfulfilled needs, faulty attributions, and assigning cause or fault to others' behaviors.

Conflict is inevitable; conflict resolution is possible with skills.

Unfulfilled Needs As we learned in Chapter 6, each party in a relationship has varying needs for inclusion, control, and openness. Those needs are complicated by the dialectic tension created by each person's contradictory needs for connection/autonomy, openness/privacy, and stability/change. The management and negotiation of needs is the most important relational work we do in the intensifying and integrating phases of a relationship, which is why it is unwise to rush through those stages.

As we struggle to achieve compatibility, we may consciously or unconsciously mask an important need. For example, you might be more affectionate than you would prefer in order to meet the affection needs of your partner. Or you subordinate your need for control because the other person requires dominance. It is almost certain that, at some point, you will find it necessary to assert your unfulfilled needs, which could throw the relationship off-balance. This is often what is occurring in the differentiating stage. Honest communication about your needs in the early stages of your relationship should assure that healthy differentiating can be achieved. So beware of your and your partner's unfulfilled needs—they are conflict escalators. Don't wait; deal with them today.

Faulty Attributions (Perception) As we discussed in Chapter 2, **attribution** refers to how we explain the events in our lives. Our sense is that we can better control what happens in our future if we understand the cause-effect relationships in our past. When we observe another's behavior, a key question we ask is: "To what should I attribute that behavior?" Consider the following example:

> Your roommate comes home, slams his books on the desk, opens the refrigerator door and slams it shut as well. You wonder what could have caused those actions. You search through your store of knowledge to arrive at a possible explanation. "Let's see. He had a major exam in calculus today; perhaps he didn't do so well. He was on the phone with his girlfriend until late last night, and, from the sound of his voice, things aren't going well there. Or maybe he is mad at me because there isn't anything in the refrigerator but a carton of outdated milk, and it was my turn to go to the store."

Each of your explanations is an attribution. Which one you settle on as the most likely will depend on a host of factors, including past experiences, your perception of your roommate, your self-concept, and any number of situational circumstances. Keep in mind that perceptions and attributions may be inaccurate; our perceptions are not always correct.

Let's extend this example further and see how perceptions and attributions can fan the flames of conflict. As the font increases, the conflict intensifies:

- Let's assume that your roommate is a math major. Your *stereotype* of math majors leads you to think, "Math majors don't fail first semester calculus exams. Besides,"—you rationalize, committing a possible *fundamental attribution error* in the process—"if he failed the exam, it's his own fault for staying on the phone so long last night."

- You engage in *projection*, imposing your own values, beliefs, and attitudes on him and concluding that his having trouble with his girlfriend is really "no big deal; there are always other fish in the sea."

- As you evaluate the possibility that your failure to go to the grocery store may be contributing to his distress, your *self-serving* bias is evoked. "I haven't had time," you tell yourself. "Besides, when it's his turn, he never goes on time."

- However, your *self-concept* includes knowing that you are a bit of a procrastinator yourself, and you feel a trifle guilty about that. You figure that it is only a matter of time before he complains about the empty refrigerator.

- You think about apologizing, but your hunch is that he will respond angrily anyway, so you decide, in your *defensiveness*, to launch a preemptive strike. "Why did you eat all the leftover pizza last night?" you shout. He glares at you. "I needed *something* to eat!" he shouts back. You were right! You knew he'd be angry and get loud. (Or was it *self-fulfilling prophecy*?)

- The battle is on. Before the evening is over you have argued about everything from the empty refrigerator to whose girlfriend is a pain-in-the-neck.

When insignificant problems are managed poorly, they can escalate out of control into an argument about a whole range of issues unrelated to the original source of conflict. Often the wounds from these arguments never heal.

Assigning Fault (Punctuation)

Conflict isn't caused by just one person in the relationship: it takes "two to tango," in other words. The problem lies in how the participants assign cause or fault to each others' behaviors. We use **punctuation** when we assign cause and fault according to our perception of whose behavior is responsible and whose behavior is the natural result. To illustrate, consider Joe and Sally. Joe is a quiet sort of guy. Sally likes to talk about her feelings toward Joe, both positive and negative. Joe would rather not. When Sally persists, Joe gets quieter. Sally criticizes Joe for his lack of responsiveness. Conflict ensues, with the usual conversation going something like this:

Sally: "I am tired of how you never want to talk."

Joe: "I'm tired of how you always criticize me."

Sally: "I wouldn't have to criticize you if you would just talk to me."

Joe: "Well, maybe I'd talk to you more if you weren't always criticizing me."

Now suppose that Joe and Sally were given a few semi-colons and periods and were asked to punctuate this stream of words describing their conflict: Sally criticizes Joe shuts down Sally criticizes Joe shuts down Sally criticizes Joe shuts down Sally criticizes Joe. See **Figure 7.2** for how Joe and Sally might differ in their punctuation of these words.

As you can see, each attributes his or her behavior to the other. To Joe, it is Sally's criticism that causes him to be silent. To Sally, it is Joe's silence that drives her to

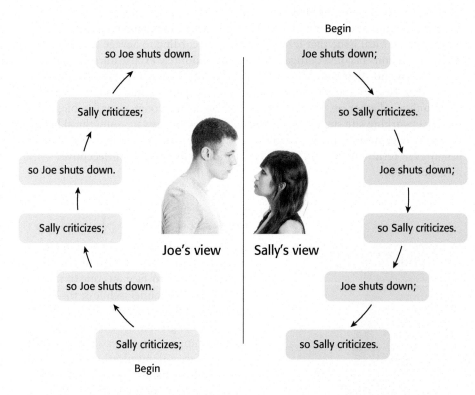

Figure 7.2 How Joe and Sally would punctuate differently.

criticize him. Each blames the other. Discrepancy in how they punctuate their stream of words has created an impasse.

Obviously, in a conflict like this, someone must make the first move toward reconciliation. However, doing so could represent capitulation and be unthinkable for the person whose dominant need is control; for the person whose primary need is affection, however, making the first move would not be a problem. As always in conflict situations, the negotiation of needs is required but definitely is not easy. So beware—punctuation that assigns fault whether used by you or your partner is a conflict escalator. Don't wait until it's too late; acknowledge and negotiate the problem today.

Unethical Behavior

No one likes to be deceived or manipulated. Conflict is sure to escalate in a relationship when deception and lying are involved. Researching the impact of deception on relationships, McCornack and Levine (1990) found that "more than two-thirds of the subjects who reported that their relationship had terminated since the time that the lie was discovered reported that the discovery of the lie played a direct role in their decision to end the relationship" (p. 131). The researchers note that the more involved and intimate we become in a relationship, the more we expect that our partner will never lie to us. So uncovering a deception is an emotional shock that increases uncertainty, lowers trust, and increases conflict.

Another type of unethical behavior relates to gossip. Gossip which involves personal interest items about people serves an important role in the workplace: it's the grease that keeps the informal communication network (the grapevine) moving (March & Sevon, 1982). Employees often find important information on the grapevine that the supervisor forgot to tell them, and, during a crisis, the grapevine is a fast way to dispense needed information. However, when gossip is negative or malicious and affects individuals, relationships, or company image, it becomes an ethical issue that leads to conflict. According to Savage (2008), when discussions become derogatory, we should politely excuse ourselves. She also recommends that personal finances and health issues are topics that should be avoided. Negative gossip about a person or company should also be avoided when online whether on your own personal site, a chat room, e-mail, a blog, or a social networking site such as *MySpace* or *Facebook*. So beware—unethical behavior involving deception or malicious gossip is sure to cause conflict in a relationship; it may even terminate it. Don't wait; take action to improve your deceptive behavior today.

Conflict and Technology

In Chapter 1, we discussed a variety of channels that are used for communicating and mentioned that face-to-face was one of the best because of its channel richness; the more codes (verbal, visual, and vocal) a channel conveys, the greater the chance of communication success. However, if the face-to-face communication channel can't be used for whatever reason and sending a written letter or memo would take too long, then you should select a channel using some type of affordable technology, such as the telephone (or cell phone), instant messaging (IM), text messaging, or e-mail. A 2005 study reported that "75% of teen-agers who go online use instant messenger" (Nadler, 2008, p. 2) instead of e-mail. E-mail is more a staple of the business world; instant messaging and text messaging are used more by students and young adults on their computers or cell phones—both can further personal and work relationships. Both can also lead to misunderstandings and conflict.

While any type of technology can be misunderstood and result in conflict, it may well be that messages sent by e-mail are the most prone to conflict. Have you ever received an e-mail message that made you mad almost instantly? Not only can e-mail make us angry, but when discussing a relatively minor conflict by e-mail, the technology itself may cause the conflict to intensify just like the conflict escalators discussed above. In fact, if we aren't extremely careful, a minor conflict can "spin out of control with angry recriminations and severely hurt feelings after a series of e-mails" (Friedman and Currall, 2003). Don't wait for a serious e-mail conflict to occur; plan now for how to avoid them. For more on how e-mail intensifies conflict and what to do about it, see the *Making Theory Practical* section on page 192.

Conflict Styles

When we experience conflicts, we often hold others responsible for their behavioral choices, forgetting that our behaviors are choices as well. In this section, we will present a number of strategies for making appropriate choices in managing relational conflict. It is important to keep in mind that for any of these strategies to be effective certain underlying assumptions must be met:

- Both parties should have some level of commitment to the relationship.
- Both should wish to resolve the conflict.
- Neither should be mentally dysfunctional.
- Neither party should be committed to leaving if things don't go well.

With these assumptions in place, the way we deal with conflict varies, depending on the situation and the relationship. For example, we manage workplace conflict differently from the way we handle conflict at home. Our approach to conflict with friends differs from conflict with a spouse. Power and intimacy differences in the relationship also play a role. In most situations, we tend to limit conflict resolution to the one or two styles with which we feel most comfortable. Basic conflict management styles include passive, aggressive, passive-aggressive, and assertive. The style that suits each of us best may be the result of how we saw conflict managed in our family while growing up, or it may be a function of our personality and basic needs. See which style you tend to use when handling conflict and potential problems.

The Passive Style

The **passive style** is adopted by people who are uncomfortable with open conflict. The message conveyed by passive behavior is, *"My needs are not important; yours are."* You will see passive communicators use the following behaviors:

- *Denial.* "What conflict? We get along great." The result of denial is that felt needs go unexpressed. Those close to the passive person remain unaware that there is conflict and, therefore, fail to meet the person's needs.
- *Avoidance.* "Let's not talk about *that*." When the conversation seems to be headed toward a touchy subject, passive people do their best to avoid it. You may recognize this tactic as one used in relationships in the circumscribing stage.
- *Accommodation.* "Whatever you think." Overt conflict is avoided because the accommodator simply gives in. This would be the favored approach of a submissive person. However, not all people who behave submissively are, in fact, low in need for control; they have just managed to keep it hidden.

The obvious advantage to the passive approach is that there is unlikely to be a lot of screaming and yelling or expression of angry feelings. The "fight-phobic" person would find this appealing. Then, too, there are times when there is no real need to invest a lot of energy in disagreeing about something. There are some issues on which people can "agree to disagree" without launching a full-scale argument. However, when an issue is troubling enough that it threatens the perception of one's partner and/or the integrity of the relationship, the passive style is not an appropriate choice.

MAKING THEORY **PRACTICAL**
DISPUTE-EXACERBATING MODEL OF E-MAIL (DEME)

Ever wonder why e-mail can make you mad so quickly? Have you ever tried to solve a conflict using e-mail only to find a minor problem escalating into a much larger one?

With the average corporate employee handling 171 e-mail messages daily (Bateman & Snell, 2009), e-mail in the workplace is not only used to dispense information, plan meetings, and solve problems, it is used to wage disputes and manage conflict. Personal experience and a careful look at e-mail research has led management experts Raymond Friedman and Steven Currall (2003) to conclude that "some structural features of e-mail make it more likely that disputes will escalate when people communicate electronically than when they communicate face-to-face or via the telephone" (p. 1326).

Theorists
In their article *Conflict Escalation*, Friedman and Currall (2003) set forth their theory of conflict escalation called the dispute-exacerbating model of e-mail or DEME. As you read the six main propositions of DEME, see if you have experienced any of these problem areas with e-mail messages (either in business or personal relationships):

- *Proposition 1: Diminished feedback leads to reduced self-correcting behavior.* Because only written words can be used to interpret meaning (there are no nonverbal or vocal cues) and feedback is delayed, it is impossible to correct minor disagreements or misunderstandings or to direct the conversation in another direction immediately upon noticing a problem. Therefore, words may be interpreted as more negative than intended, and the other party may be seen in a more negative light—especially if the parties have little or no history working together.

- *Proposition 2: Diminished feedback leads to reduced information.* Relationships don't occur instantly; people learn about each other over time. Without this time factor, the parties have a reduced sense of each other and minimal information to reduce uncertainty. As a result, the interpersonal bond is slow to form, yet emotions are intensified and supportive responses are missing (no cues that would normally motivate a supportive comment).

- *Proposition 3: Minimal social cues lead to communication that is more serious and less friendly.* The desire to be socially acceptable is less of a deterrent, and the norms of politeness and cooperation may be ignored when using e-mail. As a result, the parties tend to be more outspoken and aggressive and less likely to empathize with each other.

- *Proposition 4: Lengthy e-mails lead to less give-and-take and more focus on perceived negative statements.* Although not all e-mails are lengthy, many people tend to put all their arguments into one long e-mail. This is called argument bundling. Getting a large group of arguments causes the receiving party to view them more negatively, and there is a good chance that his or her anger will increase as each argument is read. Also, when responding to a large number of points, it is easy to overlook some of them and concentrate on the ones that appear to be the most negative.

- *Proposition 5: Excess attention to e-mail as it is read several times and an equally long response is planned leads to heightened anger and increased commitment to one's own view.* Reading the e-mail several times builds anger and diminishes the possibility of compromise, as it becomes clear that the other party intended everything that was said.

- *Proposition 6: Strength-of-relationship ties may lead to a moderating affect on the conflict.* The stronger the relationship ties and/or the more certain it is that both parties will be working together in the future, the greater the chance that a moderating effect will occur. People are more likely to give each other "the benefit of the doubt" if they know each other well or are in the same in-group. They are also more likely to be friendly and seek compromise.

PRACTICAL APPLICATION
Because of the risk of conflict escalation, Friedman and Currall suggest that "e-mail is not the preferred way to manage disputes" (p. 1342). But if e-mail is the only feasible channel, then there are ways to minimize conflict:

1. When receiving e-mail, be aware that comments you perceive as negative may not be intended as

negative. Use perception checking and be ready to apologize if a misunderstanding occurs.

2. When sending e-mail, edit all your messages carefully. Even a relatively calm statement "can be easily misinterpreted as being more aggressive than intended" (p. 1342). Think of possible ways that your statement could be interpreted, and reword it several times if needed.

3. Think carefully before deliberately sending negative comments. If you are feeling unusually aggressive or angry, make sure you really want to make that response. How would you feel if it were sent to you?

4. If you have a prior relationship with the other person and/or will likely be working with them again in the future, mention it; social ties help to reduce conflict.

5. When people get angry they tend to become overly logical in their arguments and forget that persuasion involves emotion as well as logic. Include emotional arguments along with your logical ones.

6. Although e-mail is not a text message, as much feedback as possible is needed during conflict. Instead of sending one long e-mail, divide the message or arguments into categories or sections and send them separately. Be sure to edit your subject line so each e-mail has a different and specific title. Sending too many arguments in one e-mail appears overwhelming and negative. If it is necessary to send one longer e-mail, preface it with one or two shorter, introductory e-mails. When sending a long e-mail, use boldfaced headings and bullets when possible to simplify the look of the message.

Key Source: Friedman, R. A., & Currall, S. C. (2003). Conflict escalation: Dispute exacerbating elements of e-mail communication. *Human Relations, 56*(11), 1325–1347.

APPLY **WHAT YOU KNOW**
RELATIONSHIPS AND CONFLICT

To apply what you know about relationships, conflict escalation, and technology, complete the following critical thinking questions below:

- In the roommate conflict over perception and attributions on page 188, could unfulfilled needs or assigning fault have played a role in the conflict escalation as well as faulty attributions? Why?

- Applying what you have learned from previous chapters, what two perception checks could be used to defuse the roommate conflict and one that could make it worse? Remember that a good perception check contains three parts (see Chapter 2, pages 39–45 for help). Share your perception checks with others.

- Think of a recent situation in your life in which conflict resulted from an e-mail message. Give a brief explanation of the situation, what main proposition of DEME was likely responsible, and what you did or could have done to defuse the situation.

The Aggressive Style

Aggressive communicators prefer to confront conflict directly in a manner that makes it clear that they are aggrieved. Their message is, "*My needs are important; yours are not.*" The **aggressive style** is marked by exaggerated verbal and nonverbal expression. Habitual explosive anger, verbal tongue-lashings, and nonverbal hostile behaviors are the hallmark of the aggressive communicator. Aggressive people are almost always people with high control needs, though not all dominant people are aggressive. Despite their hostile behaviors, aggressive people may actually need affection. Their aggression, in fact, may be a sort of temper tantrum brought on when they feel that they are being thwarted in their attempts to get their needs met. Aggressive behavior may succeed in getting one's needs attended to; however, as you can imagine, it has the potential to do untold damage to the relationship. Aggressive communication, like all communication, is irreversible—once it's been said, you can't wipe it away.

The Passive-Aggressive Style

In our list of conflict management styles, the **passive-aggressive style** deserves a special place. The message of the passive-aggressive communicator is, *"I'll pretend that I think your needs are important to me, but they really aren't."* Passive-aggressive people are angry but seldom own up to their personal feelings. This does not mean that they will allow their partners' perceived transgressions to go unpunished. Far from it! They do not play the role of passive doormat! On the other hand, they do not want to be accused of being a mean aggressive. So they devise a way to punish their transgressor in such a subtle and obscure way that for their partners to call attention to what they are doing would be to appear overly sensitive, humorless, or aggressive themselves. Passive-aggressive people can then get pleasure in casting themselves in the role of innocent victims.

Here are a few examples of passive-aggressive tactics:

- *The silent treatment.* When someone asks if you are upset, a passive-aggressive behavior would be to respond with a wide-eyed and perplexed facial expression, followed by a brief wounded look, and then an obvious attempt to compose your face again into a study of wonderment that the other would think such a thing.

- *The innocent approach.* You might also take the innocent approach by saying something like "You mean I did that wrong? I was just trying to help."

- *The joking approach.* You could make a cruel joke at your partner's expense (whether in public or private) and then chide the partner for lack of humor when s/he appears hurt.

Have you observed these tactics being used in the past? There are many other similar tactics used by passive-aggressive persons. To be fair, sometimes people develop a passive-aggressive style in order to counter their partners' habitual aggressions. The issue is control; the passive-aggressive person may not know how to get control in more productive ways. However, some people enjoy their passive-aggressive game; they especially enjoy it if they can induce their partners to overreact to such a degree as to lose personal control. However, make no mistake about it: passive-aggressive behavior is often nasty and is always emotionally dishonest. **Emotional dishonesty** is not owning up to your feelings and then punishing your partner because your needs were not met.

The Assertive Style
Although we are reluctant to claim that any one communication skill or behavior is "the best" approach to handling conflict, the **assertive style** of conflict management has so much to commend it that it should be cultivated by everyone. Assertive communicators look for conflict resolutions that will satisfy both parties. The message conveyed by assertive communicators is:

"My needs are important to me, but your needs are just as important." They encourage others to express their needs and are genuinely interested in what others have to say. At the same time, they openly and honestly express their own needs but do not resort to manipulation to get their own way. Assertive communicators demonstrate that their primary concern is the health of their relationships. For suggestions on using the assertive style, see the *Developing Skills* feature on page 196.

Conflict Outcomes

From our previous description of relationships and conflict, you may have concluded that a positive outcome is too idealistic to be expected. However, a satisfying resolution should be attainable with effort and an awareness of conflict outcomes (Weaver, 1984). In most cases, the assertive communication style—because it considers both your own needs and those of your partner—is usually the best method.

Win-Win

The most desirable outcome is a **win-win** solution in which both parties are able to get their needs met. Although it may be unreasonable to expect that all parties will get *all* their needs met, assertive communicators prefer that all parties get their major needs met when possible. Communicators often give up on this possibility too soon. Assume that you and your spouse are in conflict over where to take your vacation. You favor a beach destination, and your spouse prefers Las Vegas. The discussion gets heated as you each insist on your choice, and you reach an impasse where only one of you can win.

The key to exploring a win-win outcome is for both of you to forget destinations for the moment and focus on the reasons for your choices. For you, the ideal vacation is one that enables you to relax, read a book or two, and soak up rays of the sun. Your spouse, however, is looking for some excitement—a lively environment, good food, and an array of entertainment options. Having identified the qualities you both desire in a vacation destination, you may now explore other destinations that would enable you both to get the kind of break you are seeking—a cruise, for example. This third option, a cruise that satisfies all your needs as well as your spouse's, would not have been considered if you had remained fixed on your initial destinations.

Compromise

Sometimes needs are such that an option cannot be found that completely fulfills the goals of both parties. If this is the case, the second-best outcome is a **compromise**. The downside of a compromise is that both parties give up something; no one is the "winner." However, both will get part of their needs met, though certainly less than in the win-win outcome. Back to the vacation example: you'll give up the sun if you can keep the relaxation; your spouse will give up the gambling as long as good food is available. If cruises make you seasick, there are plenty of other options that feature both good food and relaxation—a satisfactory compromise. Although compromise is viewed as a second choice, all conflict styles from passive to assertive use it when needed.

LEARNING OBJECTIVE

7.4 What are several possible outcomes to conflict, and which outcomes usually result from the passive, aggressive, passive-aggressive, and assertive conflict styles?

A cruise was a win-win outcome for this couple.

DEVELOPING SKILLS
HOW TO COMMUNICATE ASSERTIVELY

Assertive communicators are able to present their ideas without causing an angry, defensive response because they use confirming messages instead of disconfirming ones (Gibb, 1961, 1970; Wilmot & Hocker, 2007).

Confirming messages convey that you value the other person and regard his or her needs as important; **disconfirming messages** imply that the other person is not valued and his or her needs are not important to you.

Think about how many of the following types of confirming messages you typically use. To become more assertive, make plans to begin using one or two additional types of confirming messages until they become almost automatic, even in emotional situations:

• *Descriptive Comments.* One of the best ways to make assertive comments is to be sure that the comments describe the *behavior* you find objectionable rather than the *character* of the person. Also, when speaking, own your feelings by using "I" in the statement. "I was surprised when you decided to invite people over without warning me" is an example of a descriptive comment. On the other hand, if you find yourself making statements that accuse or blame the other person, you are making *evaluative* comments. This type of comment usually includes the word "you" and causes people to become defensive.

• *Problem-Solution Comments.* Assertive comments take a problem-solution approach rather than an "I-know-best" approach. This approach indicates that you regard the other's needs and preferences as being equally important to yours and that your goal is to find a win-win solution when possible. Saying, "Let's discuss how we should go about making social plans in the future" is an assertive approach.

Saying, "I'm not going to entertain your guests anymore unless you give me advance warning" takes a control approach that is certain to cause a defensive reaction.

• *Equality Comments.* Assertive comments imply that you regard the other person to be equally as capable as you of rational thought and moral judgment. "I'm really interested in how you came to that decision" is an example of communication that emphasizes equality. Of course, you have to say this with sincerity and not with a smirk or critical tone of voice. However, if you were to say, "Well, I wouldn't have done that to you!" you are suggesting that your intelligence, judgment, and moral character are superior.

• *Spontaneous Comments.* Assertive communicators are more likely to enter the discussion with no preset agenda. They are willing to make their judgments as they go, based on whatever gets revealed and reply with comments that are honest, open, and spontaneous. Before making comments, however, you will want to make sure you understand the other person's frame of reference and that you don't make spur-of-the-moment comments that could hurt someone's feelings. Ask questions; don't assume. Once the situation and feelings are clear, then you can respond. Aggressive, and especially passive-aggressive, communicators are more likely to have a planned strategy; they have determined the outcome they desire, and they have devised a strategy for achieving it.

• *Open Comments.* Assertive comments make it clear that you are giving your opinion but that you are open to negotiation and even change. This is an important idea if you genuinely desire to hear and understand others' points of view while also gaining their respect for your own. When you convey that your idea is the only correct view —as the aggressive communicator does— you are communicating that you are closed to any other points of view.

• *Empathetic Comments.* Assertive communicators make empathetic comments that show that they care rather than taking a neutral position that shows indifference and says, "I don't care." When people say that they are unwilling to accommodate you because they have a policy and they don't make exceptions to their policy, they are communicating neutrally. They seem to be saying, "There's nothing special about you." To be sure, there are often situations in which policies must be adhered to. However, even in those cases, the relationship is more likely to benefit if you change your verbal and nonverbal elements slightly: "I wish I could do that for you, but I can't. I regret that it might be upsetting to you, but I cannot feel good about the unfairness to others if I make an exception for you."

Win-Lose

Sometimes, however, your needs truly are mutually exclusive. You crave New York City, but your spouse needs mountain air. In such a situation, you may have to settle for a **win-lose** outcome. As the label suggests, one of you gets your needs met, and the other does not. Both the aggressive and the passive communicator often prefer this method. It may be hard, at first glance, to see how this could be an acceptable alternative for an aggressive communicator, particularly if s/he is the "loser." However, there is a way to convert this objectionable outcome into one that satisfactorily resolves the conflict—add a word to the label for this outcome: *Equitable win-lose.* Equity is fairness. An equitable win-lose is achieved when partners agree and honor the agreement that one will "win" this one, but the other will win the next.

Lose-Lose

The least satisfactory outcome is the **lose-lose** outcome. This is the result when both party's focus is: "If my needs aren't met, then yours won't be either" (e.g., "That's fine; we just won't go on a vacation this year"). This is a particularly virulent form of relational gamesmanship, sometimes part of the repertoire of the passive-aggressive communicator: "Maybe you should just go on your own vacation. I'll just stay here and work to pay for it." We can see that the goal here is to retaliate and to punish the other. Striving for this sort of outcome will extend the conflict, generating negative feelings that will linger for a long time and may be impossible to overcome.

APPLY **WHAT YOU KNOW**
RELATIONSHIPS AND CONFLICT OUTCOMES

To apply what you know about relationships and conflict, answer these critical thinking questions:

- Which conflict style (passive, aggressive, passive-aggressive, or assertive) do you use more often? Why do you think this is the case?

- Select a television or movie character that is a good example of each of the conflict styles and explain your reasons for the choices.

- Which conflict outcome do you seem to use more often? Why? Give an example of a recent situation when the conflict outcome occurred.

CHAPTER SUMMARY

As this chapter has stressed, maintaining successful relationships, especially during conflict, requires knowledge and skill. You can determine your knowledge of relationships and conflict by checking the skills and learning objectives presented in this chapter.

Summary of **SKILLS**

Check each skill that you now feel qualified to perform:

- ❏ I can evaluate one or more of my relationships to determine which stage of development or deterioration is involved and make changes for improvement as needed.
- ❏ I can identify any conflict escalators present in my relationships and work to minimize their effects as well as assess my typical conflict style.
- ❏ I can communicate assertively by using confirming messages and learn to use the win-win method to solve conflicts.
- ❏ I can manage my interpersonal relationships and conflicts in a flexible manner by applying some of the communication tips provided in this chapter.

RELATIONSHIPS **AND YOUR CAREER**

7.5 What information and skills covered in this chapter relate specifically to your career?

Managing interpersonal relationships and conflict will be of special importance to you in your career. The following career features take a look at interpersonal relationships specifically as they relate to careers in business, education, and healthcare. Whatever career you choose, the following information should interest you.

SPOTLIGHT ON **RELATIONSHIPS AND CONFLICT**

BUSINESS

Aggressive communicators—especially the bully—can make relationships miserable in the work environment. Steve Adubato gives some great advice for handling bullies in his book *Make the Connection* (2006, pp. 170–171):

- Work on making your body language strong and confident. Bullies pick their victims from people "with poor posture, downcast eyes, and a drooping head."

- Tell your colleagues, who can serve as a buffer and make sure you are not left in isolation—the preferred situation of the bully.

- Don't ignore bullies; confront them. Ignoring them just makes them angry and more determined: "Hey, Sam, lay off. I'm not interested in what you think" or "Your comments are unacceptable. I'd appreciate it if you would stop."

- Practice confronting the bully using your mirror. Effective communication of all types requires practice.

EDUCATION

Conflict in the classroom can disrupt learning and hamper the quality of relationships between the teacher and students. Mottet et al. (2006) discuss a study by Boice (1996, p. 463), where both teachers and students ranked the same three student misbehaviors as the most disturbing. Do you agree?

1. Students who converse so loudly during class that neither the teacher nor other students can be heard

2. Students who confront the teacher with sarcastic comments or groans

3. Students who make unpredictable and highly emotional outbursts causing the class to become uncomfortable

To minimize conflict, create a positive classroom climate including (Mottet et al., p. 20):

- Making assignments enjoyable.

- Being optimistic and enthusiastic.

- Treating students with respect.

- Appearing relaxed and comfortable.

- Showing interest and caring.

HEALTHCARE

Although 90% of patients want Internet access to their doctors, only 10–15% of physicians use it regularly (Roter, et al., 2008). In "Can E-Mail Messages between Patients and Physicians Be Patient-Centered?" Roter answered the following concerns:

- *Can e-mail remain patient-centered?* Statements used by 72% of physicians and 59% of patients were task related (information & questions); other statements "were used to express and respond to emotions and to build a therapeutic partnership" (p. 84). Note: Although doctors talk twice as much as patients in face-to-face sessions, patients wrote twice as much in e-mail messages.

- *Can conflict be handled effectively by e-mail?* Patients made complaints of their doctor in 8% of their statements. Physicians responded to the criticisms "with empathy or apologies," and some suggested that the issue "be resolved by phone or in person" (p. 84), which seemed to please the patients.

CAREER MOMENT **INTERPERSONAL SKILLS**

In many instances, job interviewers are more interested in your interpersonal skills than they are in your computer skills or knowledge of your field. Therefore, when you are interviewing for your ideal job, your communication and interpersonal skills will give you an edge whether that job is in communication, business, education, healthcare, or in such other fields as engineering, law, accounting, dental hygiene, or criminal justice.

Having this basic communication course on your resume is good, but having an additional course or two is even better. It would show that you are really concerned with communication, and that you have advanced skills that make you especially desirable as a job candidate. Employers know that they can polish your knowledge and skills of the job, if needed. However, training you to be an effective communicator is much more difficult and, in some cases, impossible. Therefore, they want to hire candidates who already know how to communicate successfully.

We would like to recommend an excellent second speech course for you to take: **Interpersonal Communication**. Improving your interpersonal skills will improve your success in the workplace, regardless of the specific field you decide to pursue. Check with your instructor or the chairperson of the communication department for specifics on taking an interpersonal communication course.

CONNECTING TO **BUSINESS**

Are you considering a business or professional career? If so, you will certainly experience conflict. Consider the following meeting between managers of departments in a large company:

- Nester, from marketing, tells the group that marketing needs two more employees to keep the company competitive.
- Joan, from computers, believes that updating the software programs would be more cost effective. Joan speaks loudly and refuses to let others give their opinions.
- Finally, Del, sales, interrupts Joan and accuses her of misinterpreting the financial figures she has been spouting.
- Rick, human resources, wants to join in but says nothing and looks at the agenda instead of at the group members.
- Joan stalks out saying that she will report this worthless meeting to upper management.

ACTIVITY

In groups of three to five, use the information in this chapter to answer the following questions:

1. What were the sources of conflict in this meeting?

2. What conflict managing styles were used by each manager, and how did each style affect the group?

3. How might the conflict be resolved?

CONNECTING TO **EDUCATION**

Are you considering a career in education? If so, you will want to develop a feeling of closeness (immediacy) with your students. One way to create a relationship with your students is through positive verbal strategies. Mottet and Richmond (1998) identified several approach/avoidance verbal variables that people use when pursuing or avoiding relationships. A more recent study (Mottet, Martin, & Myers, 2004) found that when instructors used verbal approach strategies, students were more motivated to communicate with them.

ACTIVITY

1. In groups of four or five, think about your own experiences with teachers and brainstorm a lengthy list of the following:

   • Comments that teachers might say that would probably make students feel more "distant" or "removed."

   • Comments that teachers might say that would probably make students feel "closer" to them.

2. Discuss which approach strategies might cause you the most difficulty and which ones would seem fairly easy.

CONNECTING TO **HEALTHCARE**

Are you considering a career in healthcare? If so, your verbal messages can have a definite effect on patients and on your relationships with them. Consider this situation:

Mr. Turner has been having pain in his right leg and has been admitted to the hospital. Tests show that he has cancer and that the leg needs to be removed. He refuses to let anyone in the room and is calling everyone "incompetent fools." It is your job to calm Mr. Turner, but he just told you that you are an idiot and ordered you from the room.

ACTIVITY

In groups, practice using confirming messages.

1. First discuss why Mr. Turner is using the aggressive conflict style—see the situation from his viewpoint.

2. Review the confirming and disconfirming messages discussed on page 196.

3. Write out verbal comments you could say to Mr. Turner that would represent disconfirming messages.

4. Now write out comments you could say to Mr. Turner that would represent confirming messages.

5. In pairs, with one of you playing Mr. Turner and one of you being the healthcare provider, role-play the situation. First use disconfirming messages; then use confirming messages.

▶ Log onto MyCommunicationLab.com to access Connecting to Psychology and Connecting to Science, Technology, Engineering, and Math—both with related activities.

Summary of LEARNING **OUTCOMES**

7.1 *What are the five stages of relationship development and the five stages of relationship deterioration?*

- Knapp's stages of relationship *development* include the initiating, experimenting, intensifying, integrating, and bonding stages.
- The stages of relationship *deterioration* include the differentiating, circumscribing, stagnating, avoiding, and terminating stages.

7.2 *What is the definition of* conflict, *what are several conflict escalators to avoid, and what theory explains why conflict often results from e-mail messages?*

- *Conflict* is an "expressed struggle between at least two interdependent parties who perceive incompatible goals, scarce rewards, and interference from the other party in achieving their goals." In order for conflict to exist, it must be outwardly expressed.
- *Conflict escalators* include unfulfilled needs, faulty attributions (perception), assigning fault or cause to others' behaviors (punctuation), and unethical behavior.
- The way that conflict relates to e-mail is discussed in the *Making Theory Practical* feature on pages 192–193.

7.3 *What are the four styles that people use in managing conflict, what is the main focus of each style, and what are some suggested ways to communicate assertively?*

- When they find themselves in conflict situations, people tend to use one of four conflict styles: passive, aggressive, passive-aggressive, and assertive.
- People who are uncomfortable with open conflict tend to use the passive style and handle conflict by denial, avoidance, or accommodation. People who prefer to confront conflict directly handle conflict in the aggressive manner with exaggerated verbal and nonverbal expressions.

People who are angry but don't want to own up to their personal feelings handle conflict in the passive-aggressive manner by devising a way to punish the other person in a subtle and obscure way by using the silent treatment, the innocent approach, or the joking approach. People who look for a resolution to conflict that will satisfy all parties involved are using the assertive style of handling conflict.

- For suggestions on how to communicate assertively, see the *Developing Skills* feature on page 196.

7.4 *What are several possible outcomes to conflict, and which outcomes usually result from the passive, aggressive, passive-aggressive, and assertive conflict styles?*

- Four main outcomes to conflict are the win-win, compromise, win-lose, and lose-lose approaches.
- Since the win-win outcome allows all parties to get major needs met, it is the preferred outcome of the assertive communicator. Other conflict styles may try this outcome, but give up too soon because it requires time and effort.
- The compromise outcome is used by all conflict styles as a second choice; the win-lose outcome is preferred by the aggressive communicator and sometimes the passive communicator; the lose-lose outcome is not desired by any conflict style, but both the passive-aggressive and the aggressive communicators use it as a form of punishment.

7.5 *What information and skills covered in this chapter relate specifically to your career (see highlighted fields of business, education, and healthcare)?*

- The *Spotlight on, Career Moment*, and *Connecting to* features highlight the importance of developing relationships and managing conflicts in the fields of business, education, and healthcare—additional fields are included online.

SOLVE IT NOW!

Taking into consideration all that you learned about relationships and conflict from this chapter, how would you analyze Patrick and Gina's communication in our opening scenario? *

- Who do you think is most at fault for their relationship difficulties and why?

- Which conflict escalator, if any, is causing the most problems: unfulfilled needs, faulty attributions, or assigning fault? Why?
- What does each person need to do to produce a win-win resolution to their conflict?
- Which assertive comments would be the most helpful for Patrick and Gina to improve their relationship now and in the future? Why?

*(Check your answers with those located in MyCommunicationLab, Scenario Analysis for Chapter 7)

The next two chapters will deal with working in groups—teamwork (especially problem-solving in teams) is one of the most important skills in business and the professions.

KEY TERMS

SKILL BUILDERS

1. Divide into all-male and all-female groups. Each group will be using the chapter opening scenario about Patrick and Gina.
• Female groups should focus on Patrick and (1) decide what specific steps and/or communication strategies he should take to salvage the relationship; (2) provide a brief reason for each suggestion; and (3) make a written copy of their ideas.
• Male groups should focus on Gina and (1) decide what specific steps and communication strategies she should take to salvage the relationship; (2) provide a brief reason for each suggestion; and (3) make a written copy of their ideas.
• Now each group should exchange written papers with a group of the opposite gender and critique the other group's suggestions and reasons using this scale:
5—Great job!
4—Some suggestions would work.
3—These suggestions are better than nothing, but. . . .
2—Ouch! Some of these suggestions show a lack of understanding.
1—Run (don't walk) to sign up for a class in gender communication!
• If time allows, open the discussion to the entire class and discuss what things surprised, shocked, or pleased you the most.

2. Critically Evaluating
Using the critical evaluation form from Chapter 1, select and evaluate an article on *relationships* or *conflict* obtained from a communication journal such as *Communication Education* (you may wish to check your library databases for articles). Be prepared to share your observations with your classmates.
3. The section on stagnating relationships included several reasons why people choose to remain in stagnating relationships. In groups, expand this list of reasons by applying social exchange theory (discussed in Chapter 6); then answer the following questions:
• What explanation does this theory offer for why couples stay in relationships that have reached the stagnating stage? List at least three reasons and explain why these arguments make sense to the couples who use them.
• Have you or anyone you know had a relationship that reached the stagnating stage? If so, which reason on your list more clearly described their experience? Be prepared to share and support your group's ideas with the class.
4. Unless we consciously made a decision to change, most of us learned our method for handling conflict from our families while growing up. Which styles did your caregivers use? Are these methods the ones that you typically use today? If yes, discuss why; if no, discuss why not.

EXPLORE SOME MORE . . .

Watch the following movies for examples of interpersonal relationships:
• *The Devil Wears Prada* (2006)—Shows Meryl Streep who plays Miranda, fashion editor of *Runway* magazine, bullying her employees. Would you say she uses the aggressive or the passive-aggressive conflict style?

• *Ambulance Girl* (2005)—Kathy Bates plays a professional woman with relationship problems who adds purpose and close relationships when she trains to be a volunteer EMT (emergency medical technician).

8 Communicating in Problem-Solving Groups

8.1 What are the differences between groups, teams, and virtual teams, and what are the three types of groups used most often? What is a service-learning project, and how do you organize one if assigned?

8.2 When making decisions, when do individual decisions work best? When do group decisions work best?

8.3 What are the characteristics of successful small groups, and what theory offers helpful advice?

8.4 What are the six steps of the group problem-solving process, what occurs in each step, and what theory is especially helpful when analyzing a problem?

8.5 What information and skills covered in this chapter relate specifically to your career (see highlighted fields of business, education, and healthcare)?

After studying this chapter you should be able to . . .

- Organize a service-learning project or a problem-solving group and effectively participate in one if the opportunity arises.
- Compare and contrast when individual or group decisions would work best to solve problems in your own life and implement each as needed.
- Describe the characteristics of successful groups, including their rules, norms, and phases, and use this information to improve your group participation.
- Put into action the steps of the group problem-solving process with success when participating in group experiences whether in business, education, or healthcare settings.

CHAPTER SUMMARY ⟩ P. 227 ⟩

SCENARIO

Sheila sat alone in the library meeting room, wondering where everyone was. Did she have the wrong place or the wrong time? She looked over the handout her Communication professor had given her when he assigned her to the group. She was unfamiliar with the concept of service learning but hoped one of the four members coming would be able to shed some light—"if they ever get here."

Darron was the next to arrive. Sheila and Darron had never really talked, just exchanged pleasantries in the hall sometimes, but she had the impression he was nice enough, though perhaps a little shy since he rarely said anything in class.

"Hey," Darron greeted her. "Sorry I'm late."

"You're not the only one late. I hope this isn't going to be a group where we waste a lot of time waiting for people to show up. That's one of the things I don't like about working in groups."

"My problem is that I usually end up doing a lot of the work because others don't take the project seriously. They basically get a free ride," Darron observed.

"I don't know why Professor Jackson doesn't let us work individually on this; we could get a lot more done in a lot less time. You can be sure we'll spend most of the time arguing and trying to agree on compromises," Sheila added.

"That's true," Darron agreed. "Hey, I don't know what we're supposed to be doing on this assignment. Have you ever heard of this 'service-learning' thing?"

Teresa entered the room at that moment and overheard Darron's question. "Oh, I have. We did a service-learning project in one of my classes a couple of semesters ago. It can really be a lot of fun, but it's certainly hard work."

"Well, let's hope some of the others know what we're supposed to do and have some great ideas to offer," Sheila said. "In the meantime, do you think we should go ahead and get started? There are three of us here, and that's a majority."

"Yeah," Darron concurred. "I want to get this meeting over with so I can meet friends for lunch. It shouldn't take long to decide what kind of project we want to do, and we can assign most of the work to the two who aren't here yet."

Teresa laughed. "That would serve them right for being late. Though I wasn't exactly punctual myself—sorry about that."

"It's okay," Sheila shrugged. "Tell us about service learning and we'll take it from there."

As you read this chapter, look for specific advice that would help the students in our opening scenario work with each other and plan their service-learning project. If you can identify the difficulties that Sheila and her classmates are having with their group and service-learning project, you will find your own group experiences, whether in a classroom, community setting, or work environment, more successful and enjoyable.

SOLVE IT NOW! 〉 P. 230 〉

Does this sound like a group you have participated in—people confused about what is expected and who's in charge, with varying expectations and knowledge levels, and with communication hampered by incompatible goals, motivation, and work ethics? The words *group* and *project* fill many people with dread. Yet working in groups is a fact of life. If you think about it, much of what is accomplished in the workplace, in education, and in civic life is the product of decision-making by groups of various sizes. If you aren't comfortable working in groups, the information in these next two chapters on group communication should have a positive influence on your career as well as your college education. Both require knowledge of small group dynamics and an ability to work in teams.

The Nature of Groups

It takes more than a collection of people to make a *group*. For example, on the first day of any class you will see a wide variety of students—a collection of people. When, if ever, during the term does that collection of people become a group? The passengers on an airplane are a collection of people—what might have to happen to make them become a group?

LEARNING **OBJECTIVE**

8.1 What are the differences between groups, teams, and virtual teams, and what are the three types of groups used most often? What is a service-learning project, and how do you organize one if assigned?

What Makes a Group?

For a collection of people to become a *group*, four distinguishing features are needed:

1. *The number of people must be small enough for everyone to actively participate.* Most college classes are too large for everyone to participate on a regular basis unless the professor breaks the class into smaller groups. This is why there are usually three to seven students in a class who do most of the talking. It would be impossible to cover the material necessary for a course if everyone had a chance to participate each day on each topic.

2. *The people must be interacting together to achieve common goals.* Just because students are in the same class does not mean they all have the same goal or reason for taking the class. Your goal might be to earn an "A"; but other students might think a "C" would be great. Even if you all wanted an "A," you wouldn't be a group unless you were interacting together to achieve the grade (study groups, research teams, tutoring sessions, and so on). So, would standing in line with several of your friends to buy tickets for a concert represent a group? If you answered no, you are correct. Although you have a common goal and are enjoying this gathering of friends, you are not working together to achieve that goal. It is also important to note that when we use the word *group*, we are not including social groups that gather informally for the purpose of enjoying time together.

3. *The people should be interacting face-to-face.* Although virtual groups are able to communicate with all members without being face-to-face (FTF), communication and understanding are more difficult without nonverbal communication and the instant feedback you get FTF. Unless the team members have worked together in the past, it is advisable that they meet FTF at least once—usually at the beginning of the project—to get to know each other's unique qualities and cultural background, establish a common frame of reference through shared experiences, and build trust. (Bock, 2003). It is also advised that in addition to the initial FTF meeting, virtual teams meet "at key points throughout the team's relationship" (Davis & Scaffidi, 2007, p. 17).

4. *The people should have a number of meetings over an extended period of time.* Groups that meet for a limited number of times—perhaps only once—may be able to solve a single task but won't have time to create history, group norms, or a feeling of identity that is important to the creativity and productivity of successful groups.

For our purposes in this chapter and the next, when we use the term **group**, we are referring to *small groups* and will use the following definition: *Small group communication involves a small number of people (usually 3–7) who have multiple face-to-face meetings over an extended period of time and who interact to achieve common goals.*

Teams and Virtual Teams

Although *teams* and *groups* are used interchangeably by many people, there is a slight difference. A group is a generic term that applies to many types and sizes of gatherings. A **team**, on the other hand, is a type of group that is "a high-performing task group whose members are actively interdependent and share common performance objectives" (Francis & Young, 1992, p. 9). In addition, "the word *team* also has come to connote closer cooperation and cohesiveness than the term *group*" (Tubbs, 2009, p. 6). In other words, a team is very much like the small group we defined above: It is relatively small; members work together closely over a period of time; they get to really know and respect each other; they share in decision making and work together to solve conflicts; they work to achieve quality and are committed to productivity (Diamond & Diamond, 2007).

A **virtual team** is similar to a small group with the exception that members "are geographically and/or organizationally or otherwise dispersed and . . . collaborate via communication and information technologies in order to accomplish a specific goal" (Zigurs, 2003, p. 340). Virtual teams have all the characteristics of a small group except for the face-to-face interaction. However, as mentioned earlier, virtual teams should meet FTF at the beginning of a project and at important junctures throughout the project when possible. This is especially important when team members do not know each other; less crucial if the members have worked together in the past.

Groups and Culture/Gender/ Ethics/Technology

There are many factors that affect how people interact in a group setting and, therefore, impact the success of a group or team. Culture is certainly one of these factors and will be discussed also in more detail later when we focus on characteristics of successful groups. In this section, we will look at all four factors that can affect a group's outcome—culture, gender, ethics, and technology.

Culture
Not all cultures approach discussions and problem solving in the same manner. Whether you work in an area that is culturally diverse or you are in an intercultural/global work group, it is important to understand the collectivist/ individualist difference of cultures discussed in earlier chapters. Recall that individualistic cultures (countries such as Canada and the United States) expect people to be task oriented and speak up when they disagree. They also tend to attack a problem from a linear approach that values reasoning and logic. Each piece of the problem is dealt with and, once an issue is decided upon, there is no need to discuss it again at a later time. However, collectivistic cultures (such as Korea, China, and Japan) are more relationship-

oriented than task-oriented and expect people to be conciliatory and concerned with face-saving of self and others (Nibler & Harris, 2003). They are more likely to approach a problem from a holistic view and reopen topics for later discussion if they feel that a new topic relates to it in some way (McDaniel, et al., 2009). Understanding these different approaches to problems can lower the frustration level of a group.

Gender

Research indicates that there are some differences in the way males and females communicate. For example, Gay (2009) summarizes it this way: "European American females use more affiliating, accommodating, and socially bonding language mechanisms, while males are more directive, managing, controlling, task focused, and action oriented in their discourse styles" (p. 359). Although these differences may cause some difficulties in problem-solving discussions, it may be gender expectations that men and women hold that cause even greater difficulties. On the other hand, while groups in the United States and other individualistic cultures normally view men and women on problem-solving teams as being equal, not all cultures have the same view. For example, American negotiating teams include both men and women and are likely to place a woman as head negotiator—ability is the key to selection (Samovar, et al., 2010). However, many countries, including Muslim countries such as Saudi Arabia, have real difficulties with women on negotiating teams, especially if they are the lead person (Hendon, et al., 1996, p. 174). Understanding possible gender differences can lower the frustration level of your group.

Ethics

Ethics is of major importance to successful problem-solving groups. Decisions must be supported with current, accurate information, and conversations should avoid use of exaggeration and plagiarism. Most countries agree with this view of ethics; however, whether gifts and bribes are considered ethical is another matter. If you find yourself on an international team, you will have to deal with this issue. While the United States government has strict guidelines on gifts and bribes, many countries view these as an important part of business. While it is important that you not offend others, Ferraro (2006) recommends that "acting ethically and with integrity is not only the right thing to do, but is also good for business and one's career over the long haul" (p. 146).

Technology

There are many types of technology that can be used by problem-solving groups, including conference calls, e-mail, instant messaging, desktop videoconferencing such as Microsoft's NetMeeting, and electronic brainstorming software. Each of these types of technology has strengths and weaknesses and should be chosen carefully. Strengths include speed of message transferral, message sharing, widespread location of group members, brainstorming of topics to generate more ideas is possible because the participant's name is omitted, and less group conflict when using videoconferencing (Fulk & Collins-Jarvis, 2001). Weaknesses include minimal or no nonverbal communication for interpreting meaning, e-mail more likely to increase conflict (see DEME theory discussion in Chapter 7), dislike of using technology by some members, and technical problems. Also, any cultural differences would only accentuate these problems. Selecting the proper technology and preparing ahead of time will improve group use of technology.

Types of Groups

Different types of groups include social groups, support groups, training groups, therapy groups, problem-solving groups, and many more. Types of groups that you may experience in organizations, in the classroom, or at work can be organized into three basic types:

1. **Learning groups**—There are many types of groups that involve learning, including study groups, focus groups, and training groups. Not only can more information be disseminated faster, but people in groups who are involved in collaborative learning are more motivated to get involved and tend to learn more information from each other.

2. **Self-maintenance groups**—Therapy groups such as grief recovery and Alcoholics Anonymous represent one type of self-maintenance group. Other types include groups that work together to maintain their understanding and use of communication, interpersonal skills, and conflict skills.

3. **Problem-solving groups**—Quality circles, task forces, and cross-functional teams are just a few of the many types of problem-solving groups. Since this type of group is used regularly by people in business, education, and healthcare, we will cover it in detail in this chapter. **Service-learning projects** like the one that Sheila and her group are planning in our opening scenario are usually problem-solving groups as well, although some might fall under the category of learning groups. To get a clearer idea of what a service-learning project is, read the *Developing Skills* feature in this chapter.

LEARNING **OBJECTIVE**

8.2 When making decisions, when do individual decisions work best? When do group decisions work best?

Individual versus Group Decisions

As the members of the group in the chapter opener observed, sometimes a few members will end up taking most of the responsibility while others do as little as possible. Group work is time-consuming as well, because discussions must take place before decisions are reached, and everyone needs to have some influence over the final outcome. Conflicts emerge, often threatening to derail any progress. Compromises are often necessary, sometimes leaving some members feeling dissatisfied with the group's ultimate decision. Certainly, the finished product of a problem-solving group does not always meet the standards of the ideal. Group work can be especially frustrating when some members engage in unproductive behaviors. It is hard to enjoy working with people who don't take the task seriously.

When Individual Decisions Work Best

For the reasons just stated, many people prefer working alone. Here are times when **individual decision making** does work best:

- *When fast decisions are needed.* When time is extremely short, a group usually won't be able to meet the deadline; however, an individual with experience and ability will be able to reach a decision in a shorter period of time. For example, in battle, commanders must often respond quickly to a developing situation. Not only do they not have time to convene a committee, they may not even have time to consult with an advisor.

- *When decisions are fairly simple or will affect only a few people* (such as ordering office supplies). As long as the individual has all the requisite information for making the decision, a group is not needed in this situation. In fact, imagine how it would bog

DEVELOPING SKILLS
HOW TO ORGANIZE A SERVICE-LEARNING PROJECT

Sheila and her group members aren't the only ones uncertain about service-learning projects. Volunteerism and service learning are often confused. The National Commission on Service-Learning offers this definition ("What Is," 2004): "Service-learning is a teaching and learning approach that integrates community service with academic study to enrich learning, teach civic responsibility, and strengthen communities."

It's important to realize that service learning is not a volunteer program where individuals from a class or campus complete a certain number of hours of volunteer work. Volunteerism is great, but it is not service learning. In other words, when students pick up trash in a park along a riverbed, they are volunteering and providing community service—but this is not service-learning. To make the park project into a service-learning project for a communication course, your group would need to do some or all of the following:

- *Use the group problem-solving process* discussed later in this chapter (see pp. 218–227) to select a project (possibly the park project) and organize it. For example, in Step 3, your group would list and rank criteria considered important in picking a service-learning project. Sample criteria might include selecting a project that: fits within the time and resources of team members, will be fun, provides a benefit to people in the community (nation, or world), is legal, is approved by the professor and campus officials, and so on. Then the criteria will be grouped into *musts* and *wants* with the wants ranked in importance. In Step 4, you will generate possible solutions (projects)—cleaning up the park could be one of them. Then in Step 5, you will apply the criteria to select the best project.
- *Get permission* from the community organization in charge as well as your professor and college volunteer department and plan steps to meet any requirements.
- *Actively participate* by completing the project (in this case, cleaning up the park).
- *Analyze what occurred and what your group did* (take pictures to show in a final PowerPoint presentation to the class).
- *Share your results* with the park service and/or community, possibly suggesting solutions for keeping the park clean.
- *Ask the community organization in charge to evaluate your group's project* and send the evaluation to your professor. A simple evaluation form will include three or four questions on a five-point continuum. Questions could include: *How well did the group meet its goals?* or *How much did the group project contribute to the community?* If the community organization had a representative in attendance on the day of the project, s/he might be asked whether the *appearance of team members* was appropriate and about the *attitude of group members* or *how group members interacted* during the project.
- *Reflect on what you learned doing the project*—about your community, yourself, the problem-solving procedure, working in groups, communication, and what the group could have done differently. Your professor will probably give your group an evaluation form to complete or a journal entry to write.
- *Present a written and/or oral report of the project* (including photos) to classmates in a class session or other planned meeting, and possibly make the meeting open to community members.

As you can see, service learning is more than volunteerism. Not only will you be extending learning outside your classroom and conducting a valuable project for people in the community, you will be learning how to use group problem solving and effective communication in a "real-life" situation. See the National Service Learning Clearinghouse at www.servicelearning.org for additional project ideas.

APPLY **WHAT YOU KNOW**
GROUPS AND SERVICE-LEARNING PROJECTS

Apply what you know about groups and service-learning projects by completing the following activities:

- Brainstorm a list of criteria (guidelines) that your group could use in evaluating which service-learning project to select if assigned one by your professor: for example, "a project that can be accomplished in the given time" or "a project that will be fun as well as informative."

- In groups of three or more, brainstorm a list of projects that could be used for service learning. Explain how they meet your criteria. Compare lists with other groups.

Figure 8.1 Use Individual Decisions

Use Individual Decisions When...
Fast decisions needed
Decisions fairly simple / affect few
Working with others is difficult

down the office procedure if a group were required to make all the minor decisions necessary to run an office.

- *When working with others is difficult.* Working alone is probably best if you have difficulty with relationships and can't handle conflict openly. As LaFasto and Larson observe (2001), a team is an "intricate network of relationships" and "it takes only one ineffective relationship to get in the way of a team's success" (p. 34). As we discussed in Chapter 7, relationships can't avoid all conflict; in fact, conflict can be productive if handled correctly. However, if conflicts are ignored or handled in a way that wastes time and energy, the relationship (and the team) suffers. See **Figure 8.1**.

When Group Decisions Work Best

However, there are many reasons that **group decision making** is preferred over decisions made by an individual (Beebe & Masterson, 2006; Pavitt, 2003; Frank, et al., 2004). Group decisions work best in the following situations:

- *When quality is essential.* One of the main advantages of working in a group is that doing so increases the possibility of a high-quality decision because groups have access to more resources. You have undoubtedly heard the expression that "two heads are better than one." An extension of that saying would suggest that three heads may be better than two. Everyone in the group has different experiences, different levels of expertise, and different viewpoints that may enable the group to examine a problem from multiple perspectives, preventing a decision that is made with only limited information.

- *When acceptance by a large number of people is needed.* When the members of a group represent different factions of an organization or issue, the decision has a greater likelihood of addressing the needs of all members of the larger group and, therefore, being acceptable to them.

- *When accuracy is crucial.* Since members can work together to spot mistakes or issues that have not been properly addressed, the potential for accuracy is improved. Scholars have concluded that "group judgments tend to be more accurate than the judgments of typical individuals" (Gigone & Hastie, 1997, p. 153).

Healthcare is one profession that makes use of team and virtual team decisions.

- *When tasks are complex or difficult.* When more people who can share responsibility are involved, tasks that require a great deal of work are easier on everyone. For instance, if a community-wide event is being planned, the number of details that must be taken care of may be beyond the abilities of one or two people to achieve. Also, the more minds are applied to a difficult task, the more likely they will find a quality solution. Healthcare is one area that has successfully employed group decisions—even virtual teams are used, as described in the *Spotlight on Healthcare* section later in this chapter.

- *When differing, strong opinions and conflict exist.* It is also best for a group to be involved in making a decision when it is important that the decision be one that is acceptable to everyone in the group. People are more likely to support a result when they have had a part in making the decision or when their interests are represented by a member of the group.

In general, groups have the edge over individuals acting alone in making high-quality decisions that are acceptable to a large group of people, especially when members are chosen with care and possess the communication skills necessary to be effective group participants.

Figure 8.2 Use Group Decisions

Use Group Decisions When...
Quality essential
Acceptance needed by many
Accuracy crucial
Tasks complex or difficult
Strong opinions and conflict exists

APPLY **WHAT YOU KNOW**
INDIVIDUAL VERSUS GROUP DECISIONS

In our opening scenario, Sheila is concerned with a group project her instructor has assigned—a service-learning project. She comments to her group: *I don't know why Professor Jackson doesn't let us work individually on this; we could get a lot more done in a lot less time.* Apply what you know about individual versus group decisions, and answer the following questions:

- Based on the text, how would you respond to Sheila's comment?
- What is your personal reaction to Sheila's comment and to service-learning projects? (See the *Developing Skills* feature earlier in the chapter or Google "service learning and college")
- Do you believe that group decisions generally produce the best decisions? Please explain. Be prepared to share your answers with a small group of classmates or the entire class.

Characteristics of Successful Small Groups

LEARNING **OBJECTIVE**

8.3 What are the characteristics of successful small groups, and what theory offers helpful advice?

We defined a small group earlier by stating four distinguishing features: (1) *small size*, (2) *face-to-face*, (3) *multiple meetings*, (4) *common goals*. In addition, there are other characteristics that are important if a small group or team is to be really successful and productive. Let's take a look at each of these characteristics.

The Optimum Size

The first question that often arises in discussing the topic of groups is "What exactly is the optimum size for a small group or team?" You probably received a hint earlier in our definition of small-group communication. To be the most productive, a small group or team should consist of at least three people. Dyads which include two people aren't suggested because when there are only two people involved, any conflict will pit one-against-one; in addition, it will take too long to research a complicated problem. With three members, you have more people power, can better represent a larger organization that is small to average in size, and have an odd number if a vote is required. Even so, scholars who study group process recommend five to seven members as the most productive size, with five considered to be the **optimum group size** for maximum participation (Kameda, et al., 1992). Five is regarded as optimal because it is large enough to provide diversity of opinion but not so large as to inhibit full participation by all. When a group becomes too large, some members may find that they have little opportunity to give input, and other members may find it easier to take a less active role.

Even NASA prefers the optimum size of five for groups on space missions.

When there are members who do not or cannot participate, the advantage of making decisions in a group is lost, and the potential for misunderstanding and conflict are much greater. Of course, there are cases in which a group would have to be larger than five to seven in order to accomplish the tasks assigned to it. A community-wide event in a large city, for example, may require a steering committee of a dozen or more people in order to ensure that all details are adequately addressed. Even then, smaller subcommittees of three to seven people who are engaged in a similar task may be formed in order to keep the group size manageable.

Small groups of three to seven members have been used successfully in many aspects of society. It is the small group that has allowed mega churches such as Saddleback Church in Anaheim, California, to grow to over twenty thousand members and still retain a close membership committed to giving and volunteering. Group members meet in each other's homes weekly to study and pray (Gladwell, 2005b). Drug and alcohol abuse programs such as Alcoholics Anonymous use the power of small groups to create a feeling of belonging and change behavior. Even Barack Obama in his campaign against Hillary Clinton harnessed the power of small groups of volunteers on the Internet through his social-networking tool called MyBo (which allowed supporters to organize themselves however they wanted). In March 2008, MyBo included over 8,000 self-organized groups (Dickinson, 2008).

Decision-Making Methods

Another characteristic of successful small groups or teams is the decision-making method used. There are many methods available, but only one is generally considered the best.

- *Decision by vote.* You may have noticed that the numbers we have mentioned—three, five, and seven—are all odd numbers, which would prevent the possibility of a tie vote. This is a valid reason for making your team an odd number, but it assumes that all members are always present and voting (which they aren't) and that the group has determined decision making should be accomplished by a majority **vote** (which isn't always true). The problem with voting as a method for deciding decisions is the people on the wrong side of the vote feel dissatisfied with the outcome. Voting makes winners and losers. Therefore, voting should be used only for minor issues or when other methods for reaching decisions haven't worked.

- *Decision by compromise.* **Compromise** is a method for making decisions that is generally considered to be better than voting because no one completely loses; however, no one completely wins either. All group members must give up something in order to reach the compromise. Although this decision-making method definitely works, it isn't considered to be the best method.

- *Decision by consensus.* The preferred method of reaching a decision is by **consensus**, or general agreement. Consensus is accomplished when all members agree on a solution to a problem. It may not be the preferred solution for some—or even any—members, but it is a decision that all members can live with and will be able to support during the implementation step. Note that consensus is different from compromise. In a compromise, no one gets completely what they wanted; in a consensus, everyone agrees that the final decision is a good one, and it may even be better than the original solutions group members first suggested.

Group Cohesiveness

Another characteristic of effective groups is **cohesiveness,** which is the quality that causes the members of the group to be attracted to the group and willing to endure despite challenges. Cohesive groups have a "culture of camaraderie" and increased feelings of "felt responsibility" toward the group (Tan & Tan, 2008, p. 104). Although groups that lack cohesiveness may be able to complete tasks, their commitment to the group and pride in belonging to the group are likely to be minimal. Teams with low cohesiveness are also likely to experience **social loafing** (tendency of group members to slack off, letting others carry the load). Social loafing is greatly reduced or eliminated in groups high in cohesiveness (Karau & Williams, 1993). Group size also makes a difference in social loafing: the larger the group, the more difficult it is to evaluate each person's performance, and the more social loafing is likely to occur.

There are also a number of factors that may contribute to group cohesiveness (See **Figure 8.3**) that can be intentionally implemented:

Figure 8.3 Cohesive Groups

Group Cohesiveness: Contributing factors include...
Shared goals
Sufficient diversity of members
Enduring bonds with limited membership
Competition with other groups

- *Shared goals.* In order for a group to be cohesive, all members of the group must "perceive that their goals can be met within the group" (Littlejohn & Foss, 2008, p. 241). You will recall from Chapter 6 that the interpersonal needs of people are *inclusion, control,* and *openness.* In other words, every member of the group must feel that s/he belongs and is accepted by the other members of the group, that s/he has some influence over group outcomes, and that s/he feels free to share ideas and opinions with other people in the group. It is the task of every person in the group to ensure that every other person in the group is able to get these interpersonal needs met. Unless that occurs, the group cannot be fully cohesive.

- *Group diversity.* Cohesiveness is more likely to occur when there is sufficient **group diversity** among group members to permit access to multiple perspectives yet sufficient similarity of values to ensure commonality of goals. If there are members of the group who operate with **hidden agendas**—personal goals that are more important to them than the group's goals—cohesiveness is damaged. Every member of the group must feel that the group's goals are important, and there must be some common vision for the group. If you are asked to be a member of a committee whose task is one that you think is trivial, you do everyone a disservice by agreeing to join.

- *Enduring bonds/limited membership.* Scholars who have studied group cohesion have observed that the members of some types of organizations are more likely to develop enduring bonds. For example, military units, athletic teams, and university fraternities, sororities, or other social organizations exhibit particularly strong group loyalty. One factor that may contribute to the cohesion of these groups is that membership is offered to a limited number of people. There is often a period of testing (boot camp for the military, two-a-days for athletic teams, and a "pledge" or provisional period for social clubs). When a group adopts a group nickname or slogan, and when the members wear symbols of their group membership, group pride is fostered.

- *Competition with another group.* Entering into competition with another group can greatly increase cohesiveness; the football team is never as cohesive as it is during the time when the players prepare for a showdown with the school's arch-rival team. While competition with an outside group may increase team unity, competitiveness within the group may be destructive to cohesiveness. For example, when there is a power struggle that emerges, or when coalitions form within the group, cohesiveness may be destroyed.

Cultural Diversity

With more and more organizations expanding into global markets in order to improve productivity, the chances are good that you may be offered the opportunity to join an international or virtual team during your career. Knowing how to handle cultural diversity is an important characteristic of successful small groups and teams. For example, when Advanced Micro Devices, a U.S.-based organization, decided to build a state-of-the-art factory in Germany, the cross-cultural teams of American, East German, and West German engineers faced several problems (Klyukanov, 2005):

- West Germans—viewed East Germans as out-of-date and the Americans as too informal and more concerned with speed than quality.
- East Germans—viewed West Germans as condescending.
- Americans—viewed West Germans as too formal and rational—unwilling to participate in valuable brainstorming sessions.

The final decision: "A different meeting format was designed that opened with an American-style brainstorming session, when input was encouraged from everyone, and concluded with a formal reflective process, when ideas were presented and summarized" (p. 235). Brainstorming ideas were posted on a board so exact meanings would be clear; meetings were held in English and German—members could present ideas in either language. As a result, the operation was "pronounced the most successful startup in the history of the company," and the microprocessor produced by the diverse engineers "was the most advanced in AMD's world-wide operations" (p. 235).

Teams that are culturally diverse are more creative and less susceptible to groupthink.

According to international expert Nancy Adler (2007), an important place to begin is by recognizing *cultural differences* (rather than pretending that they don't exist) and developing a *mutual respect* for all cultures on the team—which the American and German team members were finally able to do. Not all cultures approach problem solving the same way, which can cause communication difficulties; however, having multicultural or international members on the team often results in more creative solutions to problems and makes the team less susceptible to groupthink (Adler, 2007).

Absence of Groupthink

Some people think that the sign of a cohesive group is a lack of conflict. They assume that when everyone agrees, the group must be especially tight-knit. In actuality, this is not the case. In truly cohesive groups, conflict is present because it is allowed. People in cohesive groups feel free to disagree with others because they do not fear that they will be punished or expelled from the group for their dissent. In fact, a group that experiences no conflict is generally not a successful group and may be experiencing a dysfunctional condition known as groupthink (Janis, 1982; 1989). **Groupthink** occurs when members of the group refrain from expressing divergent viewpoints for fear of being sanctioned or because they like the group so much that they don't want to risk causing the group any discomfort. If you have ever been in a situation where you found yourself in disagreement with what you perceived to be the view of everyone else in the group, but you chose not to express your opinion for fear that you would be ridiculed or regarded as "not a team player," you may have been in the midst of groupthink. The problem with groupthink is that the apparent group unity may be an illusion. Although you may not be the only person who holds your view, it appears to you that you are. However, it is likely that you have experienced an instance in which all it took for a decision to be reversed was for one person to venture an opposing opinion. At that point others may have jumped in and said, "You know, I was worried about that, too." For more on groupthink, see the *Making Theory Practical* feature on page 216.

Rules, Norms, and Phases

The final characteristic of successful small groups deals with the structure of groups. Effective groups operate with certain standards of conduct, called *rules* and *norms*, and move through several fairly predictable steps, called *phases*.

Group rules are *explicit standards of conduct* that are clearly spelled out—either orally or in writing. Rules may include the location and time of meetings, membership requirements, expected behaviors, and attendance policies. Rules are powerful; if people violate them, the group will take action—violators usually will be sanctioned or punished in some way. **Group norms**, on the other hand, are *implicit standards of conduct*. They are not spelled out but simply emerge over time. For example, if one member arrives late to the meeting and no one comments on the tardiness, someone else is likely to do the same thing at another time. If the lateness still goes unnoticed, others will eventually perceive that punctuality is not required, and soon no one will feel a need to arrive on time—lateness has become an acceptable norm. Although they are not as easily recognized because they have never been discussed, norms are just as powerful as rules. Sometimes people are unaware of the existence of a norm until it is violated. Even then, you might have a hard time explaining why the offending behavior was wrong; you just know that "that's not how we do things."

Sometimes, as in the cartoon on page 217, people recognize that an unproductive norm has developed. The negative norm developed by the constantly tardy group described above is likely to become noticed as one that interferes with optimal group functioning. The problem is how you, as an effective group member, can encourage reversal of the unproductive norm. Imagine that you are the chairperson of the "Constantly Tardy Group." Should you start chastising tardy members when they arrive? Should you decide to just start meetings exactly on time? Either of these actions could backfire. Even though you are the chair, your attempts to alter the norm may be seen as a violation, particularly if everyone else is satisfied with the way things are. New leaders who try to make wholesale changes in the way a group operates often create resentment. Therefore, it is a good idea to approach the task of altering an unproductive norm carefully. New leaders

MAKING THEORY **PRACTICAL**
GROUPTHINK THEORY

Have you ever been a member of a small group that you really enjoyed yet observed one of the following occur?

• You disagreed with someone's comment, but kept your opinion to yourself.

• Members were feeling unsettled about a complaint presented by an outsider until someone described the outsider in a stereotypical way, making everyone laugh; then the uncertainty seemed to disappear.

• You started to mention a possible problem area for consideration but changed your mind when you realized that you were the only one with doubts.

If so, you were probably involved in a condition that can occur in highly cohesive groups called *groupthink*.

Theorist

Irving Janis and his colleagues developed groupthink theory to explain a negative aspect that can occur in highly cohesive groups that exert pressure on members to maintain the high level of cohesiveness (Janis, 1982; 1989). Janis defined groupthink as "a mode of thinking that people engage in when they are deeply involved in a cohesive ingroup, when members' strivings for unanimity override their motivation to realistically appraise alternative courses of action" (1982, p. 9). In other words, friendship and the good of the group take precedence over critical analysis of problems and alternatives.

Groupthink: Defective Analysis

Although members of cohesive groups generally feel comfortable enough around each other to disagree and express their opinions openly, when self-esteem needs become too important, highly cohesive groups become involved in groupthink. When this happens, faulty and even disastrous decisions may be the result, such as the decision made by a NASA group discussing the possible wing damage to the space shuttle Columbia from a piece of foam that flew off during liftoff (Borenstein, 2006). Although numerous engineers were concerned and wanted to analyze the situation critically, program managers guilty of several symptoms of groupthink kept the engineers from being heard. As a result, seven astronauts were killed when the shuttle exploded upon reentry. In hindsight, the decision not to hear the engineers was obviously a poor one. The Columbia Accident Investigation Board Report of August 2003 contained this statement: "We are convinced that the management practices overseeing the Space Shuttle Program were as much a cause of the accident as the foam that struck the left wing" (CAIB, p. 11).

Groupthink Symptoms

According to Janis, there are eight symptoms that predict groupthink and its faulty analysis of issues (Hogg & Hains, 1998; Janis, 1989):

• *Illusion of invulnerability*—feeling that the group couldn't possibly be wrong.

• *Group rationalization*—all group members making the same excuse: "We didn't have the money needed to expand our analysis."

• *Illusion of morality*—believing the group decisions will be moral, without delving into possible negative consequences:

"Of course our aid to the homeless will be effective—we are good, moral people aren't we?"

• *Shared stereotypes*—laughing at outsiders with dissenting opinions and minimizing the importance of their position: "You know how those engineers are!"

• *Self-censorship of dissenting opinions*—failing to offer differing opinions which might be disagreeable to the group: "I'm sure glad I didn't mention that idea."

• *Direct pressure*—pressure applied by the leader or members when a group member does insist on presenting a dissenting opinion: "I know you didn't really mean to upset the group, Mary. Now, let's get back to our discussion."

• *Shared illusion of unanimity*—failing to voice doubts by mistakenly believing everyone is in agreement: "I can see that we are all in agreement on that issue—let's move to the next topic."

• *Mind guarding*—protecting the group from hearing possibly upsetting information.

PRACTICAL APPLICATION

Even one person in a group can make a difference in how a group evaluates problems and solutions. Whether you are a member or a leader, you can be on the lookout for problems and suggest that the group implement one or more of these helpful techniques for defusing groupthink (Janis, 1989; Littlejohn & Foss, 2008):

1. Encourage a discussion of opposing views by asking everyone to brainstorm why some people might not approve of a particular decision.

2. Appoint someone to act as a "devil's advocate" and offer possible disadvantages to a proposed decision.

3. Invite outsiders and experts whose views differ from the majority group opinion to a meeting to present their perspectives.

4. If you are the leader, make sure everyone feels free to disagree by waiting to present your ideas until everyone else has spoken.

Primary Source: Irving L. Janis, *Groupthink: A Psychological Study of Foreign Policy Decisions and Fiascoes*, (2nd ed.), 1982. Boston: Houghton Mifflin.

are often well-advised to take some time to become a part of the group before attempting to make significant changes. Remember, too, that groups are more likely to accept decisions when they have participated in making them. Once tardiness is discussed and a new procedure is enacted by the group, the norm becomes an explicitly stated rule.

Not only are successful groups aware of the role of rules and norms, they are also aware that groups progress through fairly predictable phases— the orientation, conflict, emergence, and reinforcement phases (Fisher, 1980). At each meeting, the group can be expected to pass through all four of these stages. In fact, in a single meeting, the group may recycle through them again and again as they tackle each new aspect of their overall goal. Once you are aware of the expected phases listed below and realize the important work that must be accomplished in each phase, you will likely feel more comfortable working in groups:

© 2005 Ted Goff

"This is the most absurd, unbelievable, pointless idea I've ever heard. I like it!"

© Ted Goff

- *Orientation Phase.* As the group begins its work, a period of orientation takes place in which members work to become comfortable with one another and to develop an understanding of the task at hand. When a group is new, the **orientation phase** may require more time but will diminish with each subsequent meeting.

- *Conflict Phase.* Once the members feel oriented, the work of the group gets under-way, and conflicts may occur any time. Recall from our discussion of cohesiveness that conflict should not be regarded as a sign of a poorly functioning group. Most conflict is desirable; indeed, if there are no disagreements, groupthink is probably occurring. On the other hand, the leader must work to ensure that the **conflict phase** does not become so intense or personal that the ability of the group to reach consensus is undermined.

- *Emergence Phase.* As the members enter the **emergence phase** they will turn from debating myriad possibilities to honing in on a limited number of ideas and examining the advantages and disadvantages of each. Assuming that conflict has been well-managed in the previous phase, members may begin to embrace options that, while they are not precisely what they prefer, are acceptable *alternatives.* Emergence is a crucial stage, particularly when the group is attempting to achieve consensus so all members will have some measure of satisfaction with the proposed solution. If consensus isn't possible and the group settles for a majority vote, don't be surprised if members of the minority side feel dissatisfied because the solution is not one they can wholeheartedly endorse and because they suffered the humiliation of defeat.

- *Reinforcement Phase.* In this final phase, members review the decisions made or the tasks accomplished, reassuring themselves that they have achieved a desirable goal. This phase is often marked by high spirits as the members achieve group solidarity and pat themselves on the back. As the leader, you should recognize this as a positive stage of group development and be careful not to interrupt it prematurely. It may appear that the group is wasting time "rehashing" the process, but, in fact, the **reinforcement phase** sets the stage for productive work in the future.

APPLY **WHAT YOU KNOW**
CHARACTERISTICS OF SUCCESSFUL GROUPS

To apply what you have learned about the characteristics of successful groups, answer these questions:

- In our opening scenario, Darron was certainly worried about social loafing. Have you ever been in a group where social loafing was a problem? Discuss any solutions your group or leader tried that were not successful; what was successful?

- Select two roles and two norms that would be important for a typical group of college students and explain your choices.

- Rank order all the characteristics of successful groups from most to least important. Explain why your number one pick is so important and give an example to support your answer.

LEARNING **OBJECTIVE**

8.4 What are the six steps of the group problem-solving process, what occurs in each step, and what theory is especially helpful when analyzing a problem?

Group Problem-Solving Process

The accomplishment of the four phases of group interaction is facilitated by a structured approach to problem solving. An effective leader provides guidance to keep the group on track. This is best achieved by systematically working through the prescribed steps of the **group problem-solving process** (**Figure 8.4**) adapted from Dewey's classic reflective thinking process (Dewey, 1910). Without structure, groups are inclined to approach problem solving in a chaotic fashion. Much time is lost if your group backtracks over topics and decisions already discussed, or introduces new options at the eleventh hour. When there is no structure, groups often begin meetings by suggesting solutions and staking out positions while skipping the first several important problem-solving steps. However, as we shall see, the proposal of solutions should be reserved for a later point, after other important tasks have been achieved.

Group Process Step 1: Identify the Problem

The first step of the problem-solving process is to *identify the problem*. Sometimes this is not difficult to do since the team may have been charged with a clearly defined mission. At other times, members may be aware of symptoms, but they may have given little thought as to what is the essence of the problem. Consider, for example, this scenario:

TOM: Okay, what exactly is the problem?

RUTH: The problem is that patients are sitting in their rooms waiting for discharge for several hours when they could have gone home already. Lunchtime rolls around, and we don't have any trays for them because they weren't ordered.

FRANK: We nurses are getting a lot of flak, because we are the ones the patients complain to. Sometimes I wish we could deactivate their call buttons—or rip them out entirely! The problem is that accounting doesn't send up the necessary forms in a timely fashion.

NORA: Accounting needs to have all the information necessary before we can issue an approval for discharge. Once patients are gone, it is difficult to track them down to make sure that we have what we need. The nursing staff is not providing us with the information we need.

FRANK: Nursing isn't accounting. We can't be responsible for the financial part of hospitalization. We already have enough to do. Besides, we can't send the information until we get it, and we are always waiting on pharmacy to issue the scripts.

Figure 8.4 Basic Steps of the Problem-Solving Process

Step 1 Identify Problem

Step 2 Analyze Problem

Step 3 Establish and Rank Criteria

Step 4 Generate Possible Solutions

Step 5 Apply Criteria and Select Best Solution

Step 6 Implement and Follow-up

JACK: Pharmacy sometimes isn't notified for several hours that a patient is being discharged. In the meantime, we have a whole hospital full of patients who need their meds. We already have enough to do without having to track down who is ready for discharge.

As you can see, each member of the group may have a different idea about what the problem is, basing their perceptions on their own areas of operation. If group members fail to discuss the problem (because they assume that everyone already knows what it is) or fail to test group agreement by putting the problem into exact words, they may not even realize there is a disagreement until much later in the process when they can't reach a decision. To save time, lay out the problem in exact words early in Step 1.

Phrase Problem as a Question Not as a Statement

When you are putting the problem into words, be sure to phrase it as a question. Questions sound more open to revision than statements and are less likely to be viewed negatively by members who have some disagreement. It is also a good idea to avoid questions that can be answered "yes" or "no," questions that indicate by the way they are worded that the group has a bias, or questions that include vague terms (Wood, et al., 2000).

APPLY **WHAT YOU KNOW**
WORDING THE PROBLEM

Now that you realize why a group should clearly identify its problem early in the discussion process, expand your understanding by (1) identifying which of the following problem statements represents the *best wording* and (2) the weaknesses of the other worded problems:

- What can we do to get nursing to be more conscientious about sending complete patient information to the accounting department after the doctor has discharged the patient?

- Delay in patient discharge should receive immediate consideration by all hospital departments.

- What action should the Hospital Improvement Team recommend to shorten the discharge time for patients?

- Should the Hospital Improvement Team order extra lunches to cover patient discharge delays?

- Who is causing the ridiculous delays in patient discharge?

Phrase the Problem as a Fact, Conjecture, Value, or Policy Question

It helps to clarify your problem if you can word it as a question of fact, conjecture, value, or policy:

- A **question of fact** seeks to determine what the present situation is. Questions of fact may be either non-controversial or controversial. A non-controversial question of fact can be answered with data that includes no controversy or disagreement. "How much did we spend last year on staff training?" is a non-controversial question of fact. However, a question such as "Is our staff training program effective?" is a controversial question of fact, because it relies on the need to hear differing viewpoints on such issues as to how effectiveness is defined and measured.

- A **question of conjecture** asks what can be anticipated in the future. Questions of conjecture are especially tricky. A typical question of conjecture is "If current trends continue, what will be the situation at some point in the future?" The problem with an answer to a question of conjecture is that it is only a "best guess." However, sound policies must take into account the future. We will discuss this thorny problem more in Step 3 of the problem-solving process.

- A **question of value** is oriented toward evaluating what course of action is best or most worthy. The answers to questions of value are entirely dependent upon the nature of the group in question. Two groups dealing with the same question of value are likely to answer differently because of the differing value systems held by members of each group. There are many values that all members of a culturally homogeneous group are likely to hold. They differ, however, in each person's value system; that is, each person may have a different way of ordering the primacy of their values. One member, for example, may place comfortable working conditions ahead of salary, while another may value salary above all else. The differing value systems among members is a big challenge for working groups.

- A **question of policy** seeks to determine what course of action should be taken. In determining a course of action (usually a change from how things are done now), a group will need to first answer one or more of the other types of questions—fact, value, and maybe even conjecture. As an example, assume that you have been appointed to a task force at work to decide what your company's policy should be with respect to telecommuting. It is easy to see that your group's problem is to make a decision about policy. However, a workable policy cannot be developed without first considering a host of other questions. In Steps 2 and 3 of the problem-solving process, we will explore how those questions come into play.

So which type of question are you most likely to use in your future problem-solving discussions? The answer is—it all depends. Some groups are charged with discussing only questions of fact (controversial ones, of course, since non-controversial questions do not require discussion), conjecture, or value. For example, selection committees are essentially answering a question of value—which candidate is the best for us to choose? However, questions of policy are often the ultimate issues with which groups must grapple, so you may use that type of question more often—keeping in mind that sound policy rests on answering other types of questions as you research the problem.

APPLY **WHAT YOU KNOW**
QUESTIONS OF FACT, CONJECTURE, VALUE, OR POLICY

Apply what you know about the four types of questions by identifying which of the following is
(a) a noncontroversial question of fact; (b) a controversial question of fact; (c) a question of conjecture; (d) a question of value; or (e) a question of policy:*

1. If the current trend in patient discharge delays continues, what are the possible ramifications including hospital finances, employee satisfaction, and patient satisfaction?

2. Is the hospital discharge procedure effective?

3. What action should the Hospital Improvement Team recommend to shorten the discharge time for patients?

4. Is the money spent when discharged patients are delayed in leaving the hospital for more than two hours a wise use of hospital money?

5. How much has the number of discharged patients delayed by more than two hours each month this year increased or decreased from each month the previous four years?

Be prepared to compare answers with a classmate or members of a small group, if asked.

* Check your answers with those located in MyCommunicationLab, *Apply What You Know* for Chapter 8.

Group Process Step 2: Analyze the Problem

Once the problem is clearly identified and worded in a way that is approved by the members, it is time to *analyze the problem*. In this step, the group first breaks the problem down by considering the issues that need to be discussed, gathers any needed information on each issue, and then discusses each issue one at a time. As you think about this step, consider again the importance of having people in your group who are capable of performing the role of analyzer.

List Issues Needing Discussion
Before you do any serious research on the topic and before the group discusses the problem, it is important to make a list of items or issues that the group will need to research and discuss. It is easier if a member writes the ideas on a marker board or flip chart so everyone can readily see them. Depending on the topic, you will want to research issues such as the following:

- Causes of the problem
- Seriousness of problem
- Laws involved
- People or companies/colleges involved
- Employee/management, community/student, local/national opinions
- Money available to use in solving problem

- Past efforts to solve problem
- Negative consequences of previous solutions
- Possible negative consequences of future solutions
- People you need to interview
- Facts you need to locate

Once your list is compiled, combine or eliminate topics whenever possible to make the list as compact yet complete as possible. Then you are ready to begin data collection.

Gather Information and Discuss
In addition to your own knowledge and that of your group members, materials can be obtained by interviewing outside experts and people involved in the problem or by using the college or community library; the Internet; or newspapers, magazines, and databases available through college or company libraries. Not only should you locate information, you must also think

carefully about it and organize both the information and your thoughts about it before sharing with your group. The more planning you do ahead of time, the faster the process when the group is together.

Apply Force-Field Analysis and Discuss
An initial process that aids analyzing the problem is to apply a step-by-step, **force-field analysis** (Lewin, 1951; Swinton, 2005):

1. *Make a list of the* pros *(driving forces) and* cons *(restraining forces) of a specific group idea, decision, desired action, or plan.* **Driving forces** are those that are moving the group toward making one or more changes to the status quo; **restraining forces** are those that are holding the group back from making any changes.

2. *Assign points to each force based on its strength.* In most cases, a 12-point scale works well with 1–4 representing *weak forces*; 5–8 representing *moderate forces*; and 9–12 representing *strong forces*.

3. *Total the scores to determine if the driving forces or the restraining forces predominate and discuss what insight they offer* to the group and its problem. If the results are unexpected, be sure to discuss whether any important factors were left out of the analysis. Failure to consider important questions of fact, value, and conjecture will likely result in an unworkable policy. For a sample force-field analysis, see Chapter 8 activities in the Web site that accompanies your text.

Once the problem has been thoroughly researched, analyzed, and discussed, the group is ready to move to Step 3.

APPLY **WHAT YOU KNOW**
USING FORCE-FIELD ANALYSIS

Apply what you know about force-field analysis to the following:

- If you are working on a group project now, use your actual topic; if not, select a problem to solve that relates to your college or community and list all the topics that your group would need to research and discuss in Step 2.

- Work with your group to complete a force-field analysis on your topic ending with a visual diagram.

- Be prepared to share and explain your diagram to other groups or your class.

Group Process Step 3: Establish and Rank Criteria

A third step in the problem-solving process involves *establishing and ranking criteria* for judging solutions. **Criteria** are standards that any possible solution must meet in order for it to be acceptable to the group. The group must determine its criteria in order for a decision to be based on logic. Without criteria, groups are likely to make decisions based on emotion, meaning that the decision is based on the personal preferences of group members. The problem here is that each member may have different preferences, resulting in discussion that is likely to veer into personal issues as opposed to what is best for the group as a whole.

When to Establish Criteria?
The best time to establish criteria is normally before any detailed investigation of possible solutions. Waiting until after options are explored to establish criteria often results in people's favoring criteria that

best meet their preferred solution. This may allow bias to creep in. For example, imagine you are in the market for a new car. If you establish criteria after visiting a car lot and falling in love with a particular vehicle, the criteria will probably relate more to your desire for a particular car rather than to your daily need to carpool to work or class. Obviously it would be better to outline the requirements that any car would have to meet before visiting the automobile dealership or planning possible solutions. Sometimes, it is impossible to avoid looking at possible alternatives ahead of time, as when a selection committee is given a list of candidates to interview. Even then, however, your group should have previously developed a job description that specifies the qualifications (or criteria) you are seeking. Note that if your group uses force-field analysis, much of the criteria will emerge from that analysis of forces, including your answers to the questions of fact, conjecture, and value arrived at by your group.

Must and Want Criteria

To illustrate the difference between must and want criteria, let's continue using the example of buying a car and assume that your family is working together to purchase a new family car. **Must criteria** are reserved for required items that are absolutely necessary—you won't buy a car without them; **want criteria** are desired but not essential items—it would be really nice if the car had these items. Each family member will participate in listing criteria. The list will be narrowed and divided into must and want criteria. A possible list of must and want criteria might include

Must Criteria:
- Must cost less than $15,000.
- Must be rated for at least 25 miles-per-gallon on the highway.
- Must include side air bags.

Want Criteria:
- Great sound system.
- Sporty-looking appearance.
- Made in America.
- MP3 player hookup.
- Automatic transmission.
- Comfortable seats for at least five people.

Looking at this list, you can probably tell which ones came from the teenagers and which ones came from the parents. As soon as this family group has brainstormed their list of criteria, eliminated some and combined others, and divided them into must and want criteria, they are ready for the more emotional discussion of how to rank and/or weigh these want criteria.

Weighing and Ranking Want Criteria

Must criteria do not need to be weighed or ranked because they are already of critical importance. Any decision that does not meet all the must criteria will be eliminated without further discussion. That is why must criteria are kept to a minimum. However, want criteria do need to be ranked in some fashion. It is at this point in a discussion that members tend to get emotional as they select the criteria they think are the most important and give their reasons why. In this case our family group buying a car might rank the want criteria from most to least important giving six points to the most important all the way down to one point to the least important (because there are six want criteria). Or they might assign each want criterion a weight of 1, 2, or 3 points:

> 3 = very important
> 2 = moderately important
> 1 = important

How would you rank or weigh the want criteria listed above? Would comfortable seats for five people rank higher than an automatic transmission or a great sound system? Once the group can come to agreement on the importance of the criteria that will be used in evaluating the solutions (cars in this case), the rest of the discussion should be completed fairly easily.

Confusing Criteria with Solutions
Groups often have problems separating criteria from possible solutions. To make sure this doesn't happen to your group, take the list of criteria and see if each one fits after this phrase: "Any decision we reach should or should not. . . ." For example, "Any decision we reach should be agreeable to the majority of the group" or "any decision we reach should cost less than $15,000"—each fits and each is a criterion. On the other hand, "Any decision we reach should be a red sports coupe" is obviously not a criterion, but a possible solution.

APPLY **WHAT YOU KNOW**
USING CRITERIA

Apply what you know about criteria to these critical thinking questions:

- Make a list of the criteria that high school or transfer students could use in selecting a college or university. Use this phrase: "Any college/university I select should or should not. . . ."
- Divide the list into must criteria and want criteria making sure to keep your must criteria to a minimum. Rank-order your want criteria from most to least important or assign each a weight of 1, 2, or 3 points according to importance. Remember that must criteria do not need to be ranked because they are already more important than any of your want criteria.
- Why do you think that members in a problem-solving discussion often fail to use criteria in reaching their decisions? Discuss at least three reasons.

Group Process Step 4: Generate Possible Solutions

The fourth step in the group problem-solving process is to *generate possible solutions*. In this stage the members of the group will suggest options that should be considered. As noted earlier, in some situations, the possible solutions—job candidates, for example—are already in place. However, in many groups, it will be the responsibility of the members to generate possible solutions. This may mean that members will have to do research outside of the group meeting. They will have to gather information and bring it to the next meeting in order for the group to have a productive discussion.

Sometimes, group members have already discovered solutions from their research done in Step 2 and are ready to generate possible solutions without additional research. In that case, the group may want to brainstorm for possible topics or use Nominal Group Technique (NGT). Effective brainstorming and effective NGT are discussed in the following sections.

Brainstorming   In instances where your group is charged with developing creative options on its own, one way to generate possible solutions is to use **brainstorming.** Brainstorming calls for group members to list spontaneously and creatively as many ideas as possible, using the following guidelines (Osborn, 1993):

- *There should be no evaluation, either positive or negative, of any idea until all ideas have been proposed.* In other words, when a member says, "We could . . ." the idea should not be met with any appraisal. There *must* be no responses such as "That's a ridiculous idea that would never work." Only supportive comments are allowed because they encourage each member to keep contributing. But the positive comments should be oriented toward support of the process as opposed to support of any particular idea.

- *List as many ideas as possible without worrying about how intelligent they sound or whether the ideas have quality.* Effective brainstormers are concerned with quantity, not quality. It's not until Step 5 that the solutions are evaluated. At that time, some will be combined with others, and some will be eliminated.

- *Accept all ideas, even the "wacky" ones.* Seemingly ridiculous ideas may serve as seeds for other creative solutions that could hold promise. These great ideas would not have been generated without the stimulation provided by the "wacky" ones.

- *Build off of other members' ideas instead of trying to make each idea unique.* For example, if your group is brainstorming gift ideas to make from scrap lumber, and someone says "birdhouse," other members should build off that idea with similar items such as doll house, dog house, or wren house, to name a few.

Nominal Group Technique   One problem with brainstorming is that more outgoing members may dominant while the quieter or shy members may contribute very little. This results in many potentially productive solutions being withheld. When ideas are coming quickly, quieter members may hesitate and find their ideas already presented by someone else. A method of generating ideas that assures equal participation from all members is called **nominal group technique** (Delbecq, et al., 1986). Nominal group technique (NGT) includes the following two steps:

1. *Each member is asked to engage in private brainstorming,* making a list of as many possible solutions as s/he can think of. After a reasonable period of time—the leader should note when no one is still actively writing ideas—the brainstorming ends.

2. *The leader then makes a master list of member ideas on a markerboard or flipchart for everyone to see.* Each member offers just one idea from her/his list at a time. Members cross off ideas on their lists once the ideas are mentioned by someone else. The process continues until all ideas on the lists have been mentioned, as well as any additional ideas that may have been spurred by someone else's contribution. Members may add to their lists as the process unfolds.

Place your master list of brainstormed ideas on a flipchart or wall board for ease of viewing by all members.

APPLY **WHAT YOU KNOW**
USING BRAINSTORMING AND NOMINAL GROUP TECHNIQUE

To apply what you have learned about brainstorming and NTG as methods for generating solutions (or problems or criteria), complete the following in small groups, if possible:

- Select a person who is fast at writing notes. Set a stop-watch to three minutes and brainstorm "any possible use for used license plates." At the end of three minutes, each group should count its list. The group with the longest list should read it out loud. The other groups should read one topic on their lists that was not mentioned earlier. Discuss how effectively each group followed the four rules for brainstorming.

- Next, each group should use NGT (see the guidelines above) to generate a list using this topic: "How can individuals help conserve natural energy?" Begin by giving each person three minutes to brainstorm a private list. Then, following the suggestions above, make a master list using the markerboard or flipchart.

- Which method (brainstorming or NGT) did the group prefer? Why? Which method generated the most items? Why?

Group Process Step 5: Apply Criteria to Select Best Solution(s)

Once your group has compiled a sufficient range of possible solutions, it is time to *apply criteria to select the best solution*. This process will likely involve a great deal of discussion, but it will be made easier if the criteria have been firmly established and weighted in Step 3. Discussion will focus on the extent to which a particular option does or does not meet the standards the group has determined are important. Using our car buying example, see **Figure 8.5** for a look at possible want criteria applied to Cars A, B, & C.

As you can see in Figure 8.5, each of the five want criteria has an assigned weight of 1, 2 or 3, as we determined in Step 3. Each car is rated on a scale of 1 to 5 on how well it meets each of these want criteria. For example, Car A must have had a great sound system because it received 5 points which were then multiplied by the assigned weight for the criterion for a total of 15 points. Once all cars are evaluated on all six criteria, their points are totaled. Car C in this example was the best solution because it had the largest number of points.

Although this process appears to take a considerable amount of time, using criteria actually decreases the time groups take to reach a quality decision. Disagreements are likely to arise as to how closely an option meets the criteria, but since most of the emotion occurred in Step 3 when the criteria were decided and ranked, this final process should be fairly straightforward. There may be situations in which weaknesses in criteria become apparent in this phase, and the group may determine that changes would be helpful. However, the leader must be sure that the group is in full agreement that modifications need to be made. It is essential that members are not swayed by one or two forceful people who are merely trying to alter the process when they see that their own favored solutions are not measuring up well against the established criteria.

Figure 8.5 Narrowing down solutions using criteria

Want Criteria	Assigned Weight	Multiplied by	Car A	Car B	Car C
Sound system	3	x	5 = 15	2 = 6	4 = 12
Sporty appearance	1	x	1 = 1	3 = 3	5 = 5
Made in America	2	x	3 = 6	4 = 8	5 = 10
MP3 player hookup	2	x	4 = 8	2 = 4	4 = 8
Automatic transmission	2	x	5 = 10	3 = 6	5 = 10
Comfortable seats for 5	3	x	3 = 9	3 = 9	5 = 15
	Total	=	49	36	60

Group Process Step 6: Implement and Follow-up

For many groups, the decision is the goal. However, in some situations, the group is also charged with *implementing the solution*. The group may have ongoing responsibilities in putting the new idea or procedure into effect. Perhaps individuals are assigned certain tasks required to make the decision work. Additional meetings may be required to update the group on what has been achieved and what remains to be done. Then, too, some groups are expected to engage in *follow-up* at some point in time. It is possible that several weeks or months may pass between meetings, but eventually the group will be asked to gather again to evaluate the progress that has been made, the extent to which the solution seems to be working, and whether any modifications are required at that point.

A structured group process such as the group problem-solving process outlined in this chapter has the best potential for arriving at well thought-out decisions. The purpose of creating groups is to allow for diversity of perspective and access to the thinking and expertise of many people. This does not guarantee a great decision, of course. Sometimes compromises have been required that result in a less-than-ideal solution, but if the group has been managed effectively and the members are all committed to the process, there is a better chance of a quality result than there might be if an individual made a decision based upon limited knowledge and perspective. The leader plays a major role in the effectiveness of the group. Successful leaders are discussed in Chapter 9.

APPLY **WHAT YOU KNOW**
USING THE PROBLEM-SOLVING PROCESS

To apply what you have learned about the problem-solving process, work in groups (if possible) to arrive at consensus answers for the following questions:

- Where in the six-step process do most groups begin? Why?

- Which steps are often omitted? What effect does this have on reaching a final decision?

- Which of the six steps do you consider to be the most important to successful group discussions? Which steps are the most enjoyable? Which steps give you the most trouble? Why?

CHAPTER SUMMARY

As this chapter indicates, communicating in problem-solving groups requires knowledge and skill. You can determine your knowledge of groups by checking the skills and learning objectives presented in this chapter.

Summary of **SKILLS**

Check each skill that you now feel qualified to perform:
- ❏ I can organize a service-learning project or a problem-solving group and am prepared to participate effectively in one if the opportunity arises.
- ❏ I can effectively decide when individual or group decisions would work best to solve problems in my own life and implement each as needed.
- ❏ I can describe the characteristics of successful groups, including their rules, norms, and phases, and implement this information to improve my participation in group situations.
- ❏ I can put into action the steps of the group problem-solving process with success when participating in group situations whether in business, education, or healthcare settings.

GROUP SKILLS **AND YOUR CAREER**

8.5 What information and skills covered in this chapter relate specifically to your career?

Communicating in problem-solving groups and teams will be of special importance to you in your career. The following Career features take a look at group skills in the workplace specifically as they relate to careers in business, education, and healthcare. Whether you are interested in one of these career fields or will be a consumer of the services of these areas, the following information should be of interest to you.

SPOTLIGHT ON **SUCCESSFUL TEAMS**

BUSINESS

Successful teams must have training and experience working together. This is especially true of airline pilots and their crews.

- *Aviation Week & Space Technology* (Scott, 2005) discusses how important teamwork is for the Blue Angels, the U.S. Navy's aerial demonstration team. Can you imagine the practice needed to perform a flawless 45-minute program with six F/A-18A Hornets flying an inch apart while pulling Gs?

- The National Transportation Safety Board (NTSB) found that "73 percent of all incidents took place on the crew's first day; 44 percent occurred on the crew's very first flight together" (Hill & McShane, 2008, p. 267).

- Hackman (2002) reports that crews that had not flown together made more mistakes on the NASA flight simulator than exhausted crews that had worked together.

EDUCATION

Educators realize that it is impossible for everyone in a class to participate, which is why they often break their classes down into smaller groups. The question is: Is there a particular size group that works best in a classroom?

- *No larger than four* in K-12 classrooms recommends Vermette (1998)—otherwise some students will sit back and let others do all the work. Groups of three or four encourage participation.

- *From two to six* suggest Abrami, et al. (1993; 1995) but give this warning: "The larger the group, the more complex communication becomes, and the more difficult it is to promote equal participation, interpersonal skill development, and, possibly, learning" (1995, p. 60).

- *From four to six* in communication classes advise Daly, Friedrich, & Vangelisti; (1990) to have adequate thoughts and ideas to improve understanding of course content.

HEALTHCARE

The Mayo Clinic regularly uses teams of experts to handle patient problems (Berry & Bendapudi, 2003). If a team is uncertain about a complicated patient problem, it will bring another expert onto the team. Virtual teams also meet when needed, as in the case of a patient with serious skin cancer "at risk for metastasis and, owing to the necessary surgery, nerve injury and disfigurement" (p. 104). An ENT MAYO specialist quickly put together a team of twenty doctors from all three of Mayo's campuses to collaborate by videoconference. In an hour and a half conference they "reached a consensus for a course of treatment, including specific recommendations on how aggressively to sample the patient's lymph nodes and how best to reconstruct the surgical wound" (p. 104).

CAREER MOMENT **PROBLEM SOLVING**

One of the most important skills to success in your career is the ability to work in teams to solve problems. Research by Smith and Forbes (1997) found that the ability to analyze and solve problems while working with others was a crucial skill for the 21st century. The NACE 2009 survey of national employers reported the following ranking of candidate qualities and skills on a 5-point scale (*Job Outlook 2009*): communication skills received 4.6 points; teamwork skills received 4.5 points; problem-solving skills received 4.3 points; and analytical skills received 4.3 points. Obviously, in addition to communication ability employers are looking for people with team and problem-solving skills. Teams are important in many fields, not just the business world. Team skills are valuable in relationships, schools and

colleges, hospitals and other healthcare facilities, volunteer organizations, local and national government agencies, and many more.

If you feel that you would like more experience in working with and leading problem-solving teams, we suggest you seriously consider enrolling for a speech course called Discussion and Small Group Communication. This course offers experience working in all types of group and team situations. It includes an understanding of how groups operate; how members and leaders interact; how to handle problem people; research and practical skill development; and practice in participating in multiple team experiences. You may find you are involved in a service-learning experience as well. Although this course is not offered on all college campuses, most communication departments do offer it. Check with your instructor or the chair of your communication department for specifics. Having knowledge of problem-solving skills will look great on your resume and help you succeed in your chosen career.

CONNECTING TO **BUSINESS**

If you are considering going into the field of business, your career may depend on how well you can manage cultural diversity in a group setting. Take the following quiz adapted from the Personal Report of Intercultural Communication Apprehension (PRICA) (Neuliep & McCroskey, 1997). Answer each question using the following scale: (1) strongly agree, (2) agree, (3) undecided, (4) disagree, or (5) strongly disagree.

ACTIVITY Answer each question on a scale from 1 to 5 and total your scores.

1. ___Generally, I am comfortable interacting with a group of people from different cultures.

2. ___ I like to get involved in group discussions with others who are from different cultures.

3. ___ I am calm and relaxed when interacting with a group of people who are from different cultures.

4. ___ I have no fear of speaking up in a conversation with a person from a different culture.

5. ___ Ordinarily I am very calm and relaxed in conversations with a person from a different culture.

6. ___ While conversing with a person from a different culture, I feel very relaxed.

7. ___ I face the prospect of interacting with people from different cultures with confidence.

Totals from 28–45 indicate intercultural anxiety; scores from 7–14 indicate intercultural confidence.

(From J. W. Neuliep and J. C. McCroskey, "The development of intercultural and interethnic communication apprehension scales," *Communication Research Reports, 14*, 385–398. Copyright © 1997. Reprinted by permission of Taylor & Francis, http://www.informaworld.com.)

CONNECTING TO **EDUCATION**

If you are considering a career in education, the chances are good that you will have the opportunity for team-teaching during your career. William Newell, lists these characteristics of an effective team-teacher: "open to diverse ways of thinking, wary of absolutism; able to admit that they do not know; good at listening; unconventional; flexible; willing to take risks; self-reflective; and comfortable with ambiguity" (Davis, 2002 p. 47).

ACTIVITY In small groups of people interested in a career in education, discuss the following topics:
- Describe a team-taught course you have taken and whether you learned more or less than in a regular course.
- Make a list of the *strengths* and the *weaknesses* of these classes.
- What could be done to avoid each weakness in classes you might teach in the future?

CONNECTING TO **HEALTHCARE**

If you are considering a career in healthcare, you will soon learn that much of what happens in healthcare today occurs in interdisciplinary teams. For example, physicians, nurses, physical therapists, and social workers may all work together to plan a patient's treatment regimen, as well as to make decisions about when patients are ready to be discharged and how follow-up care should be managed. The success of these interdisciplinary teams depends upon the ability of members on the team to bring their unique perspective while also respecting the views of others on the team without "turf" battles and power struggles (Ellingson, 2005).

ACTIVITY Using your personal experience, articles from your college's databases, and an Internet search for the topic "healthcare teams," make a list for each of the following potential team members including their unique perspectives and possible problem areas: general physicians, nurses, social workers, public healthcare workers, specialists (e.g., oncologists), physical therapists, pharmacists, others.

▶ Log onto MyCommunicationLab.com to access Connecting to Psychology and Connecting to Science, Technology, Engineering, and Math—both with related activities.

Summary of LEARNING **OUTCOMES**

8.1 *What are the differences between groups, teams, and virtual teams, and what are the three types of groups used most often? What is a service-learning project, and how do you organize one if assigned?*

- A *group* is more than a collection of people. A group involves three to seven people who have multiple face-to-face meetings over an extended period of time and who interact to achieve common goals.

- The three types of groups most often used are learning groups, self-maintenance groups, and problem-solving groups.

- A *team* is a type of group usually found in the work setting that has closer cooperation and cohesiveness than most groups; a *virtual team* is a team that has members that are dispersed by location and so must collaborate via the Internet or other technologies to accomplish specific goals.

- A service-learning project is a group that "integrates community service with academic study to enrich learning, teach civic responsibility, and strengthen communities." See the *Developing Skills* feature on page 209 for pointers on organizing a service-learning project.

8.2 *When making decisions, when do individual decisions work best? When do group decisions work best?*

- Individual decisions work best when fast decisions are needed, when the decisions are fairly simple and will affect few people, and when working with others is difficult due to the people involved or your own communication skills.

- Group decisions work best when quality is essential, acceptance by a large number of people is needed, accuracy is crucial, tasks are complex or difficult, and strong opinions and conflict exist in the group.

8.3 *What are the characteristics of successful small groups, and what theory offers helpful advice?*

- Successful small groups have an optimum size (5 to 7), prefer making decisions by consensus rather than by vote or compromise, have cohesive members who avoid social loafing, avoid thinking that involves groupthink, use cultural diversity to improve productivity, and are aware of

the roles that rules, norms, and phases play in a successful group discussion.

- Groupthink theory offers valuable tips to group members in the *Making Theory Practical* feature in this chapter. Look for types of defective analysis used by groups and eight symptoms of groupthink.

8.4 *What are the six steps of the group problem-solving process, what occurs in each step, and what theory is especially helpful when analyzing a problem?*

- The six steps of the group problem-solving process include: (1) identify the problem; (2) analyze the problem; (3) establish and rank criteria; (4) generate possible solutions; (5) apply criteria to select the best solutions; and (6) implement and follow-up on solutions.

- In *Step 1*, the problem is narrowed, clarified, and worded so that everyone understands and approves it. In *Step 2*, the problem is divided into issues, each issue is researched and then discussed with the group arriving at an understanding on each issue. In *Step 3*, the group decides on specific criteria that they will use in evaluating possible solutions to the problem, divides the criteria into musts and wants, and weighs and/or ranks the want criteria. In *Step 4*, possible solutions are generated using brainstorming or NGT. In *Step 5*, the criteria from Step 3 are applied to each solution in order to select the best solution or solutions. In *Step 6*, the selected solutions are implemented and followed-up to make sure that implementation was successfully completed.

- Force-field analysis is an especially helpful procedure for analyzing the forces for change and the forces against change of a problem in Step 2.

8.5 *What information and skills covered in this chapter relate specifically to your career (see highlighted fields of business, education, and healthcare)?*

- The *Spotlight on, Career Moment*, and *Connecting to* features highlight the value of listening in the fields of business, education, and healthcare—additional fields are included online.

SOLVE IT NOW!

Taking into consideration all that you learned about problem-solving from this chapter, how would you analyze Sheila and her group in our opening scenario? *

- How well did Sheila's group meet the optimum size for a successful group?

- What did the attendance at the meeting indicate about the group's cohesiveness and social loafing? If you were Sheila, Darron, or Teresa, what would you do to improve the situation?

- What specific rules do you think the group should have? What norms do you think Darron is expecting? Why?

- Imagine that you were giving the group an explanation of a service-learning project. Write a summary in five to seven sentences that would clarify what is expected.

- What specific problem-solving skills would you recommend for Sheila and her group that should help them with group discussions now and in the future?

*(Check your answers with those located in MyCommunicationsLab, Scenario Analysis for Chapter 8)

KEY TERMS

brainstorming	p. 225	group diversity	p. 213	nominal group technique	p. 225	reinforcement phase	p. 217
cohesiveness	p. 213	group norms	p. 215	optimum group size	p. 211	restraining forces	p. 222
compromise	p. 212	group problem-solving process	p. 218	orientation phase	p. 217	self-maintenance groups	p. 208
conflict phase	p. 217	group rules	p. 215	problem-solving groups	p. 208	service-learning projects	p. 208
consensus	p. 212	groupthink	p. 215	question of conjecture	p. 220	social loafing	p. 213
criteria	p. 222	hidden agenda	p. 213	question of fact	p. 220	team	p. 206
driving forces	p. 222	individual decision making	p. 208	question of policy	p. 220	virtual team	p. 206
emergence phase	p. 217	learning groups	p. 208	question of value	p. 220	vote	p. 212
force-field analysis	p. 222	must criteria	p. 223			want criteria	p. 223
group	p. 206						
group decision making	p. 210						

SKILL BUILDERS

1. Taking into consideration all that you have learned about small groups, think about your past group experiences and determine three things you have done right and three things you need to improve. Which task and maintenance roles do you typically perform? Which dysfunctional role are you most guilty of? Be prepared to share your answers with your classmates.

2. Critically Evaluating

Using the critical evaluation form from Chapter 1, select and evaluate an article on *effective teams* or *virtual teams* obtained from a communication journal. (You may wish to check your library databases for articles; Communication and Mass Media Complete through EBSCOHost references the major speech communication journals). Be prepared to share your observations with your classmates.

3. Do you recall the PRCA-24 communication apprehension quiz you took at the beginning of the semester? Take a look at your scores again (see the *Developing Skills* feature in Chapter 1). If your total score was above 65 or any subtotal was above 18, then you suffer some anxiety in communicating with others; a total score over 80 or any subtotal over 24 indicates you had high anxiety at the time you took the survey. High anxiety communicators are likely to experience difficulties in their careers as well as in their personal relationships. To revisit your PRCA-24 responses as they relate to team scores, do the following:

- Being as objective and honest as possible, answer the following questions indicating the degree to which each statement now applies to you. Answer using this scale (but don't try to remember what you said the first time):

(1) Strongly Agree (2) Agree (3) Are Undecided (4) Disagree (5) Strongly Disagree

____1. I dislike participating in group discussion.
____2. Generally, I am comfortable while participating in a group discussion.
____3. I am tense and nervous while participating in group discussions.
____4. I like to get involved in group discussions.
____5. Engaging in a group discussion with new people makes me tense and nervous.
____6. I am calm and relaxed while participating in a group discussion.
____To total the group subscale, begin with 18 points. Subtract your scores for questions 1, 3, and 5. Then add the scores for 2, 4, and 6.

- Compare your group subtotal (which is the best indicator of group anxiety) to your previous score. Do you see any differences in your group score? Keep in mind that the lower your scores, the more confident you are.

4. In small groups of three to seven, use your personal experiences of working in teams in the classroom setting, clubs or organizations, or in the work environment to discuss your answers to this question: *What single change or recommendation would make the most improvement in the quality and success of the typical small group or team*? Make sure all group members get a chance to express an opinion and work for a consensus decision. Share your decision and the reasons for it with another group or your class.

9 Becoming Effective Group Members and Leaders

After studying this chapter you should be able to . . .
- Analyze the member characteristics, roles, and responsibilities that you use effectively and those that need improvement.
- Analyze the leadership characteristics and responsibilities that you use effectively and those that need improvement.
- Enhance your skills as an effective leader using the tips offered by the leadership theories and approaches presented.
- Build effective group member and leadership skills as they relate to your career.

CHAPTER SUMMARY 〉 P. 255 〉

SCENARIO

Andrea scanned the faces of the four people sitting around the conference table. She was slightly acquainted with two of the people on her committee but knew the other two well. They worked in her division and had been on previous committees with her. Max, the oldest member, had been angry when she had received a promotion that he wanted, but she hoped his resentment was a thing of the past now that she had been moved out and he had taken her place. She also knew that Galina was lobbying to be moved from Max's group and suspected there was tension between them.

Andrea had been surprised when President Sutherland selected her to chair the Technology Upgrade Committee. She hoped the group could work together and produce a proposal that would impress Mr. Sutherland. She figured she already had an ally in Galina and decided the best strategy would be to woo one of the members she didn't know well; that would make three-against-two if a conflict developed, assuming that Max would choose to oppose her.

Rosa was excited to be a part of this committee. She knew that developing a plan for upgrading the company's technology was an important assignment, and, as the only member from IT on the committee, she figured her opinions would be sought. While she didn't know any of the members very well, she had always found it easy to work with people, and she assumed that this group would be no different. She knew that Andrea had a reputation for being assertive, but Rosa was confident she could hold her own and gain the support of the others as soon as they were aware of her expertise.

D'Andre smiled to himself. He had overheard a conversation between his supervisor and Mr. Sutherland concerning the centralized system they favored. He figured that when Sutherland learned D'Andre had championed that very plan, his promotion would be a sure thing. People who disagreed with Mr. Sutherland were usually overlooked when promotions were made. Now all he had to do was propose Mr. Sutherland's plan first and then remain committed to that position.

Galina had been on two committees with Andrea, so she was delighted to find herself on yet another. It was important for her to be noticed by Andrea since she was determined to get transferred to her group. Andrea was a very popular supervisor, always responsive to her subordinates' needs and willing to go to bat for them when problems arose. Galina had been on the verge of quitting several times since Max had been named to head their team. Maybe taking a leadership role in this committee would be her ticket out.

Max was taking measure of the others as he leaned back in his chair. This was going to be an easy group to influence, he decided. Galina knew better than to cross him, since she needed his approval to get a bonus next month. D'Andre was young and ambitious; logic suggested that he would be eager to please the most senior member of the committee. Rosa was an unknown quantity; as far as Max knew, this was her first major committee assignment. Besides, she seemed quiet. Max figured that she wouldn't try to influence anybody—which, of course, meant that the majority would align with him. Nothing would give Max more pleasure than to see Andrea have to swallow her pride. She might think she was top dog because she had been chosen chair, but Max would change that. No way would he let her run this show.

Max leaned forward. "I think it is time for us to get started," he announced. He smiled inwardly when he noted Andrea's cocked eyebrow and surprised look.

As you read this chapter, see if you can determine which type of power each member in our opening scenario seems to have and what task and maintenance roles each is performing. In addition, what does Andrea, the appointed leader, need to do to ensure that this group is successful—including which leadership style to use and how she should handle any dysfunctional member roles. By analyzing this opening scenario, you should be able to analyze real-life group situations in which you will find yourself in the future.

SOLVE IT NOW! 〉 P. 258 〉

How would you like to be the appointed leader of this team? Based on what you just read in this opening scenario, who do you think is the most likely to take control of this first meeting? It will be a bumpy road, but if Andrea understands about leadership, problem-solving, and member needs, she should be able to guide this group to an effective decision. Of course, the personal goals and hidden agendas expressed by individuals in the opening scenario could turn into dysfunctional roles and cause the group to stray from the task at hand.

Characteristics of Effective Group Members

LEARNING **OBJECTIVE**

9.1 What are the characteristics of effective group members, and what role do they play in successful groups?

The success of a group is directly related to the members that are in it. So, if you were given the task of selecting people to serve on a committee or team, what type of person would you select? Let's begin our search for the answer to this question by looking at some general characteristics of effective group members.

Keeping an Open Mind

Effective group members are open-minded to ideas, solutions, and people. Yes, they are familiar with the topic and have done some preliminary research and have even thought about possible problem areas and problem people before coming to the group meeting. However, that does not mean that they have already made up their minds. Nothing slows down group process more than members who come with minds so closed that they are no longer willing to consider opposing ideas. In fact, some ineffective members are so closed-minded that they don't even listen carefully to ideas that differ from their own.

Just because members are open-minded doesn't mean that there will be no conflict. Most effective group discussions experience some conflict as members openly express their views and concerns. This type of conflict can actually stimulate group members to generate ideas and solutions that they might never have thought of if the group was in complete agreement from the beginning. It is really exciting to be in a discussion where many differing viewpoints are expressed and yet, by the end of the session, the group comes to a consensus decision that is really better than any of the individual opinions expressed. There is a kind of excitement and sense of satisfaction in the air as the group leaves the meeting. So, if you have the responsibility for picking group members, look for open-mindedness as an important characteristic.

Preparing and Participating Effectively

Another characteristic of effective group members is that they prepare before meetings and participate actively during meetings. Effective group members prepare for every group meeting the same way they would prepare for an exam or an interview by a local newscaster. Yes, it is true that if members came to meetings unprepared, the meetings would still continue; however, they would take much longer and would be less likely to achieve a high degree of success. You have no doubt been in long, boring meetings like this, haven't you? Either there was no business needing discussion and, therefore, no reason for holding a meeting, or the members were unprepared. When members are unprepared, it takes most of the scheduled time just to bring everyone up to speed on the issues, leaving very little time for solving the problem. So more meetings have to be scheduled, and on and on it goes.

Effective group members not only prepare ahead of time, they also participate effectively during meetings. There is more to effective participation than just talking; group members should work with the leader and each other to fulfill the formal and informal roles needed for successful group process. If you have ever been in a meeting and thought to yourself, "Why doesn't someone cut off that dominator and get this discussion moving?" or "Half of the group hasn't said a thing today. I wonder what's wrong?"—you have identified important group roles that need to be performed. You can improve your effectiveness as a participant by learning to use both the task and maintenance roles that will be discussed later in this chapter. So, when picking group members look for people who are prepared and participate effectively.

Using the Problem-Solving Procedure Effectively

It is amazing how many people have little concept of how to organize a successful group—whether they are in business, education, healthcare, or other career fields. They have even fewer skills when it comes to problem solving. Yet, as indicated by the *Career Moment* feature in the previous chapter, teamwork and problem-solving skills are two of the most sought-after qualities employers look for when interviewing job candidates. Group members with little knowledge of problem solving usually begin by discussing solutions and stating what solution they think is best. As you know by reading the group problem-solving process discussed in Chapter 8, possible solutions should be Step 4 in the process—after identifying the problem, analyzing the problem, and establishing criteria. Beginning a discussion with solutions almost guarantees that the group will either experience drawn-out conflict or will settle for groupthink with little or no discussion of alternative courses of action. Effective group members, on the other hand, know how to use the problem-solving procedure effectively. These are the people you want to include in your search for effective group members.

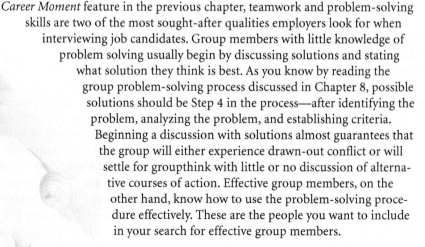

Handling Conflicts Effectively

Conflict is inevitable in successful group discussions, but the way members handle the conflict makes all the difference. Generally, the passive, aggressive (as shown in the photo), or passive-aggressive styles of handling conflict discussed in Chapter 7 are to be avoided. However, the assertive style of responding to conflict is the most successful because feelings and opinions can be openly and honestly expressed by all members. The goal of the assertive group member is to reach a win-win resolution to conflict that will be agreeable to all members of the group. (If a win-win resolution isn't possible, a compromise may be needed.) Also, the assertive group member is careful to use confirming, supportive messages rather than the disconfirming, defensive messages used by aggressive and passive-aggressive members. Effective group members use the assertive types of comments included in the *Developing Skills* feature on page 196. When selecting members for your group, look for people who can solve conflicts effectively and are interested in win-win solutions.

APPLY **WHAT YOU KNOW**
GROUP MEMBER CHARACTERISTICS

Expand your understanding of the member characteristics of small groups by considering these questions:

- Based on your experience, which member characteristics do you think are the most important? Why?

- Identify at least one specific member characteristic that you plan to work on to make yourself a more effective group member. Why is improvement needed?

Effective Member Roles

One characteristic of effective group members is that they participate effectively and use group roles as needed. **Group roles** are categories of behaviors enacted by individuals. They include both *formal roles* (specified) and *informal roles* (developed over time). As you read about each role, see which ones you typically use in groups and which ones you need to improve if you are to be a more effective group member. (See **Figure 9.1**.)

Formal Roles

There are some roles that are formal, meaning that they are specified. One such **formal role** is the chairperson. The person who is assigned or elected to be the "chair" is expected to provide certain consistent contributions to the group especially as related to agenda setting and arranging for a recorder:

- The **agenda setter** is one important formal role provided by the chairperson who develops an agenda or formal plan for the meeting. When planning the agenda, effective chairpersons need to consider in advance which topics are likely to generate conflict and which people are likely to dominate and whether the agenda can be arranged to moderate discussion of any potentially controversial issues.

- The **recorder,** who will take notes on what was discussed during the group's meeting and on any decisions that were reached, is another important formal role. Groups that

9.2 What are the roles that members should exhibit and the roles they should avoid in successful groups, and what are some suggestions for working with dysfunctional members in the group setting?

fail to keep a record of what transpired during a meeting often find themselves confused or in disagreement at the next meeting. For this reason, many groups require that minutes of the meeting be published and distributed to group members by an official secretary or a person appointed by the chair.

Although the formal roles just described are certainly important, it is the informal, unassigned task and maintenance roles discussed next that determine the real success of a group. Just as norms emerge over time, **informal roles** emerge as individuals experiment with various roles. For example, imagine that you observe a task or people problem in a group meeting and step in to correct it by enacting a particular role. If your attempt is successful and is accepted by the other members of the group, you likely will try it again later when a similar problem occurs. Eventually the group will come to rely upon you (and maybe one or two others) to perform that specific role. Typically each individual will perform several roles during the life of the group, depending on the situation and members present. Keep in mind that the roles you take on in one group may not be the roles you play in the next. Roles that are needed for group success but not performed by any group member are considered to be the responsibility of the chairperson. More authoritarian leaders may feel it is their job to perform most task and maintenance roles; more democratic leaders appreciate active group participation. As you read the next sections, identify which task and maintenance roles you have successfully performed previously in a group and one or two that you wish to try in your next group involvement.

Figure 9.1 Small Group Roles

Formal Roles	Agenda Setter and Recorder
Task Roles	Information/Opinion Giver and Seeker, Analyzer, Expediter, and Clarifier
Maintenance Roles	Supporter, Harmonizer, Tension Reliever, and Gatekeeper
Dysfunctional Roles	Dominator, Deserter, Blocker, Aggressor, and Showboat

Task Roles

One important category of informal roles are the **task roles** (Benne & Sheats, 1948; Keyton, 1999), behaviors that individuals exhibit in a group that assist the group in achieving its goals. Task roles help the group get the job done (**Figure 9.2**).

- An important task role is the **information/opinion giver,** who provides the group with substance for discussion by reporting research findings and giving opinions on the information as well as on other members' comments. This role is one that every member should take on. If there are members in the group who do not offer information and opinions, they really are not fully participating in the group. To perform this role effectively, you will need to research the topics on the agenda and listen carefully to others during each discussion.

- The **information/opinion seeker** is a group member who makes sure all members get a chance to share their information and opinions with the group. People who find it easy to offer information and opinions sometimes get so involved that they ignore the fact that others have not participated. An information/opinion seeker might say, "Jason, what do you think about this idea" or "Let's make sure we hear from everyone on this issue—who hasn't had a chance to give an opinion yet?" To perform this role effectively, you may need to talk less and observe more. Watch for nonverbal cues to tell you when others would like to speak.

- The **analyzer** is a group member who is able to spot relevant issues and show how information and ideas fit with other information the group is considering. The person who is adept at analytical thinking is able to recognize when information is missing or when other issues that have not been addressed should be investigated. When decisions begin to emerge, the analyzer is able to test the suitability of the decision. A group that lacks an analyzer is in danger of making an ill-formed decision because issues that

Figure 9.2 Task Roles

Task Role	Definition
Information/ opinion giver	Offers ideas, research, and suggestions related to the problem or task
Information/ opinion seeker	Makes sure that all group members get a chance to share their ideas and opinions
Analyzer	Identifies issues and relates new information to known information
Expediter	Helps keep discussion on track by initiating, pointing out deadlines and digressions
Clarifier	Ensures that everyone understands the ideas being discussed

should have been discussed may become apparent only after the solution fails. To perform the task role of analyzer effectively, you will need to enjoy analyzing facts but not persist in revisiting ideas endlessly. It may help to think out loud by presenting pros and cons for the group to consider.

- The **expediter** is a group member who keeps the discussion on track by suggesting how to get started, reminding the group of deadlines, and pointing out when the group is digressing. Because members with a variety of agendas will assume this role at different times, it is important not to let expediting become the main goal of the group. For example, a person could serve as expediter merely to get the meeting over in order to attend to personal business (hidden agenda) when, in fact, moving on could mean failing to look at important issues. To be an effective expediter, you must keep the group on track (avoiding hidden agendas, of course) while realizing that sometimes a topic that seems to be a digression may actually be introducing an issue that needs to be discussed, a relevant digression. The key is to keep a balance between the role of expediter and the role of analyzer.

- Finally, the **clarifier** is a group member who ensures that everyone is clear on what is being discussed, what decisions have been made, and what members' comments mean. The clarifier will do a lot of paraphrasing. "So, John, you are saying . . ." "So, we have decided to . . . Is that right?" You can see that the role of clarifier needs to work closely with the role of recorder; in fact, the recorder may do clarifying during the meeting as well when documenting the key topics that are discussed. Without a clarifier, people in the group may become confused, sometimes misunderstanding and assuming disagreement (or agreement) where there is none. To be an effective clarifier, your goal will be to make as sure as possible that everyone fully understands the issues and what is happening.

Now that we have covered the roles that assist the group in achieving its task, let's look at the roles that help the group to maintain cohesiveness. These roles are oriented toward helping members get their interpersonal needs met.

Maintenance Roles

In addition to the informal task roles, groups also need another category of informal roles called maintenance roles (Benne & Sheats, 1948; Keyton, 1999). **Maintenance roles** are the behaviors that individuals exhibit in a group that help the group preserve its cohesiveness; maintenance roles help the group members feel good about being a part of the group (**Figure 9.3**).

- The **supporter** is a group member who affirms the contributions of others by complimenting their ideas, expressing appreciation for their participation, and generally making everyone feel included and respected. If you offer an idea and no one responds—your idea seems to be ignored—you will not be eager to offer

Figure 9.3 Maintenance Roles

Maintenance Role	Definition
Supporter	Affirms and compliments the contributions of others
Harmonizer	Reconciles conflicts among members
Tension Reliever	Uses humor to maintain a relaxed group atmosphere
Gatekeeper	Controls the flow of communication for equal participation

new ideas. The supporter prevents this from happening. To effectively perform this important maintenance role, you need to be a good listener and help build cohesiveness by demonstrating respect and appreciation for the ideas of others.

- A second maintenance role is the **harmonizer,** who reconciles conflict that occurs in the group. Recall that conflict is not always a negative thing. It is important to avoid groupthink (discussed in Chapter 8) so that everyone in the group will feel free to express dissenting views. However, conflict that is poorly handled can threaten group unity. Conflict can lead to alliances and coalitions that cause a rift in the group. The harmonizer helps to prevent this by finding ways to manage conflict. To be an effective harmonizer, facilitate conflict management by looking for win-win outcomes or, if that fails, good compromises. If you can encourage the group to find third options that enable both sides to achieve all or some of their needs, group cohesiveness can be preserved.

- The **tension reliever** is a group member who uses a variety of techniques (such as humor) to maintain group harmony and keep a relaxed atmosphere. Although the tension reliever works along with the harmonizer, this person's role goes beyond easing tensions created by personal conflicts to dealing with such other sources of tension as being stuck with no new ideas, facing an immediate deadline, or being tired from lengthy deliberations. To be an effective tension reliever, you should be able to spot these moments in the life of the group and suggest ways of reducing or eliminating the tension. For example, you might suggest a break, recommend a period of brainstorming in which wildly creative ideas are encouraged, or make a funny remark that causes everyone to laugh—who can remain tense after a moment of genuine laughter?

A good tension reliever helps maintain group harmony and keep a relaxed atmosphere.

- The final maintenance role is the **gatekeeper,** who controls the flow of communication. The gatekeeper ensures that everyone has an opportunity to be heard and that no one is dominating the conversation. This is a role that nearly anyone can learn to take on as needed. To be an effective gatekeeper, you first will need to be aware of who has contributed, who has not, and who has said too much. It is amazing how many group members are completely unaware of who is doing what. Next, you occasionally address a silent member and ask for an opinion. Just because people say little doesn't mean they have nothing to say; they may be having a hard time finding the opportunity to share it. The most difficult task of being a gatekeeper is tactfully cutting off those performing dysfunctional roles (to be discussed next) so that everyone has an equal opportunity to participate.

You can see that task and maintenance roles are important to the success of any group discussion. However, at any one time there needs to be a balance of the roles—too few or too many will cause problems. It is also essential that you avoid role fixation. This occurs when someone continues to assume a role even when that role is no longer needed. Also note that members who possess **role diversity**—the ability to assume multiple roles—have the potential to be especially influential to the group. If you have the communication skills necessary to perform all of these roles, if you are able to spot when the absence of a particular role is threatening the productivity or cohesiveness of the group, and if you are able to supply the needed role at the right time for it to be accepted by the members—you will be regarded as a leader. Leadership will be discussed in greater detail in the next chapter.

Dysfunctional Roles

We have discussed the formal, assigned roles and the informal, unassigned task and maintenance roles of groups. All of these roles are functional, meaning they are desirable because they contribute to the effectiveness of the group. However, you will run into groups with members who adopt undesirable roles. These **dysfunctional roles** are nonfunctional behaviors that interfere with either the attainment of the group's goals or the sense of group cohesiveness. We will look at five major dysfunctional roles (Benne & Sheats, 1948; Keyton, 1999). Keep in mind that even effective communicators can take on one of these roles if the situation is stressful and their emotional involvement is great enough. As you read about these roles, identify the one(s) that you are most likely to use by habit or in moments of stress (**Figure 9.4**).

Dominator
The **dominator** tends to monopolize the discussion. Dominators have an opinion on every subject and will usually give it before anyone else gets a chance to speak. In addition, they always have a comment to make about everyone else's ideas, often with a negative slant as they point out any errors. Dominators make others feel that their contributions are not as valuable although this is usually an unintended result of their talkativeness. Often times, the dominator is really involved and excited about the topic and has prepared and researched carefully. In fact, dominators may just be better prepared than other members and not even be aware that they are dominating.

Deserter
The **deserter** withdraws from the discussion due to lack of preparation, uncertainty, or anxiety. The direct opposite of the dominator, the deserter rarely, if ever, offers a thought or any information, leaving the rest of the group to carry the weight of the discussion. Deserters cause concern because no one can be sure what they think— they may have an excellent idea that never gets brought into the discussion.

Blocker and Aggressor
Two other dysfunctional roles are the blocker and aggressor. The **blocker** is the person who stubbornly refuses to allow the group to move forward for a variety of possible reasons: desire to overanalyze the topic, need to prove that s/he is right, or refusal to compromise. "What do you mean, 'Put it to a vote?' We haven't even begun to discuss the reasons for this problem," says the blocker. In a similar manner, the **aggressor** slows the discussion by criticizing and insulting group members and their ideas; there is no tact shown—just sarcasm and hostility. It may be that aggressors personally dislike or are jealous of those they criticize. "I can't believe you think that would

Figure 9.4 Dysfunctional Roles

Dysfunctional Role	Definition
Dominator	Monopolizes the conversation
Deserter	Withdraws from the conversation
Blocker	Refuses to allow the group to move forward
Aggressor	Criticizes and insults group members and their ideas
Showboat	Constantly draws attention to self

© 2003 Ted Goff

"Is this the committee you get to be on when no one else wants you on their committees anymore?"

© Ted Goff

be a good solution. Only an idiot would suggest something like that!" Interestingly, while taking potshots at everyone else, the aggressor often has no real solution to offer.

Showboat

A final dysfunctional group role is the **showboat**. This person is the one who is constantly drawing attention to self, often by clowning around, telling jokes, launching into stories of personal exploits, and generally distracting others. If you were to call the showboat out, you would probably hear this story: "I was just trying to be a tension-reliever." However, if you think about it, instead of relieving tension, this person is creating tension by failing to take the group's task seriously. As amusing as they may sometimes be, showboats are frustrating to have as group members.

It is important to eliminate the dysfunctional roles in your group if you hope to accomplish your task in an efficient and effective manner and at the same time encourage group cohesiveness. When groups accomplish their tasks and feel a sense of group pride, members find that group work is very satisfying and rewarding. It is every member's responsibility to ensure that the group functions optimally. For suggestions on how to work with dysfunctional members as well as how to minimize your own use of dysfunctional roles, see the tips in the *Developing Skills* feature on page 244.

Now that you know what makes an effective group member, let's look at group leadership. Perhaps you have wondered: Are leaders born or made? Is leadership something that I can learn? What would it take for me to become an effective leader? This part of the chapter will offer some insight into these questions with the intent of helping you develop your leadership skills.

APPLY **WHAT YOU KNOW**
TASK, MAINTENANCE, AND DYSFUNCTIONAL ROLES

Groups need members to perform a variety of task and maintenance roles in order to be successful. At the same time, the fewer dysfunctional members in your group, the more successful it will be. To apply what you know about group roles, answer the following questions and be prepared to share them with your class:

- Which *task role* would you say is the most important to the success of a small group? Give an example to explain your answer.
- Which *maintenance role* would you say is the most important to the success of a small group? Why?
- Which *dysfunctional role* causes the most problems in a group discussion? Why?

LEARNING **OBJECTIVE**

9.3 What are the characteristics of effective group leaders and what role do they play in successful groups?

Characteristics of Effective Group Leadership

If your professor asked you and your classmates to raise a hand if you considered yourself to be a leader, would your hand go up? What would be the difference between those who raised a hand and those who did not? Let's begin our search for the answer to this question and other questions about leadership by looking at some general characteristics of effective group leaders.

Using Power Effectively

As the opening scenario indicates, there is a close relationship between leadership and power. **Power** is the ability to exert influence over others. As **Figure 9.5** indicates, there are five different types of power that can be exerted in groups (French & Raven, 1959):

- **Reward power**—ability to provide desired benefits.
- **Coercive power**—ability to punish.
- **Legitimate power**—ability to influence based on a position you hold.
- **Expert power**—ability to provide knowledge or skills.
- **Referent power**—ability to influence based on your charisma.

The higher a person's status (rank or position), the more likely group members are to perceive the person as having power (Sell et al., 2004). In western cultures, the notion of power is often viewed with suspicion and mistrust. The concern is that people who possess power over others will use that power unethically and with little regard for others as they pursue their own goals. Power implies domination. The term *leadership,* which is viewed more positively than *power,* implies the ability to exert influence in a cooperative effort. Therefore, **leadership** is seen as "a process whereby an individual influences a group of individuals to achieve a common goal" (Northouse, 2007, p. 3). In other words, leadership is the exercise of one's power with the goal of meeting the needs of the group. Kirkman and Rosen (1999) reviewed 112 teams and found that leadership "was the single-most important predictor of the teams' success" (Tubbs, 2009, p. 234). Leadership recognizes the transactional nature of communication, in which each party affects and is affected by the other. A leader cannot exercise power without the consent of those led.

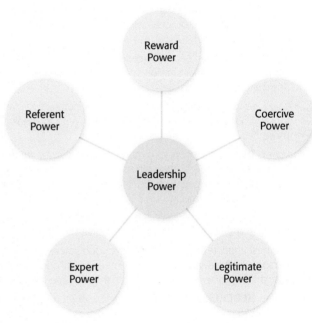

Figure 9.5 Types of Power

Sharing Responsibility

Leadership is not always invested in one person. In effective group situations, leadership is shared, with one person achieving greater influence over others in one situation while another person gains greater influence as the situation changes. Or as Bales in his classic *Interaction Process Analysis* (1950) found, most effective groups have both a task-oriented and a maintenance/relationship-oriented leader—two different people concentrating on different aspects of the group process. One may be the **nominal leader,** who is the person who has been formally designated as the leader or chairperson; the other may be the **emergent leader,** who acquires influence by performing task or maintenance roles as needed. Recall in our discussion of member roles, we noted that people who have the quality of role diversity—the ability to assume a variety of roles over time—will gain more enduring influence as they are able to step in and provide the role that is in greatest need at the moment. Some groups, in fact, are constructed without anyone named to lead the group. "Leaderless groups," however, do not truly function without a leader; effective groups have leadership that emerges over time from one or more members.

DEVELOPING SKILLS
HOW TO WORK WITH DYSFUNCTIONAL MEMBERS

One of the most frustrating things about being in a group is dealing with dysfunctional members. You can't sit back and wait for the leader to handle the situation—all group members need to take an active role in assisting with problem members. Here are some suggestions on handling dysfunctional behaviors for you to try out in your next group meeting. Or if you are one of these dysfunctional people, here are some suggestions for you as well:

If you are a **DOMINATOR** *or are in a group with a dominator, try these suggestions:*
- If you are speaking more than others in your group, there is a good chance you are dominating. Wait until others have spoken before giving your opinions; concentrate on a task or maintenance role; and listen carefully.

- Usually a good gatekeeper is needed to move the conversation along. When asking a question, avoid making direct eye contact with dominators as it encourages speaking.

- If you are in a group with two or more dominators, try establishing this rule: For each new topic introduced, each member gets one minute to speak. Once everyone gets a turn, move back to an open-discussion format.

If you are a **DESERTER** *or are in a group with a deserter, try these suggestions:*
- If you are speaking less than others or not at all, there is a good chance that you are a deserter. Plan to present a specific piece of research and a written summary as a handout. Practice ahead of time.

- If you have both dominators and deserters in your group, try arranging the seating to place the quiet members between more talkative members.

- The best antidote for the deserter is a good gatekeeper who can tactfully draw the quiet person into the discussion and give needed encouragement. To get deserters involved, assign them to serve as group recorder or to write group ideas on the markerboard.

If you are a **BLOCKER** *or* **AGGRESSOR** *or are in a group with a blocker or aggressor, try these suggestions:*
- If you catch yourself feeling irritated by people in your group, giving (or wanting to give) hostile or personal putdowns, or arguing in a stubborn manner for longer than ten minutes, you may well be a blocker or aggressor. Say something like, "Let me think about this for a minute" and then cool down and force yourself to listen to what the others are saying.

- This might be a good time for the *tension reliever* to establish a more relaxed atmosphere, a *supporter* to affirm previous contributions of members, or the *gatekeeper* to summarize and move the conversation to another person or topic.

- If your group contains a person known to be a blocker or aggressor, try assigning the role of recorder to that person (an important role that might help fulfill their need for control yet leave little time for arguments) or arrange to sit the blocker or aggressor directly beside the leader or gatekeeper.

- Listen to the blocker and aggressor respectfully as you would to all group members. Strive for a win-win conflict resolution.

If you are a **SHOWBOAT** *or are in a group with a showboat, try these suggestions:*
- If you are spending more time cracking jokes than concentrating on the topic being discussed, you are probably a showboat. Switch to the role of *tension reliever* and only add humor when needed. Also, is it possible that you are not prepared for the meeting and are disguising this fact with your distractions? Carefully prepare for future meetings.

- An effective way to deal with showboats is to find some way to assign them a simple but important task. Once they feel that they can play useful roles, their behavior may change.

Benefiting from Culture/Gender/Technology/Ethics

Effective leaders acknowledge the effects that culture, gender, technology, and ethics can have on groups and work to make these potential differences become benefits to the group.

Leadership and Culture/Gender

From 1972 to 2002, women involved in leadership roles in organizations in the United States increased from 18 to 46 percent (Porterfield & Kleiner, 2005), but, by 2003, senior management positions were held by only 16 percent of women in the United States (Bellar et al., 2004). This is a worldwide problem, according to the Grant Thornton International Business Report (2007), noting that women occupy only 22 percent of top business positions worldwide. The Philippines tops the list with women in 50 percent of top positions, followed by the Netherlands (13%), Germany (12%), Luxembourg (10%) and Japan (7%). (See **Figure 9.6.**)

According to the most recent survey by the Government Accountability Office (GAO Highlights, 2006), there were slight diversity increases at the management level in the financial services industry between 1993–2004, while white women saw a slight increase from 36.7% to 37.4%, and white men experienced a decrease from 52.2% to 47.2%. The graph in Figure 9.6 and the bullets below summarize data from the report:

- Overall minority men and women in management in the financial services industry: 11.1 to 15.5%
- African Americans: 5.6 to 6.6%
- Asians: 2.5 to 4.5%
- Hispanics: 2.8 to 4.0%
- American Indians: 0.2 to 0.3%

A long-held belief is that female leaders are more relationship- and people-oriented while male leaders are more task- and job-oriented (Kabacoff, 1998). Do men and women really have different leadership styles, or is this a stereotype? According to Thorne et al., (1983), "very few expected sex differences have been firmly substantiated by empirical studies" (p. 13). It appears that a leadership style that is a blend of both the traditionally masculine and traditionally feminine characteristics (called an **androgynous** style) is what works best in today's world (Claes, 2006; Wood, 2009). As you read about various leadership theories coming next, note how often task roles (traditionally masculine) and maintenance roles (traditionally feminine) are introduced as being important roles that leaders and team members should perform for productive small group problem-solving results.

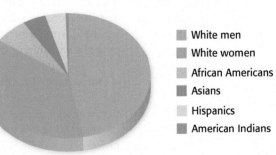

Figure 9.6 Management Positions in 2004

- White men
- White women
- African Americans
- Asians
- Hispanics
- American Indians

Leadership and Technology

As globalization continues, and team members and leaders become even more scattered across distance and time zones—a flexible, electronic-savvy form of leadership used with virtual teams, called **e-leadership,** is needed. Today "fewer than one in four managers at global companies work in the same location as their team" (Butler, 2008). For example,

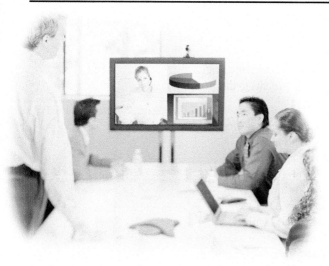

in December of 2007, IBM held a four-day, online conference involving 300 professionals from 10 different countries discussing 5 subthemes related to new technologies. Each subtheme was led by an expert from one of four countries—Canada, India, the United Kingdom, and the United States (Hamilton, 2008).

Although research is in the early stages, here are some suggestions for leaders of virtual teams (Allen, 2008; Branson et al., 2008; Butler, 2008; Gibson & Cohen, 2003):

• Be open to ambiguity, uncertainty, and calculated risk-taking.

• Delegate and encourage—don't micro-manage. Each member should know what other members are working on to feel connected.

• Select team members who are skilled in the specific task and in interpersonal communication—training may be needed.

• Meet virtually one-on-one with each member to establish trust and a personal feeling—phone calls and instant messaging are viewed as friendly.

• Rotate conference calls and virtual meetings to vary across time zones, so no one is continually inconvenienced.

• Since virtual teams tend to consider less information when making decisions than face-to-face groups, it is important to inform teams about virtual limitations and encourage information gathering.

• Encourage members to give ideas in a low-context manner that is complete and explicit—especially if the team is culturally diverse and has no previous experience working together. (Refer to Chapter 1 for a discussion of low- and high-context cultures.)

Leadership and Ethics

Ethics is another issue that can affect groups and their leaders. As we noted earlier, the notion of power and leadership is often regarded with suspicion and mistrust—especially in western cultures. Therefore, ethical leadership in western societies always takes into account the needs of followers and leaves followers with the freedom of choice.

One strategy for ensuring that you function as an ethical leader is to adopt the "leader as servant" perspective (Greenleaf, 2002; Senge, 2006). This implies that you see your role as one in which you facilitate the development of the members of your group—as human beings as well as participants in the group process. This does not mean that you must silence your own views. It does mean that you should offer your ideas as a participant and not as the final arbiter. You will still be regarded as an influential member, but you will temper your contributions with the realization that your ideas are simply "one among many." At all times, you will seek to encourage others, and you will work to serve their interests and needs. Those needs include the interpersonal needs that have been discussed previously: inclusion, control, and affection. They may also include practical needs, such as consideration of others' time schedules and unforeseen difficulties. Servant leaders put their followers first, seeing them as the most important part of the group. Interestingly, in doing so, the servant leader is usually regarded by the members as the most important member of the group and viewed as "first among equals."

Expand your understanding of the characteristics of effective small group leaders by considering these questions:

- Based on your experience, how has culture, gender, technology, and ethics changed the traditional view of leadership? Give an explanation for at least one area.

- Identify at least one specific leader characteristic that you plan to work on to make yourself a more effective group leader. Why is improvement needed?

Becoming an Effective Leader

LEARNING **OBJECTIVE**

9.4 What are the theories and/or approaches to becoming an effective leader that offer productive ways of building leadership skills, and what practical tip does each offer for real-world application?

One of the most productive ways to build leadership skills is to look at some of the theories that have been advanced to explain how and why some people are able to exert leadership while others are not. Each of the theories has specific tips to offer as you consider your leadership strengths and weaknesses.

Leadership Traits

One theory to explain why some people emerge as leaders is **leadership traits,** which makes the assumption that leaders are born—that is, some people simply possess the traits that cause others to look to them for leadership. This may seem to be an appealing idea. You have probably observed people who appeared to influence others with no real effort. However, since the early 1900s scholars like Stogdill (1948) have examined over 25,000 research studies and books looking for traits associated with leadership. They examined such traits as intelligence, physical attractiveness, stamina, sociability, confidence, verbal skills, enthusiasm, and others but found no single trait or set of traits that consistently appeared in all leaders but not in followers. Researchers (Kellett et al., 2006; Kouzes & Posner, 2002) found a difference between successful and less successful leaders. Successful leaders seem to have more of the following:

- Adaptability
- Ambition
- Creativity
- Desire to lead
- Fair-mindedness
- Focus on empowerment

- Inspiration
- Rapid information processing
- Self-confidence
- Supportiveness
- Technological knowledge
- Trustworthiness

The question is, were leaders who show some of these qualities born with them, or did they acquire them through experience or by modeling after mentors or family members? Most experts now believe that effective leaders are trained, not born with innate abilities. The more leadership experience people gain, the better their leadership skills become. For example, interviewing numerous business leaders, Conger (2004) found that family and experiences had influenced leadership development more than formalized training. So, if you want to learn to be a leader, should you try to achieve the traits listed above? Yes, but don't expect to accomplish them overnight; it will take dedication and hard work.

Practical Tip: Even if you don't have previous experience at leadership and haven't had family members or friends to use as models, you now know that leadership is a trained skill. Therefore, if you see certain traits that you would like to develop, begin working on one or two of them realizing that change comes slowly. Fortunately, while you are working on these long-term leadership qualities, there is a more time-conscious approach explained in the function theory discussed next.

Leadership Functions

We now recognize that leadership is less about what a person *is* than what a person *does*. Most experts agree with professionals like Rudy Giuliani, former mayor of New York, whose leadership skills were so valuable after the terrorist attacks on September 11, 2001. "Leaders are made," said Giuliani in a speech to the Urban Land Institute. "Everything is about the lessons they learn, the things they focus on, the people they copy" (Silverman, 2004, p. 2).

When we look at what successful leaders do, we find that they perform both task and maintenance roles (also referred to as functions)—in other words, they focus on the job *and* the people (Sayles, 1993). The theory of **leadership functions**, then, explains that people emerge as leaders by fulfilling needed task roles (roles that assist the group in achieving its goals) and maintenance roles (roles that help the group preserve its cohesiveness and maintain harmony among members) discussed earlier in this chapter. *Task roles* include such behaviors as information/opinion giver, information/opinion seeker, analyzer, expediter, and clarifier; *maintenance roles* include such behaviors as supporter, harmonizer, tension reliever, and gatekeeper.

"Leaders are made," says former mayor of New York, Rudy Giuliani. "Everything is about the lessons they learn, the things they focus on, the people they copy."

Practical tip: While you are working on long-term leadership traits, concentrate on recognizing and performing task and maintenance roles as well. Many of these you already use on a regular basis; some you will need to practice in order to use effectively. Keep in mind that to be an effective leader, you don't have to perform all the roles yourself. Encourage group members to share in leadership responsibility by performing various roles themselves. This will give you more time to observe the group and to fulfill the roles that are not being handled by other members. It's difficult to guide a group through a detailed discussion while observing member reactions, making sure that everyone is getting a chance to participate, and handling conflicts all at the same time. Sharing leadership roles means a more effective group process.

APPLY **WHAT YOU KNOW**
USING LEADERSHIP TRAITS AND FUNCTIONS

Apply what you know about leadership traits and functions by completing at least one of the following:

- Take another look at the list of traits that research indicates are more often used by successful leaders. In your experience, which two of them do you think would make the most importance to group members? On a scale from 1 (low) to 5 (high), rate yourself as you stand now on each of these two traits. How likely do you think it would be for you to see an improvement in one year from now? Two years from now? Five years from now?

- Take another look at the list of task and maintenance roles from the member section at the first of this chapter. Which two from each category are you already comfortable using? From each category, select one that needs a bit of practice. Plan to use these roles in class discussions or in a group project until you feel comfortable with them. Don't wait for someone else to give direction; if you think a role is needed, jump in and do it!

Leadership Styles

Another perspective from which to view your leadership skills is to consider **leadership styles** (also called the three-dimension theory of leadership). The three leadership styles most frequently studied are *authoritarian*, *democratic*, and *laissez-faire* (White & Lippitt, 1968):

- The **authoritarian leader** is the one who essentially makes the decisions and imposes them upon the group. Although group hostility can be up to thirty times greater with an authoritarian leader (Manz & Sims, 2001), there are some definite advantages: decisions are made more quickly which is good when time is at a premium, and extremely large groups need the control provided by this leadership style. Also, the authoritarian style works best when the group's tasks are relatively simple.

- The **democratic leader** participates with the group in deliberating and decision making; members are empowered to actively participate. Member satisfaction is usually greater with a democratic leader, and members are less resistant to accepting changes when they have played a role in the decision making. On the other hand, effective democratic leadership requires training and patience and allowing others to participate in the decision making is time-consuming. The democratic style works best when tasks are detailed or complicated and when group approval is needed for a decision.

- The **laissez-faire leader** turns the whole process over to the group with little or no further involvement. This works well when the members are trained professionals who need little guidance. However, most groups need some guidance and as a result experience low satisfaction and low productivity with laissez-faire leaders.

The best way to conceptualize the three leadership styles is to think of them as positions along a continuum, with the authoritarian and laissez-faire styles at the extreme ends of the continuum, and the democratic style in the center (**Figure 9.7**).

There are, of course, other points all along the continuum where leaders may fall.

Practical Tip: Flexibility allows for the best results. So, when working to select a leadership style, consider (1) the style you feel the most comfortable using, (2) the best style for the situation, and (3) the style that fits the needs and expectations of your specific group. Contingency theories discussed next offer more advice on selecting the best leadership style.

Figure 9.7 The Three-Dimensional Theory of Leadership

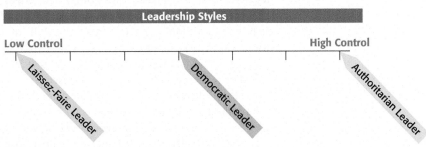

APPLY **WHAT YOU KNOW**
LEADERSHIP STYLES

Expand your understanding of leadership styles by answering the following critical thinking questions about authoritarian, democratic, and laissez-faire groups:*

1. Which leadership style would take the most time to reach a decision? Why?

2. Which leadership style would take the shortest time to develop commitment to the decision? Why?

3. Which leadership style would take the longest time to implement a decision? Why?

*(Check your answers with those located in MyCommunicationLab, Apply What You Know for Chapter 9.)

Contingency Leadership

When examining leadership styles, the question often arises as to which style is "best." For people in the United States it is tempting to assert that the democratic style is the optimal position. However, it is not difficult to think of instances in which the authoritarian style is preferred. Military commanders, for example, in combat find it necessary to rely on an authoritarian style. Most contemporary thinkers on the subject adopt a **contingency leadership** approach when answering the question of which style is best. Contingency theorists hold that there is no "best" style, but that the appropriate style is contingent (or dependent) upon the nature of the situation. We will look at two contingency theories: Fiedler's **situational contingency theory** and Hersey and Blanchard's **situational leadership theory**.

Contingency Model

One of the first and probably best known contingency theories was developed by Fred Fiedler (1967, 1996). Fiedler believed that there were two types of leaders—task-oriented leaders and people-oriented leaders. Fiedler's research focused on when each leadership style worked best. He found that leadership effectiveness depended on three situations or contingencies:

- *Leader-member relations* (whether team members like and trust the leader).
- *Task structure* (whether the jobs, goals, and procedures are clearly structured).
- *Position power* (whether the leader has power to reward and punish).

Fiedler's research discovered that *task-oriented leadership worked best* in two extreme situations: (1) when all three situations were positive—leader well-liked, tasks structured, and leader with power; or (2) when all three situations were negative—leader disliked, tasks poorly defined, and leader with little power. A task orientation works in situation 1 because the members are knowledgeable and like each other and don't especially need the skills of a people leader. A task orientation works in situation 2 because structure and guidance are more important than liking the leader. (See **Figure 9.8.**)

Fiedler was especially interested to discover that *people-oriented leadership worked best* when all three situations were moderately favorable—leader moderately liked, task moderately defined, and leader with some power. In this situation, a people-oriented leader with good interpersonal skills is needed to inspire members to better task completion and generally create a positive environment.

It was Fiedler's belief that very few leaders are good at both task and people orientations; they have a definite preference for one or the other. Asking them to be flexible and change from one style to the other rarely works. Therefore, Fiedler suggested that leaders should be selected to fit the situation: if all three situations

Figure 9.8 Contingency Model

	Relations	Task Structure	Position Power	Best Style
If	Leader is liked	Task structured	Leader has strong power	Task Orientation
If	Leader is disliked	Task unstructured	Leader has weak power	Task Orientation
If	Leader is moderately liked	Task moderately structured	Leader has some power	People Orientation

are positive or all three are negative, a task-oriented leader should be selected; if all three situations are only moderately favorable, a people-oriented leader should be selected. Once the situation in the group changes, leadership should also change.

Practical Tip: Are you more of a people person or a task person? If you are thinking that your task and people skills aren't equally effective, Fiedler's theory may shed light on how to improve your leadership abilities—research the group ahead of time and only agree to be the leader if the group fits your leadership style and abilities. If you have both task and people skills, use the approach that fits the specific group situation as described by Fiedler. If you aren't sure which you are, take Fiedler's Least Preferred Coworker scale (LPC) in the *Connecting to Business* feature in the Career section of this chapter.

Situational Model
Another prominent example of the contingency approach was proposed by Hersey and Blanchard (Hersey et al., 2007). Unlike Fiedler, these researchers believe that good leaders *can* change styles. According to Hersey and Blanchard, when leaders determine the appropriate leadership style for any given situation, they should consider whether group members are (1) able and/or (2) willing. If members of the group are *able*, they understand the task that needs to be done and possess all the required skills and training to meet the objectives. If group members are *willing*, they are confident in their abilities and eager and motivated to do the task.

To handle a group with a mix of ability and willingness, Hersey and Blanchard offer four leadership styles—delegating, participating, selling, and telling—and suggest that the styles be used in the following situations:

- When a group is ↑ able and ↑ willing = **Delegate** (leader turns over major responsibility for decision making to the group).
- When group is ↑ able but ↓ unwilling = **Participate** (leader shares, encourages participation, and facilitates group process).
- When group is ↓ unable but ↑ willing = **Sell** (leader explains task and gives group chance to ask questions to improve understanding).
- When group is ↓ unable and ↓ unwilling = **Tell** (leader gives detailed instructions and provides close supervision).

According to this theory, a leader who misreads the group and uses the wrong style can expect to "hurt morale and performance" (Daft, 2008). Daft tells of a new president of Harvard University who chose to use the telling style with professors who were knowledgeable and willing and expecting to be partners in decision making. The result was "serious conflict with some faculty members and eventual demands for his ouster" (p. 500).

Practical Tip: In this leadership model, Hersey and Blanchard are suggesting that leaders can change styles depending on the needs of their group. This would certainly be more flexible than having to pick your group to fit your predetermined style. However, this means that you will have to know your group and determine how able and willing they are to complete their assigned task. Some groups may need close supervision and others will prefer to work basically alone. Of course, you will want to adjust to the changing needs of the group when new tasks are undertaken.

APPLY **WHAT YOU KNOW**
USING LEADERSHIP CONTINGENCIES

Apply what you know about contingency theories of leadership by answering at least one of the following:

1. Fiedler believes that very few people are good at both task and people leadership, so asking them to be flexible rarely works. Do you agree with him? Why or why not?

2. Hersey and Blanchard suggest that leaders can change styles if they consider the ability and willingness of their group members. Which leadership styles (delegating, participating, selling, or telling) do think is used most often in small groups? Give an example.

Transformational Leadership

The leadership theories discussed up to this point are called *transactional* because leaders "clarify the role and task requirements of subordinates, initiate structure, provide appropriate rewards, and try to be considerate of and meet the social needs of subordinates" (Daft, 2008, p. 505). In other words, transactional leadership involves transactions between leaders and employees: an employee fulfills a request of a leader and the leader responds with a reward. The problem with transactional leadership is that risk and personal involvement usually are not encouraged on the part of the leader or the subordinates. Yet to survive in today's fast-paced world that is filled with constant change, risk and personal involvement are essential. The only way that change will occur fast enough is if employees feel part of the "family" and begin taking an active role beyond the everyday transactions.

According to Bass (1985; see also Bass & Avolio, 1997), it is the transformational leader who is especially suited for innovation, creativity, and change. **Transformational leadership** inspires employees of the company to "go beyond their self-interests or expected rewards for the good of the team and the good of the organization" (Bass & Riggio, 2006, p. 104). An example of a leader with transformational qualities is Richard Kovacevich, CEO of Wells Fargo (Daft, 2008). Kovacevich has inspired employees to care enough to be accountable for the company's success. Slogans such as "Mind share plus heart share equals market share" remind employees that for success to occur, they must apply both their minds and their hearts. As a result, Wells Fargo has developed into one of the largest and most successful banks in the country.

Practical Tip: You may not feel that you have the ability to become a transformational leader, and it may be that you need more experience working as a leader before you consider the transformational leadership style. Don't let that frustrate you. You have plenty of time to develop the skills needed before moving to this level of leadership. To get an idea of how likely you are to become a transformational leader, take the Transformational Leadership Scale included in the *Making Theory Practical* feature on page 254.

APPLY **WHAT YOU KNOW**
USING TRANSFORMATIONAL LEADERSHIP

Apply what you know about transformational leadership theory by answering the following critical thinking questions:

- Make a list of current and past leaders who seem to fit the definition of transformational leader. Is there a good balance of women and cultural minorities? Discuss.

- Lee Iacocca, in his book *Where Have All the Leaders Gone?* (2007), makes the statement that "the courageous, dedicated leaders who are committed to the good of society" seem to have disappeared. Do you agree with Iacocca? If so, what has caused this change in leadership?

Responsibilities of Members and Leaders

LEARNING **OBJECTIVE**

9.5 What are the responsibilities that members and leaders should be prepared to take in a successful group?

A successful group outcome requires the efforts of all group members as well as the leader. Here is a list of **member responsibilities** and another one of **leader responsibilities** that you can follow before, during, and after group meetings to make sure you are assisting your group in every way possible.

Member Responsibilities

Implement these member responsibilities.

Before the meeting:

- Reread minutes from previous meeting to make sure you completed all tasks.
- If unable to attend, contact the group chairperson and plan for a substitute if needed.
- As you arrive at the meeting, silence your cell phone.

During the meeting:

- Take an active role by asking questions, clarifying, summarizing, and listening.
- Take notes, even if you aren't assigned to be the recorder.
- Remain open to others' suggestions and avoid hostility or dysfunctional behaviors.
- When conflicts develop, work to help find win-win solutions.
- Assist the leader so everyone feels included, and the group stays on track.

After the meeting:

- Keep a file of notes/materials from all meetings; complete all assignments.
- Read minutes when distributed and communicate any errors or omissions.
- Do not work outside of the group to influence others to your point of view about any unresolved issues.
- Do not repeat what other group members have said in group meetings.
- If you are asked about the group, keep all your comments positive.

Leader Responsibilities

Try these leadership responsibilities:

Before the meeting:

- Decide whether to call a meeting—use e-mail when possible.
- Plan and distribute an agenda after asking members for their input.
- Anticipate possibilities of conflict without deciding how these conflicts should be resolved.

During the meeting:

- Stick to the agenda and keep everyone on track.
- Follow the steps of the effective problem-solving process (discussed in Chapter 8).
- Facilitate involvement of all members while minimizing dysfunctional roles.
- Manage conflict with win-win outcomes or workable compromises.

MAKING THEORY **PRACTICAL**
TRANSFORMATIONAL LEADERSHIP THEORY

Have you ever admired a person so much that you were willing to do anything he or she asked? Did this person inspire you to greater enthusiasm and productivity than you thought possible? Were you awed by this person's vision of the future?

If you answered "yes" to these questions, this person was probably a transformational leader. So far, this chapter has covered many theories of leadership, each offering you some helpful pointers for developing your own leadership skills. Transformational leaders build on other leadership styles but go beyond to offer creativity, change, and a vision of the future.

Theorist

Bernard Bass, a leadership and small group theorist and psychologist, began with an idea first mentioned by James Burns (1978), conducted multiple research studies on transformational leaders, and published his results in his 1985 book, *Leadership and Performance Beyond Expectations*. Bass describes transformational leadership as a charismatic type of leadership where "followers seek to identify with the leader and emulate him or her" (Bass & Riggio, 2006, p. 5). In addition to arousing strong emotions and loyalty through charisma (which is not enough by itself, warns Bass), the transformational leader also makes a "profound effect" on others by building trust, acting with integrity, inspiring others, encouraging innovative thinking, and mentoring people's development (Bass, 1985; Bass and Avolio, 1997).

PRACTICAL APPLICATION

Although it might be difficult for you to become charismatic if you aren't already, Bass feels that leaders can be trained to become transformational. Of course, the first step is to determine what transformational behaviors you already use on a regular basis. To do that, take the Transformational Leadership Scale below—each of the questions represents an important behavior of transformational leaders.

TRANSFORMATIONAL LEADERSHIP SCALE[*]

Instructions: Rate your leadership (or the leadership of another person) by how often you or they engage in the following seven behaviors.

Scale: rarely or never 1 2 3 4 5 very frequently or always

1.____ Communicates a clear and positive vision of the future to team members.
2.____ Treats members as individuals, supports and encourages their development.
3.____ Gives encouragement and recognition to members.
4.____ Fosters trust, involvement and cooperation among team members.
5.____ Encourages questioning assumptions and thinking about problems in new ways.
6.____ Is clear about values; practices what he/she preaches.
7.____ Instills pride and respect in others and inspires them by being highly competent.

Score: Total your points_____ (scores can range from 7–35).

- A score of 26–35: You make extensive use of transformational leadership, meaning you are visionary, innovative, supportive, participative, and respected by others.

- A score of 16–25: You make some use of transformational leadership; however, any scores of 1 or 2 do not fit this leadership style, and you may want to make some changes.

- A score of 7–15: You make little or no use of transformational leadership. Your leadership style is probably a transactional one instead.

[*]This scale was adapted from the Global Transformational Leadership scale (GTL), a short measure of transformational leadership developed by Carless et al., (2000).

Key Sources: Bass, *Leadership and Performance Beyond Expectation,* 1985; Burns, *Leadership,* 1978.

- Offer your views as appropriate, but avoid dominating the group.
- Reserve time at the end of the meeting to summarize and preview the next meeting.
- Express appreciation for group members' cooperation and hard work.

After the meeting:

- Reflect on what happened during the meeting; formulate ideas for any problems.
- Be available to group members for consultation about tasks for the next meeting.
- Accomplish any tasks that are your responsibility.
- Keep notes on ideas that should be included in the agenda for the next meeting.

CHAPTER SUMMARY

As this chapter indicates, becoming effective group members and leaders requires knowledge and skill. You can determine your knowledge of successful groups by checking the skills and learning objectives presented in this chapter.

Summary of **SKILLS**

Check each skill that you now feel qualified to perform:
- ❏ I can analyze the member characteristics, roles, and responsibilities that I use effectively and work to improve my member skills in at least two additional areas.
- ❏ I can analyze the leadership characteristics and responsibilities that I already use effectively and work to enhance my skills in at least two new areas.
- ❏ I can improve my skills as an effective leader by applying tips from at least two leadership theories or approaches.
- ❏ I can put into action new group member and leadership responsibilities and skills as they relate to my career.

Summary of LEARNING **OUTCOMES**

9.1 *What are the characteristics of effective group members, and what role do they play in successful groups?*

- Characteristics of effective group members include open-mindedness; willingness to prepare for discussions; knowledge of groups and the group problem-solving process; knowledge of conflicts and the willingness to handle them effectively.

- Characteristics of effective group members play an important role in a group's success. Group discussions are difficult enough even with effective members. Without effective members, the process will be extremely slow and may not work at all.

9.2 *What are the roles that members should exhibit and the roles they should avoid in successful groups, and what are some suggestions for working with dysfunctional members in the group setting?*

- Roles that members should utilize in successful groups include: (1) *formal roles* (agenda setter and recorder); (2) *task roles* (information/opinion giver and seeker, analyzer, expediter, and clarifier); and (3) *maintenance roles* (supporter, harmonizer, tension reliever, and gatekeeper).

- Roles that members should avoid using in successful groups include the *dysfunctional roles* (dominator, deserter, blocker, aggressor, and showboat).

- Suggestions for working with dysfunctional members are located in the *Developing Skills* feature on page 244.

9.3 *What are the characteristics of effective group leaders, and what role do they play in successful groups?*

- Characteristics of effective group leadership include leaders who use power effectively, share responsibility with group members, and work to make culture, gender, technology, and ethics a benefit to the group.

LEADERSHIP **AND YOUR CAREER**

LEARNING **OBJECTIVE**

9.6 What information and skills covered in this chapter relate specifically to your career?

Communicating effectively as a group member or a leader will be of special importance to you in your career. The following *Spotlight on, Career Moment,* and *Connecting to* Features take a look at members and leaders in the workplace specifically as they relate to careers in business, education, and healthcare. Whether you are interested in one of those career fields or will be a consumer of the services of these areas, the following information should be of interest to you.

SPOTLIGHT ON **GROUP MEMBERS & LEADERS**

BUSINESS

American managers and their employees do not perceive the leadership role of management in the same way. For example, Karlins and Hargis (1988) investigated 52 large organizations and found the following:

- Most managers (88 percent) divided their time equally between task and maintenance issues—realizing the importance of both tasks and people.

- However, most employees (85 percent) reported that their managers were much more interested in tasks than people.

When group members feel that their needs and concerns are not important to the leader, the motivation and success of the group is diminished. Employees tend to remember negative feelings and events longer than they do positive feelings (Dasborough, 2006), making this difference in perception even more important.

EDUCATION

As Searby & Shaddix in their article "Growing Teacher Leaders in a Culture of Excellence" (2008) point out, teachers do not typically see themselves as leaders—yet even when they are not in a formal leadership position, teachers still lead. Compare the following list of what leaders do with what teachers do (p. 36): Leaders . . .

- Ask tough questions.

- Have competent credibility.

- Set the tone for meetings and discussions.

- Are willing to learn new information and share it.

- Mentor others one-on-one.

- Interpret reality for others.

- Anticipate other's needs and meet them without being asked.

- Ask, "What is our purpose?"

- Support others emotionally and professionally.

- Ask, "Is this consistent with our values and beliefs?"

HEALTHCARE

In many helping professions such as healthcare, leadership is often referred to as mentoring. According to Tamparo & Lindh in their book *Therapeutic Communications for Health Care* (2008), the problem with mentoring is determining how much is enough. Some healthcare professionals give so much that they become "disillusioned and suffer burnout," while others protect themselves by remaining detached and appear "rude or disinterested" to their clients (p. 9). Successful mentors answer "Yes" to each of the following questions—can you?

- Do you genuinely enjoy helping people?

- Can you enjoy assuming a "servant" role for those you help?

- Can you be open to people and accept their differences?

- Can you be firm, yet gentle?

- Can you resist feeling dismayed or rejected when unable to "save" a client?

CAREER MOMENT **EFFECTIVE TEAM MEMBERS**

According to LaFasto and Larson (2001), in their book *When Teams Work Best,* even the U.S. Department of Labor has "identified teamwork as one of five workplace skills that should be taught more aggressively in public schools" (p. xvii). Of course, not all groups are successful. Some teams fail due in large part to poor training. You can learn to be an effective team member beginning with this course in communication. Researchers have found that college students who join small study groups experience "increased student achievement, increased persistence through courses and programs, and more favorable learning-related attitudes" (Cooper, 1998, p. 3). We suggest that you learn to work in a team by joining one or more study groups while in college.

In fact, Harvard Business School thinks study groups are important enough to assign each student to a learning team of five to six  people during orientation. According to their Web site (www.hbs.edu/case/study-groups.html): "Some Learning Teams meet in the morning before class to discuss the cases, share expertise, and sharpen arguments to strengthen communication and persuasion skills" (The Case Method).

CONNECTING TO **BUSINESS**

If you are considering going into a business or professional field, you will want to determine and polish your leadership skills. One way to assess your leadership style is to take Fiedler's *Least Preferred Coworker* scale (LPC) by Fiedler & Chemers (1974).

ACTIVITY Think of a coworker that you dislike working with. Answer each question by circling the number that most closely describes this person on each pair of adjectives. Total the circled responses—scores can range from 18 to 96.

Pleasant	8 7 6 5 4 3 2 1	Unpleasant	Gloomy	1 2 3 4 5 6 7 8	Cheerful
Friendly	8 7 6 5 4 3 2 1	Unfriendly	Open	8 7 6 5 4 3 2 1	Guarded
Rejecting	1 2 3 4 5 6 7 8	Accepting	Backbiting	1 2 3 4 5 6 7 8	Loyal
Tense	1 2 3 4 5 6 7 8	Relaxed	Untrustworthy	1 2 3 4 5 6 7 8	Trustworthy
Distant	1 2 3 4 5 6 7 8	Close	Considerate	8 7 6 5 4 3 2 1	Inconsiderate
Cold	1 2 3 4 5 6 7 8	Warm	Nasty	1 2 3 4 5 6 7 8	Nice
Supportive	8 7 6 5 4 3 2 1	Hostile	Agreeable	8 7 6 5 4 3 2 1	Disagreeable
Boring	1 2 3 4 5 6 7 8	Interesting	Insincere	1 2 3 4 5 6 7 8	Sincere
Quarrelsome	1 2 3 4 5 6 7 8	Harmonious	Kind	8 7 6 5 4 3 2 1	Unkind

CONNECTING TO **EDUCATION**

If you are considering a career in education, not only will you need to be a good leader, but you have a wonderful opportunity to train other leaders. In the *21 Irrefutable Laws of Leadership* (Maxwell, 1998), Law #13 is the Law of Reproduction or "It takes a leader to raise up a leader" (p. 133). In a study of numerous leaders, Maxwell found that 85% of them became leaders because of the influence of other leaders. This is true in every field. For example, Maxwell notes that in the NFL in 1998, 15 head coaches had worked directly or indirectly with Bill Walsh or Tom Landry (former Super Bowl winning coaches).

ACTIVITY Form two groups of three to five people interested in education and discuss the following:

1. Which of the many leadership styles discussed in this chapter do you think would make the best teachers? Select at least two and list several reasons for each choice.

2. If you decided on the field of education because of the influence of past teachers, what did they do that encouraged you? Was it a leadership role?

3. How is it possible for an educator to train leaders in fields other than education? Be specific.

CONNECTING TO **HEALTHCARE**

If you are considering a career in nursing (or another area of healthcare), you need to get ready for change. According to Grossman & Valiga (2005), "Professional nurses can no longer think of themselves as 'just nurses.' Nurses are increasingly expected to provide leadership, whether they hold staff positions or are vice presidents, nurse practitioners, or nurse educators" (p. 66). Transactional leadership no longer works in today's world; instead, transformational leaders are needed. So nurses must: follow their dreams, be articulate, chart their own growth as well as followers' growth, establish trusting relationships, assess their strengths and weaknesses, and constantly seek new ways of doing things (p. 68).

ACTIVITY Form groups of three to five people interested in healthcare to answer these questions:

• What does it mean for nurses to think of themselves as "just nurses"? Is this attitude true of other healthcare professionals as well? Why or why not?

• Describe the typical "dream" or "vision" that motivates most nurses. Is this dream shared verbally, or is it generally kept secret?

• Name two specific things that will have to change if nurses are to become transformational leaders.

▶ Log onto MyCommunicationLab.com to access Connecting to Psychology and Connecting to Science, Technology, Engineering, and Math—both with related activities.

- If used correctly, leadership is "the single-most important predictor of the teams' success" (Tubbs, 2009, p. 230). Effective group leaders (leaders with the characteristics described) have more effective groups.

9.4 *What are the theories and/or approaches to becoming an effective leader that offer productive ways of building leadership skills, and what practical tip does each offer for real-world application?*

- The theories and/or approaches to becoming an effective leader include the following: leadership traits, leadership functions, leadership power, leadership styles, leadership contingencies, and transformational leadership.

- A summary of the practical tips for each leadership theory can be found in the Practical Tip paragraph at the end of each theory: leadership traits on p. 247; leadership functions on p. 248; leadership styles on p. 249; contingency leadership on p. 251; situational

leadership on p. 251; transformational leadership on page 252. For specifics on transformational leadership, see the *Making Theory Practical* feature in this chapter.

9.5 *What are the responsibilities that members and leaders should be prepared to take in a successful group?*

- Member and leader responsibilities can be organized into before, during, and after meetings.

- For a specific list of responsibilities for each category, see page 253.

9.6 *What information and skills covered in this chapter relate specifically to your career (see highlighted fields of business, education, and healthcare)?*

- The *Spotlight on*, *Career Moment*, and *Connecting to* features highlight the value of listening in the fields of business, education, and healthcare—additional fields are included online.

SOLVE IT NOW!

Taking into consideration all that you learned about becoming effective group members and leaders from this chapter, what advice can you give Andrea in our opening scenario?*

- What task, maintenance, and dysfunctional roles were performed or appeared likely to occur by the group members in the opening scenario?

- What advice can you give Andrea on maintaining control while still empowering the group members to participate and effectively solve problems?
- Which leadership approach discussed in this chapter do you think would work best for Andrea with this particular group? Why?
- What specific group skills would you recommend for Andrea that would improve her leadership and communication skills now and in the future?

*(Check your answers with those located in MyCommunicationLab, Scenario Analysis for Chapter 9)

KEY TERMS

agenda setter	p. 237	e-leadership	p. 245	leader responsibilities	p. 253	referent power	p. 243
aggressor	p. 241	emergent leader	p. 243	leadership	p. 243	reward power	p. 243
analyzer	p. 238	expediter	p. 239	leadership functions	p. 248	role diversity	p. 240
androgynous	p. 245	expert power	p. 243	leadership power	p. 243	showboat	p. 242
authoritarian leader	p. 249	formal role	p. 237	leadership styles	p. 249	situational contingency theory	p. 250
blocker	p. 241	gatekeeper	p. 240	leadership traits	p. 247	situational leadership theory	p. 250
clarifier	p. 239	group roles	p. 237	legitimate power	p. 243	supporter	p. 239
coercive power	p. 243	harmonizer	p. 240	maintenance roles	p. 239	task roles	p. 238
contingency leadership	p. 250	informal role	p. 238	member responsibilities	p. 253	tension reliever	p. 240
democratic leader	p. 249	information/ opinion giver	p. 238	nominal leader	p. 243	transformational leadership	p. 252
deserter	p. 241	information/ opinion seeker	p. 238	power	p. 243		
dominator	p. 241	laissez-faire leader	p. 249	recorder	p. 237		
dysfunctional roles	p. 241						

SKILL BUILDERS

1. Taking into consideration all that you have learned about leadership and the problem-solving process, think about your past group experiences and what leadership and power roles you usually perform. Which advice do you think will be the most helpful? Were there any suggestions in this chapter that would not seem to help you personally? Be prepared to share your answers with your classmates.

2. Critically Evaluating

Using the critical evaluation form from Chapter 1, select and evaluate an article on *Leadership* obtained from a communication journal such as *Communication Education.* (You may wish to check your library databases for articles. *Communication and Mass Media Complete* in EBSCOHost is an excellent database for communication articles.) Be prepared to share your observations with your classmates.

3. Videotape a segment of a problem-solving discussion. Which step(s) of the group problem-solving process were you in? Evaluate the strengths and weaknesses of the discussion. What one change would result in a big improvement in the discussion?

4. Consider the *leadership* of teams and committees of which you have been a member. In groups, share the answers to one or more of the following questions:
- Which leadership style was most often used? Why do you think this style was the style of choice?
- Give an example of an effective group leader and explain what made this person so effective.
- Give an example of an ineffective group leader and explain what made this person so ineffective.
- Do college students use different leadership styles from those typically found in the business and professional world? If so, why?

5. In small groups, discuss the following: Prior to the presidential election of 2008, Barack Obama used the Internet to organize thousands of small groups of supporters (Schifferes, 2008). Many of these groups were composed of college students and young adults who were inspired to work long, unpaid hours going door-to-door campaigning for Obama (Dickinson, 2008). The efforts of these groups are credited for Obama's wins against Hillary Clinton in the primaries. Based on what you know about transformational leadership, would you describe Obama as a transformational leader? Why or why not?

6. Society depends on people in small groups finding answers to some very crucial questions such as *what to do in case of a massive world-wide epidemic (pandemic) of an extremely deadly virus.* In small groups, discuss one of the following subcategories. Instead of appointing a leader, all group members should take the task and maintenance roles as needed. When finished, discuss how successful the discussion was and why:
- Given the great efficiency of available transportation and certain panic to get to loved ones, how could a quarantine be enforced?
- If a cure is found, who gets the treatment first—the citizens of the country of origin, the wealthy, the educated, people with valuable trades or crafts, medical providers, infants, farmers, or others?
- After billions die, how should the remaining unclaimed wealth be distributed? How should abandoned land be allotted?
- With a few million people left on earth, what effect will this have on the type of government needed? How will freedom be kept and totalitarianism avoided? What leadership style will be the most important during these times?

EXPLORE SOME MORE . . .

1. One of our favorite films for viewing all types of group participants and leadership is *12 Angry Men* (1957), with Henry Fonda as the only juror who votes for acquittal when a vote is taken at the beginning of jury deliberation of a murder trial. There is a more recent version (1997), but we prefer the original, black-and-white version.

2. Looking for a good book that includes great advice on leadership or team process? We suggest you read:

- *The 21 Irrefutable Laws of Leadership* by John C. Maxwell (Thomas Nelson, Inc., 1998)

- *The Five Dysfunctions of a Team* by Patrick Lencioni (Jossey-Bass, 2002)

- *When Teams Work Best: 6000 Team Members and Leaders Tell What It Takes to Succeed* by Frank LeFasto and Carl Larson (Sage, 2001)

- *Service Learning* by Margit Watts (Prentice-Hall, 2007)

- *The Joy of Teaching* by Gene E. Hall, Linda F. Quinn, and Donna Gollnick (Allyn & Bacon, 2007)

10 Public Speaking: Getting Started

10.1 What is the definition and what are the causes and types of speaker anxiety?

10.2 What are the seven techniques for building speaker confidence, which are best, and how does uncertainty reduction relate to anxiety?

10.3 What are the five steps in preparing a successful speech, and which is the most important?

10.4 What are the three types of audience analysis, and what are some tips for effectively analyzing an audience?

10.5 What speaking skills covered in this chapter relate specifically to your career (see highlighted fields of business, education, and healthcare)?

After studying this chapter you should be able to . . .

- Pinpoint your level of public speaking anxiety by using the PRSCA.
- Manage your communication anxiety using one or more of the seven techniques presented.
- Prepare a short speech following the five steps spelled out in the chapter.
- Improve your analysis of an audience by using demographic, attitude, and situational analysis.

CHAPTER SUMMARY 〉 P. 283 〉

SCENARIO

Aaron stared into space, his chin resting on both hands, elbows firmly planted on the top of his desk. "Where to start?" he thought.

He found himself wishing that he hadn't agreed to do this presentation, though he knew that as parents of children with asthma, his audience would be eager for any information that he could supply from his vantage point as a respiratory therapist. He felt perfectly competent dealing with patients one on one, but even just thinking about doing a presentation in front of a group of people made him nervous.

Aaron rose from his desk and surveyed the books on his shelves. He had a pretty thorough reference library on the topic of asthma and other respiratory disorders. However, for the most part, they were highly technical publications written for the health professional. Quoting from those sources would be like speaking to his audience in a foreign language. He leafed through the pages of the largest of his books, wondering if any of the charts and models it contained would be useful to the listeners. He sighed and replaced the book on the shelf. How could he figure out what information and visuals to use until he knew what he was going to talk about?

He wished the hospital's Coordinator of Patient Education and Support Services had been more specific when she asked him to do a presentation for the Parents of Children with Asthma. He wondered how old their children were and how long they had been diagnosed. He didn't know if the PCA members were new to the group or had been attending for a long time. What if they already knew everything he had to say?

Aaron felt overwhelmed. He knew that he was a well-trained and competent respiratory therapist, but public speaking was outside of his comfort zone. On the other hand, he was excited to think about how he could be useful to a group of anxious parents and, by extension, to their children. This really was a great opportunity—if he could just manage his nervousness and figure out where to start.

Like Aaron, you may be feeling some similar anxieties about the individual or team presentations required in your class. Most people do have some anxiety when it comes to speaking in front of others. For that reason, we are starting this chapter off by taking a look at confidence building, including several successful techniques that people use to manage their speech anxiety. Then we will turn our attention to another concern expressed in the opening scenario—where to start when planning a presentation—and cover five clear-cut steps. We will concentrate on the first and most important step in developing effective presentations: audience analysis. Armed with these ideas, you should be ready to develop effective presentations for classroom assignments for this course, as well as for future situations in which you are called upon to speak to an audience.

SOLVE IT NOW! ❭ P. 284 ❭

Are you expecting to work in a field where you will never be asked to give a speech? Many people assume that only teachers, preachers, and politicians have to give speeches. This is probably what Aaron in our opening scenario assumed. However, no matter what profession you enter, the chances are good that, as you advance in your career, you will be expected to make presentations.

As you read this chapter, see if you can find specific communication tips to offer Aaron and other beginning speakers to build their confidence and get started in planning a presentation.

Understanding the Nature of Anxiety

LEARNING **OBJECTIVE**

10.1 What is the definition and what are the causes and types of speaker anxiety?

The prospect of speaking to an audience is often the source of great anxiety. From time to time, survey organizations reveal research findings indicating that speaking in public is the number one or number two fear of adults. A Gallup poll conducted in 2001 ranked fear of speaking second behind fear of snakes (Brewer, 2001). Another survey by Richmond and McCroskey (1992) found that 95 percent of Americans have some degree of speaker anxiety—so you are not alone.

What Is Speaker Anxiety?

There are many terms that are used to refer to the discomfort that most people feel when confronted with the need to speak to an audience: communication apprehension, stage fright, **speaker anxiety,** or speaker reticence. No matter what you call it, most people agree that it doesn't feel good. Although some people feel almost no nervousness when addressing audiences, they are in the minority and are probably confident simply because they have given speeches so often. Likely, their initial attempts were just as fraught with anxiety as ours are.

Not every culture experiences anxiety in the same way or to the same degree. For example, as long as they don't have to speak in English, Puerto Ricans seem to have less anxiety than American speakers (McCroskey et al., 1985). On the other hand, both the Chinese (Zhang et al., 1996) and the Chinese in Taiwan (Hsu, 2004) are more anxious about speaking than Americans.

In Chapter 1, you took the PRCA-24 (Personal Report of Communication Anxiety) to determine your level of anxiety in a variety of situations. James McCroskey (1982), the creator of the PRCA-24, has another survey called the **PRSCA** that highlights public speaking. If you wish to take this survey, please see the Skill Builders section at the end of this chapter. Remember that the survey can be only as accurate as you are in answering the questions.

What Causes Speaker Anxiety?

Although there are many reasons that speakers feel anxiety, there are two major causes—the situation and/or the person. Sometimes your fear may come from a situation you find threatening or an internal feeling you have about speaking, or both. As you read, see if you can determine which type of anxiety is giving Aaron in our chapter opener the most problems.

© 1995 Ted Goff

"In this seminar we'll discuss a simple technique for over-coming your fear of speaking in public."

© Ted Goff

Anxiety Caused by the Situation

Speaker anxiety may be nothing more than the situation. **Situational anxiety** (also called "state anxiety") is anxiety created by a new, different, or unexpected situation. A score from 18–23 in the public subtotal on the PRCA-24 is a good indication of situational anxiety. All of us have some situational anxiety although it differs from person to person. For example, some people are comfortable speaking to a small work group but get nervous when making presentations to large groups. Some people get nervous speaking to a group of strangers while others are more nervous speaking to people they know. You might find that seeing a camera while having a speech taped or knowing that you will be evaluated on a class or work presentation makes a speaking situation unusual and, therefore, frightening. If so, by the time you are taped or evaluated on a second speech, you will feel more confident. One of your authors recalls a gifted teaching colleague who had no nervousness about teaching her students or even speaking to the state legislature about issues related to public education in her state; however, making a short presentation to her colleagues terrified her. In her case, it was the specific situation that engendered anxiety, as opposed to a more generalized fear that some people have about public speaking.

APPLY **WHAT YOU KNOW**
SITUATIONAL ANXIETY

Think about situations that cause you anxiety and situations that do not—make a list of each. Would speaking before a class of 30–100 or more students cause anxiety, but speaking before a small group of 10 would not?

- Once you have added approximately 10 items to each list, see if you can determine any commonalities in each listing.

- Why do you feel comfortable in some situations but not in others?
- What could you do to change how you feel?
- Compare your observations with those of one or more classmates.

Anxiety Caused by Internal Feelings

For some people, apprehension about speaking in public—or about communicating in general—is caused by more than the situation; it is an internal feeling they carry with them called **trait anxiety**. Trait anxiety (such as the fear of looking foolish or feeling totally inadequate as a speaker) is something some speakers experience regardless of the situation. If the speaker feels inadequate as a speaker, it won't make much difference whether the audience is large or small, whether the audience includes familiar people or strangers, or whether the speaker sits or stands—he or she still feels inadequate. A score higher than 24 on the Public subtotal of the PRCA-24 or a total PRCA score higher than 80 are indicators of trait anxiety.

Some trait anxiety is learned. Researchers (Beatty, 1988; McCroskey & Beatty, 1998) have suggested there are three characteristics that indicate learned trait anxiety: (1) a feeling of *dissimilarity*—that they are different from others (less effective, more nervous, and so on); (2) a *negative speaking history*—they remember prior negative speaking experiences, even as far back as elementary school; and (3) a feeling of *subordinate status*—that they aren't as smart as others and know less about their topic than others (even audience members).

For some people, trait anxiety also may be inborn. Some contemporary scholars have embraced the communibiological perspective in studying why some people are predisposed to anxiety about communicating. Based on neurobiological evidence, **communibiology** scholars (Beatty et al., 1998; McCroskey & Beatty, 2000) suggest that genetic factors play a primary role in determining whether a person is comfortable in interacting with other people. Other communication scholars such as Condit (2000) suggest that biology is only one factor, that situational factors are also significant, and that most people can develop some level of comfort in communication if motivated to do so. Biopsychologists lend support to Condit's position and suggest that behaviors (including speaker anxiety) are based on three factors: past experiences, situations as we view them, and our "genetic endowment" (Kimble, 1989; Pinel, 2006, p. 23).

The idea to keep in mind is that nearly everyone feels some anxiety in at least some situations involving communication with others. You may feel that your anxiety is unique, and that no one else you know shares your apprehension. However, almost everyone feels some nervousness, especially about public speaking. The trick is learning how to manage your anxiety so that it does not interfere with your ability to communicate effectively. For most people, some level of nervousness actually serves a positive purpose because it facilitates performance. If you have ever participated in any competitive activity or any of the performing arts, you can probably remember how nervous you felt before a big game or an important performance. In truth, the nervousness you feel enables you to rise to the occasion and to produce your best efforts. Therefore, your goal should be not to eliminate all anxiety but to minimize and manage it.

Building Speaker Confidence

In this section, we will introduce several techniques that public speakers have found to be beneficial in managing their natural anxiety (see **Figure 10.1**). Keep in mind that the best results occur when you use "the widest possible combination of methods" to manage your anxiety (Allen et al., 1989, p. 63; see also Kelly & Keaten, 2000). Also, don't expect instant results; overcoming inborn traits or longstanding patterns of thought will require work.

LEARNING OBJECTIVE

10.2 What are the seven techniques for building speaker confidence, which are best, and how does uncertainty reduction relate to anxiety?

Be Prepared

One of the most obvious techniques to build speaker confidence is to be prepared. If you have put in the necessary effort to prepare your presentation and have practiced it until you feel comfortable, you will be able to remind yourself truthfully that you have done all you can to be ready. It's interesting to note that people with high communication anxiety tend to prepare less rather than more for their presentations (Daly et al., 1995). Maybe they feel that they are going to do a poor job anyway, so why waste the time preparing? If you are one of these people, please

Figure 10.1 Seven Techniques for Building Speaker Confidence

Managing Your Anxiety
1. Be prepared.
2. Engage in skills training.
3. Use positive imagery.
4. Enjoy deep breathing and relaxation.
5. Apply cognitive restructuring.
6. Become audience-centered.
7. Practice speaking often.

note that Lily Walters, a consultant and author of *Secrets of Successful Speakers* (1993), estimates up to a 75 percent drop in anxiety for speakers who carefully prepare their presentations.

When you do practice your presentation, don't forget to practice aloud, on your feet, and, when possible, in an environment similar in size to the actual room in which you will speak. Once you feel somewhat comfortable, add some friends and family as an audience. Smith & Frymier (2006) found that students who practiced in front of an audience were more effective speakers than those who practiced alone. They also found that practicing in front of four or more people was better than having only one to three people as an audience. Whether this advice works for you will depend on your own comfort level; you may prefer to practice alone.

Part of being prepared is getting enough rest the night before the presentation. Many people also find that arriving early and interacting with a few members of the audience reduces their jitters. This interaction is especially helpful during the presentation when you want to look for people to engage in eye contact.

Engage in Skills Training

Another way to increase speaker confidence is through **skills training,** which involves setting reasonable speaking goals, learning the necessary skills needed to reach those goals, and judging the success of the speaking goals (Phillips, 1991). In other words, you are more likely to feel comfortable about public speaking if you have acquired the knowledge about how to develop an organized speech, prepare appropriate visuals, and practice effective delivery techniques. A recent study by Duff and colleagues (2007) found that enrolling in a communication course that teaches public speaking skills was as successful in reducing speaking anxiety as other treatment methods. Reading this chapter on speaking and the ones that follow and applying the practical tips offered is an excellent beginning to building your speaker confidence.

Use Positive Imagery

Can you imagine an effective golfer such as Tiger Woods preparing for a putt by visualizing the ball missing the cup, or an NFL quarterback preparing for a game by visualizing himself lateraling the ball and having it completely miss the running back? This seems ridiculous, doesn't it? Yet speakers often imagine themselves feeling nervous, having a dry mouth, or forgetting what to say. If this sounds like you, try building your confidence by using positive imagery instead. When using **positive imagery** (also called **visualization**), you must use images that are detailed, positive, and vivid. Begin by imagining yourself preparing for the event, and see each action with as much detail as possible. For example, imagine yourself dressing for the event, arriving at the site, chatting with others before the speech, rising to begin, using the performance behaviors that are associated with effective delivery, responding to audience feedback, concluding and accepting applause, and feeling a sense of accomplishment. The more vividly you imagine each positive detail, the more useful this method is. It is based on the notion that when your mind vividly records these images, it is *as if* you have actually done them. Then, on the day of your presentation, your mind directs you to the same sort of successful performance you have visualized.

Researchers have found that imagining giving a successful speech has many of the same benefits as actually giving a successful speech, and this method is both easy to use and long lasting (Ayres et al., 1997; Porter, 2003; Zagacki et al., 1992). Although researchers have found that positive imagery is effective with both situational and trait anxiety (Ayres et al., 1998), it is especially good for people with high communication apprehension—so high that the thought of giving a speech causes them to experience a feeling that is close to panic. Using positive imagery with deep breathing and relaxation as discussed below is even more beneficial. One of our students commented that positive imagery is like recording over the negative tapes you have of yourself and replacing them with positive ones.

Enjoy Deep Breathing and Relaxation

Another way to improve your confidence is to practice using deep breathing and relaxation. **Deep breathing** simply involves taking a breath through your nose, holding your breath as you count from one to three, and then slowly exhaling through your mouth as you feel your tension gradually draining away. Deep breathing slows your heart rate and decreases that butterfly feeling in your stomach—you feel more in control (Pletcher, 2000). Hamilton (2000) estimates that deep breathing can lower anxiety by as much as 15 percent. You can test this estimate by first taking your pulse and blood pressure at a booth found at most pharmacies; then try several rounds of deep breathing; then retake your pulse and blood pressure. Note the drop in beats per minute and the change in your overall blood pressure.

It is easier to give an effective speech if you relax first. **Relaxation** begins by alternately tensing and relaxing each muscle group in your body. Follow this by inhaling deeply and then exhaling forcefully to rid your body of all tension. Once you have achieved a state of relaxation, begin to visualize yourself successfully delivering your speech. As mentioned earlier, relaxation is especially good for people with high communication apprehension—the apprehension that causes a feeling of panic. These techniques allow successful mental practice before the anxiety of a "real" audience. Muscle relaxation is also useful during the actual presentation. You may experience physical symptoms, such as rapid heart rate, shallow breathing, dry mouth, sweaty palms, rubbery knees, and butterflies in the stomach. It is important to realize that these sensations are the natural reaction to the increased adrenaline produced by your body in any moment of stress. Taking a deep breath and relaxing when you experience these symptoms can help you gain control. See the instructions for relaxation in the *Connecting to Healthcare* activity at the end of this chapter.

Apply Cognitive Restructuring

For many people, the basis of their anxiety is in the way they think about an event and the way they talk to themselves about it. The technique of **cognitive restructuring** is basically a way of reframing your perception of a feared stimulus into a more positive one. According to psychologist Albert Ellis (2004), it is not the events in our lives that cause our emotions; it is the way we think about those events. Consider this example: If you have ever dated someone for a considerable length of time, and then your relationship falls apart, what is your emotional response? For some people, such an event is devastating. They see it as rejection and as evidence that they are unlovable. By contrast, other people might regard the event as just the way things go; the relationship was a learning experience, but now it is time for a fresh start. What is the difference between these two reactions? It is not the event; the event was the same. The difference is in how the two people thought about the event.

The notion behind cognitive restructuring is that you can choose to change the way you think about a situation. This requires an awareness of the self-talk in which you engage. Dr. Ellis points out that much of our self-defeating self-talk is based on irrational beliefs. Three of these beliefs identified by Dr. Ellis and his students have particular relevance to public speaking:

- I am not a worthwhile person unless I am completely competent in all things at all times.
- I am not a worthwhile person unless I am loved and approved of by all people at all times.
- Life is awful and upsetting unless I am in control of all situations.

The irrational belief that you must be completely competent gives rise to the expectation that you must be perfect. The truth is that you do not have to give a perfect speech. Telling yourself that you must be perfect causes you to overreact to mistakes and to any sign of nervousness that you feel. This, then, causes additional anxiety. In effect, you develop anxiety about your anxiety! The belief that you must be loved and approved of at all times causes you to think that if anyone doesn't fully enjoy your speech, the speech is a total failure. In reality, it is likely that there will be some people who don't particularly like your speech. This, however, does not mean that it is a failure. Believing that you must be in control at all times is also irrational. Unexpected things happen; expect them. Believing that total control is essential causes you to overreact to small mistakes, once again making your speech seem a failure.

In order to overcome this sort of negative and self-defeating self-talk, you must learn to recognize those moments when you are engaging in that sort of intrapersonal communication based on irrational beliefs, and you must learn to challenge those beliefs. It is good to begin to develop a number of positive affirmations that you can use to substitute for the negative statements you tell yourself. "I know I will mess up" should be replaced with "If I prepare well and practice in advance, I will be able to handle anything that happens unexpectedly."

APPLY **WHAT YOU KNOW**
IRRATIONAL VERSUS POSITIVE SELF-TALK

Think about the negative statements you typically say to yourself when something goes wrong—especially when it comes to public speaking. Make a list of three to five of them.

- For each negative statement, determine what irrational belief you have that causes you to make the statement and what emotional reaction you have to this belief.

- Replace each negative statement by writing out a positive statement based on a rational belief. The next time something goes wrong, try using one of your new statements. Think about how this new self-talk feels and if your reaction is more positive.

- What suggestions would you give Aaron in our opening scenario for improving his self-talk?

MAKING THEORY **PRACTICAL**
UNCERTAINTY REDUCTION THEORY

- *Passive observation of the person communicating with others* (e.g., how the professor talks with other students in class)
- *Passive observation of the person in a different setting* (e.g., how the professor communicates outside of class)
- *Active but indirect search for information* (e.g., asking another student for information about the professor)
- *Active interaction with the person* (e.g., asking the professor questions; self-disclosing with the goal of getting a reciprocal disclosure from the professor)

When we first meet people—whether an individual, someone in a group, or a speaker—we likely experience some uncertainty and even anxiety. Who would have thought that it's not just the speaker who feels that way? Audience members, too, feel various degrees of uncertainty and some even experience anxiety. For example, consider a student audience on the first day of class (Friedrich & Cooper, 1990). Because they don't know much about the professor and may be unfamiliar or anxious with the course material, their concerns may include the following:

"Is this professor approachable; what if I need help?"

"Will assignments and exams be difficult?"

"If there is group work, will I fit in with my classmates?"

"What exactly does this course cover, and will it be interesting?"

Theorist
According to Charles R. Berger, developer of **uncertainty reduction theory** (Berger & Calabrese, 1975; Berger, 1997), people improve their communication with others by being able to predict the actions and behaviors of others. Uncertainty keeps us from being able to make these predictions and makes us uncomfortable or even anxious. Berger's theory describes the ways that communicators gather information about others with the goal of reducing uncertainty and increasing predictability.

Gathering Information
When we meet someone we don't know the first thing we do is gather information about that person. Berger says we search for information in the following ways:

PRACTICAL USES
Now that you know that speakers aren't the only ones to experience uncertainty and anxiety, change the focus from your personal anxiety to what you as a speaker can do to provide needed information to ease uncertainty in your audience (Berger & Kellermann, 1983; Littlejohn & Foss, 2008). For example, with an unknown audience:

- Arrive early and interact with a few members as they arrive—speak on general topics as well as your speech topic. This chance for active interaction as well as passive observation of your speaking with others should provide information and reduce uncertainty.
- Give an introduction to your topic that makes the purpose and specific content of your presentation clear.
- Communicate attraction and affiliation—perhaps to the point where additional information may be unnecessary (Littlejohn & Foss, p. 150).
- Have someone the audience likes and respects introduce you.
- Begin your presentation with strong nonverbal expressions of attraction including smiles, open gestures, and friendly vocal variety.
- Use the information and names of those you meet prior to the speech (or during your audience analysis) to build affiliation with your audience. Let them know of interests, experiences, behaviors, or expectations you have in common.

Primary Source: Berger, C. R., & Calabrese, R. J. (1975). Some explorations in initial interaction and beyond: Toward a developmental theory of interpersonal communication. *Human Communication Research, 1,* 99–112.

Become Audience Centered

Another approach to confidence building involves developing the capacity to be audience centered. Being **audience centered** means focusing on the audience to determine whether they are understanding your ideas rather than worrying about yourself and the impression you are making. Many people are more nervous than they need to be because they focus too much on the performance aspect of a speech. A speech is more than a performance; it is communication. As is true of all communication, a speech should focus on the needs of your audience. If you think of your speech only as a performance, you will be overly conscious of the impression you are making on others; this is being *self centered*. People who are focused on what others think of them are often anxious. However, people who are focused on helping others—helping others to understand or to make changes that will be beneficial to others—rarely have time to worry about how they are coming across. Genuine concern for others almost always reduces anxiety.

In fact, although you may not be aware of it, audience members also feel some uncertainty and anxiety of their own (see this chapter's *Making Theory Practical* feature on page 269). Concentrating on ways to reduce audience anxiety is a sure way to relieve any personal anxiety you may have as a speaker.

Practice Speaking Often

Finally, as has already been noted, many successful public speakers have learned to enjoy the process only after giving many, many presentations. *Take advantage of opportunities to speak*. Each speaking opportunity, you should remind yourself, is another chance to develop your skills. Few people are "naturals," requiring no honing of skills. Most accomplished speakers can tell tales of embarrassing moments that were great learning experiences. As with any new skill, continued practice leads to greater and greater success. You probably did not do a perfect swan dive the first time you jumped off the diving board. Over time, however, you can attain greater competence until, amazingly, you may find yourself enjoying the experience of public speaking.

The techniques for managing anxiety that we have just discussed are helpful whether your anxiety is mild or serious, trait or situational. Speaker confidence by itself does not guarantee speaker competence. Successful speakers must be able to prepare an effective presentation.

APPLY **WHAT YOU KNOW**
UNCERTAINTY REDUCTION THEORY

Apply what you know about uncertainty reduction theory by completing the following activity. Be prepared to share your list and comments with the class.

- Prepare a list of suggestions for things that you would like to see college professors do and say to reduce uncertainty and anxiety of students during the first day (or week) of class and/or prior to presenting new assignments.

- Who do you think is in most need of this list—professors in their first year or experienced professors? Explain your reasoning.

- What would you recommend that Aaron in our opening scenario do to ease the uncertainty of his audience (and himself) during his upcoming presentation?

An Overview: Five Steps in Preparing a Successful Speech

LEARNING **OBJECTIVE**

10.3 What are the five steps in preparing a successful speech, and which is the most important?

Preparing a speech for delivery to an audience is a clear-cut five-step process, as indicated in **Figure 10.2**:

The steps include: (1) analyzing the audience; (2) developing your topic, purpose, and thesis; (3) gathering your materials; (4) organizing your main points; and (5) practicing your speech.

We are providing a brief look at all five steps in this opening chapter on speaking with the hope that you will find them helpful in the event that your instructor wishes to assign a short speech or two to get you up and running in gaining public speaking skills. Because audience analysis is so important, we will discuss it in detail later in this chapter; the remaining four steps will be analyzed in more detail in following chapters.

Figure 10.2 Five Steps to a Successful Speech

STEP 1
AUDIENCE ANALYSIS

STEP 2
TOPIC SELECTION

STEP 3
MATERIAL GATHERING

STEP 4
ORGANIZING

STEP 5
PRACTICING

Step 1: Analyzing Your Audience and the Situation

The first step—*audience analysis*—is the most important since it will influence all of the decisions you make in completing the other four steps. Your audience's demographics (characteristics) and attitudes, as well as how they interact with the specific situation, are all part of audience analysis and are important if you are to communicate effectively with them and their frames of reference. *Speakers' failure to analyze their audiences effectively is the number one reason that speeches fail to meet their goals* (St. John, 1995). We will look in more detail at audience analysis before we leave this chapter.

Step 2: Developing Your Topic, Purpose, and Thesis

The second step is to *develop your topic, purpose, and thesis*. Sometimes your topic is assigned; other times you are able to choose your own. The best way to choose a topic that will interest your audience is to choose one that interests you. Think

There are many successful ways to practice a speech.

about the things that you enjoy doing or learning about. It is important that you choose a topic that you know enough about to speak knowledgeably about it. You also need to narrow it enough to fit the time allotted.

All speeches have a purpose. The three general purposes are to inform, to persuade, and to entertain. Make sure you are clear as to which of these is your dominant purpose, although a speech may accomplish more than one. You also need to develop a thesis, which is a simple statement, in as few words as possible, of the central point you wish to convey in your speech. (*Step 2 is developed further in Chapter 11.*)

Step 3: Gathering Materials

The third step is to *gather your materials*. Begin by thinking about what you already know about the topic and organizing these ideas in a rough-draft outline. Expand your base of knowledge by looking at other materials. The type of materials you consult will depend upon your topic, but, in general, you are trying to find materials that will add interest to your speech, will clarify difficult concepts, or will prove any claims you make. (*Step 3 is developed further in Chapter 11.*)

Step 4: Organizing Your Main Points

The fourth step is to *organize the materials you gathered*. You need to divide your topic into two to five main points. The shorter your speech, the fewer points you should use. Each point needs to flow naturally from the previous point, and all points must relate to the topic by expanding on it. You should also plan an interesting way to introduce the topic to your audience and a memorable way to conclude. (*Step 4 is developed further in Chapter 12.*)

Step 5: Practicing Your Speech

Finally, you should *practice your delivery*. You should practice out loud, several times, timing the speech to make sure you stay within the time limit. You may wish to practice with a friend who can offer constructive feedback. In any case, you should pay attention to using a voice that is loud enough to be heard and demonstrates your enthusiasm for your topic. You should also practice using good posture and appropriate gestures, though gestures should not be planned in advance. Most elements of good delivery are accomplished acceptably if you are well-prepared and if you are genuinely enthusiastic about your topic. (*Step 5 is developed further in Chapter 13.*)

APPLY **WHAT YOU KNOW**
PREPARING A SUCCESSFUL SPEECH

Apply what you know about speech preparation by answering the following questions:

- Which of the five steps in preparing a successful speech are the most difficult for you (if you have given speeches before) or sound like they would be the most difficult (if you haven't given speeches before)? Give an example to clarify your answer.

- Whether you are speaking in a team or speaking as an individual, which of the following do you think would be the most important for a successful speech: content, visual aids, or performance? Explain your answer by referring to Aaron in the scenario, to a personal presentation, or to a presentation you have observed.

Although each of these steps will be covered in greater detail in the chapters that follow, from this discussion you should be able to see that developing an effective presentation is a process that involves systematically applying the principles of effective communication in general. If you know what your message is, if you choose verbal and nonverbal symbols that do not create noise for your listener, and—above all—if you keep your listener's needs in mind, you will be able to deliver an effective presentation.

Audience Analysis: A More Detailed Look

Public speaking is like any other form of communication: You cannot know *how* to approach your listeners until you know something *about* them and the situation. Although your audience may be diverse, they still share many characteristics. For example, because people have limited attention spans, they are more likely to remember things that are well-organized and repeated. By considering this and other aspects of audience analysis, you can make appropriate decisions in planning your speech. As Figures 10.2 and **10.3** indicate, the process of analyzing your audience overarches all of the other speech preparation steps.

LEARNING **OBJECTIVE**

10.4 What are the three types of audience analysis, and what are some tips for effectively analyzing an audience?

Figure 10.3 Speech Preparation Step #1

STEP 1
AUDIENCE ANALYSIS
- Demographic Analysis
- Attitude Analysis
- Situational Analysis

STEP 3
MATERIAL GATHERING

STEP 4
ORGANIZING

STEP 5
PRACTICING

We are dividing audience analysis into three parts: demographic analysis, attitude analysis, and situational analysis. You will need to do all three, but most speakers begin with demographic analysis—perhaps because it is one of the most obvious to determine.

Demographic Analysis

When we speak of **audience demographics,** we are talking about the statistical characteristics of the group. Some examples of the demographic characteristics of an audience include:

- age
- cultural heritage
- educational background
- occupation
- race
- religious orientation

- gender
- geographical location
- marital and parental status
- sexual preference
- socioeconomic class
- various group affiliations

Some of these characteristics will be more important than others with respect to your particular speech. For example, if you wanted to give a speech about how to save money now for later retirement, age and occupation would be important considerations; group affiliations and religious orientation would probably not be as important. Cultural heritage could also be important—people from different cultures may have different perspectives on the value of saving. To make sure your speech shows *cultural sensitivity,* do your homework. It is wise to give full consideration to as many demographic variables as possible in order to have a basis for your attitude analysis.

Although conducting a demographic analysis may be relatively easy for your classroom speeches (you can look around and figure out such factors as age, race, culture, and the like), not all demographic characteristics are visible. So don't wait until the day of the speech to consider them. In non-classroom presentations, find someone who is familiar with the group and ask that person as many questions as possible. Never assume anything. Do not, for example, assume that being asked to speak to the YMCA (which stands for Young Men's Christian Association) means that you will be speaking to a group consisting solely of men. Ask. You do not want to be surprised.

APPLY **WHAT YOU KNOW**
CONDUCTING A DEMOGRAPHIC ANALYSIS

Using the members of your class as your audience (or the members of a club or organization), complete the following:

- Conduct the demographic portion of the audience analysis form in Figure 10.9. Although an exact speech topic isn't necessary for a demographic analysis, it would be good to have a possible topic in mind—perhaps one that you are thinking about using for an upcoming class presentation.

- Which of these demographic characteristics do you think would be especially important if you are speaking about music or art? About business, healthcare, or education? About social problems?

- Which demographics would likely be of special importance to Aaron in our opening scenario? Why?

Attitude Analysis

Although audience demographics are important, they are only part of analyzing your audience; you also need to know your audience's attitudes. We began with audience demographics because audience attitudes are often closely related to demographics. An **attitude** is a feeling of likes or dislikes (approval or disapproval) toward a person, idea, or an event. Attitudes are based on beliefs, which are based on values. There are three major factors to consider about your audience's attitudes: their attitude about your topic, about you (the speaker), and about attending the speech. We will discuss each of these separately, but realize that audiences are not easily categorized along these dimensions. They are not all interested in your topic or all uninterested. It is best, then, to think about your audience's attitudes as falling along a continuum ranging from extremely interested to extremely disinterested, or somewhere in between. You may find that some members of your audience will fall at every point along the continuum. However, there is some reason that this group of people is congregated here at this time, which suggests that they do have some commonalities. For that reason, they will tend to cluster at one point or another on the continuum. *It is to the point at which they cluster that you will aim your speech.*

Attitudes toward Your Topic

Your audience will have a general attitude about your topic. When considering what that attitude is, you will need to think about their level of interest in the topic, their level of knowledge about the topic, and, in the case of persuasive speeches, their level of agreement with your position on the topic. Let's examine each of these.

Interest Your audience comes to the speech either predisposed to be interested in your topic, or not interested, or somewhere in between. It is important to know where they fall along the continuum (**Figure 10.4**). Let's say that you are giving a speech to a group of college students about how to apply for financial aid. Your demographic analysis would likely suggest that because of their ages and because of their status as college students, they likely to have a high degree of interest. However, if you were to deliver a speech about care giving for elderly parents to this same audience, the demographics would suggest a lower or neutral level of interest. Knowing this, you would need to find a way to stimulate their interest in your topic very early in the speech.

Keep in mind that even uninterested audiences can become interested—if you do a good job. For example, I may not think I am interested in football, but I may become interested once you point out that football season is approaching and that I have

Figure 10.4 Audience Attitude toward Topic

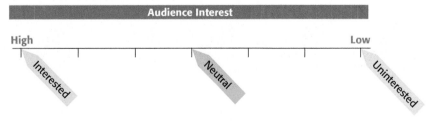

two choices: I can be frustrated and alone while my friends are watching the games, or I can join them by using three simple techniques that you will discuss in your speech. Now, you have grabbed my interest. Chapter 12 will discuss specific methods for stimulating audience interest that you can use in your speech introductions.

Knowledge You must also discover the level of audience knowledge about your topic (**Figure 10.5**). If your audience knows very little about your topic, you will need to focus on basic principles; if your audience is knowledgeable about your topic, you can explore more technical information. For example, assume you are planning a speech about football to your class. If your demographic analysis reveals that the majority of your audience is female, you might have reason to suspect that many of your listeners have only a basic understanding about the game. Trying to cover the intricacies of the spread offense or the cover-two

Figure 10.5 Audience Attitude toward Topic

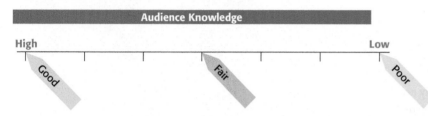

defense may not be feasible. However, if you discover that most of your male and female classmates already know football basics, giving a speech that explains how many players are on the field and how they are divided into offense and defense would likely bore and even insult your listeners. Therefore, you will have to decide what to include in your speech that will make it interesting for everyone regardless of their level of knowledge.

Agreement When you prepare a persuasive speech, you have an additional factor to consider about your audience's attitude toward the topic. You must draw some conclusions, based on the audience's demographics, about their level of agreement with your position. Again, your audience will not always be in agreement on a controversial topic. Some may be highly in favor of your position, others strongly opposed, and others neutral (**Figure 10.6**). You must, however, find out as much as you can about your audience in order to make a judgment about where they are likely to fall along the continuum ranging from strongly in favor to strongly opposed. For example, knowing whether your audience members are registered to vote and whether they are registered as Democrats, Republicans, Independents, or "other" could give you an idea of audience attitudes on some topics.

If you have determined that, based on the demographics, your audience is likely to be strongly in agreement with you, your task will be to reinforce their beliefs. This is the situation that political candidates find themselves in as they attend rallies during their campaigns. People who attend a politician's speech are usually

Figure 10.6 Audience Attitude toward Topic

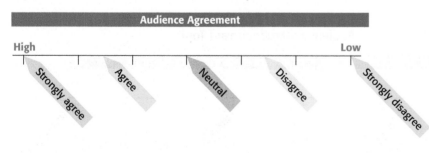

there because they are supporters. However, in some situations the candidate may willingly agree to address an audience that is likely to be hostile to her/his views. In this case, the candidate must develop a persuasive strategy that will not alienate listeners. It is unlikely that the candidate will cause the hostile audience to completely change their position based on that one speech. Therefore, the candidate's goals need to be realistic. We will discuss this idea further in Chapter 14 when we deal with persuasion. In addition, when your analysis leads you to believe that your audience is likely to be neutral, it is important for you to determine why they are neutral. This, too, will be addressed more thoroughly in the persuasion chapter.

Attitudes toward You (the Speaker)

Does your audience already know who you are? Do they already know about your background with respect to your topic? Is their attitude toward you positive or negative (**Figure 10.7**)? The issue here is speaker credibility, or *ethos*. Your **credibility** rests upon the audience's perception of your competence, your character, and your charisma. In other words, for you to be perceived as credible, your audience must know that you know what you are talking about, they must believe that you are trustworthy, and they must see you as someone who is enthusiastic, sincere, and dynamic.

Sometimes your credibility is a given. In future speeches, you may find that you are asked to speak on a topic related to your expertise. Sometimes your audience will have come to the speech

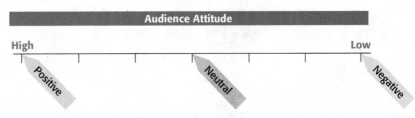

Figure 10.7 **Audience Attitude toward Speaker**

precisely because of your acknowledged expertise. At other times, your audience may not know much about your credentials, but someone will introduce you to the audience and provide the audience with information about your background that will help to build your credibility in their eyes. In general, if your demographic analysis of your audience suggests that you do not have initial credibility—a perception of your competence, character, and charisma that the audience holds before you even begin to speak—you will need to plan how to demonstrate your credibility early in your speech. No matter what your audience's initial perceptions are, you will have to continue to build on your credibility throughout the speech by demonstrating your knowledge, your fairness, your interest in their needs, and your genuine enthusiasm for your topic.

Attitudes toward Being There

A third attitude that must be addressed is your audience's attitude toward being there. Basically audiences are voluntary, involuntary, or accidental (**Figure 10.8**). Each type of audience poses its own challenges:

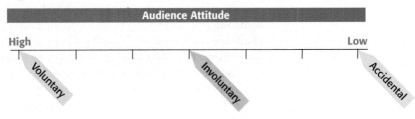

Figure 10.8 **Audience Attitude toward Attendance**

Voluntary Members. The **voluntary audience** is present because there is something about the topic, the speaker, or the occasion that has drawn them there. In other words, they are there because they want to be; they may even have paid to be there. A speaker presenting a message to such an audience has a great deal more latitude than when dealing with other audience types. However, there is always the challenge of giving the listeners what they were anticipating. Failure to consider their needs can cause them to be especially disappointed, which may then affect your credibility in the future.

Involuntary Members. The **involuntary audience** is particularly challenging because they are there because they have to be—someone in authority has decreed that they must be present. Keep in mind that one of the characteristics of ethical communication is that it must not remove a listener's choices. Since involuntary audiences are not there of their own volition, some of their choices have already been removed. The ethical speaker should not further erode their freedom of choice. For example, if you are giving a speech opposing abortion to an audience that did not willingly choose to be there, and if your demographic analysis suggests that there may be many people there who are strongly in favor of a woman's right to choose, and if your demographic analysis indicates that there may be people in the audience who would find your topic upsetting in some way, it is absolutely unacceptable to subject your audience to verbal or visual elements that would create emotional distress. If you are doing this same presentation to a voluntary audience—an audience that knew beforehand what the topic would be and what the speaker's position is—many of the constraints would be removed. This is an important audienceattitude, and your ability to conform to the standards of ethical communication rests upon your careful consideration of this factor. Recall that in Chapter 1 we defined ethics as *a system of moral principles that governs the conduct of people in relationship to others.*

Accidental Members. The **accidental audience** contains members who were merely going about their daily lives and happened to wander into an area where someone was attempting to drum up an audience for one reason or another. The challenge with accidental members is to get them to stop and pay attention. People have many competing demands on their time, and listening to a speech may not be high on some people's list of priorities. Although this type of speaking situation is relatively less common than the others we have discussed, it does occur from time to time, such as when evangelists or politicians set up a public address system in a well-traveled location on campus.

DEVELOPING SKILLS
HOW TO CONDUCT AN AUDIENCE ANALYSIS

By analyzing audience demographics, audience attitudes, and the situation, you will be in a better position to make decisions on many things:

- How best to *narrow and focus your topic* (Chapter 11);
- The most *effective research and supporting materials* to use (Chapter 11);
- The best way to *organize* your ideas (Chapter 12 for informative topics; Chapter 14 for persuasive topics);
- The most effective *delivery and visual aids* (Chapter 13);
- The most persuasive *arguments* to use (Chapter 14).

Everything you do in a speech depends on the audience.

When Analyzing a Classroom Audience

You probably already know many facts about your classmates—so you have a start on your demographic analysis. Also, you have a heads-up on the situational analysis since your speech will likely occur in the classroom, and you are already familiar with the basic room set-up. However, don't assume. Conduct a brief survey of facts you need to know using the questionnaire below at least a week before the speech.

When Analyzing Groups outside the Classroom

When speaking to groups outside the classroom, start by asking demographic, attitude, and situational questions of the person who asked you to speak. In addition, ask for the names and e-mail addresses of two or three audience members to contact. Arriving at the speech site early will allow you to meet some of the audience members and find additional beliefs and interests you have in common.

Although you may not actually be able to give the following questionnaire (**Figure 10.9**) to potential audience members outside the classroom, use it to organize your notes and remind yourself of important items to ask the person in charge as well as any audience members you speak with by e-mail.

Figure 10.9 Audience Analysis Form

Audience Analysis Form
—To use in gathering information whether by e-mail, phone, or in person—

Demographic Analysis:
_____% Men; _____% Women; _____% Married; _____% Living together; _____% with Children
Number in each age group: _____17–20; _____ 21–25; _____ 26–30; _____ 31+
States or countries lived in: _____
Different cultural heritages represented: _____
Clubs and organizations: _____
College majors (or minors): _____
Hobbies/Interests: _____
Other: _____

Attitude Analysis:
1. Attitude toward topic:
   Interest in topic: _____ interested _____ neutral _____ uninterested
   Knowledge of topic: _____ good _____ fair _____ poor
   Agreement with topic:
   _____ Strongly agree _____ Agree _____ Neutral _____ Disagree _____ Strongly disagree
2. Attitude toward speaker:
   Attitude toward me: _____ positive _____ neutral _____ negative
3. Attitude toward attendance:
   _____% Voluntary _____% Involuntary _____% Accidental

Situational Analysis:
Number of people expected: 5–10 _____ 11–20 _____ 21–30 _____ 31–40 _____ 41+ _____
Maximum time allotted for speech: _____ Preferred length: _____
Room set-up: _____ Audience in chairs _____ Audience at tables _____ Speaker on stage
_____ Speaker on level with audience _____ Lectern available
Equipment available: _____ Lectern/podium _____ Microphone _____ Laptop computer
_____ Presenter mouse/remote _____ Internet connection _____ Wall screen _____ Other
Q&A expected: _____ Yes _____ No _____ Unknown
Questions audience may have about topic: _____
_____
Key ways topic could benefit audience: _____

SPEAKING SKILLS **AND YOUR CAREER**

LEARNING **OBJECTIVE**

10.5 What speaking skills covered in this chapter relate specifically to your career?

The introduction to public speaking in this chapter—including confidence building, types of presentations, steps to preparing a speech, and audience analysis—offers many skills that will be of special importance to you in searching for and developing your career. The following career features take a look at how important public speaking is in the workplace and specifically to careers related to business, education, and healthcare.

SPOTLIGHT ON **AUDIENCE ANALYSIS**

BUSINESS

For businesses that deal with cross-cultural communication, audience analysis is critical. Chuck Williams in *Effective Management* (2008) suggests that one way to improve understanding when communicating with people from other countries or cultures is to determine how they show emotions. Are they more affective or neutral?

- *Affective cultures*—openly display their emotions. For example, business people from Egypt, Spain, Italy, or France openly show both positive and negative emotions. They would likely consider people who do not show emotions as cold or indifferent.

- *Neutral cultures*—mask their emotions. For example, for business people from Hong Kong, China or Japan, it is unacceptable to show strong emotions because emotions can "disrupt harmony and lead to conflict" (p. 393). They would likely consider people who show emotions as less reliable.

EDUCATION

Effective teachers use the categories of audience analysis discussed in this chapter to analyze audiences they may speak to. In the *School Library Media Activities Monthly* (September, 2004), Callison and Lamb point out that teachers must work with more audiences than just their students; other audiences include "parents, community members, and colleagues" (p. 34). Each audience is different, and messages must be adjusted to achieve successful communication with each.

If the instructor has done a good job obtaining demographic, attitude, and situational audience information and used this information to improve communication, there are signs that their message is being received and appreciated. For example (p. 37):

- Listeners appear relaxed.

- They lean forward in interest.

- Their eye contact is more direct.

- They smile and nod their heads in approval.

HEALTHCARE

When teaching healthcare practices or procedures, it is critical that nurses analyze their audience carefully. Berman et al. in *Fundamentals of Nursing* (2008) warn that just because a client makes direct eye contact and uses head nods and smiles doesn't mean that s/he understand your instructions or will follow them (p. 506).

- If the client is from a collectivistic culture that is concerned with "saving face," showing a lack of understanding would be considered rude. Also, asking questions or indicating confusion could cause the professional to lose face. These clients need to know that asking questions is a good thing.

- If the client is from a culture that is more concerned with the present than the future, preventative measures may not be considered important. Focus on "short-term" problems instead of prevention of future problems.

CAREER MOMENT **SPEAKING SKILLS FOR THE WORKPLACE**

Think about the career you are working toward. What skills and qualities do you think employers in your field think are essential? The most recent survey from NACE (*Job Outlook* 2009) again places *communication skills* (writing and speaking) as the qualities/skills most sought after by employers. Not only are communication skills the most desired skills for new hires, the survey also notes that communication skills are the "number one skill that is most-lacking in new college graduate hires" (p. 24). This year's survey participants also noted that "presentation skills, teamwork skills, and overall interpersonal skills" were lacking in new hires.

So, where do you rank in the eyes of a potential employer? Do you know how to prepare and present a quality speech?

The final chapters in this text cover everything you need to know not only to answer this question effectively, but to actually select, prepare, and present an excellent presentation. If you would like to have additional practice in speaking and would like to add real polish to your speaking abilities, you may want to take an additional communication course that focuses specifically on speaking, such as Public Speaking. Check with your professor for more information.

CONNECTING TO **BUSINESS**

Whether speaking to work groups or dealing with people individually, it is important to "know the demographics of your workforce" (*Employee Retention Survey*, 2000). A survey of 667 workers by BridgeGate, LLC, found the following factors likely to improve employee retention: a raise—valued more by workers aged 18–24 (54% vs. 46% for all workers); flexible work schedules—valued more by women than men (12% vs. 11.6%); stock options—valued more by men (17% vs. 6%); training opportunities—valued more by younger employees (5% vs. 4%); benefits—valued more by those with only a high school education (19% vs. 10%); benefits—valued more by older workers (22% of workers over 55; vs. 18% for all workers).

ACTIVITY

1. In groups of five to seven, make a list of 10–15 benefits that workers might find attractive today, approximately a decade after the original survey. Rank these benefits from most to least preferred for female workers; for male workers; for workers between the ages of 18–25; for workers over the age of 35.

2. What major life changes occur between the ages of 25 and 35 that may account for these differences? Do they differ for men and women?

3. Which groups do you think have more uncertainty and anxiety about their jobs? How could a speaker reduce those anxieties?

CONNECTING TO **EDUCATION**

When assigning team presentations as an educator, you should be aware that team members have difficulty accurately assessing the success of contributions to a group presentation. Luo et al. (2005) use attribution theory to shed light on the problem. A study found that when the team received positive feedback, they assessed themselves and others equally. When the team received negative feedback, members were more likely to blame poor performance on the assignment and more likely to blame "internal causes" for poor performance of team members (pp. 69–70). A discussion of attribution tendencies would help team members be less subjective.

ACTIVITY

1. Review attribution theory as discussed in Chapter 2.

2. In groups of four or five, brainstorm possible attributions that team members use to explain performance *when receiving negative feedback* (such as "My team wasn't prepared").

3. Select two or three of the most threatening attributions from your list and discuss ways to make them less threatening.

4. As a teacher, is there a way to minimize the effect of attribution error in team presentation evaluations? Give examples.

CONNECTING TO **HEALTHCARE**

You will need to teach progressive relaxation to your patients—especially if you go into nursing. Relaxation is considered to be a mind-body therapy designed to bring about healing (Berman et al., 2008, p. 338). It also helps patients feel less anxious and more in control and includes the following steps (adapted from p. 339): sit comfortably with feet flat on the floor; begin by tensing your right fist, then relax it. Be aware of how tension feels; repeat the process with your left fist; now, tense and relax both fists together. Concentrate on how good relaxation feels; next tense and relax both fists and both arms; use the tension-relaxation process with each muscle group in the body moving to the chest, shoulders, neck, forehead, and jaw muscles. Then move to the toes, ankles, knees, legs, buttocks, groin, and stomach; each time you relax a muscle group, work on feeling completely relaxed.

ACTIVITY In groups of three, practice the procedure.

1. How would you explain the importance of relaxation to a group of skeptical patients? Be specific.

2. Now, take turns being the healthcare provider in charge and present the process to your group members. Coach

them if you notice a problem. Members should ask questions and play the role of patients.

3. Discuss how the relaxation exercise made you feel and why.

APPLY **WHAT YOU KNOW**
CONDUCTING AN ATTITUDE ANALYSIS

Using the members of your class as your audience (or the members of a club or organization), complete the following:

- Conduct the attitude portions of the audience analysis form in Figure 10.9 and select an exact speech topic to complete the

analysis. If you don't have a topic in mind for one of your own speeches, use Aaron's topic from our opening scenario.

- Which of these attitude characteristics do you think would be especially important for your topic or Aaron's topic? Why?

Situational Analysis

It's easy to see how audience demographics and attitudes can affect the success of a presentation, but many people overlook the importance of the situation (or occasion). Your first situational consideration is to determine why there is a need to address your audience. For example, poor analysis of the situation by Queen Elizabeth after the death of Princess Diana on August 31, 1997, caused a negative international reaction to the Royal Family (Benoit & Brinson, 1999). In fact, her personal approval rating dropped to 28 percent prior to Diana's funeral. The Queen, wanting to give the family a chance to grieve in private, remained at Balmoral Castle, where they were on holiday when the tragedy occurred. She did not make a public statement or return to London. The Queen completely misread how her silence would be judged by English citizens and people around the world. Newspapers carried such headlines as "Show Us You Care," and "Your People Are Suffering. Speak to Us Ma'am" (p. 146). As a result, the Royal Family returned to London and the Queen gave an unprecedented televised talk to her people the night before Diana's funeral (for more on this incident, see *Skill Builders* at the end of this chapter). See additional situational items to consider in the *Developing Skills* feature on page 279.

Your understanding of a particular situation will guide you in many aspects of your speech preparation. For example, some occasions carry with them certain expectations. If you are the best man at your friend's wedding, the toast you may be asked to give should conform to certain standards: it should be brief, heartfelt, in good taste, and not cause undue discomfort or embarrassment to the bride or the groom. After-dinner speeches, eulogies, panel presentations—whatever the occasion, you should take time to learn the accepted protocols for that type of speech.

APPLY **WHAT YOU KNOW**
CONDUCTING A SITUATIONAL ANALYSIS

Using the members of your class as your audience (or the members of a club or organization), complete the following:

- Conduct a situational analysis using the appropriate section of the audience analysis form in Figure 10.9. Select the same topic you used for the attitude analysis in the previous activity.

- Which of the situational characteristics do you think would be especially important for analyzing the audience on your topic or Aaron's topic? Why?

- Be prepared to share your completed analysis form with the class if asked.

CHAPTER SUMMARY

Becoming an effective, confident speaker is hard work, but it can be done with effort. You can determine your basic knowledge of public speaking by checking the skills and learning objectives presented in this chapter.

Summary of **SKILLS**

Check each skill that you now feel qualified to perform:

- ❑ I can pinpoint my public speaking anxiety as being either situational or trait and explain to others the definition and causes of speaker anxiety.
- ❑ I can manage my communication anxiety, using one or more of the seven techniques presented.
- ❑ I can prepare a successful speech by following the five steps spelled out in the chapter.
- ❑ I can effectively analyze an audience by using demographic, attitude, and situational analysis.

Summary of LEARNING **OUTCOMES**

10.1 *What is the definition and what are the causes and types of speaker anxiety?*

- Speaker anxiety refers to the discomfort people often feel when confronted with the need to speak to an audience.
- Anxiety is caused by a new or unexpected situation (situational anxiety) or by a person's internal feelings (trait anxiety).

10.2 *What are the seven techniques for building speaker confidence, which are best, and how does uncertainty reduction relate to anxiety?*

- Techniques for building speaker confidence include preparation, skills training, positive imagery, deep breathing and relaxation, cognitive restructuring, audience-approach, and speaking experience.
- Different techniques work for different people; therefore, the most success is usually obtained by using a combination of methods.
- Uncertainty reduction theory, discussed in the *Making Theory Practical* feature, includes ways to reduce anxiety by being able to predict and explain the behavior of others.

10.3 *What are the five steps in preparing a successful speech, and which is the most important?*

- The five steps in preparing a successful speech include 1) Analyzing the audience; 2) Developing your topic, purpose, & thesis; 3) Gathering materials; 4) Organizing the content; and 5) Practicing your speech.
- The first step is the most important because what you find out about your audience will influence all the decisions you make in the other planning steps—that is, everything you do in your speech depends on your audience.

10.4 *What are the three types of audience analysis, and what are some tips for effectively analyzing an audience?*

- Successful audience analysis includes demographic analysis, attitude analysis, and situational analysis.
- Tips for effective audience analysis are included in this chapter's *Developing Skills* feature.

10.5 *What speaking skills covered in this chapter relate specifically to your career (see highlighted fields of business, education, and healthcare)?*

- The *Spotlight on, Career Moment,* and *Connecting to* features highlight the value of listening in the fields of business, education, and healthcare.

SOLVE IT NOW!

Taking into consideration all that you learned about confidence building and speech preparation from this chapter, how would you analyze Aaron's concerns in our opening scenario? *

- Which techniques would you suggest to Aaron to build his speaking confidence? Why do you suggest those specific techniques in his case?

- Write three to five specific questions that Aaron should ask the Coordinator of Patient Education and Support Services to determine important demographic character-istics about his audience?

- How would you explain to Aaron the importance of attitude and situational analysis?

- What specific communication goals would you recom-mend for Aaron that would improve his speaking ability now and in the future?

*(Check your answers with those located in MyCommunicationLab, Scenario Analysis for Chapter 10)

The next chapter will look at choosing a speech topic and finding supporting material you will use in your presentation.

KEY TERMS

accidental audience	p. 278	communibiology	p. 265	PRSCA	p. 263	uncertainty reduction theory	p. 269
attitude	p. 275	credibility	p. 277	relaxation	p. 267	visualization (positive	
audience centered	p. 270	deep breathing	p. 267	situational anxiety	p. 264	imagery)	p. 266
audience demographics	p. 274	involuntary audience	p. 278	skills training	p. 266	voluntary audience	p. 278
		positive imagery (visualization)	p. 266	speaker anxiety	p. 263		
cognitive restructuring	p. 267			trait anxiety	p. 264		

SKILL BUILDERS

1. To determine your public speaking anxiety, take the follow-ing PRPSA questionnaire and compare your scores with those you received from taking the PRCA-24 in the *Developing Skills* section of Chapter 1. If your score shows some anxiety, deter-mine which anxiety reducing techniques discussed in this chapter would be the most helpful to you.

The Personal Report of Public Speaking Anxiety
(Richmond & McCroskey, 1992)

Directions: Answer each of the following questions using this scale: **Strongly agree = 5; Agree = 4; Undecided = 3; Disagree = 2; Strongly Disagree = 1.** Don't think of just one situation but answer the questions as they apply to your average speaking experience.

1. While preparing for giving a speech, I feel tense and nervous.

2. I feel tense when I see the words *speech* and *public speech* on a course outline when studying.

3. My thoughts become confused and jumbled when I am giving a speech.

4. Right after giving a speech, I feel that I have had a pleasant experience.

5. I get anxious when I think about a speech coming up.

6. I have no fear of giving a speech.

7. Although I am nervous just before starting a speech, I soon settle down after starting and feel calm and comfortable.

8. I look forward to giving a speech.

9. When the instructor announces a speaking assignment in class, I can feel myself getting tense.

10. My hands tremble when I am giving a speech.

11. I feel relaxed while giving a speech.

12. I enjoy preparing for a speech.

13. I am in constant fear of forgetting what I prepared to say.

14. I get anxious if someone asks me something about my topic that I do not know.

15. I face the prospect of giving a speech with confidence.

16. I feel that I am in complete possession of myself while giving a speech.

17. My mind is clear when giving a speech.

18. I do not dread giving a speech.

19. I perspire just before starting a speech.

20. My heart beats very fast just as I start a speech.

21. I experience considerable anxiety while sitting in the room just before my speech starts.

22. Certain parts of my body feel very tense and rigid while giving a speech.

23. Realizing that only a little time remains in a speech makes me very tense and anxious.

24. While giving a speech I know I can control my feelings of tension and stress.

25. I breathe faster just before starting a speech.

26. I feel comfortable and relaxed in the hour or so just before giving a speech.

27. I do poorer on speeches because I am anxious.

28. I feel anxious when the teacher announces the date of a speaking assignment.

29. When I make a mistake while giving a speech, I find it hard to concentrate on the parts that follow.

30. During an important speech I experience a feeling of helplessness building up inside me.

31. I have trouble falling asleep the night before a speech.

32. My heart beats very fast while I present a speech.

33. I feel anxious while waiting to give my speech.

34. While giving a speech, I get so nervous I forget facts I really know.

Scoring:

Step 1: Add the scores for items 1-3, 5, 9–10, 13–14, 19–23, 25, 27–34. _____

Step 2: Add the scores for items 4, 6–8, 11–12, 15–18, 24, and 26. _____

Step 3: Use this formula to determine your final score: PRPSA = 132 minus the total from Step 1 plus the total from Step 2.

Analysis: Your scores on the PRPSA can range between 34–170. Scores below 85 suggest practically no anxiety; scores from 85–92 suggest a low level of anxiety; scores between 93–110 suggest moderate anxiety; scores from 111–119 suggest a moderately high anxiety; and scores between 120–170 suggest a very high level of anxiety.

2. Critically Evaluating

Using the critical evaluation form from Chapter 1, select and evaluate an article on *speaker anxiety* obtained from a communication journal such as *Communication Education* (you may wish to check your library databases for articles). Be prepared to share your observations with your classmates.

3. As mentioned earlier, poor audience analysis by Queen Elizabeth after the death of Princess Diana on August 31, 1997, caused a negative international reaction to the Royal Family. In groups, search for (1) more detail on the reason that Queen Elizabeth II decided to keep a low profile after Diana's death, (2) how she and her advisors so misjudged the attitudes of the British people, and (3) why she ultimately changed her mind and returned to London and made a speech the night before the funeral. Research as many of the following as possible:

- Watch the movie *The Queen* with Academy Award winner Helen Mirren playing Queen Elizabeth II.

- Watch the Queen's Tribute to Princess Diana—the complete speech is available at *YouTube.com* by typing in "Diana Princess of Wales Tribute."

- Search for newspaper stories about the reaction of the British people, using the databases available through your campus or city libraries.

- Read the following article: "Queen Elizabeth's image repair discourse: Insensitive royal or compassionate queen?" by Benoit and Brinson (1999) in the *Public Relations Review, 25(2),* 145–151.

Discuss what type of attitude analysis discussed in this chapter (and overlooked by the Queen) was largely responsible for the public reaction and how her speech helped solve the problem.

EXPLORE SOME MORE . . .

1. To listen to one of the 100 Best Speeches of the Twentieth Century (such as "I Have a Dream" by Martin Luther King, Jr.), go to http://www.AmericanRhetoric.com and click on Top 100 Speeches. Also, click on Movie Speeches for speeches such as Coach Herb Brooks: Address to 1980 U.S. Olympic Hockey Team before Playing the Soviets—delivered by Kurt Russell in the movie, *Miracle*; or the President's Address to the U.S. pilots in the movie, *Independence Day*—delivered by Bill Pullman.

2. Looking for a good book that includes great advice on making quality presentations? We suggest you read *Riding the Waves of Culture: Understanding Cultural Diversity in Business* (2nd. Ed) by Fons Trompenaars and Charles Hampden-Turner (London: Micholas Brealey Publishing, 2000). Check in your college library's database collection for NetLibrary or elibrary which are ebook collections.

11 Selecting a Topic and Gathering Supporting Materials

After studying this chapter you should be able to . . .
- Use brainstorming and cognitive mapping to select and narrow a quality speech topic.
- Write a clear purpose and thesis statement for a speech.
- Create a rough-draft outline and use it to locate research information from credible sources.
- Identify effective types of supporting materials and incorporate them into your speeches.

CHAPTER SUMMARY 〉 P. 312 〉

SCENARIO

Ebony was the first person Keith saw when he finally got out of Professor Lee's class. He was relieved that she had waited. "You're really going to have to help me with this one!" he exclaimed, rolling his eyes.

Puzzled, Ebony asked, "What do you mean? All we have to do is come up with some topics we'd like to speak on this semester."

"That's easy for you. You actually like public speaking. You probably have a list of fifteen topics already, while I haven't come up with one suitable idea yet."

"Well, begin by jotting down things you know something about. I'm going to talk about my favorite topic . . ."

"Let me guess," Keith interrupted. "Clothes. Or the latest fashions."

"You know me so well," she laughed. "Our first assignment is an informative speech. Think of something you're really interested in and know a lot about and that you'd like us to know about, too. Then teaching us about it will be easy. But I think the speech you will really enjoy is the persuasive one. All you have to do is to convince us you're right about an issue that's important to you—should be easy for you, given how argumentative you are," she teased.

"Ha! ha!" Keith pretended to be insulted. "It's one thing to spout my opinion in Government class, but something else to have to back up every argument with enough evidence to prove I'm right. And as far as the 'teaching' thing is concerned, what do I know that anyone else would be interested in? I'm not an expert on much of anything. I mean, all I do is go to class and study and work. Who would be interested in that?"

"Hey, I've known you for a long time. You've done lots of interesting stuff," Ebony insisted.

"Well, maybe," Keith shrugged.

"Come on. Let's get some coffee and work on this. We'll come up with something," Ebony said reassuringly.

Keith, in our chapter opener, is uncertain about how to prepare presentations for his speech class. Although he has the advantage of knowing his audience, at this point, he is stuck somewhere in the second step of speech preparation. As you read this chapter, identify at least three major skills that Keith will need to accomplish his goal of choosing interesting topics and finding quality supporting materials.

SOLVE IT NOW! ⟩ P. 313 ⟩

It is important to remember that audience analysis should be every speaker's overarching concern throughout the process of developing a presentation. Every decision you make from now on will be made on the basis of who you perceive your listeners to be. With this in mind, we are ready to discuss both the second and third steps in preparing a speech.

Developing Your Topic, Purpose, and Thesis

LEARNING **OBJECTIVE**

11.1 What are the guidelines for selecting a topic, and what are the differences between a general purpose, a specific purpose, and a thesis statement?

The second step of the speech development process is topic selection, which includes developing your topic, your purpose, and your thesis (**Figure 11.1**).

Topic Selection

Topic selection is the first part of developing your topic. You will often find, as you prepare presentations in the future, that your general topic will be established by the person who has asked you to speak. If you are doing a presentation as part of your work, your supervisor will undoubtedly specify the topic you are to address. If you are asked to do a presentation for a civic or professional organization, the likelihood is that the program chairperson will suggest at least the general topic in advance. If you are speaking publicly before a city council or similar governing body, your topic will most likely be related to a concern you have that has brought you to the meeting. However, in your classroom presentations, it is likely that you will be asked to choose your own topics. Whether choosing your own topic or developing a presentation around a topic that has been assigned to you, always make your audience your first consideration.

Select a Topic of Interest to You If you are like most beginning public speakers, you may be concerned about how you can choose a topic that will be interesting to your audience. The answer is easier than you might think: *Talk about something you know about and care about.* If you choose a topic that relates to a special interest of yours, the chances are great that you will be more enthusiastic about your topic than you would be about an assigned topic, and your enthusiasm for your topic will most likely cause your audience to be interested in it as well. However, the way you develop your topic should take into consideration the needs of your audience.

Figure 11.1 Step 2: Topic Selection

- STEP 1 AUDIENCE ANALYSIS
- STEP 2 TOPIC SELECTION
- STEP 3 MATERIAL GATHERING
- STEP 4 ORGANIZING
- STEP 5 PRACTICING

- Developing your topic
- Developing your purpose
- Developing your thesis

Select a Topic of Value to Your Audience and Situation

To choose a topic and to develop it for your particular audience and situation, set aside some time to do some personal brainstorming.

Brainstorm for Topics Begin by making some lists; you might title these "Hobbies/Interests," "Academic Major/Career/Job," and "Political/Social Issues." Remember that the first rule of brainstorming is to avoid making judgments; if an idea occurs to you, write it down. Don't stop to consider whether it is a good idea or not; just write it down. If you focus, you will find that it does not take long for ideas to begin to come to you as fast as you can write them down, as one idea builds upon another. Keith from our opening scenario was worried about finding good speech topics; when he began brainstorming, however, he was amazed at the number of topics he found—see his list in the sample in **Figure 11.2**

You will note that the majority of these topics could be appropriate for either informative or persuasive speeches, depending on your intent. For example, music as a broad topic could be narrowed to explaining informatively any of a number of aspects of the subject. However, it could also be narrowed to discuss persuasively school vouchers, marketing to minors, effects of certain music genres on society, and a host of other controversial issues related to music.

Create a Cognitive Map Once you have a fairly good list, pull out one of the topics you have identified and construct what is called a **cognitive map,** as Keith does in **Figure 11.3.** Your purpose here is to think of as many ideas as you can that are related to the topic you have chosen. This, too, is a brainstorming process, and ideas should not be censored. Write these ideas around your central idea.

Continue with a Second Cognitive Map Once you have found a sizable number of ideas surrounding the key topic, pull out one of those and begin the cognitive mapping process again as Keith does in **Figure 11.4.** Notice that some of these topics lend themselves more to persuasion; therefore, Keith will need to select one that is appropriate to his assignment.

Continue this process several more times until you begin to see your topic being narrowed to include only a few related points. When deciding which term to pull out of a cognitive map for additional mapping, keep your audience in mind. For example, if you are very knowledgeable about diabetes as Keith is, and if you could talk about any aspect of the disease, you should think in terms of the information that would be most interesting or useful to your audience, based on their levels of knowledge and interest. By using the cognitive mapping strategy, you will soon be able to focus your topic more narrowly into a speech that will interest you and your audience and can be covered in the allotted time.

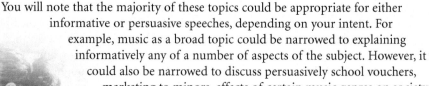

When you brainstorm for topics, begin with those that interest you. This woman should definitely have photography on her list.

APPLY **WHAT YOU KNOW**
BRAINSTORMING AND COGNITIVE MAPPING

Now that you have a good idea of the process of topic selection, check your understanding by completing the following:

- Develop your own brainstorming list of speech topic areas, using Keith's list as a model.

- Select one of the topics from your brainstorming list and create a series of cognitive maps to gradually narrow that topic for possible use in your next speech assignment.

Figure 11.2 Keith's Brainstorming List of Topics

HOBBIES/INTERESTS	ACADEMIC MAJOR/ CAREER/JOB	POLITICAL/SOCIAL ISSUES
Sports	History & Political Science	Gun Control
Travel	Geography	War
Birth Order	Kinesiology	Legalization of Marijuana
Child-Rearing	Sales & Marketing	Drinking Age
Grilling	Economics	Stem Cell Research
Health	Banking	Terrorism
Genealogy	Teaching	School Vouchers
Music	Insurance	Volunteerism
Photography	Medicine	Global Warming
Egyptian Mummies	Food Service	Socialized Health Care
Astronomy	Retail	Binge Drinking
Computers	Science & Technology	Smoking Bans

Figure 11.3 Keith's First Cognitive Map

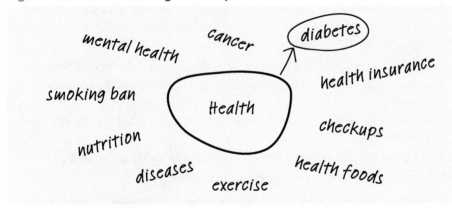

Figure 11.4 Keith's Second Cognitive Map

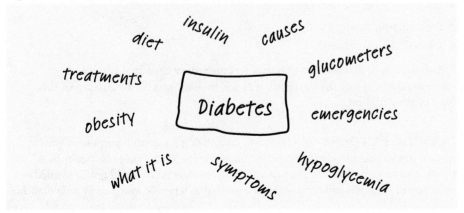

Purpose

Another part of developing a topic is to clarify both your general and specific purposes. The **general purpose** identifies the type of speech you plan to give (informative, persuasive, or entertaining) and your **specific purpose** is a statement about what you want the listeners to be able to accomplish as a result of your speech.

General Purpose
Speeches are presented for one of three general purposes: to inform, to persuade (which includes speaking to convince, or actuate), or to entertain. The purpose of an **informative speech** is to create understanding. When you take a topic (including a person, thing, event, place, problem, or concept) and clarify, expand, or teach it to your audience, you are giving an informative speech. Examples of topics for informative speeches include the following:

- Current theories of the causes of climate change
- How healthcare is provided in Cuba
- Keeping business blogs safe
- Teaching children with ADHD
- Dream interpretation

The purpose of a **persuasive speech** is to influence the values, beliefs, attitudes, or behaviors of others. Therefore, when you select a controversial topic and deliberately attempt to change the way others believe or behave, you are giving a persuasive presentation. Persuasive speeches include the *speech to convince* where you ask for audience agreement and the *speech to actuate* where you want the audience to do more than just agree—you want them to take a specific action. Examples of topics for persuasive speeches include the following:

- HPV vaccinations should be administered in public schools with other vaccinations.
- Pharmaceutical companies should be restricted in advertising new drugs directly to consumers.
- Exploration of alternative fuel sources is better left to the free market rather than funded by government.
- Disabled war veterans should be better compensated by the U.S. government.
- Vending machines should remain in elementary schools.

A **speech to entertain** is presented in situations where it is necessary to build or maintain a lighthearted mood, such as an after dinner speech. Examples of topics for entertaining speeches include the following:

- Music: the good, the bad, and the ugly
- Teaching your teenager to drive
- Taking Fido on vacation

Although speeches to entertain may be commonly used in a variety of contexts, the scope of this textbook will not include specific discussion of this type of presentation.

Since your speeches are likely to be informative or persuasive, this text will concentrate on these two types.

Specific Purpose
In addition to recognizing the general purpose of your speech, you should also clarify its specific purpose. You should state this clearly in as simple a sentence as possible. Your specific purpose statement should not be worded as a reflection of what *you* will do; it should be worded in terms of *your goal for your audience.*

In other words, it should reflect what you are aiming for your audience to be able to do when your speech is concluded.

Your specific purpose statement, then, will not say, "I will inform my audience about . . ." Instead, it should say, "After listening to my speech, my audience will . . ." What follows the "will" is a verb or verb phrase, and its nature will depend upon the general purpose of your speech. If you are doing an informative speech, you will use a verb that reflects a desired outcome of informing someone: "After listening to my informative speech, my audience will . . ." should be followed with a verb such as "know" or "understand." Other informative outcomes are that your audience will "be able to" perform some action: design, build, create, list, recognize, perform, and the like. Examples of *specific purpose statements for an informative speech* are as follows:

- After listening to my informative speech, my audience will *know* the qualities required to be an effective coach for children's sports.

- At the conclusion of my informative speech, my audience will *understand* the value of compounding interest.

- After listening to my informative speech, my audience will *be able to build* a Purple Martin birdhouse.

- As a result of my informative speech, my audience will *know how to perform* CPR on an adult.

Specific purpose statements for persuasive speeches use different types of verbs from those used for informative speeches. That is because the desired outcomes of a persuasive speech are different. When you persuade someone, you are attempting to get them to strengthen or change their values, beliefs, attitudes, or behaviors or to take an action. The verb you use, therefore, will reflect one of those goals:

- After listening to my persuasive speech, my audience *will strengthen their belief* that corporate CEOs who engage in unethical business practices should be prosecuted to the fullest extent of the law.

- After listening to my persuasive speech, my audience *will oppose* amnesty for illegal immigrants.

- After listening to my persuasive speech, my audience *will believe* that school vouchers are the best way to ensure fairness in access to quality education.

- After listening to my persuasive speech, my audience members *will sign* a form to authorize donation of their organs upon death.

It is always a wise idea to commit your specific purpose to writing and to keep the statement before you—or at least clearly in your mind—as you go about the remaining steps in the speech development process. Doing so will pinpoint what you are trying to accomplish and will help you avoid the tendency to stray from that purpose.

APPLY **WHAT YOU KNOW**
PURPOSE STATEMENTS

Now that you have a good idea of what a specific purpose statement is, check your understanding by completing the following:

- Write a specific purpose statement for one of the ideas generated by Keith in his second cognitive map that you think would make a good *informative speech.*

- Write a specific purpose statement for one of the ideas generated by Keith in his first cognitive map that you think would make a good *persuasive speech.*

- Write a specific purpose statement for one of the ideas you generated in your latest cognitive map that could be used to help you prepare your next speech assignment.

Thesis Statement

The final component of the second step in the speech development process is to determine your thesis. A **thesis statement** is usually one or two sentences, worded as simply as possible, that captures the **central idea** you want the audience to remember about your speech. It also serves as a preview of your **main points.** A thesis statement differs from a specific purpose statement in several important ways:

- A purpose statement is *primarily a working tool* to keep you on track and focused on what you are trying to accomplish and how it will benefit your audience. Purpose statements are usually *not stated aloud when you deliver your speech* because that would call attention to the mechanics of your speech, which you don't want to do.

- Thesis statements, by contrast, are *directly stated* at the end of your introduction prior to moving to the body of your speech. They are designed to get the audience on track, so they can follow your ideas during your speech.

Here are some examples to illustrate how your topic, general purpose, specific purpose, and thesis are related:

TOPIC: **How to make a high-quality, custom-fit Halloween costume**

GENERAL PURPOSE: To inform

SPECIFIC PURPOSE: After hearing my speech the audience will understand how to prepare an inexpensive yet original Halloween costume.

THESIS: Creating an inexpensive and original Halloween costume can be easily accomplished by purchasing the fabric and pattern, fitting and cutting the fabric, and assembling the costume.

TOPIC: **Spanking as a Means of Discipline**

GENERAL PURPOSE: To persuade

SPECIFIC PURPOSE: After hearing my presentation, audience members will believe in the negative effects of spanking children and will no longer use spanking as a method of discipline.

THESIS: Parents should avoid spanking children as a form of discipline because it is ineffective and potentially damaging. Spanking models hitting as a way to solve problems, lowers a child's self-esteem and confidence, seldom improves behavior, and promotes long-lasting anger.

Notice, in the second example above, that the thesis presents the central argument of a persuasive speech and is followed by a **preview** sentence—a statement that forecasts the main points that will be covered in the body of the speech. By contrast, in the first example, the thesis and preview are accomplished in a single sentence. Either is an acceptable approach; the goal is both to communicate the central idea and to preview the main points as simply and concisely as possible.

It is to your advantage to settle on the main ideas in your thesis/preview as soon as possible. It may not be possible to finalize them until after your research, but knowing what your key points will be enables you to develop a rough-draft outline (discussed below) and focus your research, saving you valuable time.

APPLY **WHAT YOU KNOW**
THESIS STATEMENTS

Now that you know what a good thesis statement is, check your understanding by completing the following:

- Using the purpose statement you wrote for Keith's informative speech, develop a thesis statement of one or two sentences.
- Using the purpose statement you wrote for Keith's persuasive speech, develop a thesis statement of one or two sentences.

- Using the purpose statement you wrote for your next speech assignment, develop a thesis statement of one or two sentences.

Gathering Materials: Begin with a Rough-Draft Outline

Having determined your topic and purpose, and having developed at least a preliminary thesis, you are now ready to find the information you need to flesh out your topic. This is the third step in developing a successful speech (**Figure 11.5**). However, please note that gathering materials really begins with outlining a rough draft of your presentation.

LEARNING **OBJECTIVE**

11.2 What is a rough-draft outline, why should it be used, and how does it differ from a final, more formal outline?

A Rough-Draft Outline Saves Valuable Time

Although preparing a rough-draft outline of your ideas may not sound like much fun, it is something that professional speakers do because it saves them valuable time. A **rough-draft outline** includes a list of the probable main points you think you will cover in your speech as well as possible supporting ideas and materials—but no introduction or conclusion. This outline will not replace the formal outline or storyboard discussed in Chapter 12. The rough-draft outline is only a working

Figure 11.5 Step 3: Material Gathering

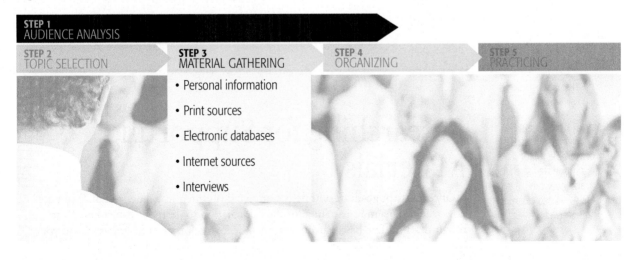

STEP 1
AUDIENCE ANALYSIS

STEP 2
TOPIC SELECTION

STEP 3
MATERIAL GATHERING

- Personal information
- Print sources
- Electronic databases
- Internet sources
- Interviews

STEP 4
ORGANIZING

STEP 5
PRACTICING

document that allows you to "see" the key ideas you plan to cover (although, during research, you may find a new idea you want to add, or you may decide to replace a key idea with one you like even better). Not only does a rough-draft outline help you "see" and organize your main points, the rough-draft outline is also the place to indicate: (1) materials you already have, (2) materials you don't have but know where to find, and (3) materials you need but don't have and will want to locate as part of your research. Indicate these materials by writing in brackets next to the points or supporting materials; for example, [history textbook], [check doctor's office for Heart Assoc. pamphlet], [find statistics], or [source?]. Knowing what to look for allows you to narrow your research and save valuable time.

If you're not sure that you really need a rough-draft outline, consider what Ebony in our opening scenario did: She knew that she wanted to talk about fashion. However, instead of jumping right into the research, she applied the same cognitive mapping strategy used by Keith. From that, she realized that she was mainly interested in fashion in the 1960s, and particularly the hippie style. Next she prepared a rough-draft outline that allowed her to identify the areas of research she needed to pursue and possible places to look for materials. Her rough draft outline then looked like the one on in **Figure 11.6** on page 297.

Ebony's thesis then, would possibly read: "In the 1960s, young people involved in the US hippie movement no longer dressed to look like miniature versions of their parents. Instead, they chose to express themselves through their own style of clothing, hair styles, and shoes."

A Rough-Draft Outline Makes Getting Opinions from Others Easier

If you aren't sure that you have included the right main points or that your supporting ideas make sense, you will want to solicit opinions from various colleagues, friends, or family members before you begin researching in detail. Handing them a rough-draft outline like the one in Figure 11.6 is sure to get you more valuable suggestions than a few scribbled notes or a written manuscript. The rough-draft outline can be read easily and rapidly, while notes or a manuscript require more time than most friends are willing to give.

APPLY **WHAT YOU KNOW**
ROUGH-DRAFT OUTLINES

Now that you have a good idea about the importance of rough-draft outlines, check your understanding by constructing a rough-draft outline for the speech you have been building throughout this chapter. Refer to Ebony's Hippie Style outline in Figure 11.6 as a model.

LEARNING OBJECTIVE

11.3 What resources are available for locating supporting materials, and how can plagiarism be avoided when using them?

Researching for Supporting Materials

Once your rough-draft outline is completed (granted it will be "rough"), you are now ready to begin researching for the information to flesh out your topic. Your rough-draft outline has helped you narrow information needing research, and you have probably even written down suggested places to look. When researching for supporting materials, such as quotations, statistics, or examples, include the following resources in your search: personal information, print sources, electronic databases, Internet sources, and interviews. Before discussing research resources, we need to stress two points.

- First, when you deliver your speech you will need to cite the sources of your supporting materials. In Chapter 13, we will give you pointers on how to verbally cite your sources, but for now, keep in mind that you must record the author, title, publication, publication date, and page numbers of any supporting materials you plan to use.

- Second, when you search for materials, use quotation marks on any information taken down word-for-word in order to avoid plagiarism (using the ideas or words of another person without giving credit). *It is your responsibility as an ethical speaker to give credit to any person whose ideas or words you have used in your presentation.*

Plagiarism has resulted in serious professional consequences for many people. Some highly publicized examples can be found in the *Spotlight on* feature later in this chapter. To avoid plagiarism in your speeches, follow the advice in the *Developing Skills* feature on page 298.

Personal Information

One of the easiest ways to avoid the temptation to plagiarize is to start researching what you already know by looking for **personal information**. If you chose the topic because it was something you were interested in and knew something about (as was suggested earlier), it is likely that you already have a great deal of information. Think about any personal experiences you, family members, or friends have had that relate to the topic. Jot down specific instances (brief examples or detailed illustrations) that you could use to support your main points. Think about past papers or reports you have written on the subject as a way to locate sources you used in the past. However, be sure to update the sources and be careful about using materials you wrote in the past exactly as written without speaking to your professor. This could be considered "self plagiarism" on some college campuses.

Keep in mind that even if you are an acknowledged expert on your topic, you should include material from other sources to support what you are saying. Using outside print or Internet sources shows the audience that you are well informed and objective and adds to your credibility.

Print Sources

Print sources, such as books, magazines, and newspapers, should always be included in your research process. Check out several of the following sources:

- *Books*: Use the online catalog at city and college libraries to search for books on your topic. If you have problems finding what you need, ask a librarian. You may be able to chat with a librarian online as well (check your campus library). Other places to search for and purchase books are your city or college bookstores, and *Amazon.com* or *eBooks.com*. If you can't locate the correct search terms, ask a librarian for the Library of Congress Subject Headings book or search for it in the online catalog.

- *Magazines and Journals*: You may prefer to browse through the magazines and journals located in your library or use one of the electronic databases (such as EBSCOhost or CQ Researcher) to search for specific magazines or articles. When possible use **refereed journals,** meaning that the articles contained in the journal

Figure 11.6 Ebony's Rough Draft Outline

U.S. HIPPIE STYLE IN THE 1960S

I. Clothing [interview grandparents for pictures]

1. Bell-bottom pants, halter tops, and headbands [freshman paper]

2. Jeans, tie-dyed t-shirts, vests, and necklaces [personal Retro poster]

II. Hair Styles

1. Long and straight [find pictures for PowerPoint slides?]

2. Beards [hair magazines for retro styles]

III. Shoes

1. Sandals [search in databases and Google for hippie sandals]

2. Platform shoes [visit shoe shop for retro shoes]

DEVELOPING **SKILLS**
HOW TO AVOID PLAGIARISM

With so many plagiarism cases in every field today, it may be that people are just not clear on what plagiarism really is. **Plagiarism** is using the ideas or words of another person (whether from a print or online source) without giving credit. Even if you cite a source, if you use the information verbatim without using quotation marks to indicate the quoted content, it is still plagiarism. A survey of medical students by Rennie and Crosby (2001) found that 56 percent of them admitted that they had used information copied/pasted from another source word-for-word and, although they listed the reference, did not use quotation marks around the copied information. Without the quotation marks, you are saying to the reader that the words are your own. Changing one or two words does not qualify as a paraphrase either—it is still plagiarism. You may have access through your college to online software such as *Turnitin.com* that allows students to check for plagiarism in speech outlines and written materials before submitting them.

In case you are not clear on what plagiarism is and what it is not, take a look at a portion of a student's outline on President Ronald Reagan's First Inaugural Address in 1980. The student was having so many problems keeping plagiarism out of her outline that we took one of her actual sources and prepared several versions of it to help her and her classmates identify plagiarism (Hamilton, 2007). Consider which of the following speaker versions are plagiarized and which are not. Before you look at the actual answers, compare your answers with those of a classmate.

Actual source material: "More than anything else, it was Reagan's exceptional communication skills that enabled him to gain control of the political agenda and change the temperature of the time" (Giuliano, 2004, p. 46).*

Speaker versions (from speech outline):

A. It was Reagan's outstanding communication skills that allowed him to gain control of the political agenda and change the temperature of the time (Giuliano, 2004).
❏ Plagiarized   ❏ Not plagiarized

B. I've read several of Reagan's speeches, and I believe that it was Reagan's amazing communication skills that allowed him to gain control of the political agenda and change the temperature of the time.
❏ Plagiarized   ❏ Not plagiarized

C. "More than anything else, it was Reagan's exceptional communication skills that enabled him to gain control of the political agenda and change the temperature of the time" (Giuliano, 2004, p. 46).
❏ Plagiarized   ❏ Not plagiarized

D. Reagan's communication skills are well known and it is those skills "that enabled him to gain control of the political agenda and change the temperature of the time" (Giuliano, 2004, p. 46).
❏ Plagiarized   ❏ Not plagiarized

E. Reagan managed to stay on top of the political scene by using outstanding communication skills
❏ Plagiarized   ❏ Not plagiarized

F. Reagan managed to stay on top of the political scene by using outstanding communication skills (Giuliano, 2004).
❏ Plagiarized   ❏ Not plagiarized

Answers on page 299

How many did you get correct? Did you have as many problems as the student who gave the speech on Reagan? Plagiarism is a serious offense that can cause you problems in your classroom speeches and in your career. Now that you have a better idea of exactly what is considered plagiarism and what is not, you might want to try the plagiarism activity located on MyCommunicationLab under Chapter 11 activities.

*Source: Giuliano, C. P. (2004). What made Ronald Reagan "the great communicator?" *The Strategist*, 46–47.

have been selected by acknowledged experts in the field. Refereed journals add credibility to your presentation. Also check out the reference section of the library for magazine indexes such as the *Index to Journals in Communication Studies*, the *Education Index*, or the *Social Science Index*.

- *Newspapers*: Current newspapers available in your library contain up-to-date information (although in abbreviated form), quotes from experts, and personal interest stories for use in your speeches. If you are looking for back issues of newspapers, an electronic database such as *LexisNexis, EBSCOhost,* or *ProQuest Newspapers* provides complete articles for your use.

- *Other Print Sources*: Also available in your library's reference section are pamphlets, files, yearbooks (such as *Facts on File Yearbook* or the *Statistical Abstract of the United States*), quotation books (such as *Bartlett's Familiar Quotations*), dictionaries (such as *Dictionary of American History*), and encyclopedias (such as *Physician's Desk Reference* or *Encyclopedia of Science and Technology*). Also, ask your librarian for government documents or special collections if they relate to your topic.

Electronic Databases

The process and quality of research has been greatly enhanced by the tremendous advances made in technology. Although *Google Scholar* or similar search engines will locate scholarly articles for you, usually you have to pay to access them. However, if you use the many **electronic databases** that your college library has purchased, you can have access to full-text articles from hundreds of professional journals at no personal cost. There are well over a hundred electronic databases that you can likely access 24/7 from your own room—just a few are listed here:

- *CQ Researcher* is great for current issues and includes a pro-con section with detailed bibliography if you need additional sources; it also includes pictures and graphs to use in your PowerPoint slides.

- *Opposing Viewpoints Resource Center* is excellent for persuasive speeches; in addition to providing articles on both sides of each topic; it includes a media section for videos and podcasts.

- *Student Resource Center* is especially good for medical topics. Also, see *MEDLINE* and *Health Source: Nursing/Academic Edition* through *EBSCOhost*.

- *EBSCOhost* covers all topics but especially helpful are its *Academic Search Complete* (with over 4,600 peer-reviewed journals), *Business Source Complete* (which is great for business topics), *Military and Government Collection* (which includes *Vital Speeches of the Day,* a journal of current speeches over a wide variety of topics), and, if your college subscribes to it, *Communication & Mass Media Complete* (with full text of over 350 journals in communication and related fields).

Internet Sources

Since 1992, the Internet has grown from a handful of users in universities to a worldwide 231.5 million active Web sites in April 2009, according to Internet researchers ("April," 2009). Even with all of these sites, *surfing the web is not the same as*

Answers:

A. Plagiarized
(source cited, but only two words changed—still using words of another as own)

B. Plagiarized
(even though words added, two words don't make a paraphrase; no source cited—even more serious than example A)

C. Not plagiarized
(however, you can't put the entire outline in quotes; limit your use of quotes)

D. Not plagiarized

E. Plagiarized
(information is paraphrased but since no source is cited, speaker took credit for idea; therefore, it is plagiarized)

F. Not plagiarized

researching the web. It's possible to spend way too much time and never find current, accurate, quality, and objective information that fits your topic. To find this type of information on the Internet, you need to know the appropriate search terms, use multiple search engines, know how to narrow your hits to a usable number, and know how to evaluate Internet sources and blogs.

Use the Appropriate Search Terms

One or two current books or refereed journal articles from an electronic database (both available from your college library) can be good ways to find keywords for your topic. You may also want to look in the Library of Congress Subject Headings book. Keep in mind that *a single keyword will never find you all the information on a topic.* For example, you could find different sites and articles, depending on whether you search for *visualization, positive imagery,* or *mental imaging.* It is also a good idea to search using the wildcard (*) added to some keywords. Although not all search engines use the asterisk, many do; using it will search for all forms of the word (for example, *swim** will search for *swim, swimming, swimmer, swimmers,* and so on).

Use Multiple Search Engines

Search engines such as *Google* or *Hotbot* are designed to search Web sites on the Internet. Keep in mind that *a single search from a single search engine will never find you all the information available;* you should conduct multiple searches and use multiple search engines.

- *Standard search engines* such as *HotBot* or *Excite* search by relevance and search more of the web.
- A *hierarchical index* such as *Yahoo!* searches in categories and is good for complex subjects.
- *Alternative search engines* use a variety of search methods. *Google* ranks by the number of links to other sites; *AskJeeves* searches by sentences instead of keywords.
- *Metasearch engines* such as *Dogpile, Surfwax,* or *Vivisimo* search other search engines. However, since these engines search only 10–50 hits of each search engine, the percentage of Web sites searched is quite low (Notess, 2006).

Narrow Hits to a Usable Number

With so many Web sites available, the number of hits you receive on any one search may be unmanageable. For example, a *Google* search of *country music* resulted in 142 million hits; obviously, the search terms needed to be narrowed. To narrow (or in some cases to expand) a search, use **Boolean operators,** which use words such as NOT, AND, OR, −, or + to specify how a search is conducted. For specific suggestions on using Boolean operators, see **Figure 11.7.**

Evaluate Internet Sources Carefully

Anyone can put information on the Internet, whether the person/group is an expert or not, and whether the person/group is biased or not. It is up to the user to evaluate Internet sources carefully to determine how credible, unbiased, accurate, and current each source is. The first rule is *always compare anything found on the Internet to similar information in one or more print sources.* Also, keep in mind that the list of references at the end of your speech outline must be as accurate as a bibliography for a report or paper. References to internet sources should list an author, date, title of article, title of the Web site, and the date that you accessed the site—basically the same information given for print sources. If this information is not available, go to another source. Specifics to check include:

Figure 11.7 Boolean Operators

Used to Narrow Search	Result	Examples of hits
1. Quotations around terms	Searches documents that use words inside quotes as a single term/phrase; does not search each word separately.	*country music* = 142,000,000 *"country music"* = 23,100,000
2. AND between words	Finds documents that use both words.	*"country music" AND singers* = 5,270,000
3. + (plus sign)	Finds documents that use either word, but not both words (leave space before plus sign, but not after)	*"country music" +singers* = 535,000
4. NOT or – between words	Excludes documents with words that follow NOT.	*"country music" NOT singers* = 3,860,000

Used to Expand Search	Result	Examples of hits
1. Wildcard * (asterisk) at end of partial word	Finds documents including all forms of the word (i.e., *speak** finds *speaking, speaker,* and *speakers*).	
2. OR between words	Finds documents that use *both* words and documents that use *either* word.	*country OR music* = 2,210,000,000

- *Is the source's information credible?* Check for the author of the article or site—credible sources are willing to indicate name, occupation/position, and experience as well as to provide a contact email address. There are many magazines and newspapers that have online sites that are definitely credible.

- *Is the source's information biased?* Every site has a purpose that should be clearly stated. It may also be clear from its title or URL—for example, is it a .com (sales), .edu (education), or .gov (government) site? For example, although *Wikipedia.com* contains some valuable information, anyone can add or delete content—possibly adding biased opinions and inaccurate information. Obviously, readers should always validate information contained from *Wikipedia* by checking other sources. Since your credibility will be reduced if you cite *Wikipedia* as your source, cite reliable databases or books instead.

- *Is the source's information accurate?* If you are reading about information or opinions that are new to you, definitely verify the information for accuracy by comparing it to database or print source information. If you notice consistent spelling errors or grammar problems, you need to be especially careful about the accuracy of information on the site. Not all sites claim to be accurate—blog sites offer opinions, not facts. Opinions could be a useful type of support for some speech topics but keep in mind that their accuracy is suspect.

This student is conducting a personal interview to gather additional information for her presentation.

- *Is the source's information current?* One of the values in using the Web is that the information may be more current than many printed sources. Articles should have dates or at least contain a last-updated link at the bottom of the site. If the site is no longer being updated regularly, or it is not clear when the material was placed on the site, you should avoid using the materials found there.

Interviews If none of the above research categories includes the type of information you need in your speech, you may want to conduct a personal interview with someone who has expertise on your topic. You may be surprised at how willing people are to share their knowledge and experiences with others. Of course, your interviewee should be someone regarded as credible by your listeners. If the audience is unfamiliar with your subject, you can demonstrate credibility by making a brief reference to your subject's relevant background when you deliver your speech.

When you contact your subject, explain the purpose of the interview, offer to meet at your subject's convenience, and estimate the time you will need. It is important to request only a reasonable amount of time, and it is even more important that you do not go over that time limit. Remember that the information you use in your speech that is acquired in an interview is only as credible as the interviewee is to your audience. A friend's personal opinion is not effective proof for an argument unless your friend happens to be a widely accepted expert on your topic. For suggestions on how to organize the interview and for the types of questions that work best, see the informational interview discussed in the Interviewing Appendix at the end of this text.

APPLY **WHAT YOU KNOW**
RESEARCHING FOR SUPPORTING MATERIALS

Now that you are familiar with good places to research for supporting materials, complete the following activity:

- Begin researching for the speech that you have been building by consulting at least one print source, one electronic database, and one Internet site.
- Find one piece of information from each source and list the information for future reference or for use in class, if assigned.

Be sure to record the title, author, source, publication date (or date accessed in case of Internet sources), and page numbers. You will need these for citations in your outline and actual presentation.

- What about *YouTube,* blogs, *Twitter,* or *Facebook*? In what situations, if any, could these be used as sources? When should they be avoided?

LEARNING OBJECTIVE

11.4 What are the types of supporting materials used in speeches, how is each defined, and why is each important?

Types and Uses of Supporting Materials

As you look through your research information (gained from personal knowledge, print sources, electronic databases, Internet sources, and personal interviews), you want to identify which specific supporting materials will be useful for your speech. Information found in **supporting materials** can support ideas in your speech by adding interest and making it more memorable, by adding clarification, or by adding proof. The type of supporting materials you choose should be based upon the analysis of your audience's needs. Adding information that would stimulate your audience's interest is important in any type of speaking but is especially important in informative speaking. Clarifying difficult or unfamiliar concepts is often necessary if you expect your audience to understand what you are saying. Proving your point is of primary concern in persuasive speeches; thus you need to choose the supporting materials that have the best chance of convincing your audience to accept your point of view. Not all types of supporting material, however, are equally effective in achieving each of these purposes.

As you can see, it is important to analyze your audience. Demographic characteristics may play an important role in helping you select supporting materials. Consider the following examples:

- *Cultural background.* As we discussed in Chapter 3, individualistic/low-context cultures such as the United States and Canada expect your supporting materials to be explicit and clearly spelled out for the audience. On the other hand, collectivistic/ high-context countries such as Mexico and Japan, who feel it is the responsibility of the listener to grasp the speaker's content, prefer indirect messages and may become offended if content is too explicit and certainly don't want topics that are embarrassing or filled with conflict. For these countries, narratives and personal examples often work better (Ting-Toomey, 2000).

- *Gender.* Also, keep in mind that men and women may find different types of supporting material more memorable. There is some evidence to suggest that men focus more on the factual elements of a message (Richardson, 1999), such as facts and statistics, while women may listen more to the personal aspects of a message (Borisoff & Merrill, 1991), such as examples and illustrations.

Let's look at several types of supporting material (see **Figure 11.8**) and how you can use them to accomplish the purposes of adding interest, clarification, and proof.

Definitions

Definitions are statements explaining the meaning of a word or idea. When you are using a term that may be unfamiliar to your audience or when you are using the term in a specific way that may differ from the audience's usual understanding, you need to provide a definition. For example, a speaker who works in construction may think that *soffits, eaves,* and *fascia* are terms that everyone knows, but how many of you could give a good definition of these terms? Or a persuasive speaker may assume that everyone means the same thing by the term *euthanasia*—but there are a wide range of meanings in use today. A clear definition is needed in both these cases. For example, see the definitions given in a speech titled "Principles and Paradoxes" by Amy Brinkley (2007), a global risk executive for Bank of America:

> A *principle* is a rule or standard of behavior, a basic truth that has intrinsic value.
>
> A *paradox* is something that is seemingly contradictory . . . but that nonetheless may be true. (p. 531)

To make her definitions even better, Brinkley could have followed them with one or two examples to clarify the definitions.

	Adds Interest	Clarifies	Proves
Definitions	No	Yes	No
Explanations	Yes	Yes	No
Examples	Yes	Yes	Yes—with additional proof
Hypothetical illustrations	Yes	Yes	No
Factual illustrations	Yes	Yes	Yes—with additional proof
Literal comparisons	Yes	Yes	Weak—need additional proof
Figurative comparisons	Yes	Yes	No
Quotations	Yes	Yes	Yes—if credible source
Statistics	Weak	Yes	Yes—if used properly

Figure 11.8 Types of Supporting Materials and Typical Uses

Explanations

Explanations occur when you verbally make a word, concept, or procedure more understandable, perhaps by outlining the causes or processes or by showing the logical relationships between ideas or objects. Explanations are used primarily to clarify. In a speech titled "Avoiding Integrity," James E. Lukaszewski (2007), Chairman and President of the Lukaszewski Group Inc., explains one way for business leaders to embrace integrity by developing what he calls "the little green book":

> Every organization needs to create a little green book that clearly identifies the wrong things to do, but also contains clear illustrations of the right way of doing things. . . . The little green book is about what to do; where to go; how to act, speak, behave, and respond with integrity; and specific guidance on what the right thing to do is, all the time. The little green book is the employee handbook to integrity. (p. 200)

By themselves, explanations are not able to serve as strong proofs, but, like definitions, they are often a necessary part of the process of proving. If, for example, you wish to support your argument that lethal injection is cruel and unusual punishment, you may need to explain what is involved in administering a lethal injection, and you may also need to establish a definition of what constitutes cruelty.

In summary, the best explanations are brief and specific; they are also effective when followed by one or two examples or comparisons.

Examples and Illustrations

Examples are brief, factual instances used to clarify and add interest and even proof to your speech content. You have probably noted in your classes or business meetings that a professor or business speaker often introduces a concept that has little or no meaning to you until an example that illustrates the concept is presented. In a speech called "Shall We Dance?" Ronald M. Davis (2008), president of the American Medical Association, used this brief example to clarify the importance of patients getting more exercise:

> Incidentally, one way to get exercise is through dancing. In fact, the state of West Virginia is combating the epidemic of youth obesity by placing the video game Dance Dance Revolution in all 765 public schools in the Mountain State. (p. 46)

Examples grab our attention because they are powerful ways to clarify and add interest to an idea or concept. Examples may contain a brief amount of detail as in the example above, or they may be presented in list form. Keep in mind that effective examples are rarely used alone—two or three are much more interesting and certainly provide more proof than a single, isolated instance. In an address called "Better Together," Muhtar Kent (2007), president and CEO of The Coca-Cola Company, used four brief examples to support his point that things have changed in 21 years:

> When I entered college, the World Wide Web was the domain of maybe a hundred doctoral students on the West Coast of the United States. Half of the Fortune 500 companies doing business then don't exist today.
>
> Back then the founders of Google and MySpace had not yet been born . . . and the guys who started Dell and eBay were just getting out of diapers. (p. 267)

Obviously, using only one of the above brief examples wouldn't have had much impact, would it?

Whereas examples are brief and present little detail, **illustrations** are detailed, vivid stories or narratives told with enthusiasm and vigor. Illustrations can be factual or hypothetical as long as you include enough detail so the audience can "see" exactly what is happening. In a speech, "Taming Hostile Audiences," given to the National Speakers Association in Washington, D.C., Larry Tracy (2005) used this illustration to support his point that a speaker must stay composed no matter what:

> I was on a panel at a major university, addressing U.S.–Latin American policy. The three other members of the panel were professors from the university, all opposed to that policy. The audience was composed primarily of students, who, in the Q&A session, were aggressive but fair.
>
> Then a man in his 40's rose, asked a "question" to which I responded. This was then followed by two more, which were loud personal attacks against my honesty. I felt my Irish temper starting to boil. My instinct was to lash back.
>
> Fortunately, for reasons I still don't understand, I did not. Instead, I said, "Look, everybody in this auditorium wants to give me a hard time, and I just can't let you have all the fun." I broke eye contact, but he kept shouting.
>
> At that point, another person shouted at the questioner, "Will you sit down and shut up? We want to get at him too." That struck me as funny—perhaps I have a perverted sense of humor—and I laughed. The audience joined in, and even my adversaries on the panel laughed. We then had a fairly civil discussion of policy issues.
>
> What would have happened if I had succumbed to the temptation of responding sharply to this man's accusations? The audience would have sided with him, I would have been booed, and the evening would have been quite unpleasant. (pp. 311–312)

Unlike examples, illustrations can be effective when used alone. Keep in mind that hypothetical illustrations are not effective as proof. However, factual illustrations can prove if paired with other supports—perhaps a second illustration if time allows, followed by a list of examples, some statistics, or a quote from an expert. For example, if you wish to prove that riding a motorcycle without a helmet is dangerous, you might use a detailed illustration of a person who suffered a serious injury riding without a helmet. Let your audience picture the weather, the road conditions, the reason the rider was in such a hurry, exactly what happened during the accident, and how the accident would have been minimal if a helmet had been worn. If time allows, add a second detailed story; if not, provide a list of examples of other motorcycle accidents that occurred during the same month—all equally as serious, all without helmets. Cite some statistics comparing injuries with and without helmets and read a quote from a motorcyclist who now wears a helmet and why. In this way, not only have you added interest and emotion to your speech, you have developed a potentially very powerful proof; you have supported the illustration and "humanized" the statistics. When used correctly, examples and illustrations (especially narratives as discussed in the *Making Theory Practical* box on page 307) increase the chances that attitude change will occur (Park et al., 2007).

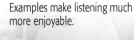

Examples make listening much more enjoyable.

Comparisons

Comparisons show similarities between a known and an unknown idea or object in order to make the unknown clear. There are two types of comparisons: literal and figurative. A **literal comparison** compares two or more items that are basically alike; for example, detailing "two ways to motivate an audience" or "three methods to solve the parking problem" or "four varieties

of apples." A **figurative comparison** includes two or more items that are basically dissimilar; for example, comparing the "variety of human beings to the variety of snowflakes" or comparing "cultural assimilation to a melting pot." Sally Mason (2007), in her speech "Gender Gap in Technology," used a figurative comparison to clarify the importance of computer skills for women who have shown less interest in them than men:

> As computer technology becomes increasingly pervasive in our society, those who are unskilled in using it will find themselves falling further and further behind. The limited computer skills of many young women today will limit their opportunities and their incomes in the same way outright discrimination limited opportunities for their grandmothers 40 years ago. (p. 161)

Keep in mind that when you use a comparison, you help an audience understand something that is complicated or unknown by likening it to something they all recognize. For example, if you are trying to inform your audience about the workings of an ant colony, you might draw an analogy to some bureaucratic organization with which your audience is likely to be familiar. Or, perhaps the reverse would apply: If you believe that your audience is likely to know a little about how ant colonies work, but you are trying to convince them that a particular bureaucracy is like an unintelligent version of an intelligent ant colony, your comparison would work the other way. In either case, your use of comparison helps your audience to understand a difficult concept by showing how it is similar to something they do understand.

It is important to note that persuasive speakers often try to prove through the use of comparison. This is often effective, but it may be used fallaciously. If the things that are being compared are not sufficiently similar to make a valid comparison possible, the speaker commits the **fallacy of false analogy**. For example, if you wish to prove that a teen curfew is a good thing for your major metropolitan city because a similar curfew enacted in a nearby suburb has had positive results, you may not be making a valid point. If the city and the suburb are not similar in most regards, the enactment of a similar curfew may not bring similar results. Good critical listeners would spot this fallacy instantly.

Quotations

Quotations (sometimes called expert testimony) may be used to support a point you have already made. **Quotations** are concise and especially well-worded statements by an outside source considered credible by your audience, which are paraphrased or read word-for-word. Quotations by famous people, past and present, are often used to provide clarification, interest, and proof to an idea. In a graduation speech titled "The American Dream," the president of Purdue University, Martin C. Jischke (2007), used this quote, which added clarification, interest, and proof to his view of the American Dream:

> I can tell you what it [the American Dream] meant to James Truslow Adams [who coined the term "The American Dream" in his book *Epic of America*]. He wrote that the American Dream is the "dream of a land in which life should be better and richer and fuller for everyone, with opportunity for each according to ability or achievement. It is not a dream of motor cars and high wages merely, but a dream of social order in which each man and each woman shall be able to attain to the fullest stature of which they are innately capable, and be recognized by others for what they are, regardless of birth or position." (p. 315)

MAKING THEORY **PRACTICAL**
FISHER'S NARRATIVE PARADIGM

When you begin to drift off during a lecture or presentation, what is one sure thing that will refocus your attention? How about a narrative or story? Would you agree that a good factual or hypothetical story—as long as it is interesting and includes vivid details—will usually cause you to shift your attention back to the speaker? Sometimes the lead-in to the story is enough to get your attention:

"Just imagine if the following happened to you . . . "
"I'll never forget my first driving lesson . . . "
"Obama explained his point with this story . . . "

Theorist:
Of the many theories about narrative, Walter R. Fisher's *narrative paradigm* (1987) may be one of the most helpful to speakers. According to Fisher, people (regardless of their cultural background) are natural storytellers (p. 64). He believes that dramatic narratives are more than just stories that add clarity and interest (although they do); effective narratives become a form of evidence that can be used in arguments to inform as well as to persuade listeners. According to Fisher, since life is a series of narratives (think of how you could describe your life through a series of stories about people, events, or things), audience members are open to viewing narratives as evidence. Narratives capture "the experience of the world, simultaneously appealing to the various senses, to reason and emotion, to intellect and imagination, and to fact and value" (p. 75).

A Quality Narrative:
In order for a narrative to work as evidence, Fisher says, it must have *narrative rationality* which involves two principles of logic: probability and fidelity.

• **Probability** *refers to whether the story sticks together in a coherent manner*—the storyline is clear; the characters behave in a reliable manner.

• **Fidelity** *refers to whether the story "rings true" to the audience*—the story sounds truthful; the story and characters are accurate historically and culturally.

Even hypothetical narratives have power as long as they include probability and fidelity.

An example of a storyteller who uses Fisher's principles of logic was former president Ronald Reagan who was labeled by the media as the "Great Communicator." Reagan's stories about America and her place in the world were "grounded in American history" and related well to the "central values of the American Dream" (p. 146), which gave them probability and fidelity in the eyes of his public. What current politicians have enhanced their credibility by using narratives?

PRACTICAL USES:
Many speakers, if asked to provide the type of evidence and logic needed for persuasion, would include supports such as statistics, factual comparisons, and quotations from authorities. Fisher's research shows that narratives and stories are used for more than just interest and clarity; they also serve as a type of evidence when the principles of logic (probability and fidelity) are applied. Narratives are an excellent way to establish a common ground between you and your audience, to build your credibility, and even to persuade. Since narratives are used in most cultures around the world, they are an excellent way to communicate with audience members from other cultures. This is especially true when there is conflict between your position and that of audience members from a more collectivistic culture where conflicts are not discussed openly. Using a narrative approach, however, is an acceptable and persuasive way to discuss conflict when a more direct approach is unacceptable (Hall, 2002).

Source: Walter R. Fisher, *Human Communication as Narration: Toward a Philosophy of Reason, Value, and Action,* 1987. Columbia: University of South Carolina Press.

Of course, to be effective, the audience must regard your source as worthy of belief. If the source is someone you know to be a recognized authority, but you fear that your audience may not be aware of the person's qualifications, it is necessary for you to provide a little bit of information to affirm your source's credibility: "According to John Smith, who is the Executive Director of the county agency on youth violence . . ." Citing when and where the source gave the information is also important—especially to establish proof: "In this week's issue of *Time* magazine, John Smith, who is the Executive Director of the county agency on youth violence . . ."

If you have personal experience with the topic, your information can be presented in the form of an explanation, an example, a narrative, a comparison, and perhaps even statistics if your experience is extensive enough—but not as a quotation. Like examples, your personal experience is just an isolated instance, so you will need to add other types of support as well.

Statistics

We have spoken of **statistics** (numbers used to show a relationship between items) several times now, and certainly they are among the first things we think of as ways to prove something. However, we have a bit of a "love/hate" relationship with statistics. On the one hand, we demand statistical proof. On the other hand, when we hear statistics, we are not always sure what they mean, and we are not sure that we trust them. We have heard that people use statistics to manipulate. We have heard that people can manipulate statistics to prove whatever they want to. Yet, we still require statistics in order to be persuaded. So, here are some guidelines for successful use of statistics.

Use Unbiased Sources

As an ethical communicator, you have the responsibility to find and use statistics that are from as unbiased a source as is possible. They should also be as current as possible. You must also understand what the statistics show, and you need to be prepared to explain that to your audience as you state the statistics or present them in visual form in a chart or graph. You must also be certain to cite the sources of any and all statistics you use.

Round Off Numbers

It is important to be accurate in your reporting of statistics, but you should not be so excruciatingly accurate that you overwhelm your audience with a string of numbers. Imagine that a persuasive speaker has just told you that the national debt was "ten trillion, eight hundred seventy-seven billion, eight hundred seventy-nine million, four hundred fifty-nine thousand, four hundred and eight dollars and fifty-six cents." By the time you heard the "fifty-six cents," would you have any recollection of what the first number was? You might remember that it had something to do with trillions, and you might even remember that it was ten trillion, but anything after that would probably be lost to you. It would be better to report this figure as "approximately 10.9 trillion."

Convert Percentages to Fractions When Possible

Similarly, when giving percentages, converting them to fractions when possible is often a wise move. Telling us that "sixty-seven point two percent" of the population agrees about something is not nearly as easy to understand as it would be if you were to say "just over two-thirds."

Statistics don't stand alone; you must explain them.

Relate Statistics to Audience It is also helpful if you can compare a statistic to something that is meaningful to your audience's frames of reference. For example, if you are talking about the number of people who died last year from a particular cause, the statistic is more powerful if you can equate it to the population of a town or city with which the audience is familiar. Another way to make your statistic more powerful is to show how many people in your actual audience would be affected by it. For example, if your statistic says that one in three people will experience a certain problem in his or her lifetime, point out to your audience that since there are 30 of them attending the presentation, the statistic is saying that approximately 10 of them will experience this problem in the future.

Cite Your Sources Statistics are potentially powerful. Certainly, the fact that they are used so often is a measure of how important they are as proof to people. However, using them ethically, making sure they are from unbiased sources, and making sure that the audience understands what the statistics mean and how they relate to the audience isn't enough. Critical listeners also expect you *to always cite the sources of all statistics that you use.* Check Chapter 13 (page 370) for guidelines on how to cite your sources. Following the suggestions you have just read about using statistics and citing sources, the president of AARP, Jennie Chin Hansen (2008), gave these remarks and cited a new report by the Institute of Medicine (IOM) in her speech, "Who Will Care For Us?":

> By 2030, one in five Americans will be age 65 or older. It is estimated that the United States will need an additional 3.5 million formal health care providers—a 35 percent increase—just to maintain the current ratio of providers to the total population . . .
>
> Yet, despite these well-documented projections, the IOM study found that the U.S. health care workforce receives little geriatric training and is not prepared to provide older patients with the best care. There is only one physician certified in geriatrics for every 2,500 older Americans and only one-third of our baccalaureate nursing programs required a course focused on geriatrics in 2005. (p. 353)

These, then, are the primary types of supporting material. You should choose those types that best accomplish your objectives: to add interest, to clarify, and to prove. No matter how much you already know about your subject, your audience will find your presentation more credible if you can back up your ideas and claims with materials from outside sources.

APPLY **WHAT YOU KNOW**
TYPES OF SUPPORTING MATERIALS

Now that you know several types of supporting materials, apply what you know by completing the following:

- Refer to Figure 11.8 on page 303 and identify which types of supporting material you selected from the sources you used in the previous activity. Label each one.

- Did you find a variety of sources? If you did not find at least three types, consult your sources again and locate additional types of supporting material.

Quality Supporting Materials and Your Career

Now it's time to relate the information in this chapter directly to your career. The *Spotlight on, Career Moment,* and *Connecting to* features offer a specific look at how locating and using quality supporting materials affects presentations in business, education, and healthcare.

SPEECH MATERIALS **AND YOUR CAREER**

LEARNING **OBJECTIVE**

11.5 What communication skills covered in this chapter relate specifically to careers?

The communication and perception skills covered in this chapter can be of special importance to you as you search for and develop a career. The *Spotlight on, Career Moment,* and *Connecting to* features relate communication skills from the chapter to success in the specific fields of business, education, and healthcare.

SPOTLIGHT ON **ETHICS AND PLAGIARISM**

BUSINESS

In May 2005, Dave Edmondson became the president and CEO of Radio Shack. In less than nine months, he was in trouble at home, overseas, and on the blogosphere for "inaccuracies on his resume and corporate biography" (Landy, 2006). His resume claimed that he had degrees in psychology and theology from Pacific Coast Baptist College in San Dimas, California. However, college records showed that he had attended only two semesters (although they admitted that they could have lost records during the move to Oklahoma) and had no degree in psychology.

While all this was taking place, the atmosphere on the blogs changed from supportive to hostile toward Edmondson. In the end, Edmondson admitted that he had "clearly misstated" his academic record and resigned (CBCNews.com, 2006).

EDUCATION

School board chairman Keith Cook, from Orange County, North Carolina (Manzo, 2004), was scheduled to give a high school commencement address. While browsing the Internet for ideas, he found a speech that compared the movie *Titanic* to real-life problems—excellent for graduating seniors. Since there was no source listed with the speech, he decided to use it liberally in his address without giving any reference.

A reporter in the audience thought he recognized the speech, which was given by Donna Shalala while she was U.S. Secretary of Health and Human Services. Cook claimed that his use of the speech was an "honest mistake" because he was under the impression that when no name is given, no credit is required (Norton, 2004). Cook stepped down as chair but remained on the board until the next election. He was not reelected.

HEALTHCARE

Cole (2007) discusses three cases of plagiarism by students applying for geriatric medicine fellowships. The 500-word applications were supposed to include a statement showing "the applicant's personal motivation for pursuing a geriatric fellowship" (p. 436). In these three cases, each student from different parts of the country had used almost identical stories about an "elderly lady with mild dementia who had been admitted to my care because she was suffering from a urinary tract infection. Starting her on a routine antibiotic, I noticed that while her physical condition improved, her spirit remained listless and depressed." Each story goes on with the applicant deciding that the woman's problem was due to loneliness. Each began giving her extra attention with amazing results.

A *Google* search using keywords "Geriatric: Personal Statement" found the Web site used by all three applicants.

CAREER MOMENT **SPEAKERS BUREAUS**

If you are thinking that the job you want for a career won't require you to make speeches—that may be true if you plan on remaining in an entry level position. However, the higher up the promotion ladder you go, the greater are the chances that you will be expected to make presentations. So why wait? Practice the speaking skills you are learning in this course by volunteering to be a part of the speakers bureau on your campus, professional organization, or business. Speakers bureaus are made up of members or employees like Mike Mullane, a shuttle astronaut for NASA. According to Mullane (2007), NASA receives "hundreds of requests a month for speakers" (p. 80).

Companies view speakers bureaus as a public relations gesture; you can use these speaking opportunities to practice. For example, Arnold Schwarzenegger learned speaking skills by volunteering to speak at numerous charity functions (Gallo, 2006). Abraham Lincoln learned to speak by standing on a stump in a field and telling stories to hired hands (Carnegie,

2003). Barbara Jordan—Congresswoman from Texas—learned to use her marvelous voice during speech competitions in high school (Crawford, 2003) and debates in college (Lind, 1996). Your college probably has speaking and debate teams that you can join—and they are more fun than a stump!

All these methods work. Just keep in mind that speaking skills don't happen overnight. This course will certainly help lay the foundation, but you will need additional practice and work to become your best. The speaking opportunities offered by speakers bureaus may be just what you need to fine-tune your skills for the workplace.

CONNECTING TO **BUSINESS**

Are you considering a business or professional career? It is important for people giving presentations in the workplace to be familiar with the copyright laws of the United States. The current copyright laws are available from the federal government, and you can get PDF or text versions at www.copyright.gov/title17. Fines for copyright infringement can be as much as $150,000 or as low as $200, depending on the severity of the infringement (Chapter 5, p. 148). To determine your knowledge of the copyright law, complete the following activity.

ACTIVITY

The Ohio Literacy Resource Center located at Kent State University has prepared an Interactive Quiz over the copyright laws. Go to http://literacy.kent.edu/Oasis/Workshops/copyquizinteractive.html and take the quiz. After taking the quiz, write a short paragraph explaining (1) what score you received from the quiz, and what the score says about your knowledge of copyright laws, (2) how the copyright laws relate to the plagiarism discussed in this chapter, and (3) what you now know about the copyright laws that you did not know before.

CONNECTING TO **EDUCATION**

As discussed in this chapter, speaking skills are essential for successful teaching. Studies indicate that when instructors make content relevant to students, students are more motivated to learn (Millette & Gorham, 2002). The survey below (adapted from Frymier & Shulman, 1995) includes ways effective teachers use supporting materials to add relevance. Take the survey for a teacher you enjoyed and again for one you did not.

ACTIVITY Complete for two instructors, using 0 = Never; 1 = Rarely; 2 = Occasionally; 3 = Often; 4 = Very Often

___1. Uses *definitions* that make content relevant to me.

___2. Uses *explanations* that make content relevant.

___3. Uses relevant *examples, illustrations, & narratives.*

___4. Uses *comparisons* familiar to me to clarify content.

___5. Offers relevant and interesting *quotations*.

___6. Uses *statistics* to make content relevant to me.

___7. Clearly states how materials relate to me/career.

___8. Relates new content to previous content.

___9. Uses own experiences to make content relevant.

___10. Uses student experiences to make content relevant.

___11. Uses class discussion to aid relevance of content.

___12. Uses current events to make class content relevant.

SCORING: Total for instructor you enjoyed_____;
total for instructor you didn't enjoy_____.
Outstanding = 43–48; Good = 38–42; Fair = 33–37

CONNECTING TO **HEALTHCARE**

Oral presentations are a key way the healthcare profession conveys important information. According to Kreps and Thornton (1992), "there are many instances where the content of health information provided by informal information sources contradicts the most recent and well-documented healthcare knowledge" (p. 124). Sometimes, the only way to introduce a new healthcare practice is to compare it to the health beliefs held by the audience. Are you aware of these beliefs and which are true and which are false?

ACTIVITY Form groups of at least three to five people interested in being healthcare professionals.

- Brainstorm a list of health beliefs over a wide range of topics—such as "chicken soup will cure a cold" or "cell phones cause cancer."

- After you have listed as many health beliefs as you can, divide them into three groups: Beliefs that are true, beliefs that are false, and beliefs you are uncertain about.

- Research the unknown beliefs using a healthcare site such as *WebMD* or conducting a search on *Google* or *Yahoo!* using the keywords *health beliefs of American people* or *health myths.* Report back with your results.

▶ Log onto MyCommunicationLab.com to access Connecting to Psychology and Connecting to Science, Technology, Engineering, and Math—both with related activities.

CHAPTER SUMMARY

As this chapter has stressed, selecting speaking topics (Step #2 in preparing a speech) and gathering supporting materials (Step #3 in preparing a speech) are skills necessary for preparing a successful speech. Not all people know how to carry out these steps or are willing to put in the effort needed to achieve a successful speech. You can determine your knowledge of these steps by checking the skills and learning objectives presented in this chapter.

Summary of **SKILLS**

Check each skill that you now feel qualified to perform:
- ❑ I can use brainstorming and cognitive mapping to select and narrow my quality speech topics.
- ❑ I can write a clear purpose and thesis statement for my speeches.
- ❑ I can create a rough-draft outline and use it to locate research information from credible sources.
- ❑ I can identify effective types of supporting materials and incorporate them into my speeches.

Summary of LEARNING **OUTCOMES**

11.1 *What are the guidelines for selecting a topic, and what are the differences between a general purpose, a specific purpose, and a thesis statement?*

- You are likely to be a successful speaker if you pick a topic that interests you and is of value to your audience. Use brainstorming and cognitive maps to select and narrow your topic.

- A *general purpose* identifies the type of speech you plan to give—informative, persuasive, or entertaining—and is not spoken aloud.

- A *specific purpose* reflects what you want your audience to be able to do when your speech is over and usually begins with, "After listening to my speech, my audience will . . ." A specific purpose is not spoken aloud but is a working tool for the speaker.

- A *thesis statement* is spoken aloud to the audience and includes one or two brief sentences that capture the central idea you want the audience to remember and provide a preview of the main points to be included in the speech.

11.2 *What is a rough-draft outline, why should it be used, and how does it differ from the final, more formal outline?*

- A rough-draft outline includes a list of the probable main points you think you will cover in your speech as well as possible supporting materials and where to find them.

- You should use a rough-draft outline because it will save you valuable time researching and make it easier to get opinions about your topic from others.

- A rough-draft outline is a working, planning document and does not include an introduction, conclusion, or transitions. The formal outline is expanded in more detail. It does include the introduction, conclusion, and transitions and is much more polished.

11.3 *What resources are available for researching supporting materials, and how can plagiarism be avoided when using them?*

- Resources for locating supporting materials include personal information, print sources, electronic databases, Internet sources, and interviews.

- Plagiarism occurs when you use the ideas or words of other people without giving them credit, so be careful to put materials taken word-for-word inside quotation marks as you research.

- Learn to avoid unintentional plagiarism by following the advice in the *How to* feature in this chapter.

11.4 *What are the types of supporting materials used in speeches, how is each defined, and why is each important?*

- Supporting materials include definitions, explanations, examples, illustrations, comparisons, quotations, and statistics.

- Definitions for each supporting material begin on page 303.

- Supporting materials are important for speech success because they add interest, clarification, and proof to your ideas. Since not all types of supporting material are equally effective in achieving these purposes, you should always use a variety of supports.

- Don't overlook the importance of narratives (a type of illustration), as explained in the *Making Theory Practical* feature. When used correctly, narratives serve as evidence and can be a persuasive type of proof for speakers to use.

11.5 *What communication skills covered in this chapter relate specifically to careers (see highlighted fields of business, education, and healthcare)?*

- The *Spotlight on, Career Moment,* and *Connecting to* features highlight the value of communication in the fields of business, education, and healthcare.

SOLVE IT NOW!

In previous chapters, you have been asked to solve a problem presented in the opening scenario. However, in this chapter, by completing the *Apply What You Know* activities, you have already solved Keith's main concerns. It's time to evaluate how well Keith applied these principles. Watch Keith's speech located in the Multimedia library for this chapter in MyCommunicationLab and answer the following questions:*

- How well has Keith narrowed his topic to be relevant to his audience?
- What are Keith's general and specific purposes?
- What is Keith's thesis, and what are his main points? How effective were they?
- How credible were Keith's sources? How effectively did he cite his sources?
- What types of supporting materials did Keith use? How would you evaluate their variety? What other types might have added interest and clarity?

*(Check your answers with those located in MyCommunicationLab, Scenario Analysis for Chapter 11).

The next chapter will continue preparing you for successful speaking by giving pointers on outlining and organizing your speeches.

KEY TERMS

SKILL BUILDERS

1. Critically Evaluating Print Materials

Using the critical evaluation form from Chapter 1, select and evaluate an article that relates to your next speech topic from one of the databases available through your college library. (If you do not have a speech assignment, find an article dealing with plagiarism.) *EBSCOhost* or *ProQuest* would be good databases to begin your search. Be prepared to share your observations with your classmates.

2. Critically Evaluating Online Materials

Conduct an online search for articles relating to your next speech topic (if you do not have a speech assignment, find an article dealing with plagiarism). Using the criteria for evaluating online sources (on pages 299–301 in this chapter), select an article that meets the criteria and is, therefore, a quality article; find one article that does not meet one or more of the criteria and, therefore, is not a quality article. Print the articles and attach them to a full page written analysis that tells specifically what is right and what is wrong with both articles. Be prepared to share your findings with your classmates. Your instructor may request that you turn in a copy as well.

3. Critically Evaluating the Problem of Plagiarism

Why do you think so many people today plagiarize? Join with four or five other students and brainstorm a list of reasons—make your list as long as possible. Once the list is completed, narrow the list (by discussion or voting) to the top five reasons. Next, take each of the five topics and consider the following:

- Determine the "why" behind each of the reasons.
- Is there a common thread that connects these reasons?
- What does the list of reasons say about the values of the American people? Are they different from what they were when your parents were in college?

Compare your list of reasons and any common thread you have found with the results of other groups. Why do you think they are similar or different?

4. Throughout this chapter, you have learned about the importance of citing sources. Review the excerpts from speeches used in this chapter and identify those excerpts that adequately cited their sources and those that did not. Compare your findings with your classmates.

12 Informative Speaking

After studying this chapter you should be able to . . .
- Select an appropriate pattern and successfully organize an informative speech.
- Prepare a quality introduction and conclusion for an informative speech.
- Apply effective transitions to an outline for an informative speech.
- Prepare a successful outline or storyboard that follows the principles given in this chapter.

CHAPTER SUMMARY 〉 P. 339 〉

SCENARIO

Jeff knew it was time to get this peer feedback meeting underway, but he hesitated. Across the table, Matunde and Amy were arranging stacks of notes. He realized that both of his teammates had done much more preparation for their informative speeches than he had. "Why don't you start first?" he asked, looking at Matunde. "You sure do have a lot of stuff there."

"Yes," responded Matunde in his pleasantly accented way. "I am not sure what Professor Shelton wants, but I have many stories to tell."

"Are you still going to talk about Kenya?" Amy inquired. "I think that would be so interesting!"

"Yes, I am," he nodded. "Kenya is something I know about and enjoy discussing. Some stories are about my family and some are about what has been happening in my country, and others are about . . . well, there are many things to tell."

"I'll bet," Jeff replied. "But since we only have six minutes, what do you plan to focus on? I mean, are you going to talk mostly about your family, or the country, or what?"

Matunde thought for a moment. "I think I must talk about some of everything. Everything is related."

Amy paused a moment before speaking. "Jeff has a point, Matunde. Professor Shelton says we must narrow our topic into just a few key ideas. I think I'm in the same boat as you are. My topic is on voting, and I have way more material than I can cover in six minutes."

"Maybe we should start with mine," Jeff suggested. "I have written down a few ideas mostly from personal experience and a little from research. If you could help me decide what my key ideas should be, that would help me figure out how much more research I need to do."

"That sounds like a good idea," Matunde agreed. "Maybe if we work on Jeff's first, we could get an idea about how to do ours."

They all adjusted their chairs so they could see Jeff's paper. "Yeah, this looks more manageable than my pile of notes," said Amy. "Let's get started."

Jeff's Speech Notes

ADHD: Attention Deficit Hyperactivity Disorder. I have it, but it was worse when I was a child. Now I am able to manage it better.

Ritalin and counseling helped me. www.kidshealth.org says using more than one way to treat is called "multimodal."

I used to feel dumber than my friends. My mom said I was actually smarter. I don't know, but I am in college now and making a good GPA.

Source: www.familydoctor.org says 4–12% of school-age children have ADHD—mostly boys.

Research says some people think it isn't really a disorder; that it is just a personality difference.

My mom says I was impulsive and always interrupted others and didn't think about what I did before I did it.

She was always experimenting with not letting me eat certain foods because she thought I was allergic to them and that was the reason I had ADHD.

My teachers said I was "hyper" and fidgeted and couldn't sit still. They also said I couldn't pay attention because I was distracted and that I never finished my work.

My dad says he thinks he has it too because he was just like me when he was a kid and still is a little like that. He gave me some research that shows it might be inherited.

The www.nimh.nih.gov website says some people with ADHD also have Tourette's or anxiety and depression; some even have bipolar, though no accurate stats for how many.

It sounds like the students in our opening scenario aren't sure what to do at this stage in their speech preparation process. As you read this chapter, pick out specific advice you would give Jeff, Matunde, and Amy to help them meet their communication goals. Doing so should help you with your own speech preparation as well.

SOLVE IT NOW! 〉 P. 342

If while reading the preceding two chapters, you have been working to build your own speech or are working on a team presentation, you may be at a similar point to the students in our opening scenario. You have gathered a great deal of information, both from what you already know about the topic and from research. Now it's time to turn all this material into a dynamite presentation—but where to start? Before we cover organizing, which is Step Four in the speech development process, let's take a brief look at informative speaking and how it differs from persuasive speaking.

Informative Speaking: Characteristics

As we discussed in Chapter 11, an **informative speech** is defined as a speech designed to create understanding about a person, thing, event, place, problem, or concept. It is important to know the characteristics of an informative speech that distinguish it from a persuasive speech.

LEARNING **OBJECTIVE**

12.1 What is the definition of *informative speaking,* and what specific factors distinguish it from a persuasive speech?

- *Speaker Intent:* One important difference between informative and persuasive speeches deals with the speaker's intent. The intent of informative speakers is to create understanding by clarifying, expanding, or teaching a specific topic to the audience. If they discuss alternatives, it is done with the intent of giving the audience new or more detailed information. No particular solution is pushed; there is no intent to persuade. On the other hand, although persuasive speakers present information to clarify arguments and update listener knowledge, their intent *is* to persuade by influencing the attitudes, beliefs, values, and/or behaviors of their listeners.

- *Supporting Information:* A second difference between informative and persuasive speeches involves how supporting information is used in a speech. Supporting materials, as discussed in Chapter 11, are designed to clarify, add interest, and prove. They include definitions, explanations, examples and illustrations, comparisons, quotations, and statistics. Informative speakers use supporting information to give the audience more unbiased choices—the more audience members know, the better life decisions they make. On the other hand, persuasive speakers use supporting information to prove that only certain beliefs or actions are acceptable. In other words, they attempt to limit audience choices.

- *Audience Information:* A third difference between informative and persuasive speeches relates to how the speaker uses information about the audience—especially psychological information. Informative speakers are interested in the psychological information (values, beliefs, attitudes, and behaviors) they gain from analyzing the audience in order to relate their topics more effectively to the frames of reference of their listeners. They are especially interested in any cultural or value differences that might keep audience members from listening to or using the information in their speeches. On the other hand, persuasive speakers use the psychological information gained from analyzing the audience so they can best determine how to influence their listeners.

- *Speaker Expectations:* A fourth difference between persuasive and informative speeches relates to speaker expectations. Effective informative speakers expect their audience members to grasp the full content of each presentation. Although they realize, of course, that audience members won't remember everything in the presentation due to poor listening habits, they hope listeners will understand the basic information by the time the presentation is completed. On the other hand, experienced persuasive speakers do not expect all audience members to make a full attitude change during a single persuasive presentation. Although information can be grasped in a single presentation, extreme attitude change takes longer—persuasion usually occurs over time. More specifics on persuasive speeches are covered in Chapter 14.

Now that we are clear on what an informative speech really is, let's look at what's involved in organizing an informative speech beginning with your rough-draft outline.

LEARNING OBJECTIVE

12.2 What are the patterns for organizing informative speeches, and when does each pattern work best?

Organizational Patterns for Informative Speeches

Organizing—the fourth step in developing a successful speech—includes two main parts: organizing and outlining (**Figure 12.1**).

The place to begin organizing is with the rough-draft outline you prepared prior to doing research. Recall that rough-draft outlines do not include introductions or conclusions—only a list of "probable" main points as well as possible supporting ideas and materials (see Chapter 11, page 297 for a sample). Hopefully you found that your rough-draft outline pinpointed the research needed, thereby saving you time. Now that your research is complete, it is time to (1) take the main points from your rough-draft outline and expand and revise them based on your audience analysis and research; (2) decide on the best organizational pattern to add interest and clarity to your topic; (3) add your introduction and conclusion; and finally, (4) use all the above to develop a final, more detailed and polished outline called a *formal outline*. The formal outline isn't just for the professor; it is for your use in checking for organizational problems and gaps in supporting material. Now that you have an idea of what is involved in this chapter, let's look at each area in more detail.

Like an essay, a speech needs to have three parts: an introduction, a body, and a conclusion. Each part needs to accomplish several purposes, but the general structure is, as

Figure 12.1 Step Four: Organizing Your Information for a Successful Speech

STEP 1 AUDIENCE ANALYSIS				
STEP 2 TOPIC SELECTION	STEP 3 MATERIAL GATHERING	STEP 4 ORGANIZING		STEP 5 PRACTICING
		• Organizational patterns		
		• Introductions		
		• Conclusions		
		• Transitions		
		• Outlining		

many Speech and English teachers like to say: First you tell us what you're going to tell us; then you tell us; then you tell us what you told us. Another way to say this is: *First you preview; then you view; then you review.*

You may be tempted to start your speech preparation by working on the introduction. However, since you really can't decide how to introduce something until you know exactly what you are introducing, begin with the body of your speech instead. Having chosen your material based on your audience analysis, you are ready to revise your rough draft as you decide which organizational patterns are most appropriate for your presentation. The patterns most commonly used in informative speeches include: chronological, spatial, topical, causal, and problem-solution. Since most speeches can be organized in a variety of ways, try the different patterns below until you find the ones most effective for organizing your specific main points—don't just settle on the first pattern you try.

Chronological (Time Order)

If your goal is to trace the history of something or to explain a process in a step-by-step sequence, you will want to choose the **chronological pattern.** In the following examples, you will see how speeches about the Ford Mustang and Planning a Vacation could be approached chronologically:

TOPIC: The Ford Mustang

I. The Mustang revealed (1965)

II. The Mustang ruined (1980s)

III. The Mustang revived (1990s)

IV. The Mustang reborn (2010)

TOPIC: Planning a Vacation

I. Deciding where to go

II. Acquiring information about your destination

III. Making arrangements

Spatial (Geographical)

If your goal is to present main points that are related to each other because of their physical or geographical location, you will want to choose the **spatial** or **geographical pattern.** When using this pattern, main points may be organized from north to south, east to west, left to right (or the reverse of each of these, if appropriate). Or you may look at the topic from outermost to innermost, nearest to farthest, top to bottom (or the reverse of these, if appropriate). In the following examples, you can see how the Ford Mustang and Vacation speech topics could be approached using a spatial pattern:

TOPIC: The Ford Mustang (*note that these are organized from outermost to innermost*)

I. The exterior styling of the Mustang

II. The interior amenities in the Mustang

III. The engine of the Mustang

TOPIC: Planning a Vacation

I. Destinations within a 100-mile radius of Springfield

II. Destinations within a 200-mile radius of Springfield

III. Destinations within a 300-mile radius of Springfield

This picture might be a good one to use with a speech on Planning Your Vacation.

Topical

When your goal is to present types, categories, aspects, features, or elements of a topic—but there is no chronological or spatial relationship among the main points—you will want to select the **topical pattern.** Deciding how to order your points in a topical pattern will depend on your audience. Points may progress from the most familiar to the least familiar, easiest to hardest, or toward a climax with the most powerful point last. Generally, the last main point should not be your weakest because you will want your ending to have impact. On the other hand, saving your most important point for last in a business presentation may not be wise, since schedules often require those who most need to hear the last point to leave early. The sample outlines below demonstrate how the Mustang and Vacation speeches might be approached topically:

TOPIC: Features of the Ford Mustang

I. Styling

II. Economy

III. Performance

TOPIC: Planning Your Vacation

I. How much time do you have?

II. How much money can you spend?

III. What do you want your vacation to accomplish?

Note that in the preceding examples, the main points could have been organized in a different order depending on what you determined about your audience's needs.

Causal (Usually Cause-Effect)

When your main points have a relationship to each other because one point is the *cause* of some phenomenon and the other point is the *effect* of it, you will choose the **causal pattern** of organization. (Note that "causal" should not be misread as "casual.") As the name of this pattern implies, it involves only two main points. A sample causal outline follows:

TOPIC: Unnecessary Infections

I. Causes:
   A. Poor hand hygiene
   B. Improper wound care

II. Effects:
   A. First, transmission of seemingly harmless microorganisms
   B. Second, appearance of infections
   C. Third, growth of infection from minor to serious

Notice that while the main points in the above example are arranged in a cause-effect pattern; the *subpoints* under each main point (the **internal organization**) are arranged using other patterns. The subpoints under main point I are ordered topically, while the subpoints under main point II are arranged chronologically. However, when you refer to the organizational pattern of a speech, you are referring to how the main points are organized, not the subpoints.

Problem-Solution

When your speech centers around reviewing a problem and offering an informative look at two or more possible solutions to the problem without taking a position on any of the solutions, you will use the **problem-solution pattern.** Be careful that you don't end up trying to persuade. Although the problem-solution pattern is most commonly used for persuasive speeches, with care it can be the basis of an excellent informative speech. The following is an example of an informative speech using the problem-solution plan:

TOPIC: STEM Majors (Science/Technology/Engineering/Math) in Serious Decline

I. Fewer students are majoring in science and math.
   A. Brief review of causes
   B. Brief review of effects
II. Informative look at some possible solutions
   A. Rigorous teacher training seminars
   B. Project Kaleidoscope
   C. Increased pay for STEM teachers
   D. Full scholarships for students in STEM majors

Use the handy guide in **Figure 12.2** to select the best pattern for your speech.

Figure 12.2 Informative Organizational Patterns

Chronological Pattern—arranged by time		
I. First step	I. 2000	I. Young
II. Second step	II. 2005	II. Middle-aged
III. Third step	III. 2010	III. Elderly
Spatial Pattern—arranged by physical location		
I. First floor	I. North	I. Left
II. Second floor	II. East	II. Center
III. Third floor	III. South	III. Right
Topical Pattern—arranged by categories or features		
I. First main point	I. Feature A	I. Important
II. Second main point	II. Feature B	II. Less important
III. Third main point	III. Feature C	III. Most important
Causal Pattern—arranged by cause/effect		
I. Cause		
II. Effect		
Problem-solution Pattern—arranged by problem/solution		
I. Problem		
II. Possible solutions		

APPLY **WHAT YOU KNOW**
ORGANIZATIONAL PATTERNS

As you have seen, informative speech topics can be approached in many different ways. Check your understanding by completing several of the following:

- Reorganize the Mustang and Vacation examples shown on page 319 into the causal and problem-solution patterns.

- Think of how you would narrow the topic of music if you were giving an informative speech and list your main points, using at least two different informative patterns.

- Experiment with two or three organizational patterns to determine which one is best for the speech you are building for this class. Construct a rough-draft outline for the approach you like best.

LEARNING **OBJECTIVE**

12.3 What are some cultural differences and preferences in speech organization, and who uses each?

Speech Organization: Cultural Differences

Keep in mind that not all cultures organize messages in the *linear* or *straight line* approach used in the United States (Lieberman, 1997), and used in the organizational patterns presented above. Americans tend to make their points clearly and move from one to the next, giving evidence and examples when needed. Lieberman (page 23) notes that speakers from the countries that speak Romance languages, such as France, tend to organize in a *straight line filled with several zig-zags* approach. They start with a basic principle but take several seemingly unrelated side paths before arriving back to the main point. Speakers from Asian countries may only hint at main points, expecting the listener to grasp the ideas from a circuitous path filled with parables and examples. In other words, they are more likely to speak using a *spiral* approach. Still other speakers, such as those from Kenya, are more likely to organize their speeches in a *bicycle wheel* approach, where "the spokes wander out repeatedly to the rim as the speaker gives an illustration, mentions a proverb, or tells a story, and then return back to the thesis at the center, though usually not exactly at the place from which they began" (Miller, 2009, p. 256). You recall that Matunde, who was introduced in our opening scenario, is from Kenya. Although he has no fear of speaking because Kenyans are used to making presentations at the many ceremonial occasions that mark everyday life (Miller, p. 252), he is confused about how to organize his presentation. You can see why Matunde is puzzled by the direct approach pattern indicated by his professor—effective Kenyan speakers would not speak in that manner. Since Kenyans value collectivism and view time from a polychromic perspective, Matunde plans to share his many stories with the audience and isn't overly worried about staying in the time limit set by his professor. This will probably cause problems for both of them.

For presentations in the United States, the linear or straight line approach is expected—especially in your classroom speeches. However, it is important to realize that organizational differences do exist and not all cultures have the same expectations when listening to speakers. In our global economy, you may have an opportunity to speak to people with different organizational expectations. If so, get advice from speakers in that culture on how to handle the difference. Knowing your audience is critical to successful speaking as we have indicated by placing Audience Analysis as Step 1 in our five steps for developing a successful presentation (see Figure 12.1 on page 318).

LEARNING **OBJECTIVE**

12.4 What functions should an effective speech introduction perform, and what are the types or guidelines for each?

Speech Introductions

The purpose of your introduction is to prepare your audience to listen to the material in the body of your speech. An introduction serves five main functions:

- *Catch the audience's attention* and direct it toward you and your topic.
- *Build rapport* by creating a feeling of good will with your audience.
- *Establish your credibility* by clarifying why you picked this topic as well as your expertise and knowledge on this topic.
- *Point out benefits to audience*—point out why the audience will benefit by listening to you.
- *Clarify central idea with thesis and preview of main points*—provide a well-worded thesis statement and summary of main points.

It is also important to note that when you accomplish one of the five functions, you can also accomplish others at the same time. For example, a narrative used as a personal anecdote (discussed later in this section) can serve to catch the audience's attention, establish your credibility, and suggest the importance of your topic to your audience—all at the same time.

Read the sample introduction from Ryan's speech on *Pirate Life* (**Figure 12.3**) and see how effective you think it is. Then let's look in detail at each of the five functions of an introduction and end by discussing when each should be used.

Figure 12.3 Ryan's Speech Introduction

I want you to imagine that the time is 1700. You are on a pirate ship and there is a massive battle going on. You're watching one of the most famous pirates, Blackbeard himself, battling it out. He gets shot in the chest at point-blank range but gets back up. He is attacked and stabbed numerous times but keeps on fighting. In fact, he sustains 20 sword wounds and 5 shots before finally going down. Even Captain Jack Sparrow in *Pirates of the Caribbean* would be impressed.

I know that I would be—in fact, I've been obsessed with pirates since I was 15 years old. I've read every book about pirates that I could get my hands on and have immersed myself in their culture. I've even started to turn the inside of my van into a kind of pirate ship.

Although pirate life was not as glamorous or as exciting as portrayed in recent movies, it is a fascinating bit of history that everyone should know about. Let's travel back in time and see what it was really like on board a pirate ship, visit with several of the most famous pirates (both male and female), and learn some pirate slang that will help you feel right at home when you watch Jack Sparrow in his next movie.

Catch Audience Attention

Generally speaking, the first words in your introduction should be attention-getting. The exception to this rule is if you are speaking to an unfamiliar audience. In that case, you might begin with rapport-building (as described above), followed by your **attention-getter.** However, an announcement of your topic is not an effective attention-getter. "My speech is about . . ." is unlikely to cause anyone to sit up and pay attention! There are many better ways to capture your audience's favorable attention without resorting to boring announcements or gimmicks, as illustrated by this chapter's cartoon. Instead, use one of the many successful types of attention-getters: questions, a startling statement, a narrative, unexpected content, or humor.

Question (Actual or Rhetorical)
Your topic may be one that lends itself to starting with a question. There are many types of questions you could use. The "How many of you have ever been fishing?" sort of question is rarely engaging. It often causes the audience to wonder if they are expected to respond and, if so, how. Typically the response will be a few hands raised tentatively as everyone looks around to see if anyone else is responding. There is also a danger that your "How many of you" question will generate a verbal response from some members of your audience, which, if you had not planned for it, may interrupt your train of thought and cause you to lose control of the situation. The best questions for attention-getters are rhetorical questions. When you think of the term *rhetorical question*, you may think it refers to one for which a questioner does not expect a response. Although that is true, that is not what makes a question "rhetorical." A **rhetorical question** provokes thought in the listener. "Have you ever stopped to wonder what you would do if you were told that you had won a million dollars?" Such a question might be a great way to introduce a topic about spending vs. investing. Listeners would pause to think about how to respond and be drawn into your topic.

© 2000 Ted Goff

"Please don't make me use another water balloon to keep your attention."
© Ted Goff

Startling Statement

Another way to start your speech is to make a **startling statement.** Perhaps you could cite a statistic that dramatically demonstrates the importance of your topic. "If today is an average day, more than three women will be murdered by their husbands or boyfriends in this country, as stated in the March 2009 issue of *Violence,* published by Texas A&M University." The source for this statement (Violence, 2009) might be followed by other statistics that emphasize the problem of domestic violence and add to your startling statement.

Narratives (Factual or Hypothetical)

One of the most engaging methods of catching your audience's attention is to tell a story. A story, or **narrative,** can be either factual (about something that really happened) or hypothetical (about something that could happen but hasn't yet). Statistics such as those above are even more compelling if they are preceded by a brief case history of a particular woman who was a victim of domestic abuse, particularly if she is someone to whom your audience members can relate. The fact is that we never outgrow our love of stories. It is important, though, that you plan the story well, using vivid language but recounting only the necessary details. Rambling stories told off-the-cuff will lose your audience and consume too much time that is better spent in developing your main points.

Audiences also enjoy hypothetical situations and stories. Asking your audience to imagine themselves in a situation involves them in your topic as participants rather than as observers. Give the same interesting details and use the same vivid language you would if relating a "real life" narrative. Barbara Bush used such a story during her 1990 commencement address to Wellesley College graduates (type in "Barbara Bush Commencement Address at Wellesley College" in www.americanrhetoric.com):

> Wellesley, you see, is not just a place but an idea—an experiment in excellence in which diversity is not just tolerated, but is embraced. The essence of this spirit was captured in a moving speech about tolerance given last year by a student body president of one of your sister colleges. She related the story by Robert Fulghum about a young pastor, who, finding himself in charge of some very energetic children, hits upon the game called "Giants, Wizards, and Dwarfs." "You have to decide now," the pastor instructed the children, "which you are—a giant, a wizard, or a dwarf?" At that, a small girl tugging at his pants leg asked, "But where do the mermaids stand?" And the pastor tells her there are no mermaids. And she says, "Oh yes there are—there are. I am a mermaid."
>
> Now this little girl knew what she was, and she was not about to give up on either her identity or the game. She intended to take her place wherever mermaids fit into the scheme of things. "Where do the mermaids stand? All of those who are different, those who do not fit the boxes and the pigeonholes? Answer that question," wrote Fulghum, "and you can build a school, a nation, or a whole world."

Sometimes you may want to use a **personal anecdote,** which is a story about something that actually happened to you. If you construct it well, your anecdote may serve to establish your credibility and, perhaps, also demonstrate your topic's importance to the audience. Just keep in mind that you should not allow your story to ramble, which is sometimes difficult when you are talking about something that happened to you.

Unexpected Behavior or Content

You may find that showing an interesting visual or engaging in some surprising behavior may focus your audience's attention. For example, if you are giving a speech about the Loch Ness Monster, you might start by saying, "Watch closely," followed by a brief video of an alleged sighting of Nessie. Or, if you are giving a speech on highway litter, beginning your speech with a photo of the clutter found on the median of a nearby highway or showing a box of the candy wrappers and fast food bags you picked up on your way to class today would grab attention. In some situations you could possibly even dump the trash on the floor as an unexpected behavior to cause your audience to wonder what will follow; obviously, however, this tactic would not be acceptable in all situations. We do suggest that you avoid using distracting gimmicks as shown in the cartoon above or other behaviors such as dropping your notes, or tripping on the way to the front of the room. These diminish your credibility as a speaker.

Humor

Many speakers like to begin with a joke or some humorous remark. Indeed, this is such a common practice that books are regularly published with titles such as *500 Great Jokes for Speakers*. Of course, by the time those books reach print, the jokes have already been used so often that they may lack the punch needed to keep an audience from groaning. If you are going to start with a joke, here are some guidelines to follow:

If you use it well, humor can be an excellent way to get audience attention.

- First, make sure the joke actually *relates to your topic*. Listeners are annoyed when they recognize that a joke has no bearing on the topic and was used only as a cheap way to generate interest.

- Second, be certain that your joke is *appropriate for your audience*. Off-color jokes are questionable, as they run the risk of alienating some of your listeners.

- Third, make sure that the joke *is funny*. Avoid jokes that relate to only a small segment of your audience so only a few people "get the point."

- Fourth, make sure you *know how to tell a joke*. As someone once said, "Some can tell 'em and some can't." If you are not a person whose humor is usually appreciated, don't take a chance with a joke. If it fails to draw laughs, your anxiety level is bound to increase.

- And finally, if you plan on using self-disparaging humor, where you become the brunt of the joke, take care—it's not as easy to use as it seems. However, according to Professor Robert Smith, who has made hundreds of presentations and is the author of *The Elements of Great Speechmaking* (2004), if you can make it appear spontaneous and sound genuine, then self-deprecating humor is one of the best.

As you choose your attention-getter, keep in mind that your goal is to catch the audience's favorable attention. You would be ill-advised to use humor, a story, startling content, or any technique that violates your audience's expectations. The point, after all, is to gain the goodwill of your audience.

APPLY **WHAT YOU KNOW**
ATTENTION-GETTERS

Now that you understand ways to gain attention in your introduction, complete the following activities:

- Select one of the sample outlines you constructed for the topic of music and create attention-getters using two or three of the techniques discussed above.

- Using the speech you are building for your class assignment, experiment with two or three attention-getting techniques to find the best one. Share your various versions with one or two classmates. Either present them orally or write them out to be read.

Build Rapport

Along with the attention-getter, it is important to establish **rapport** with your audience—a feeling of liking or closeness. This is especially important if the audience does not know you. Depending on your topic, it may be possible to combine getting attention and establishing rapport. If not, you will need to include material in your introduction that demonstrates your positive attitude toward your listeners. For example, if you are asked to address a civic organization where you are not a member, it may be useful to begin your speech with remarks about how pleased you are to have the opportunity to address them and how much you admire the mission of their organization. You might begin your speech with something like the following:

> It is a great pleasure to have the opportunity to speak to you today. I have long admired the mission of your organization; in fact, almost every day I talk with someone who has benefited from your group's generosity.

If the audience already knows you, though—as is true of your classroom audience— you should begin with your attention-getter.

Establish Credibility

Citing personal experience with your topic—as this speaker has from building his own home—is a good way to establish credibility.

Establishing **credibility**—why your audience should consider you a good source of information on your topic—is important if you want audience attention and respect. What do you know about the topic? What experience do you have with it? Why are you interested or concerned with this subject? Even if the audience knows you, don't assume that they know about your expertise on this topic. Remember that you may have been able to establish your credibility as a part of your attention-getter. When that is not the case, you might interject a statement such as the following after your attention-getter:

> My own first experience with building a home for my family wasn't nearly as stressful as many of my friends told me it would be. In fact, since then I have served as general contractor on two homes.

If you will be introduced to the audience by someone else, be sure to include information that relates to your training or experience as related to your topic in the short biography you provide.

Point Out Benefits to Audience

Just because they laughed at your opening humor doesn't mean the audience will continue to listen unless you show how your topic will benefit them personally. Audience analysis is the key to the detail needed in this step of your introduction. Sometimes you can safely assume that your audience knows how the material affects or benefits them. If you are speaking to your class about financial aid for college, it is safe to assume that they are aware of your topic's relevance. However, if you plan to encourage them to begin investing for retirement, other financial obligations probably seem more pressing, and retirement seems far away. In this instance, you will need to demonstrate early in your speech that the issue of retirement planning should not be postponed. Since it is human nature to be most interested in issues that have immediate relevance, link your topic to current needs of your audience.

Clarify Central Idea with Thesis and Preview of Main Points

Many speakers do a good job with introducing their general topic but fail to make their central idea or position clear. When the central idea is not clear, audience confusion distracts from careful listening. The only time omitting your central idea is recommended is in a persuasive speech where audience analysis has indicated a strong opposition to your position. In that case it's probably a good idea to take a back-door approach and wait until later in the speech to state your exact position. Usually, however, including a good thesis statement in an informative speech is recommended. Ending your introduction with a good thesis statement and preview not only makes your purpose and main points clear, it serves as an effective transition into the body of your speech.

You will recall from Chapter 11 that a thesis and preview can be accomplished in a single sentence, or, for the sake of clarity, may be stated in two sentences. The following is an example of a single sentence that accomplishes both goals:

> Recognizing the symptoms of skin cancer is best accomplished by knowing the three types: Basal cell, squamous cell, and malignant melanoma.

When Each Function Should Be Used

There are instances in which you will not need to include all the above steps in your introduction. For example, if you are familiar with your audience and already enjoy a cordial relationship with them, you will not need to devote much time to *rapport-building*. This is likely to be true of your classroom speeches, as you may have already spent many weeks together, interacting in person (or online, if you are taking your course via distance learning). Similarly, if your audience already knows that you are an authority on your topic, you will not need to spend much time establishing your *credibility*. As you can see, the extent to which you include material in your introduction aimed at establishing rapport, building credibility, and stimulating interest in your topic, depends entirely upon your audience analysis. If you have any doubt, it is better to devote some time to achieving those purposes rather than to assume that they are already accomplished. All introductions, however, must include attention-getters and previews of your main points.

One final point: Remember that the introduction should be a relatively brief part of your speech, probably no more than 10–15 percent of your total speech time. Also remember that the first 45 seconds or so will likely be your most anxious moments. Therefore, it is a good idea to have your introduction very well prepared. Once you are that far into your speech you will have become acclimated to speaking to the group, and any nervousness typically begins to subside.

APPLY **WHAT YOU KNOW**
EFFECTIVE INTRODUCTIONS

Apply what you know about quality introductions by completing the following:

- Design an introduction for an upcoming classroom speech by using all the elements discussed above.

- Exchange written introductions with a classmate and share feedback.

- If audience benefits seems weak, interview several class members for suggestions on what might motivate them about your topic.

LEARNING OBJECTIVE

12.5 What functions should an effective conclusion perform, and what are the guidelines for each?

Speech Conclusions

The third part of your speech is the conclusion. Conclusions serve two functions: to summarize your main points (essentially a restatement of your thesis and preview) and to make your speech memorable. Conclusions should take no more than ten percent of your total speech time. Read Ryan's conclusion to his speech *Pirate Life* (**Figure 12.4**) and see how effective you think it is. Then let's look in detail at each of the two functions of a conclusion: a summary of main points and a memorable ending.

Figure 12.4 Ryan's Speech Conclusion

> I hope you've learned a few things about the life of a pirate today. We found that being on board ship was no treat unless you happen to really like eating hardtack. We visited several pirates including Mary Reed, Black Bart, and Henry Morgan, who was actually knighted instead of hung. And we learned some real pirate slang with words still used today.
> Just remember that it is much better to "splice the main brace" than it is to "dance the hempen jig."

Summary of Main Points

Your summary reminds your audience of your central idea and the main points you covered, which is one important way to help your audience retain the information you have provided. Although some people find it helpful to begin their summary "In conclusion," a well-designed summary statement should make it clear to your audience that you are ending your speech, without calling attention to the mechanics of your speech. Some examples of ways to lead into your summary statement include:

- So, today we have talked about the three types of skin cancer: basal cell, squamous cell, and malignant melanoma.

- Fortunately, a properly attended campfire rarely spreads out of control. However, your children should be prepared in case their clothing catches on fire by knowing these three easily remembered steps: Stop, Drop, and Roll.

- I think you can see that knowing a little more about dreams, why we have them, and what they tell us about ourselves can help you view your sleep time as more than a period of physical rest.

Memorable Ending

Your memorable closing can be accomplished in many ways. Often speakers end their speeches by using a quotation from a person who is widely recognized and respected by the audience. A good quotation will be relatively brief—perhaps one to three sentences—and should be worded in a particularly memorable way that ties together the material you presented in the body. Often good quotations are humorous, dramatic, or philosophically insightful. They should not be mere recitation of facts; they should be stated in an especially poetic or apt way.

You can also end in a memorable way by returning to a story that you used as an attention-getter, perhaps only now revealing the ending of the story or that the story is about someone they know—perhaps even you. Concluding in this way creates an appealing unity to your speech. Earlier we looked at the attention-getter from Barbara Bush's 1990 commencement address to Wellesley College. Note how she related back to her introduction and tied it in with her conclusion:

> For 50 years, it was said that the winner of Wellesley's annual hoop race would be the first to get married. Now they say the winner will be the first to become a CEO. . . . Both of those stereotypes show too little tolerance for those who want to know where the mermaids stand. . . . So I want to offer a new legend: the winner of the hoop race will be the first to realize her dream—not society's dreams—her own personal dream.
>
> And . . . who knows? Somewhere out in this audience may even be someone who will one day follow in my footsteps, and preside over the White House as the President's spouse—and I wish *him* well.

Like attention-getters in an introduction, memorable closings may use visual images. You may want to conclude with a humorous reference, possibly to some situation you shared with the audience or something you alluded to earlier in the speech. You could also construct your own quotable statement. You should not use the conclusion to introduce new ideas or evidence. And the closing thought should not be merely a repetition of points you have already made. Furthermore, your final parting thought should not be abrupt, leaving your audience to wonder if your speech is over, or end with the words, "That's it" or "That's all I have." The key to an effective closing thought is that it should be highly memorable: dramatic, poignant, humorous, clever, insightful, or powerful.

Questions and Answers (Q&A)

When you are permitting time for Questions & Answers after your speech, it is much better to divide your conclusion into its two parts, inserting the **Q&A** between the summary and the final parting thought. If you tack the Q&A onto the speech after the memorable parting thought, your true parting words will be "Thank you for your questions." This is hardly a memorable way to end your speech! Therefore, when using Q&A, your conclusion will sound something like this:

Now that we have looked at *(main point I)*, *(main point II)*, and *(main point III)*, I hope you understand the importance of *(your topic)*. Perhaps you have some questions. *(Take questions here.)* Thank you for your questions. When I think about . . . *(whatever your final thought is, goes here, and it should end memorably)*.

If your professor has assigned you to include Q&A in your informative presentation, you may be concerned about how to handle that part of your speech. We will address this issue in greater detail in Chapter 13.

APPLY **WHAT YOU KNOW**
EFFECTIVE CONCLUSIONS

Apply what you know about quality conclusions by completing the following:

- Design a possible conclusion for an upcoming classroom speech by using all the elements discussed above. Make sure

your conclusion includes a summary and memorable parting thought.

- Exchange your written conclusion with a classmate and share feedback. If time allows, practice your conclusion out loud in front of a classmate, friend, or family member.

Now that you have organized your main points and added an introduction and conclusion, the next important part of your speech is to add needed transitions to help the audience move easily through your speech.

LEARNING **OBJECTIVE**

12.6 What are transitions, and what are some suggestions for using them effectively in a speech?

Speech Transitions

A final element in planning your speech is how you move from one main point in your body to another main point. The sentences that allow you to do this are known as **transitions.** They should be planned in advance and added to your outline; if they are not, they will too often be little more than an announcement of your next main point. Another typical (but poor) transition is "Next . . ." or "Secondly . . ." These phrases are better than no transition at all, but they are not the most effective way to construct a bridge that links your main points to each other. You recall that Amy in our opening scenario was planning to speak on voting. In the following outline, Amy has begun the process of expanding her rough-draft outline into a formal outline and has added her transitions to connect her main points:

 I. Voting is a privilege that people worked hard to receive.
 A. Boston Tea Party (factual illustration)
 B. Black voting rights (quote by Martin Luther King, Jr.)
 C. Women voting rights (quote by Susan B. Anthony)
 D. Iraqi voting rights (recent news video clip)

Transition: Voting is indeed a privilege. Although you may think that you don't care who becomes governor or even president, the issues that these officials help decide may affect you as well as the things and the people you care about most.

 II. Voting affects all of us.
 A. A federal example
 B. A state example
 C. A local example

Transition: As you can see, voting does affect important issues in our lives—but you may be thinking that your single vote doesn't really matter; but it does!

 III. One vote does count!
 A. Texas admitted to the union by just one vote.
 B. Andrew Jackson saved from impeachment by one vote.
 C. Kennedy won over Nixon in 1960 by less than one vote per precinct.
 D. The electoral votes from Florida decided by 537 out of 6 million votes won the 2000 election for Bush.

Amy's transitions make use of **internal summaries** which recap previous points and **previews** which forecast or lead smoothly into points to come. In other words, as you move from main point I to main point II, you should first briefly summarize main point I, and then forecast what will be addressed in main point II. When you get to main point III (where applicable), you should recap main points I and II before previewing main point III. Transitions that accomplish this bridging in an artful way are more enjoyable and feel more like a part of the speech. For example, the following transition is acceptable:

Now that we have explored (first main point), we are ready to look at (second main point).

However, this next transition is more artful and more enjoyable to hear:

So, now that you have put all your money into purchasing the best quality supplies for your project, you don't want to just put those supplies into storage in your basement; you want to get this project built. Building a birdhouse is a relatively simple process that involves . . .

Then, when you move to your third main point, you could say,

You have now put all those expensive supplies to work and you have constructed the finest birdhouse in America. But you'll never know if it is a great birdhouse until you see birds flocking to it. So now it's time to . . .

Transitions are important in written essays but they are even more important in a speech. If readers get lost, they can always go back and reread. Listeners, however, cannot go back and relisten. It is the speaker's responsibility to make sure that the audience can follow the important ideas in the presentation. Transitions also include built-in repetition that enables an audience to remember main points long after the speech is over.

APPLY **WHAT YOU KNOW**
EFFECTIVE TRANSITIONS

Apply what you know about quality transitions by completing the following activity:

- Design a quality transition between each of your main points using your rough-draft outline completed earlier in this chapter.

- Show the rough-draft outline to one or more classmates, asking them to make suggestions for improving the clarity of your transitions if needed. Return the favor, if the classmate wishes.

Although it may seem that you are ready to begin practicing your presentation, there is one part of organizing we have yet to cover—outlining. Making a final, more polished, formal outline is extremely helpful in spotting those last-minute organization problems that need to be resolved.

Speech Outlining

When you write papers for your English or History classes, do you start with an outline? If not, you are missing the real purpose of using an outline. If you are wondering why you need an outline, see if the following makes sense.

Why Bother with Outlines?

There are actually several important reasons to prepare an outline as part of your speech organization. Let's take a brief look at each reason.

LEARNING **OBJECTIVE**

12.7 What are the types of and important reasons for preparing an outline, what is a possible alternative to an outline, and what are the six principles for effective outlining?

DEVELOPING SKILLS
HOW TO ORGANIZE USING STORYBOARDS

Storyboarding is a planning tool typically used by cartoon designers, producers of commercials, or advertising agencies to provide a graphic look at each step or frame in a video or multimedia production. This approach helps with brainstorming, makes sure everyone is clear on what is planned, and makes it easy to locate problem areas and make changes. Although there are many software programs to aid in storyboarding (such as *Macromedia Director, Hypercard,* or *StoryBoardQuick*), for the speaker's purposes, it is just as easy to sketch your own storyboards as Amy did in **Figure 12.5**.

Figure 12.5 Amy's Sample Storyboard

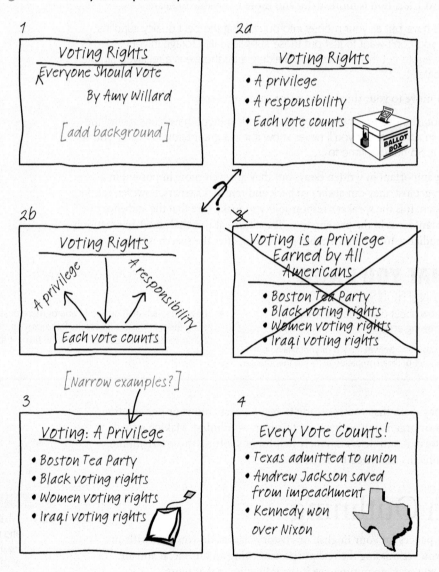

Basically, you take one or more sheets of paper and draw six to nine rectangles on them. Then begin to fill in each rectangle with a title, main points, clipart or drawings, charts or graphs, and so on. Don't try to be perfect—this is a way to brainstorm and organize. You can always come back and revise, cross out, move, and polish your first efforts. The blank space above and below the slides is an excellent place to put ideas, revision plans, or team member comments, if you are giving a team presentation.

In addition to the software mentioned earlier, one way to give you flexibility in what you put on each slide is to use *PowerPoint* software to create a rough draft of each storyboard, slide, or rectangle. By using *PowerPoint*, you can create a wide variety of charts for your statistics that look better than drawing them by hand. You can print off thumbnail copies of your slides that look like storyboards by using the following steps:

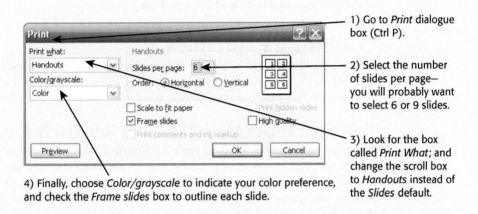

1) Go to *Print* dialogue box (Ctrl P).

2) Select the number of slides per page—you will probably want to select 6 or 9 slides.

3) Look for the box called *Print What*; and change the scroll box to *Handouts* instead of the *Slides* default.

4) Finally, choose *Color/grayscale* to indicate your color preference, and check the *Frame slides* box to outline each slide.

If you have a real dislike of outlining, are working with a team, or are just looking for a more visual way to organize, preparing storyboards is a good place to begin. Note: Using *PowerPoint* storyboards is also a good way to organize your notes to prepare for exams. A study comparing students who studied for quantum physics by writing summaries of the material with students who prepared *PowerPoint* slides of the material found that the *PowerPoint* group scored significantly better on tests (Gunel et al., 2006).

It's Easier to Conceptualize Your Ideas

An outline is basically a map for your presentation. It allows you to conceptualize the way your speech will flow, pulling the ideas and information that belong together into a cohesive structure. Without a map, you would probably find yourself spending extra time backtracking to see if you had included certain ideas. If you aren't clear, your listeners won't be either.

It's Easier to Organize and Move Points Around

When you outline it is easy to confirm that your ideas are organized. For example, if you are presenting the seven steps necessary to build a birdhouse, an outline will reveal that you may need to combine some ideas to make it manageable. For example the first two steps can be subpoints related to preparing to build the birdhouse (drawing up plans and gathering the necessary materials), the next three steps can be subpoints related to constructing the birdhouse, and the final two steps can be subpoints related to finishing the project. This would give you three main points, with all of the seven steps presented as subpoints.

It's Easier to Get Help from Others

In order to make any valuable comments on your speech content, your friends would have to take the time to read the entire manuscript before making comments. However, if you handed them an outline, in just a few moments, they would be able to ask questions and make helpful suggestions and even make comments on your sources.

A visual form of organizing and outlining called storyboarding is another way to get helpful suggestions on your speech from others. If you find organizing and outlining difficult, try storyboarding described in the *Developing Skills* feature on pages 332–333. Many people find storyboarding an effective alternative to outlining because of its visual qualities. Even if your instructor requires a full outline, storyboarding can still be useful for planning.

Outlining Principles

Effective outlining requires the use of several simple **outlining principles.** See how many of these guidelines for effective outlining you already use on a regular basis (and will probably use automatically in your storyboards without realizing it).

Principle 1: Use Main Points of Relatively Equal Value

Your main points represent two or more key ideas that are subdivisions of your overall topic and should be developed to similar degrees. You should not develop one point with extensive detail and support while barely discussing the next. Certainly, there are times that one main point will require a little more detail than another, but the difference should not be so great that the main points are significantly out of balance.

Beginning speakers often treat a definition as a main point. This is a mistake. For example, if your topic is *Euthanasia,* you will undoubtedly need to define that word for your listeners so they know exactly what you are talking about. However, giving a definition requires only a few seconds. Remember that a definition is a type of supporting material that helps you develop a main point; it is not a main point by itself.

Principle 2: Include at Least Two Items per Level

Whether dealing with main points, **subpoints** (ideas used to support the main points), or sub-subpoints (ideas or supporting materials used to support the subpoint), the first rule of outlining usually applies: If there is a 1, there should be a 2; if there is an A, there should be a B. Each of the elements in an outline is a division of the previous element. If you find yourself with only one part, you can usually expand it or combine it with another point.

Principle 3: Use Parallel Structure   The second rule of outlining

concerns parallel structure. **Parallel structure** means that your main points are worded in a similar manner grammatically or syntactically. For example, if one point begins with a noun, all points at that level should begin with a noun; if one point is a complete sentence, then all points at that level should be complete sentences. It is also advisable for subpoints to be worded using parallel structure. Here are some ways to word main points or subpoints in a parallel manner:

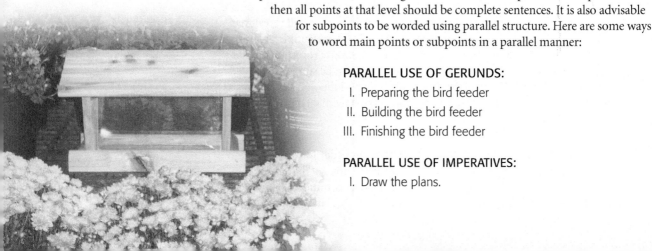

PARALLEL USE OF GERUNDS:

   I. Preparing the bird feeder

  II. Building the bird feeder

 III. Finishing the bird feeder

PARALLEL USE OF IMPERATIVES:

   I. Draw the plans.

II. Gather the materials.

III. Construct the bird feeder.

PARALLEL USE OF QUESTIONS:

I. Is global warming a real phenomenon?

II. Does global warming affect human life?

III. Can global warming be prevented?

PARALLEL SYNTAX (similar wording that repeats a key word or phrase):

I. The signs of global warming

II. The dangers of global warming

The following example illustrates a lack of parallel wording. There is an organizational structure, but, because it is not parallel, it is less clear and less coherent than the examples above:

NOT PARALLEL—MIXED CONSTRUCTIONS:

I. Is global warming a real phenomenon?

II. The signs of global warming

III. How global warming affects you

Principle 4: Don't Use Roman Numerals for Introduction, Body, or Conclusion   When outlining a speech, it is advisable to treat the Introduction, the Body, and the Conclusion as separate units. Such an outline would look like this:

INTRODUCTION:

I. Attention-getter

II. Credibility builder

III. Interest stimulator

IV. Thesis and preview

BODY:

I. First main point

II. Second main point

III. Third main point

CONCLUSION:

I. Summary

II. Memorable final thought

The reason for this suggestion is practical. It is easier for you, the speaker, to recognize the first main point in your body when it is designated with the Roman numeral I rather than with the Roman numeral II.

Principle 5: Use Standard Outline Numbering   It is also wise to make sure that you understand the sequence of numerals and letters for each level of subordination in an outline. They are as follows:

    I. Roman numeral: The main point

      A. Capital letter: The first subpoint

        1. Arabic numeral: Supporting material and subdivision of the first subpoint

          a. Lower-case letter: Supporting material and subdivisions of the first sub-subpoint

            i. Lower-case Roman numeral; used for very fine details

            ii. Lower-case Roman numeral; second detail under a

Principle 6: Use Generous Indentations

Please note the generous use of indentation. Outlines are not of much use if all of the symbols of subdivision are aligned at the left margin. One of the benefits of outlines is that the subdivision of ideas is visually clear, which is achieved through proper indentation.

Types of Outlines

There are three basic types of outlines: the rough-draft outline, the formal outline, and the speaking outline. It is important not to get these types confused.

- *Rough-draft outline.* When you begin to work on your speech you will use a **rough-draft outline** in which you sketch out the basic structure of your presentation, as discussed in Chapter 11.

- *Formal outline.* Once you have gathered supporting materials to flesh out your ideas and prove your assertions, and determined the organizational structure you will use, it is time to construct a more thorough, **formal outline** that includes much more detail than the rough-draft outline. Amy has begun to flesh out her outline and add transitions in the outline on page 330. A completed formal outline used by Ryan is located in **Figure 12.6** on pages 337–338. Some speakers also use the formal outline in the initial stages of practicing their speeches.

- *Speaking outline.* Once you reach the final stages of your practice and are ready for the actual presentation, you will want to reduce your formal outline to a **speaking outline** (as Amy has done in **Figure 12.7**). This outline consists of only the key words and phrases that will remind you of the points you wish to make and should contain as few words as possible. Only quotations, statistics, citations, and transitions should be written out in full, and these only in order to ensure accuracy. Many speakers move from a speaking outline to no outline for the actual speech. If you use quality visual aids, such as *PowerPoint* slides, you generally won't need a speaking outline at all. Speaking outlines will be covered in more detail in the next chapter on practicing presentations.

Figure 12.7 First Note Card from Amy's Speaking Outline

#1

"Voting Rights"

Introduction

- Remember 2004 election results with Bush & Kerry? (explain)
- Voting interests me because...
- 3 Aspects of voting (Preview) Vis #1

Body

I. Voting: A Privilege Vis #2

  A. Boston Tea Party

    --History

    --Fight for rights

  B. Black Voting Rights

    --MLK, JR.

    --Bloody Sunday, 1965

    --Voting Rights Act, 1965

    --Reaction to LBJ's speech and bill

[Quote from Pauley, 1998]

Figure 12.6 Ryan's Pirate Life Outline

"The Pirate Life"

General Purpose: To inform

Specific Purpose: After hearing my speech, the audience will be better educated on the real life of past pirates, rather than the image portrayed in books and movies.

The Pirate Life
- Life on board
- Famous pirates
- Pirate slang

INTRODUCTION

I. *Attention-getter:* Story of Blackbeard's last battle and death, which includes his getting shot 5 times and suffering 20 severe sword wounds before he finally died.

II. *Qualification:* Since I was age 15, I've been obsessed with pirates and have read many books on the subject.

III. *Audience Motivation:* You see a pirate's life in the movies, but, by taking a look at the real life of a pirate, you can know what it's really like.

IV. *Thesis:* [*Visual #1*] Although pirate life was not as glamorous or as exciting as portrayed in recent movies, we will travel back in time and see what it was really like on board a pirate ship, visit with several of the most famous pirates (both male and female), and learn some pirate slang that will help you feel right at home when you watch Captain Jack Sparrow in his next movie.

Introduction:
Ryan begins his speech with an illustration about Blackbeard's last battle. He lets people know how much he likes the topic by mentioning that he has read numerous books on the topic, and he states his thesis and preview of main points.
Q: *Do you think Ryan did enough to motivate his audience to want to listen?*

BODY

I. Understanding the life of a pirate starts with life on the ship. [*Visual #2*].
   A. Food
      1. Lengths of the voyages were determined by the amount of food available (Matthews, 2006).
      2. Examples of food: salted meats like beef and pork, hardtack, and oatmeal.
   B. Drink
      1. Beer, rum, cider, and water
      2. Popular drink: Grog—rum, hot water, lemon, and sugar
      3. Among the drinks, fresh water was a rarity.
   C. Crew
      1. Crews of 20–300; ships were usually crowded, depending on when the loot was obtained.
      2. Duties and titles ranged from Captain to boatswain, gunner to surgeon, to cabin boy.

Transition: Now that we've seen that life on board a pirate ship was less than glamorous, let's meet some real pirates (both men and women).

Life On Board
- Food: hardtack & salted meats
- Drink: beer, wine & cider
- Crew: 20-300 members

First Main Point:
In Ryan's first main point, he paints a pretty grim picture of the life on board ship by looking at the food, drink, and crewmates.
Q: *What types of supporting materials did Ryan use to support his first point? Did they add enough interest, clarity, and proof for you?*

II. Successful pirate ships were due to the famous pirates who ran them. [*Visual #3*]
   A. Bartholomew Roberts
      1. Nicknamed Black Bart. Had no liking for alcohol, which some suspect is why he became one of the most successful pirates of his era (Breverton, 2004).
      2. Captured over 400 ships in the space of 3 years. That's an average of 1 ship every 3 days for 3 years.
      3. His philosophy in life was "a merry life and a short one" and he accomplished that dying in a battle with the British.
   B. Henry Morgan
      1. Started out as a commissioned privateer during the English Spanish war. The war ended, and he continued to pirate Spanish vessels and became one of the most successful pirates (Konstam, 2005).

Famous Pirates
- Bartholomew Roberts
- Henry Morgan
- Mary Read

2. He was captured and held for 2 years, but, instead of standing trial, he was knighted and later became the governor of Jamaica.
3. He was later thrown out of office due to a shift of political powers and died leaving the location of his vast treasure unknown.

C. Mary Reed

1. Famous woman pirate who started out in the navy disguised as her brother and later joined the life of piracy upon being captured by pirates (Gosse, 1924, p. 154).
2. Joined forces with another fellow female pirate named Anne Bonny.
3. Known for exposing her chest in battle to distract her enemy and to show them that they were about to be killed by a woman.

Transition: So far, we've examined what life on board a pirate ship was really like and met several of the most famous pirates (including one woman). Let's end our look at the pirate life by learning some hearty pirate slang.

III. Understanding pirates requires learning the tongue of a pirate. [*Visual #4*]

A. *Dance the hempen jig*—to hang from ropes made of hemp.
B. *Jack Ketch*
  1. Jack Ketch was the hangman.
  2. To dance with Jack Ketch was also used as a term meaning "to be hung."
C. *Kiss the gunner's daughter*—to be flogged while bending over one of the ship's guns.
D. *Splice the main brace*—to take a drink.
E. *Cat-o-nine tails*
  1. A whip with nine lashes used for flogging.
  2. "To let the cat out of the bag" also derived from this term.

#4

Pirate Slang
- Dance the hempen jig
- Jack Ketch
- Kiss the gunner's daughter
- Splice the main brace
- Cat-o-nine tails

CONCLUSION

I. I hope you've learned a few things about the life of a pirate today. We found that being on board ship was no treat unless you happen to really like eating hardtack. We visited several pirates, including Mary Reed, Black Bart, and Henry Morgan, who was actually knighted instead of hung; and we learned some real pirate slang with words still used today.

II. Just remember that it is much better to "splice the main brace" than it is to "dance the hempen jig."

REFERENCES

1. Breverton, T. (2004). *Black Bart Roberts: The greatest pirate of them all.* Gretna, LA: Pelican Publishing.
2. Gosse, P. (1924). *Pirate's Who's Who.* New York: Burt Franklin. Accessed February 31, 2009 at http://books.google.com/books?id=rlXe67Wp2sIC&printsec=frontcover&dq=intitle:Pirates&lr=&as_brr=1&sig=ACfU3U0D5upNxlmnm3o-fAadcx9r0bBa5w.
3. Konstam, A. (2005). *History of Pirates.* Newport Pagnell, England: Mercury Books.
4. Matthews, John. (2006). *Pirates.* New York: Atheneum Books.

Source: "The Pirate Life" by Ryan Elliot. Reprinted by permission.

Second & Third Main Points:
Ryan did a good job of limiting his topic to only three main points—narrowing a topic is always a difficult task.
Q: *Do you think that five slang terms was the right amount?*

Transitions:
Ryan's transitions into his second and third main points are clear and interesting. By adding them to his formal outline, he shows their importance.
Q: *How big a role do you think his transitions played in the success of his presentation? Rate them on a scale of 1 to 5.*

Visual Aids:
Although he began with 10 visual aids, Ryan did a good job using only the most important slides.
Q: *Did you like Ryan's visual aids? (Check Chapter 13 for what makes a good visual aid.)*

Conclusion:
There are two main points in the conclusion of an informative speech—the summary and the memorable thought.
Q: *Does Ryan's conclusion effectively summarize and leave the audience thinking about the speech? What else should he add?*

References:
Ryan cited his sources during his presentation to add to his already broad knowledge on the topic.
Q: *Do you think Ryan's sources were good enough to give his speech credibility and add proof?*

APPLY WHAT YOU KNOW
EFFECTIVE OUTLINING

Apply what you know about outlines by completing the following activity:

- Design a formal outline for the speech you are working on or plan to give in the near future.

- Ask a classmate to make suggestions for improving the clarity of your outline. Return the favor, if the classmate wishes.
- Prepare a brief speaking outline and share with a classmate.

CHAPTER SUMMARY

Understanding the basic communication process is the first step toward becoming a competent communicator. You can determine your knowledge of the communication process by checking the skills and learning objectives presented in this chapter.

Summary of **SKILLS**

Check each skill that you now feel qualified to perform:
- ❑ I can select an appropriate pattern and successfully organize an informative speech.
- ❑ I can prepare a quality introduction and conclusion for an informative speech.
- ❑ I can apply effective transitions to an outline for an informative speech.
- ❑ I can prepare a successful outline or storyboard that follows the principles given in this chapter.

Summary of LEARNING **OUTCOMES**

12.1 *What is the definition of informative speaking, and what specific factors distinguish it from persuasion?*

- An informative speech is defined as *a speech designed to create understanding about a person, thing, event, place, problem, or concept.*
- The four specific factors that distinguish informative speaking from persuasion include speaker intent, supporting information, audience information, and speaker expectations.

12.2 *What are the patterns for organizing informative speeches, and when does each pattern work best?*

- The basic organizational patterns for informative speeches include chronological, spatial, topical, causal, and problem-solution.
- The *chronological* pattern works best when tracing the history of something or explaining a process in a step-by-step sequence; *spatial* works best when main points are related by their physical or geographical location; *topical* works best when presenting types, categories, aspects, features, or elements of a topic that have no chronological or spatial relationships; *causal* works best when one point is the cause of some phenomenon and the other point is the effect of it; and *problem-solution* works best when explaining a problem and offering an informative look at one or more possible solutions.

12.3 *What are some cultural differences and preferences in speech organization, and who uses each?*

- Cultural differences in speech organization include the linear approach, the zig-zag pattern, the circuitous path or spiral approach, and the bicycle-wheel approach.
- The linear approach is preferred by many individualistic cultures such as the United States; the zig-zag pattern is used by Romance countries such as France; the circuitous path or spiral approach is preferred by many collectivistic cultures such as Japan; the bicycle-wheel approach is used in Kenya.
- The importance of selecting the appropriate pattern, especially in light of cultural differences, is explained in the *Making Theory Practical* feature for this chapter.

12.4 *What functions should an effective speech introduction perform, and what are the types or guidelines for each?*

- An effective introduction includes several functions: catch audience attention, build a feeling of goodwill, establish credibility, point out the benefits of your speech, and clarify your central idea with a thesis and preview of main points.
- When each function should be used depends entirely on your specific audience. Also, an effective introduction should take no more than 10–15 percent of your total speech time. See pages 322–327 for additional guidelines.

ORGANIZATION **AND YOUR CAREER**

LEARNING **OBJECTIVE**

12.8 What informative skills covered in this chapter relate specifically to your career?

The following career features take a look at how important informative speaking and organization are in the workplace and specifically to careers related to business, education, and healthcare. Whether you are interested in one of those career fields or will be a consumer of the services of these areas, the following information should be of interest to you.

SPOTLIGHT ON **THE IMPORTANCE OF ORGANIZATION**

BUSINESS

Organizing a sales presentation begins with a clear knowledge of the customer—your audience. Use the system for organizing questions called **ADAPT** (Ingram et al., 2008), which moves from open to specific questions to relate your product to the customer and transition right into the presentation or sale:

- **A = Assessment questions** seek general information—"Who is involved in making this purchase decision?"

- **D = Discovery questions** look for problems or frustrations—"How do you feel when . . . ?"

- **A = Activation questions** seek to uncover the seriousness of any problems—"What problems does this cause?"

- **P = Projection questions** help the customer imagine how much better things could be without these problems—"If we could_____, would it help you_____?"

- **T = Transition questions** confirm the customer's desire to solve the problem—"Would you be interested in pursuing an arrangement with our company?"

EDUCATION

There is a direct relationship between teachers who give clear, organized explanations and presentations and student learning—the better the teacher's organization, the more the students learn (Comadena et al., 2007; Evertson & Emmer, 2009). Also, in most cases, there is an advantage to presenting ideas clearly at the beginning of a presentation. In the *Academic Leader*, a newsletter for deans and department chairs, Strikwerda (2006) suggests that it is important to "Get the main points out very quickly. You put the audience at ease immediately if you show that you know what you are going to talk about" (p. 6).

Strikwerda also offers an interesting piece of advice for potential educators: Save all your speeches, identifying the date, audience, and what parts of the speech did and did not work. Assessing your individual and team presentations in this manner is an excellent way to evaluate your strengths and weaknesses.

HEALTHCARE

In order for the dissemination of healthcare information to be effective, health communication writers Kreps and Thornton (1992) recommend the following: "the messages presented should be well-organized and persuasive to successfully influence the health beliefs, attitudes, values, and behaviors of audience members" (p. 126). They suggest the following basic organization (p. 129):

1. Secure attention.
2. State a problem or need.
3. Offer a solution.
4. Help the audience visualize the desirability of the solution.
5. Invite definite action.

The key ideas presented in each step need to be "replicated and reinforced" in multiple methods. For example, a procedure explained orally should be reinforced through a visual aid showing each step or a model that can be manipulated by the speaker.

CAREER MOMENT **POLISHING YOUR SPEAKING SKILLS**

As mentioned earlier, oral and written skills rank number one in the list of skills that employers look for in job candidates; they also rank as the number one skill most lacking in today's candidates (Job Outlook 2009). The problem is so bad that "states spend nearly $250 million a year on remedial writing training for government workers" (Daft, 2008, p. 576). Daft also notes that "30 percent of all business memos and e-mails are written simply to get clarification about an earlier written communication that didn't make sense to the reader" (p. 577).

In these turbulent times, one way to make yourself more attractive to interviewers is to develop your writing and speaking abilities. Since both writing and speaking benefit from organizational and outlining skills, the content discussed in this chapter is a good place to begin to enhance your employability skills. Don't

overlook the use of *PowerPoint* slides since they help with organization and retention, as mentioned in this chapter's *Developing Skills* feature.

An other way to improve your organization skills is to work with scrambled outlines. Go to MyCommunicationLab activities for Chapter 12 and look for the four scrambled outline exercises. Time yourself on each outline and notice how each one takes you less and less time as your skills in organizing improve. Don't take a casual approach to your chosen career; stand out from the pack by improving your communication and organizing skills.

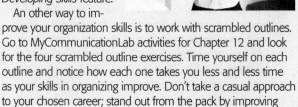

CONNECTING TO **BUSINESS**

If you are considering a business or professional career, speaking skills will be essential. However, as our *Career Moment* indicated, the speaking and writing skills that are the most sought after by employers are lacking in the typical college graduate. Organization is one of these skills that employees don't have—if you can learn to organize a speech, you can effectively organize a written report. To determine more about organization in the workplace, complete the following activity.

ACTIVITY Interview three to five business managers and ask them the following questions. Be prepared to report back to your classmates:

1. What are the main organizational problems you see in spoken and written reports?

2. What organizational patterns (list the informative patterns for them) are used the most often in your company. Why are they the most effective?

CONNECTING TO **EDUCATION**

If you are considering a career in education, your ability to organize your course materials will make a difference in student learning and satisfaction. The best student learning occurs when you show students how your content fits into organizational systems they already understand (Mottet et al., 2006, p. 26). One way to learn how to make content relevant is by thinking back over how instructors you had in the past organized their materials and/or lectures.

ACTIVITY In groups of four or five discuss the following questions:

1. Share memories of an instructor who poorly organized class materials or lectures. Specifically, what did that instructor do or not do that caused the problem? How did this instructor's poor organization affect you and your learning? Share your memories with your group members.

2. Share memories of an instructor you would select as a role model for effective organization of course content and lectures. What did that instructor do that made organization clear and enjoyable? How did this instructor's effective organization affect learning?

3. Make a list of at least five guidelines for beginning teachers to follow when organizing their courses and/or lectures.

CONNECTING TO **HEALTHCARE**

If you are considering a career in healthcare, you will likely have many opportunities to present information to patients. Whether patients understand and recall your information may depend on how well you organize what you say in the patient interview. According to Stewart and Cash (2008), "In a typical 20-minute interview, less than 2 minutes is devoted to information giving" (p. 394), and, of that information, patients may remember no more than two items.

ACTIVITY In groups of three to five people, answer the following questions:

1. Based on information from this text, brainstorm a list of guidelines for organizing your questions and information when interviewing a patient. For example, you might suggest beginning with an open-ended question such as "Tell me about your symptoms." Each additional question becomes less open and more specific, which allows you to follow-up on any problem areas noticed in the patient's answer to the first question.

2. Make sure your list includes ways to help the patient remember the information covered in the interview.

3. Be prepared to share your list of guidelines with other groups or the class.

▶ Log onto MyCommunicationLab.com to access Connecting to Psychology and Connecting to Science, Technology, Engineering, and Math—both with related activities.

12.5 *What functions should an effective conclusion perform, and what are the guidelines for each?*

- A successful conclusion includes two main functions: to summarize your main points (essentially a restatement of your thesis and preview) and to make your speech memorable.

- An effective conclusion should take no more than 10 percent of your total speech time. See pages 328–330 for additional guidelines.

12.6 *What are transitions, and what are some suggestions for using them effectively in a speech?*

- Transitions—including internal summaries and previews—are words used to effectively move the audience from one point in your speech to another.

- Instead of using "Next" or "Secondly," try using longer transitions to add interest as well. See pages 330–331 for additional guidelines.

12.7 *What are the types of and important reasons for preparing an outline, what is a possible alternative to an outline, and what are the six principles for effective outlining?*

- There are three types of outlines used in preparing a speech: the rough-draft outline, the formal outline, and the speaking outline.

- There are three important reasons for preparing one or more outlines as you build your speech: First, it's easier to conceptualize your ideas; second, it's easier to organize and move points around; third, it's easier to get help from others.

- A possible alternative to outlining is to use a tool called storyboarding, illustrated in the *Developing Skills* feature in this chapter.

- The six principles of effective outlining include: 1—using main points of relatively equal value; 2—including at least two items per level (except in rare circumstances); 3—use parallel structure; 4—don't use roman numerals for the introduction, body, or conclusion; 5—use standard outline numbering; and 6—use generous indentations.

12.8 *What informative skills covered in this chapter relate specifically to your career (see highlighted fields of business, education, and healthcare)?*

- The *Spotlight on, Career Moment*, and *Connecting to* features highlight the value of communication in the fields of business, education, and healthcare.

SOLVE IT NOW!

Taking into consideration all that you have learned about organization from this chapter, what advice would you give Jeff in our opening scenario about how to organize and outline his speech?*

- Looking at Jeff's ideas for information to be covered in his speech (see his notes in the opening scenario), which organizational pattern do you think would make the best use of his information?

- Construct an outline to show how you would place Jeff's information in a speech, using the pattern you selected above. Start by listing the main points.

- Add transitions between each main point in Jeff's outline and suggest a possible successful attention-getter.

- What would you suggest for an effective attention-getter and a memorable ending for Jeff's speech?

- Based on information in this chapter, what communication goals should Jeff adopt that would help his speech preparation the most? Why?

*(Check your answers with those located in MyCommunicationLab, Scenario Analysis for Chapter 12)

The next chapter will continue preparing you for successful speaking by covering effective verbal and visual delivery.

KEY TERMS

attention-getter	p. 323	internal summaries	p. 331	Q&A	p. 329	speaking outline	p. 336
causal pattern	p. 320	narrative	p. 324	rapport	p. 326	startling statement	p. 324
chronological pattern	p. 319	outlining principles	p. 334	rhetorical question	p. 323	storyboarding	p. 332
credibility	p. 326	parallel structure	p. 334			subpoints	p. 334
formal outline	p. 336	personal anecdote	p. 324	rough-draft outline	p. 336	topical pattern	p. 320
informative speech	p. 317	previews	p. 331			transitions	p. 330
internal organization	p. 320	problem-solution pattern	p. 321	spatial (geographical) pattern	p. 319		

SKILL BUILDERS

1. If we haven't convinced you yet that outlines are important, try organizing with color (Hearn, 1999). The whole purpose of an outline is to help you easily see the divisions of your speech and tell whether any changes need to be made. Writing your speech out in manuscript form makes it almost impossible to analyze your organization—an outline is definitely an improvement; an outline using color-coding is even better. It allows instant visualization of how your ideas relate.

Begin by selecting several colors to use on your outline, e.g., black, dark blue, green, purple, brown, orange, and red. If any object in your speech is normally seen in a particular color, using that color will make the point easier to remember than selecting an atypical color (Allen, 1990). Each section of your speech outline should be in a different color; use a shadow around text in lighter colors. For example:

I. **Use red (color #1) for each main point.**

  A. **Use dark-blue (color #2) for second-level heads or supporting materials.**

    1. **Select another color (color #3) for the third-level heads or supports.**

    2. **Continue with same color.**

  B. **Back to dark-blue for subpoint B.**

    1. **Color #3 indicates supporting materials on this third level.**

      a. **New color (color #4) for fourth-level supporting materials.**

      b. **Continue same color.**

    2. **Back to color #3 for level-three heads or supports.**

    3. **Continue with same color.**

II. **Back to red for your second main point (first-level head).**

  A. **Dark blue (color #2) to indicate supporting materials.**

    1. **Color #3 for third-level heads.**

    2. **Continue with same color.**

  B. **Back to dark blue (color #2) for second-level heads.**

  C. **Continue with same color.**

2. Critically Evaluating Print Materials Using the critical evaluation form from Chapter 1, select and evaluate an article that relates to outlining or organization from one of the databases available through your college library. *EBSCOhost* or *ProQuest* would be good databases to begin your search. Be prepared to share your observations with your classmates.

3. In groups select one of the following topics:

- Attention Deficit Hyperactivity Disorder (ADHD)
- Buying and Selling Textbooks on *Amazon*
- Wasted Food in America
- The NFL Draft
- Guidelines for Purchasing a Dog (or Cat)
- Svalbard Global Seed Vault

Have each group member do a little research to become familiar with the topic (if needed); then, at a scheduled time, complete the following:

1. Decide on possible main points—the speech may be either informative or persuasive.

2. Decide on each step of the speech introduction.

Be prepared to present your introduction to the class (one student could present the entire introduction, or each step could be presented by a different student). The class should evaluate each introduction by suggesting two things they especially liked and two things that could use some improvement. If time allows, each group could make the suggested changes and present their introduction a second time. Discuss whether the changes improved the overall introduction and why.

EXPLORE SOME MORE . . .

1. To listen to one of the 100 Best Speeches of the Twentieth Century, go to http://www.AmericanRhetoric.com and click on Top 100 Speeches. Most speeches are available in audio, video, and manuscript form.

2. To read current presentations given by speakers from a variety of professions, go to your college or library database called *EBSCOhost* and search in *Academic Search Complete* or the *Military and Government Collection* for *Vital Speeches of the Day*. Select a speech and critique the organizational pattern that was used, the introduction and conclusion.

3. Looking for a good book that includes great advice on making quality presentations? We suggest you read *The Elements of Great Speechmaking: Adding Drama & Intrigue* by Robert V. Smith (2004, University Press of America), *Presenting to Win: The Art of Telling Your Story* by Jerry Weisman (2006, Pearson Education), and *Perfect Speeches for all Occasions* by Matt Shinn (Random House Books, 2010).

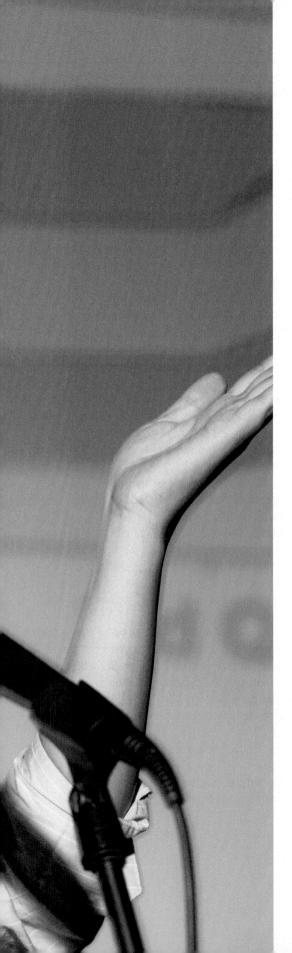

13 Adding Visuals and Practicing Your Presentation

After studying this chapter you should be able to . . .
- Identify various types of visual aids including PowerPoint and prepare several of them so they communicate effectively and look professional.
- Adapt your delivery method, visual aids, and speech content to different audience types.
- Evaluate your personal verbal and nonverbal delivery and apply text suggestions for any needed improvements.
- Cite your sources appropriately during a presentation.

CHAPTER SUMMARY ⟩ P. 368

"Hey, Val, thanks so much for giving me a ride," Amina said as she slipped in and buckled up. "I'll return the favor once my car is running."

"No problem. Say, since we're going to the same place every day, would you be interested in carpooling?" Valerie asked.

"Sounds great to me," Amina agreed. "How's your student teaching going?"

"So far, so good. But all I've been doing is observing; next week, I do my first real teaching. I'll have to admit I'm a little nervous about it."

Amina nodded. "Same here. I present Monday, so I know what I'll be doing all weekend. I have to use PowerPoint slides with my lecture, and I certainly don't want to be one of those presenters who just reads word-by-word from slides, usually bad ones, and bores everyone to death. Do you think most teachers practice their lectures?"

"I figure they probably did when they were student teaching," Valerie suggested. "Surely after they've been teaching a while, they don't have to actually practice. I have noticed though, that my best teachers do seem to be using up-to-date information and PowerPoint slides, so I would assume that they do have to work all the time on making their presentations better. I do my first presentation on Tuesday, and my big concern is how to make equations interesting to high-schoolers."

"You know what?" Amina responded. "I know the stereotype that math teachers are boring, but, honestly, my high school algebra teacher was really good. He made us enjoy math, and, trust me, that was no small feat!"

"What did he do that made the difference? This speaking to large groups is new to me, and I could sure use some tips," Valerie admitted.

"I'm not sure how to explain it," Amina replied. "For one thing, he seemed to really like his subject a lot."

Valerie nodded. "I've had teachers like that, too. I mean, I'm sure they all must enjoy their subject, but some are better at communicating it."

Amina nodded in agreement. "You know, in our Education classes we're always talking about 'best practices.' Maybe what we need to do is pinpoint exactly what makes the great teachers different. Being an expert in their field isn't enough. Somehow the good teachers are able to help their students find the subject interesting as well as informative. I think it's all in how they communicate. Why don't we think about the really good teachers we've had and see if we can find some common traits? Then we can get together this weekend and compare notes."

"Great idea! Want to meet for lunch tomorrow?" Valerie asked as she pulled up to Amina's apartment.

"Works for me," said Amina as she opened the car door. "I'll call you in the morning, and we can decide where to meet. Thanks again for the ride."

Amina has recognized an important truism about public speaking: No matter how well you know your material, you still have to make it interesting to your audience. Although she and Valerie may not have stopped to think about how good speech delivery happens, they clearly know that it matters. As you read this chapter, work to identify the skills and behaviors that Valerie and Amina—and you—will find useful in making presentations to classes and planning PowerPoint visuals for future audiences.

SOLVE IT NOW! ⟩ P. 372 ⟩

By this point in your speech preparation—as with the students in our opening scenario—you have given careful consideration to your topic and purpose and you have developed a thesis that includes the main ideas you will cover. You have gathered sufficient material to make your speech interesting and to clarify difficult concepts, and, if your speech is persuasive, you have found data that will enable you to prove your arguments. Now it is time to turn your attention to the final step—practicing your speech for an effective verbal and nonverbal delivery, including using visual aids effectively. Let's begin by looking at how you develop the visual aids you will use in your speech.

Preparing Quality Visual Aids

The skill with which you use **visual aids** (such as flipcharts, objects, or computer-generated visuals like PowerPoint) reinforces or distracts from your message and your credibility. Visual aids are appropriately named because they should "aid" your presentation of information—not replace it. Instead, some speakers use so many visual aids that the audience becomes distracted or even bored; others put way too much information on their visuals and read directly from them; still others load their computer visuals with so many pictures, silly clipart, and motion that they lose credibility as a speaker. We will address these problems in this section on preparing quality visual aids so that they will be an aid to both you and your audience.

LEARNING **OBJECTIVE**

13.1 What are the general types of visual aids, how are they used in a speech, and what are the design principles and general guidelines for using PowerPoint effectively?

Types of Visual Aids

Many types of visual aids are available for a speaker to use to illustrate or support points in a speech. We will look at those that are used most often: audiovisual aids; computer-generated visuals; flip charts and posters; handouts, models, and objects; and markerboards and chalkboards.

- **Audiovisual aids**—including sound bites, video clips, movie clips, podcasts of music, speeches, or procedures from the following: PowerPoint clipart, library databases (such as *Opposing Viewpoints* or *eLibrary*), *Google's YouTube,* DVDs, or CDs. Effective audiovisual aids should last no longer than thirty seconds. If you are using PowerPoint, inserting these audiovisual aids directly into your slides or linking to them makes a smooth, professional presentation.

- **Computer-generated visuals**—prepared on software programs such as PowerPoint and usually shown on wall screens. They can be shown on a computer (if your audience is small enough) or posted to the Internet for audience convenience. Tips for creating and using PowerPoint are included later in this chapter.

When used well, objects add interest and clarity to a presentation.

- **Flip charts and posters**—used on self-standing or table easels for groups of no more than 25. Even with a small audience it is important to make sure your print is large enough to be read easily (test your visual for readability in a room similar in size to your actual speech room), and it is important that you stand to the side so you won't block the visual from the audience.

- **Handouts and objects**—used to add a personal touch to your presentation. If the object is too small to be viewed easily by the audience, place it on a document camera which will magnify the image onto a wall screen, or photograph it or a similar object for use on PowerPoint. Passing objects around the audience should normally be avoided because it distracts from what you are saying. Handouts can also be distract-ing—people will read them instead of listening to you. Unless you want the audience to refer to the materials, it is usually best to wait until the end of the presenta-tion to distribute them. Most handouts merely serve as a reminder of speech content. To use them to improve listener learning, handouts should "complement rather than duplicate a PowerPoint presentation" (Kinchin, 2006). In business settings, however, when a large amount of material is presented and will be referred to at a later date, distributing duplicates of your PowerPoint slides might be useful.

- **Markerboards and chalkboards**—available in most speaking situations but should be your last choice. Your back will be toward the audience while you are writing on the boards, and your voice will be more difficult to hear since it is projected away from the audience rather than toward them.

General Guidelines for Using Visual Aids Successfully

The purpose of using visual aids is to help you communicate your ideas—not to replace you, but to "aid" you. Although there are always exceptions to any rule, the following guidelines should help you create and use visuals successfully:

- *Strive for professionalism.* Your specific audience will determine how professional you need to be, but mistakes such as spelling errors and inappropriate pictures always take away from your professionalism. When using computer-generated visuals (e.g., PowerPoint), work for consistency by using the same background color and design as well as placing photos or clip art in the same general location on each visual. When using posters or models or other types of visuals, make sure that these, too, are professional in appearance and in the way they are managed.

- *Strive for simplicity.* No more than one-fourth of what you plan to say in your speech should appear on your visuals—so keep them simple and easy for the audience to read. Also, simplicity requires that you have no more than one idea per visual and that you limit the total number of visuals used (one or two for each main point should be plenty). Even if you are using flip charts, posters, or objects, keep in mind the saying, "Less is more." An audience can be overwhelmed with too much of anything. Especially limit the use of motion and sound if you are using PowerPoint—hand clapping or spinning objects may seem unique the first time we hear or see them but become progressively more annoying each time they are used.

- *Strive for clarity*. Nothing is more frustrating for audience members than to have a speaker say, "As you can clearly see . . ." when the object is too small to be seen, or the text is too small to be read. To ensure clarity of text when using a chalkboard, markerboard, poster, or flipchart, make your capitals approximately 3 inches high and your basic text approximately 1.5 inches high. Titles on PowerPoint slides (or other computer-generated visuals) should be no smaller than 40 points—larger is better. The text for main points generally should be at least 26 to 32 points, and text on charts should be at least 18 points.

© Randy Glasbergen.
www.glasbergen.com

"You have been accused of cruel and abusive behavior. Is it true you made your staff sit through a PowerPoint presentation?"

© 2005 by Randy Glasbergen.

The color of your text is another way to improve the clarity of your visuals. If you are using a flipchart or white markerboard, avoid pastel colors—use dark colors such as blue or black instead. When using computer-generated visuals, remember that light backgrounds require dark-colored text; darker backgrounds require light-colored text. One light color that has excellent clarity is yellow. In fact, according to researchers, the color yellow is remembered better than any other color (Bynum et al., 2006). Avoid the color combination of red and brown, which look the same at a distance. For additional clarity, add a shadow that outlines the text and any figures used—especially if the text or figures are fairly light and need to stand out from the background. Finally, when practicing your speech, check the clarity of your visuals and make any needed corrections. For additional clarity tips, see the general design principles included in the *Making Theory Practical* feature later in this chapter.

Another way to achieve clarity in use of your visuals is to make sure your audience understands what the visual is telling them. Don't assume that they understand the significance of the data. For example, you might show a graph and then say,

> "As you can see by this data from the Pew Internet and American Life Project, 2004, almost as many Americans between the ages of 18–29 receive their news from comedy TV shows as receive it from the nightly network news. This is additional evidence of the need for college students to be taught to distinguish between credible news sources and entertainment. Clearly we need an emphasis on media literacy."

- *Prepare for possible problems*. Most problems that occur with visuals relate to technology problems at the site or with your computer-generated slides. To minimize problems, be sure to try your presentation on several other computers. It's possible that you think you have saved your presentation to a CD or USB flash drive but, when trying it out on another computer, find that you actually saved it to your hard drive instead. It's also possible that you think all your pictures and photos are working, only to click on a slide during your presentation to find a large X where that special photo should be. Avoid this situation by rehearsing your presentation complete with the visuals and by putting your PowerPoint presentation into a file and embedding any special pictures, fonts, or sounds into the same file. Finally, bring at least one backup with you and send your presentation to your e-mail account so that you can access it from the Internet in case of problems.

MAKING THEORY PRACTICAL
BASIC DESIGN PRINCIPLES

One of the reasons that so many visual aids (especially those made using PowerPoint) are so boring and confusing is because they are no longer produced by art departments. Instead, as Tad Simons, past editor-in-chief of *Presentations Magazine* said in an interview with *Presentations.com* (Bajaj, 2004), "people without a lick of design sense are out there creating their own slides, inflicting their ineptness on unsuspecting audiences everywhere" (¶ 13). For example, if you aren't sure about the answers to the following questions, you could use some design training:

- Is it a good idea to double space between main points?
- What should you do to give your slides a clean, professional appearance?
- What elements, other than pictures, are sure to create a definite visual attention-getter?

Author
Robin Williams in *The Non-Designer's Design Book* (2008) has identified four **basic design principles.** These principles— contrast, repetition, alignment, and proximity—will improve the appearance, clarity, and professionalism of all types of text and graphic visual aids. There is no need for "wimpy" visuals when you can use the following design principles to make them into "wow" visuals:

Contrast
The idea behind contrast is to avoid elements on the page that are merely *similar*. If the elements (type, color, size, line thickness, shape, space, etc.) are not the *same,* then make them *very different.* Contrast is often the most important visual attraction on a page—it's what makes a reader look at the page in the first place.

Repetition
Repeat visual elements of the design throughout the piece. You can repeat colors, shapes, textures, spatial relationships, line thicknesses, fonts, sizes, graphic concepts, etc. This develops the organization and strengthens the unity.

Alignment
Nothing should be placed on the page arbitrarily. Every element should have some visual connection with another element on the page. This creates a clean, sophisticated, fresh look.

Proximity
Items relating to each other should be grouped close together. When several items are in close proximity to each other, they become one visual unit rather than several separate units. This helps organize information, reduces clutter, and gives the reader a clear structure (Williams, 2008, p. 13).

PRACTICAL USES
If you want your visuals to be noticeably more professional-looking, Williams's basic design principles provide the answer. To illustrate these four principles, let's use a simple PowerPoint visual (**Figure 13.1**):

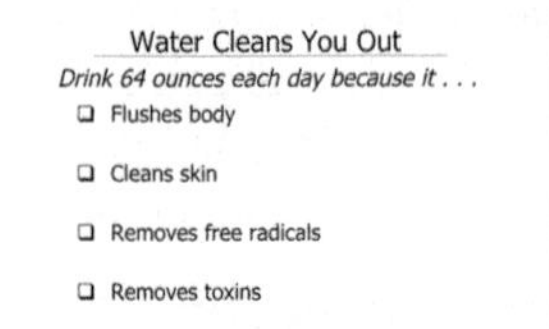

You may be thinking that this visual looks pretty good—it doesn't have too many words, and the typeface is large enough to read. Although these points are true, this visual doesn't follow the basic design principles for the following reasons:

**Figure 13.1
Ineffective Visual**

Water Cleans You Out
Drink 64 ounces each day because it . . .
❑ Flushes body
❑ Cleans skin
❑ Removes free radicals
❑ Removes toxins

- There is *no contrast*. Everything on the visual is in Tahoma typeface, and although the title is 36 points, it doesn't stand out from the subtitle in 30-point type or the main points in 32-point type. There is no color or boldface to contrast, and even the empty bullets are bland. Basically your eyes don't know where to look.

- There is *no repetition* (except for the bullets). Organization is strengthened by repeating visual elements—e.g., repeating the color of a title in the bullets and the clipart, including a line at the top of the visual that appears someplace else in the slide, or matching the boldface in the title with boldfaced words in the text or a dark element in a photo. Other than the bullets, there is no repetition in this visual.

- *Alignment* is weak. Although centering is a form of alignment (as used by the title, underline, and subtitle), it is not carried through to the main points. The most professional visuals have visual alignment on the left and right sides as well as at the top and bottom. Professional visuals also have **white space** (space with nothing in it) around all outside edges that also adds to the visual organization of the slide. Although this visual has white space, it has too much on the right side with no structural purpose. The only things that align on this visual are the bullets, but they don't align with anything else. Alignment gives a visual that "clean, sophisticated, fresh look."

- *Proximity* is missing. Proximity means that items that go together should be grouped together and should appear visually as a unit. In this visual the main points are double spaced which makes them look like separate items instead of a unit. This is also the reason that the bars in a chart or bar graph should be wider than the space between them. Using some space between text items and figures to give structure to the information on your slides helps the audience grasp the content on the visual faster. In fact, Mayer (2001) in his **contiguity principle** says that audiences learn better when pictures on slides are placed immediately next to the information they represent.

The following visual (**Figure 13.2**) is a possible way that this original visual could be revised using Williams's basic design principles. It is a definite improvement, isn't it?

In this revised visual, your eyes now know where to look, and it grabs your attention.

Figure 13.2
Effective Visual

- It definitely has *contrast* with typeface size, color, and boldness. The title typeface is Rockwell Extra Bold 60 points, which contrasts with the main points in Century at 32 points.
- *Repetition* occurs with the use of blue in the title, bullets, and clipart; the use of similar lines to accent the title and clipart, and the match of a second color in the subtitle with the color of the lines.
- *Alignment* on the right and left gives a clean, pleasing structure to the visual. Notice that both lines and the clipart align on the right side and that the bullets, subtitle, title, and title underline align on the left side. The white space is even on all sides, which avoids a cluttered look. Also notice that the bottom line not only aligns with the clipart and title underline on the right side, it also aligns with the word *toxins* in the last main point. Nothing on a visual should be randomly placed if you want that professional look.
- Finally, the main points look like a unit because now they have *proximity* but are not so close that they appear crowded.

With the help of Williams's basic design principles, you now should be able to answer the three questions asked at the beginning of this feature and use these principles to produce professional visual aids of your own.

- *Focus on the audience during your presentation.* No matter what type of visual aids you plan to use, beware that inexperienced speakers tend to look at the visuals more than the audience. Rehearse your presentation, looking at your visuals as little as possible while making direct eye contact with your audience. If using a flipchart or poster on an easel, stand beside the visual so that you don't block the audience's view. If using a computer, look at the computer's screen instead of turning to look at the wall screen. If you need to point to an object on the screen, step back beside the screen. In that way, when you point, you won't have to turn your back to the audience. Practice using a laser pointer and/or a remote presentation mouse that allows for flexibility of movement or, better yet, **highlight** the words that you want emphasized directly in your PowerPoint slides. Do not read word-for-word from your visuals or sound too formal—just talk to the audience in a conversational voice. According to the **personalization principle** (Mayer, 2001), audiences actually learn more when speakers use a conversational delivery.

Using PowerPoint Successfully

One of the most used software programs for computer-generated visual aids is Microsoft's PowerPoint. In fact, it is estimated that more than 30 million PowerPoint presentations were given daily using PowerPoint 2003 (Goldstein, 2003). Thinking of all the boring, poorly designed presentations we have seen, it seems obvious that just because PowerPoint is so easy to use doesn't mean that people should use it without training in design. In fact, Sandberg (2006) says that "bad PowerPoint presentations cost companies $252 million a day in wasted time" (p. B1).

Each of the following sample slides contains design strengths as well as design problems that limit effectiveness (based on principles from Holcombe & Stein, 1996 and Paradi, 2007). Note each problem and its solution for use in your own slide preparations.

Figure 13.3 Slide A

Problem Slide A (Figure 13.3)

- **Problem 1:** *There are way too many words*—just looking at this slide will cause the audience to stop listening. **Solution:** *Limit information to what can be read in six seconds or less— "the Rule of Six."* Use no more than six lines of text and no more than six words per line if you want your audience to grasp the content in six seconds. Why six seconds? Because longer than six seconds and your audience moves from a listening mode into a reading mode. As we mentioned in Chapter 4 on listening, audiences can't read and listen at the same time. They can switch back and forth between listening and reading but they can't do both simultaneously.

- **Problem 2:** *The text is in all caps*—this really slows down comprehension (Adams & Dolin, 2001). **Solution:** *Use upper and lowercase text for main points (and titles).* With all caps there is not the instant recognition that is provided by the dot of the letter "i" or the "t" or "g" that extend above and below words. Save all caps for the occasional word you want to emphasize.

- **Problem 3:** *Main points are in complete sentences*—unnecessary words also slow comprehension. **Solution:** *Main points should be phrases or single words—not complete sentences.* Complete sentences take too long to decipher and indicate to the audience members that this presentation is likely to be really boring. If the speaker reads each of these main points word-for-word, it is even more annoying. Don't forget that making your main points parallel also speeds audience comprehension. For example, the first three points in Slide A could be revised into parallel phrases:

  - Prescription drugs—$200 billion per year
  - Health benefits—dropped by many employers
  - Expensive drugs—hurting the elderly

- **Problem 4:** *The title is missing.* **Solution:** *All slides should have an identifying title.* Without a title or heading, Slide A is confusing—figuring out what the subject is takes so much effort the audience is likely to tune out. Even if your slide is basically a picture or chart, it still needs a title to aid comprehension.

- **Strength 1:** *The background color is pleasing—better than stark white.* There is nothing wrong with using a light or pale background such as cream, beige, or light blue; however, a stark white background can be hard on the eyes. Also, select a dark text when using a light background; use a light text (such as white or yellow) when using a dark background. If you aren't sure about the quality of the wall screen or the lighting in the room, stick with lighter backgrounds; if the equipment is good, a dark background can be very effective.

- **Strength 2:** *The photo "anchors" the main idea of the slide.* Photos and clipart should be chosen with care because humans have an amazing capacity to remember pictures (Nickerson, 1980), especially if the pictures are vivid (Hishitani, 1991). Selecting a picture with no strong connection to your topic just to have a picture is a roadblock to memory. Because Slide A refers to prescription drugs, this colorful photo of pills ready to be dispensed **anchors** the topic to the photo. Later when the audience tries to remember the points on the slide, the photo of pills will jog their memories. To illustrate the recall power of pictures, think of an exam you have taken where you couldn't remember a specific fact. However, you were sure that the information was on the left side of the page under a cartoon. Once you remembered the specific cartoon (the visual anchor in this case), the chances are that you also recalled the missing fact.

Problem Slide B (Figure 13.4)

- **Problem 1:** *Text color makes main points extremely hard to read.* **Solution:** *Use a light color with a defining shadow to make text stand out clearly in front of a busy or multicolored background.* Using the wrong color for your text can make it difficult or impossible to read. In this situation, yellow text would not only stand out but would add repetition with the yellow flowers; the title and bullets could be a different color—white, perhaps.

- **Problem 2:** This is another example of using *way too many words!* **Solution:** *Follow the Rule of Six and use fewer words* (see Slide A). Instead of the seven lines of text used on slide B, one line per bullet would allow for faster audience comprehension. Fewer words would also allow for use of a larger typeface, making the text easier to read.

- **Strength:** *Using a picture as the background is a good idea.* In this slide on water gardens, the picture of a water garden adds interest and clarity to the speech. However, in most cases, it is better to use the *washout* feature on PowerPoint to fade the background, allowing the text to stand out.

Figure 13.4 Slide B

Problem Slide C (Figure 13.5)

- **Problem 1:** *The title uses a distracting, difficult-to-read typeface.* **Solution:** *Use a simple, readable typeface.* There are so many fun typefaces available with PowerPoint that it is easy to get carried away. The script with curlique typeface used in slide C may be cute, but is difficult to read and doesn't seem to fit with the content of biting dogs or the background design. The fastest typeface to read is a sans serif typeface such as Arial, Tahoma, or Verdana. A **sans serif typeface** has a clean, geometric look without any finishing strokes or extending lines that are found on **serif typefaces,** such as Times New Roman or Century. Serif typefaces can be used for your main points and are especially good when the text is small as on charts or the legend that accompanies a chart.

- **Problem 2:** *The title includes too many words.* **Solution:** *Limit the title to essential words only—use a subtitle if more information is needed.* A good title should instantly

Figure 13.5 Slide C

grab attention and make the focus of the slide clear. According to Peoples (1996), an effective visual aid looks like "a billboard on an interstate highway that people can read going by at 65 mph" (p. 249). The title of your slide should be like that part of the billboard that first grabs the attention of those passing by. A good title for Slide C would be "Why Dogs Bite" or "Biting Dogs." If the speaker planned to use three main points in the speech about dogs—Breeds, History, and Behavior—the title might read, "Dog Behavior" with a subtitle of "Why some dogs bite." To see how a subtitle might look, go back to Figures 13.1 and 13.2 and look at the slides on ineffective and effective design principles or the "No Child Left Behind" slide below.

- **Problem 3:** *The text used for the main points is too small for easy reading.* **Solution:** *Increase the text size to 26 or 32 points and remove all unnecessary words.* The text in Slide C is 16 points—much too small for an audience to read easily. The only place where you could use text this small is the credit line under a photo. Even the text on a pie chart should be at least 18 points. By removing the sentences and leaving only the essential words, the text size in this visual could be increased to at least 26 points and probably larger, depending on the typeface selected.

- **Problem 4:** *This slide includes nothing to aid memory of content.* **Solution:** *Add a close-up picture of a dog showing its teeth ready to bite.* Photos and clipart if selected carefully do more than add color and interest to a speech: they serve as anchors to help improve the chances that listeners will be able to recall the information you are presenting.

- **Problem 5:** *The slide is rather dull.* **Solution:** *Try using an alternative to bullets to add variety.* Although bullets focus audience attention on the main points, they may not be as interesting as other methods of presenting information such as graphs, pictures, or dropdown boxes. Look at the sample slides in **Figure 13.6** to see other ways of presenting information that you may want to try. The information on each of these slides could have been presented as bullets. Do you think these alternative approaches add more interest?

Figure 13.6 Alternatives to Bullets on PowerPoint Slides

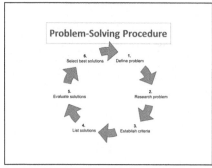

APPLY **WHAT YOU KNOW**
POWERPOINT SLIDES

Apply what you know about quality PowerPoint slides by completing the following:

- Take two of the sample slides A, B, or C above and revise them into more successful slides that follow the design principles and solutions presented in this chapter.

- Print copies of your revised slides to share with other class members or the entire class, if asked by your professor.
- Compare your slides with the revised slides located on MyCommunicationLab under Chapter 13.

Once your visual aids are completed, it is time to practice using them as you rehearse your speech, making sure that the content, visuals, and delivery work together for a smooth, confident presentation.

Preparing for a Specific Audience

13.2 What are the four general audience types, the four methods for delivering a speech, and the best delivery styles for each audience?

Delivery is the act or manner of communicating your ideas to others. If your delivery is effective, it reinforces your message; if it is ineffective, it distracts from it. Practicing your speech is the secret to great delivery. **Verbal delivery** includes the actual words the audience hears you say and the language style you use when saying them. **Nonverbal delivery** includes what the audience sees you doing as you speak (making eye contact, using gestures, standing comfortably and securely, and appearing confident) in addition to the vocal sounds or paralanguage that affect your words including your volume, rate, and tone of voice.

The key to effective speech practice begins with audience analysis—you must identify your audience type in order to select the delivery method that will communicate with them best. Recall that audience analysis is the first of the five steps to a successful speech (**Figure 13.7**). Although practicing your speech is the final step, it is attached to and under the umbrella of audience analysis.

Figure 13.7 **Practicing Your Speech**

STEP 1
AUDIENCE ANALYSIS

STEP 2
TOPIC SELECTION

STEP 3
MATERIAL GATHERING

STEP 4
ORGANIZING

STEP 5
PRACTICING

- Practice using visuals
- Choose delivery method for specific audience
- Practice verbal, physical, and vocal delivery
- Practice citing sources

The whole point of audience analysis is to adapt your speech to each specific audience. Different audiences require different delivery methods if you hope to keep their interest, aid their memory, or convince them to accept your proposal or advice.

Identify Audience Type

According to Elsea (1985), there are four general types of audiences: friendly, neutral, uninterested, and hostile. The **friendly audience** includes people who know and like you or who like your topic. Delivery for the friendly audience should be warm and relaxed with plenty of gestures, eye contact, and vocal variety—PowerPoint with pictures works well. The **neutral audience** includes people who are looking for facts and information and view themselves as objective. Delivery for the neutral audience should appear authoritative and credible with small gestures—use nothing flashy and keep your visuals professional looking (see the section on visual aids earlier in this chapter). The **uninterested audience** includes people who would rather not be here and probably plan to take a mental vacation. Delivery for the uninterested audience should include large gestures and plenty of entertaining, colorful visuals— if you wish to use PowerPoint, make sure your audiovisual equipment is of good enough quality that you don't have to darken the room. Finally, the **hostile audience** includes people who have an attitude against you and/or your topic and who might even ridicule you if given a chance. Delivery for the hostile audience should be slow and controlled. Avoid personal references, humor, or any question-and-answer session, if possible.

An audience evaluation will help you determine your audience type. Refer back to the sample audience analysis form in Chapter 10.

Select Best Delivery Method

All speech types (informative, persuasive, or entertaining) may be classified according to the method of delivery chosen. Speeches generally are delivered using one of these four methods: manuscript, memorized, impromptu, or extemporaneous. Once you have analyzed your audience and determined which type audience is likely to attend your presentation, you are ready to select the best delivery method to use. Each method has its uses and its challenges, but, with careful rehearsal, any one can be successful.

Manuscript Speech A **manuscript speech** is one that is prepared in advance and written exactly as you intend to deliver it. The word choice is set with the intent to avoid deviating from the manuscript. There are often situations for which a manuscript speech is essential. For example, the President of the United States and officials of organizations often use manuscripts to avoid misspeaking.

Manuscript speeches, however, do pose challenges with effective delivery. The most important problem is that when you read word for word, you will normally sound canned and flat, which is not engaging to an audience. This is particularly true of the novice speaker who doesn't realize how much rehearsal it takes to be able to read a manuscript and make it sound natural. An additional challenge is handling the pages of your manuscript unobtrusively. If you are ever required to deliver a speech from a manuscript, remember it is very important that you practice over and over until you can adhere to the text while maintaining eye contact and can manage your notes smoothly.

Sometimes beginning speakers unintentionally deliver a manuscript speech because they rely too heavily on their notes. Whether this is from nervousness or a lack of practice, the result is the same—the speech is boring to the audience. Of course, this problem is unlikely to occur if your speaking notes provide a skeleton outline that includes only keywords and phrases.

Memorized Speech

A **memorized speech**, like a manuscript speech, is carefully crafted in advance, but is delivered from memory; you have no manuscript at the lectern. There are instances when this delivery method is useful; for example, if you are required to give the same speech over and over. The key to a good memorized speech is to appear to be speaking spontaneously (as though you had not written your words out in advance). This is important if your audience is one that may mistrust the sincerity of a speaker who follows a prepared script—a hostile audience, for instance.

However, there are some obvious problems with memorized speeches. First, like manuscript speeches, unless they are presented by an experienced speaker, they often sound canned. In addition, inexperienced speakers often worry they may forget what to say next, which creates additional speaker anxiety. If delivering a speech from memory is essential, practice until it is embedded in your brain while striving for a natural-sounding delivery. Miller (2005) suggests that it takes one hour of serious work to memorize one minute of your manuscript. However, if you are willing to invest the time and effort, it is possible to give an effective memorized speech.

Impromptu Speech

The **impromptu speech** method of delivery allows for little preparation since you speak about a topic after having only a few moments to organize your thoughts. You have probably already encountered this method. For example, in the midst of a class discussion, the teacher or another student turns to you and says, "What is your opinion?" Or at a meeting, the chairperson unexpectedly calls upon you to update the group on the progress of your project. The fact is that life is full of impromptu speech opportunities, and the ability to "think on your feet" is a skill highly prized among people who aspire to career advancement or social adeptness.

The secret to giving an effective impromptu speech is knowing how to use the few moments you have before speaking. Do not think about what you are going to *say*; think about what you are going to *talk about*. There is a fine distinction here that you must understand to be a good impromptu speaker. Don't think about the words or details of what you want to say because once you begin to speak, you won't remember them anyway. Instead, think about the topic. Quickly outline in your head one or two major ideas you want to cover. Also quickly devise a funny comment or some other way to open your speech— perhaps picking up on some "theme" that was introduced earlier— and some way to conclude memorably. In other words, a good impromptu speech sounds a lot like any good speech: it has an introduction, a body, and a conclusion, and good transitions between points. Having used your few moments of preparation to decide on the two or three key ideas you will discuss, you simply improvise as you speak. Introduce one idea and elaborate on it, summarize, and then move to the next idea and elaborate on it.

If people are looking at you expectantly, but you are not yet certain of your points, here are two ways to stall, suggested by Stone and Bachner (1994): (1) Open by giving some background material; or (2) begin with the word "because" (such as, *because* this is such an important topic, and *because* there are so many different opinions on this topic, I feel . . .). Once you have mastered the art of impromptu speaking, you may find that you actually enjoy it. However, since you should never use the impromptu style when the audience expects a polished speech, this style is not recommended for any of the audience types discussed above.

Extemporaneous Speech The method that most speakers and audiences prefer is the **extemporaneous speech,** a carefully researched, organized, and practiced presentation that sounds conversational rather than read or memorized. Unlike impromptu speeches, an extemporaneous speech is well prepared. However, it is less likely to sound "canned," as manuscript and memorized speeches often do. The extemporaneous speech is the method most used in public speaking situations today and will be the primary focus in this chapter. Even those who speak in more formal settings usually try to appear as if they are speaking extemporaneously, probably because the this style comes across as more honest and candid.

The challenge to extemporaneous speaking is maintaining a conversational tone and getting your ideas across without memorizing the speech. After practicing several times, you may find that certain wording "sticks" because it continues to be the most efficient and effective way to convey your thoughts. But other language will change, and, each time you deliver the speech to a new audience, it may change yet again. This is actually the strength of this method of delivery. Because your words have not been preset, you are free to adapt to the needs of your audience as you speak. If they seem puzzled or confused, you can rephrase an idea. If they seem to be catching on quickly, you can skip ahead.

As you can see, each of the delivery methods has its usefulness as well as its challenges. No matter which delivery method you decide is best or your professor requests, you will need to rehearse multiple times and pay attention to the many behaviors that constitute effective verbal and nonverbal delivery discussed next.

APPLY **WHAT YOU KNOW**
DELIVERY METHODS

Apply what you know about delivery methods by completing the following:

- Look for "Informative speech or presentation" on *YouTube* and select a speech that sounds interesting.

- Identify which delivery method was used and how successfully it was used. Give specifics.

- Under what circumstances might a different delivery method have been better? Explain your answer.

- Based on the speech, what type audience do you think the speaker was addressing? Why?

LEARNING **OBJECTIVE**

13.3 What are some guidelines for choosing effective language, and what are the important aspects of physical delivery that help speakers communicate their messages?

Practice Your Verbal and Nonverbal Delivery

From the moment your audience hears your first words and takes their first look at you, you have begun the process of establishing your credibility, your status, and even your persuasiveness (Knapp & Hall, 2007). Therefore, both your verbal delivery (the words you use) and your nonverbal delivery (your physical appearance) deserve some important consideration.

Pick Words Carefully

As speakers, we know that language has the power to affect others' perceptions of us. We also know how easy it is to be misunderstood or misinterpreted because of our differing frames of reference. In addition, it's important to remember that the words we use can also clarify our ideas (or create confusion), and they can add interest and enjoyment (or create boredom). Therefore, here are a few quick guidelines for picking your words (keeping in mind that they all depend on the audience analysis you conducted):

- *Keep your language simple*—avoid jargon or highly technical terms unless you provide definitions.

- *Make your delivery relatively informal*—using such pronouns as *I* and *we* makes it seem more like a personal conversation with the audience. Maya Angelou, known for her excellent speaking ability, used an informal delivery style during her eulogy for Coretta Scott King on February 7, 2006 (to hear the complete speech go to americanrhetoric.com and type in "Maya Angelou" in the search box):

  > I speak as a sister of a sister. Dr. Martin Luther King was assassinated on my birthday. And for over 30 years, Coretta Scott King and I have telephoned, or sent cards to each other, or flowers to each other, or met each other somewhere in the world.
  >
  > We called ourselves "chosen sisters," and when we traveled to South Africa or to the Caribbean or when she came to visit me in North Carolina or in New York, we sat into the late evening hours, calling each other "girl." It's a black woman thing, you know. And even as we reached well into our seventh decade, we still said "girl."

- *Use specific, concrete language that paints a picture in the minds of your listeners*—even if you are using visual aids. Researchers (Bryden & Ley, 1983; Richardson, 2003) have found that concrete, vivid language is easier for listeners to remember. For example, "A large, menacing, black roach with twitching feelers inched toward her" is easier to remember than "an insect crawled toward her."

- *Use enthusiastic, forceful language.* Remember that, when you are in front of an audience, you will need to be a little louder than usual, just to sound normal. The same is true with enthusiasm—you need to be more enthusiastic than usual just to sound normal when you are in front of an audience. Enthusiasm and forcefulness are especially important during persuasive speeches. Maya Angelou is also an excellent example of a speaker who uses forceful language when she speaks, as you will notice if you listen to one of her speeches.

- *Avoid using language that calls attention to the mechanics of your speech.* There are certain words and phrases that are best omitted from your speech, such as "my topic is" or "my first main point" or "my next point" or "in conclusion." In a well-constructed speech, your thesis, transitions, and summary will signal to your audience that you are moving from one section of your speech to another without your having to announce it.

Maya Angelou is known for her delightful informal delivery style.

Use Direct Eye Contact

Eye contact may be the most important visual aspect of delivery. Novice speakers often report that the idea of having to look at their audience is a major source of anxiety. However, eye contact is the way you make a connection with your audience. It is also the way you monitor your audience's responses, which enables you to make the necessary adjustments as you continue your speech. Moreover, audiences simply do not respond well to speakers who do not look them in the eye or who look over their heads (just in case you were thinking of that as an option).

To be effective, eye contact should be frequent, sustained, and directed toward all members of the audience. Certainly, it is acceptable to glance at your notes occasionally to make sure you are on track or to ensure the accuracy of a quotation. However, you should be so familiar with the material that you are able to deliver it with as much eye contact as possible. Fleeting glances in the direction of the audience do not constitute eye contact—make sure that you distribute eye contact to the entire audience. One good technique is to think of the audience as consisting of several groupings of people. As you rehearse, practice directing your eyes to one grouping and strive to look at each person in that grouping at least once before shifting your attention to another grouping of audience members.

Use Effective Facial Expressions

Facial expression, as we learned in Chapter 5 on nonverbal communication, is a powerful way to communicate and convey emotions. For starters, your facial expression should convey a sincere interest in the audience and enthusiasm for the topic. In addition, at various points, your face needs to register emotions that are appropriate for the material being discussed. When talking about a serious subject, your face should reflect the gravity of the topic. If you are one of those people who register their nervousness with a kind of perpetual smile or threat of a smile, attempt to reduce any self-consciousness by rehearsing your speech often enough to feel confident and to involve yourself fully in the topic. Keep in mind that the best facial expressions are those that arise naturally from your interest in the audience and the topic; planned facial expressions almost always look artificial.

Monitor Posture, Gestures, and Movements

Another important type of nonverbal delivery requiring practice involves posture, gestures, and movement. Let's look at each of these in more detail.

Posture   As we learned in Chapter 5, your posture can convey information about you to a listener, particularly with respect to your level of confidence (Pincus, 2007). A relaxed and open posture, with an erect torso and shoulders back, tells the audience that you are comfortable with yourself and with the speaking situation. It is important to begin your speech by establishing a secure body position. Your weight should be evenly distributed on both feet (not on one hip called the "college stance"), and your feet should be placed in a position that provides stability for you. For most people, having one foot slightly in front of the other feels more secure than having them positioned side by side and prohibits frequent and repeated weight-shifting or swaying. If you are prone to distracting movements while speaking, placing one foot slightly in front of the other while keeping your weight on both feet makes it more difficult to cross your feet at the ankles, tap one foot, or swing your leg. Adopting this posture should also prevent you from leaning on the lectern as the speaker in this photo is doing.

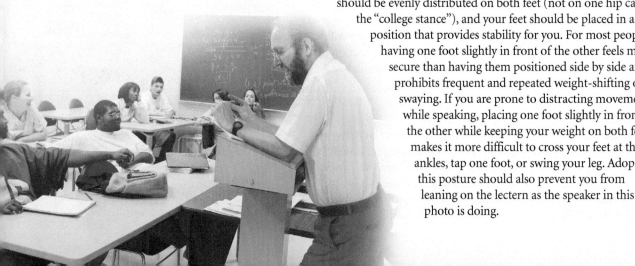

Gestures
The best gestures are those that arise naturally from what you are saying. Be careful about planned gestures as they can look artificial and detached from what you are saying. Generally speaking, it is wise to position your arms so that your hands are above the level of your waist. If you are speaking without a lectern or notes, this might mean that you begin with one hand resting lightly in the palm of the other. If you are speaking with a lectern, you may wish to rest your hands "lightly" on the lectern in order to give them a launching position for the gestures that will arise from what you say. Avoid stuffing hands into your pockets, clasping them behind your back, gripping the edge of the lectern with them, or letting them hang limply at your side. Although it's a good idea to use gestures when you practice, once you begin the actual speech, do not think about gestures at all. If you have practiced using them, they will tend to arise spontaneously, as appropriate.

Gestures and Culture
Although gestures add clarity to your message, be aware that not all cultures appreciate or expect the same gestures—so know your audience. Take, for example, the "Hook 'em Horns" gesture that represents the Texas Longhorn, the mascot at the University of Texas. During his second inauguration, George W. Bush and his wife gave this gesture as a sign of respect as the UT band marched past. Unfortunately, this gesture, which means either "Satan" or "cuckold" to people in other countries, caused quite a stir when televised around the world ("Bush Shocks Foreigners," 2006). The size of your gestures can also communicate different messages: small, controlled gestures are considered polite and professional by Japanese audiences; Greek and Italian audiences expect more sweeping gestures (Eckert, 2006, p. 48).

Movements
If the situation allows for it, movement can be very effective in a speech. If you are required to deliver your speech in an auditorium from behind a lectern with an attached microphone, you may not have the option of moving. However, in smaller rooms, or in situations where the microphone can be removed and carried with you, you may find that changing your position from time to time adds interest and prevents the speech from seeming static. However, movement must always be purposeful. It is not wise to pace or sway because this demonstrates nervousness. Instead, use movement at appropriate points in the speech, such as during transitions. Remember when you use a transition, you are moving from one main idea to another, and it makes perfect sense to plan and rehearse moving at that time. You can also use movement to reinvolve parts of your audience when you sense that their interest is temporarily waning. By moving toward a group, you draw them back into the situation. Watch out for too much repetition or nervous "tics," such as repeatedly scratching your nose or pulling your ear, smoothing your hair, tugging on clothing, tapping the lectern, or fidgeting in any way. Make sure that you are comfortable using the pointer or the computer mouse so that having one in your hand does not cause you to play with it. Videotape yourself while rehearsing to catch possible problems.

Monitor Clothing and Grooming
Although clothing and grooming may not seem as important as either eye contact, facial expressions, or gestures, your appearance does send a message to your audience. In general, your clothing should suit both your needs and the expectations of the audience, and it should serve to enhance or maintain your credibility with the audience. If you aren't sure about a particular outfit, stick with the more conservative styles (Damhorst & Fiore, 2000) and remember that the darker the outfit, the more authority it conveys (Damhorst & Reed, 1986). Jewelry should be subtle and not distracting.

Baseball caps or other headgear should be avoided unless it is part of a uniform you are wearing or required by your religion. In general, though, caps and hats often obscure your face—in particular your eyes—and sometimes promote a too-casual attitude that detracts from your credibility. The same is true about grooming and hairstyles. Hair should be clean, neat, and fixed so it won't fall into your face. If you suspect a problem with your hair, ask your friends or family to watch you rehearse and to give you honest feedback.

APPLY **WHAT YOU KNOW**
VERBAL AND PHYSICAL DELIVERY

Apply what you know about physical delivery by answering the following critical thinking questions:

- Which guidelines for effective word choices do you think are the most important in classroom speeches? Why?

- How important do you think clothing, posture, gestures, and movement are to a successful classroom speech? Why?

- Go to MyCommunicationLab for Chapter 13 and evaluate one of the sample speeches, looking for the speaker's verbal and physical delivery. What suggestions do you have to make the speech more successful?

The visual aspects of speech delivery are all related to how we communicate nonverbally. As you will recall, a large percentage of the meaning of a message is conveyed by the nonverbal code. Therefore, it is important to attend to these nonverbal aspects of presenting a speech. However, speeches also involve speaking aloud, which means that your voice is also important. We will turn our attention now to the aspects of your delivery that your audience hears and will focus on yet another nonverbal category: vocal delivery or paralanguage.

LEARNING **OBJECTIVE**

13.4 What are the four attributes of the human voice, how do they impact speech delivery, and what other vocal elements can interfere with effective delivery?

Practice Your Vocal Delivery (Paralanguage)

A speech is not a performance—it is the way you make direct contact with your audience. It is the way your sincerity and enthusiasm for your topic shine through. Your **vocal delivery** is the primary medium by which you make contact with your listeners. In fact, Decker and Denney (1993) in their book *You've Got to Be Believed to Be Heard*, suggest that audiences won't really listen to you unless you make emotional contact with them, convincing them that you are likable and believable. One recent political figure who makes emotional contact with his listeners using his compelling speaking voice is President Barack Obama.

From your own experience, you can undoubtedly point to speakers whose voices capture and hold your attention. Most people would agree that the speaker's voice is an important factor in our willingness to attend to a presentation. Certainly, there are some people who seem to be blessed with a splendid vocal instrument while others have less remarkable voices. All of us, however, can improve our chance of speaking effectively by working to use the voice we have to its best effect. As you read the following vocal attributes, see which ones you need to improve.

Pitch

Pitch, which refers to the relative highness or lowness of a vocal tone, is one of the four key attributes of the human voice. No one will enjoy listening to you if you use a **monotone,** which is speaking with a single pitch or a very narrow range of pitches. The monotonous speaker conveys a lack of energy and enthusiasm and leaves listeners wondering why they should be interested since the speaker doesn't seem interested. To be an effective speaker, vary your pitch to convey your ideas with enthusiasm. Another fairly common misuse of pitch is called **upspeak** and occurs when you habitually end each sentence on an upward inflection, sounding as if you are asking a question or are uncertain. Effective speakers make declarative statements that end in downward inflections, conveying confidence and authority.

Rate

A second attribute of the human voice is **rate**, which refers to the speed at which words are delivered. In the public speaking context, it is important for you to speak slowly enough to allow your audience to understand what you are saying but fast enough to hold the audience's attention. Keep in mind that a slightly faster speech rate conveys mastery of your subject. It also enhances your credibility and gives the audience less time to daydream. The best way to ensure an appropriate speech rate is to practice your speech out loud many times in advance so that you feel confident in your ability to articulate your ideas.

No matter what rate you use, there will be times that your listeners will benefit from the use of pauses in your speech. A **pause** is a live silence, either short or long. A well-timed pause will allow your idea to be absorbed by the listeners, can be used to focus attention on your next word or idea, or may be used for dramatic effect. In addition, a pause before a transitional statement directs audience attention to your next key idea.

Volume

The third attribute of the human voice is **volume**—the loudness or softness of your speaking voice. It is, of course, essential that you speak loud enough to be heard comfortably by all listeners. The issue here is how you project your voice. Vocal projection is like throwing a ball. Just as you would exert enough physical energy to deliver the ball to the intended catcher, so your voice needs to be aimed at the listeners sitting farthest from you. Have a friend or family member give you feedback on your speaking volume during a rehearsal session.

Emphasis

Emphasis uses all three of the vocal attributes discussed thus far: *pitch* (usually higher), *rate* (usually slower), and *volume* (usually louder). Vocal **emphasis** is using your voice to signal important words or ideas that you don't want your audience to miss. Emphasis is similar to underscoring or boldfacing a word in print: it draws attention to the idea and conveys importance to the topic.

President Obama uses his speaking voice to make emotional contact with his listeners.

Vocal Quality

The fourth attribute of the human voice is **vocal quality**, which refers to the quality of the sounds you produce when you speak. The best quality voices are those that can be described as **resonant**, meaning that you produce your voice with adequate breath support, using a relaxed throat and clear articulation. Improving vocal quality is not an easy task. The first time you hear your recorded voice is likely to be a disheartening experience. We all sound different to ourselves from how we do to others because we hear ourselves through sound waves traveling through the air and sound waves traveling through our facial tissues and bones. But listen objectively to your voice, and you can determine what areas of vocal production you need to improve. Many schools offer courses in Voice and Diction that are designed to help you polish your vocal quality or overcome particular deficiencies (see *Career Moment* on page 370).

Articulation

In addition to the four attributes of the human voice discussed so far, speakers should be mindful of their use of **articulation,** which refers to the shaping of speech sounds by use of the articulators. When someone tells you to "speak up," the problem may be partially inadequate volume, but also it may be a sign that you are not using good articulation. Listeners grow impatient with speakers who use sloppy articulation and may interpret this problem as an unwillingness to communicate, which would damage your credibility. In addition, if you speak at a fairly rapid rate, good articulation is essential for understanding. Good articulation requires that you actively use your lips and tongue so that speech sounds can be produced with clarity and crispness. See **Figure 13.8** for some common articulation errors.

Pronunciation

Just as it is important for you to produce speech sounds clearly, it is also important that you pronounce words correctly. **Pronunciation** refers to the act of saying a word using the accepted standards of the language group. Discovering the proper pronunciation is not always easy, as dictionaries sometimes differ with each other as to which of two or three accepted pronunciations are preferred. However, it is worth the trouble to make sure that the pronunciation of a word you use is at least one of those that is regarded as acceptable by educated members of your language community. Incorrect pronunciation is damaging to a speaker's credibility.

Sometimes you know that you need to look up a word to find out how it is pronounced. For example, if you are planning to refer to a drug used in the treatment of a health condition, you will need to consult a medical dictionary to check the pronunciation of an often difficult polysyllabic word. It is essential that you practice saying it aloud so often that it rolls off your tongue without stumbling. However, you

Figure 13.8 Some Common Articulation Errors

Problem	Example
Adding sounds:	Hard "g" added to "ng" words: "sing-ging"
Omitting sounds:	"gimmie" for "give me"
Omitting syllables:	"probly" for "probably"
Substituting sounds:	"dis" for "this" or "wif" for "with"
Reversing sounds:	"aks" (sounds like "ax") for "ask"
Dropping endings:	Especially "ing" as in "goin" or "doin"
Slurring sounds & syllables:	"awono" for "I don't know"
	"gonna" for "going to"
	"skonon" for "What's going on?"

may be unaware that you are mispronouncing other common words that you use every day. The pronunciation you use is obviously the one you think is correct—otherwise you wouldn't be using it. In **Figure 13.9** you will see examples of some frequently mispronounced words. Check yourself on those words; do you say them the right way or the wrong way? This is another instance in which it would be wise to ask someone whose language usage you know to be correct to help you spot your mispronunciations. You might also want to do a *Google* search for Internet sites that list other commonly mispronounced words; almost everyone could use a pronunciation checkup.

Figure 13.9 Frequently Mispronounced Words

This way:	Not this way:
Across	Accrost
Athlete (2 syllables)	Athuhlete (3 syllables)
Escape	Excape
Height	Heighth
Iran ("i" as in "sit")	I ran
Larynx ("inks")	Larnyx ("nix")
Library	Liberry
Mirror (2 syllables)	Mere (1 syllable)
Nuclear	Nukyular
Often (t is silent)	Off ton
Realtor	Reluhter
Salmon (l is silent)	Salmon
Similar	Simular
Washington	Warshington

Vocal Dysfluencies

Just as you should avoid the use of distracting physical mannerisms, so you should avoid the use of **vocal dysfluencies** (or interferences) that interrupt the fluent delivery of language, such as vocal tics or fillers that people make from habit or nervousness. Vocal tics include a wide array of vocal dysfluencies that you may do unconsciously, such as repeated clearing of the throat or smacking noise. Vocal fillers are even more noticeable than vocal tics. "Uh," "you know," "I mean," "OK?," "you see?" "like," "stuff like that," and "what not" are examples of fillers that, on the face of it, look like language but do not convey any meaningful information except that the speaker is uncertain, anxious, or ill-prepared. The best way to avoid using them in a speech is to rehearse out loud many times. The surer you are about what you will say, the less likely you will feel the need to fill in the silence with "like" or "uh." As we have discussed so many verbal and nonverbal aspects of delivery, you may feel a little overwhelmed. It does seem like there is a lot to remember. Just as a novice golfer finds herself standing at the tee and thinking "Feet; Stance; Grip; Swing; Hips; Elbows; Follow-through," so the novice speaker—like Amina in our opening scenario—may grow anxious thinking "Eye contact; Facial expression; Gestures; Pitch; Volume."

Actually, the key to effective presentations can be summed up by saying: "Enthusiasm." If you are talking about a topic that truly excites you, and if you can generate excitement about sharing information and opinions with your audience, your enthusiasm will overcome any minor "errors" you may make in your speech. Enthusiastic speakers rarely fail to use appropriate facial expressions and gestures. Enthusiastic speakers typically do not speak in a monotone, and they usually speak with appropriate rate, volume, and articulation.

APPLY **WHAT YOU KNOW**
VOCAL DELIVERY

Apply what you know about physical delivery by answering the following:

- Select a recording device such as your cell phone, voice mail, or computer, and read a short passage from your textbook. Listen to your delivery as objectively as possible and evaluate the effectiveness of your speaking voice. Which aspects of your voice could use some improvement?

- Next, record yourself speaking in a conversational voice about something that happened to you today. Compare your conversational voice with your reading voice, and note any differences. What improvements would you make in your conversational voice?

- Develop a plan for how you can work on improving your voice. Select one key area to work on before your next speech.

Although verbal and nonverbal aspects of delivery are definitely noticeable to your audience and affect their attitude toward you and your topic, how you cite your sources during the speech also makes a difference.

LEARNING **OBJECTIVE**

13.5 Why is it important to cite sources during a presentation, and what are the basic guidelines for citing them?

Practice Citing Your Sources

There are important reasons for citing sources during a presentation. For one thing, it can add to your credibility as a speaker (O'Keefe, 1998)—it shows that you are prepared and know what you are talking about. Also, people tend to be more persuaded when they are aware that evidence supports an argument (Reynolds & Reynolds, 2002) and are even more likely to be persuaded if the speaker gives the qualifications of the source (O'Keefe, 1998).

Even so, when it comes to citing sources, inexperienced speakers usually make three major mistakes—you have undoubtedly seen these in class presentations:

- First, *some speakers list their sources only in their outlines*, thinking that now they have done everything necessary when it comes to research and don't need to cite any sources. The problem here is that the audience does not have a copy of the outline and can only guess at the sources used.

- Second, *some speakers think that speaking is the same as writing a paper*, so they wait until the end of the speech to show a PowerPoint slide listing all of their references. Few speakers actually read the list, and most show it for five to ten seconds, which is not enough time for the audience to read more than one source. However, the main problem with presenting sources at the end of a speech is that it is too late to do much good. The audience has already decided what they believe and whether you know what you are talking about. To be effective, sources need to be cited at the time the information or quotation is given.

- Third, *some speakers orally present so much information with each citation that it is awkward to follow and becomes distracting*. The audience begins to listen to *how* the speaker cites the sources and misses the importance of the citation.

DEVELOPING **SKILLS**
HOW TO ORALLY CITE YOUR SOURCES DURING YOUR PRESENTATION

Basic rule 1: *Anytime you cite statistics in a speech*, you need to orally cite where you found the information, including the date the statistics were compiled. If there is no date, don't use the statistics unless you can verify them in another source.

Basic rule 2: *Anytime you quote or paraphrase someone*, you need to orally cite where you found the information, including something about the person you are citing (don't assume everyone already knows). Also, making the source and the source's qualifications clear will add to the persuasiveness of your speech.

Basic rule 3: *Anytime you present a significant fact*, you need to orally cite where you found the information, including the date of the source. If you are using a Web site that has no date, cite the date the site was last updated. If there is no recent update on the site, don't use it.

Carefully researching your speech topic is a good thing—but effective sources won't do your credibility or the credibility of your topic any good unless the audience is aware of them. As mentioned earlier, waiting until the end of your speech to show a list of sources isn't very effective—the positive impact your sources could have on your credibility and persuasiveness has been lost. Therefore, it is much better if you orally cite each source during the speech when you first introduce the source. Any later mention of the same source can be abbreviated.

Since your audience does not have a list of references or your outline in front of them, all they know is what you tell them—so the question is: How much information about the sources should you give? Exactly how detailed your oral citations should be will depend on your professor and your audience. However, in general, give enough information that audience members can find the source on their own if they want to later but don't include so much that it becomes awkward or distracting (VerLinden, 1996).

Consider the following citation examples based on guidelines suggested in online articles by James Madison University and Eastern Illinois University*:

- "Dr. Robert Smith, Provost and Vice Chancellor for Academic Affairs at the University of Arkansas, has written a book in which he offers all the speaking techniques he has used in hundreds of presentations over the years. In this 2004 book, *The Elements of Great Speechmaking*, Smith provides this unforgettable advice: . . ."

- "Guest show host Larry King, who has interviewed over 30,000 guests during his career, was himself interviewed on the April 11, 2007, television show *60 Minutes* by none other than Mike Wallace. When asked how he would sum up his 50-year career, King replied, ' . . .'"

- "Do you typically find most statistics boring? Well, you will find the latest tornado statistics for our state anything but boring. According to the U.S. Disaster Center's statistics published this week, . . ."

- "In a personal interview conducted on April 3, 2008 with Joyce Otoupal, president of the local chapter of the American Cancer Society, I learned that . . ."

To test your knowledge about orally citing sources, go to the *Skill Builders* at the end of this chapter and complete activity 4.

*Oral Citations at http://www.lib.jmu.edu/gold/citingspeech.doc; Tips for Oral Citations at http://www.eiu.edu/~assess/TipsOralCites%20.doc.

APPLY **WHAT YOU KNOW**
CITING SOURCES

Apply what you know about source citation by completing the following:

- Select two sources you plan to use in one of your next speeches, and write each one exactly the way you plan to deliver it orally. Be sure to follow the suggestions in the sections above.

- Practice delivering each source so that it feels and sounds natural. Deliver your sources for one or two classmates and get their suggestions on whether you need to make any improvements.

- If asked by your professor, share one of your planned citations with the class.

LEARNING OBJECTIVE

13.6 What important advice should speakers keep in mind as they begin final preparation for a speech?

Citing sources requires careful practice. Decide how to cite them, write them down, and then practice saying them until they flow easily. The correct way to cite oral sources is covered in the *Developing Skills* feature in this chapter.

Final Preparations before Your Speech

In this chapter we have discussed the preparation of visual aids as well as the verbal, physical, and vocal components of effective speech delivery. Now let's discuss some final tips to help you feel prepared and confident for your presentation.

- **Tip 1**: *Practice out loud several times, and time your speech each time.* A quick mental run-through is not adequate; you will not feel prepared and confident if you have not heard yourself speaking your words out loud several times.

- **Tip 2**: *Practice your speech in several ways, if possible.* Some people find that practicing in front of a mirror is helpful; others find that audio or video recording equipment works best. You might also have family or friends who would be willing to serve as an audience; if so, let them know what type of feedback you are seeking.

- **Tip 3**: *Prepare for a Q & A session carefully even though you obviously can't practice it.* If someone asks a question that you can't answer, maintain your poise while admitting that you do not know the answer. Then suggest a source for the information and move on to the next question. (Be sure to review the suggestions in Chapter 12 for how to end your speech after the Q & A is finished.)

- **Tip 4**: *Use the night before your presentation wisely.* Prepare all of the materials you will need; double check the operation of your visuals; use positive imagery to see yourself giving a confident presentation; and get to bed early.

- **Tip 5**: *Be enthusiastic.* Audiences are very forgiving of speakers who seem to like what they are talking about, like their listeners, and enjoy being there. Ironically, if you maintain this attitude, you might find that you actually do enjoy public speaking.

CHAPTER SUMMARY

As this chapter has stressed, preparing visuals aids and practicing your presentation (Step #5 in preparing a speech) is important to becoming a confident and professional speaker. Being able to identify areas needing improvement and then knowing how to improve them requires techniques discussed in this chapter. You can determine your knowledge of these techniques by checking the skills and learning objectives presented in this chapter.

Summary of **SKILLS**

Check each skill that you now feel qualified to perform:

❑ I can identify various types of visual aids, including PowerPoint, and prepare them so they communicate effectively with my audience.

❑ I can adapt my delivery method, visual aids, and speech content to communicate with different audience types.

❑ I can evaluate my verbal and nonverbal delivery and apply text suggestions for any needed improvement.

❑ I can appropriately cite my sources during my presentations.

Summary of LEARNING **OUTCOMES**

13.1 *What are the general types of visual aids, how are they used in a speech, and what are the design principles and general guidelines for using PowerPoint effectively?*

- The most typically used visual aids include: audiovisual aids, computer-generated visuals, flip charts and posters, handouts and objects, and marker-boards and chalkboards.

- In using visual aids strive for professionalism, simplicity, and clarity while preparing for possible problems and focusing on your audience. Find suggestions for each of these areas on pages 348–354.

- The design principles for using PowerPoint are explained in the *Making Theory Practical* feature. The principles include contrast, repetition, alignment, and proximity.

- Suggestions for using PowerPoint successfully are explained by looking at problem slides and suggested solutions to each problem (see pages 352–354). Problems include using too many words, putting text into all caps, using complete sentences, leaving off the title, using inappropriate background colors and pictures, and many more.

13.2 *What are the four general audience types, the four methods for delivering a speech, and the best delivery styles for each audience?*

- The four audience types include the friendly, neutral, uninterested, and hostile audiences.

- The four methods for delivering a speech include the manuscript speech, the memorized speech, the impromptu speech, and the extemporaneous speech.

- Most audiences, speakers, and professors prefer the extemporaneous speech, which is a carefully researched, organized, and practiced presentation that sounds conversational rather than read or memorized. The extemporaneous style of delivery works best for all audience types with the exception of the hostile audience.

- The manuscript speech, which is written and spoken word for word, should be used only if the situation requires that no deviation of language occur, such as in a presidential speech, where the text of the speech has already been distributed to the press. The memorized speech, which is carefully crafted in advance but delivered from memory, should be given only if the speech will be given multiple times or if your credibility might be damaged by the presence of a manuscript or notes—such as in the case of a hostile audience. The impromptu speech occurs when you are required to speak about a topic after having only moments to organize your thoughts, such as in a meeting when you are asked to give an update on a procedure with no prior warning.

13.3 *What are some guidelines for choosing effective language, and what are the important aspects of physical delivery that help speakers communicate their messages?*

- Guidelines for choosing language carefully include keeping your language simple, relatively informal, specific and concrete, enthusiastic, and forceful. At the same time, make sure that you avoid using language that calls attention to the mechanics of your speech.

- Important aspects of delivery include eye contact, facial expressions, posture, gestures, movement, clothing, and grooming.

13.4 *What are the four attributes of the human voice, how do they impact speech delivery, and what other vocal elements can interfere with effective delivery?*

- The four attributes of the human voice include *pitch* (the highness and lowness of vocal tones), *rate* (the speed of speech), *volume* (the softness and loudness of the speaking voice), and *vocal quality* (the quality of the sounds you produce).

- Additional vocal elements that contribute (or detract) from a speaker's delivery include *emphasis* (using the voice to signal important words or ideas

DELIVERY **AND YOUR CAREER**

13.7 What visual aid and delivery skills from this chapter relate specifically to your career?

The following *Spotlight on*, *Career Moment*, and *Connecting to* features take a look at how important quality visuals and effective delivery is in the workplace and specifically to careers related to business, education, and healthcare. Whether you are interested in one of those career fields or will be a consumer of the services of these areas, the following information should be of interest to you.

SPOTLIGHT ON **LANGUAGE AND VERBAL DELIVERY**

BUSINESS

An article in *Women in Business* called "Speak Out" (Luckert, 1991) notes that speaking skills are crucial to be successful in today's business world and offers the following suggestions for rehearsing a speech:

- Rehearse the entire speech once for six days in a row.
- Practice wearing the actual clothes you plan to wear during your speech to become comfortable with them.
- Practice using your visual aids and any "props" you plan to use.
- Rehearse using a microphone—many women have soft volume.
- Videotape yourself to make sure you sound conversational.
- Practice standing tall and making direct eye contact.
- Watch the tendency to smile, especially when the topic is serious.

EDUCATION

The National Literacy Trust of London (2005) stated that children entering school for the first time show a decreased ability in speaking and listening skills. The director of the Trust, Neil McClelland, warns that "most brain development occurs between birth and the age of two, so babies and toddlers need a quality linguistic environment just as much as they need nourishing food" (Garner, 2002, ¶5). When reading to babies and toddlers, parents and educators in daycare or preschool should consider the following suggestions (Gestwicki, 2007, pp. 69–70):

- Select a book with simple pictures that both you and the children will enjoy.
- Rehearse reading aloud, varying your tone and facial expressions.
- Read slowly enough so the children can create mental images.
- Stop at a place that builds anticipation for what will happen when next you resume reading.

HEALTHCARE

Doctors and nurses have a tendency to use jargon and confusing language when talking or writing instructions to patients. This is especially confusing for patients with limited reading ability or limited knowledge of English. An article in *Internal Medicine News* (Silverman, 2003) had these interesting facts:

- Medical personnel's failure to use plain language costs over $73 billion each year in the U.S. (¶ 2).
- Problems in reading increase "the risk of hospitalization by 53%" and lead to "higher rates of diabetic complications, amputations, and heart attack" (¶ 5).
- Communication problems between healthcare providers and patients occur more often when the patient has a serious illness and is feeling emotional.
- To help with language problems, ask patients to paraphrase or "teach-back" the information received.

CAREER MOMENT **PERFECTING YOUR SPEAKING VOICE**

There are many careers that require a pleasing speaking voice, such as acting, radio or television broadcasting, advertising, business, law, and even teaching. Would you like to change or polish your speaking voice? Perhaps you have a southern drawl or a northern twang or maybe an accent that you would like to soften. You might need to change your vocal quality by working on your resonation, articulation, pronunciation of certain sounds, pitch, or volume. These changes would be especially helpful if your native language is not English, and people have problems understanding you. Each of these problem areas could be changed for the better, giving you more vocal flexibility, if you enrolled in a speech course called **Voice and Diction** (or Voice and Articulation, on some college campuses).

Voice and Diction courses give you instruction and practice in communicating effectively using your voice. The course identifies specific physiological or environmental speaking patterns and habits that you might wish to alter. Speech techniques will

be introduced through a variety of interesting exercises. Of course, habits don't change without hard work, but, with practice, you will be able to improve your communication ability in your chosen career and your confidence as a speaker.

Another course that would give you practice in improving your speaking voice is called **Oral Interpretation**. If you are planning a career in elementary education, this course would give you valuable literature selections and class exercises to enhance your teaching. For more details on either of these courses, see your professor or the chairperson of the Communication department. Don't wait until later to make a decision that will improve your speaking voice and your career success.

CONNECTING TO **BUSINESS**

If you are considering going into sales, you will definitely need to develop effective verbal and nonverbal delivery skills. You may communicate face-to-face for some sales and give formal presentations at other times. To see if you are the type of person who would do well in sales, take the following quiz adapted from Ivancevich & Duening (2007, p. 433). If most of your answers are 1 or 2, sales is for you; if mostly 5 or 6, sales is probably not for you.

ACTIVITY Answer each question on this scale: Strongly agree 1 2 3 4 5 6 Strongly disagree

1. Even without direct supervision, I would work just as hard.
2. I am willing to work long hours.
3. I enjoy trying hard to please people.
4. I am organized and plan my daily schedule.
5. I can be flexible if the situation requires it.
6. When under pressure, I try to remain calm.
7. I can speak to groups of people.
8. I don't think being late for appointments is good.
9. I listen carefully to others and ask them questions.
10. I find problems and tasks interesting and exciting.

CONNECTING TO **EDUCATION**

If you are considering a career in education, your ability to use effective verbal and nonverbal delivery will be important no matter what age level you teach. The *Spotlight on* feature in this chapter discussed the importance of reading to babies and toddlers and provided suggestions for how to read to them (Gestwicki, 2007). One way to learn to use your physical appearance and vocal skills when reading or speaking is to practice reading children's books.

ACTIVITY Form two groups of at least two students, and complete the following steps:

1. Each group should select a children's book and take turns reading to another group. Gestwicki suggests:
   - *Pat the Bunny* by D. Kunhardt, Golden Books, 2001.
   - *Miffy at the Zoo* by D. Bruna, Big Tent Entertainment, 2004.
   - *If You Give a Mouse a Cookie* by L. Numeroff, et al., 1985.
2. Practice reading using your vocal delivery (vary your pitch, rate, volume, emphasis, and vocal quality) to make the char-

acters come alive. Also rehearse using good eye contact, facial expressions, and gestures. Use the book as a visual and show some of the pictures.
3. When you are ready, each group should present its book to another group, who should play the role of children.
4. Each group should critique the other by suggesting two things that were especially good, and two things needing some changes.

CONNECTING TO **HEALTHCARE**

If you are considering a career in healthcare, you will want to pick your words carefully and pay attention to your paralanguage (tone, pitch, and emphasis). For example, if you work with elderly patients, be sure to avoid using Elderspeak (Berman et al., 2008) such as calling elderly adults *honey, darling*, or *sweetie*, using the pronoun *we* inappropriately, such as, "Are we ready to take our walk?"; or using baby talk with slow speech, short sentences, simple words, and exaggerated pitch variety.

ACTIVITY

Form a group of at least three to five students in your class who are interested in being healthcare professionals. Each group should brainstorm additional examples of Elderspeak. Discuss why you think many people speak to elderly adults in this manner and how you think this makes elderly people feel.

If you formed more than one group, share your group's list and answers with other groups or your entire class.

▶ Log onto MyCommunicationLab.com to access Connecting to Psychology and Connecting to Science, Technology, Engineering, and Math—both with related activities.

that you don't want your audience to miss), *articulation* (the clarity of vocal sounds), *pronunciation* (saying words using the accepted standards of a cultural or geographic group), and *vocal dysfluencies* (distracting vocal tics or fillers such as "uh").

13.5 *Why is it important to cite sources during a presentation, and what are the basic guidelines for citing them?*

- Citing sources during a presentation adds to your credibility as a speaker and improves your persuasiveness. Speakers often make the mistake of putting their sources in their outline or on the final slide of their presentation—neither of these add to a speaker's credibility or persuasiveness.

- Cite your sources any time you use statistics, any time you quote or paraphrase someone, and any time you cite a significant fact. Specific guidelines are found in the *Developing Skills* feature in this chapter.

13.6 *What important advice should speakers keep in mind as they begin final preparation for a speech?*

- Tip 1: Practice out loud several times, and time your speech each time.
- Tip 2: Practice your speech in several ways, if possible.
- Tip 3: Prepare for a Q & A session carefully, even though you obviously can't practice it.
- Tip 4: Use the night before your presentation wisely.
- Tip 5: Be enthusiastic.

13.7 *What visual aid and delivery skills covered in this chapter relate specifically to your career (see highlighted fields of business, education, and healthcare)?*

- The *Spotlight on, Career Moment,* and *Connecting to* features highlight the value of communication in the fields of business, education, and healthcare.

SOLVE IT NOW!

Taking into consideration all that you learned about confidence building and speech preparation from this chapter, what visual aid and delivery advice would you recommend to Amina and Valerie in our opening scenario that would help them prepare for their student teacher presentations?*

- What audience type are Amina and Valerie likely to experience in the high schools when they give their first student-teaching presentations?

- Based on that audience type, what specific suggestions would you recommend when they prepare their PowerPoint presentations? What would you recommend that they avoid?

- Based on the audience type, what specific suggestions would you give Amina and Valerie for their delivery—including both verbal and nonverbal suggestions?

- How important do you think it will be for Amina and Valerie to cite sources during their presentations? Why?

*(Check your answers with those located in MyCommunicationLab, Scenario Analysis for Chapter 13)

The next chapter will continue preparing you for successful speaking by giving pointers on how to be persuasive.

KEY TERMS

SKILL BUILDERS

1. Taking into consideration all that you have learned about rehearsing a presentation, think about your past speaking experiences and determine which areas covered in this chapter you need to concentrate on the most when rehearsing your upcoming speeches. Which rehearsal advice did you find the most helpful? Were there any suggestions in this chapter that would not seem to help you personally? Be prepared to share your answers with your classmates.

2. Critically Evaluating

Using the critical evaluation form from Chapter 1, select and evaluate an article on *Using PowerPoint* obtained from a communication journal such as *Communication Education* (you may wish to check your library databases for articles). Be prepared to share your observations with your classmates.

3. Based on your personal experiences giving speeches or observing other give speeches, discuss your answers to these questions with others in a small group:

- What delivery problems are the most common? Why do you think these are so prevalent?

- Why do college students rehearse very little or skip rehearsal altogether?

- Which of the most annoying characteristics relating to PowerPoint do you see most often? What additional characteristics not mentioned in this chapter would you add to the list?

- Looking at the sample Problem Slides A–C covered in this chapter, which PowerPoint problems seem to be the most annoying and why? Do the solutions suggested seem likely to help? What other solutions would you suggest?

4. In groups, determine which of the following source citations is most effective and which is least effective and why. Revise the best into one that is even better and be prepared to share why it is better with your class. Check out the original source at www.cbsnews.com/stories/2004/04/19/health/main612476.shtml.

Researchers say that college-aged students are sleep deprived because they get only six to seven hours of sleep per night but really need nine hours.

- James Clack, Duke University director of counseling and psychological services, in an April 2004 CBS News report entitled "Help for Sleep-Deprived Students," says that the typical student gets only six to seven hours of sleep a night but needs nine hours. This deprivation leads to stress and lowered academic performance.

- According to Professor James Clack of Duke University, the typical student gets only six to seven hours of sleep a night instead of the nine hours research says they need.

- A 2004 CBS News report says that the typical student who gets between six to seven hours per night is sleep deprived.

- How many of you get less than six hours of sleep each night? An April 19, 2004, Associated Press article reported that the typical college-aged student should be getting nine hours of sleep each night. You won't be surprised to learn than most students get between six and seven hours instead.

EXPLORE SOME MORE . . .

1. To listen to one of the 100 Best Speeches of the Twentieth Century (such as "I Have a Dream" by Martin Luther King, Jr.), go to http://www.AmericanRhetoric.com and click on Top 100 Speeches.

- Also, click on Movie Speeches for speeches such as Coach Herb Brooks's "Address to 1980 U.S. Olympic Hockey Team before Playing the Soviets," delivered by Kurt Russell in the movie *Miracle;*

- "President's Address to the U.S. Pilots" in the movie *Independence Day,* delivered by Bill Pullman.

2. Looking for a good book that that includes great advice on making quality presentations and PowerPoint? We suggest you read:

- *Lend Me Your Ears: All You Need to Know about Making Speeches and Presentations* by Max Atkinson (Oxford University Press, 2009);

- *Beyond Bullet Points: Using Microsoft PowerPoint to Create Presentations that Inform, Motivate, and Inspire* by Cliff Atkinson (Microsoft Press, 2005).

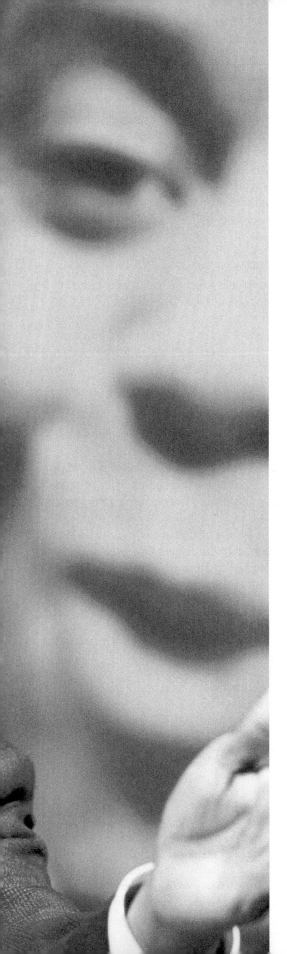

14 Persuasive Speaking

After studying this chapter you should be able to . . .
- Use social judgment theory to build an argument that will change the minds of your audience.
- Identify fallacious arguments in others' speeches and avoid them in your own.
- Plan and present a successful persuasive speech, using one or more of the persuasive organizational patterns.
- Apply the persuasive appeals successfully to a variety of audiences.

CHAPTER SUMMARY ⟩ P. 401 ⟩

"There's something missing in this presentation, but I can't decide what it is." Anh put her notes on the desk and looked up with a worried frown at her assistant, Mike. "This may be our one chance to persuade these students that Pets for the Environment needs and deserves their help."

"We have plenty of interesting facts and illustrations that relate to college students, but will they be interested enough to volunteer to help us? That's what we need—their help," Mike agreed.

"Something is missing. I'm really concerned that this won't be persuasive enough. I think we both agree that since Pets for the Environment is the newest nonprofit in the state, the students probably have never heard of it and may not even understand how much nonprofit organizations depend on volunteers. We do need to give them lots of facts," Anh replied.

Mike nodded his head. "That's true. But I don't think just facts will be enough. We have to make them care enough to want to volunteer."

"You don't think the facts will persuade them?" Anh asked. "When I heard about the number of pets that have died or become ill from the chemicals in pet food, toys, flea collars, and yards, I was persuaded that something had to be done."

"You know, I think it was more than just the numbers that persuaded you," Mike suggested. "I think it was the fact that pets and children were involved and that chemicals harm both pets and children. I think you had an emotional response to the facts you heard."

"You may be right," Anh conceded. "But will that be true of this audience? Most college students don't have pets or children. It's great that the Independent Students Association invited me to speak at its next meeting. Now what can I add to our presentation that will help persuade these students to volunteer to help save pets and children from dangerous chemicals?"

Anh and Mike in our opening scenario are right to be concerned about their presentation because persuasion is not the same as information. Their goal—and yours, if you are giving a persuasive speech—is to learn what is involved in persuasion and then to develop a successful persuasive presentation. As you read this chapter, identify at least three persuasive tips that could help Anh and Mike in their task to give a persuasive presentation to an unknown college audience.

SOLVE IT NOW! P. 405

We are bombarded by persuasive messages every day. Unless you just this second rolled out of bed, it is almost certain that you have been the target of multiple persuasive messages already by radio, television, Internet, billboards, and even your cell phone. As we discussed in Chapter 3, it is important to learn how to listen critically to persuasive messages to avoid being manipulated. However, it is also important to learn how to formulate persuasive messages so we can influence others effectively and ethically. Let's begin our discussion by looking at the nature of persuasion and how it differs from information.

Understanding Persuasion

LEARNING **OBJECTIVE**

14.1 What is the definition of persuasion, how do persuasive speeches differ from informative speeches, and what specific factors affect persuasion?

Training in persuasion has been around since ancient times when Aristotle, a Greek philosopher and teacher, defined **rhetoric** as "the faculty of discovering in every case the available means of persuasion" (Aristotle, 1926). Most rhetoricians agree that his all-encompassing treatise, *The Art of Rhetoric*, set the stage for all books on persuasion since that time. For a more modern definition, let's look at the speaking overview in Chapter 10 (p. 271): **persuasion** occurs when a speaker crafts messages with the intent of influencing the values, beliefs, attitudes, or behaviors of others.

Differences between Persuasive and Informative Speeches

One way to clarify persuasion is to contrast it with informative speaking, which we discussed in Chapter 12. Let's look at some key differences in detail.

Role of Speaker Intent
While the intent of the informative speaker is to create understanding by clarifying, expanding, or teaching a specific topic to the audience, the intent of a persuasive speaker is to present information in order to change the way the audience thinks or acts. By using logical, ethical, and emotional appeals (without trickery or control), persuasive speakers work to influence the attitudes, beliefs, values, and/or behaviors of their listeners. Presenting information and then telling your audience members to make up their own minds is not persuasion. In individualistic cultures such as the United States, speakers will be more persuasive if they take an explicit approach and state exactly which position they are advocating. O'Keefe (1990) offers this summary of research: "The overwhelmingly predominant finding is that messages that include explicit conclusions or recommendations are more persuasive than messages without such elements" (p. 160). In the section on persuasion and culture in this chapter, we will suggest a different approach to take with audiences from collectivistic cultures.

Role of Supporting Information
While informative speakers use supporting information to give the audience several unbiased choices, persuasive speakers use supporting information to prove that only certain beliefs or actions are acceptable. In other words, they attempt to limit audience choices. Note that persuasion does not involve trickery or coercion. Ethical speakers do not make up or withhold information or plagiarize sources. Instead, persuasive speakers use honest logic and evidence, establish truthful credibility, and use ethical emotional appeals to convince audience members that their positions are the only correct ones. Pay particular attention to the supporting materials especially designed for proof (see Figure 11.8 on page 303 for specifics).

Role of Psychological Information
While informative speakers use psychological information (values, beliefs, attitudes, and behaviors) gained from analyzing the audience so they can relate their topics more effectively to the frames of reference of their listeners, persuasive speakers use the psychological

information so they can best determine how to persuade their listeners. Without this knowledge, as summarized in **Figure 14.1**, their chances of being persuasive are greatly diminished.

Keep in mind that values are extremely difficult to change—especially in a single persuasive speech. *Values* are tied up with culture, and people do not take kindly to having their values attacked. It is more effective to indicate that you respect the audience's values and that, in fact, your values are consistent with theirs; then you can show them how your proposal fits in with those values. Knowing an audience's values helps you determine their beliefs and attitudes, which are more open to change than values. Look to see if a *belief* that relates to your topic might be based on faulty information or even lack of knowledge; if so, you can correct or explain this situation in your presentation. You are likely to find a wider range of *attitudes* in your audience than beliefs or values. Since attitudes lead to behaviors, you will want to spend most

Figure 14.1 Analyze your audience's values, beliefs, attitudes, and past behaviors.

Values
Principles a person holds as important
- Values may include family, wealth, ambition, health, security, or group achievement.
- Values are influenced by culture. For example, people in the individualistic cultures generally value the rights of the individual, while the members of collectivistic cultures are more likely to value the welfare of others.
- A person's value system is significant because it is the basis for his or her belief system.

Beliefs
What we hold to be true even if we can't prove that they are true
- Your beliefs are shaped by your values. For example, if you value family over ambition, you may believe that parents should put children ahead of personal career.
- Your beliefs are important because they are the foundation for your attitudes.

Attitudes
Leanings or predispositions to feel positively or negatively about an idea
- Attitudes are shaped by your values and beliefs. For example, if you value family over ambition and believe that a parent should put children ahead of personal career, your attitude toward having one parent staying at home with the children is probably positive.
- Your attitudes are important because they influence your behaviors.

Behaviors
Actions taken and justified from our values, beliefs, and attitudes
- Future behaviors are indicated by looking at our attitudes. For example, with the values, beliefs, and attitudes discussed above, you would be likely to take the behavior of staying at home with your children or doing whatever was necessary to ensure that your spouse was able to stay at home until the children were in school
- The stronger your attitudes, the more likely the behavior.

of your time in determining audience attitudes that relate to your topic, to you as a speaker, and to attendance at the speech. Follow the attitude analysis advice in Chapter 10, using the attitude analysis questions in Figure 10.9 on page 279. Once you have determined probable audience attitudes, you can work on changing them or strengthening them by using the logical, ethical, and emotional appeals covered later in this chapter.

Role of Speaker Expectations
A fourth difference between persuasive and informative speeches relates to speaker expectations. Effective informative speakers expect their audience members to grasp the full content of each presentation. Of course, as we discussed in Chapter 3 on listening, audience members won't remember everything in the presentation, but at least the chances are good that they will understand the basic information by the time the presentation is completed. On the other hand, experienced persuasive speakers do not expect audience members to make extreme attitude changes during a single persuasive presentation. If you are expecting this, you will be very disappointed—most people who are persuaded make small jumps in opinion change. Change usually continues over time rather than in one instant and dramatic occurrence. To get as much attitude change as possible, it is important to analyze your audience carefully so you will know which arguments are likely to be the most successful. Social judgment theory has some very practical advice for persuasive speakers, including how to determine which listeners are most likely to be persuaded (see *Making Theory Practical* feature on page 380).

Factors That Affect Persuasion
There are many factors that affect persuasion, but the ones that are especially important to speakers include culture, gender, ethics, and technology. Just as you would have to consider your parents and their attitudes if you were going to try to persuade them that you should move into an apartment off campus, so you will need to keep your audience's attitudes in mind when you attempt to persuade them as well. Pay particular attention to how culture, gender, ethics, and technology may affect audience attitudes. Let's take a brief look at each of these factors.

Culture
When it comes to persuading people, values are all important. Showing how your proposal fits in with the audience's values makes persuasion more likely. The problem is that different cultures often have different values. Several times in this text, we have mentioned the differences between individualistic and collectivistic cultures and low- and high-context cultures and the role these cultural variables play in the way messages and speakers are perceived. Those from collectivistic/high-context cultures, such as Mexico and Pacific Rim nations, are more likely to be persuaded with an indirect approach. Those from individualistic/low-context cultures, such as Great Britain and the United States, generally react positively to a more direct persuasive approach. Acuff (1993) points out that Eastern European countries, such as Russia or Poland, are even more direct in their communication than are Americans.

Power distance (Hofstede, 2001) is another cultural variable that affects persuasion. Audiences from high power distance cultures, such as Mexico and most Arab countries, view inequality and power differences as part of the status quo—as such, they are more likely to be persuaded by speakers with high status and authority and view a lone person making a presentation as having low status. On the other hand, audiences from low power distance countries, such as the United States or Australia, who value equality and shared decisions, are more likely

MAKING THEORY PRACTICAL
SOCIAL JUDGMENT THEORY

To help understand what the attitudes of your audience mean to you, the speaker—especially the views of those who are opposed to your position—let's take a look at **social judgment theory**. Your audience's attitudes toward your topic may fall anywhere from *strongly agree* to *strongly disagree* on this continuum:

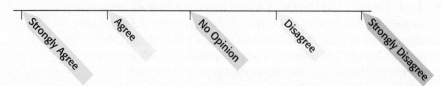

Theorists

Social judgment theory, developed by Sherif et al. (1965), proposes that on any issue there will be a range of positions. Where someone stands on a particular issue (such as gun control) will determine how likely that person is to be persuaded by a speaker's position. Social judgment theory says that in making a judgment, listeners will compare the speaker's view with their own position (called an **anchor**), which is based on their existing feelings and prior experiences concerning the issue. The more ego-involved they are with their preferred position, the less likely they are to be persuaded by another view. To be **ego-involved** means that the preferred position or anchor is closely tied to the person's self-identity.

Principles of Theory

To illustrate social judgment theory, let's continue with the issue of gun control. Imagine that there are nine different positions on the topic ranging from 1: *All citizens should be allowed to own a firearm of their choice in order to protect*

themselves all the way to #9: *Only military and law enforcement officers should be allowed to own guns*. Imagine that the speaker plans to take position #9. Whether you are persuaded by this speaker's position will depend largely on your existing views on gun control and where you stand in the continuum of the nine positions.

According to social judgment theory, the continuum of possible positions on a topic (such as the nine positions on gun control) can be divided into the following categories for each audience member:

• *Anchor* (**X**)—a person's most preferred position.

• *Latitude of Acceptance* (**LA**)—those positions that are acceptable; a person's anchor (**X**) falls within this range.

• *Latitude of Rejection* (**LR**)—those positions that are totally unacceptable; extreme positions on one or both ends of the continuum could be included here.

• *Latitude of Noncommitment* (**LN**)—those positions that are tolerable and trigger only neutral feelings.

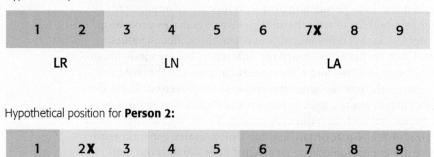

According to social judgment theory, *people who are highly ego-involved in their position will be the most resistant to change*. For example, a person who is strongly conservative and holds to a "strict interpretation" of the Constitution, is likely to have a *narrow latitude of acceptance*, meaning that

he or she would most likely be willing to consider only a limited number of the nine positions (see Person #2 above). On the other hand, people who have minimal ego-involvement in their position are more likely to have a *wide latitude of acceptance* (see Person #1 above).

Another principle of social judgment theory suggests that *persuasive messages tend to get distorted by listeners*. When listeners hear information that supports arguments that fall within their latitude of acceptance, they are likely to *assimilate* that information so that it seems closer to their anchor position than it truly is. On the other hand, when the information falls into the listeners' latitude of rejection, they are likely to *contrast* it so that it seems further from their position than it might actually be. In either case, little persuasion occurs. In the first situation, listeners will perceive that the new information merely confirms what they already believe. In the second situation, the new information is rejected.

PRACTICAL USES

So what does social judgment theory tell you about a strategy for your persuasive topic?

• First of all, persuasion is difficult, and analyzing your audience is crucial.

• Second, the arguments that have the greatest potential to lead to a change in beliefs will be those that represent small to moderate differences between your position and the listeners' anchor positions.

• Third, the strategy that is most likely to be productive is to argue for acceptance of a position that is, perhaps, no more than two positions away from your listeners' anchor positions.

So, how would you apply social judgment theory to our gun control example above? Since the speaker's position is number 9, there is a good chance of persuading an audience made up mostly of people such as Person #1, who is only two positions away. However, it is unlikely that the speaker will persuade an audience made up mostly of people such as Person #2 for three reasons:

• Person #2 is seven positions away from the speaker's position—this degree of change is highly unlikely.

• The speaker's position falls into the latitude of rejection for Person #2.

• Person #2 is likely to be ego-involved with the anchor position since he or she has a narrow latitude of acceptance and a wide latitude of rejection.

Therefore, as a speaker, your challenge is to determine where the majority of your audience is located along the continuum of positions for your topic. Although you can expect your listeners to hold varying positions on your topic, the majority of audience members will tend to cluster at a limited number of points. It is to these people that you will aim your persuasive efforts.

In our hypothetical case above, if your audience is clustering around Person #2's anchor position—remember that your position is #9—it would probably be wise to ask for a less radical position change from your audience than you would prefer. If you can move your listeners even one position closer to your position, then you are paving the way for subsequent persuasive speakers to move them even further along the continuum toward the position you actually hold.

Finally, keep in mind one more principle from social judgment theory: when the speaker's position falls in the audience's latitude of rejection, it is possible that a **boomerang effect** may result, meaning that instead of moving toward your position, the original opinion is strengthened. This, of course, is not what you want.

Source: Sherif, C. W., Sherif, M., & Nebergall, R. E. (1965). *Attitude and attitude change: The social judgment-involvement approach*. Philadelphia, PA: W. B. Saunders.

to be persuaded by a good idea presented by any competent person, regardless of the person's status or the number of people making the presentation. Effective persuasive speakers are aware of cultural differences and are able to relate their proposals across cultures.

Gender   Although gender differences may play less of a role in persuasion, listeners expect male and female speakers to fit into socially acceptable cultural values. According to Canary & Dindia (1999), in the American culture, men are generally considered to be more persuasive than women. They note that men are generally expected to be more outwardly aggressive and to use strong persuasive appeals, while women are expected to be less aggressive and use less intense persuasive appeals. At the same time, gender plays little role when Americans select the members of a negotiation team—experience and knowledge of the issues are more important. However, this approach causes persuasive problems since "there is no question that international business negotiations are dominated by men" (Acuff, 1993, p. 92). Effective speakers must be aware of the gender expectations and values of their audience.

Ethics

Ethical standards are also related closely to the values of a culture. In 2009, as the United States faced a serious economic crisis, numerous examples of financial fraud were uncovered, including those of Bernard Madoff, whose "ponzi scheme" cost Americans $50 billion or more, and Paul Greenwood and Stephen Walsh, who misappropriated approximately $553 million. Even so, Americans value honesty and ethics and expect their speakers to be ethical. To add to their credibility, persuasive speakers must be especially careful to research all sides of the topic, include only factual information to support their arguments, and accurately cite their sources. Persuasive presentations are not performances made for entertainment. Since, as a persuasive speaker, you can influence the beliefs, attitudes, and actions of your listeners, you have a heavy responsibility for honesty and accuracy. You must avoid plagiarism, distortion, exaggeration, fallacious reasoning, false supporting materials, and manipulative use of emotion in your presentations. Adapting to your audience does not mean falsifying information; it means putting your arguments into a form that will give them the best chance of being listened to. Although persuasive speakers do try to limit their arguments to what an audience will view as acceptable, there is no coercion or trickery in persuasion. The audience has a right to critically evaluate your information and to make their own decisions.

Technology

According to Charles Larson in *Persuasion* (2010), "It is clear that the Internet is changing the structure of persuasion as perhaps no other medium has since television. . . . it has democratized the voices of the individual . . ." (p. 362). E-commerce is growing by 33 percent a year (Ingram et al., 2008); everyone from individuals to small bed-and-breakfasts to large corporations from countries around the world advertise and sell their products online; millions of bloggers and users of *Facebook* and *YouTube* influence friends and strangers alike. Both factual and fallacious information on every conceivable topic is available almost instantaneously through technology such as *Google*, blogs, podcasts, e-zines (e-mail magazines), mobile phones, iPhones, and on and on. We are bombarded with hundreds of persuasive messages each day, and the need to carefully assess the credibility of these sources continues to grow as technology grows.

APPLY **WHAT YOU KNOW**
UNDERSTANDING PERSUASION

Apply what you know about persuasive speeches and how they differ from informative ones by completing the following critical thinking questions:

- Consider these values held by people of various cultures—group harmony, authority, self-reliance, belonging, equality, and patience. Select the value that you hold most strongly and use it to complete the following activity. First, list a *belief* that

comes from this value; next, list an *attitude* that comes from that belief; and finally, list a *behavior* you engage in because of that attitude.

- Using the belief that you just identified, apply social judgment theory to identify an additional belief that would fall into your latitude of acceptance and another one that would fall into your latitude of rejection.

Types of Persuasive Speeches

LEARNING **OBJECTIVE**

14.2 What are the two types of persuasive speeches, and what are the differences between them?

The two types of persuasive speeches introduced in Chapter 11—speeches to convince and speeches to actuate—differ in the way they appeal to audience values, beliefs, attitudes, and behaviors. The question that you, as a potential persuader, need to wrestle with is this: What am I trying to do with my message? Do I want my message to convince the audience to agree with a particular position, or do I want my message to move the audience to take a particular action?

Speech to Convince

If your goal is to convince, you will be asking for the audience to agree with your position on a particular topic. To succeed, you may need to convince them to form a new belief or change a previous belief:

- *Form a New Belief.* In this case, you are trying to get the audience to form an opinion where none existed previously. Perhaps they really don't have any belief on the topic so that your position falls in their latitude of noncommitment. This could be from lack of interest or lack of knowledge. It is up to you to present detailed and novel information and emotional appeals that will convince them that a new belief is in their best interests.

- *Change a Previous Belief.* Depending on where your audience's attitudes fall on the continuum from *strongly agree* to *strongly disagree* on your position, you may attempt to get the audience to change one of their beliefs. For example, if your audience believes that their community is safe, they won't be interested in raising money to hire new law enforcement officials. You will first need to convince your audience through the use of evidence, logic, and examples that the community is not safe—that is, you want the listeners to alter their previously-held belief to a more realistic one.

Another way to encourage listeners to change a previous belief begins with establishing a **common ground** between you and your audience by showing areas where you have similar interests, problems, or background. Then, if you can show that you used to have a belief similar to theirs but were forced to change that belief due to new evidence or a realization that the belief was based on false information, your audience may be persuaded to change their belief as well.

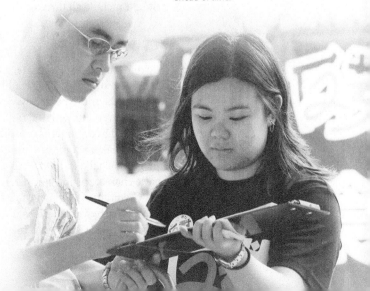

To establish common ground with your audience you may need to interview one or more of them ahead of time.

Speech to Actuate

In the **speech to actuate,** not only do you want your audience to agree with your position, you want them to take a specific action, such as voting. This is a more difficult goal to achieve because people are not easily motivated to act. In a speech to actuate, you may want the audience to do one of the following:

- *Continue a behavior*—such as continue donating money to a worthy cause; continue exercising three times a week; continue writing letters opposing the school board's actions on testing; continue using a designated driver at parties with alcoholic beverages.

- *Discontinue a behavior*—such as discontinue driving home after drinking even if they don't feel drunk; discontinue plagiarizing on assignments even if they think the assignment is busywork; discontinue getting less than seven hours of sleep most nights.

- *Adopt a new behavior*—plan a will before the summer is over; adopt their pets from a pet rescue organization instead of paying for puppies from a breeder; volunteer to help with a nonprofit organization at least ten hours each semester.

Recall that behavior is linked to attitude, which is linked to beliefs, which are linked to values. Long-lasting behavior change is not accomplished without some attention to the other principles to which behavior is linked. Smoking cessation, for example, is difficult to influence if the listeners value pleasure (or whatever smoking represents to them—rebelliousness, freedom of choice, the feeling of companionability with others in their social circle, or the like) more than they value health.

APPLY **WHAT YOU KNOW**
SELECTING YOUR SPEECH TYPE

Apply what you know about types of persuasive speeches by completing the following:

- Locate the brainstorming list of speech topics you prepared in Chapter 11, using Keith's list as a model (see Figure 11.2, page 291). If you can't find the list, prepare a new list of topics specifically related to persuasive speeches.

- Identify two topics that would make speeches to convince and two topics that would make speeches to actuate. Select topics that you feel strongly about and are interested in selecting as candidates for your persuasive speech.

- Select the best topic from each category, and write either a specific purpose or thesis statement for each topic.

LEARNING **OBJECTIVE**

14.3 According to Aristotle, what are the three primary means of persuasion, and how do they help you build effective persuasive appeals?

Persuasive Appeals That Really Persuade

According to Aristotle, there are three primary "means of persuasion," or types of **persuasive appeals**: *ethos*, *logos*, and *pathos*. You have encountered these terms in Chapter 3 as we discussed the topic of critical listening. **Ethos** deals with your credibility as a speaker; **logos** refers to the evidence and reasoning you use to add proof to your arguments; and **pathos** refers to your ethical use of emotion to get your audience personally involved in your topic. If you really want to be persuasive, your speech should include all three of these persuasive appeals.

Speaker Credibility (Ethos)

If you want to be persuasive, your audience must perceive you to be someone worthy of belief—in other words, a credible person. According to researchers, the more credible you are, the more persuasive you likely will be (O'Keefe, 1990). Listeners who have low ego-involvement with the topic are especially influenced by speaker credibility and less interested in arguments or evidence. On the other hand, listeners who are ego-involved in the speaker's topic are more impressed by evidence and logic than speaker credibility (Eagly & Chaiken, 1993; Petty & Cacioppo, 1996). A credible speaker is one with three basic characteristics: competency, trustworthiness, and charisma.

Credibility begins in the introduction of your speech when you share with the audience why your topic is important to you as well as what knowledge and experience you have with the topic. In other words, you explain what makes you *competent* to speak on this subject. If you have some expertise, the audience is more likely to listen—the first step toward being persuaded. In addition to your comments in the introduction, you can establish competence by demonstrating that you understand the issues (citing quality sources), that you have thoroughly investigated the data (by looking at both sides of the issue), and that your expertise can be relied upon (giving personal examples or narratives). Avoid using dysfluencies, such as "uhs" or poor articulation. These can hurt how audience members judge your competency (McCroskey & Young, 1981). On the other hand, a professional appearance can add to your competency (Behling & Williams, 1991) and so can your use of professional-looking visual aids (Seiler, 1971; Vogel et al., 1990), as discussed in Chapter 13.

To establish credibility you must also convince the audience that you are **trustworthy**—a person of good character. This is accomplished by, among other things, acknowledging other points of view (Chaiken, 1986), orally citing the sources of all of your information, and indicating that you have been fair in your analysis of the subject. You also increase the chances of being perceived as trustworthy by demonstrating your concern for the audience's needs—in other words, by being a person of goodwill. If you have a personal stake or will benefit in some way by successfully persuading your listeners, you may be perceived as more trustworthy if you acknowledge that fact but then go on to demonstrate that your primary concern is in meeting the audience's needs. Be careful with your delivery because poor eye contact, poor articulation, and a monotone voice can also make listeners question your trustworthiness (Addington, 1971).

A credible speaker is one with three basic characteristics: competency, trustworthiness, and charisma.

Finally, ethos involves **charisma**, which is that quality that causes people to be drawn to you. It is a quality that some people seem just naturally to possess. But charisma is also something that you can build, primarily through how you deliver your speech. The speaker who is clearly passionate about the topic and genuinely enthusiastic about speaking to the audience is likely to be seen as more charismatic than the speaker who appears to be delivering the speech because of having been coerced into doing so.

Evidence and Reasoning (Logos)

To be persuasive you need more than just credibility, you also need to show you are using effective evidence and reasoning. **Evidence** includes the statements and opinions presented in the form of statistics, definitions, illustrations, and other types of supporting materials that back up your position. **Reasoning** is a process that ties your evidence together in an orderly manner so that your conclusion logically follows from the evidence (Kahane & Cavender, 2002). **Figure 14.2** includes a review of three types of reasoning: inductive, deductive, and causal.

In order to accomplish logos appeals:

- *Include research from all sides of your selected issue.* You can't be sure that your position is supported by evidence until you look at all sides of the issue. Also, you need this information in order to effectively **refute** arguments against your position.

- *Present the evidence that is used to support each position and orally cite your sources for the evidence or data.* According to O'Keefe (1998, p. 67) there is "a significant persuasive advantage for messages providing information source citations." Some audience members have difficulty identifying evidence (Bettinghaus & Cody, 1997). Since they can't be persuaded if they don't know evidence exists, it is important to let your listeners know that important evidence is being presented (Reynolds & Reynolds, 2002). It's also a good idea to use logical-sounding phrases such as "as a result" or "based on this evidence, it is logical to conclude" (Bettinghaus & Cody, 1997).

Figure 14.2 Three Types of Reasoning

Types of Reasoning
Inductive Reasoning–begins with arguments and evidence that leads up to a conclusion.
• Good when audience is strongly opposed or hostile to topic.
• Preferred by collectivistic, high context cultures (like Mexico or Japan).
Deductive Reasoning–begins with the conclusion and then offers specific evidence and arguments to support that conclusion.
• Good when audience agrees with topic.
• Good when some members may have to leave before end of speech (i.e., a business meeting).
Causal Reasoning–shows a relationship or link between two problems, solutions, or items indicating that one caused the other.
• Prove the relationship with evidence.
• Or use logic to prove a probable relationship exists.

- *Use sound reasoning; avoid using fallacious reasoning.* Not everyone is able to examine the data and draw conclusions from the evidence that are logically correct. It is your responsibility as an ethical communicator to avoid making claims that are not based on logical reasoning. Unfortunately, some speakers use **fallacious reasoning**—arguments with fallacies or flaws in the reasoning. Some of the most common types of fallacious reasoning are listed and briefly discussed in **Figure 14.3**. Although we don't include every type of fallacy here, this partial list should help you to recognize that strong arguments are part of the logos of the message and should be based on sound reasoning.

When preparing your persuasive speech avoid using fallacious reasoning. Critical listeners in your audience would pick up on your use of fallacies and consider you less credible. Those who are not as aware may be fooled, but to attempt to manipulate them by using fallacious reasoning is unethical on your part.

Audiences need to hear the fruits of your research, and they must be allowed to follow your reasoning. However, credibility and well-reasoned evidence are not enough to persuade most audiences—a third persuasive appeal is also needed.

Emotional Appeal (Pathos)

Most audiences need more than sound evidence delivered by a trustworthy person to be persuaded. Speakers must also use *emotional appeals*, or pathos. In other words, your listeners may be convinced that your findings are trustworthy, that your cause is just, and that you are a good person who has only their interests at heart, but unless you move them emotionally, they may not be persuaded. This doesn't mean that they will all reach for their hankies; it does mean that they will feel personally connected to your topic and position. There are many ways to move people emotionally. Visual images may arouse an emotional response. Stories about the plight of a person, especially a person with whom your audience can identify or for whom audiences typically feel a high degree of concern, are often quite effective in generating emotional responses.

In addition to meeting the control, openness, and inclusion needs discussed in Chapter 6, an emotional appeal in a persuasive speech is usually positive, often causing the audience to feel excited or sympathetic. However, it is possible to use negative emotional appeals—called **fear appeals**—that cause the audience to feel afraid or worried. Although false fear appeals, such as unethical exaggeration, are to be avoided, ethical fear appeals

Figure 14.3 Fallacious Reasoning

Ad hominem—"argument against the person" is the type of reasoning used when the speaker attacks a person instead of the person's argument. For example, if you told your audience that they should not believe your opponent because of some personal circumstance or trait that is irrelevant to the topic, it would appear that you are trying to divert your audience's attention from the merits of the opponent's argument. "You cannot believe Ms. Jones' statement that her proposal will save tax dollars; after all, she has been married three times!"

Ad populum—asserts that an idea is true because most people think it is true. This fallacy is often effective because many of us want to fit in with the majority. If you told your audience that something was true because "everyone else" was doing or believing it, you would be using *ad populum* or "bandwagon." Just because several people believe something to be true, doesn't make it true.

Ad verecundiam—is an appeal to authority that claims that an idea must be true because some esteemed person claims it is true, even though the issue at hand is out of that person's area of expertise. When you quote the opinion of a Hollywood celebrity on a topic other than their field of knowledge and experience, you run the risk of using an *ad verecundiam* fallacy.

Begging the question—occurs if you try to prove that a claim is true by using the claim itself as proof. This type of reasoning is circular reasoning that is missing any proof. For example: "Many of us have heard the charges recklessly made by Mayor Griswold's opponents that she is in the pocket of certain special interest groups. We all know that this can't be true. We know her. We know her character. We know that she would never put herself in this position."

Hasty generalization—occurs when you base your conclusion on only isolated examples or too few examples. Imagine a speaker using the following argument:

• Last year in our own city a student was caught carrying a handgun
• A survey of one inner-city school found that 10 percent of students bring handguns to school
• It is obvious that our state needs to install metal detection equipment in every school in the state.

Unless the above conclusion is supported with more inclusive research, it is certainly a hasty generalization.

Post hoc—occurs when speakers assert that because event A occurred shortly before event B, B must have been caused by A, even though no clear evidence is presented linking the two events. For example, if you were to present evidence that instances of cancer increased shortly after the introduction of aspartame into diet drinks and concluded that this proved that aspartame causes cancer, you would be using a *post hoc* argument that is potentially fallacious.

Straw man—occurs when you try to prove the validity of your position by attacking an exaggerated or misrepresented version of an opponent's argument instead of the opponents' actual position. It is easier to defeat this straw man argument than the *real* position. Although it appears that you have won a victory over the opponent, the real position has not been addressed. For example, legislators often vote in favor of bills that are quite complex, including provisions that require additional expenditure of taxes. A legislator may choose to characterize her opponent's support of a bill as a "vote for higher taxes," which few people like to see. The straw man is defeated, but the actual position, which is much more complex, is ignored.

can be persuasive. Research indicates that arousing a high level of fear is more persuasive than low or medium levels of fear (Sutton & Eiser, 1984). Persuasion is most effective if, after arousing a significant level of fear, you follow with an explanation of how likely the consequence is to actually happen and what the audience can do to minimize it or to stop it from occurring (Maddux & Rogers,

1983). If the audience members think that they are personally unable to overcome barriers to solving the problem, they are less likely to be persuaded. For more on fear appeals, see the *Spotlight on Healthcare* later in this chapter.

There are many other contributions to the study of persuasion introduced by Aristotle in *The Art of Rhetoric*. However, these three ideas—ethos, logos, and pathos—are among the key principles that can be used in guiding a speaker in the construction of a persuasive speech. As you prepare your presentations, whether you are doing individual speeches or working on a team presentation, you must make sure that all three of these appeals are adapted carefully to your audience.

APPLY **WHAT YOU KNOW**
PERSUASIVE APPEALS

Apply what you know about persuasive appeals and complete the following:

- Use the sample persuasive speech in this chapter (pp. 398–400) or select one of the persuasive speeches on

MyCommunicationLab for Chapter 14. Identify one use of ethos, one of logos, and one of pathos.

- Identify any instances of fallacious reasoning, and label the specific type.

LEARNING **OBJECTIVE**

14.4 What are the seven persuasive patterns covered in this chapter, and what are the most appropriate speaking uses for each?

Persuasive Organizational Patterns

The way you organize your persuasive speech will determine how effective it is. Let's look at seven of the most effective persuasive patterns, dividing them into three categories to clarify when they are the most useful.

Persuasive Pattern for Arguments: Statement of Logical Reasons

If your goal is to present a logical, straightforward argument to your audience, the statement of logical reasons pattern is especially effective (see **Figure 14.4**).

The statement of logical reasons pattern, which is a persuasive variation of the topical pattern (see Chapter 12), is one of the easiest and most elegant persuasive plans you can use. Its success will depend—as all speeches do—on your audience and on the material you are using. Since the **statement of logical reasons pattern** is directly persuasive, it works well if the majority of your audience agrees with you or is close to agreeing with you. However, if your audience is likely to be strongly opposed to your position or hostile to you, you will probably want to select a different pattern. In this plan, you are essentially stating, "This is what I believe and here is why." Your position is clearly stated in the introduction, and your three to five main points are the reasons for your belief. The subpoints are the evidence to support each belief. Here is the pattern template and a speech example:

Figure 14.4 Persuasive Pattern for Arguments

Statement of Logical Reasons
I. First logical reason
II. Second logical reason
III. Third logical reason

PATTERN TEMPLATE:

Topic and Position: Thesis stated in introduction with your position stated clearly.

   I. My first reason for believing as I do (subpoints will present evidence to support)

  II. My second reason for believing as I do (subpoints will present evidence to support)

 III. My third reason for believing as I do (subpoints will present evidence to support)

SAMPLE TOPIC:

Topic: Capital Punishment.

Position: We should all support capital punishment.

   I. Capital punishment helps to deter crime.

  II. Capital punishment saves taxpayer money when it is properly applied.

 III. Capital punishment is consistent with the teachings of the great religions.

As in the topical pattern that we learned in Chapter 12, arrangement of main points will depend on what you believe will be most effective with your audience. It is usually recommended that you put your least powerful point in the middle of your speech if possible. If your topic lends itself to exposing the weaknesses of another person's arguments, see the refutation pattern located on MyCommunicationLab for Chapter 14.

APPLY **WHAT YOU KNOW**
ARGUMENTS PATTERN

Now that you have an understanding of the statement of logical reasons pattern that is most often used for speeches, complete the following:

- Using the topic of "Use of Taxpayer Money to Finance Construction of Professional Sports Arenas" or the persuasive topic you plan to use in your next speech, list and organize possible main points and some subpoints in the *statement of logical reasons pattern*.

- Share your outline with some classmates and get their opinion on how effective this pattern might be.

Persuasive Patterns for Problems and Solutions

If your goal is to persuade your audience on how to solve a problem, there are three patterns that work especially well: problem-solution, progressive questions, and comparative advantages (see **Figure 14.5**).

Problem-Solution
Although the **problem-solution pattern** can be used in an informative speech, it is most commonly used in persuasive speeches. For this pattern to be persuasive, you must convince the audience that the problem is a serious one and that your solution(s) will solve the problem. Please note that in this pattern, you must develop both the problem and the solution more or less equally. If you plan to mention the problem only briefly (perhaps because you think

Figure 14.5 Persuasive Patterns for Problems and Solutions

Problem-Solution Pattern
I. Problem presented
II. Solution presented
Progressive Questions Pattern
I. Question #1 asked and answered
II. Question #2 asked and answered
III. Question #3 and more as needed
Comparative Advantages Pattern
I. Plan A is ineffective
II. Plan B is much better

the audience already understands it thoroughly) and spend the majority of your time explaining why they should adopt your proposed solution, you will be using another pattern from among those we will be discussing shortly. For now, just remember you are NOT using the problem-solution pattern unless you are actually spending a significant portion of the body discussing the problem. The following is an example of a persuasive speech using the problem-solution pattern:

PATTERN TEMPLATE:

Topic: Thesis stated in introduction

    I. Statement of problem

        A. We see the effects all around us.

           1. Effect #1

           2. Effect #2

           3. Effect #3

        B. We know what causes it.

           1. Cause #1

           2. Cause #2

    II. Statement of solution

        A. How it works

        B. Benefits

SAMPLE TOPIC:

Topic: Air Pollution

This photo showing automobile-caused pollution would work well as a computer visual introducing the main points of a speech on air pollution.

Position: We can solve air pollution if we adopt a three-prong plan of action.

    I. Air pollution is a serious national problem.

        A. We see the effects all around us.

           1. Smog and pollution

           2. Plant damage and crop losses

           3. Human asthma and lung conditions

        B. We know what causes it.

           1. Automobiles and other users of fossil fuels

           2. Power plants and factories

    II. Air pollution can be solved if we adopt these plans of action.

        A. Drive hybrid cars or cars that get over 30 miles per gallon.

        B. Use alternate means of transportation at least twice per week.

        C. Improve inspection procedures for plants and factories.

Progressive-Questions[1]

In the progressive-questions pattern, the speaker walks the audience through the problem-solving process, beginning with the problem and ending with a solution by asking and answering a series of questions in a sequence that logically follows the thought patterns of the audience. The **progressive-questions pattern** organizes the main points of the speech, using questions of fact, conjecture, value, and policy—review these question types in

[1] Developed by one of your authors, Bonnie Creel.

Chapter 9. Sound policy will be developed best when all four of these questions are included. Likewise, a speaker is able to advocate more effectively for a policy if these questions are answered to the audience's satisfaction. Your progressive main points or questions could include the following:

- *What is the current situation?*—a noncontroversial question of fact. The speaker presents data that describe a current problem for which no policy exists, or for which the current policy has apparently been ineffective.

- *How did we get into this situation?*—a controversial question of fact. It typically seeks to establish causality when people disagree about the causes of the problem.

- *What will happen if we maintain the status quo?*—a question of conjecture. Using projections from reliable sources, the speaker will predict a worsening problem if something is not done to change the situation.

- *Why is maintaining the status quo unacceptable?*—a question of value. The competent speaker will have used audience analysis to identify the values that are most deeply held by the audience and will attempt to show that the current situation does not meet those values.

- *What should be our course of action?*—a question of policy. In this final main point, the speaker will make a recommendation to accept a proposed policy, often as a replacement for a policy currently in place.

Although the order and type of questions can be changed, as needed, for various audiences, the above questions and order are used the most often. Following is the pattern template and one topic example for the progressive-questions pattern:

PATTERN TEMPLATE:

I. What is the situation or problem?

II. How did we get into this situation or problem?

III. What can we expect in the future?

IV. Why is the status quo unacceptable?

V. What should be our course of action or policy?

SAMPLE TOPIC:

Topic: Cervical Cancer
Position: Cervical cancer can be decreased if states take the proper action.

I. The current situation includes an increase in rates of cervical cancer.

II. We got into this situation because increasing numbers of young women are having unprotected sex with multiple partners at younger ages.

III. In the future, we can expect even greater numbers of cervical cancer caused by the human Papilloma virus.

IV. The status quo is unacceptable because there is an effective and safe vaccine that will protect against HPV, and because parents who neglect to provide this for their daughters, for whatever reason, are endangering public health.

V. Our course of action should involve states' requiring the vaccine against HPV for all girls from age 12 as a condition of enrollment in public schools.

The questions could be worded in many different ways. Remember that the goal of the progressive questions pattern is to answer the questions in a sequence that logically follows the thought patterns that are most likely to be persuasive to your audience. Also, when you use questions of fact, conjecture, value, and policy in your presentation, policy is more soundly developed and more likely to be persuasive.

Comparative-Advantages

The **comparative-advantages pattern** is an excellent way to organize your persuasive speech when your audience agrees that there is a problem needing to be solved but disagrees on how best to solve it. In this situation, you do not need to spend much time proving that there is a problem (as you would if you were using the problem-solution pattern). Rather, a comparative-advantages pattern will compare and contrast various solutions demonstrating that your plan has more (or more desirable) advantages, and fewer (or less undesirable) disadvantages than any of the other plans. There are at least two ways to do this shown in the following pattern templates; see also the topic example for comparative advantages pattern:

PATTERN TEMPLATES:

Approach 1:

 I. First plan

  A. Advantages of plan 1

  B. Disadvantages of plan 1

 II. Second plan (the last plan is generally the one you favor)

  A. Advantages of plan 2 (or disadvantages first, if you prefer)

  B. Disadvantages of plan 2 (or advantages)

Approach 2:

 I. Advantages (or you may choose to do disadvantages first)

  A. First plan

  B. Second plan

 II. Disadvantages (or advantages)

  A. First plan

  B. Second plan

SAMPLE TOPIC:

Topic: Recycling
Position: Curbside recycling is superior to drop-off recycling for citywide implementation.

(Note: This pattern assumes everyone is already in agreement that some sort of recycling program needs to be offered. Therefore, no discussion of the problem is needed—only of the possible solutions.)

 I. Plan 1: Having drop-off locations around the city is a flawed option.

  A. There are some advantages to drop-off recycling:

   1. No investment in extra truck maintenance would be required.

   2. Properties already owned by the city could serve as drop-off sites.

B. However, there are significant disadvantages to this plan:

  1. The cost for staffing at drop off sites will be expensive.

  2. Because drop-off recycling is inconvenient for citizens, fewer homes will recycle resulting in more trash in remaining landfills.

II. Plan 2: Curbside recycling is the superior option.

A. There is one disadvantage: Extra use of trucks will require additional maintenance of trucks.

B. However, there are significant advantages to this plan:

  1. Residents are significantly more likely to recycle with the convenience of curbside pickup.

  2. There will be significantly less trash in our remaining landfills.

  3. Money received from recycled materials sold to local companies will not only pay for the extra truck maintenance, it will provide for a new city park.

One significant benefit of the comparative-advantages pattern is that it shows your audience that you have considered both sides. This adds to your credibility, especially in the competence and character dimensions. If structured well, this plan can be used with audiences you think are likely to be opposed to your position. By using comparative advantages, you can acknowledge that each plan has both advantages and disadvantages, which demonstrates that you have been fair and even-handed in your analysis of both positions. Obviously, this strategy will work only if you can truly prove that your plan solves the problem more effectively than the other plan. This pattern, by the way, is also good when you are expecting the audience to be exposed to **counter-persuasion**—that is, you anticipate that they will hear the other side at some point (maybe just before or after your speech). By showing the negatives of the other view and the positives of your view, you have prepared them to be less easily swayed by the opposing view. You have "inoculated" them (McGuire, 1985; Szabo & Pfau, 2002). For more on inoculation theory, see the *Developing Skills* feature in this chapter.

Persuasive Pattern for Policy and Action: The Motivated Sequence

If your goal is to persuade the audience to change a policy or to take a particular action, the motivated sequence is one of the best patterns to use (see **Figure 14.6**).

The **motivated-sequence pattern** designed by Alan Monroe in the 1930s (Gronbeck et al., 1994) is a variation of the problem-solution pattern that doesn't end with convincing the audience; it actuates the audience to take a specific action. One typical use of the motivated sequence pattern is to "sell" someone something: a product, a process, an idea, or an action.

It is important to realize that, unlike all of the other patterns we have looked at, this one *does not need a separate introduction and conclusion*; those functions are accomplished within the five main points of the pattern: attention, need, satisfaction, visualization, and call to action. Here is a template of the pattern and a topic example:

Figure 14.6 Persuasive Pattern for Policy and Action

Motivated Sequence
I. Attention
II. Need
III. Satisfaction
IV. Visualization
V. Action

PATTERN TEMPLATE:

I. Call *attention* to the fact that there is a problem (attention-getter to open).

II. Prove that this is a serious problem that *needs* to be solved.

III. Tell us your proposed solution to *satisfy* the problem.

IV. *Visualize* the improved situation if we adopt your plan, and/or the worsening situation if we don't.

V. Call us to the specific *action* you want us to take (conclude in a memorable way).

As you can see, the first two main points correspond to the "problem" step in the problem-solution pattern, and the last three main points take care of the "solution" step, adding the element of the call to action.

SAMPLE TOPIC:

Topic: Seat Belts
Position: A national bill advocating zero tolerance for unbuckled children should be implemented.

I. Almost half of the children killed in traffic crashes are not buckled in their seats.

II. Unbuckled children remain a serious problem in the United States today.

   A. Restrained children have an 80% lower risk of fatal injury.

   B. Each year, there are over 7,600 children killed in vehicle accidents.

   C. Most accidents happen within 5–20 miles from home.

III. A zero tolerance for unbuckled children bill should be implemented nationwide.

IV. If all children were buckled in every time they rode in a car, the number of children killed in car accidents could be reduced by 50 percent.

V. Sign my petition to our Congressional representatives today urging them to vote for a new seatbelt law.

Keep in mind that you can use the motivated sequence as your overall organizational pattern while also incorporating elements of the other patterns as ways to structure each of these steps. For example, your *satisfaction* step could be structured using statement of logical reasons and your *visualization* step could be structured by using comparative advantages. Other options could also be used.

APPLY **WHAT YOU KNOW**
POLICY AND ACTION PATTERN

Now that you have an understanding of the organizational pattern that is most often used for speeches that focus on policy or call to action, complete the following:

- Using the topic of "Standardized Testing as a Requirement for Graduation," create a rough-draft outline to reflect how you might construct the speech using the motivated-sequence pattern. Try to include subpoints as well as main points.

- If you are beginning to develop a persuasive speech for your class, experiment with whether your topic might work in the motivated-sequence pattern. If not, which persuasive pattern do you think will work best? Why?

DEVELOPING **SKILLS**
HOW TO USE INOCULATION THEORY

Wouldn't it be great if, once your arguments have convinced an audience, they would remain immune to having their opinions changed by any information or counterattacks they might hear later? Inoculation theory (McGuire 1964; 1985) describes a process that makes people resistant to being persuaded. According to McGuire, you can make people immune to accepting ideas in the same way a shot or vaccination makes them immune to disease. For example, before the flu season, you take a shot containing a weakened amount of flu virus which causes your body to build antibodies against the flu. In the future, if you are infected, your body will recognize the virus, attack, and defeat it. According to McGuire, ideas work in a similar manner. Helping your audience look at opposing arguments or the pros and cons of certain ideas allows them to build counterarguments to use when they are faced with these or similar arguments later.

So how can you use this approach in a speech? Let's assume that your topic is a "hot" one in the media, and you feel fairly sure that audience members will hear the other side of the issue from later speakers. To help build immunity against opposing ideas, as a speaker you can present one or two typical arguments that may be used to oppose your position. You can briefly look at these arguments and then refute them with logic and evidence showing why they are based on inaccurate evidence, are built on faulty reasoning, or are just flat out wrong. You are stimulating the production of counterarguments so that when the audience hears one of these arguments, they will resist being persuaded. In fact, researchers have found that even if a new argument is presented that you did not mention, immunity often carries over as well to these new arguments in sort of a "broad blanket of protection" (Pfau, 1997, pp. 137–138).

Remember, if you want to build immunity to counterarguments in your audience, it takes more than just mentioning opposing arguments—you have to specifically refute them. Unless your audience already agrees with your position or the topic is a new one that is unlikely to be mentioned in the news, presenting your side then mentioning and refuting the arguments opposed to your position is a good approach for building audience resistance to future attacks. It has been used successfully to inoculate teenagers against smoking (Pfau al., 1992) and used successfully in politics—for example when Bill Clinton used inoculation theory in 1992 to foil anticipated Republican attacks against his record as governor of Arkansas (Pfau & Burgoon, 1988). You can do more than just give a persuasive speech and hope that your audience will remain persuaded; you can use inoculation theory and gain a degree of certainty.

APPLY **WHAT YOU KNOW**
PROBLEMS AND SOLUTIONS PATTERNS

Now that you have an understanding of the organizational patterns that are most often used for speeches that focus on problems and solutions, complete the following:

- Using the topic of "Graduated Drivers' Licenses for Teen Drivers," select one of the organizational patterns presented in this section and create a rough draft outline to reflect how you might construct the speech. Try to include subpoints as well as main points.

- Select another of these patterns and experiment with how you might use it to approach the speech from a different angle. Which pattern do you think works best, and why?

- If you are beginning to develop a persuasive speech for your class, experiment to determine whether your topic might work well with one or more of these patterns.

We have examined seven different organizational patterns that work well for persuasive speeches. Before you decide on one for your persuasive speech, look carefully at all the patterns and pick the one that is best suited for your topic and audience and that fits your personal preferences.

LEARNING **OBJECTIVE**

14.5 Which persuasive patterns are most appropriate when the majority of the audience agrees, disagrees, is neutral, or has opinions that vary widely?

Adapting Organizational Patterns to Audiences

As we have pointed out repeatedly in this text, you cannot make any meaningful decision about how to communicate without carefully considering your audience. You want audience members to adjust their values/beliefs/attitudes/behaviors to your ideas. But to do so, you must figure out how to adjust your ideas to meet their needs.

One way to adjust to your audience's needs is to select an organizational pattern that is particularly effective in presenting your arguments in a way that will take into account where your audience is when you begin your presentation. While you can use many patterns in a variety of situations, as a speaker you should be aware that certain patterns are especially effective in certain situations. In this section, we will suggest some patterns you might want to consider, depending on the characteristics of your specific audience. We are not suggesting that these are the only patterns that are useful in each case; we are merely highlighting those organizational schemes that you may find especially useful.

When the Audience Favors Your Position

Sometimes, your audience analysis will suggest to you that your audience members are already likely to be in favor, possibly strongly in favor, of your position. In this case, your goal is to reinforce their beliefs and focus on the positive.

To do so, you should not merely repeat what they already know. You must find new and compelling information that will strengthen their perception that the beliefs you share are sound. A speech that focuses on demonizing the opponent or making derogatory comments about the opposing position may backfire. Audiences that already believe as you do are more likely to respond to a speech that is more positive in tone. *Use the statement of logical reasons pattern* as it allows you to accomplish what you need to accomplish in an uncomplicated and straightforward manner. You persuade by showing several logical reasons why the desired position is the correct position, belief, action, or behavior. "We believe this, and we believe it because we have seen _____, and because we _____, and because we know that _____."

If your audience is likely to strongly oppose your position, be sure to refer to social judgment theory in planning your arguments.

When the Audience Opposes Your Position

When your audience analysis reveals that your audience is opposed or strongly opposed to your position, your goal is to change beliefs. It is important to be realistic about what you will be able to achieve with your speech.

One way to understand an audience that opposes your position is by referring to social judgment theory (see the *Making Theory Practical* feature in this chapter). Recall that the arguments likely to be the most persuasive will be those that represent small to moderate discrepancies between the listener's anchor position and the new proposition. This is because persuasion is incremental, meaning that opinions are generally formed over a long period of time. The likelihood that your speech alone will change the strongly held beliefs of an audience is minimal. In many cases, your most realistic expectation would be that you might be able to move your audience along a continuum from *strongly opposed* to your position to a point at which they are willing to consider positions that oppose theirs. Your hope, then, would be that subsequent persuasive messages, delivered by you or by other sources, would continue to move that audience toward your favored position.

There are two organizational patterns that may be useful when your audience is likely to be initially opposed to your position.

- *Statement of logical reasons* may work, as long as your reasons offer new information that may fall inside your audience's latitude of acceptance.

- *Comparative advantages* is a pattern that may be useful, especially if you are fair in acknowledging the strengths of the opposing position while at the same time stressing the superiority of your position.

When the Audience Is Neutral toward Your Position

There are, inevitably, situations in which your audience analysis suggests that your audience members are likely to be neutral in their attitudes toward your topic. This is helpful information only if you investigate further to determine why they are neutral.

There are three basic reasons that audiences may be neutral. The first is that they are *ignorant*. In other words, they do not know anything about your topic. They do not know what stem cells are or why they are controversial. If this is the situation you face, your persuasive plan will have to include presentation of sufficient information to permit the audience to understand the issue. However, sometimes the audience members are well acquainted with the topic, having heard arguments both pro and con. Their neutrality is based on the fact that they are *undecided*. They are sitting on the fence, and they have not decided which side they will choose to stand on. Your goal in this instance is to demonstrate the superiority of your position, showing how the results can affect the audience personally. A third reason that audiences may be neutral is that they are *apathetic*. They don't really care. To persuade this group, you must motivate them to care. Human nature being what it is, the best way to make people care is to show them how the issue affects them. The best organizational pattern depends on the cause for the neutrality:

- The *progressive-questions pattern* works well when the audience is neutral because of *ignorance*. It is also suited for audiences that are neutral due to *apathy*; audiences that are apathetic probably don't think that a serious problem exists.

- The *comparative-advantages pattern* is particularly useful when audience members are aware of the topic but are still *undecided*.

When the Audience Opinions Vary Widely

In audiences with a wide variety of opinions, aim your arguments (design your strategy) to appeal to the point at which the audience tends to cluster (see social judgment theory). If your audience is made up of a balanced number of listeners who agree, have no opinion, and disagree the statement of logical reasons can be especially helpful. The logical reasons pattern is more moderate and likely to relate to all without offending anybody and can strengthen those who already agree or are leaning that way.

Sample Student Speech

Now that we have discussed how to prepare an effective persuasive presentation, read this sample persuasive speech by Jessica Peters. The speech was transcribed from the video taken during her actual speech. As you read this speech, see if you can determine whether it was a speech to convince or a speech to actuate. Also, what organizational pattern did Jessica use? Do you think it was the best pattern for her topic? What suggestions for improvement would you make?

Expired Tires

by Jessica Peters

INTRODUCTION:
In her introduction, Jessica grabs our attention by telling us what happened when she got her driver's license at the age of 16. She then gives a factual illustration of four young men on a camping trip and a quotation from a 20/20 correspondent to show the seriousness of her topic—Expired Tires. She then previews the main areas she will cover in her speech.

Q: *Did Jessica motivate you to want to listen to her speech? What else might she have done in her introduction to grab your attention?*

When I turned 15 I could not wait to get my license. Unfortunately my dad could. We spent the entire spring before my 16th birthday studying cars. But the one thing that my dad didn't teach me is the one thing that most dads don't know to teach their daughters. While crazy drivers and car accidents are taught as the most dangerous component of driving the fact is that the tires on your car are actually the most dangerous aspect a driver ever overlooks.

"In July of 2003 four young men took a dream camping trip to Canada. Everything seemed great. The location, the equipment, and the time had been selected perfectly. Even the car had been checked for safety on the road. It seemed that everything was prepared. But on July 21 two of the four young men were killed in a car accident. The accident was caused by the fact that the car being driven rested on tires that had aged past their expiration dates." In fact according to Chief Correspondent Brian Ross on a July 2008 20/20 program called Aged Tires, "the tires were nine years old." Expired tires is a problem that many Americans face each and every day but overlook because no one has taken the time to explain the issue of aged tires. So today that is just what I will do by first, examining the issue of expired tires, then taking a look at what the tire industry plans to do about this problem, before finally learning what we can do to better protect ourselves on the road ahead.

PROBLEM:
Jessica uses a variety of interesting supporting materials to persuade us of the seriousness of the problem.

Q: *How many different types of supporting materials can you identify?*

Jessica also does a good job of citing her sources in the speech instead of waiting until the end to give us a list of her references as some speakers do. She was obviously aware that if she waited, the persuasive value of her sources would be much less.

According to AA1Car.com, an automotive diagnostics Web site last visited on October 5, 2008, the issue first came to light in late 2003 when a private safety group called Strategic Safety asked the National Highway Traffic and Safety Administration, known as the NHTSA, to investigate the issue of aging tires. Because expired tires cause blow outs both Strategic Safety and NHTSA took a deeper look into accidents caused by an old tire blowing out. In that same year Strategic Safety "documented twenty car accidents caused by an old tire blowing out." Reportedly ten of the twenty accidents resulted in fatalities, meaning that a little more than five years ago the average driver had only a 50% chance of surviving an accident caused by expired tires.

Many of you may be thinking that surely you could tell the difference between a brand new tire and an old tire easily. There must be a distinct, physical difference, right? Wrong. A twenty-year-old tire can be and is being sold alongside 'brand new' tires each and every day. And from the outer appearance of the tire no one can tell the difference. But we should remember that looks can be deceiving. While a fifteen- or even twenty-year-old tire may look just as new as a tire fresh from the manufacturer, the inside of the tire is slowly deteriorating over time, allowing the expired tire to dry out and begin cracking.

According to Sean Kane, vehicle safety advocate, "over 100 deaths in the U.S. have been attributed to aged tires that dried out and lost their treads even though they appeared to be safe." The deterioration process works like this. William D. Siuru, journalist for *New Car Buying Guide* on September 27, 2008, states that "the causes of tire deterioration are natural aging and oxidation as well as ultraviolet and ozone damage." Wisegeek.com on September 27, 2008, explains that "oxidation is one thing that causes metal to rust and freshly cut apples to turn brown." Siuru further explains that "both light and heat cause oxidation and can create enough damage to cause a slow leak or early tube failure". But oxidation is not the only problem. Siuru's article continues to explain that "ozone attacks rubber, causing it to crack perpendicular to any applied stress." When a driver takes his car, with its aged tires, for a spin the heat of the road combined with the heat being generated by the increasing speed causes the tire to melt and wear in small amounts. As the combination of internal deterioration, speed, and heat progress, the tire is literally waiting for its moment to cause a tremendous blowout. So if this problem has been around for years, then why is this the first time that so many Americans are hearing about it?

Some say that the American tire industry doesn't want to deal with the effects of cleaning up their "mess." It would be too much trouble to track down all of the aged tires in America. However, on 20/20 Brian Ross states that Britain "strongly recommends" a six–year tire replacement of all British tires. In fact in an interview with Brian Ross, Sean Kane states that the issue of expired tires "is known by everyone but the American consumer." However, SafetyResearch.net on June 18, 2009, states that many tire and American manufacturers like Bridgestone–Firestone, Ford Motors, and Daimlerchrysler all recommend that tires should have expiration dates, yet Britain is the only country to take advantage of this recent information making many American consumers wonder why exactly this information is being passed up. Brian Ross questions, "Are British consumers better informed than Americans?" Perhaps so, but regardless, if the American Tire Manufacturers know that tires should be replaced every six years then what exactly is preventing them from protecting the American consumer?

In the 20/20 interview with Brian Ross, Dan Zieliksia, Representative of the American Rubber Manufacturer Association, states that he sees no way for Britain to come to the conclusion of six-year expirations. But when asked if he had looked into Britain's explanation for six-year expiration dates he replied with, "Umm . . . I have not." Even though Zieliksia is a member of the same Rubber Manufacturer Association as the British. And to make the situation worse, Brian Ross states that "Ford Motors, an American manufacturer, asked the Federal Government to impose a six-year expiration date on tires." And, according to safetyresearch.net accessed on April 16, 2009, in 2006 Ford Motors added a "six-year tire replacement recommendation regardless of tread wear," to their official Web site and all owners' manuals. This information makes the consumer wonder why this vital information is being passed up, especially when the tire industry's fellow manufacturers believe that there is a necessity for tire expiration dates. So if the American tire industry does not acknowledge this problem then what can we, the consumer, do to better protect ourselves?

The answer to that question is a very simple one. In fact we all have had the answers right at our fingertips for years. On the inside of every tire is a code that represents when that specific tire was manufactured, allowing the owner to learn just how old their "new" tires are.

Though the code may be a bit intimidating at first, it is actually quite simple to understand. In the photo here you can see the code that is imprinted on the inside of the tire. If you will notice the code says "4005" [Visual Aid of a car tire]. The year the tire was manufactured is always the last number of the code, which represents the final number of said year. For example if a tire was made in 1991 its code will

Q: How would you evaluate Jessica's job of citing her references? Did she give too little, too much, or just the right amount of information? How smoothly was she able to move back-and-forth between speech content and citations ?

One way that Jessica helps convince us of the seriousness of her topic is by comparing what the American consumer knows with what the British consumer has been told by the tire manufacturers.

Q: *How effective do you think this approach was?*

SOLUTION/ACTION:
Jessica gives us a solution to the problem of old and expired tires that we can implement ourselves.

Q: *Did this part of Jessica's speech persuade you to run out and take a look at your own tires to make sure that you don't have a "ticking time bomb" on your car?*
Q: *What do you think about Jessica's choice to use the problem-solution pattern of organization? Would another pattern have worked better?*

VISUALS:
In this speech, Jessica did not use PowerPoint. Instead, she used only one photo of a tire that she placed on a flip-chart and kept covered until she was ready to refer to it.

Q: *What do you think? Was one visual aid enough? Why or why not?*

end with the number "1" or if a tire is made in 2003 the number printed will be "03." Therefore, we can see that the tire in this photo was made in 2005 because it ends with the numbers zero and five. The first numbers represent the week of the year in which the tire was made. This tire has the numbers "4" and "0," meaning that this tire was made in the 40th week of the year 2005.

A surprisingly easy code to crack, yet it has been hidden from the American consumer for years. And I do mean hidden. In an interview by Brian Ross for the 20/20 program, Sean Kane states that the code system "was never devised for the consumer to decode." Making some of the most important numbers in your life the most secretive and confusing to understand. Robert Moore, father of one of the young men mentioned at the beginning of this speech, states for 20/20 that "these tires are like ticking time bombs." But armed with this information we can all make better choices on our future tire purchases and check the tires we have currently.

I understand that life gets crazy and that we don't always get to that Saturday project. But if that Saturday project meant life or death, I bet we would make the time. So I am asking you now—make the time to check the codes on your tires because things don't always go as planned. They certainly didn't for those four young men on their camping trip. Today we have examined the issue of expired tires, then taken a look at the inaction of the tire industry, before finally learning what we can do to better protect ourselves on the road ahead. I know I will be teaching my friends and family how to better protect themselves and I hope now you will do the same.

REFERENCES:
Jessica used a variety of quality sources in her speech.

Q: *Which of her sources do you think are the most persuasive? Were there any that you would suggest could have been omitted?*

REFERENCES*

1. Brian Ross; abcnews.go.com/blotter; October 5, 2008.

2. Watch out for old tires. AA1Car.com; October 5, 2008 Accessed at http://www.aa1car.com/library/tire_expire.htm.

3. Sean Kane quoted from Joseph Rhee. (2008, June 3). New warning: 'Catastrophic failure' discovered in aged tires. abcnews.go.com Accessed October 5, 2008 at http://abcnews.go.com/Blotter/story?id=4988518& amp;page=1.

4. William D. Siuru; How to store spare tires. newcarbuyingguide.com; Accessed September 27, 2008 at http://www.newcarbuyingguide.com/index.php/news/main/4560/event=view.

5. What is oxidation? *Wisegeek.com*; Accessed September 27, 2008 at http://www.wisegeek.com/what-is-oxidation.htm.

6. Dan Zieliksia; abcnews.go.com; October 5, 2008.

7. Tire aging tests, data and policies continue to emerge. Safety Research & Strategies, Inc. (Safetysearch.net). Accessed April 16, 2009 at http://www.safetyresearch.net/2006/10/01/tire-aging-tests/.

8. Robert Moore; abcnews.go.com; October 5, 2008.

*1, 6, and 8 come from a 20/20 program on July 24, 2008. "Aged Tires: A Driving Hazard. Brian Ross Investigates."

Final Thoughts from the Authors

If there is one principle that we hope has been sufficiently stressed in this chapter, it is that everything you do in planning your persuasive strategy is dependent upon your audience analysis. You, of course, are a human being, so the ideas and structures that are effective in motivating you are one clue to what may be useful in reaching your audience. However, people are individuals, and individuals differ from one another in often significant ways. Audiences are groups of individuals, gathered together due to certain commonalities, but individuals nonetheless. A speaker must account for those individual differences and keep them uppermost in mind during the process of preparing a persuasive presentation.

The goal of this textbook has been to stress this same principle as it applies to all communication. We hope that you have seen throughout your reading that communicating for success—success in public speaking, group participation, interpersonal relationships, careers, and life in general—is greatly enhanced when you take an other-centered approach. When your communication is aimed not just at getting your own needs met, but also at ensuring that others' needs are seen as equally important, your chances of developing good relationships are much greater.

We have tried to introduce you to the knowledge, values, and skills that are central to becoming a competent communicator. We hope you have also acquired some new skills that you can use to your benefit and the benefit of others. You can accomplish mastery of these and other skills, as well as develop a greater depth in your understanding of communication, by exploring other courses offered by the Communication department at your college. Whether you take another course or not, remember that effective communication is a goal worth striving for every day and in every aspect of your life. We wish you well as you continue to communicate for success.

CHAPTER SUMMARY

As this chapter has stressed, persuasion is difficult, and the skills needed to be persuasive require serious practice. However, since the need for persuasion is present in all phases of life, these skills are worth the effort. You can determine your knowledge of language by checking the skills and learning objectives presented in this chapter.

Summary of **SKILLS**

Check each skill that you now feel qualified to perform:
- ❑ I can use social judgment theory to build an argument that will help change the minds of my listeners.
- ❑ I can identify fallacious arguments in others' speeches and avoid them in my own speeches.
- ❑ I can plan and present a successful persuasive speech, using one or more of the persuasive organizational patterns.
- ❑ I can apply persuasive appeals to a variety of audience types.

PERSUASION **AND YOUR CAREER**

LEARNING OBJECTIVE

14.6 What persuasive skills covered in this chapter relate to your career?

The persuasive skills covered in this chapter can be of special importance to you as you search for and develop a career. To illustrate this point, we will highlight the fields of business, education, and healthcare (other career fields are included on the website that accompanies this text).

SPOTLIGHT ON **PERSUASIVE SPEAKING**

BUSINESS

In advice for persuasive speaking, in *Interpersonal Skills in Organizations* (de Janasz et al., 2002), effective speakers are urged to organize in two ways:

- First, make your key concepts clear so the audience will have an agenda or "framework" for your speech content. Include this agenda as a handout or present it on a PowerPoint slide, so there is no confusion in the minds of your audience.

- Second, present your main arguments at the beginning, so they will serve as "a road map," and the audience will "know where you're heading and why" (p. 180).

EDUCATION

Educators need to use fear appeals with care. "Anyone who plagiarizes in this class will fail the course" is a message containing threat or fear appeals. Kearney et al. (1984) found that fear appeals resulted in less learning and in students developing negative feelings toward the instructor. Sprinkle et al. (2006) reported:

- Students were motivated *least* by fear appeals used alone; the *most* by *efficacy* used alone.

- When fear appeals were followed by efficacy statements, higher student motivation occurred than when fear appeals were used alone. Also, students were significantly more likely to ask for help on a speech from instructors who used both fear and efficacy statements rather than fear alone.

HEALTHCARE

Persuasive health messages are most effective when they contain ideal guidelines (Murray-Johnson & Witte, 2003):

1. *Cues to action* direct listener attention.

2. *Motivational appeals* convince listeners that there is a threat to their well-being if they fail to adopt the recommended action, and that the consequences will be severe.

3. *Assurance of "response efficacy"* demonstrates that a recommendation will work.

4. *Assurance of "self-efficacy"* persuades listeners that "they can."

5. *Removal of barriers* acknowledges that barriers exist but can be overcome.

6. *Emphasis on benefits* outweigh any negative problems.

7. *Acknowledgment of social norms* shows that new behavior will be accepted by friends.

CAREER MOMENT **SPEAKING SKILLS AND YOUR CAREER**

By now you have already given a speech or are close to giving one—probably an informative speech or maybe a team presentation—and may be preparing to give a persuasive speech as well. Because this course includes all types of communication skills in addition to speaking, two speeches may be all you will give. Once you have completed the second speech, you will be amazed by how much you learned and improved. However, you will probably notice some areas that still need improvement. And, of course, unless you actively search for speaking opportunities after leaving this course, you may never get the opportunity to make these improvements. In fact, your old habits which are lurking in the background, may return all too soon.

Wouldn't it be nice, while all your speaking skills are still fresh, to be able to work on them and polish them until you feel really comfortable with them?

Consider taking a public speaking course offered at your college or university. Public Speaking is a transferable, regular college course that begins where this course ends. Usually, you

will give between four and six different types of presentations (such as informative, persuasive, manuscript, oral reading, after-dinner speech, team presentation, and special occasion speeches) that expand your knowledge of and skills at speaking. When you have completed that course, you will be ready to prepare and present effective speeches in the workplace. Not only will you have perfected your speaking skills, but you will now have two communication courses on your resume, thus showing employers that you did more than take a required communication course—you have proof of motivation and commitment to successful communication, which will benefit you throughout life.

CONNECTING TO **BUSINESS**

Are you considering a business or professional career? Your success may well depend on your persuasive abilities—both oral and written. If you are writing a persuasive message to be sent by memo or e-mail, the *direct approach* often used in oral presentations may not be the best method to choose. According to Lesikar and colleagues (2008), an *indirect approach* is best in sales or personal issues when the receiver is likely to be resistant or even hostile. Instead of beginning with the request, the message leads up to the request by making the importance and benefits of the request clear.

ACTIVITY:

- In groups of 3–5 persons, make a list of possible reasons that using the indirect approach is more successful than the direct approach when attempting to persuade by memo or e-mail a resistant or even hostile person. Use the information in Chapters 10–14 in making your list.

- Which persuasive appeal (*logos, pathos,* or *ethos*) do you think would be essential to turning the reader from resistance to enthusiasm? Give an example.
- Which organizational patterns presented in this chapter do you think would be the most successful for an indirect approach? A direct approach? Why?

CONNECTING TO **EDUCATION**

Are you considering a career in education? Your success may well depend on your ability to motivate and persuade. Educators sometimes confuse persuasion with control—there is no force or coercion in persuasion. Educational psychologist Anita Woolfolk (2010) points out that students of all ages learn more when they are allowed self-determination and autonomy in the classroom. In fact, "controlling environments tend to improve performance only on rote recall tasks" (p. 381). In an effort to be persuasive, teachers may use controlling language such as *have to, need to,* or *ought to,* which undermines motivation.

ACTIVITY:

- On your own paper, list four or five courses in which you have learned the most in either high school or college. Was your learning due more to your own self-motivation or to the motivation of the teachers? How effective were these teachers at persuasion and motivation?

- In groups of 3 or 4, discuss which persuasive appeal (*logos, ethos,* or *pathos*) you think would help motivate students in the classroom. Give examples when possible.
- Which persuasive patterns do you think would be the most successful if used by teachers in the classroom? Why?

CONNECTING TO **HEALTHCARE**

Are you considering a career in healthcare? If so, your success and the welfare of your clients may well depend on your persuasive abilities. In the *Spotlight on Health* feature, seven guidelines are outlined for the development of effective persuasive health messages. Murray-Johnson and Witte (2003) suggest that no particular order is needed but that the more guidelines used the more persuasive the message becomes. Guidelines #3 and #4 are often assumed but need to be made clear—that the treatment is effective and that it is something that the client can do fairly easily.

ACTIVITY: (Work by yourself or in a group)

- Select a speech topic that advocates a health behavior change (e.g.., smoking cessation or weight loss) and assume that you will be speaking to a group of people who are in need of this health change.
- Identify some of the specific barriers to self-efficacy ("I don't think I can do it") that might be discouraging to these listeners.

- Create a brief outline for a persuasive speech using the motivated-sequence pattern.
- Decide where in the outline to place each of the seven guidelines for effective health messages.
- If time allows, have each group member present a step in the speech outline to the other group members as though they were the actual audience.

▶ Log onto MyCommunicationLab.com to access Connecting to Psychology and Connecting to Science, Technology, Engineering, and Math—both with related activities.

Summary of LEARNING **OUTCOMES**

14.1 *What is the definition of persuasion, how do persuasive speeches differ from informative speeches, and what specific factors affect persuasion?*

- Persuasion occurs when a speaker crafts messages with the intent of influencing the values, beliefs, attitudes, or behaviors of others.

- Persuasive speeches differ from informative ones based on (1) the intent of the speaker; (2) the supporting material used; (3) how the psychological information is used; and (4) the expectations of the speaker.

- What a persuasive speaker can expect from an audience is explained in the *Making Theory Practical* feature that looks at the practical applications of social judgment theory (pages 380–381).

- Specific factors that affect persuasion are culture, gender, ethics, and technology. See pages 379–384 for specifics.

14.2 *What are the two types of persuasive speeches, and what are the differences between them?*

- The two types of persuasive speeches are the speech to convince and the speech to actuate.

- In the speech to convince, you are trying to get your audience to agree with your position by either forming a new belief or changing a previous belief.

- In the speech to actuate, you are trying to get your audience not only to agree with you but also to take a specific action, such as to continue a behavior, discontinue a behavior, or adopt a new behavior.

14.3 *According to Aristotle, what are the three primary means of persuasion, and how do they help you build effective persuasive appeals?*

- Aristotle's three primary means of persuasion include *ethos* (your credibility as a speaker), *logos* (the evidence and reasoning you use to add proof to your arguments), and *pathos* (your ethical use of emotion to get your audience personally involved in your topic).

- Credibility is persuasive if you show your audience that you are *competent* to speak on the topic, that you are a *trustworthy* person of good will, and finally, that you have *charisma,* as shown by your enthusiasm for the topic and for your audience. Evidence and reasoning are persuasive if you use good reasoning (inductive, deductive, and causal reasoning), cite your evidence, and avoid use of fallacious reasoning. Emotion can be persuasive if you use the hierarchy of needs to relate personally with your audience and if you use fear appeals with care.

14.4 *What are the seven persuasive patterns covered in this chapter, and what are the most appropriate speaking uses for each?*

- The five persuasive patterns include the statement of logical reasons, problem-solution, progressive question, comparative advantages, and motivated sequence.

- The statement of logical reasons pattern uses an explicit approach that clearly presents three to five logical reasons.

- Three patterns are used with problems and solutions: the *problem-solution* pattern discusses the problem by presenting the effects and causes; then one or more solutions are presented to solve the problem. The *progressive-questions* pattern walks the audience through a series of questions and answers, from the problem to the final solution. The *comparative-advantages* pattern is effective when the problem is already known to audience members but they cannot agree on a solution—the speaker compares possible solutions or plans showing how one plan is better than the others.

- A practical approach to counter-persuasion (inoculation theory) is described in the *Developing Skills* feature in the problem-solving patterns.

- The *motivated-sequence pattern* is used when you want the audience to change a policy or take a particular action.

14.5 *Which persuasive patterns are most appropriate when the majority of the audience agrees, disagrees, is neutral, or has opinions that vary widely?*

- When the audience favors your position, consider using the statement of logical reasons pattern.

- When the audience opposes your position, consider using the statement of logical reasons or comparative-advantages pattern.

- When the audience is neutral, consider using the progressive questions or comparative-advantages patterns.

- When audience opinions vary widely, consider using the statement of logical reasons pattern.

14.6 *What persuasive skills covered in this chapter relate specifically to careers (see highlighted fields of business, education, and healthcare)?*

- The *Spotlight on, Career Moment*, and *Connecting to* features highlight the value of communication in the fields of business, education, and healthcare.

SOLVE IT NOW!

 Taking into consideration all that you learned about persuasive communication from this chapter, what tips would you give Anh and Mike from our opening scenario? *

- What specific advice would you give Anh and Mike about the differences between an informative and a persuasive speech? Would you recommend that they plan to give a speech to convince or a speech to actuate? Why?

- What advice does the social judgment theory offer in this situation?
- Which one or two persuasive organizational patterns would you suggest they use and why?
- What specific *communication goals* would you recommend for Anh and Mike that would improve their persuasive skills now and in the future?

*(Check your answers with those located in MyCommunicationLab, Scenario Analysis for Chapter 14)

KEY TERMS

ad hominem	p. 387	comparative-advantages pattern	p. 392	inoculation theory	p. 395	reasoning	p. 385
ad populum	p. 387			logos	p. 384	refute	p. 385
ad verecundiam	p. 387	counter-persuasion	p. 393	motivated-sequence pattern	p. 393	rhetoric	p. 377
anchor	p. 380	deductive reasoning	p. 386			social judgment theory	p. 380
attitudes	p. 378			pathos	p. 384		
begging the question	p. 387	ego-involved	p. 380	persuasion	p. 377	speech to actuate	p. 383
		ethos	p. 384	persuasive appeals	p. 384	speech to convince	p. 383
behaviors	p. 378	evidence	p. 385	post hoc	p. 387	statement of logical reasons pattern	p. 388
beliefs	p. 378	fallacious reasoning	p. 386	power distance	p. 379		
boomerang effect	p. 381	fear appeals	p. 386	problem-solution pattern	p. 389	straw man	p. 387
causal reasoning	p. 386	hasty generalization	p. 387			trustworthy	p. 385
charisma	p. 385	inductive reasoning	p. 386	progressive-questions pattern	p. 390	values	p. 378
common ground	p. 383						

SKILL BUILDERS

1. Critically Evaluating

Using the critical evaluation form from Chapter 1, select and evaluate an article on *persuasion or persuasiveness* obtained from a database or a communication journal such as *Communication Education*. Be prepared to share your observations with your classmates.

2. Reread this chapter's *Making Theory Practical* feature on social judgment theory. In groups of three to five, complete the following:

- First, list the nine positions on gun control on a board or flipchart so all can see.
- Next, each individual should take the nine positions and determine (1) the preferred position (anchor), (2) which positions fall into the latitude of acceptance, (3) which positions fall into the latitude of noncommitment, and (4) which positions fall into the latitude of rejection.

- Without getting into an argument or trying to persuade each other, indicate the anchor position for each group member with an X next to the list on the board.
- Finally, by each of the nine positions, indicate how many group members listed the position as LA (latitude of acceptance), LN (latitude of noncommitment), or LR (latitude of rejection). Based on social judgment theory and your group's position results, determine how persuasive a speaker likely would be with this position: Only military and law enforcement personnel should be allowed to carry guns. Why? Be prepared to share your list and comments with the class.

3. You should be alert to instances of fallacious reasoning. Take the front section of a local newspaper and read several articles looking for examples of fallacious reasoning listed in Figure 14.3. When you locate at least five problems in reasoning, decide which types you think are the most serious and the least likely to be identified by readers or speakers. Share your examples and analysis with the class.

Appendix

Communicating Successfully in the Interviewing Context

LEARNING **OBJECTIVES**

A.1 What makes a quality interview, what are several different types of interviews, and what four responsibilities are needed for an effective interview?

A.2 What is an informational interview and what are the benefits of informational interviewing?

A.3 What are the interviewee responsibilities and the interviewer responsibilities in the employment interview?

After studying this chapter you should be able to . . .

- Identify the importance of interviewing as well as the different types of interviews and use this information in planning a job hunt.
- Effectively organize and conduct an informational interview.
- Effectively organize and plan questions to ask in an employment interview and incorporate them into interview experiences.
- Effectively plan answers to standard and behavioral interview questions.

APPENDIX SUMMARY〉 P. 416

Interviewing is a communication skill that is likely to be of importance to your career or profession. We have mentioned interviewing at least three times in this text as an important communication skill: (1) In Chapter 1, interviewing was discussed as a type of context; (2) in various *Career Moments* in the text, interviewing was mentioned as a way to find and compare information on various possible jobs or careers—called informational interviewing; and (3) in Chapter 12, interviewing was mentioned as a way to find additional information for a speech when researching databases and Internet sources failed to find the exact statistic or fact needed. In this appendix, we will take a more detailed look at the interviewing process and offer some tips on how to use it effectively.

Interviewing: An Overview

Let's begin our discussion of interviewing by defining it and looking at what makes a quality interview.

LEARNING **OBJECTIVE**

A.1 What makes a quality interview, what are several different types of interviews, and what four responsibilities are needed for an effective interview?

What Makes a Quality Interview?

An **interview** is a specific communication context that occurs when two parties—the interviewer and interviewee—ask and answer questions with a specific purpose in mind. This definition contains several important aspects needed to make a quality interview.

- *Specific communication context* implies that the communication skills learned throughout this text apply as much to interviewing as to other contexts. In other words, effective interviewers are effective communicators.

- *Two parties* implies that at least two people are involved—one interviewer and one interviewee. However, *party* may refer to more people as well. For example, one interviewer may simultaneously question several interviewees as occurs when an American Airline's interviewer screens applicants for the position of flight attendant. Or several interviewers may question a single interviewee as occurs when city board members question a contractor who has bid to make revisions to city hall. In some cases, there are multiple interviewers and interviewees, which occurred when members of a Congressional hearing interviewed in 2009 the CEOs of several automobile manufacturers who were asking for government bailout money.

- *Ask and answer questions* implies that skills for both asking and answering questions are needed to make an effective interview. It is not just the interviewer who asks questions—in most interviews, both parties are asking questions and seeking information. For example, while the interviewer is trying to decide if the applicant will make a good addition to the team, the applicant is trying to decide if the company is a place he or she really wants to work.

- Finally, *specific purpose in mind* implies that an interview doesn't just happen on the spur of the moment; effective interviews require prior thought and careful planning by both parties. It also implies that there are many different purposes or types of interviews. The most important types of interviews for those planning or advancing a career are the *informational interview,* in which you seek information about a specific job from a variety of people related to that position, and the employment interview where you actually apply for a position—each of these will be covered in detail in following sections. The informational interview can also be used to disseminate and gather specific information needed for any number of purposes such as a report or presentation, which was discussed in Chapter 11. Informational and employment interviews are used whether you are in business, education, healthcare, or a variety of other career areas.

Other important types of interviews include the following (Stewart & Cash, 2008):

1. The *survey interview* is used by researchers, manufacturers, and journalists to collect data and "establish a solid base of fact from which to draw conclusions, make interpretations, and determine courses of action" (p. 141). Survey interviews can be conducted in person, by telephone, by mail, and even through the Internet.

2. The *recruiting interview* is used by companies, the military, colleges and universities, and sports teams to attract talented individuals to apply with them for a future position—in some cases the selection and commitment occur on the spot.

3. The *performance interview* is used by businesses and nonprofit organizations as a way to assess and encourage quality performance and goal setting of employees at all levels of the organization. Promotion, reward, discipline, and even termination may be tied to these performance reviews.

4. The *persuasive interview* is used by sales personnel, marketing specialists, or fund-raisers as a way to sell a product, change an attitude, or collect money. Persuasive interviewers are more likely to be successful if they can show how their product, idea, or cause will also benefit the interviewee in an important and ethical way.

5. The *healthcare interview* is used by healthcare providers as a way to present and gather accurate information, establish a feeling of trust and caring, and efficiently handle medical problems. The most successful healthcare interviews, as indicated in the various *Spotlight on* and *Career Moment* sections of this text, occur when the patient is allowed to take an active role.

In all the situations just mentioned, effective interviewing allows for a timely exchange of information with a wide range of goals. Without effective, quality interviewing, all of these situations would be much more difficult.

Interviewer and Interviewee Responsibilities

In order for an interview to be effective, both the interviewer and the interviewee must take an active role. Although their roles will be somewhat different depending on the type of interview, both parties begin with the same four responsibilities: communicate effectively, prepare thoroughly, participate actively, and listen carefully. Which responsibilities can you perform effectively and which need some improvement?

Responsibility 1: *Communicate Effectively* When both interview parties are effective communicators, the interview is much more productive, especially when it comes to handling frame of reference differences. As an interviewee, if you know what the other party wants and can communicate how you are able to satisfy those wants, you will be more successful. For example, the *California Job Journal* What Employers Want, (2009) says that all employers want and look for five characteristic traits in the people they hire: Integrity—bases decisions on what's good for others; likability—uses effective people skills; stability—is not a job hopper; flexibility—is able to adapt to change; and compatibility—fits in with other colleagues. As you prepare for your all-important employment interviews, plan ahead how you will incorporate into your answers any of these characteristics that relate to you. Other important communication skills include such things as using narration with well-organized, personal stories that support and prove your points; using nonverbal skills such as effective voice, gestures, and eye contact that show your enthusiasm for the position; and maintaining courtesy where you leave the interview with a handshake and a thank you (Civiello, 2009).

Interviewers also need to relate to the frame of reference and wants of their applicants especially when interviewing today's student right out of college. According to Stewart and Cash (2009, pp. 186–187), today's applicants are less interested in salary and benefits than their predecessors and more interested in training, supervision with feedback, and working in a diverse yet friendly and enjoyable environment. They want interviewers "to ask them relevant, open questions and give them opportunities for self-expression" without interruptions or pressuring them. Also, as Civiello notes (p. 16), they are technologically savvy and enjoy networking with others. Effective interviewers should plan ahead to meet the wants of current applicants because their impression of your company will depend on how they relate to you—the first person they meet.

Responsibility 2: *Prepare Thoroughly* Effective communication

obviously requires careful preparation by both parties. As an interviewee, start by making a list of your own skills and qualities using suggestions from books like *What Color Is Your Parachute* updated each year by Richard Bolles (2009). Pay particular attention to the helpful workbook in Chapter 11 of his book. You will also find his Web site full of valuable tips (www.thejobhuntersbible.com). Once you have a clear picture of your skills and qualities, the next step is to figure out what jobs, careers, and companies are the best fit for your abilities and what job and location would give you the most enjoyment. Think about typically asked questions that will be covered later under the employment interview and how you can best answer these questions by highlighting your skills and qualities. John Lees, in *How to Get a Job You'll Love* (2008), suggests that interviewees should organize their answers to typical interviewer questions into mininarratives. Although these narratives should not be memorized, they should begin with a brief situation or problem; describe how you or a team handled the problem; state the outcome in specifics when possible (i.e., sales increased by 10 percent); and conclude with what you learned from the experience and what you might do differently in future situations.

Interviewers also need to prepare for each interview carefully. They should know as much as possible about the situation, the person to be interviewed, and the type of interview, such as employment, persuasive, or healthcare. In the case of a job interview, be sure to know the exact job requirements, and plan a series of questions that will help determine how well the applicant meets or exceeds each requirement. Read the letter of application and accompanying paperwork to get a feel for the applicant and how best to relate to them. Make sure that all questions are job related and avoid any questions that could be considered unlawful (specifics covered in a later section).

Responsibility 3: *Participate Actively* In most cases, inter-

viewing is a two-way street, meaning that both parties should actively ask and answer questions. This may be less true in the first interview where the interviewer takes more control, but even then, the interviewee is expected to ask pertinent questions. In an ideal world, the interviewer knows what skills and qualities are important for the job and asks the correct questions to find important information. However, if your interviewer does not ask questions that tap into your skills and competencies, it is up to you to structure your answers so you can present the information and qualities that you think the interviewer needs to know in order to fairly assess you. Keep in mind that as an interviewee, you have a real interest in the company and the job; your future happiness and career depend on accepting the right job. If you don't take an active role in the interview process by asking probing questions, you are abdicating your decision-making ability. Also, asking questions shows the interviewer that you have a real interest in this particular job. Asking about specific aspects of the job, how he or she would describe the ideal employee, how creative you are allowed to be, how employee appraisals and feedback sessions are handled, and what Internet access is allowed are just a few of the possible questions interviewees might wish to ask.

Responsibility 4: *Listen Carefully* Listening, as discussed in Chapter 3, is essential in an effective interview. If you can determine which listening style (people, action, content, or time oriented) the other person prefers, you will be better able to communicate with them. Recall from Chapter 3 that people-oriented listeners prefer to receive personal examples while a content-oriented listener is looking for detailed facts and evidence. Your responses to questions will be more positively received if you meet the listening expectations of the other party. Because the applicant is likely trying to be persuasive, interviewers need to listen critically for the applicant's credibility, logic, and appeals to emotion by probing observations and paraphrasing for clarity and confirmation.

APPLY **WHAT YOU KNOW**
INTERVIEWING OVERVIEW

Apply what you know about interviewing to these critical thinking questions:

- Think of a quality interview that you have been in as an interviewee and discuss what made it so effective. Which of the aspects in our definition of an *interview* played a role in this success? What additional aspects did you observe? Which aspect do you think was most responsible for the interview's success? Why?

- Which of the four interviewer/interviewee responsibilities do you think will be your strongest? Which one do you think will need the most improvement? Explain your reason for each choice.

- Brainstorm a list of your *skills* and another list of your *qualities*. Place a check by one skill and one quality that you think are most likely to get you the job of your choice. Place a check by one skill and one quality that could cause you some problems during an interview.

Now that we have looked at some general but valuable advice about interviewing, let's conclude this appendix by looking in detail at two regularly used interview types: the informational interview and employment interview.

LEARNING OBJECTIVE

A.2 What is an informational interview and what are its benefits?

Informational Interviewing

One of the most valuable types of interviews is the informational interview, especially for the college student or recent graduate.

What Is an Informational Interview?

An **informational interview** is an interview used to disseminate and/or gather specific information in a timely fashion in a variety of settings. Examples of an informational interview used to provide facts would be a supervisor explaining specific company procedures to a newly hired employee or a nurse showing a patient how to change a bandage. An example of an informational interview used to gather pieces of information would be an educator or student interviewing an expert about new facts that could be used in a presentation/lecture or a potential job candidate questioning a lawyer about the requirements and duties of a legal assistant. Keep in mind that, in an informational interview, you are the interviewer.

Informational Interviews: Presentation Context When you are using the informational interview to gain or verify information for a presentation, you will be interviewing people who are experts in some aspect of your speech topic. For example, suppose your speech topic was on childhood obesity and that

your research was leading you to suspect that the high-fat, high-calorie snack foods children eat while watching television, playing video/computer games, and even at school were contributing to the problem. You have found many magazine and journal articles discussing the problem and citing research studies. But you want to know what the local elementary schools are doing about the problem and what they allow in their vending machines. When you interview the principals of several schools, you are conducting informational interviews. You will want to make sure you are organized and ask the right types of questions—see suggestions for both later in this appendix. Plan the specific questions you will ask ahead of time and bring them with you to the interview. However, be flexible if the discussion brings another question to mind that you had not previously considered. You may want to tape record the interview, if allowed, to use as a backup, but you will want to take brief notes as well. Be aware that if you plan to quote something the subject said verbatim, you will need to make sure you get the exact wording during the interview. You may find that you will need to settle for paraphrasing, in which case it helps if you paraphrase frequently during the interview to verify the accuracy of your understanding. Any time you quote, paraphrase, or refer to ideas you gained from an interview in your speech, you must cite your interviewee. If you are looking for proof, it will be only as good as the expert you interviewed.

Informational Interviews: Job Context

When you use the informational interview to discover information about a potential job, you will be interviewing people who work in a similar position, people who hire for the position you think you want, people who work for a specific company that interests you, or people who have valuable information and can refer you to people to interview next. These interviews should last no longer than 15 minutes. Each time you interview one of these people, you are discovering valuable information and making important contacts—you are **networking**. You are not applying for a job; you are researching about the job by asking a variety of questions:

- What does the job involve?
- What challenges or problems come with this position?
- Any changes or new developments anticipated?
- Is experience and training required for the position?
- What type of resume is preferred?
- What is the typical salary range and benefits new employees receive?
- What typical interview questions are most applicants asked?
- What organizations or associations do most employees join?
- Which journals or trade magazines do employees read?

For the beginning job applicant, or anyone planning a career change, or even a person seeking a big promotion, the informational interview is a must. In each of these situations, the more information you have, the better your chances of making the right impression and giving quality answers to tough questions. If you have done your homework, there should be very few surprises during a job interview.

Benefits of Informational Interviewing

There are many advantages to conducting an informational interview whether you are using it to gather information for a presentation or to plan a career and prepare for a job interview.

Benefits for the Speech Researcher

Verifying information is one of the main benefits of informational interviewing for the person researching for a presentation. You will undoubtedly find quality information by using current books and looking for magazine and journal articles in the databases located in your college or local libraries. However, your audience will be more interested and will find information more persuasive if you can verify that your research relates directly to your state or community. The best way to do this is through informational interviews you personally conduct.

Finding additional or missing information is another important benefit of informational interviews especially if your topic is so recent that not much has been written on it yet. Check with your librarian, community centers, local agencies and organizations, and well-known businesses for the names of local people that have expertise on your topic. Don't be hesitant to contact these people—they will likely be honored that you consider them to be an expert and will help you in any way possible.

Benefits for the Job Hunter

For the job hunter, *finding available jobs* that you really like may be the biggest benefit of informational interviewing. The number-one way that people find jobs is through networking (Bolles, 2009; *Weddles' Newsletter*, 2009); and the number-one way you find people to network with is through informational interviewing. As Gladwell says in *The Tipping Point: How Little Things Can Make a Big Difference* (2002), relying only on the people you know is a mistake because their circle of friends is about the same as yours. It is your acquaintances that are the most help to you because they can introduce you to people that you don't yet know. Each informational interview introduces you to new people that may have the perfect job for you. Both Bolles and Weedles recommend that you conduct several informational interviews prior to actually beginning a job hunt—effective interviewers take the time to conduct from 5 to 10 (or more) of these valuable interviews.

Reducing the length of a job hunt is another important benefit of informational interviews. Once you begin the job hunt, the length of time it takes you to find the perfect job is inversely related to the number of people you see each week. If you interview with only two people each week, your job hunt could take as long as a year; however, if you interview with approximately 20 people each week, you may find the perfect job in as little as 90 days (Weinstein, 1993). Where do you find these interview opportunities? You find many of them from the referrals and leads you gained during your informational interviews.

Gaining interviewing confidence is another important advantage of informational interviews. After conducting from 5 to 10 informational interviews, the fear and mystery of the interview process is gone. Your first few interviews may be a bit rocky, but as you gain practice and information, you will gain confidence as well. Recall from the discussion of confidence building in Chapter 10 that preparation, skills training, and positive imagery are effective ways to gain speaking confidence—they also work with interviewing confidence. Informational interviews give you both preparation and skills training in effective interviewing. By being an interviewer, you get a good idea of what interviewers look for, and you can answer questions more effectively. Using positive imagery (also called visualization) is another effective way to build your interviewing confidence. Imagine yourself feeling confident and relaxed during an interview. Imagine yourself using all that valuable information gained from the informational interviews to structure quality answers to the questions asked by the interviewer. The mystery is gone and you can concentrate on giving relaxed, detailed answers that will present your skills and qualities in the best possible light.

APPLY **WHAT YOU KNOW**
INFORMATIONAL INTERVIEWING

To apply what you know about informational interviewing, answer the following questions:

- Select a career job you might like to have between six months and five years from now, and think of two types of people that you could interview about the position (such as a lawyer to find out about the position of legal assistant). List at least three questions

that you would like to ask that would help you prepare for the position or help you decide what career you would like to pursue.

- Which of the benefits would be most likely to encourage you to conduct several informational interviews? What might keep you from actually conducting an informational interview? Explain your reasons.

Employment Interviewing

LEARNING **OBJECTIVE**

A.3 What are the inter-viewee responsibilities and the interviewer responsibilities in the employment interview?

Interviewing skills play an important role in your ability to communicate in an **employment interview** whether you are the interviewee or the interviewer. Both the interviewee and interviewer have responsibilities in an effective employment interview.

Interviewer Responsibilities

In addition to communicating, preparing, participating, and listening carefully, the interviewer is responsible for asking questions effectively and organizing efficiently.

Asking Questions Effectively   To get the information from others that you need, you have to ask the right questions. Whether you are conducting an employment interview or an informational interview, the only way to be sure you will get the right information is to know what types of questions to ask. For example, don't ask a direct question if you want the detailed answer that comes with an open question. The following guidelines will help you develop the proper questions needed to conduct an interview that is both efficient and productive:

- Use **direct questions** if you want a brief answer or a yes-or-no answer. Direct questions are useful for gathering basic data, for verifying facts, and for relaxing nervous candidates. Examples include: "How long have you been working in the healthcare field?" "Is a four-year college degree required to work in this field?" "I see your mailing address is _____. Can you still be reached at this address?"

- Use **closed questions** if you want to limit answers to the choices provided in your question such as "Which type of employees are the most successful at this company: those who are always punctual; those who show the most initiative; or those who are the most loyal?" After the question is answered, you could ask the interviewee to explain why they chose the answer they did and what it says about the management style of the company. If worded carefully, closed questions can stimulate creative thinking and a lively discussion. The results can also be used to compare companies or interviewee responses.

- Use **open-ended questions** if you want to get richer, more detailed information. Open-ended questions are broad questions that allow the applicant to expand on any approach they wish. As such, applicant answers can be time consuming but will usually get you much more information. "How did you come to be interested in oncology?" or "Describe the main weakness you see in applicants right out of college" would be examples of open-ended questions. Therefore, unless you are pretty sure that you already know the information and just need some verification through a direct question, begin interviews with open-ended questions and follow them with direct questions as needed.

- Use **follow-up questions** when you want to probe for additional information or need clarification of an idea such as: "That's interesting. Could you tell me what happened that caused you to change your views on that?" Follow-up questions are especially useful in eliciting narratives or stories from applicants and they may relax the applicant as well. If you are looking for information to use in a presentation or report, narratives and stories can be used to add interest to your speech.

- Use **verbal and nonverbal probes** to encourage people to include more information without your having to ask more questions. Verbal probes could include comments such as, "Really?" "Interesting," and "Tell me more." Nonverbal probes could encourage talk by leaning forward in your chair, maintaining direct eye contact, and smiling; they could discourage talk by breaking off eye contact and shuffling papers on the desk.

- Avoid **unlawful questions** in order to comply with federal and state guidelines. The Equal Employment Opportunity Commission (EEOC.gov) uses two guidelines to determine the legality of interview questions that you should follow as well: (1) all questions must be job related, and (2) all applicants for a position must be asked the same basic questions. Asking where you were born or what religious holidays you observe would be unlawful because they are not job related; having a different list of questions to ask minorities, women, people over 50, and men would be unlawful because all candidates should be asked the same questions. The objective of these laws and guidelines is to give all persons—regardless of race, sex, national origin, religion, age, disabilities, and marital status—the same chance to prove that they are qualified based on "bona fide occupational qualifications" such as experience, skills, and education and not on non-job-related traits. When interviewers determine what job-related qualities are necessary for a job and ask questions based on those qualities, the interview process is much more effective.

Organizing an Efficient Interview

In addition to asking quality questions, you will get the most information from an interview if it is well organized. A good interview has the same three parts as a good speech—an introduction, a body, and a conclusion:

- *The Introduction* is the opening section of your interview. Begin by introducing yourself, thanking the person for consenting to the interview, and briefly explaining your purpose and how long you anticipate the interview will take. It's a good idea to establish rapport with interviewees to relax them and encourage them to give quality answers.

- *The body* of the interview is where you will ask your questions. Effective interviewers organize their questions ahead of time into categories. For example, plan to ask all questions that relate to the job and its responsibilities together; questions that relate to salary and benefits together; and questions that relate to education, training, and experience together. If you already have a good deal of information on a particular category from the resume or application form, you may want to organize the questions in that category using the *inverted funnel sequence*—meaning that you begin with closed or direct questions and end with open questions. The inverted funnel is also effective when the interviewee is hostile or quite nervous—brief, direct questions have a calming effect. If you know only minimal information on a particular applicant, use the *funnel sequence* that begins with open-ended questions and ends by narrowing down to a direct or closed question. The most typical method of organization is the funnel sequence and the most often used type of question is the open-ended one.

- *The conclusion* is the final section of your interview. It is a good idea to end with a summary of the areas covered, and when the applicant can expect to hear from you. Also, ask the applicant if they have any questions they would like to ask. If you are the interviewee, be sure to have some quality questions ready to ask. As the interviewer, be sure to bring the interview to an end on schedule, shake hands, and express your gratitude for your interviewee's time.

Interviewee Responsibilities

In addition to communicating, preparing, participating, and listening carefully, the interviewee is responsible for preparing for different types of interviewers and preparing for both standard and behavioral questions.

Preparing for Different Types of Interviewers

Not all interviewers use the same approach to the employment interview. You will feel more comfortable if you are prepared for a variety of different interview types. The basic approaches used by interviewers include the following (Stewart & Cash, 2008):

- The *structured* or *directive approach* is used by interviewers who are very organized and plan to ask a lot of questions in a fairly short period of time. As a result, their questions tend to be more direct and closed and they take control over the interview. You will have less of an opportunity to give creative responses and will find it more difficult to use any planned narratives.

- The *nonstructured* or *nondirective approach* is used by interviewers who plan to share control of the interview with you. They are not as concerned with time and will generally ask more open-ended and probing questions. They want you to give detailed answers and you will have time to incorporate the narrative approach discussed earlier into your answers. Use this opportunity to include your skills and qualities that you think are a good fit with the position. Expect them to ask several behavioral questions (covered in the last section) to see if you can think on your feet. Take your time and give thoughtful answers.

- The *combination approach* is used by interviewers who move from structured to unstructured approaches, depending on the category being discussed or the comfort level of the applicant. They may use the structured approach for topics that lend themselves to facts and short answers and move to the unstructured approach for topics needing a more detailed, thoughtful answer. In some cases, the interviewer wished to throw the applicant off base to see how they can handle pressure. Don't let the switching confuse you—take your time and concentrate on making sure you present yourself in a confident, controlled manner.

Preparing for Both Standard and Behavioral Questions

The most typically asked questions are called **standard questions** because they relate to the applicant's basic skills and qualities. Standard questions include: "Where do you expect to be five years from now?" or "How would your colleagues describe your leadership ability?" Although you don't want any answers memorized, the best interviewees plan possible answers to standard questions ahead of time and may even practice answers until they flow smoothly. Lists of standard questions are available in interviewing books such as Bolles (2009).

The best interviewers also ask tough **behavioral questions**, which assess the applicant's creativity and ability to handle real-life situations. Interviewees may be able to give canned answers to standard questions, but will have to think on their own when answering most behavioral questions. The object is to see if you can demonstrate a skill instead of just saying you have the skill. Behavioral questions include: "Go to the front of the room and sell this ruler to me; when you are finished, tell me how you organized the sales pitch." Or "How would you handle a team member that always seems to agree with the group when they are together, but after meetings sends e-mail to the boss saying how ineffective the group is and how embarrassed he was by them and then singles out a person from the group to criticize?" When answering questions, pull from your personal experiences when possible; keep your answers job related; use Lees' (2008) approach discussed earlier: summarize the situation, state how you handled it or would handle it (give the specific outcome if there was one), conclude with what you learned from the experience, and possible changes you might make in the future.

APPLY **WHAT YOU KNOW**
EMPLOYMENT INTERVIEWING

To apply what you know about employment interviews, answer these questions:

- Take the three questions that you listed for the informational interviewing *Apply What You Know* box and identify what type question each was. If you can't identify the type, it probably needs to be rewritten—rewrite the question(s) into a clear, quality question.

- Put the three questions into either the funnel or the inverted funnel sequence—how effective would that sequence be in a real interview using those questions? Explain why.

- Select one of the standard questions and one of the behavioral questions listed as samples in the preceding text and write out your answer for each question.

APPENDIX SUMMARY

As this appendix has stressed, interviewing involves a series of skills. You can determine your interviewing ability by checking the skills and learning objectives presented in this chapter:

Summary of **SKILLS**

Check each skill that you now feel qualified to perform:
- ❏ I can identify the importance of interviewing as well as the different types of interviews and use this information in planning a job hunt.
- ❏ I can effectively organize and conduct an informational interview.
- ❏ I can effectively organize and plan questions to ask in an employment interview and incorporate them into my interview experiences.
- ❏ I can effectively plan answers to standard and behavioral interview questions.

Summary of LEARNING **OUTCOMES**

A.1 *What makes a quality interview, what are several different types of interviews, and what four responsibilities are needed for an effective interview?*

- A quality interview takes place in a specific communication context, involves at least two parties, involves asking and answering questions, and has a specific purpose in mind.

- Types of interviews include the informational, employment, survey, recruiting, performance, persuasive, and healthcare interviews.

- Four responsibilities for effective interviews includes communicate effectively, prepare thoroughly, participate actively, and listen carefully.

A.2 *What is an informational interview and what are its benefits?*

- An informational interview is an interview used to disseminate and/or gather specific information in a timely fashion in a variety of settings.

- Benefits to the informational interview include finding available jobs, reducing the length of a job search, and gaining interviewing confidence.

A.3 *What are the interviewer responsibilities and the interviewee responsibilities in the employment interview?*

- Interviewer responsibilities include asking questions effectively and organizing efficiently.

- Interviewee responsibilities include preparing for different types of interviewers and preparing for both standard and behavioral questions.

KEY TERMS

References

Abrami, P. C., Chambers, B., Poulsen, C., Howden, J., D'Apollonia, S., Simone, C. D., Kastelorizios, K., Wagner, D., & Glashan, A. (1993). *Using cooperative learning.* Montreal, Quebec: The Centre for the Study of Classroom Processes.

Abrami, P. C., Chambers, B., Poulsen, C., Simone, C. D., D'Apollonia, S., & Howden, J. (1995). *Classroom connections: Understanding and using cooperative learning.* Toronto: Harcourt Brace & Company Canada, Ltd.

Acuff, F. L. (1993). *How to negotiate anything with anyone anywhere around the world.* New York: American Management Association.

Adams, J. M., & Dolin, P. A. (2001). *Printing technology* (5th ed.). Albany, NY: Delmar.

Addington, D. W. (1971). The effects of vocal variations on ratings of source credibility. *Speech Monographs, 38,* 242–247.

Adler, N. J. (2007). *International dimensions of organizational behavior* (5th ed.). Cincinnati, OH: South-Western.

Adubato, S. (2006). *Make the connection: Improve your communication at home and at work.* New York: Barnes & Noble, Inc.

Albom, M. (1997). *Tuesdays with Morrie.* New York: Doubleday.

Allen, C. K. (1990). Encoding of colors in short-term color memory. *Perceptual and Motor Skills, 71,* 211–215.

Allen, M. (2008, May). Leading the virtual team. *Associations Now, 4(5),* 18.

Allen, M., Hunter, J., & Donohue, W. (1989). Meta-analysis of self-report on the effectiveness of public speaking anxiety treatment techniques. *Communication Education, 38,* 54–76.

Alter, K., Rank, E., Kotz, S. A., Toepel, U., Besson, M., Schirmer, A., & Friederici, A. D. (2003). Affective encoding in the speech signal and in event-related brain potentials. *Speech Communication, 40(1–2),* 61–70.

Altman, I., & Taylor, D. (1973). *Social penetration: The development of interpersonal relationships.* New York: Holt, Rinehart & Winston.

Andersen, P. A., & Wang, H. (2009). Beyond language: Nonverbal communication across cultures. In L. A. Samovar, R. E. Porter, and E. R. McDaniel. *Intercultural communication: A reader* (12th ed.) (pp. 264–281). Boston, MA: Wadsworth.

Angelou, M. (2006, February 7). Remarks at the funeral service for Coretta Scott King. *American Rhetoric.com.* Accessed at http://www.americanrhetoric.com/speeches/mayaangeloueulogyforcorettaking.htm.

Antheunis, M. L., Valkenburg, P. M., & Perer, J. (2007). Computer-mediated communication and interpersonal attraction: An experimental test of two explanatory hypotheses. *CyberPsychology & Behavior, 10(6),* 831–835.

April 2009 Web Server Survey. (2009). Accessed April 8, 2009, from http://news.netcraft.com/archives/web_server_survey.html.

Argetsinger, A. & Roberts, R. (2007, May 13). Oprah Winfrey's Degrees of Communication at Howard. *Washington Post,* D03. Accessed from http://www.washingtonpost.com/wp–dyn/content/article/2007/05/12/AR2007051201168.html.

Argyle, M. (1973). The syntaxes of bodily communication. *International Journal of Psycholinguistics, 2,* 78.

Aristotle. (1926). *The art of rhetoric.* J. H. Freese (Trans.). Cambridge, MA: Harvard University Press.

Arundale, R. B. (2005). Pragmatics, conversational implicature, and conversation. In K. L. Fitch & R. E. Sanders (Eds.), *Handbook of language and social interaction* (pp. 41–66). Mahwah, NJ: Lawrence Erlbaum.

Associated Press. (2006, August 31). RadioShack layoff notices are sent by e-mail. *The New York Times.com.* Accessed at http://www.nytimes.com/2006/08/31/business/31radio.html.

Atkinson, C. (2005). *Beyond bullet points: Using Microsoft PowerPoint to create presentations that inform, motivate, and inspire.* Redmond, WA: Microsoft Press.

Atkinson, M. (2009). *Lend me your ears: All you need to know about making speeches and presentations.* New York: Oxford University Press.

Axtell, R. E. (2007). Essential do's and taboos: The complete guide to international business and leisure travel. Hoboken, NJ: Wiley.

Ayres, J., Heuett, B., & Sonandre, D. A. (1998). An examination of whether imaging ability enhances the effectiveness of an interview designed to reduce speech anxiety. *Communication Education, 43,* 252–258.

Ayres, J., Hopf, E. S., & Ayres, D. M. (1997). Visualization and performance visualization: Applications, evidence, and speculation. In J. Daly, J. C. McCroskey, J. Ayres, T. S. Hopf, and D. M. Ayres (Eds.), *Avoiding communication: Shyness, reticence, and communication apprehension* (2nd ed.) (pp. 401–422). Cresskill, NJ: Hampton.

Bainton, G. (1890). The art of authorship. Accessed January 2009 from http://www.bartleby.com/73/540.html.

Bajaj, G. (2004, March 26). An interview with Tad Simmons. *Presentations.com.* Accessed November 21, 2006 at http://www.indezine.com/products/PowerPoint/personality/tadsimons.html.

Bales, R. F. (1950). *Interaction Process Analysis: A method for the study of small groups.* Reading, MA: Addison-Wesley.

Barak, A., & Gluck-Ofri, O. (2007). Degree and reciprocity of self-disclosure in online forums. *CyberPsychology & Behavior, 10(3),* 407–417.

419

Barker, L., Edwards, R., Gaines, C., Gladney, K., & Holley, R. (1981). An investigation of proportional time spent in various communication activities by college students. *Journal of Applied Communication Research, 8,* 101–109.

Barker, L. L., & Watson, K. W. (2000). *Listen up: How to improve relationships, reduce stress, and be more productive by using the power of listening.* New York: St. Martin's Press.

Barnard, W. (1991). Group influence and the likelihood of a unanimous majority. *Journal of Social Psychology, 131(5),* 607–614.

Barnlund, D. C. (1970). A transactional model of communication. In K. K. Sereno & C. D. Mortensen (Ed.). *Foundation of communication theory* (pp. 98–101). New York: Harper & Row.

Barraket, J. & Henry-Waring, M. S. (2008, June 1). Getting it on(line): Sociological perspectives on e-dating. *Journal of Sociology, 44(2),* 149–165.

Barzini, L. (1983). *The Europeans.* New York: Penguin Books.

Bash, D. P., & Webel, C. P. (2008). *Peace and conflict studies* (2nd ed.). Thousand Oaks, CA: Sage.

Bass, B. M. (1985). *Leadership and performance beyond expect*ations. New York: Free Press.

Bass, B. M., & Avolio, B. J. (1997). Full range leadership development: *Manual for the multifactor leadership questionnaire.* CA: Mind Garden.

Bass, B. M., & Riggio, R. E. (2006). *Transformational leadership* (2nd ed.). Mahwah, NJ: Lawrence Erlbaum.

Bateman, T. S., & Snell, S. A. (2009). *Management.* Boston: McGraw-Hill.

Baxter, L., & Montgomery, B. (1996). *Relating: Dialogues & dialectics.* New York: Guilford Press.

Beatty, M. J. (1988). Situational and predispositional correlates of public speaking anxiety. *Communication education, 37(1),* 28–39.

Beatty, M. J., McCroskey, J.C., & Heisel, A. D. (1998). Communication apprehension as temperamental expression: A communibiological paradigm. *Communication Monographs, 65,* 197–219.

Beebe, S. A., & Masterson, J. T. (2006). *Communicating in small groups: Principles and practices* (8th ed.). Boston: Pearson Education.

Behling, D. U., & Williams, E. A. (1991). Influence of dress on perceptions of intelligence and expectations of scholastic achievement. *Clothing and Textiles Research Journal, 9(4),* 1–7.

Bellar, S. I., Helms, M., & Arfken, B. (2004). The glacial change: Women on corporate boards. *Business Perspectives, 16(2),* 30–38.

Benne, K. D., & Sheats, P. (1948). Functional roles and group members. *Journal of Social Issues, 4,* 41–49.

Benoit, W. L., & Brinson, S. L. (1999). Queen Elizabeth's image repair discourse: Insensitive royal or compassionate queen? *Public Relations Review, 25(2),* 145–151.

Bente, G., Donaghy, W. C., & Suwelack, D. (1998). Sex differences in body movements and visual attention: An integrated analysis of movement and gaze in mixed–sex dyads. *Journal of Nonverbal Behavior, 22(1),* 31–58.

Berger, B. A. (2005). *Communication skills for pharmacists* (2nd ed.). Atlanta, GA: APHA Publications.

Berger, C. R. (1997). Producing messages under uncertainty. In J. O. Greene (Ed.), *Message production: Advances in communication theory* (pp. 221–244). Mahwah, NJ: Lawrence Erlbaum.

Berger, C. R., & Calabrese, R. J. (1975). Some explorations in initial interaction and beyond: Toward a developmental theory of interpersonal communication. *Human Communication Research, 1,* 99–112.

Berger, C. R., & Kellermann, K. A. (1983). To ask or not to ask: Is that a question? In R. Bostrom (Ed.), *Communication Yearbook 7* (pp. 342–368).

Berman, A., Snyder, S. J., Kozier, B., & Erb, G. (2008). *Fundamentals of nursing: Concepts, process, and practice* (8th ed.). Upper Saddle River, NJ: Pearson Prentice-Hall.

Berry, L. L., & Bendapudi, N. (2003). Clueing in customers. *Harvard Business Review, 81(2),* 100–106.

Bettinghaus, E. P., & Cody, M. J. (1997). *Persuasive communication* (5th ed.). New York: Holt, Rinehart & Winston.

Beyea, S. C. (2004). Improving verbal communication in clinical care. *AORN Journal, 79(5),* 1053–1054. [Association of Operating Room Nurses]

Birdwhistell, R. L. (1970). *Kinesics and context: Essays on body motion communication.* Philadelphia: University of Pennsylvania Press.

Blakeman, M. et al. (1971). *Job-seeking skills reference manual* (3rd ed.). Minneapolis: Minnesota Rehabilitation Center.

Bock, W. (2003). Some rules for virtual teams. *The Journal for Quality and Participation, 26(3),* 43.

Boice, R. (1996). Classroom incivilities. *Research in Higher Education, 37,* 453–486.

Bolles, R. N. (2009). What color is your parachute? 2009: A practical manual for job-hunters and career-changers. Berkeley: Ten Speech Press.

Boorstin, D. J. (1983). *The discoverers.* New York: Random House. Borenstein, S. (2006, July 11). Experts: NASA's shuttle program is back. *Associated Press* News Release. Accessed May 31, 2009 at http://www.foxnews.com/printer_friendly_wires/2006Jul11/0,4675,SpaceShuttle,00.html1.

Borenstein, S. (2006, July 11). Experts: NASA's shuttle program is back. Associated Press News Release. Accessed May 31, 2009 at http://www.foxnews.com/printer_friendly_wires/2006Jul11/0,4675,SpaceShuttle,00.html1.

Borisoff, D., & Merrill, L. (1991). Gender issues and listening. In D. Borisoff & M. Purdy (Eds.), *Listening in everyday life: A personal and professional approach* (pp. 59–850. New York: University Press of America.

Boyle, R. C. (1999). A manager's guide to effective listening. *Manage, 51(1),* 6–7.

Branson, L., Clause, T. S., & Sung, C. (2008). Group style differences between virtual and f2f teams. *American Journal of Business, 33(1),* 65–70.

Brewer, G. (2001, March). Snakes top list of Americans' fears. Gallup News Service. Accessed at http://www.gallup.com/poll/1891/snakes-top-list-americans-fears.aspx.

Brinkley, A. W. (2007). Unambiguous leadership in ambiguous times. *Vital Speeches, 73(12),* 531–533.

Brown, M. B. (2000). Diagnosis and treatment of children and adolescents with attention deficit/hyperactivity disorder. *Journal of Counseling and Development, 78,* 978–987.

Brownell, J. (2006). *Listening: Attitudes, principles, and skills* (3rd ed.). Boston: Allyn and Bacon.

Bryden, M. P., & Ley, R. G. (1983). Right hemispheric involvement in imagery and affect. In E. Perecman (Ed.), *Cognitive processing in the right hemisphere* (pp. 116–117). New York: Academic.

Buckman, R. (1992). *How to break bad news: A guide for health care professionals*. Baltimore, MD: Johns Hopkins University Press.

Building listening skills with Asian folktales. (2007, March 18). Education-World.com. Accessed April 26, 2007, at http:// www.education-world.com/a_lesson/04/lp340-04.shtml.

Burgoon, J. K. (1983). Nonverbal violations of expectations. In J. M. Wiemann and R. P. Harrison (Eds.), *Nonverbal interaction* (pp. 11–77). Beverly Hills, CA; Sage

Burgoon, J. K. (1993). Interpersonal expectations, expectancy violations, and emotional communication. *Journal of Language and Social Psychology, 12*, 30–48.

Burgoon, J. K. (1994). Nonverbal signals. In M. L. Knapp and G. R. Miller (Eds.), *Handbook of interpersonal communication* (pp. 229–285). Newbury Park, CA: Sage.

Burgoon, J. K., Berger, C. R., & Waldron, V. R. (2000). Mindfulness & interpersonal communication, *Journal of Social Issues, 56(1)*, 105–127.

Burgoon, J. K., & Hoobler, G. D. (2002). Nonverbal signals. In M. L. Knapp and J. A. Daly (Eds.). *Handbook of Interpersonal Communication* (3rd ed.) (pp. 240–299). Thousand Oaks, CA: Sage.

Burgoon, J. K., & Le Poire, B. A. (1993). Effects of communication expectations, actual communication, and expectancy disconfirmation on evaluations of communicators and their communication behavior. *Human Communication Research, 20*, 75–107.

Burns, J. M. (1978). *Leadership*. New York: Harper & Row.

Bush shocks foreigners with 'Satanic' sign. (2005, January 21). Associated Press. Accessed at http://www.foxnews.com/story/0,2933,145062,00.html.

Business Wire. (2000, May 1). BridgeGate Survey 2000. *Bridgegate.com*. Accessed at http://www.bridgegate.com/clients/1d.htm.

Employee retention survey reveals Americans favor cash over flextime; in second annual bridgeGate report, employees seen changing their minds about workplace perks. (2000, July 26). *Business Wire*. Accessed at http://findarticles.com/p/articles/mi_m0EIN/is_2000_July_26/ai_63683414.

Butler, K. M. (2008). Virtual Reality: Most teams work remotely, increasing need for different processes. *Employee Benefit News, 22(2)*, 57.

Bynum, C., Epps, H. H., & Kaya, N. (2006). Color memory of university students: Influence of color experience and color characteristic. *College Student Journal, 44(4)*, 824–831.

(CAIB) *Columbia Accident Investigation Board*. (2003, August). Report Volume 1. Washington, DC: Government Printing Office.

Callison, D., & Lamb, A. (2004, September). Audience Analysis. *School Library Media Activities Monthly, 21(1)*, 34–39.

Calnan, A. C. T., & Davidson, M. J. (1998). The impact of gender and its interaction with role and status on the use of tag questions in meetings. *Women in Management Review, 13*, 19–36.

Canary, D. J., & Dindia, K. (1999). Sex differences and similarities in communication. Lawrence Erlbaum.

Caputo, J. S., Hazel, H. C., & McMahon, C. (2000). *Interpersonal communication: Competency through critical-thinking*. Boston: Allyn & Bacon.

Carless, S. A., Wearing, A. J., & Mann, L. (2000). A short measure of transformational leadership. *Journal of Business and Psychology, 14(3)*, 389–405.

Carnegie, D. (2003). *Public speaking and influencing men in business*. Whitefish, MT: Kessinger Publishing.

Carrere, S., & Gottman, J. M. (1999). Predicting divorce among newlyweds from the first three minutes of a marital conflict discussion. *Family Process, 38(3)*, 293–301.

Carton, J. S., Kessler, E. A., & Pape, C. L. (1999). Nonverbal decoding skills and relationship well-being in adults. *Journal of Nonverbal behavior, 23*, 91–100.

The Case Method. (2008). *Harvard Business School*. Accessed July 14, 2008 from www.hbs.edu/case/study-groups.html.

CBCNews.com. (2006, February 17). Radio shack CEO apologizes for resume errors. Accessed June 7, 2006 at http://www.cbc.ca/story/business/national/2006/02/16/radio-060216.html.

Chaiken, S. (1986). Physical appearance and social influence. In C. P. Herman, M. P. Zanna, & E. T. Higgins (Eds.), *Physical appearance, stigma, and social behavior: The Ontario symposium* (Vol. 3, pp. 143–177). Hillsdale, NJ: Erlbaum

Chou, H., & Yeh, Y. (2007). Conflict, conflict management, and performance in ERP teams. *Social Behavior and Personality, 35(8)*, 1035–1048.

Christensen, C. R. (1991). Every student teaches and every teacher learns. In C.R. Christensen, D. A. Garvin, and A. Sweet (Ed.). *Education for judgment: The artistry of discussion leadership* (pp. 99–119). Boston: Harvard Business Press.

Civiello, M. (2009, February). Communication counts in landing a job. T + D, 63(2), 82–83.

Claes, M. T. (2006). Women, men, and management styles. In P. J. Dubeck & D. Dunn (Eds.), *Workplace/women's place: An anthology* (3rd ed.. pp. 83–87). Los Angeles: Roxbury.

Cole, A. F. (2007, June). Plagiarism in graduate medical education. *Family Medicine, 39(6)*, 436–438.

Collier, B., & Wilson, M. J. (1994). What does a graduate need?: Evidence from the careers and opinions of CFOs. *Financial Practice & Education, 4(2)*, 59–65.

Comadena, M. E., Hunt, S. K., & Simonds, C. J. (2007). The effects of teacher clarity, nonverbal immediacy, and caring on student motivation, affective and cognitive learning. *Communication Research Reports, 24*, 241–248.

Condit, C. M. (2000). Culture and biology in human communication: Toward a multi-casual model. *Communication Education, 49(1)*, 7–24.

Conger, J. A. (2004). Developing leadership capability: What's inside the black box? *Academy of Management Executive, 18*, 136–139.

Cook, G. I., Marsh, R. L., & Hicks. J. L. (2003). Halo and devil effects demonstrate valenced-based influences on source-mentoring decisions. *Consciousness and Cognition, 12,* 257–278.

Cooper, J. (1998, Spring). Cooperative learning in college science, mathematics, engineering, and technology. *Cooperative Learning and College Teaching, 8,* 1–8.

Cooper, L. O. (1997). Listening competency in the workplace: A model for training. *Business Communication Quarterly, 60(4),* 75–84.

Corman, S. R., Trethewey, A., & Goodall, B. (2007, April 3). A 21st century model for communication in the global war of ideas: From simplistic influence to pragmatic complexity. *Consortium for Strategic Communication (CSC).* Report #0701, Arizona State University. Accessed September 27, 2008 at http://comops.org/article/114.pdf.

Cowan, N. (2001). The magical number 4 in short-term memory: A reconsideration of mental storage capacity. *Behavioral and Brain Sciences, 24,* 87–14.

Crawford, A. F. (2003). *Barbara Jordan: Breaking the barriers.* Houston: Halcyon Press.

Credo. (2009). Credo for Communication Ethics. *The National communication Association* (Natcom.org). Accessed from http://www.natcom.org/index.asp?bid=514.

Crews, J. M., Cao, J., Lin, M., Nunamaker, J. F., Jr., & Burgoon, J. K. (2007). A comparison of instructor-led vs. web-based training for detecting deception. *Journal of STEM Education, 8(1–2),* 31–40.

Cullen, L. T. (2006, March 26). SATs for J-O-B-S. Time.com Accessed at http://www.time.com/time/magazine/article/0,9171,1176994,00.html.

Daft, R. L. (2008). *Management* (8th ed.). Mason, OH: Thomson South-Western.

Daft, R. L., & Marcic, D. (2006). *Understanding management* (5th ed.). Mason, OH: Thomson South-Western.

Daly, J. A., Friedrich, G., & Vangelisti, A. (1990). *Teaching communication: Theory, methods, and research.* Hillsdale, NJ: Erlbaum.

Daly, J. A., Vangelisti, A., & Weber, D. J. (1995). Speech anxiety affects how people prepare speeches: A protocol analysis of the preparation process of speakers. *Communication Monographs, 62,* 383–397.

Damhorst, M., & Fiore, A. M. (2000).Woman's job interview dress: How the personnel interviewers see it. In M. L. Damhorst, A. Miller, & S. O. Michelman (Eds.), *The meaning of dress* (pp. 92–97). New York: Fairchild.

Damhorst, M., & Reed, J. A. P. (1986). Clothing, color value and facial expression: Effect on evaluations of female job applicants. *Social Behavior and Personality, 14(1),* 89–98.

D'Anna, C.A., Zechmeister, E. B., & Hall, J. W. (1991) Toward a meaningful definition of vocabulary size. *Journal of Reading Behavior,* 23(1), 109–122.

Dasborough, M. T. (2006). Cognitive asymmetry and employee emotional reactions to leadership behaviors. *Leadership Quarterly, 17,* 163–178.

David, C., & Baker, M. A. (1994). Re-reading bad news: Compliance-gaining features in management memos. *The Journal of Business Communication, 31(4),* 267–290.

Davis, D. C., & Scaffidi, N. M. (2007). *Leading virtual teams.* Conference Papers—International Communication Association, 2007 Annual Meeting, 1–25.

Davis, J. R. (2002). *Interdisciplinary courses and team teaching: New arrangements for learning.* Westport, CT: ORYX Press.

Davis, R. M. (2008, January). Shall we dance? *Vital speeches, 74(1),* 43–46.

Decker, B., & Denney, J. (1993). *You've got to be believed to be heard.* New York: St. Martin's.

de Janasz, S. C., Dowd, K. O., & Schneider, B. Z. (2002). *Interpersonal skills in organizations.* Boston: McGraw-Hill.

Delbecq, A. L., Van de Ven, A. H., & Gustafson, D. H. (1986). *Group techniques for program planning: A guide to nominal group and delphi process.* Westport, CT: Green Briar.

Dewey, J. (1910). *How we think.* Boston: Heath.

Diamond, L. E., & Diamond, H. (2007). *Teambuilding that gets results: Essential plans and activities for creating effective teams.* Naperville, IL: Sourcebooks.

Dickinson, T. (2008, March 20). The machinery of hope: Inside the grass-roots field operation of Barack Obama, who is transforming the way political campaigns are run. Ronningstone.com. Accessed July 12, 2008 from http://www.rollingstone.com/news/coverstory/obamamachineryofhope.

Duff, D. C., Levine, T. R., Beatty, M. J., Woolbright, J., & Park, H. S. (2007). Testing public anxiety treatments against a credible placebo control. *Communication Education, 56(1),* 72–88.

Doyle, A. (NA). The interview advantage: How to use nonverbal communication to impress. *About.com.* Accessed at http://jobsearch.about.com/od/interviewsnetworking/a/nonverbalcomm.htm.

du Pre, A. (2000). *Communicating about Health: Current Issues and Perspectives.* Mountain View, CA: Mayfield.

Duval, T. S., & Silva, P. J. (2002). Self-awareness, probability of improvement, and the self-serving bias. *Journal of Personality and Social Psychology, 82,* 49–61.

Eagly, A. H., & Chaiken, S. (1993). *The psychology of attitudes.* Fort Worth, TX: Harcourt Brace Jovanovich.

Eckert, S. (2006). *Intercultural Communication.* Mason, OH: South-Western.

Edwards, R. (1990). Sensitivity to feedback and the development of the self. *Communication Quarterly, 38,* 101–111.

Ekman, P. (1965). Communication through nonverbal communication: A source of information about an interpersonal relationship. In S. S. Thompkins & C. E. Izard (Eds.), *Affect, Cognition and Personality.* New York: Springer.

Ekman, P. (1994). Strong evidence for universals in facial expressions: A reply to Russell's mistaken critique. *Psychological Bulletin, 115*, 268–287.

Ekman, P. (2003). *Emotions revealed: Recognizing faces and feelings to improve communication and emotional life*. New York: Times Books.

Ekman, P., & Friesen, W. V. (1969). The repertoire of nonverbal behavior: Categories, origins, usage, and coding. *Semiotica, 1*, 49–98.

Ekman, P., & Friesen, W. V. (1971, April). Constants across cultures in the face and emotion. *Journal of Personality and Social Psychology, 17*, 124–129.

Ekman, P., & Friesen, W. V. (1999). Hand movements. In L. K. Guerrero, DeVito, J. A., & Hecht, M. L. (Eds.), *The nonverbal communication reader: Classic and contemporary readings* (2nd ed.). Prospect Heights, IL: Waveland Press.

Ekman, P., & O'Sullivan, M. (1991). Who can catch a liar? *American Psychologist, 46*, 913–920.

Elashmawi, F., & Harris, P. R. (1998). Multicultural management 2000. Houston, TX: Gulf Publishing.

Eldred, J. (2007, January). Speaking, listening, learning. *Adults Learning*, 7.

Elfenbein, H. A. (2006). Learning in emotion judgments: Training and the cross-cultural understanding of facial expressions. *Journal of Nonverbal Behavior, 30(1)*, 21–36.

Ellingson, L. L. (2005). *Communicating in the clinic: Negotiating frontstage and backstage teamwork*. Cresskill, NJ: Nampton Press.

Ellis, A. (1994). Rational emotive behavior therapy approaches to obsessive-compulsive disorder (OCD). *Journal of Rational-Emotive & Cognitive Behavior Therapy, 12*, 121–141.

Ellis, A. (2004). *Rational emotive behavior therapy: It works for me—it can work for you*. Amherst, New York: Prometheus Books.

Elsea, J. E. (1985, September). Strategies for effective presentations. *Personnel Journal, 64*, 31–33.

Employee retention survey reveals Americans favor cash over flextime; in second annual bridgegate report, employees seen changing their minds about workplace perks. (2000, July 26).

Ethics Quick Test. (2009). The TI Ethics Quick Test. Accessed September, 2009 from http://www.ti.com/corp/docs/company/citizen/ethics/quicktest.shtml.

Evertson, C. M., & Emmer, E. T. (2009). *Classroom management for elementary school teachers* (8th ed.). Boston: Allyn & Bacon.

Farquharson, B. (2006, October). Listen to me. *Graphic Arts Monthly*, 61.

Feeley, Th. H., Hwang, J., & Barnett, G. A. (2008). Predicting employee turnover from friendship networks. *Journal of applied Communication Research, 36(1)*, 56073.

Ferraro, G. P. (2006). *The cultural dimension to international business* (5th ed.). Upper Saddle River, NJ: Pearson Prentice-Hall.

Ferriss, T. (2007). *The 4-hour workweek: Escape 9–5, live anywhere, and join the new rich*. New York: Crown.

Fiedler, F. E. (1967). *A theory of leadership effectiveness*. New York: McGraw-Hill.

Fiedler, F. E. (1996). Research on leadership selection and training: One view of the future. *Administrative Science Quarterly, 41*, 241–250.

Fiedler, F. E., & Chemers, M. (1974). *Leadership and effective management*. Glenview, IL: Scott, Foresman.

Fink, H. (2007). Tell it like it is: Essential communication skills for engineers. *Industrial Engineer, 39(3)*, 44–48.

Fisher, B. A. (1980). *Small group decision making* (2nd ed.). New York: McGraw-Hill.

Fisher, R. P. & Geiselman, R. E. (1992). Memory enhancing techniques for investigative interviewing: The cognitive interview. Springfield: Charles C. Thomas.

Fisher, W. R. (1987). *Human communication as narration: Toward a philosophy of reason, value, and action*. Columbia: University of South Carolina Press.

Francis, D., & Young, D. (1992). *Improving work groups* (2nd ed.). San Diego, CA: Pfeiffer.

Frank, M. G., Feely, T. H., Paolantonio, N., & Servoss, T. J. (2004). Individual and small group accuracy in judging truthful and deceptive communication. *Group Decision and Negotiation, 13*, 45–54.

French, J., & Raven, B. (1959). The bases of social power. In D. Cartwright, (Ed.), *Studies of Social Power*, pp. 150–167. Ann Arbor, MI: Institute for Social Research.

Friedman, R. A., & Currall, S. C. (2003). Conflict escalation: Dispute exacerbating elements of e-mail communication. *Human Relations, 56(11)*, 1325–1347.

Friedrich, G. W., & Cooper, P. (1990). The first day. In J. A. Daly, G. W. Friedrich, and A. L. Vangelisti (Ed.), *Teaching communication: Theory, research, and methods* (pp. 237–246). Hillsdale, NJ: Lawrence Erlbaum Associates.

Friedrichsen, M., & Milberg, A. (2006, June). Concern about losing control when breaking bad news to terminally ill patients with cancer: Physicians' perspective. *Journal of Palliative Medicine, 9(3)*, 673–682.

Frymier, A. B., & Shulman, G. M. (1995). 'What's in it for me:' Increasing content relevance to enhance students' motivation. *Communication Education, 44*, 40–50.

Fulk, J., & Collins-Jarvis, L. (2001). Wired meetings: Technological mediation of organizational gatherings. In F. M. Jablin and Putnam, L. L. (Eds.), *The new handbook of organizational communication: Advances in theory, research, and methods* (pp. 624–663). Thousand Oaks, CA: Sage.

Gallo, C. (2006, May 22). Terminate your public speaking fears. *Business Week Online*. Accessed from EBSCO Publishing.

GAO Highlights. (2006, June). Overall trends in management-level diversity and diversity initiatives, 1993–2004. *Government Accountability Office*. Accessed July 15, 2008 from http://www.gao.gov/cgi-bin/getrpt?GAO–06–617.

Garner, R. (2002, August 3). Children's speaking skills in decline. Bridges4kids.org. Accessed August 6, 2008 from http://www.bridges4kids.org/articles/8–02/UKIndy8–3–02.html.

Garretson, C. (2009, April 13). Economy changing work game for 'Gen Y.' *Network World, 26*(14), 1 and 16.

Gay, G. (2009). Culture and communication in the classroom. In L. A. Samovar, R. E. Porter, & E. R. McDaniel (Eds.), *Intercultural Communication* (pp. 347–364). Boston: Wadsworth Cengage Learning.

Gestwicki, C. (2007). *Curriculum in early education.* Clifton Park, NY: Thomson Delmar Learning

Gibb, J. R. (1961). Defensive communication. *Journal of Communication, 11,* 141–148.

Gibb, J. R. (1970). Sensitivity training as a medium for personal growth and improved interpersonal relationships. *Interpersonal Development, 1,* 6–31.

Gibson, C. B., & Cohen, S. G. (2003). *Virtual teams that work: Creating conditions for virtual team effectiveness.* San Francisco, CA: Jossey-Bass.

Gigone, D., & Hastie, R. (1997). Proper analysis of the accuracy of group judgments. *Psychological Bulletin, 121,* 149–167.

Gladwell, M. (2002). The tipping point: How little things can make a big difference. New York: Little, Brown & Co.

Gladwell, M. (2005a). *Blink: The power of thinking without thinking.* New York, NY: Little, Brown and Company.

Gladwell, M. (2005b, September 12). The cellular church: How Rick Warren's congregation grew. *The New Yorker, 81*(27), 60–67. Accessed July 8, 2008 from EBSCOHost Database.

Glass, P. (2002, July-September). Turn off that racket. *Sssh! Listen Up!* Accessed at http://www.highgain.com/newsletter/back-issues/e_news_july_september_02/hg-enews-july_sept_02.html.

Goldstein, M. (2003). It's alive! The audience, that is, but some presenters don't seem to know it. *Successful Meetings, 52*(2), 20.

Goodman, S. R., & Leiman, A. (2007). *College admissions together: It takes a family.* Dullas, VA: Capital Books (IPM).

Gordon, R. G., Jr. (ed.). (2005). *Ethnologues: Languages of the World, 15th ed.* Dallas: TX.: SIL International. Online version: http://www.ethnologue.com/.

Gorham, J. (1988). The relationship between verbal teacher immediacy behaviors and student learning. *Communication Education, 37,* 40–53.

Gorham, J., & Christophel, D. M. (1990). The relationship of teachers' use of humor in the classroom to immediacy and student learning. *Communication Education, 37,* 40-53.

Gottman, J. M., & Levenson, R. (2000, August). The timing of divorce: Predicting when a couple will divorce over a 14-year period. *Journal of Marriage and the Family, 62,* 737–745.

Grant Thornton International Business Report. (2007, March). Four in ten businesses worldwide have no women in senior management. *International Business Report* (IBR). Accessed July 17, 2008 from http://www.internationalbusinessreport.com/Press-room/2007/women-in-senior-management.asp.

Greenleaf, R. (2002). *Servant leadership* (reissued from 1977). Mahwah, NJ: Paulist Press.

Grice, H. P. (1975). Logic and conversations. In P. Cole, & J. Morgan (Eds.), *Syntax and Semantics* (vol. 3, pp. 41–58). New York: Academic.

Gronbeck, B. E., McKerrow, R. E., Ehninger, D., & Monroe, A. H. (1994). *Principles and types of speech communication* (12th ed.). New York: HarperCollins College.

Grossman, S. C., & Valiga, T. M. (2005). *The new leadership challenge: Creating the future of nursing* (2nd ed.). Philadelphia, PA: F. A. Davis Company.

Guerrero, L. K., & Anderson, P. A. (1991). The waxing and waning of relational intimacy: Touch as a function of relational stage, gender and touch avoidance. *Journal of Social and Personal Relationships, 8,* 147–165.

Guffey, M. E. (2007). Essentials of business communication (7th ed.). Mason, OH: South-Western.

Gunel, M., Hand, B., & Gunduz, S. (2006). Comparing student understanding of quantum physics when embedding multimodal representations into two different writing formats: Presentation format versus summary report format. *Science Education, 90*(6), 1092–1112.

Hackman, J. R. (2002, July). New rules for team building. *Optimize,* 50–62.

Hall, B. J. (2002). *Among cultures: the challenge of communication.* Fort Worth: Harcourt.

Hall, E. T. (1973). *The silent language.* Garden City, NY: Anchor.

Hall, E. T. (1976). *Beyond culture.* New York: Doubleday.

Hall. E. T. (1983). Proximics. In A. M. Katz and V. T. Katz (Eds.), *Foundations of nonverbal communication: Readings, exercise, and commentary* (pp. 5–27). Carbondale: Southern Illinois University Press.

Hall, E. T., & Hall, M. R. (1990). *Understanding cultural differences: Germans, French, and Americans.* Yarmouth, ME: Intercultural Press.

Hall, J. A. (1984). *Nonverbal sex differences: Communication accuracy and expressive style.* Baltimore: Johns Hopkins University Press.

Hamilton, C. (2007, November). Tips & tools for fighting plagiarism in traditional and online communication classes. Presented at the NCA national convention in Chicago.

Hamilton, C. (2008, April). In Practice IBM: Virtual worlds unite virtual teams. *Chief Learning Officer, 7*(4), 48.

Hamilton, D. (2000, March). Prepare and practice. *Officepro,* 14.

Hansen, J. C. (2008). Who will care for us? *Vital Speeches, 74*(8), 352–357.

Hansen, M. V., & Allen, R. G. (2002). *The One Minute Millionaire.* New York: Harmony Books.

Hardey, M. (2002). Life beyond the screen: Embodiment and identity through the Internet. *The Sociological Review, 50*(4), 570–585.

Hayakawa, S.I. (1949). *Language in thought and action.* New York: Harcourt, Brace and Company, 235–236.

Hearn, R. (1999). *Teaching speech organization and outlining using a color-coded approach.* Paper presented at the annual meeting of the Western States Communication Association in Vancoucer, British Columbia on February 19–23.

Heath, D. (1991). *Fulfilling lives: Paths to maturity and success.* San Francisco: Jossey-Bass.

Hechinger, J. (2008, September 18). College applicants, beware: Your Facebook page is showing. *Wall Street Journal, 252*, D6.

Heider, F. (1958). *The Psychology of Interpersonal Relations.* New York: Wiley.

Help for sleep–deprived students. (2004, April 19). The Associated Press. Accessed April 23, 2007 at http://www .cbsnews.com/stories/2004/04/19/health/main12476.shtml.

Hendon, D. W., Hendon, R. A., & Herbig, P. (1996). *Cross-cultural business negotiations.* Westport, CT: Quorum Books.

Herrick, J. A. (1995). *Argumentation: Understanding and shaping arguments.* Scottsdale, AZ: Gorsuch Scarisbrick.

Hersey, P., Blanchard, K., & Johnson, D. E. (2007). *Management of organizational behavior* (9th ed.). Upper Saddle River, NJ: Prentice-Hall.

Heslin, R. (1974, May). Steps toward a taxomony of touching. Paper presented to the annual meeting of the Midwestern Psychological Association, Chicago, IL.

Hess, U., Senécal, S., Kirouac, G. Herrera, Philippot, P., & Kleck, R. E. (2000). Emotional expressivity in men and women: Stereotypes and self-perceptions. *Cognition and Emotion, 14*, 609–642.

Hill, C. E., & McShane, S. L. (2008). *Principles of Management.* Boston: McGraw-Hill.

Hishitani, S. (1991). Vividness of image and retrieval time. *Perception and Motor Skills*, 73, 115–123.

Hofstede, G. J. (1984). *Culture's consequences.* Beverly Hills, CA: Sage.

Hofstede, G. J. (2001). *Culture's consequences: comparing values, behaviors, institutions and organizations across nations* (2nd ed.). Thousand Oaks, CA: Sage.

Hofstede, G. J. (2005). *Cultures and organizations: Software of the mind.* New York: McGraw Hill.

Hogg, M. A., & Hains, S. (1998). Cohesiveness and groupthink. *European Journal of Social Psychology, 28*, 323–341.

Holcombe, M. W., & Stein, J. K. (1996). *Presentations for decision makers* (3rd ed.). New York: Van Nostrand Reinhold.

Holm, J. H. (1981). *Business and professional communication.* Boston: American Press.

Hosek, C. A., Phelps, B. J., & Jensen, J. (2004, Summer). Average sleep times among undergraduate college students. *Psi Chi Journal, 9(2)*.

Hsu, C. (2004, Fall). Sources of differences in communication apprehension between Chinese in Taiwan and Americans. *Communication Quarterly, 52*, 370–390.

Hubbell, A. P, & Chory-Assad, R. M. (2005). Motivating factors: Perceptions of justice and their relationship with managerial and organizational trust. *Communication Studies, 56(1)*, 47–70.

Iacocca, L. (2007). *Where have all the leaders gone?* New York: Scribner.

Ingram, T. N, LaForge, R. W., Avila, R. A., Schwepker Jr., C. H., & Williams, M. R. (2008). *Professional selling: A trust-based approach* (4th ed.). Mason, OH: South-Western.

Ingram, T. N., Schwepker, C. H., & Hutson, D. (1992, August). Why salespeople fail. *Industrial Marketing Management, 21*, 225–230.

Ishak, N. M., Mustapha, R. B., & Nadzir, N. R. (2002). Personality profiles of college students in technical and non–technical fields: Implications for workforce readiness. *International Journal of Vocational Education and Training. 10(2)*, 61–72.

Ivancevich, J., & Duening, T. (2007). *Business principles, guidelines, and practices* (2nd ed.). Mason, OH: Thomson.

Ivy, D. K., & Backlund, P. (2008). *Gender speak: Personal effectiveness in gender communication* (4th ed.). Boston: Pearson Allyn & Bacon.

Janis, I. L. (1982). *Groupthink: A psychological study of foreign policy decisions and fiascoes* (2nd ed.). Boston: Houghton Mifflin.

Janis, I. L. (1989). *Crucial decisions: Leadership in policymaking and crisis management.* New York: Free Press.

Janusik, L., & Wolvin, A. (2007). *24 hours in a day: A communication time study update.* Paper presented at the annual meeting of the National communication Association, Chicago, IL.

Jaska, J. A., & Pritchard, M. S. (1994). *Communication ethics: Methods of analysis* (2nd ed.). Belmont, CA: Wadsworth.

Jischke, M. C. (2007). The American dream: What is it? Who is it? *Vital Speeches, 73(7)*, 314–315.

Jobs Outlook (2006, October 27). *The Seattle Times.* Accessed November 7, 2006 at http://seattletimes.nwsource .com/html/education/2003326317_collwebfuturemajors .html.

Job Outlook 2007. (2007). What are you doing after graduation? *National Association of colleges and Employees* (NACE). Accessed at http://www.naceweb.org.

Job Outlook 2008 Survey. (2008). The perfect candidate. National Association of Colleges & Employers (NACE). Accessed at www.jobweb.com/joboutlook/2007/default .htm. Must be a member to access.

Job Outlook 2009. (2009). How employers view candidates (1-42). *National Association of colleges and Employees* (NACE). Accessed at http://www.naceweb.org.

Johnson, D. D. (1995). Color adaptation for color deficient learners. *Visual Arts Research, 21*, 26–41.

Jones, S. E., & Yarbrough, A. E. (l985). A naturalistic study of the meanings of touch. *Communication Monographs*, 52, 19–56.

Kabacoff, R. L. (1998). *Gender differences in organizational leadership: A large sample study.* Paper presented at the meeting of the American Psychological Association, San Francisco, CA.

Kabat-Zinn, J. (2007). *Arriving at your own door: 108 Lessons in Mindfulness.* New York: Samuel Wiser.

Kahane, H., & Cavender, N. (2002). *Logic and contemporary rhetoric: The use of reason in everyday life* (9th ed.). Belmont, CA: Wadsworth.

Kameda, T., Stasson, M. F., David, J. H., Parks, C., & Zimmerman, S. (1992). Social dilemmas, subgroups, and motivational loss in task-oriented groups: In search of an "optimal" team size. *Social Psychology Quarterly, 55*, 47–56.

Kanter, D., & Mirvis, P. (1990). *The cynical American: Living and working in an age of discontent and disillusionment.* San Francisco: Jossey-Bass.

Karau, S. J., & Williams, K. D. (1993). Social loafing: A meta-analytic review and theoretical integration. *Journal of Personality and Social Psychology, 65,* 681–706.

Karlins, M., & Hargis, E. (1988). Inaccurate self-perception as a limiting factor in managerial effectiveness. *Perceptual and Motor skills, 66,* 665–666.

Kavilanz, P. B. (2007, March 28). Study: TV ads = higher obesity risk for kids. CNN Money.com. Accessed October 24, 2007, at: http://cnnmoney.com/2007/03/27/news/companies/kaiserchildren_tvads/index.htm.

Kearney, P., Plax, T. G., Richmond, V. P., & McCroskey, J.C. (1984). Power in the classroom IV: Alternatives to discipline. In R. Bostrom (Ed.), *Communication yearbook 8* (pp. 724–746). Beverly Hills, CA: Sage.

Kellett, J. B., Humphrey, R. H., and Sleeth, R. G. (2006). Empathy and the emergence of task and relations leaders. *Leadership Quarterly, 17,* 146–162.

Kelly, L., & Keaten, J. A. (2000). Treating communication anxiety: Implications of the communibiological paradigm. *Communication Education, 49,* 45–57.

Kelner, M. J., & Bourgeault, I. L. (1993). Patient control over dying: Responses of health care professionals. *Social Science and Medicine, 36(6),* 757–765.

Kent, M. (2007, June). Better together: Life lessons. *Vital Speeches, 73(6),* 266–268.

Keyton, J. (1999). *Group communication: Process and analysis.* Mountain View, CA: Mayfield.

Kimble, G. A. (1989). Psychology from the standpoint of a generalist. *American Psychologist, 44(3),* 491–499.

Kinchin, I. (2006). Developing PowerPoint handouts to support meaningful learning. *British Journal of Educational Technology, 37(4),* 647–650.

Kirkman, B. L., & Rosen, B. (1999). Beyond self-management: Antecedents and consequences of team empowerment. *Academy of Management Journal, 42,* 58–74.

Klyukanov, I. E. (2005). *Principles of intercultural communication.* Boston: Pearson Education.

Knapp, M. L., & Daly, J. A. (2002). *Handbook of interpersonal communication* (3rd ed.). Thousand Oaks, CA: Sage.

Knapp, M. L., & Hall, J.A. (2007). *Nonverbal communication in human interaction* (5th ed.). Belmont, CA: Wadsworth.

Knapp, M. L., & Vangelisti, A. L. (2008). *Interpersonal communication and human relationships* (6th ed.). Boston: Allyn & Bacon. ISBN-13: 978-0205543724

Knee, C. R., Patrick, H., & Lonsbary, C. (2003). Implicit theories of relationships: Orientations toward evaluation and cultivation. *Personality and Social Psychology Review, 7(1),* 41–55.

Korzybski, A. (1950). *Manhood of Humanity* (2nd ed.). New York: Institute of General Semantics.

Kosslyn, S. M., & Rosenberg, R. S. (2006). *Psychology in context* (3rd ed.). Boston: Allyn & Bacon.

Kouzes, J. M., & Posner, B. Z. (2002). *The leadership challenge* (3rd ed.). San Francisco: Jossey-Bass.

Krames,J. A. (2003). *What the best CEO's know: 7 exceptional leaders and their lessons for transforming any business.* New York: McGraw-Hill.

Kreps, G. L. (1990). *Organizational communication* (3rd ed.). New York: Longman.

Kreps, G. L., & Thornton, B. C. (1992). *Health communication theory & practice.* Prospect Heights, IL: Waveland Press.

Krieger, J. L. (2005). Shared mindfulness in cockpit crisis situations. *Journal of Business Communication, 42(2),* 135–167.

LaFasto, F., & Larson, C. F. (2001). *When teams work best.* Thousand Oaks, CA: Sage.

Lakhani, D. (2009). *How to Sell When Nobody's Buying.* Hoboken, NJ: Wiley.

Landy, H. (2006, February 14). RadioShack CEO's resume in question. Star-Telegram.com Accessed May 23, 2006 at http://www.dfw.com/mld/dfw/13867927.htm?template=contentModules/printstory.jsp.

Lapakko, D. (1996). Three cheers for language: A closer examination of a widely cited study of nonverbal communication. *Communication Education, 46(1),* 63–67.

Larson, C. U. (2010). *Persuasion: Reception and Responsibility* (12th ed.). Boston: Wadsworth Cengage Learning.

Laswell, H. D. (1948). The structure and function of communication in society. In L. Bryson (Ed.), *The communication of ideas.* New York: Harper & Row.

Lazarev, S. (2007). Moldovan [Cyrillic Alphabet].Omniglot.com. Accessed August 15, 2007 from http://www.omniglot.com/writing/moldovan.htm.

Lees, J. (2008). *How to get a job you'll love* (5th ed.). Berkshire, UK: McGraw-Hill Professional.

Le Roux, J. (2002). Effective educators are culturally competent communicators. *Intercultural Education, 13(1),* 37–48.

Lencioni, P. (2002). *The five dysfunctions of a team.* Hoboken, HJ: Jossey-Bass.

Lepper, H. S., Martin, L. R., & DiMatteo, M. R. (1995). A model of nonverbal exchange in physician-patient expectations for patient involvement. *Journal of Nonverbal Behavior, 19 (4),* 207–222

Lesikar, R. V., Flatley, M. E., & Rentz, K. (2008). *Business Communication* (11th ed.). Boston: McGraw-Hill Irwin.

Lewin, K. (1951). *Field Theory in Social Science.* New York: Harper and Row.

Lewis, J. R., Bates, B. C., & Lawrence, S. (1994). Empirical studies of projection: A critical review. *Human Relations, 47(11),* 1295–1319.

Lieberman, D. A. (1997). *Public Speaking in the Multicultural Environment* (2nd ed.). Boston: Allyn & Bacon.

Lind, M. (1996, February 12). TRB from Washington: Jordan's rules. *The New Republic, 214(7),* 6.

Littlejohn, S. W., & Foss, K A. (2008).*Theories of human communication* (9th ed.). Belmont, CA: Thomson Wadsworth.

Liverpool, UK. (2007, April 24). TV food adverts increase obese children's appetite by 134%. University of Liverpool Press Resease. Accessed October 24, 2007 at: http://www.lib.ac.uk/newsroom/press_releases/2007/04/obesity_ads.htm.

Luckert, L. (1991). Speak out. *Women in business, 43(3)*, 12–14. Accessed from Academic Search elite.

Lukaszewski, J. E. (2007, May). Avoiding integrity: The greatest vulnerability for American business Leadership. *Vital Speeches, 73(5)*, 196–200.

Luntz, Frank I. (2007). *Words that work: It's not what you say, it's what people hear*. New York, NY: Hyperion Books.

Luo, L., Bippus, A. M., & Dunbar, N. E. (2005, October). Causal attributions for collaborative public speaking presentations in college classes. *Communication Reports, 18(2)*, 65–73.

Madaus, J. W. (2008). Employment self-disclosure rates and rationales of university graduates with learning disabilities. *Journal of Learning Disabilities, 41(4)*, 291–299.

Madden, M., & Lenhart, A. (2006, March 5). Online dating. Pew Internet & American Life Project. Washington, DC. Accessed August, 9, 2008 from http://www.pewinternet.org/pdfs/PIP_Online_Dating.pdf.

Maddux, J. E., & Rogers, R. W. (1983). Protection motivation and self-efficacy: A revisited theory of fear appeals and attitude change. *Journal of Experimental Social Psychology, 19*, 469–479.

Manz, C. C., & Sims, H. P. (2001). *The new superleadership*. San Francisco: Berrett–Koehler.

Manzo, K. K. (2004, June 16). N.C. School Board chairman resigns over plagiarism. *Education Week, 23(40)*, 4.

March, J., & Sevon, G. (1982). Gossip, information, and decision making. In L. Sproull & P. Larkey (Eds.), *Advances in information processing in organizations* (Vol. I). Greenwich, CT: JAI Press.

Marchese, M. (2001). Matching management practices to national culture in India, Mexico, Poland, and the U.S. *The Academy of Management Executive, 15(2)*, 130–132.

Marcic, D. (1995). Personality Assessment: Jung's Typology and the Myers-Briggs Type Indicator. In R. L. Daft & D. Marcic. *Understanding Management* (5th ed., pp. 401–403). Mason, OH: Thomson Southwestern.

Martin, M. M., Myers, S. A., & Mottet, T. P. (1999). Student motives for communicating with their instructors. *Communication Education, 48*, 155–164.

Mason, S. (2007, April). Gender gap in technology. *Vital Speeches, 73(4)*, 159–163.

Maxwell, J. C. (1998). *The 21 irrefutable laws of leadership*. Nashville, TN: Thomas Nelson, Inc.

Mayer, R. R. (2001). *Multimedia learning*. New York: Cambridge University Press.

McCornack, S. A., & Levine, T. R. (1990, June). When lies are uncovered: Emotional and relational outcomes of discovered deception. *Communication Monographs, 57(2)*, 119–139.

McCown, J. A., Fischer, D., Page, R., & Hamant, M. (2001). Internet Relationships: People Who Meet People. *Cyber Psychology & Behavior, 5(4)*, 593–596.

McCroskey, J. C. (1982). *An Introduction to Rhetorical Communication*, 4th ed. Englewood Cliffs, NJ: Prentice-Hall.

McCroskey, J. C., & Beatty, M. J. (1998). Communication apprehension. In J.C. McCroskey, J. A. Daly, M. M. Martin, & M. J. Beatty (Eds.), *Communication and personality: Trait perspectives* (pp. 215–231). Cresskill, NJ: Hampton Press, Inc.

McCroskey, J. C., & Beatty, M. J. (2000). The communibiological perspective: Implication for communication in instruction. *Communication Education, 49*, 1–6.

McCroskey, J. C., Fayer, J. M., & Richmond, V. O. (1985). Don't speak to me in English: Communication apprehension in Puerto Rico. *Communication Quarterly, 33(3)*, 185–192.

McCroskey, J. C., Richmond, V. P., & McCroskey, L. L. (2006). *An introduction to communication in the classroom: The role of communication in teaching and training* (pp. 62–64). Boston: Allyn & Bacon.

McCroskey, J. C., & Young, T. J. (1981). Ethos and credibility: The construct and its measurement after three decades. *Central States Speech Journal, 32*, 24–34.

McDaniel, E. R., Samovar, L. A., & Porter, R. E. (2009). Understanding intercultural communication: The working principles. In L. A. Samovar, R. E. Porter, & E. R. McDaniel (Eds.), *Intercultural Communication* (pp. 6–17). Boston: Wadsworth Cengage Learning.

McEvoy, S. P., Stevenson, M. R., McCartt, A. T., Woodward, M., Haworth, C., & Palamara, P., et al. (2005). Role of mobile phones in motor vehicle crashes resulting in hospital attendance: A case-crossover study. British Journal of Medicine, 331, 428–436.

McGuire, W. J. (1964). Inducing resistance to persuasion: Some contemporary approaches. In L. Berkowitz (Ed.), *Advances in experimental social psychology* (Vol. 1, pp. 191–229). New York: Academic Press.

McGuire, W. J. (1985). Attitudes and attitude change. In G. Lindzey and E.Aronson (Eds.), *Handbook of social psychology*, Vol. 2 (3rd ed., pp. 287–288). New York: Random House.

McKenna, K. Y. A., & Bargh J. A. (2000). Plan 9 from cyberspace: the implications of the Internet for personality and social psychology. *Personality and Social Psychology Review, 4(1)*, 57–75.

Menzel, K. E., & Carrell, L. J. (1999). The impact of gender and immediacy to talk and perceived learning. *Communication Education, 48*, 31–40.

MetLife.com. (2006). The MetLife Study of Employee Benefits Trends: Findings from the 2005/2006 National Survey of Employers and Employees. Accessed August 8, 2008 from http://www.metlife.com/WPSAssets/33495295001161801070V1FMetLifeStudyofEmployeeBenefitsTrendsexp0307.pdf.

Miller, G. A. (1994). The magical number seven: Some limits on our capacity for processing information. *Psychological Review, 101*, 143–352.

Miller, A. N. (2009). Public speaking patterns in Kenya. In L.A. Samovar, R. E. Porter, and E. R. McDaniel (Eds.), *Intercultural communication: A reader* (pp. 251–259). Boston, MA: Wadsworth Cengage Learning.

Miller, G. A. (1994). The magical number seven: Some limits on our capacity for processing information. *Psychological Review, 101*, 143–352.

Miller, G. R., & Stiff, J. B. (1993). *Deceptive communication.* Newbury Park, CA: Sage.

Miller, J. B. (2005). Practicing the ancient art of *memoria* in the modern classroom. *Communication Teacher, 19(2)*, 48–52.

Millette, D. M., & Gorham, J. (2002). Teacher behavior and student motivation. In J. L. Chesebro & J. C. McCroskey (Eds.), *Communication for teachers* (pp. 141–154). Boston: Allyn & Bacon.

Morreale, S., Rubin, R. B., & Jones, E. (1998). Speaking and listening competencies for college students. National Communication Association (natcom.org). Accessed at http://www.natcom.org/nca/files/ccLibraryFiles/FILENAME/000000000085/College%20Competencies.pdf.

Mottet, T. P., Martin, M. M., & Myers, S. A. (2004). Relationships among perceived instructor verbal approach and avoidance relational strategies and students' motives for communicating with their instructors. *Communication Education, 53(1)*, 116–122.

Mottet, T. P., & Richmond, V. P. (1998). An inductive analysis of verbal immediacy: Alternative conceptualization of relational verbal approach/avoidance strategies, *Communication Quarterly, 46(1)*, 25–40.

Mottet T. P., Richmond, V. P., & McCroskey, J. C. (2006). *Handbook of instructional communication: Rhetorical and relational perspectives.* Boston: Allyn and Bacon/Pearson.

Mottet T. P., Parker-Raley, J., Beebe, S. A., & Cunningham, C. (2007). Instructors who resist "college lite": The neutralizing effect of instructor immediacy on students' course-Workload Violations and perceptions of instructor credibility and affective learning. *Communication Education, 56(2)*, 145–167.

Mullane, M. (2007). *Riding rockets: The outrageous tales of a space shuttle astronaut.* New York: Scribner.

Murray–Johnson, L., & Witte, K. (2003). Looking toward the future: Health message design strategies. In T. L. Thompson, A. M. Dorsey, K. I. Millier, & R. Parrott, (Eds.) *Handbook of health communication,* (pp. 473–495). Mahwah, N.J.: Lawrence Erlbaum Associates.

Nadler, R. (2008). Text Messaging Craze. *CollegeOutlook.net.* Accessed August 10, 2008 from http://www.collegeoutlook.net/co_ca_on_campus_c.cfm.

National Literacy Trust. (2005, February). Why do many young children lack basic language skills? A discussion paper prepared by the National Literacy Trust's Talk to your Baby campaign. Accessed April 19, 2008 from http://www.literacytrust.org.uk/talktoyourbaby/discussionpaper.pdf.

Navarro, J., & Karlins, M. (2008). *What every "body" is saying: An ex-FBI agent's guide to speed-reading people.* New York: Harper Collins.

Neuliep, J. W. (2005). *Intercultural communication: A contextual approach.* Thousand Oaks, CA: Sage.

Needleman, S. E. (2008, August 3). Employers to college-age applicants: No 'thanx.' Wall Street Journal. Star-Telegram, 16E.

Neuliep, J. W., & McCroskey, J. C. (1997). The development of Intercultural and interethnic communication apprehension scales. *Communication Research Reports, 14(2)*, 145–156.

Nibler, R., & Harris, K. L. (2003). The effects of culture and cohesiveness on intragroup conflict and effectiveness. *The Journal of Social Psychology, 143(5)*, 613–631.

Nichols, M. P. (1995). *The lost art of listening: How learning to listen can improve relationships.* New York: Guilford Press.

Nickerson, R. S. (1980). Short-term memory for complex meaningful visual configurations: Demonstration of capacity. *Canadian Journal of Psychology, 19*, 155–160.

Northouse, P. G. (2007). *Leadership: Theory and practice* (4th ed.). Thousand Oaks, CA: Sage.

Norton, C. (2004, June 14). Board opts not to censure member. *Herald Sun.com.* Accessed August 9, 2006, at http://www.heraldsun.com/orange/10–490970.html.

Notess, G. R. (2006, April 4). Meta search engines. *Search Engine Showdown.com.* Accessed at http://www.searchlngineshowdown.com/multi.

Novinger, T. (2001). *Intercultural communication: A practical guide.* Austin: University of Texas Press.

O'Keefe, D. J. (1998). Justification explicitness and persuasive effects: A meta-analysis review of the effects of varying support articulation in persuasive messages. *Argumentation and Advocacy, 35*, 61–75.

O'Keefe, D. J. (1990). *Persuasion: Theory and research.* Newbury Park, CA: Sage.

Oral citations. (nd). James Madison University. Accessed at http://www.lib.jmu.edu/gold/citingspeech.doc.

Organ, D. W. (2001, September). Listening can be dangerous. Business Horizons, 10–11.

Osborn, A. F. (1993). *Applied imagination* (3rd ed.). Buffalo, NY: Creative Education Foundation.

Overholt, A. (2004a, April). Are you a polyolefin optimizer? Take this quiz. *Fast Company, 81*, 37–38.

Overholt, A. (2004b, November). Personality tests: Back with a vengeance. *Fast Company, 88*, 115–117.

Panko, R. R., & Kinney, S. T. (1992). Dyadic organizational communication: Is the dyad different? *System Sciences, 4*, 244–252.

Paradi, D. (2007). Top three problems? *ThinkOutsideTheSlide.com.* Accessed September 23, 2007, at http://www.thinkoutsidetheslide.com/survey2007.

Parents forced to subject children to drugs. (2000, September 18). *Health Watch, 5(20)*, 4–5.

Park, H. S., Levine, T. R., Westerman, C. Y., Orfgen, T., & Foregger, S. (2007). The effects of argument quality and involvement type on attitude formation and attitude changes: A test of dual–process and social judgment predictions. *Human Communication Research, 33*, 81–102.

Paul, R., & Elder, L. (2003). *The miniature guide to critical thinking: Concepts & tools.* Dillon Beach, CA: The Foundation for Critical Thinking.

Pavitt, C. (2003). Do interacting groups perform better than aggregates of individuals? *Human communication Research, 29,* 592–599.

Pawlik–Kienlen, L. (2007, November 30). Am I an introvert? A simple test to determine introversion or introverted personalities. Suite101.com. Accessed July 30, 2008 from http://behavioural–psychology.suite101.com/article.cfm/am_i_an_introvert

Pearce, W. B. (2005). The coordinated management of meaning (CMM). In W.B. Gudykunst (Ed.), *Theorizing about Intercultural Communication* (35–54). Thousand Oaks, CA: Sage.

Pearce, W. B., & Cronen, V. (1980). *Communication, action, and meaning: The creation of social realities.* New York: Praeger.

Peck, S. (1996). Conversation Openers. Accessed from http://www.dallas.net/~scotpeck/saleswebpage/conver.htm.

Peoples, D. A. (1996). *Presentations plus: David People's proven techniques* (rev. ed.). New York: Wiley.

Perusse, B. (2008, February 2). Old rockers pay the price for years of noise. Montreal Gazette. Accessed October 5, 2008 at http://www.canada.com/topics/technology/story.html?id=c37008ef–4aab–49d8–be03–82431e499736

Petrie, K. J., Booth, R. J., & Pennebaker, J. W. (1998). The immunological effects of thought suppression. *Journal of Personality and Social Psychology, 75,* 1264–1272.

Petronio, S. (1991). Communication boundary management: A theoretical model of managing disclosure of private information between martial couples. *Communication Theory, 1,* 311–335.

Petty, R. E., & Cacioppo, J. T. (1996). *Attitudes and persuasion: Classic and contemporary approaches.* Boulder, CO: Westview.

Pexman, P. M., Glenwright, M., Krol, A., & James, T. (2005). An acquired taste: Children's perceptions of humor and teasing in verbal irony. *Discourse Processes, 40(3),* 259–288.

Pfau, M. (1997). The inoculation model of resistance to influence. In G. A. Barnett & F. J. Boster (Eds.), *Progress in communication sciences* (Vol. 13, pp. 133–171). Greenwich, CT: Ablex.

Pfau, M., & Burgoon, M. (1988). Inoculation in political campaign communication. *Human Communication Research, 15,* 91–111.

Pfau, M., Van Bockern, S., & Kang, J. G. (1992). Use of inoculation to promote resistance to smoking initiation among adolescents. *Communication Monographs, 59,* 213–230, *20,* 413–430.

Phillips, G. M. (1991). *Communication incompetencies: A theory of training and performance behavior.* Carbondale: Southern Illinois University Press.

Philpott, G. M. (1983). The relative contribution to meaning of verbal and nonverbal channels of communication: A metaanalysis. Unpublished master's thesis. University of Nebraska.

Pincus, A. (2007, July 18). The presentation imperfect. *Business Week Online.* Accessed at Academic Search Elite.

Pinel, J. P. J. (2006). *Biopsychology* (6th ed.). Boston: Allyn & Bacon.

Pinker, S. (1994) *The Language Instinct: How the Mind Creates Language.* New York: William Morrow and Company.

Pletcher, B. (2000). Plan of reaction: Finding calm from stress lies just a deep breath away. Fort Worth Star-Telegram, January 10, 11.

Pornsakulvanich, V., Haridakis, P., & Rubin, A. (2008). The influence of dispositions and Internet motivation on online communication satisfaction and relationship closeness. *Computers in Human Behavior, 24(5),* 2292–2310.

Porter, K. (2003). *The mental athlete: Inner training for peak performance in all sports.* Champaign, IL: Human Kinetics.

Porterfield, J., & Kleiner, B. H. (2005). A new era: Women and leadership. *Equal Opportunities International, 24(5),* 49–56.

Punyanunt-Carter, N. M. (2006). An analysis of college students' self-disclosure behaviors on the Internet. *College Student Journal, 40(2),* 329–331.

Rabin, M. D., & Cain, W. S. (1986). Determinants of measured olfactory sensitivity. *Perception & Psychophysics, 39,* 281–286.

Rakovski, C. C., & Levy, E. S. (2007, June). Academic dishonesty: Perceptions of business students. *College Student Journal, 41(2),* 466–481.

Reisner, R. (1993, June). How different cultures learn. *Meeting News, 17,* 31.

Rennie, S. C, & Crosby, J. R. (2001). Are "tomorrow's doctors" honest? Questionnaire study exploring medical students' attitudes and reported behaviour on academic misconduct. *BMJ, 22,* 274–275

Rester, C.H., & Edwards, R. (2007). Effects of sex and setting on students' interpretations of teachers' excessive use of immediacy behaviors. *Communication Education, 56 (1),* 34–53.

Reynolds, R. A., & Reynolds, J. L. (2002). Evidence. In J. P. Dillard and M. Pfau (Eds.), *The persuasion handbook: Developments in theory and practice* (pp. 427–444). Thousand Oaks, CA: Sage.

Richardson, H. L. (1999). Women lead in style. *Transportation & Distribution, 40(4),* 78–82.

Richardson, J. T. (2003). Dual coding versus relational processing in memory for concrete and abstract words. *European Journal of Cognitive Psychology, 15(4),* 481–509.

Richmond, V. P., & McCroskey, J. C. (1992). *Communication: Apprehension, avoidance, and effectiveness* (3rd ed.). Scottsdale, Arizona: Gorsuch Scarisbrick, Publishers.

Richmond, V. P., & McCroskey, J. C. (1998). *Nonverbal communication in interpersonal relationships* (3rd ed.). Boston: Allyn & Bacon.

Riessman, C. (1990). *Divorce talk: Women and men make sense of personal relationships.* New Brunswick, NJ: Rutgers University Press.

Rinn, A. N, & Nelson, J. M. (2009). Preservice teachers' perceptions of behaviors characteristic of ADHD and giftedness. *Roeper Review, 31(1)*, 18–26.

Rodriguez, V., Valdes-Sona, M., & Freiwald, W. (2002). Dividing attention between form and motion during transparent surface perception. *Cognitive Brain Research, 13*, 187–193.

Roediger, H.L., & Thorpe, L.A. (1978). The role of recall time in producing hypermnesia. *Memory & Cognition, 6(3)*, 296–30

Roloff, M. E. (1981). *Interpersonal communication: The social exchange approach*. Beverly Hills, CA: Sage.

Roloff, M., Janiszewski, C. A., McGrath, M. A., & Manrai, L. A. (1988). Acquiring resources from intimates: When obligation substitutes for persuasion. *Human Communication Research, 14*, 364–396.

Rosenfeld, P. (1997). Impression management, fairness and the employment interview. *Journal of Business Ethics, 16(8)*, 801–808.

Ross, L. D. (1977). The intuitive psychologist and his short–comings: Distortions in the attribution process. In L. Berkowitz (Ed.), *Advances in Experimental Social Psychology*, Vol. 10 (pp. 173–220). New York: Academic.

Roter, D. L., Larson, S., Sands, D. Z., Ford, D. E., & Houston, T. (2008). Can e-mail messages between patients and physicians be patient-centered? *Health Communication, 23(1)*, 80–86.

Rourke, B. P., Young, G. C., & Leenaars, A. (1989). A childhood learning disability that predisposes those afflicted to adolescent and adult depression and suicide risk. *Journal of Learning Disabilities, 21*, 169–175.

Safeer, R. S., & Keenan, J. (2005). Health literacy: The gap between physicians and patients. *American Family Physician, 72(3)*, 463–468.

Salopek, J. J. (1999). Is anyone listening? Training & development, 53(9), 58–59.

Samovar, L. A., Porter, R. R., & McDaniel, E. R. (2010). *Communication between cultures* (7th ed.). Boston, MA: Wadsworth, Cengage Learning.

Sandberg, J. (2006, November 14). Tips for PowerPoint: Go easy on the text; please, spare us. *The Wall Street Journal*, B1.

Sapir, E. (1921). *Language: An introduction to the study of speech*. New York: Harcourt, Brace & World.

Saunders, M. D. (2001). Who's getting the message? Helping your students understand in a verbal world. *Teaching Exceptional Children, 33(4)*, 70–74.

Savage, J. L. (2008, June 4). Avoiding workplace gossip: Proper business conduct. *Suite101.com*. Accessed August 13 from http://businessethics.suite101.com/article.cfm/avoiding _workplace_gossip.

Sayles, L. R. (1993). *The working leader*. New York: Free Press.

Schab, F. R., & Crowder, R. G. (1989). Accuracy of temporal coding: Auditory-visual comparisons. *Memory & Cognition, 17*, 384–397.

Schifferes, S. (2008, June 12). Internet key to Obama victories. BBCNews. Accessed July 19 from http://news.bbc.co.uk/1/hi/technology/7412045.stm.

Schirmer, A., & Simpson, E. (2008). Brain correlates of vocal emotional processing in men and women. In K. Izdebski (Ed.). *Emotions in the Human Voice* (pp. 76–86). San Diego: Plural Publishing. Accessed October 5, 2008 at www.uga.edu/scnlab/Schirmer_Simpson_revised.pdf.

Schramm, W. (1965). *The process and effects of mass communication*. Urbana: University of Illinois Press.

Schubert, J. (2007, Winter). Engaging youth with the power of listening. *Reclaiming Children and Youth*, 15(4), 227–228.

Schutz, W. C. (1992, June). Beyond FIRO-B—three new theory derived measures—Element B: behavior, element F: feelings, element S: self. *Psychological Reports, 70 (3)*, 915–937.

Schutz, W. C. (1958). *FIRO: A three-dimensional theory of interpersonal behavior*. New York: Rinehart.

Scott, W. B. (2005, March 21). Blue Angels. *Aviation Week & Space Technology*, 162(12), 50–57.

Scotti, D.J., Driscoll, A. E., Harmon, J., & Behson, S. J. (2007, March/April). Links among high performance work environment, service quality, and customer satisfaction: An extension to the healthcare sector. *Journal of Healthcare Management, 52(2)*, 109–124.

Searby, L, & Shaddix, L. (2008). Growing teacher leaders in a culture of excellence. *Professional Educator, 32(1)*, 35–43.

Seiler, W. J. (1971, Winter). The conjunctive influence of source credibility and the use of visual materials on communication effectiveness. *Southern Speech Communication Journal, 37*, 174–185.

Sell, J. M., Lovaglia, F., Mannix, E., Samuelson, C., & Wilson, R. (2004). Investigating conflict, power, and status within and among groups. *Small Group Research, 35(1)*, 44–72.

Senge, P. M. (2006). *The fifth discipline: The art & practice of the learning organization*. New York: Doubleday.

Shand, M. A. (1994). Annotated bibliography of vocabulary-related word produced by the Johnson O'Connor Research Foundation, Inc. Johnson O'Connor Research Foundation, Inc. Accessed January 9, 2008 from http://www.jocrf.org/research/tech_reports.html.

Shannon, C., & Weaver, W. (1949). *The mathematical theory of communication*. Urbana: University of Illinois Press.

Sharf, Barbara. 1984. *The physician's guide to better communication*. Glenview, IL.: Scott, Foresman.

Sherif, C. W., Sherif, M., & Nebergall, R. E. (1965). *Attitude and attitude change: The social judgment-involvement approach*. Philadelphia, PA: W. B. Saunders.

Sills, J. (2006). When personalities clash. *Psychology Today, 39(6)*, 61–62.

Silverman, J. (2003, September 1). Improve health literacy by using plain language. *Internal Medicine News, 36(17)*, 68.

Silverman, S. D. (2004, November 4). Giuliani opens ULI conference with tips on leadership. *Commercial Property News*. Accessed July 6, 2008 at http://www.allbusiness.com/operations/facilities-commercial-real-estate/4411858–1.html.

Sloan, T., Daane, C. J., & Giesen, J. (2004, September 1). Learning styles of elementary preservice teachers. *College Student Journal*, 494–500.

Smith, J. E., & Forbes, J. B. (1997). A challenge for the 21st century: How to select who will lead and manage in business. Presented at the annual conference of the Society for the Advancement of Management, Las Vegas, NV.

Smith, R. V. (2004). *The elements of great speechmaking: Adding drama & intrigue*. Lanham, MD: University Press of America.

Smith, T. E., & Frymier, A. B. (2006, February). Get "real": Does practicing speeches before an audience improve performance? *Communication Quarterly, 54*, 111–126.

Snapshot: Personal electronic devices owned by students. (2008, January 8). Campus Technology. Accessed September 29, 2008 at http://www.campustechnology.com/articles/57155.

Sprinkle, R., Hunt, S., Simonds, C., & Comadena, M. (2006). Fear in the classroom: An examination of teachers' use of fear appeals and students' learning outcomes. *Communication Education, 55(4)*, 389–402.

St. John, S. (1995, September). Get your act together. *Presentations, 9*, 26–33.

Stanley, P. (2008, October 31). Lessons from a 2-year college "master class." *Chronicle of Higher Education*, Section B.

Stevens, K. K., Houser, M. L., & Cowan, R. L. (2009). R U able to meat me: The Impact of students' overly casual email messages to Instructors. Communication Education, 58(3), 303–326.

Stewart, C. J., & Cash, Jr., W. B. (2008). *Interviewing: Principles and Practices* (12th ed.). Boston: McGraw-Hill.

Stogdill, R. M. (1948). Personal factors associated with leadership: *A survey of the literature. Journal of Psychology, 25*, 35–71.

Stone, J., & Bachner, J. (1994). *Speaking up: A book for every woman who wants to speak effectively*. New York: Carroll & Graft.

Strayer, D. L., Drews, F. A., & Crouch, D. J. (2006). A comparison of the cell phone driver and the drunk driver. *Human Factors*, 48, 381–391.

Strikwerda, C. (2006, February). Jokes and quotes: Tips on public speaking for hardworking deans. *Academic Leader, 22(2)*, 1, 6.

Sutton, S. R., & Eiser, J. R. (1984). The effect of fear-arousing communications on cigarette smoking: An expectancy-value approach. *Journal of Behavioral Medicine, 7*, 13–33.

Suzuki, R., Buck, J. R., & Tyack, P. L. (2006). Information entropy of humpback whale songs. *Journal of the Acoustical Society of America, 119(3)*, 1819–1866.

Swinton, L.(2005, February 8). Kurt Lewin's force field analysis: Decision making made easy. *Management for the Rest of Us.com*. Accessed July 10, 2008 from http://www.mftrou.com/Lewins-force-field-analysis.html.

Szabo, E. A., & Pfau, M. (2002). Nuances in inoculation: Theory and applications. In J. P. Dillard & M. Pfau (Eds.), *The persuasion handbook: Developments in theory and practice* (pp. 233–258).Thousand Oaks, CA: Sage.

Tan, H. H., & Tan, M. L. (2008). Organizational citizenship behavior and social loafing: The role of personality, motives, and contextual factors. *The Journal of Psychology, 142(1)*, 89–108.

Tamparo, C. C., & Lindh, W. Q. (2008). *Therapeutic communications for health care* (3rd.). Clifton Park, NY: Thomson Delmar Learning.

Tannen, D. (1995). The power of talk: Who gets heard and why. *Harvard Business Review, 73(5)*, 138–149.

Thibaut, J. W., & Kelley, H. H. (1959). *The social psychology of groups*. New York: Wiley.

Thompson, H. L. (2000). FIRO Element B and Psychological Type, Part I: Why FIRO Element B? *Bulletin of Psychological Type, 23(2)*, 18–22.

Thorne, B., Kramarae, C., & Henley, N. (1983). *Language, gender, and society*. Cambridge, MA: Newbury House.

TI Ethics Quick Test. (2009). Texas Instruments. Accessed May 30, 2009 at http://www.ti.com/corp/docs/company/citizen/ethics/quicktest.shtml.

Timm, P. R. (1986). *Managerial communication: A finger on the pulse* (2nd ed.). Englewood Cliffs, NJ: Prentice-Hall.

Ting-Toomey, S. (1985). Toward a theory of conflict and culture. In W. B. Gudykunst, L. Steward, & S. Ting–Toomey (Eds.), *Communication, culture, and organizational processes* (pp. 71–86). Beverly Hills, CA: Sage.

Ting-Toomey, S. (1988). Intercultural conflict styles: Face-negotiation theory. In Y. Yun Kum and W. Gudykunst (Ed.), *Theories in Intercultural Communication* (pp. 213–235). Newbury Park, CA: Sage.

Ting-Toomey, S. (1999). *Communicating across cultures*. New York: The Guilford Press.

Ting-Toomey, S. (2000). Managing Intercultural conflicts effectively. In L. A. Samovar & R. E. Porter (Eds.), *Intercultural Communication: A Reader* (9th ed.), (388–400). Belmont, CA: Wadsworth.

Ting-Toomey, S. (1992). *Cross-cultural face-negotiation: an analytical overview*. Address to the Pacific Region Forum at Simon Fraser University. Accessed August 2, 2008 from http://www.cic.sfu.ca/forum/ting–too.html.

Ting-Toomey, S., & Kurogi, A. (1998). Facework competence in intercultural conflict: An updated face-negotiation theory. *International Journal of Intercultural Relations, 22*, 187–225.

Tips for oral citations. (nd). Eastern Illinois University. Accessed at http://www.eiu.edu/~assess/TipsOralCites%20.doc.

Tracy, L. (2005, March 1). Taming hostile audiences: Persuading those who would rather jeer than cheer. *Vital Speeches, 71*, 306–312.

Trenholm, S., & Jensen, A. (2006). Interpretive competence: How we perceive individuals, relationships, and social events. In J. Steward (Ed.) *Bridges Not Walls*, 9th. ed. (pp. 177–188). Boston: McGraw-Hill.

Trevino, L. K., & Nelson, K. A. (2004). *Managing Business Ethics* (3rd ed.). Hoboken, NJ: Wiley.

Trompenaars, F., & Hampden-Turner, C. (2000). *Riding the waves of culture: Understanding cultural diversity in Business* (2nd. ed). London: Nicholas Brealey Publishing.

Tubbs, S. L. (2009). *A systems approach to small group interaction* (10th ed.). Boston: McGraw-Hill.

Varner, I., & Beamer, L. (1995). *Intercultural communication in the global workplace*. Chicago: Irwin.

VerLinden, J. G. (1996, Spring). A critique of source citations in forensic speeches. *National Forensic Journal,* 23–36.

Vermette, P. J. (1998). *Making cooperative learning work: Student teams in K–12 classrooms.* Upper Saddle River, NJ: Merrill.

Violence (2009, March). Texas A&M Student Activities, Department of Education in Action, 1 (3).1. Accessed April 9, 2009 from http://studentactivities.tamu.edu/files/LSC%20Social%20Issues%20Newsletter%20–%20March%2009.pdf

Vogel, D. R., Dickson, G. W., & Lehman, J. A. (1990, July 27). Persuasion and the role of visual presentation support: The UM/3M study. In M. Antonoff (Ed.), *Presentations that persuade. Personal Computing,* 14.

Walker, L., & Sakai, T. (2006, December). A gift of listening for Hawaii's inmates. *Corrections Today,* 58–61.

Wall Street Journal Workplace-Ethics Quiz (1999, October 21). *The Wall Street Journal,* B1. In M.

Wall Street Journal Workplace-Ethics Quiz (1999, October 21). The Wall Street Journal, B1. In M. Shurden, S. Shurden, & D. Cagwin, A Comparative Study of Ethical Values of Business Students: American Vs. Middle Eastern Cultures. Paper delivered to the 2008 ABR & TLC Conference Proceedings in Orlando, Florida. Accessed September 10, 2008 from http://www.cluteinstitute-onlinejournals.com/Programs/Disney_2008/Article%20317.pdf.

Walters, L. (1993). *Secrets of successful speakers.* New York: McGraw-Hill.

Walther, J. B., Slovacek, C. L., & Tidwell, L. C. (2001). Is a picture worth a thousand words? Photographic images in long-term and short-term computer-mediated communication. *Communication Research, 28,* 105–134.

Wanzer, M. B., Frymier, A. B., Wojtaszczyk, A. M., & Smith, T. (2006). Appropriate and inappropriate uses of humor by teachers. *Communication Education, 55 (2),* 178–196.

Watson, K. W., Barker, L. L., & Weaver, J. B. III. (1995). The listening styles profile (LPS-16): Development and validation of an instrument to assess four listening styles. *International Journal of Listening, 9(1),* 1–13.

Weaver, J. B., Richendoller, N. R., & Kirtley, M. D. (1995, November). *Individual differences in communication style.* Paper presented at the annual meeting of the Speech Communication Association. San Antonio, TX.

Weaver II, R. L. (1984). *Understanding business communication.* Englewood Cliffs, NJ: Prentice-Hall.

Weddle, P. D. (2009, March 31). The Weak Link Syndrome. Weddle's Job Seeker Newsletter. Accessed at http://www.weddles.com/seekernews/issue.cfm?Newsletter=242.

Weinstein, B. (1993). *Resumes don't get jobs: The realities and myths of job hunting.* New York: McGraw-Hill.

Weissman, J. (2006). *Presenting to win: The art of telling your story.* Upper Saddle River, NJ: Pearson Prentice-Hall.

What is service-learning? (2004). National Service-Learning Clearinghouse, Accessed July 14, 2008 from http://www.servicelearning.org/what_is_service-learning/service-learning_is/index.php.

White, R., & Lippitt, R. (1968). Leader behavior and member reaction in three "social climates." In D. Cartwright and A. Zandor (Eds.), *Group dynamics* (3rd ed., pp. 318–335). New York: Harper & Row.

Whorf, B. L. (1956). *Language, thought, and reality.* J. B. Carroll (Ed.). New York: Wiley.

Williams, C. (2008). *Effective Management* (3rd ed.). Mason, OH: South-Western.

Williams, J. M. (2002). Technical communication, engineering, and ABET's engineering criteria 2000: What lies ahead? *Technical Communication, 49(1),* 89–95.

Williams, R. (2008). *The non-designer's design book* (3rd ed.). Berkeley, CA: Peachpit.

Wilmot, W. W., & Hocker, J. L. (2007). *Interpersonal conflict* (7th ed.). New York: McGraw-Hill.

Wolff, F. I., Marsnik, N. C., Tracey, W. S., & Nichols, R. G. (1983). *Perceptive listening.* New York: Holt, Rinehart & Winston.

Wolvin, A. D., & Coakley, D. G. (1981). A survey of the status of listening training in some fortune 500 corporations. *Communication Education, 40,* 152–164.

Wolvin, A. D., & Coakley, D. G. (1988). *Listening* (3rd. ed.). Dubuque, IA: W.C. Brown.

Wood, J. T. (2009). *Gendered lives: Communication, gender, and culture* (8th ed.). Belmont, CA: Thomson Wadsworth.

Wood, J. T., & Inman, C. C. (1993). In a different mode: Masculine styles of communicating closeness. *Journal of applied communication research, 21,* 279–295.

Wood, J. T., Phillips, G. M., Pedersen, D. J., & Young, K. S. (2000). *Group discussion: A practical guide to participation and leadership* (3rd ed.). Prospect Heights, IL: Waveland.

Woolfolk, A. (2010). *Educational psychology* (11th ed.). New York: Prentice Hall.

Wu, S., Miao, D., Zhu, X., Luo, Z., & Liu, X. (2007). Personality types of Chinese dental school applicants. *Journal of Dental Education, 71(12),* 1593–1598.

Zagacki, K. S., Edwards, R., & Honeycutt, J. M. (1992, Winter). The role of mental imagery and emotion in imagined interaction. *Communication Quarterly, 40,* 56–68.

Zhang, Y., Butler, J., & Pryor, B. (1996). Comparison of apprehension about communication in China and the United States. *Perceptual and Motor Skills, 82.* 1168–1170.

Zigurs, I. (2003). Leadership in virtual teams: Oxymoron or opportunity? *Organizational Dynamics, 31,* 339–351.

Zunin, L., & Zunin, N. (1994). *Contact: The first four minutes* (Rev. ed.). New York: Ballantine.

Glossary

6-person concept (Barnlund) A concept that shows that when two people are talking, there are actually six separate entities involved

Abstracting When we make a statement about something, we select only certain aspects of the thing we are describing and leave out other aspects

Accentors Nonverbal behaviors used to emphasize a verbal message, such as pounding your fist to indicate how serious the topic is

Accidental audiences Audience members who were merely going about their daily lives and happened to wander into an area where someone was attempting to drum up an audience for one reason or another

Acquaintances People with whom you share small talk in the experimenting stage. These relationships may go no further, but are important in getting your inclusion needs met.

Action model A model that views the communication process as a linear transmission of messages and identifies the following important components of the communication process: sender, message, code, encoding and decoding, channel, receiver, and noise

Active strategy A strategy for seeking information and reducing uncertainty where a person solicits information from others who are acquainted with a specific person to see if this other person's impressions match their own

Adaptors Nonverbal behaviors that are displayed without our conscious awareness, such as rubbing the nose due to nervousness

Ad hominem A flaw in reasoning that occurs when a speaker attacks a person instead of the person's argument

Ad populum A flaw in reasoning that asserts that an idea is true because most people think it is true

Ad verecundiam A flaw in reasoning that occurs when a speaker appeals to authority saying that an idea must be true because some esteemed person claims it is true, even though the issue at hand is out of that authority person's area of expertise

Advising responses Responses used by empathic listeners when they propose a solution to a person's problem. Advising responses should be avoided in most cases.

Affect displays When nonverbal behaviors reveal emotions that are behind our own spoken messages or the emotions we feel in response to another's message

Affiliation A feeling of belongingness expressed by some messages

Agenda setter The group member (usually the chairperson) who develops an agenda or formal plan for the meeting, including the time and place, how the meeting will be conducted, and what topics will be discussed

Aggressive style Used by communicators who prefer to confront conflict directly in a manner that makes it clear that they are aggrieved. Their message is, "My needs are important; yours are not."

Aggressor A group member who criticizes and insults other group members and their ideas. There is no tact shown, just sarcasm and even hostility.

Alignment A basic design principle that calls for all design elements to have some visual connection with another element on the page

Allness Statements that imply that the verbal expression has captured the totality of a person, object, or event

Ambiguous Meaning that is unclear and usually caused by multiple meanings, intentionality, or cultural differences

Ambiguous figures Figures that are organized so that they can be viewed as more than one object due to the figure-ground contrast

Ambivert A person who blends the styles of an introvert and an extrovert

Analyzers Group members who are able to spot the relevant issues and take new information that is brought to the group and help determine how that information fits with other information

Anchor Refers to a listener's most preferred position on a particular topic when used as part of social judgment theory (Chapter 14)

Anchor Refers to a photo, drawing, or piece of clipart that helps audience members recall the content of a visual aid when used as a memory aid (Chapter 13)

Androgynous Communication style that includes a balance between the traditional masculine and feminine characteristics—used especially in effective leadership of small groups and teams

Articulation The shaping of speech sounds by use of the articulators such as the lips, teeth, tongue, gum ridge, hard palate, soft palate, and jaw

Artifacts Objects we surround ourselves with and display to others

Assertive style Used by communicators who believe that "My needs are important, and your needs are equally important." They handle conflict by looking for a solution that will satisfy both parties.

Attention-getter Way to grab the interest of your audience at the beginning of a presentation

Attitude A feeling of like or dislike (approval or disapproval) toward a person, idea, or an event. Speakers are especially interested in audience attitudes toward the topic, the speaker, and the event.

Attribution How we explain the events in our lives in an attempt to control and understand the future

Attribution theory A theory that describes how the typical listener processes information and uses it to explain behaviors of self and others

Avoiding stage The fourth stage of relationship deterioration, which is usually brief and involves limited communication with no depth or breadth; face-to-face communication is averted when possible

Audience-centered Focusing on the audience members and whether they are understanding rather than on yourself and the impression you are making

Audience demographics Those bits of information that constitute the statistical characteristics of the audience

Authoritarian leader One who essentially makes the decisions and imposes them upon the group

Basic design principles Contrast, repetition, alignment, and proximity that will improve the appearance, clarity, and professionalism of all types of text and graphic visual aids

Begging the question A flaw in reasoning that occurs if you try to prove that a claim is true by using the claim itself as proof

Behavioral descriptions Being more precise by adding language to indicate the specific actions to which you are referring

Behavioral questions Tough questions that assess the applicant's creativity and ability to handle real-life situations and require applicants to think on their own without a canned answer

Behaviors Actions taken and justified from our values, beliefs, and attitudes

Beliefs What we hold to be true even if we can't prove that they are true. Beliefs serve as the foundation for attitudes.

Blocker A group member who stubbornly refuses to allow the group to move forward by over-analyzing, arguing to get his/her own way, or refusing to compromise

Bonding stage In this fifth and final stage of relationship development, partners make a formal public statement of commitment to the relationship

Boolean operators Guidelines or joining words, such as NOT, AND, OR, – or +, that specify how a search is conducted

Boomerang effect When a speaker's position falls in the audience's latitude of rejection, audience members are likely to become less persuaded by the speaker instead of more persuaded

Brainstorming A method of spontaneously and creatively generating as many ideas as possible

Breadth of disclosure Establishing a range of topics you can discuss with your relational partner without revealing the "real you" still safe in the core

Causal pattern Used to organize either informative or persuasive speeches when your points have a relationship where one is the *cause* and the other is the *effect*. For informative speeches, cause-effect is most often used, while effect-cause is often used with persuasive speeches.

Causal reasoning Reasoning that shows a relationship or link between two problems, solutions, or items indicating that one caused the other

Central idea A simple statement that captures the thesis of your speech

Channel The means of transmitting code including the five senses and various media such as face-to-face, telephone, or text messages

Charisma A speaker quality that includes enthusiasm and warmth that inspires an audience to exceptional motivation

Chronemics A category of nonverbal communication that includes the study of how we conceptualize, arrange, and use time

Chronological pattern Used to organize informative speeches when your main points are arranged by time, such as steps in a particular order (first to last) or by date

Circumscribing stage In this second stage of relationship deterioration, partners figuratively "draw a circle around" touchy subjects that they agree to avoid, and the relationship shrinks in intimacy

Clarifier Group members who ensure that everyone is clear on topics being discussed, decisions reached, and what other member's comments mean

Closed questions A multiple-choice question where interviewee answers are limited to the choices provided in the question. If worded carefully, closed questions can stimulate creative thinking and a lively discussion.

Closure A law of organization that says that incomplete figures tend to be closed or filled-in to represent a whole object when we perceive them

Co-constructed meanings Meanings that are not embedded in the language used but are created by the people interacting within a particular context from within each person's frame of reference

Co-culture Smaller groups of people who are bound by shared values, beliefs, attitudes, rules, and norms and interact with those of the larger culture

Code The verbal and nonverbal symbols used to represent a message (idea, thought, or feeling)

Coercive power Power derived from the ability to punish or to threat possible punishment

Cognitive restructuring A way of reframing your perception of a feared stimulus into a more positive one

Cohesiveness The quality that causes the members of the group to be attracted to the group and willing to endure despite challenges

Collectivistic cultures Cultures who are oriented to the welfare of the group (community, tribe, clan, etc.) and value group connection, interdependence, cooperation, consensus, meeting one's obligations, and fitting in

Common ground Showing areas where you have similar interests, problems, or background with your audience

Communibiology The belief that genetics plays a primary role in determining whether a person is comfortable in interacting with other people or experiences anxiety

Communication The transactional process by which people, interacting in a particular context, negotiate the meanings of verbal and nonverbal symbols in order to achieve shared understanding

Communication choices Decisions about how messages will be conveyed as well as how others' messages will be interpreted

Comparative advantages pattern A persuasive pattern where main points are organized by comparing and contrasting various solutions, demonstrating that your plan has more (or more desirable) advantages, and fewer (or less undesirable) disadvantages than any of the other plans

Comparisons Show similarities between a known and an unknown idea or object in order to make the unknown clear

Compromise This conflict outcome—where both parties agree to give up something in order to reach a decision—works if a win-win is not possible

Computer mediated communication (CMC) The way people communicate via computers

Confirming messages Messages that reflect the value of the other person and generally evoke supportive responses. The messages include the descriptive, problem-solution approach, equality implied, spontaneous, open to change, and empathetic messages.

Conflict An expressed struggle between at least two interdependent parties who perceive incompatible goals, scarce rewards, and interference from the other parties in achieving their goals

Conflict phase The stage of a problem-solving discussion where the work of the group gets underway, and conflicts may occur any time

Connotative meaning Personal meanings of words that are based on the images and emotions aroused by a word

Consensus A group decision made when all group members agree on a particular decision; may not be the preferred decision for all members but one that all members can live with

Content paraphrase A paraphrase in your own words that focuses on the information or content contained in the speaker's entire message

Context The situation in which a particular communication takes place. Contexts include intrapersonal, interpersonal, group, organizational, public, and mass communication situations to name a few.

Contingency Contingency theorists hold that there is no "best" leadership style, but that the appropriate style is contingent (or dependent) upon the nature of the situation

Contingency leadership Includes the contingency model and the situational model based on the situational contingency theory by Fiedler and the situational leadership theory by Hersey and Blanchard

Contiguity principle Audiences learn better when pictures on visuals are placed immediately next to the information they represent

Contradictors When we say something sarcastically or signal to a listener with paralanguage, facial expressions, or gestures that we mean the opposite of what our words would seem to mean

Contrast A basic design principle that calls for avoiding elements on the page that are merely similar

Control The need to feel that we have some influence over our own lives as well as the lives of others; one of the basic needs in Schutz's FIRO-B

Conversational principles (Grice) Effective contributions to conversational dialogue must meet four criteria: quality, quantity, relevancy, and manner

Counter-persuasion When the audience is exposed to arguments on the other side of the topic

Credibility Audience perception of your competence, your character, and your charisma that is important in informative and persuasive presentations; effective speakers introduce their credibility during the introduction of their speech

Criteria Standards or checklist that any possible solution must meet in order for it to be acceptable to the group and be used to determine the best out of a list of possible solutions

Critical listening This type of listening is needed when the speaker's goal is to persuade you and your goal must be to evaluate the credibility of the speaker and of the message

Culture A system of values, beliefs, attitudes, rules, and norms shared by a group of people

Culture bound How meanings of nonverbal communication are interpreted based on a person's culture, often resulting in ambiguity

Dating A way to avoid abstracting and allness by indicating *when* (giving a date) the statement was true in your experience

Decoding The process the receiver goes through in attempting to interpret or make sense of the symbols included in a message

Deductive reasoning Reasoning that begins with the conclusion and then follows with specific evidence and arguments to support it

Deep breathing Controlled, deep breaths that slow your heart rate making you feel more in control—used by systematic desensitization

Defensive listeners People who seem to be easily offended and tend to interpret innocent remarks as though they were criticisms

Definitions Statements explaining the meaning of a word or idea

Delivery The act or manner of communicating your ideas to others

Democratic leader A leader who participates with the group in deliberating and decision-making

Denotative meaning Meanings of words that are found in dictionary definitions

Depth of disclosure Deciding, when beginning to reveal your attitudes and beliefs, to assess whether there is sufficient similarity between the two of you to serve as a basis for a more substantial relationship

Deserter Group members who withdraw from the discussion due to lack of preparation or anxiety

Devil Effect Occurs when a negative assessment of a person with respect to one central trait leads to the assumption of other negative traits, whether observed or not

Dialect A variation in a spoken language specific to a particular social or cultural group or geographic region like the "r" sound in Boston

Dialectical tension The dynamic interplay of contradictory needs within a person

Dichotomize Drawing arbitrary distinctions between people or groups

Diction The manner in which each speech sound is uttered producing clearly articulated or slurred sounds

Differentiating stage In this first stage of relationship deterioration, expressed feelings are more negative, comments are centered on the need for autonomy and individuality rather than similarities, and areas of incompatibility assume great significance

Direct questions Brief questions asking for a yes or no or a brief answer that are useful for gathering basic data, for verifying facts, and for relaxing nervous candidates

Disaffiliation A feeling of a lack of connection expressed by some messages

Discloser Person who has a high need for openness in relational communication

Disconfirming messages Messages that deny the worth of the other party and generally evoke defensive responses. These messages include the evaluative, control approach, superiority implied, strategic and manipulative, closed to change, and neutral messages.

Display rules Differences in the extent to which cultures permit the expression of emotions by nonverbal means

Dominant A person with high control needs

Dominator Group members who tend to monopolize the discussion

Driving forces In force-field analysis, these are forces that are moving the group to make a certain decision or to move in a particular direction

Dyad Two people communicating with each other

Dysfunctional roles Nonfunctional behaviors that interfere with either the attainment of the group's goals or the sense of group cohesiveness; these roles include the dominator, deserter, blocker, aggressor, and showboat

Ego-involved To be ego-involved means that the audience member's preferred position or anchor is closely tied to the person's self-identity. The more ego-involved a person is, the more difficult they are to persuade.

e-Leadership A flexible, electronic-savvy form of leadership needed for virtual teams

Electronic databases expensive research sources like EBSCOhost, CQ Researcher, or LexusNexis that are available through libraries and usually include complete text

Emblems Gestures that do not require any verbal message in order to be understood, such as raising the palm of the hand to indicate "stop"

Emergence phase The stage in a problem-solving discussion where discussion turns from debating myriad possibilities to honing in on a limited number of ideas, and examining the advantages and disadvantages of each

Emergent leader The person who has the most influence over the group—may or may not be the designated leader

Emotional dishonesty Involves not owning up to your feelings and then punishing your partner for failure to divine your needs

Empathic listening A type of listening that is needed when a sender's goal is to get help to cope with or solve a problem and your goal is to listen with empathy and see the world from the sender's frame of reference

Empathy Occurs when you put yourself in other people's frames of reference—try to walk in their shoes; see the situation through their eyes

Emphasis Sound that signals the importance of word by using *pitch* (usually goes higher), *rate* (usually goes slower), and *volume* (usually grows louder)

Employment interview A hiring process used to locate quality workers. In a quality employment interview, both the interviewee and the interviewer have the responsibility of asking and answering questions.

Encoding The process the sender goes through in choosing symbols used in a message

Environment Another word for context; the part of the communication context that relates specifically to the physical surroundings in which the communication occurs

Ethics A system of moral principles that governs the conduct of people and their relationships with others

Ethnocentrism The assumption that one's own cultural perspective is superior to that of others

Ethos Refers to speaker credibility and includes three characteristics: competence, character, and charisma

Euphemisms Other words or phrases used in place of words or phrases that might be considered offensive, unpleasant, or taboo

Evidence The statements and opinions presented in the form of statistics, definitions, illustrations, and other types of supporting materials that support your position

Examples Brief, factual instance used to clarify, add interest and even proof to your speech content

Explanations Statements that make a word, concept, or procedure more understandable, perhaps by outlining the causes or processes, or by showing the logical relationships between ideas or objects

Expectancy violations theory (Burgoon) Explains the meanings that people attribute to nonverbal behaviors of others that violate our expectations

Expediter Group members who initiate the process suggesting how to go about getting started, remind the group of deadlines, and point out when the group is digressing—all designed to keep the discussion on track

Experimenting stage This second stage of relationship development involves small talk on low-risk topics in an effort to find areas of mutual interest and to get to know each other

Expert power The ability to influence by virtue of one's knowledge or skills

Expressive communication Communication with the goal of establishing and maintaining harmonious relationships. Women are often considered to be expressive communicators.

Extemporaneous speech A speech that is carefully researched and organized but is neither read nor memorized. Instead, it is enthusiastic and conversational, with only a very few notes used, if any.

External noise Distractions in the environment, such as loud sounds or unusual movement in your surroundings, that cause you to be unable to effectively compose your thoughts as you speak to others or make it difficult to decode the messages you are receiving

Extrovert A person with high inclusion needs

Facial expression The movement or position of the muscles of your face

Fallacious reasoning Flaws in reasoning such as *ad hominem, ad verecundiam*, or hasty generalization

Fallacy of false analogy When the things that are being compared are not sufficiently similar to make a valid comparison possible

Fear appeals Negative emotional appeals that cause the audience to feel afraid or worried

Feedback The verbal and visual response of the receiver to the sender's message

Feelings paraphrase A paraphrase in your own words that focuses on the emotions that you detect underneath the content of the message

Fidelity Concept from the narrative paradigm which refers to whether the story "rings true" to the audience. The story sounds truthful; the story and characters are accurate historically and culturally.

Figurative comparison Includes two or more items that are basically dissimilar such as comparing the variety of human beings to the variety of snowflakes or comparing an apple to an orange

Fillers Words or phrases that are inserted into a sentence usually to replace a natural pause but contribute nothing to the verbal meaning of the sentence such as "uh" or "you know"

FIRO-B (Schutz) People have three basic needs (inclusion, control, and openness) that are represented in different degrees—thus, each person has a "fundamental interaction and relationship orientation" or FIRO that is expressed through personal "behavior" or B

First impressions A problem in perception where we cling to original impressions to such a degree that we fail to alter those impressions when new information is received

Focused listening Listening that occurs when someone listens without thinking about personal views, makes no judgments, and only speaks to clarify what the speaker is saying

Follow-up questions Questions that enable the interviewer to probe for expansion of ideas. They are especially useful in eliciting narratives and stories.

Force-field analysis A method used by groups to analyze the *pros* (impelling forces) and *cons* (restraining forces) of a specific group idea, decision, desired action or plan

Formal outline A fully developed and detailed outline consisting of the introduction and conclusion, main points, supporting materials, and transitions

Formal roles Roles that are specified, such as the chair, agenda setter, or recorder

Frame of reference An individual perspective and view of the world that differs from other views due to such factors as self-concept, values, beliefs, attitudes, culture, gender, and age

Friendly audience Audience composed of people who know you and like you or who like your topic

Fundamental attribution error The tendency to overestimate the role that a person's character plays on behavior while underestimating the role of the situation

Gatekeeper Group members who control the flow of communication

Gaze Another word for eye contact which is the way we make visual connection with another through the use of our eyes

Gender Refers to the cultural and psychological constructions of social roles and personal identity and are classified by the terms *masculine, feminine,* or *androgynous.* Gender is not the same as the term *sex,* which refers to biological characteristics that are classified as male or female.

General purpose A statement or single word that identifies the type of speech you plan to give (informative, persuasive, or entertaining)

Gestures Kinesic movements involving the arms and hands; often referred to as body language

Group A small number of people (usually 3–7) who have multiple face-to-face meetings over an extended period of time and who interact to achieve common goals

Group communication Sometimes referred to as "multiple dyads," in which three or more people interact with each other in order to accomplish a meaningful objective

Group decision making Decisions made using a group of people when the following items are important or present: quality, acceptance by many, accuracy, complex task, or conflict

Group diversity Occurs when there are enough differences among group members to permit access to multiple perspectives yet sufficient similarity of values to ensure commonality of goals

Group problem-solving process A systematic process involving six steps that when used cuts the chaos and allows a group to reach a decision faster and with less emotion

Group roles Categories of behaviors enacted by individuals in a group. Groups contain both formal rules (specified) and informal rules (developed over time)

Groupthink A dysfunctional condition that occurs when members of the group refrain from expressing divergent viewpoints for fear of being sanctioned or because they like the group so much that they don't want to risk causing the group any discomfort

Halo effect Occurs when a positive assessment of a person with respect to one central trait leads to the assumption of other positive traits, whether observed or not

Haptics A category of nonverbal communication that refers to the study of touching behavior

Harmonizer A group member who reconciles conflicts among members in productive ways including compromise or mediation if needed

Hasty generalization A flaw in reasoning that occurs when a conclusion is based on only isolated examples or too few examples

Hidden agenda When a group member is more committed to personal goals than to the group's goals but fails to make this position known

Hierarchy of needs Human needs with the bottom needs being the most basic and which must be satisfied first. Beginning with the most basic, the needs include: physical, safely, social, self-esteem, and self-actualization.

High-context cultures Cultures in which people's understanding of what is being communicated is based on the nature of the physical situation. High-context cultures tend to be fairly collectivistic, and listen by paying less attention to the actual words spoken and more to the context such as the groups to which the speaker belongs (community, family, or organizations), the speaker's status and age, the background and history of the topic or situation, and the speaker's nonverbal gestures and expressions.

Hostile audience Audience composed of people who have an attitude against you and/or your topic who might even ridicule you if given a chance

Illustrations Detailed, vivid stories or narratives told with enthusiasm and vigor

Illustrators Behaviors that complement the meaning intended by a words such as pointing in the correct direction

Imitation listening Pretending to listen by exhibiting behaviors that are commonly associated with good listening, while simultaneously attending to some other stimulus in the environment or to your intrapersonal dialogue

Impersonal communication The exchange of verbal and nonverbal symbols in order to send or receive information between people who are polite yet distant and relate to each other from the roles or positions they hold

Imprecise language Words or phrases that lack sufficient clarity to guide interpretation

Impression management The choices that we make about how we speak and behave in order to affect what others think of us; the "face" or image that we present to a given person at a given time

Impromptu speech Where you speak about a topic having had only moments in which to organize your thoughts

Inclusion: The need to feel that we belong and to interact with others.

Indexing A way to avoid abstracting and allness by acknowledge the *differences* that may exist between people within a group or between a person at one point in time and another point in time

Individual decision making Decisions made by a single individual when the following situations are present: fast decision needed, decisions are fairly simple, decisions affect few people, working with members is difficult

Individualistic cultures Cultures oriented toward the accomplishments of the individual person and value such concepts as independence, self-reliance, competition, personal opinion, personal rights, and reaching one's full potential

Inductive reasoning Reasoning that begins with arguments and evidence that lead up to a conclusion or position

Inference A conclusion that is drawn from something you observe

Informal roles Unassigned task and maintenance roles that emerge as individuals fulfill needs of the group

Information/opinion giver Group members who provide the group with substance for discussion by reporting research findings and giving opinions

Information/opinion seeker Group members who provide the group with substance for discussion by seeking out research and opinions from other group members

Information overload Occurs when an abundance of messages all compete for your attention

Informational interview An interview used to disseminate and/or gather specific information in a timely fashion in a variety of settings

Informational listening The type of listening that is required when the sender's goal is to convey information and the receiver's goal is to comprehend the information

Informative speech A speech in which you take a topic (including a person, thing, event, place, problem, or concept) and create understanding by clarifying, expanding, or teaching it to your audience

Initiating stage This first stage toward developing a relationship is very brief, lasting only long enough to form a quick first impression, to determine if additional communication is desired by both, and to assess how best to move forward

Inoculation theory Describes a process where listeners are presented with a brief look at opposing arguments and the refutation for those arguments in an effort to make audience members resistant to being persuaded by hearing those and other opposing arguments sometime in the future

Instrumental communication Communicating with the purpose is of accomplishing some goal—men are often considered to be instrumental communicators

Insulated listening When we don't hear what we don't want to hear so we don't have to deal with it

Integrating stage In this fourth stage of relationship development, both the partners as well as others refer to the communicators as a social unit—people expect to see them together

Intensifying stage In this third stage of relationship development, a relationship begins to become truly interpersonal as communicators explore ways in which they are both similar and complementary, build trust through self-disclosure, share past stories, and build new experiences that will become stories in the future

Interaction model A communication model that views communication as message exchange or a circular process involving feedback. The interaction model is a more accurate view of communication than the action model strategy.

Intercultural communication Interaction with people from different cultures

Internal noise Refers to any number of things that you may be experiencing physiologically or psychologically that cause you to have difficulty listening to messages

Internal organization Organization *within* a main point (meaning that the subpoints supporting a main point may be organized in either a topical, chronological, spatial, or causal pattern as well)

Internal summaries Words or sentences that recap previous points

Interpersonal communication Communication that occurs "between people"

Interpretation The process of attaching meaning to words, acts, or events in our environment and using the process to make predictions about future events or behaviors

Interpreting responses Responses used by empathic listeners that offer the speaker another way to view some aspect of the situation

Interview A specific communication context that occurs when two parties—the interviewer and interviewee—ask and answer questions with a specific purpose in mind. Types on interviews include: informational, employment, healthcare, performance, persuasive, recruiting, and survey.

Intimacy The closeness in a relationship that is achieved by the mutual sharing of intellectual, emotional, and physical aspects of oneself

Intrapersonal communication Communication that occurs within a person—"self-talk." It is how people think when they are alone, and how they process messages even when they are communicating with others.

Introvert A person with low inclusion needs

Involuntary audiences Audience members who are present at your speech because they have to be; because someone in authority has decreed that they must be present

Jargon A specialized vocabulary of a particular group (professional groups or a co-cultural group)

Judging responses Responses used by empathic listeners when they try to make a person feel better with platitudes or by minimizing their concerns by using statements such as, "Don't worry; everything will be okay," "You shouldn't feel that way," or "That's not a problem." Judging responses should be avoided.

Kinesics The category of nonverbal communication comprised of body language. Kinesics includes these types of nonverbal communication: eye contact, facial expressions, posture, gestures, and movement.

Laissez-faire leader One who turns the decision over to the group with no, or almost no, involvement in the process

Language Refers to a more-or-less formally established collection of spoken words and/or symbols that has meaning for a specific group of people

Laws of organization Several ways the brain groups visual and vocal stimuli into patterns discovered by Gestalt psychologists. Some patterns include proximity, similarity, and closure

Leader responsibilities Specific responsibilities that leaders should perform before, during, and after meetings

Leadership The ability to exert influence in a cooperative effort; the exercise of one's power with the goal of meeting the needs of the group

Leadership functions Based on the leadership function theory that people emerge as leaders by fulfilling needed task roles (roles that assist the group in achieving its goals) and maintenance roles (roles that help the group preserve its cohesiveness and maintain harmony among members)

Leadership power From French and Raven's bases of power theory—the ability to influence the behavior of others rests upon the degree to which a person possesses one or more of the five bases of power, which include reward, coercive, legitimate, expert, and referent power

Leadership styles There are three different leadership styles—authoritarian, democratic, and laissez-faire. Each one has strengths and weaknesses.

Leadership traits A style of leadership based on the trait theory that holds that leaders have natural born leadership abilities

Lean medium channel A communication medium that carries only one code and does not permit the reception of nonverbally encoded messages

Legitimate power The ability to exert influence because of the position one holds, either by birth, appointment, or election

Lexicon A formal system of written characters representing the spoken words of a language system

Listening The active process of constructing meaning from spoken messages through attention to the verbal and nonverbal codes that accompany them

Literal comparison Compares two or more items that are basically alike, such as two ways to motivate an audience, three methods to solve the parking problem, or four varieties of apples

Literal listening Listening that occurs when attention is given only to the content level of the message while ignoring the relational level of meaning. Literal listening is considered to be insensitive.

Logos Evidence and reasoning that supports any claim the speaker makes

Long-term memory Stored memory that lasts a lifetime; referred to as LTM

Lose-lose This conflict outcome—"If I can't win, you won't either"—should be avoided

Low-context cultures Cultures in which people's understanding of what is being communicated is based on the nature of the physical situation. Low-context cultures tend to be fairly individualistic. In low-context cultures, people listen carefully to the actual words spoken and give only minor attention to the context in which the message occur.

Main points The key ideas that subdivide the body that will be covered during a speech

Maintenance roles The behaviors that individuals exhibit in a group that help the group preserve its cohesiveness and maintain harmony among members

Manuscript speech A speech that is prepared in advance and committed to writing exactly as you intend to deliver it. It is then read word-for-word but should not sound like it is being read—thus the need for practice.

Marking An example of racist or sexist use of language where a person's race, ethnicity or gender are referred to when those characteristics are irrelevant

Mass communication Communication where a single individual or company sends a message to a receiver who is not immediately present

Member responsibilities Specific responsibilities that members should perform before, during, and after meetings

Memorized speech A speech that is carefully crafted in advance but delivered from memory

Message The idea, thought, or feeling one wishes to convey through communication

Meta-communication Communication about communication—people talk about their communication and what they like about how the other person communicates

Microexpressions Fleeting movements of the face that may last only a fraction of a second

Mindfulness Deliberately paying attention (conscious awareness) to your thought processes in a non-judgmental way. Used by communicators who do not

respond instinctively but respond thoughtfully and think about what they are doing and recognize that they are, at all times, making choices in how to encode and decode messages.

Model of relationship stages (Knapp) A model that shows how relationships develop, are maintained, and deteriorate. The model is especially applicable to intimate relationships such as those you enjoy with close friends or romantic partners.

Model of social penetration (Altman & Taylor) A way of looking at the process of disclosure as you work toward achieving intimacy in a relationship—social penetration. Stages begin with layer 1— superficial orientation; move to layer 2—exploratory exchange; then to layer 3—affective exchange; and finally, to layer 4—stable/intimate exchange.

Models Visual representations of the component parts of real processes

Monochromic Cultures that view time as a commodity that must be managed and are usually individualistic and low-context cultures

Monopolizing Refers to the act of hogging the conversation without allowing the other person to contribute

Monotone Speaking with the voice on a single tone or a very narrow range of pitch

Motivated-sequence pattern A five-step method of organizing a persuasive speech from introduction to action

Must criteria Criteria that are absolutely necessary in picking a solution. Any decision that does not meet all the must criteria will be eliminated without further discussion

Myers-Briggs Type Indicator A licensed instrument for checking your personality type; also known as MBTI

Narrative A factual or hypothetical story with enough detail to catch the attention of the audience

Narrative Paradigm Effective narratives can become a form of evidence used in arguments to inform as well as persuade listeners

Need The motivating force that influences our human behavior

Negotiated meaning The concept that meaning doesn't exist on its own but results from give and take and compromise as the communicators arrive at a meaning for various symbols in order to accomplish their goals

Neutral audience Composed of people who are looking for facts and information and view themselves as objective

Noise Anything that interferes with successfully sending and receiving messages

Nominal group technique (NGT) A method of generating ideas that assures equal participation from all members

Nominal leader The person who has been formally designated as the leader

Nonverbal code The part of a message that encompasses anything and everything that isn't language (such as gestures, posture, facial expressions, eye contact, and the vocal elements that accompany words, including tone of voice, volume, rate, and pitch)

Nonverbal communication Any symbolic behavior, other than written or spoken language, that is either intentionally or unintentionally sent, and is interpreted as meaningful by the receiver

Nonverbal delivery What the audience sees about your physical appearance (such as eye contact, gestures, and appearance) and the vocal sounds they hear that accompany your words (such as volume, rate, or tone of voice)

Nonverbal learning disorder Known as NLD, this disorder refers to the inability to interpret nonverbal messages accurately or the likelihood that the visual parts of messages will go unrecognized

Norms The implied standards of acceptable behavior in a given situation or context; rules that are not clearly spelled out but are "known" or "assumed"

Open-ended questions Broad, general questions like "What happened during the accident?" that allow the interviewee complete freedom on what to answer

Openness The need to express our inner thoughts and feelings with others; one of the basic needs in Schutz's FIRO-B

Operational definitions Being more precise by your adding language to describe what you mean by the terms you use

Optimum group size The ideal size for a group to be the most productive—five to seven people—is large enough to provide diversity of opinion but not large enough to inhibit full participation by all

Organization Discovering the recognizable patterns in the stimulus and recoding them in a form that is simple enough to remember and use

Organizational communication Communication involving individuals, dyads, and groups communicating with other individuals, dyads, and groups. Messages penetrate several layers and, therefore, are often very complicated and ripe for distortion.

Orientation phase The beginning phase in a problem-solving discussion where members work to become comfortable with one another and to develop an understanding of the task at hand

Outlining principles Guidelines for making effective speech outlines

Paralanguage The combination of the aspects of voice production that accompany spoken language, such as the tone of voice, which may enhance or modify the meaning of the words uttered. It is the vocal sounds that accompany words; a type of nonverbal communication.

Parallel structure (in outlining) When your main points are worded in a similar manner grammatically or syntactically—if one is a single noun, all points should be a single noun; if one is a phrase, all the points should be phrases, etc.

Paraphrasing A statement in your own words, sometimes phrased in the form of a question, which reflects to senders the gist of what you heard them say

Passive-aggressive listening A type of listening that occurs when someone listens very intently to the sender's message for the purpose of attacking the sender, often by using the sender's words against him or her, as soon as the remarks are completed

Passive-aggressive style Used by communicators who believe "I'll pretend that I think your needs are important to me, but they're not," and use subtle and manipulative ways to handle conflicts. Some of their tactics include the silent treatment, the innocent approach, and the joking approach.

Passive strategy A strategy for seeking information and reducing uncertainty where a person sits back and observes how another person interacts with others

Passive style Used by communicators who feel that other people's needs are more important than their own and tend to avoid conflict by using denial, avoidance, or accommodation

Pathos Appeals to emotion as a way to be persuasive

Pause A live silence (either short or long) that is not filled with "uhs" or "ums"

Perception The process by which individuals become aware of, organize, and interpret information received though their senses

Perception checking A verbal request for feedback to determine whether your interpretation of someone's behavior (based on something they said or a nonverbal response) is accurate

Perceptual constancy Looking for consistency between what we have experienced in the past and what we are experiencing in the present

Personal anecdote A story about something that actually happened to the speaker

Personal information The best place to begin research-ing for a speech is with what you already know

Personalization principle Explains that audiences actu-ally learn more when speakers use a conversational delivery instead of a formal one

Persuasion Occurs when a speaker crafts messages with the intent of influencing the values, beliefs, attitudes, or behaviors of others

Persuasive appeals Three means of persuasion—logic (logos), credibility (ethos), and emotion (pathos)—used to connect with the audience and persuade them

Persuasive speech a speech where you select a contro-versial topic and deliberately attempt to change the way others believe or behave

Phonological rules Rules that deal with how words sound when spoken

Physiological factors A possible impairment of a sen-sory organ that can interfere with accurate perception of stimuli

Physiological noise An internal noise from some physi-cal condition that gets in the way of effective sending or receiving of messages

Pitch Part of paralanguage that relates to the relative highness or lowness of a vocal tone as it occurs on a musical scale

Plagiarism Using the ideas or words of another person without giving credit

Plus-2 concept (Hamilton) An "other orientation" to Barnlund's 6-person concept. Therefore, instead of 6 entities involved when two people are talking, we have added two more: your view of how the other person sees himself and the other person's view of how you see yourself. By putting yourself in the other person's frame of reference, you have added empathy.

Polarizing terms Terms that assert that the thing dis-cussed must be either of one kind or of its opposite kind

Polychromic Cultures that view time as a fluid and flex-ible and not to be managed. These cultures tend to be more collectivistic and high-context than mono-chromic cultures

Positive imagery (visualization) Creating a positive, vivid, and detailed mental image of yourself while giving a successful and confident speech

Post hoc A flaw in reasoning that occurs when speakers assert that because event A occurred shortly before event B, B must have been caused by A, without pre-senting clear evidence linking the two events

Posture A kinesic cue that includes the position, align-ment, and carriage of your body

Power The ability to exert influence over others

Power distance The way a particular culture views equality versus inequality and the importance of sta-tus and authority

Pragmatic rules Language rules (usually unstated and which we come to understand largely through context) that allow us to understand the meaning that we are expected to attach to a phrase or sentence

Preparation outline The expanded and polished ver-sion made from your rough-draft outline

Preview A statement that forecasts the main ideas you plan to cover in your speech and leads smoothly into points to come

Print sources A type of research that includes books, magazines and journals, newspapers, and other sources available in hard copy from a library

Probability Concept from the narrative paradigm that refers to whether the story sticks together in a coher-ent manner—the storyline is clear; the characters behave in a reliable manner

Problem-solution pattern Used to organize informative and persuasive speeches where the main points include a discussion of the problem followed by a look at possi-ble solutions (for informative speeches) and suggestion of the best solutions (for persuasive speeches)

Progressive-questions pattern (Creel) A persuasive pattern where main points are organized by asking and answering a series of questions in a sequence that logically follows the thought patterns of the audience

Projection Our tendency to assume that others possess the similar traits, motivations, and reactions that we do

Pronunciation Refers to the act of saying a word using the accepted standards of the language group

Proxemics The ways that people use social distance in interaction including intimate, personal, social, and public distances

Proximity A law of organization that says that objects that are close together tend to be grouped together when we perceive them; also, a design element for visual aids that says that items relating to each other should be grouped closely together

PRSCA The Personal Report of Speech Communication Anxiety is a form designed by Richmond & McCroskey (1992) to determine the level of anxiety felt in a variety of speaking situations

Psychological factors Factors such as strong emotion, outlook on life (generated by one's personality traits), present circumstances and moods that interfere with accurate perception of words, actions, or events

Psychological noise An internal noise related to your thoughts and emotions that gets in the way of effective sending or receiving of messages

Public communication Communication in a "one-to-many" situation in which a single speaker addresses a defined audience as exemplified by an oral presentation

Punctuation Assigning fault and cause according to our perception of whose behavior is responsible and whose behavior is the natural result

Q & A Answers given to audience questions at the end of a speech and followed with a final summary and memorable ending to refocus audience attention back to the central ideas of the speech

Questioning A type of cross-examination used to gain understanding or additional information

Question of conjecture A way to phrase a problem that asks what can be anticipated in the future

Question of fact A way to phrase a problem that is either non-controversial or controversial and seeks to determine what the present situation is

Question of policy A way to phrase a problem that seeks to determine what course of action should be taken

Question of value A way to phrase a problem that is oriented toward evaluating what course of action is best or most worthy

Quotation A concise and especially well-worded statement by an outside source considered credible by your audience. It may be paraphrased or read word-for-word.

Racist language The intentional use of epithets or terms that tend to imply the inferiority of persons who are not members of the dominant culture; also occurs when a person's race, ethnicity or gender are referred to when those characteristics are irrelevant to the message (called marking)

Rapport A feeling of liking or closeness established between the speaker and audience during the introduction of a speech

Rate Part of paralanguage that relates to the number of words uttered per minute. Rate is one of the four key attributes of the human voice.

Rational-emotive behavior therapy A cognitive behavior therapy that helps people change irrational self-talk beliefs that lead to distortions in how they view themselves, their competence, and their essential worthiness

Reasoning A process that ties your evidence together in an orderly manner so that your conclusion logically follows from the evidence

Receiver The person toward whom a particular message is aimed

Receiver apprehension A response that can occur when listeners become frightened or confused by messages from speakers who seem to have an abundance of knowledge about topics that are not part of our own day-to-day experience such as political or academic speakers. The fear is that we cannot comprehend what is being said.

Reciprocity Engaging in communication that is not one-sided because both parties participate

Recorder The group member who takes notes on what was discussed during the group's meeting and on any decisions that were reached

Refereed journals Journals that contain articles that have been selected by acknowledged experts in the field

Referent power The ability to influence others because others regard you as well-liked and charismatic

Reflected appraisal The way we think others see us (reflected by their words or reactions) is often the way we see ourselves

Reframe Recasting or reframing a communication situation from the perspective of the communication partner

Refute The process of presenting arguments that oppose other arguments

Regulators The use of nonverbal behaviors to control the flow of verbal messages

Reinforcement phase The stage in a problem-solving discussion where members review the decision made or the task accomplished, reassuring themselves that they have achieved a desirable goal

Relational messages Messages that convey information about how you view your relationship with the other person with respect to power and connection

Relative terms Terms which derive their meaning by specifying their relationship to other factors

Relaxation Alternatively tensing and relaxing each muscle group in your body until you reach a state of relaxation—used as part of systematic desensitization

Repetition A basic design element that says to repeat visual elements such as lines, text size, and color of the design throughout the piece; also a stylistic device where words, phrases, or sentences are repeated several times

Resonant voice A quality, rich voice produced with adequate breath support and a relaxed throat, as well as active use of the articulator

Restraining forces In force-field analysis, these are the forces that restrain the group from making the necessary changes or imposing restrictions on how they can accomplish their objectives

Reward power The ability to influence someone because the leader has the resources to provide benefits that others desire

Rhetoric A form of speech training introduced by Aristotle and defined as" "the faculty of discovering in every case the available means of persuasion"

Rhetorical questions Questions that are intended to make the audience think of possible answers; the speaker does not want any answers given out loud or audience members to raise their hands to answer

Rich medium channels Channels that convey both verbal and nonverbal information are *rich* channels. Channels that convey only one channel are considered to be *lean* because they convey less information.

Role diversity When a group member has the ability to assume multiple task and maintenance roles

Rough-draft outline Includes a list of the probable main points you think you will cover in your speech as well as possible supporting ideas and materials—but no introduction or conclusion

Rules Explicit group standards of acceptable behavior that are explicitly spelled out in a given situation or context

Sans serif typeface A clean, geometric typeface, such as Arial or Tahoma, that is easy to read—especially good for titles

Search Engine Various systems for searching websites on the Internet (such as *Google, Yahoo,* or *HotBot*)

Selection The process of choosing which stimulus, among all those present in the environment, to pay attention to (also called *selective attention*). We are more likely to select a stimulus that is intense, that changes, that is novel or unexpected, and has the potential to meet our needs.

Selective distortion The process of an individual's expectations or fears deceiving the senses into reporting a false stimulus as real

Selective listening Occurs when we hear what we want to hear

Selective perception The process of choosing which stimulus, among all those present in the environment, to pay attention to

Self-concept A person's overall understanding of who he or she is

Self-disclosure A sharing of personal observations, feelings, and thoughts with another in a relationship

Self-esteem The degree to which a person sees self as valuable and worthwhile

Self-fulfilling prophecy Occurs when you predict the outcome of an anticipated event, and then engage in the behaviors that insure that outcome

Self-image The picture we have of ourselves

Self-monitoring A mental process used by mindful communicators who are aware of what they are doing verbally and nonverbally as well as how others are responding to them

Self-reflection An introspective process in which you have conscious awareness of what you are doing and thinking at the moment as well as a fairly accurate view of how others view you

Self-serving bias Occurs when we tend to accept responsibility for positive outcomes in our life, but deny responsibility for negative outcomes

Self-talk The intrapersonal messages we send to ourselves about ourselves

Semantic noise An internal noise affecting successful sending or receiving of messages that occurs because people use language for which meanings are not shared

Semantic rules Language rules that dictate the range of meanings that a particular language group assigns to a particular word

Sender The person who initiates the communication process

Serif typeface A typeface with finishing strokes or extending line, such as Times New Roman or Century

Service-learning project A group that "integrates community service with academic study to enrich learning, teach civic responsibility, and strengthen communities"

Sexist language The intentional use of terms that tend to imply the inferiority of persons who are not members of the dominant culture

Short-term memory Memory that holds information for 30 seconds or less unless we take notes or rehearse the information in some way; referred to as STM

Showboat A group member who constantly draws attention to self, often by clowning around, telling jokes, launching into stories of personal exploits, and generally distracting others

Similarity A law of organization that says that objects that look similar tend to be grouped together when we perceive them

Situational anxiety Anxiety created by a new, different, or unexpected situation

Situational contingency theory (Fiedler) Theory that claims that whether task-oriented or people-oriented styles are best depends on three contingencies or situations: leader-member relations, clarity of task structure, and position power

Situational leadership theory When leaders determine the appropriate leadership style for any given situation, they should consider two factors: the extent to which the members of the group are *able* and the extent to which they are *willing*

Skills training A method of managing anxiety which involves setting reasonable speaking goals, learning the necessary skills needed to reach those goals (such as preparing and presenting a successful speech), and judging the success of the speaking goals

Social exchange theory (Thibault & Kelley) The issue of rewards and costs that affect our decision to initiate, develop, and maintain relationships

Social judgment theory A theory that proposes that on any issue there will be a range of positions. Where you stand on a particular issue (such as gun control) will determine how likely you are to be persuaded by a speaker's position

Social loafing The tendency of group members to slack off, letting others carry the load. This is especially prevalent in large groups and groups with low cohesiveness

Spatial (or geographical) pattern used to organize informative speeches when your main points are arranged by their physical or geographical location in space such as from north to south, east to west, left to right, first floor to top floor (or the reverse of each of these if appropriate)

Speaker anxiety refers to the discomfort that most people feel when confronted with the need to speak to an audience

Speaking outline Brief notes usually arranged in outline format but containing only key words and phrases

Specific purpose A statement beginning with: "After hearing my speech, my audience will. . ."

Speech to actuate A persuasive speech in which you persuade an audience to do more than just agree—you motivate them to take a specific action

Speech to convince A persuasive speech where you ask for audience agreement

Speech to entertain Speeches presented in situations where it is necessary to build or maintain a light-hearted mood such as an after-dinner speech

Speech to inspire A persuasive speech in which you take audience members (who already agrees with you and may have even taken actions in the past) and persuade them to work even harder and become more motivated, enthusiastic, or productive

Stages of development The stages that relationships follow as they develop and are maintained. These stages proposed by Knapp include initiating, experimenting, intensifying, integrating, and bonding.

Stages of deterioration The stages that relationships follow as they deteriorate. These stages proposed by Knapp include differentiating, circumscribing, stagnating, avoiding, and terminating.

Stages of listening The stages that listeners go through when listening including attending, understanding, responding, and remembering

Stagnating stage This third stage of relationship deterioration, where communication is limited to superficial topics; may be brief or may last indefinitely

Standard questions Interview questions that relate to the applicant's basic skills and qualities and allow applicant to prepare ahead of time

Startling statement A type of attention-getter where the speaker gives unusual statistics or makes a statement that startles the audience

Statement of logical reasons pattern A persuasive pattern where main points are organized according to a list of logical reasons for your position

Statistics Numbers used to show a relationship between items

Stereotyping Making assumptions about people based on our perceptions of the groups to which they belong

Stimulus Internal or external data that bombard us each moment that are picked up by our five senses

Storyboarding A planning tool typically used by cartoon designers, producers of commercials, or ad agencies that provides a graphic look at each step or frame in a video or multimedia production

Straw man A flaw in reasoning that occurs when you try to prove the validity of your position by attacking an exaggerated or misrepresented version of an opponents' argument instead of the opponent's actual position

Stylistic devices Speaking techniques that include making your ideas memorable either by arranging sentences in unusual ways or by giving words an unusual meaning

Submissive A person with low control needs

Subpoints Points that support the main ideas

Supporters Group members who affirm the contributions of others by complimenting them on their ideas, expressing appreciation for their participation, and generally making everyone feel included and respected

Supporting materials Information used to support ideas in your speech by adding interest, adding clarification, or adding proof

Supporting responses Responses used by empathic listeners as they let the speaker know that they are concerned and willing to invest the time and energy required to listen

Symbol Something that represents something else, such as a word that represents an idea or a facial expression that represents a mood

Symbolic language Words don't have meanings; they are merely symbols that represent ideas, feelings, objects, or events in our experience.

Syntactic rules Language rules that deal with how words are combined in sentences

Task roles The behaviors that individuals exhibit in a group that assist the group in achieving its goals

Team Similar to a group but with closer cohesiveness and cooperation; often used in the business environment

Tension reliever A group member who uses a variety of techniques (including humor) to maintain group harmony and a relaxed atmosphere

Terminating stage The final stage of relationship deterioration in which the relationship ends

Territoriality The space we claim for ourselves in a given situation

Theory of linguistic relativity (Sapir-Whorf hypothesis) Theory that asserts that the way a culture (or nation) thinks is related to the grammatical structure of the language that the culture speaks

Thesis statement Usually one or two sentences, worded as simply as possible, that captures the central idea you want the audience to remember about your speech. Sometimes used to refer to the central argument of a persuasive speech.

Time binding A characteristic of humans that allows them the ability to accumulate and communicate knowledge of the past in order to live in the present and shape the future

Topical pattern Used to organize informative speeches when your main points represent types, categories, aspects, features, elements but do not have a chronological, spatial relationship, or cause-effect relationship

Trait anxiety An internal anxiety (such as the fear of looking like a fool or feeling inadequate as a speaker) that the speaker experiences regardless of the situation

Transaction model The most accurate model of communication where communicators both send and receive simultaneously, both parties are responsible for the outcome of the interaction, and each affects and is affected by the other

Transactional process An exchange in which both parties are responsible for the outcome of the interaction and each affects and is affected by the other

Transformational leadership Based on a theory developed by Bernard Bass that claims that there are special leaders who are especially suited for innovation, creativity, and change. These leaders inspire employees to put aside self-interests and rewards and, instead, to work for the good of the team or organization.

Transitions Sentences that allow you to move smoothly from one main point in your speech body to another main point

Trigger words Verbal expressions that arouse emotions to such an extent that internal psychological noise is created

Uncertainty reduction theory (Berger & Calabrese) A theory that suggests that people engage in passive, active, and interactive communication strategies in order to gather information about other people to predict their actions and behaviors

Uninterested audience Audience composed of people who would rather not be here and probably plan to take a mental vacation as soon as possible

Unlawful questions Questions that do not comply with state and federal (EEOC) guidelines. These guidelines designed to give all persons—regardless of race, sex, national origin, religion, age, disabilities, and marital status—the same chance to prove that they are qualified for a job based on experience, skills, and education and not on non-job-related traits.

Upspeak Where the speaker habitually ends each sentence on an upward inflection, sounding as if a question is being asked; contrasts with *downspeak,* where each sentence ends with a falling inflection, sounding as if a statement is being made

Values Principles that a person holds as important; the basis for a person's beliefs, attitudes, and behaviors

Verbal code The part of a message that is language (including written or spoken words)

Verbal communication The exchange of meanings by the use of the written or spoken symbols of a language system

Verbal delivery The actual words the audience hears you say and the style you use when saying them

Verbal/nonverbal probes Short words or gestures used to encourage applicants to include more information without the interviewer having to ask more questions

Virtual team A team that has members that are dispersed by location so must collaborate via the Internet or other technologies to accomplish specific goals

Visual aids Flipcharts, objects, or computer-generated visuals designed to clarify, simplify, and reinforce the verbal message

Visual delivery Using things the audience can see, such as gestures or facial expressions; also called *physical delivery*

Visual illusions Something that fools the senses—we think that line A is longer than line B, but that is because our eyes are not completely reliable (actually both lines are the same length. See Figure 2.4 (p. 47) for examples of visual illusions.

Visualization creating a positive, vivid, and detailed mental image of yourself giving a successful and confident speech; also called *positive imagery*

Vocal delivery The primary medium by which your ideas and feelings are transmitted

Vocal dysfluencies Behaviors that interrupt the fluency of the spoken message, such as stammering, false starts, repetitions of sounds, clearing of the throat, or use of fillers such as "uh"; also known as *vocal interferences*

Vocal interferences Behaviors that interrupt the fluency of the spoken message, such as stammering, false starts, repetitions of sounds, clearing of the throat, or use of fillers such as "uh"; also known as *vocal dysfluencies*

Vocal quality The manner of production of your voice that may be nasal, breathy, strident, or hoarse. Vocal quality is one of the four key attributes of the human voice.

Volume The part of paralanguage that refers to the relative loudness or softness of a speaking voice. Volume is one of the four key attributes of the human voice.

Voluntary audiences Audience members who are present at your speech because they want to be; they may even have paid to be there

Vote One way that decisions are made by group members

Want criteria Criteria that are desired but not essential. Want criteria need to be rated or ranked in some fashion.

White space Space with nothing in it that equally goes around all outside edges of a computer-generated visual to add an organized look

Win-lose When preferred outcomes are mutually exclusive, a win-lose decision may be best—one person wins this time (and one loses), but the next time the reverse will be true (the losing party this time will be the winning party the next time)

Win-win A conflict outcome in which both parties are able to get all of their needs met

Withholder A person whose need for openness in relational communication is low

Word A speech sound or series of speech sounds combined into a single unit that conveys meaning

Zones Proxemic zones or distances in the North American culture that indicate relationships: intimate, personal, social, and public distances

Photo Credits

Name Index

Subject Index